The Modern Law of Negligence

The Modern Law of Negligence

Second Edition

R A Buckley MA, D Phil
of Lincoln's Inn, Barrister
Professor of Law, University of Reading

Butterworths
London, Dublin, Edinburgh
1993

United Kingdom	Butterworth & Co (Publishers) Ltd, 88 Kingsway, LONDON WC2B 6AB and 4 Hill Street, EDINBURGH EH2 3JZ
Australia	Butterworths, SYDNEY, MELBOURNE, BRISBANE, ADELAIDE, PERTH, CANBERRA and HOBART
Belgium	Butterworth & Co (Publishers) Ltd, BRUSSELS
Canada	Butterworth Canada Ltd, TORONTO and VANCOUVER
Ireland	Butterworth (Ireland) Ltd, DUBLIN
Malaysia	Malayan Law Journal Sdn Bhd, KUALA LUMPUR
New Zealand	Butterworths of New Zealand, Ltd, WELLINGTON and AUCKLAND
Puerto Rico	Equity de Puerto Rico, Inc, HATO REY
Singapore	Butterworths Asia, SINGAPORE
USA	Butterworth Legal Publishers, AUSTIN, Texas; BOSTON, Massachusetts; CLEARWATER, Florida (D & S Publishers); ORFORD, New Hampshire (Equity Publishing); ST PAUL, Minnesota; and SEATTLE, Washington

All rights reserved. No part of this publication may be reproduced in any material form (including photocopying or storing it in any medium by electronic means and whether or not transiently or incidentally to some other use of this publication) without the written permission of the copyright owner except in accordance with the provisions of the Copyright, Designs and Patents Act 1988 or under the terms of a licence issued by the Copyright licensing Agency Ltd, 90 Tottenham Court Road, London, England W1P 9HE. Applications for the copyright owner's written permission to reproduce any part of this publication should be addressed to the publisher.

Warning: The doing of an unauthorised act in relation to a copyright work may result in both a civil claim for damages and criminal prosecution.

© Butterworth & Co (Publishers) Ltd 1993

A CIP Catalogue record for this book is available from the British Library.

First edition 1988

ISBN 0 406 01029 3

Typeset by Doyle & Co, Colchester
Printed and bound in Great Britain by
Mackays of Chatham PLC, Chatham, Kent

Preface to second edition

The five-year period which has elapsed since the publication of the first edition of this book has been a remarkable one. The extent of recovery of economic loss was drastically curtailed by the spectacular decision of a seven-member House of Lords, in *Murphy v Brentwood District Council*, to overrule the relatively recent decision of the House itself in *Anns v London Borough of Merton*. Other major House of Lords cases on the economic loss front included *D & F Estates v Church Commissioners*, and significant decisions on the liability of auditors (*Caparo Industries v Dickman*) and surveyors (*Smith v Bush*). Moreover, the demise of *Anns v London Borough of Merton* has implications for the very structure of the law of negligence extending well beyond the confines of economic loss. Another important decision of the House of Lords arose out of the Hillsborough football stadium disaster, and involved reconsideration of the law relating to nervous shock or psychiatric damage. Numerous decisions of the Court of Appeal included notable cases on the Fatal Accidents Acts, and on the defences to a negligence action. Nor was the legislature inactive: considerable changes in the relationship between tort damages and social security payments, for example, were introduced in 1989 and consolidated in the Social Security Administration Act 1992.

The purpose of this edition, like the first, is to provide a critical statement of the law of negligence placing particular emphasis upon contemporary authorities and current concerns. Much of the text has therefore been rewritten so as to accord prominence, where appropriate, to the many judicial pronouncements which have been made since 1988. The text was completed at the end of February 1993 and does, it is hoped, include all significant developments up to that time.

RAB

Preface to first edition

The past quarter of a century has been a period of rapid change in the law of negligence. The scope and structure of the tort have been subjected to analysis and development, often at the highest judicial level, in decisions which have frequently proved controversial. The purpose of this book is to provide a fresh and critical exposition, for all concerned with this major area of the law. The treatment is one which, while seeking to be comprehensive, attempts to give particular emphasis to the themes and concerns which characterise the contemporary scene. I have therefore drawn wherever possible, for the purposes of illustration and quotation, upon recent cases and judicial pronouncements; even for familiar propositions usually associated with judgments from earlier periods.

Alongside, but largely separate from, the conceptual debate which has enlivened judicial consideration of the law of negligence, have been calls for radical reform, or even abolition, of the role of the law of tort in compensating victims of personal injury. Nevertheless the possibility of far-reaching change in the near future now seems rather more remote than it perhaps did a decade ago. But reform of some kind is necessary, and must surely take place sooner or later. It may turn out, however, to be on lines rather different from those envisaged by advocates of a major expansion of State activity in this area. Although this book is primarily concerned with the existing law these important issues are touched upon, particularly in the final chapters.

I am greatly indebted to Mr R W M Dias, Fellow of Magdalene College, Cambridge, and Mr M H Matthews, Fellow of University College, Oxford; both of whom read through various parts of the book in draft. I am grateful to them for saving me from a number of serious errors, and also for valuable suggestions for improvement. For the errors that remain I alone am responsible. Miss J Ray, and her staff in the Law Faculty Office at Oxford, typed several chapters before my slow initiation into the mysteries of word-processing proved adequate to the task of completing the rest. I am also grateful to the Publishers, not least for agreeing to relieve me of the burden of preparing the Index and Tables. Finally, the book could not have been written had not the Principal and Fellows of Mansfield College granted me sabbatical leave, at intervals to fit in with the timetable for its preparation.

R A B

Contents

Preface to the second edition   v
Preface to the first edition   vi
Table of Statutes   xvii
Table of Cases   xxi

PART ONE   THE STRUCTURE OF THE MODERN LAW

Chapter 1   Liability for carelessness   3
The changing fortunes of foreseeability   3
    Generalisation: its rise and fall   3
    Omissions   7
    Generalisation gives way to 'pragmatism'   10
    'Proximity' and 'policy'   11
The erosion of traditional immunities   15
    Negligent misstatement and economic loss   15
    Lawyers   15
    Buildings   15
Factors which can limit liability   17
    'Floodgates' argument   17
    Conflicting interests   17
    Public policy and the sanctity of life   19
    Illegal or anti-social conduct by the plaintiff   20
    Existing law   23
    Legislative or administrative solution more suitable?   24
    Alternative remedy more appropriate?   25
Nervous shock   26

Chapter 2   Evaluation of conduct   30
Foreseeability and objectivity   30
    Incapacity normally disregarded   30
The measurement of risk   32
    Degree of probability   32
    Gravity of harm   33
    Utility of the defendant's conduct   34
    Extent of the precautions necessary for protection   34
Care and its quality   35
    Protection of minorities   35

vii

Relevance of common practice　36
　　　Carelessness not to be inferred from subsequent adoption
　　　　of protective measures　36
　　　'Errors of judgment'　37
Proof of negligence　37
　　　Causation　37
　　　Res ipsa loquitur　40

Chapter 3　Remoteness of damage　44
Related issues distinguished　44
　　　Remoteness and causation　44
　　　Scope of the chapter　44
　　　Remoteness of damage and measure of damages　45
The foreseeability test　45
　　　Background　45
　　　The present state of the law　47
　　　Effect of extraneous circumstances　49
Intervening act by the plaintiff　53
　　　Remoteness occasionally relevant　53
　　　'Dilemma' situations　54
　　　Suicide cases　55
　　　Rescue　55
Intervention by third parties　56
　　　'Deliberate and mischievous' acts　56
　　　Negligence　59

Chapter 4　Assumption of risk, contribution and exclusion　61
Scope of the chapter　61
Assumption of risk　61
　　　Knowledge not enough　61
　　　Relationship with the duty of care　64
Contributory negligence　65
　　　Background　65
　　　Basis of apportionment　67
　　　Where the plaintiff contributes to the severity of his damage　70
　　　Contributory negligence by children　72
　　　Contributory negligence and contract　74
Contribution between wrongdoers　75
　　　Where more than one is liable　75
　　　When contribution can be claimed　76
　　　Assessment of contribution　80
Exclusion of liability　81
　　　Exclusion by contract　81
　　　Non-contractual disclaimers　82
　　　Non-contractual disclaimers and the Unfair Contract
　　　　Terms Act　84

Contents ix

PART TWO   NEGLIGENCE AND ECONOMIC INTERESTS

Chapter 5   Liability for negligent misstatement   89
The impact of *Hedley Byrne*   89
   The concept of the 'special relationship'   89
   Types of misstatement   91
Proving breach of duty   92
   Where delicate professional judgments are involved   92
   Knowledge or skill   93
   Standard of care   94
Public policy   95
   Advocate's immunity   95
   Witnesses   98
   Arbitrators and mutual valuers   98
Social occasions   100
   Liability only in very exceptional cases   100
Claims by third parties   101
   Fear of indeterminate liability   101
   Surveyors and solicitors   102
   Third party in negotiation with recipient of advice   103
   References   105
   Auditors and the extent of liability   105
Omissions   108
   Focus upon questions of law   108
Disclaimers of liability   111
   When possible   111
   Requirements   112
   Effect of the Unfair Contract Terms Act   112
Contributory negligence   114
   Relevance of the defence   114
   Law Reform (Contributory Negligence) Act 1945   114

Chapter 6   Financial loss caused by careless acts   116
The background to the modern law   116
   Fear of multiplicity of claims   116
   Effect of *Hedley Byrne*   117
   A false dawn   118
Where the plaintiff's property is reduced in value by the defendant's negligence   119
   Older approach still valid   119
   An exception?   123
Where the plaintiff suffers economic loss which is consequential upon injury or damage to a third party   126
   Traditional approach reasserted   126
   Confirmation of orthodox view   128
   Possibility of exceptions to the general rule rejected   129
Other cases of economic loss   133
   Recovery still possible in some cases   133
   Acts, statements, and purposes   134

x *Contents*

    Statutory powers   135
    Losses due to failure to insure   135
    Recovery of economic loss in public nuisance   136
    Abolition of actions for loss of services   136

PART THREE DAMAGES AND THEIR ASSESSMENT

Chapter 7 The making of awards in personal injury cases   139
Heads of damage   139
    Special damages   139
    General damages   140
Mitigation   143
    Plaintiff's state of knowledge   143
    Onus of proof   144
Subsequent events   145
Provisional damages   147
    Other procedures for postponing assessment   148
Interest   148

Chapter 8 Damages recoverable for personal injury   150
Non-pecuniary loss   150
    Pain and suffering   150
    Reduced life expectancy   151
    Loss of amenity   152
    Relevance of awards in other cases   153
    Catastrophic injury cases   154
    Unconscious plaintiffs   155
    Effect of inflation   156
Financial loss   156
    Calculation of future lost earnings   156
    Damages for the 'lost years'   161
    Relevance of gains   162
    Relationship with state benefits: Social Security
        Administration Act 1992, Part IV   164
    Tax   165
    Pension contributions not recoverable   166
Cost of care   166
    General calculation   166
    Living expenses sometimes deductible   168
    Care by relatives   169
Structured settlements   170
Scope for reform   171
    Future of tort as a compensation system   171
    Computation of damages   172
    Specific reforms   172

Contents   xi

Chapter 9   Cases involving death   174
Survival of causes of action   174
   Law Reform (Miscellaneous Provisions) Act 1934   174
Claims by dependants   176
   Background   176
   Who can claim   176
   The dependants   177
   How damages are assessed   179
   Loss of services of mother   185
   Interest   187
   Apportionment   187
   Disregard of benefits   189
   Public policy   190
Damages for bereavement   191
   Fixed sum to be awarded to spouses or parents   191
   Funeral expenses   193

Chapter 10   Property damage and other losses   195
Chattels   195
   'Restitutio in integrum'   195
   Repair or difference in value?   195
   Loss of use   197
   Other losses   198
   Gains by the plaintiff   199
Land and buildings   200
   Reinstatement or difference in value   200
   Gains   202
   Negligent surveys   203
   Date of assessment   204
   Additional losses   205
New areas of recovery   206

Chapter 11   Limitation of actions   208
General principles   208
   Time limits   208
   Limitation and dismissal for want of prosecution   210
Personal injuries   212
   Special time limit   212
   Date of knowledge   213
   Discretion to override the time limit   216
Concealment of the cause of action   220
   Start of period postponed   220
Latent damage in cases other than personal injury   221
   Background   221
   Latent Damage Act 1986   223

xii   Contents

PART FOUR   NEGLIGENCE AGAINST A STATUTORY BACKGROUND

Chapter 12   Negligence and the exercise of statutory powers   229
The problem of discretion   229
   The early decisions   229
   The policy and operational distinction   231
   The policy 'immunity'   233
   Justiciability of government decisions   235
Factors which bear upon liability   237
   Competing public interests   237
   Statutory purpose   240
   Carelessness and policy   242
Public and private law   245

Chapter 13   The action for breach of statutory duty   248
The nature of liability   248
   Introduction   248
   Background   249
The scope of the Act   253
   Protection of a 'class'   253
   Relevance of provision in the Act for a penalty   256
   A new presumption suggested   260
   The relevance of fault   261
Defences and relationship with criminal liability   263
   Contributory negligence and volenti non fit injuria   263
   Where no offence has been committed   263
Reform?   264
   An express provision?   264
   Difficulties with the Law Commission's proposal   265

Chapter 14   Employers' liability to their employees   266
The common law duty   266
   Introduction   266
   Tort and contract   267
   Safe system of work   268
   Defective equipment   274
   Non-delegable duty   275
Statutory duties   277
   Introduction   277
   Dangerous machinery and the duty to fence   278
   Floors and access   282
   Ventilation and extraction of fumes and dust   284
   Injury caused by lifting heavy loads   287
   Provision of safety equipment   288
   Causation and contributory negligence   289
Relationship between statutory and common law duties   292
   Separation   292

Contents xiii

PART FIVE SPECIAL AREAS OF LIABILITY

Chapter 15 Professional negligence 297
General principles 297
   Standard of care 297
Medical negligence 299
   Difficulties of proof 299
   Relevance of common practice 301
   Where there are differing professional schools of thought 303
   The duty to warn 303
   Contractual negligence 306
Lawyers 307
   Advocate's immunity 307
   Types of claim 307
   Tort and contract 310
Land, valuation and construction 314
   The 'property' professions 314
   Valuation 314
   Design and construction 316
Financial services 317
   Accountants 317
   Investment advice 318

Chapter 16 Liability of occupiers 319
The scope of 'occupation' 319
   What can be 'occupied'? 319
   Who is an 'occupier'? 319
Liability to visitors 320
   Persons qualifying as 'visitors' 320
   The 'common duty of care' 321
   Entry pursuant to a contract 324
   Warnings, volenti, and contributory negligence 325
   Employment of independent contractors 326
   Property damage 328
Liability to persons other than visitors 329
   Persons covered by the Occupiers' Liability Act 1984 329
   The nature of the duty imposed by the 1984 Act 330
Exclusion of liability 332
   Visitors and non-business occupiers 332
   Persons other than visitors 334
   Visitors and business occupiers 334
When the Acts do not apply 335
   Relationship with ordinary negligence 335
   Liability of non-occupiers 337
   Users of the highway 338
   Where liability has been excluded 339
Landlords and the Defective Premises Act 1972, s 4 340

Chapter 17 Defective products 343
The common law 343
  Introduction 343
  The duty 345
  Intermediate inspection 346
  Proof of negligence 348
  Economic loss 349
Strict liability: The Consumer Protection Act 1987 351
  Background 351
  Strict liability 351
  'Products' and 'producers' 352
  Agricultural products 353
  'Defect' 354
  Defences 355
  Contributory negligence, exclusion and limitation of liability 356
  Damage 357
  Evaluation 358

Chapter 18 Vicarious liability 360
Introduction 360
  Background 360
  Who is a servant? 361
  Borrowed servants 364
The course of employment 365
  Wrongful method of performance 365
  The master's indemnity 370
Independent contractors and non-delegable duties 371
  The concept of non-delegable duty 371
  'Collateral negligence' 377
'Agents' 378
  Special type of non-delegable duty upon car-owners in
    certain cases 378
  Other situations? 380

PART SIX TORT, THE STATE AND THE FUTURE

Chapter 19 Insurance and state provision 385
Introduction 385
The role of insurance 386
  Negligence: appearance and reality 386
  Road Traffic Act 388
  The Motor Insurers' Bureau 389
  Employers' liability 391
  Where the holder of a liability policy is insolvent 391
Injury at work 392
  Background and structure 392
  Accidents and diseases 393
  Disablement benefit 393
Vaccine damage 394

Criminal injuries   394
   Basis of compensation   394
   Nature of awards   395
   Is the Scheme justifiable   395

Chapter 20 Reform?   397
Criticisms of the existing system   397
   Introduction   397
   Inefficiency   397
   Arbitrariness   398
   Insurance and the moral basis of negligence   399
Various proposals for reform   400
   The Pearson Commission   400
   The New Zealand Scheme   403
   Proposals by members of the Oxford Centre for Socio-Legal Studies   404
   Focus upon disease   405
   Possible changes in the burden of proof   406
   Extension of strict liability   407
Conclusions   409

Index   413

Table of Statutes

References to *Statutes* are to Halsbury's Statutes of England (Fourth Edition) showing the volume and page at which the annotated text of the Act may be found.

Page references printed in **bold** type indicate where the section of an Act is set out in part or in full.

	PARA
Accident Rehabilitation and Compensation Insurance Act 1982 (New Zealand)	20.11
s 3, 5, 7	20.12
Administration of Justice Act 1969	
s 22	7.04, 7.13
Administration of Justice Act 1982 (11 *Statutes* 1087; 13 *Statutes* 586; 45 *Statutes* 676)	9.22, 9.27; 20.10
s 1(1)(a), (b)	8.02
2	6.27
3	9.04, 9.26
(1)	9.16, 9.18, 9.21, 9.29
4	9.02
(2)	8.14, 8.15
5	8.25
6	7.11; 8.31
15	7.13
Brighton and Chichester Railway Act 1844	
s 274	13.07
Building Act 1984 (35 *Statutes* 782)	12.04
Civil Liability (Contribution) Act 1978 (13 *Statutes* 577)	4.18; 17.09; 18.14
s 1(1)	4.18
(3)	4.19, 4.22
(4)	4.20
(5)	4.21, 4.22
2(1), (2)	4.24
(3)	4.25
3	4.18
4	4.23
6(1)	4.18
7(2)	4.18
Companies Act 1985 (8 *Statutes* 104)	
Pt VII (ss 221-256)	5.20
s 651	19.11

	PARA
Companies Act 1989 (8 *Statutes* 819)	
s 141	19.11
Congenital Disabilities (Civil Liability) Act 1976 (45 *Statutes* 654)	1.19
s 1	1.19
(2)(b)	1.19
2	1.19
4(5)	1.19
Consumer Protection Act 1987 (39 *Statutes* 188)	6.08; 17.01, 17.14
s 1(1)	17.14
(2)	17.18, 17.20
(c)	17.19
(3)	17.18
2	**17.15**, 17.17, 17.18
(1)	17.16
(2)	17.16, 17.18
(3)	17.16
(4)	**17.20**
(5)	17.17
3	17.21
(1)	17.18, 17.21, 17.22
(2)	17.21
4	17.24
(1)(a)	17.24
(c)(i), (ii)	17.24
(e)	17.23
(f)	17.18, 17.24
5	17.01, 17.27
(1)	17.26
(2)	17.22, 17.26
(4)	17.26
6	17.27
(4)	17.25
7	17.25
Sch 1	17.25

xviii *Table of Statutes*

	PARA
Contagious Diseases (Animals) Act 1869	13.07
County Courts Act 1959	
s 97A	7.13
Courts and Legal Services Act 1990 (11 *Statutes* 1211)	
s 62(1)	5.09
Criminal Justice Act 1982	19.17
Criminal Justice Act 1988	19.17
s 108-114	19.15
Sch 6	19.15
Sch 7	19.15, 19.16
Defective Premises Act 1972 (31 *Statutes* 195)	1.22; 6.06, 6.08
s 1	1.13
4	1.13; **16.38**
6(3)	16.39
Employers' Liability (Compulsory Insurance) Act 1969 (16 *Statutes* 181)	
s 1(1)	14.14; **19.09**
Employers' Liability (Defective Equipment) Act 1969 (16 *Statutes* 70)	14.01, 14.15
s 1(1)	**14.13**
Factories Act 1937	14.27
s 25, 26	14.27
Factories Act 1961 (19 *Statutes* 449)	13.03; 14.18, 14.33
s 4	14.30
(1)	**14.29**
12	14.19
(1), (3)	14.20
13	14.19, 14.21
14	14.19, 14.23
15	14.19
16	14.19, 14.25
28	14.26
(1)	**14.26**, 14.27, 14.28
(2)	14.26
29(1)	**14.26**, 14.27, 14.28
(2)	14.33
63(1)	**14.30**, 14.31, 14.33
72(1)	14.32
176(1)	14.21
Fair Trading Act 1973 (47 *Statutes* 125)	13.19
Fatal Accidents Act 1976 (31 *Statutes* 202)	
s 1(1)	9.05
(3)	**9.06**
1A	**9.26**
2	9.05
3(1)	9.21
(3)	9.18
(4)	9.16
(5)	9.29
4	9.22
5	4.25; 9.05
Gasworks Clauses Act 1871	13.06
Guard Dogs Act 1975 (2 *Statutes* 351)	13.19

	PARA
Health and Safety at Work Act 1974 (19 *Statutes* 620)	14.17
s 15	14.17
47(2)	14.17
(3)	13.18
53(1)	14.18
Sch 1	14.18
Highway Traffic Act RSO 1980 (Ontario)	
s 167	**20.16**
Highways Act 1980 (20 *Statutes* 135)	
s 58	16.35
Hotel Proprietors Act 1956 (24 *Statutes* 299)	16.14
Housing (Homeless Persons) Act 1977	13.12
Latent Damage Act 1986 (24 *Statutes* 707)	11.23, 11.25
s 3	11.25
4	11.28
Law Reform (Contributory Negligence) Act 1945 (31 *Statutes* 185)	3.14; 4.09, 4.16, 4.24; 5.32, 5.33; 9.05; 13.17; 14.34; 16.12; 17.09, 17.25
s 1	4.07, 4.25
(1)	**4.07**, 4.08; 5.33
Law Reform (Husband and Wife) Act 1962 (27 *Statutes* 608)	18.02
Law Reform (Limitation of Actions, &c.) Act 1954	11.01, 11.03
Law Reform (Married Women and Tortfeasors) Act 1935 (27 *Statutes* 602)	17.09; 18.14
s 6	4.18
Law Reform (Miscellaneous Provisions) Act 1934 (17 *Statutes* 312)	
s 1	9.02
(1)	9.01
(2)	9.02
(a)	8.14
(c)	9.29
Law Reform (Miscellaneous Provisions) Act 1971 (31 *Statutes* 194)	
s 4	9.18
Law Reform (Personal Injuries) Act 1948 (45 *Statutes* 648)	8.19, 18.01
s 1(1)	14.01
2(1)	7.06, 8.19
(4)	8.24
Limitation Act 1939	11.21, 11.22
s 26(b)	11.22
Limitation Act 1963	11.08, 11.09
Limitation Act 1975	11.03, 11.08, 11.15
s 2D	11.01
Limitation Act 1980 (24 *Statutes* 648)	11.01
s 2	11.01

Table of Statutes xix

	PARA
Limitation Act 1980—contd	
s 10	4.19
11	11.08, 11.17, 11.18
(4)	11.01, 11.08
11A	17.25
(3)	17.25
12(1)-(3)	11.20
13	9.21
(1)	11.20
14	11.09
(1)	**11.09**, 11.14
(a)	11.10
(b)	11.09
(c)	11.12
(2)	**11.10**
(3)	**11.13**
14A	11.25, 11.26
14B	11.25, 11.27
28	11.03
32	11.21
(1)(b)	11.21
33	11.15, 11.17, 11.20
(1)	11.01, 11.06, 11.15
(3)	11.16
(a)	11.16
(b)	11.16
(c)-(f)	11.16
35(3)	11.04
38(2)-(4)	11.03
London Government Act 1963 (26 Statutes 412)	
Sch 9 Pt III	
para 13(1)	12.13
15(1), (2)	12.13
Mental Health Act 1959 (28 Statutes 616)	11.03
Merchant seamen (1844)	
s 18	13.02
Mineral Workings (Offshore Installations) Act 1971 (29 Statutes 515)	13.19
s 9(3)	13.18
11(4)	13.18
Misrepresentation Act 1967 (29 Statutes 724)	
s 2	5.07
(1)	4.16
Motor Vehicles (Passenger Insurance) Act 1971	
s 1	19.05
National Assistance Act 1948	
s 29(5)	8.24
National Health Service Act 1946 (30 Statutes 714)	12.10
National Parks and Access to the Countryside Act 1949 (32 Statutes 67)	
s 60	16.18
(1)	16.18

	PARA
Occupiers' Liability Act 1957 (31 Statutes 188)	16.01, 16.04, 16.12, 16.18, 16.19, 16.21, 16.23, 16.28, 16.30, 16.31, 16.32, 16.35, 16.36, 16.37, 16.39
s 1(1)	16.06, 16.20, 16.32
(2)	16.02, 16.04, **16.05**
(3)(a)	16.01
(b)	16.14
(4)	16.18
(5)	16.27
(6)	16.26
(7)	16.19
2(1)	16.24
(3)	16.07
(b)	16.08
(4)	**16.10, 16.13**
(a)	16.11, 16.22
(b)	16.06, 16.13
(5)	**16.11**, 16.22
(6)	16.04
3(1)	16.09, 16.26
(2), (4)	16.09
4	16.38
5(1)	16.09
Occupiers' Liability Act 1984 (31 Statutes 213)	16.01, 16.07, 16.16, 16.17, 16.18, 16.19, 16.22, 16.27, 16.32, 16.35, 16.36, 16.37
s 1(1)(a)	16.32
(2)	16.01
(a)	16.02
(3), (4)	**16.20**
(5), (6)	16.22
(7)	**16.35**, 16.36
(9)	16.01, 16.23
2	16.24, 16.29
Occupiers' Liability (Scotland) Act 1960	
s 2(1)	16.24
Offices, Shops and Railway Premises Act 1963 (19 Statutes 570)	14.18
s 7(1)	14.29
16	14.26
17	14.19
23(1)	14.32
Policyholders Protection Act 1975 (22 Statutes 81)	
s 6	19.09
Powers of Criminal Courts Act 1973 (12 Statutes 584)	19.17
Public Health Act 1936 (35 Statutes 140)	1.05; 6.05; 12.04
Road Traffic Act 1930 (38 Statutes 104)	19.05
Road Traffic Act 1960 (38 Statutes 138)	
s 151	4.26
Road Traffic Act 1972	19.07

Table of Statutes

Road Traffic Act 1988 (38 *Statutes*
  823) 19.07
  s 143......................... 4.04
    (1)....................... 19.05
    145......................... 19.05
    149......................... 19.05
    (2)............ 4.03, 4.04, 18.12
    151......................... 19.06
    (5)....................... 19.06
    152(1), (2).................... 19.06
Safety of Sports Grounds Act 1975
  (35 *Statutes* 578) 13.19
Social Security Act 1985 (40 *Statutes*
  339)
  s 23.......................... 19.14
Social Security Act 1989 (41 *Statutes*
  429) 8.19, 8.20; 20.09
  s 22.......................... 8.20
  Sch 4 .... 8.19, 8.20
Social Security Administration Act
  1992 (40 *Statutes* 783) 7.06;
                                 8.20; 20.09
  Pt IV (ss 81-104) 8.18, 8.19, 8.20
Social Security (Consequential Provisions) Act 1992 (40 *Statutes*
  1012) 8.20
  Sch 2 .... 8.19
Social Security Contributions and
  Benefits Act 1992 (40 *Statutes*
  492)
  s 94(1)....................... 19.12
    103......................... 19.13
Suicide Act 1961 (12 *Statutes* 311)
  s 1 ....1.21; 9.25
Supreme Court Act 1981 (11 *Statutes* 966)
  s 32A........................ 7.11

Supreme Court Act 1981—*contd*
  s 35A......................... 7.13
    69(3)....................... 8.04
Third Parties (Rights Against Insurers) Act 1930 (4 *Statutes* 688)
  s 1 .... 19.10
Transport Act 1962 (36 *Statutes*
  245)
  s 43(7)....................... 4.26
Unfair Contract Terms Act 1977 (11
  Statutes 220) 4.26;
                         6.11; 16.28, 16.29,
                                 16.34; 17.06
  s 1 .... 4.26
    (1)(c) 16.24, 16.28
    (3) 5.29; 16.30
      (a) 6.11
      (b) 16.24, 16.28
    2(1) 4.26, 4.31; 5.29; 6.11;
                            14.02; 16.24; 16.28
    (2) 4.26, 4.31; 5.29; 6.11;
                                   16.28
    (3) 4.30, 4.31
    11(1)....................... 4.26
    (3) 4.31; 5.29; 16.28
    13(1)....................... 5.31
    14..................... 4.26, 16.28
Vaccine Damage Payments Act 1979
  (35 *Statutes* 632) 19.14
Waterworks Clauses Act 1847 (49
  Statutes 14) 13.16
Wills Act 1837 (50 *Statutes* 150) .. 15.18
Workmen's Compensation Act 1897: 19.11

Table of Cases

PARA

A

A M F International Ltd v Magnet Bowling Ltd [1968] 2 All ER 789, [1968] 1 WLR 1028, 112 Sol Jo 522, 66 LGR 706 .... 16.02, 16.13, 16.14, 16.15
Abbott v Isham (1920) 90 LJKB 309, 124 LT 734, 85 JP 30, 37 TLR 7, 18 LGR 719 .... 13.15
Ackbar v C F Green & Co Ltd [1975] QB 582, [1975] 2 All ER 65, [1975] 2 WLR 773, 110 Sol Jo 219, [1975] 1 Lloyd's Rep 673 .... 11.08
Addie (Robert) & Sons (Collieries) Ltd v Dumbreck [1929] AC 358, [1929] All ER Rep 1, 98 LJPC 119, 140 LT 650, 45 TLR 267, 34 Com Cas 214, HL ... 16.17, 16.32
Admiralty Comrs v SS Chekiang [1926] AC 637, [1926] All ER Rep 114, 95 LJP 119, sub nom The Chekiang 135 LT 450, 42 TLR 634, 17 Asp MLC 74, 32 Com Cas 91, HL... 10.04, 10.05
Adsett v K and L Steelfounders and Engineers Ltd [1953] 2 All ER 320, [1953] 1 WLR 773, 97 Sol Jo 419, 51 LGR 418, CA 14.30
Aitchison v Page Motors Ltd (1935) 154 LT 128, [1935] All ER Rep 594, 52 TLR 137.. 18.09, 18.22
Al-Kandari v J R Brown & Co [1987] QB 514, [1987] 2 All ER 302, [1987] 2 WLR 469, 131 Sol Jo 225, [1987] NLJ Rep 36, [1987] LS Gaz R 825; revsd [1988] QB 665, [1988] 1 All ER 833, [1988] 2 WLR 671, [1988] Fam Law 382, 132 Sol Jo 462, [1988] NLJR 62, [1988] 14 LS Gaz R 50, CA 15.18
Al Nakib Investments (Jersey) Ltd v Longcroft [1990] 3 All ER 321, [1990] 1 WLR 1390, [1991] BCLC 7, [1990] NLJR 741, [1990] 42 LS Gaz R 36 .... 5.23
Al Saudi Banque v Clark Pixley (a firm) [1990] Ch 313, [1989] 3 All ER 361, [1990] 2 WLR 344, [1990] BCLC 46, 5 BCC 822, [1990] 10 LS Gaz R 36.... 5.20
Albert v Motor Insurers' Bureau [1972] AC 301, [1971] 2 All ER 1345, [1971] 3 WLR 291, 115 Sol Jo 588, [1971] 2 Lloyd's Rep 229, [1972] RTR 230, HL : 19.07
Albrighton v Royal Prince Alfred Hospital [1980] 2 NSWLR 542, CA 18.19
Alcock v Chief Constable of South Yorkshire Police [1992] 1 AC 310, [1991] 3 WLR 1057, sub nom Jones v Wright [1991] 3 All ER 88, [1991] NLJR 635, CA; affd sub nom Alcock v Chief Constable of South Yorkshire Police [1992] 1 AC 310, [1991] 4 All ER 907, [1991] 3 WLR 1057, 136 Sol Jo LB 9, [1992] 3 LS Gaz R 34, 8 BMLR 37, HL 1.25
Alexandrou v Oxford (1990) Times, 19 February, CA 1.18
Aliakmon, The. See Leigh and Sillivan Ltd v Aliakmon Shipping Co Ltd, The Aliakmon
Allen v Aeroplane and Motor Aluminium Castings Ltd [1965] 3 All ER 377, [1965] 1 WLR 1244, 109 Sol Jo 629, CA 14.24
Allen v Bloomsbury Health Authority [1993] 1 All ER 651 .... 10.17
Allen v Sir Alfred McAlpine & Sons Ltd [1968] 2 QB 229, [1968] 1 All ER 543, [1968] 2 WLR 366, 112 Sol Jo 49, CA.................................. 11.06
Allison v Corby District Council (1979) 78 LGR 197, [1980] RTR 111, [1980] JPL 671.. 12.10
Aluminium Products Pty Ltd v Hill [1981] Qd R 33 .... 15.17, 15.18
Ancell v McDermott (1992) 137 Sol Jo LB 36, [1993] NLJR 363, [1993] 11 LS Gaz R 46, CA 1.18, 12.10
Anderson (W B) & Sons Ltd v Rhodes (Liverpool) Ltd [1967] 2 All ER 850 : 5.02, 5.06
Andrews v Freeborough [1967] 1 QB 1, [1966] 2 All ER 721, [1966] 3 WLR 342, 110 Sol Jo 407, CA.. 8.06

xxii Table of Cases

Andrews v Hopkinson [1957] 1 QB 229, [1956] 3 All ER 422, [1956] 3 WLR 732,
  100 Sol Jo 768 .... 17.07
Andros Springs (Owners) v Owners of World Beauty, The World Beauty [1969]
  P 12, [1968] 3 WLR 929, sub nom The World Beauty, Owners of Steam
  Tanker Andros Springs v Owners of Steam Tanker World Beauty [1968]
  2 All ER 673, 112 Sol Jo 879, [1968] 1 Lloyd's Rep 507; on appeal sub nom
  Andros Springs (Owners) v Owners of World Beauty, The World Beauty
  [1970] P 144, [1969] 3 WLR 110, sub nom The World Beauty, Owners of
  Steam Tanker Andros Springs v Owners of Steam Tanker World Beauty
  [1968] 3 All ER 158, 113 Sol Jo 363, [1969] 1 Lloyd's Rep 350, CA 10.08
Anns v Merton London Borough Council [1978] AC 728, [1977] 2 All ER 492,
  [1977] 2 WLR 1024, 141 JP 526, 121 Sol Jo 377, 75 LGR 555, 5 BLR 1, 243
  Estates Gazette 523, 591, [1977] JPL 514, HL 1.01, 1.03, 1.05, 1.14, 6.04,
                                                          6.05, 6.08, 12.04, 12.05,
                                                          12.10, 12.11, 12.13,
                                                          12.15, 12.19, 13.08
Arenson v Casson Beckman Rutley & Co [1977] AC 405, [1975] 3 All ER 901,
  [1975] 3 WLR 815, 119 Sol Jo 810, [1976] 1 Lloyd's Rep 179, 125 NLJ 1192,
  HL 1.13, 1.17, 5.10, 5.13
Argentino, The. See Gracie (Owners) v Argentino (Owners), The Argentino
Argy Trading Development Co Ltd v Lapid Developments Ltd [1977] 3 All ER
  785, [1977] 1 WLR 444, 120 Sol Jo 677, [1977] 1 Lloyd's Rep 67 .... 5.24
Argyll (Duchess) v Beuselinck [1972] 2 Lloyd's Rep 172.................... 15.19
Argyll (Duchess of) v Duke of Argyll [1967] Ch 302, [1965] 1 All ER 611, [1965]
  2 WLR 790 .... 13.11
Arlidge v Islington Corpn [1909] 2 KB 127, 78 LJKB 553, 100 LT 903, 73 JP
  301, 25 TLR 470, 7 LGR 649 .... 12.16
Armagas Ltd v Mundogas SA, The Ocean Frost [1986] AC 717, [1986] 2 All ER
  385, [1986] 2 WLR 1063, 130 Sol Jo 430, [1986] 2 Lloyd's Rep 109, 2 BCC 99,
  197, [1986] NLJ Rep 511, [1986] LS Gaz R 2002, HL 18.13
Ashdown v Samuel Williams & Sons Ltd [1957] 1 QB 409, [1957] 1 All ER 35,
  [1956] 3 WLR 1104, 100 Sol Jo 945, CA 16.24, 16.31
Ashmore Benson Pease & Co Ltd v A V Dawson Ltd [1973] 2 All ER 856, [1973]
  1 WLR 828, 117 Sol Jo 203, [1973] 2 Lloyd's Rep 21, [1973] RTR 473, CA .. 13.10
Ashton v Turner [1981] QB 137, [1980] 3 All ER 870, [1980] 3 WLR 736, 124 Sol
  Jo 792, [1981] RTR 54 .... 1.20, 16.20
Aslan v Clintons (1984) 134 NLJ 584 .... 15.16
Associated Provincial Picture Houses Ltd v Wednesbury Corpn [1948] 1 KB 223,
  [1947] 2 All ER 680, [1948] LJR 190, 177 LT 641, 112 JP 55, 63 TLR 623, 92
  Sol Jo 26, 45 LGR 635, CA 12.16
Aswan Engineering Establishment Co v Lupdine Ltd (Thurgar Bolle, Third
  Party) [1987] 1 All ER 135, [1987] 1 WLR 1, 130 Sol Jo 712, [1986] 2 Lloyd's
  Rep 347, [1986] BTLC 293, [1986] LS Gaz R 2661, CA 17.13, 17.22
Atkinson v Newcastle and Gateshead Waterworks Co (1877) 2 Ex D 441,
  [1874-80] All ER Rep 757, 46 LJ Ex 775, 36 LT 761, 42 JP 183, 25 WR 794,
  CA 13.02, 13.08, 13.10
Attia v British Gas plc [1988] QB 304, [1987] 3 All ER 455, [1987] 3 WLR 1101,
  131 Sol Jo 1248, [1987] BTLC 394, [1987] NLJ Rep 661, [1987] LS Gaz R
  2360, CA 1.25
A-G (on the relation of Paisley) v St Ives RDC [1960] 1 QB 312, [1959] 3 All ER
  371, [1959] 3 WLR 575, 103 Sol Jo 659; affd [1961] 1 QB 366, [1961] 1 All
  ER 265, [1961] 2 WLR 111, 125 JP 119, 105 Sol Jo 87, 59 LGR 105, CA ... 13.06
Attree v Baker (1983) Times, 18 November 9.13
Austin Rover Group Ltd v HM Inspector of Factories [1990] 1 AC 619, [1989]
  3 WLR 520, [1990] ICR 133, [1989] IRLR 404, sub nom Mailer v Austin
  Rover Group plc [1989] 2 All ER 1087, HL 14.22, 14.28
Automatic Woodturning Co Ltd v Stringer [1957] AC 544, [1957] 1 All ER 90,
  [1957] 2 WLR 203, 101 Sol Jo 106, 55 LGR 77, HL 14.22
Auty v National Coal Board [1985] 1 All ER 930, [1985] 1 WLR 784, 129 Sol Jo
  249, CA 8.10
Avery v London and North Eastern Rly Co [1938] AC 606, [1938] 2 All ER 592,
  107 LJKB 546, 159 LT 241, 54 LT 241, 54 TLR 794, 82 Sol Jo 582, 31
  BWCC 133, HL 9.21

B

B v Islington Health Authority [1991] 1 QB 638, [1991] 1 All ER 825, [1991]
2 WLR 501, [1991] 1 FLR 483, [1991] Fam Law 361; affd sub nom Burton
v Islington Health Authority [1993] QB 204, [1992] 3 All ER 833, [1992]
3 WLR 637, [1992] 2 FLR 184, [1993] Fam Law 19, [1992] NLJR 565,
[1992] 17 LS Gaz R 51, CA 1.10, 1.19
Bacon v Cooper (Metals) Ltd [1982] 1 All ER 397 .... 10.08
Badham v Lambs Ltd [1946] KB 45, [1945] 2 All ER 295, 115 LJKB 180, 173 LT
139, 61 TLR 569, 89 Sol Jo 381.. 13.02
Bagot v Stevens, Scanlan & Co Ltd [1966] 1 QB 197, [1964] 3 All ER 577, [1964]
3 WLR 1162, 108 Sol Jo 604, 2 BLR 67, [1964] 2 Lloyd's Rep 353 .... 11.29
Bailey v Barking and Havering Area Health Authority (1978) Times, 22 July.. 9.19
Bailey v Rolls Royce (1971) Ltd [1984] ICR 688, CA 14.11, 14.32
Baiona, The. See Unitramp SA v Jenson & Nicholson (S) Pte Ltd, The Baiona
Baker v Ollard and Bentley (a firm) (1982) 126 Sol Jo 593, CA 11.05
Baker v T E Hopkins & Son Ltd [1958] 3 All ER 147, [1958] 1 WLR 993, 102 Sol
Jo 636; affd [1959] 3 All ER 225, [1959] 1 WLR 966, 103 Sol Jo 812, CA ... 3.18
Baker v Willoughby [1970] AC 467, [1969] 2 All ER 549, [1969] 2 WLR 489, 113
Sol Jo 37, CA; revsd [1970] AC 467, [1969] 3 All ER 1528, [1970] 2 WLR 50,
114 Sol Jo 15, HL 7.10
Balfour v Barty-King, Hyder & Sons (Builders) Ltd, Third Parties [1957] 1 QB
496, [1957] 1 All ER 156, [1957] 2 WLR 84, 101 Sol Jo 62, [1956] 2 Lloyd's
Rep 646, 168 Estates Gazette 697, CA................................... 18.17
Ball v LCC [1949] 2 KB 159, [1949] 1 All ER 1056, 113 JP 315, 65 TLR 533, 93
Sol Jo 404, 47 LGR 591, CA 1.01, 17.02
Bank of Nova Scotia v Hellenic Mutual War Risks Association (Bermuda) Ltd,
The Good Luck [1990] 1 QB 818, [1989] 3 All ER 628, [1990] 2 WLR 547,
[1989] 2 Lloyd's Rep 238, [1990] 10 LS Gaz R 34, CA; revsd [1992] 1 AC 233,
[1991] 3 All ER 1, [1991] 2 WLR 1279, [1991] 2 Lloyd's Rep 191, [1991]
NLJR 779, HL 1.05
Banque Keyser Ullmann SA v Skandia (UK) Insurance Co Ltd [1990] 1 QB 665,
[1989] 3 WLR 25, 133 Sol Jo 817, [1988] NLJR 287, [1989] 26 LS Gaz R 33,
sub nom Banque Financière de la Cité SA v Westgate Insurance Co Ltd
[1989] 2 All ER 952, [1988] 2 Lloyd's Rep 513, CA; affd sub nom Banque
Financière de la Cité SA (formerly Banque Keyser Ullmann SA) v Westgate
Insurance Co Ltd (formerly Hodge General and Mercantile Co Ltd) [1991]
2 AC 249, [1990] 2 All ER 947, [1990] 3 WLR 364, 134 Sol Jo 1265, [1990]
2 Lloyd's Rep 377, [1990] NLJR 1074, HL 1.05, 5.22, 5.25
Barkway v South Wales Transport Co Ltd [1950] AC 185, [1950] 1 All ER 392,
114 JP 172, 66 (pt 1) TLR 597, 94 Sol Jo 128, HL 2.15, 13.13
Barnett v Chelsea and Kensington Hospital Management Committee [1969]
1 QB 428, [1968] 1 All ER 1068, [1968] 2 WLR 422, 111 Sol Jo 912 .... 2.12, 3.23
Barnett v Cohen [1921] 2 KB 461, [1921] All ER Rep 528, 90 LJKB 1307, 125 LT
733, 37 TLR 629, 19 LGR 623 .... 9.15
Barnett v H and J Packer & Co Ltd [1940] 3 All ER 575 .... 17.08
Barrett v Lounova (1982) Ltd [1990] 1 QB 348, [1989] 1 All ER 351, [1989]
2 WLR 137, 133 Sol Jo 121, 57 P & CR 216, 20 HLR 584, [1988] 2 EGLR 54,
[1988] 36 EG 184, [1989] 15 LS Gaz R 39, CA 16.39
Basildon District Council v J E Lesser (Properties) Ltd [1985] QB 839, [1985]
1 All ER 20, [1984] 3 WLR 812, 128 Sol Jo 330, 8 Con LR 89, [1984] LS Gaz
R 1437, 1 Const LJ 57 .... 4.16
Batty v Metropolitan Property Realisations Ltd [1978] QB 554, [1978] 2 All ER
445, [1978] 2 WLR 500, 122 Sol Jo 63, 245 Estates Gazette 43, 7 BLR 1, CA: 1.14,
6.04, 11.29
Baxter v F W Gapp & Co Ltd and Gapp [1939] 2 KB 271, [1939] 2 All ER 752,
108 LJKB 522, 160 LT 533, 55 TLR 739, 83 Sol Jo 436, CA 10.13, 15.22
Beach v Reed Corrugated Cases Ltd [1956] 2 All ER 652, [1956] 1 WLR 807, 100
Sol Jo 472, [1956] TR 215, 35 ATC 126, 49 R & IT 757................... 8.21
Beaman v ARTS Ltd [1949] 1 KB 550, [1949] 1 All ER 465, 65 TLR 389, 93 Sol
Jo 236, CA 11.22
Beard v London General Omnibus Co [1900] 2 QB 530, [1900-3] All ER Rep 112,
69 LJQB 895, 83 LT 362, 48 WR 658, 16 TLR 499, CA 18.10

xxiv Table of Cases

Beddall v Maitland (1881) 17 Ch D 174, [1881-5] All ER Rep Ext 1812, 50 LJ Ch
  401, 44 LT 248, 29 WR 484 .... 13.02
Behrens v Bertram Mills Circus Ltd [1957] 2 QB 1, [1957] 1 All ER 583, [1957]
  2 WLR 404, 101 Sol Jo 208 .... 9.07
Bell v Department of Health and Social Security (1989) Times, 13 June 14.26
Bell v Peter Browne & Co [1990] 2 QB 495, [1990] 3 All ER 124, [1990] 3 WLR
  510, [1990] NLJR 701, CA 11.05, 11.29, 15.15, 15.17, 15.18
Bell-Booth Group Ltd v A-G [1989] 3 NZLR 148 .... 5.19
Benham v Gambling [1941] AC 157, [1941] 1 All ER 7, 110 LJKB 49, 164 LT
  290, 57 TLR 177, 84 Sol Jo 703, HL 8.02, 9.27
Benn v Kamm & Co Ltd [1952] 2 QB 127, [1952] 1 All ER 833, [1952] 1 TLR 873,
  CA 14.22
Bennett v Rylands Whitecross Ltd [1978] ICR 1031 .... 14.28
Bennett v Tugwell [1971] 2 QB 267, [1971] 2 All ER 248, [1971] 2 WLR 847, 115
  Sol Jo 289, [1971] 1 Lloyd's Rep 333, [1971] RTR 221 .... 4.02, 4.04, 4.05, 4.29
Benson v Biggs Wall & Co Ltd [1982] 3 All ER 300, [1983] 1 WLR 72n 9.21
Berrill v Road Haulage Executive [1952] 2 Lloyd's Rep 490 .... 10.04
Best v Samuel Fox & Co Ltd [1952] AC 716, [1952] 2 All ER 394, [1952] 2 TLR
  246, 96 Sol Jo 494, HL 6.27
Bhoomidas v Port of Singapore Authority [1978] 1 All ER 956, [1978] 1 WLR 189,
  121 Sol Jo 816, [1978] 1 Lloyd's Rep 330, PC 18.06
Billings (A C) & Sons Ltd v Riden [1958] AC 240, [1957] 3 All ER 1, [1957] 3
  WLR 496, 101 Sol Jo 645, HL 16.10, 16.34
Bird v Pearce (Somerset County Council third party) (1978) 76 LGR 597, [1978]
  RTR 290; affd (1979) 77 LGR 753, [1979] RTR 369, CA 12.10, 12.11
Birkett v Hayes [1982] 2 All ER 710, [1982] 1 WLR 816, 126 Sol Jo 399, CA ... 7.13
Birkett v James [1978] AC 297, [1977] 2 All ER 801, [1977] 3 WLR 38, 121 Sol
  Jo 444, HL 11.06
Birmingham Corpn v Sowsbery (1969) 113 Sol Jo 877, 67 LGR 600, [1970] RTR
  84 .... 10.04
Birmingham Corpn v West Midland Baptist (Trust) Association Inc [1970] AC
  874, [1969] 3 All ER 172, [1969] 3 WLR 389, 133 JP 524, 113 Sol Jo 606, 67
  LGR 571, 20 P & CR 1052, 211 Estates Gazette 527, 629, HL 10.14
Black v Carricks (Caterers) [1980] IRLR 448, CA 14.32
Black v Fife Coal Co Ltd. See Butler (or Black) v Fife Coal Co Ltd
Bloomstein v Railway Executive [1952] 2 All ER 418, 96 Sol Jo 496 .... 16.13
Blyth v Bloomsbury Health Authority (1987) Times, 11 February, CA 15.11
Bohdal v Streets [1984] Tas R 82 .... 3.19
Bolam v Friern Hospital Management Committee [1957] 2 All ER 118, [1957]
  1 WLR 582, 101 Sol Jo 357 .... 2.09, 15.01, 15.07, 15.09, 15.10
Bolton v Puley (1982) 267 Estates Gazette 1160 .... 10.12, 10.16
Bolton v Stone [1951] AC 850, [1951] 1 All ER 1078, [1951] 1 TLR 977, 95 Sol
  Jo 333, 59 LGR 32, HL 2.04, 12.08
Bonnington Castings Ltd v Wardlaw [1956] AC 613, [1956] 1 All ER 615, [1956]
  2 WLR 707, 100 Sol Jo 207, 54 LGR 153, 1956 SC (HL) 26, 1956 SLT 135 : 2.13, 14.35
Booth & Co (International) Ltd v National Enterprise Board [1978] 3 All ER
  624 .... 13.12
Boothman v British Northrop (1972) 13 KIR 112, CA 4.08
Bottomley v Bannister [1932] 1 KB 458, [1931] All ER Rep 99, 101 LJKB 46,
  146 LT 68, 48 TLR 39, CA...................................... 1.14
Bourgoin SA v Ministry of Agriculture, Fisheries and Food [1986] QB 716,
  [1985] 3 All ER 585, [1985] 3 WLR 1027, [1985] 1 CMLR 528; on appeal
  [1986] QB 716, [1985] 3 All ER 585, [1985] 3 WLR 1027, [1986] 1 CMLR
  267, 129 Sol Jo 828, [1985] LS Gaz R 3534, CA................... 12.15, 12.16
Bourhill v Young. See Hay (or Bourhill) v Young
Bovenzi v Kettering Health Authority [1991] 2 Med LR 293 .... 15.05
Bowen v Paramount Builders (Hamilton) Ltd [1977] 1 NZLR 394 .... 6.04
Bowes v Sedgefield District Council [1981] ICR 234, 125 Sol Jo 80, CA 14.28
Box v Midland Bank Ltd [1979] 2 Lloyd's Rep 391; revsd [1981] 1 Lloyd's Rep
  434, CA 5.28
Boyle v Kodak Ltd [1969] 2 All ER 439, [1969] 1 WLR 661, 113 Sol Jo 382, HL : 13.03,
                                                                            13.17

Bradburn v Great Western Rly Co (1874) LR 10 Exch 1, [1874-80] All ER Rep
    195, 44 LJ Ex 9, 31 LT 464, 23 WR 48 .... 8.17
Bradford v Robinson Rentals Ltd [1967] 1 All ER 267, [1967] 1 WLR 337, 111
    Sol Jo 33 .... 3.09
Bradley v Eagle Star Insurance Co Ltd [1989] AC 957, [1989] 1 All ER 961,
    [1989] 2 WLR 568, [1989] ICR 301, 133 Sol Jo 359, [1989] 1 Lloyd's Rep 465,
    [1989] BCLC 469, [1989] NLJR 330, [1989] 17 LS Gaz R 38, HL 19.10
Braham v J Lyons & Co Ltd [1962] 3 All ER 281, [1962] 1 WLR 1048, 106 Sol Jo
    588, 60 LGR 453, CA 14.28
Brew Bros Ltd v Snax (Ross) Ltd [1970] 1 QB 612, [1970] 1 All ER 587, [1969]
    3 WLR 657, 113 Sol Jo 795, 20 P & CR 829, CA 1.14
Brice v Brown [1984] 1 All ER 997, 134 NLJ 204 .... 3.10
British Celanese Ltd v A H Hunt (Capacitors) Ltd [1969] 2 All ER 1252, [1969]
    1 WLR 959, 113 Sol Jo 368 .... 6.12
British Railways Board v Herrington [1972] AC 877, [1972] 1 All ER 749, [1972]
    2 WLR 537, 116 Sol Jo 178, 223 Estates Gazette 939, HL 1.09, 16.07, 16.17,
                                                              16.32, 16.33, 16.36
British School of Motoring Ltd v Simms [1971] 1 All ER 317, 135 JP 103, [1971]
    RTR 190 .... 4.08
British Transport Commission v Gourley [1956] AC 185, [1955] 3 All ER 796,
    [1956] 2 WLR 41, 100 Sol Jo 12, [1955] 2 Lloyd's Rep 475, [1955] TR 303, 34
    ATC 305, 49 R & IT 11, HL 8.21
Brooke v Bool [1928] 2 KB 578, [1928] All ER Rep 155, 97 LJKB 511, 139 LT
    376, 44 TLR 531, 72 Sol Jo 354, DC 18.17
Brooks v J and P Coates (UK) Ltd [1984] 1 All ER 702, [1984] ICR 158 .. 11.19, 14.29,
                                                                          14.30
Broom v Morgan [1953] 1 QB 597, [1953] 1 All ER 849, [1953] 2 WLR 737, 97
    Sol Jo 247, CA 18.02
Brown v Allied Ironfounders Ltd [1974] 2 All ER 135, [1974] 1 WLR 527, 118 Sol
    Jo 294, HL 14.32
Browning v War Office [1963] 1 QB 750, [1962] 3 All ER 1089, [1963] 2 WLR 52,
    106 Sol Jo 957, [1962] 2 Lloyd's Rep 363, CA 8.17
Bryanston Finance Ltd v de Vries [1975] QB 703, [1975] 2 All ER 609, [1975]
    2 WLR 718, 119 Sol Jo 287, CA 4.18
Buchan v Ortho Pharmaceutical (Canada) Ltd (1984) 46 OR (2d) 113, 8 DLR
    (4th) 373; affd (1986) 54 OR (2d) 92, 25 DLR (4th) 658, CA 2.05
Buck v English Electric Co Ltd [1978] 1 All ER 271, [1977] 1 WLR 806, [1977]
    ICR 629, 121 Sol Jo 13 .... 11.11, 11.18, 11.19
Buckland v Guildford Gas Light and Coke Co [1949] 1 KB 410, [1948] 2 All ER
    1086, 113 JP 44, 93 Sol Jo 41, 47 LGR 75 .... 16.33
Buckley v John Allen and Ford (Oxford) Ltd [1967] 2 QB 637, [1967] 1 All ER
    539, [1967] 2 WLR 759, 111 Sol Jo 136 .... 9.18
Buckpitt v Oates [1968] 1 All ER 1145 .... 4.04
Budden v BP Oil Ltd (1980) 124 Sol Jo 376, [1980] JPL 586, 130 NLJ 603, CA : 1.23
Burfitt v A and E Kille [1939] 2 KB 743, [1939] 2 All ER 372, 108 LJKB 669,
    160 LT 481, 55 TLR 645, 83 Sol Jo 419, 37 LGR 394 .... 17.02
Burgess v Florence Nightingale Hospital For Gentlewomen [1955] 1 QB 349,
    [1955] 1 All ER 511, [1955] 2 WLR 533, 99 Sol Jo 170 .... 9.07, 9.08
Burnett v British Waterways Board [1973] 2 All ER 631, [1973] 1 WLR 700,
    117 Sol Jo 203, [1973] 2 Lloyd's Rep 137, CA 4.02, 16.25
Burns v Edman [1970] 2 QB 541, [1970] 1 All ER 886, [1970] 2 WLR 1005, 114
    Sol Jo 356, [1970] 1 Lloyd's Rep 137 .... 1.20, 7.03, 9.15, 9.25, 9.29
Burns v Joseph Terry & Sons Ltd [1951] 1 KB 454, [1950] 2 All ER 987, 114 JP
    613, [1951] 1 TLR 349, 94 Sol Jo 837, 49 LGR 161, CA 14.21
Burns v MAN Automotive (1987) 61 ALJR 81 .... 3.12
Burton v Islington Health Authority. See B v Islington Health Authority
Butler (or Black) v Fife Coal Co Ltd [1912] AC 149, [1911-13] All ER Rep Ext
    1221, 81 LJPC 97, 106 LT 161, 28 TLR 150, 5 BWCC 217, HL 13.10
Bux v Slough Metals Ltd [1974] 1 All ER 262, [1973] 1 WLR 1358, 117 Sol Jo
    615, [1974] 1 Lloyd's Rep 155, CA 14.06, 14.38
Buxton v North Eastern Rly Co (1868) LR 3 QB 549, 9 B & S 824, 37 LJQB 258,
    18 LT 795, 32 JP 661, 16 WR 1124 .... 13.07

xxvi *Table of Cases*

C

CBS Songs Ltd v Amstrad Consumer Electronics plc [1988] Ch 61, [1987] 3 All
  ER 151, [1987] 3 WLR 144, 131 Sol Jo 534, [1987] RPC 429, [1987] LS Gaz
  R 1243, CA; affd [1988] AC 1013, [1988] 2 All ER 484, [1988] 2 WLR 1191,
  132 Sol Jo 789, [1988] RPC 567, HL 13.01, 13.02
Cakebread v Hopping Bros (Whetstone) Ltd [1947] KB 641, [1947] 1 All ER 389,
  [1948] LJR 361, 177 LT 92, 63 TLR 277, 91 Sol Jo 219, CA 13.17
Callow (F E) (Engineers) Ltd v Johnson [1971] AC 335, [1970] 3 All ER 639,
  [1970] 3 WLR 982, 114 Sol Jo 846, HL 14.19, 14.23, 14.24
Caltex Oil (Australia) Pty Ltd v Dredge Willemstad (1976) 136 CLR 529, 51
  ALJR 270, 11 ALR 227 .... 5.03, 6.04, 6.13, 6.16
Canadian National Rly Co v Norsk Pacific SS Co (1992) 91 DLR (4th) 289 .. 6.13, 6.21
Canadian Pacific Rly Co v Lockhart [1942] AC 591, [1942] 2 All ER 464, 111
  LJPC 113, 167 LT 231, PC 18.12
Canadian Pacific Steamships Ltd v Bryers [1958] AC 485, [1957] 3 All ER 572,
  [1957] 3 WLR 993, 101 Sol Jo 957, [1957] 2 Lloyd's Rep 387, HL.......... 13.06
Candler v Crane Christmas & Co [1951] 2 KB 164, [1951] 1 All ER 426, [1951]
  1 TLR 371, 95 Sol Jo 171, CA 5.16, 5.20, 5.23
Candlewood Navigation Corpn Ltd v Mitsui OSK Lines Ltd, The Mineral Transporter, The Ibaraki Maru [1986] AC 1, [1985] 2 All ER 935, [1985] 3 WLR
  381, 129 Sol Jo 506, [1985] 2 Lloyd's Rep 303, PC 1.02, 1.03, 5.21,
                                                              6.04, 6.12, 6.14
Caparo Industries plc v Dickman [1989] QB 653, [1989] 1 All ER 798, [1989] 2
  WLR 316, 133 Sol Jo 221, [1989] BCLC 154, 4 BCC 144, [1988] NLJR 289,
  [1989] 11 LS Gaz R 44, CA; on appeal [1990] 2 AC 605, [1990] 1 All ER 568,
  [1990] 2 WLR 358, 134 Sol Jo 494, [1990] BCLC 273, [1990] BCC 164, [1990]
  NLJR 248, [1990] 12 LS Gaz R 42, HL 1.02, 1.03, 1.07, 1.08, 1.10, 5.01, 5.02,
                                                5.03, 5.17, 5.20, 5.21, 5.23, 15.26
Capps v Miller [1989] 2 All ER 333, [1989] 1 WLR 839, [1989] RTR 312, CA ... 4.12
Carberry v Davies [1968] 2 All ER 817, [1968] 1 WLR 1103, 112 Sol Jo 445, CA: 18.25
Carmarthenshire County Council v Lewis [1955] AC 549, [1955] 1 All ER 565,
  [1955] 2 WLR 517, 119 JP 230, 99 Sol Jo 167, 53 LGR 230, HL .. 1.06, 3.19, 12.05
Carradine Properties Ltd v D J Freeman & Co (1982) 1 PN 41, 126 Sol Jo 157,
  CA... 15.16
Carroll v Andrew Barclay & Sons Ltd [1948] AC 477, [1948] 2 All ER 386,
  [1948] LJR 1490, 64 TLR 384, 92 Sol Jo 555, HL 14.21
Carslogie SS Co Ltd v Royal Norwegian Government [1952] AC 292, [1952]
  1 All ER 20, [1951] 2 TLR 1099, 95 Sol Jo 801, [1951] 2 Lloyd's Rep 441, HL: 10.05
Cartledge v E Jopling & Sons Ltd [1963] AC 758, [1963] 1 All ER 341, [1963]
  2 WLR 210, 107 Sol Jo 73, [1963] 1 Lloyd's Rep 1, HL 11.05, 11.08
Cartwright v GKN Sankey Ltd (1972) 12 KIR 453, 116 Sol Jo 433, [1972]
  2 Lloyd's Rep 242, 122 NLJ 450; revsd (1973) 14 KIR 349, CA 14.29, 14.30
Cassidy v Ministry of Health [1951] 2 KB 343, [1951] 1 All ER 574, [1951] 1
  TLR 539, 95 Sol Jo 253, CA 15.05, 18.03, 18.19
Caswell v Powell Duffryn Associated Collieries Ltd [1940] AC 152, [1939] 3 All
  ER 722, 108 LJKB 779, 161 LT 374, 55 TLR 1004, 83 Sol Jo 976, HL...... 13.17
Caswell v Worth (1856) 5 E & B 849, 26 LTOS 216, 20 JP 54, 2 Jur NS 116,
  4 WR 231, 119 ER 697, sub nom Casswell v Worth 25 LJQB 121 .... 13.10
Cattle v Stockton Waterworks Co (1875) LR 10 QB 453, [1874-80] All ER Rep
  220, 44 LJQB 139, 33 LT 475, 30 JP Jo 791 .... 6.01, 6.12
Cavalier v Pope [1906] AC 428, 75 LJKB 609, 95 LT 65, 22 TLR 648, 50 Sol Jo
  575, HL 1.14
Cavanagh v Bristol and Weston Health Authority [1992] 3 Med LR 49 .... 15.07
Cavanagh v Ulster Weaving Co Ltd [1960] AC 145, [1959] 2 All ER 745, [1959]
  3 WLR 262, 103 Sol Jo 581, [1959] 2 Lloyd's Rep 165, HL 2.09, 14.07, 15.07
Central Asbestos Co Ltd v Dodd. See Smith v Central Asbestos Co Ltd
Century Insurance Co Ltd v Northern Ireland Road Tranport Board [1942] AC
  509, [1942] 1 All ER 491, 111 LJPC 138, 167 LT 404, HL 18.09
Chadwick v British Transport Commission (or British Railways Board) [1967]
  2 All ER 945, [1967] 1 WLR 912, 111 Sol Jo 562...................... 1.25
Chambers v Goldthorpe [1901] 1 KB 624, [1900-3] All ER Rep 969, 70 LJKB
  482, 84 LT 444, 49 WR 401, 17 TLR 304, 45 Sol Jo 325, CA 5.13

Chan Wai Tong v Li Ping Sum [1985] AC 446, [1985] 2 WLR 396, 129 Sol Jo
  153, PC 8.12
Chandler v DPP [1964] AC 763, [1962] 3 All ER 142, [1962] 3 WLR 694, 106 Sol
  Jo 588, 46 Cr App Rep 347, HL 1.09
Chappell v Cooper [1980] 2 All ER 463, [1980] 1 WLR 958, 124 Sol Jo 544, CA   11.06,
  11.17
Charlton v Forrest Printing Ink Co Ltd [1980] IRLR 331, CA 1.24
Chatterton v Gerson [1981] QB 432, [1981] 1 All ER 257, [1980] 3 WLR 1003,
  124 Sol Jo 885 .... 15.10
Chaudhry v Prabhakar [1988] 3 All ER 718, [1989] 1 WLR 29, 133 Sol Jo 82,
  [1988] NLJR 172, [1989] 6 LS Gaz R 44, CA 5.14
Cherry Ltd v Allied Insurance Brokers Ltd [1978] 1 Lloyd's Rep 274 .... 5.24
Chester v Waverley Municipal Council (1939) 62 CLR 1 .... 1.25
Chin Keow v Government of Malaysia [1967] 1 WLR 813, 111 Sol Jo 333, PC .. 15.01
Ching v Surrey County Council [1910] 1 KB 736, 79 LJKB 481, 102 LT 414, 74
  JP 187, 26 TLR 355, 54 Sol Jo 360, 8 LGR 369, CA 13.15
Chipchase v British Titan Products Co Ltd [1956] 1 QB 545, [1956] 1 All ER
  613, [1956] 2 WLR 677, 100 Sol Jo 186, 54 LGR 212, CA 14.39
Chowdhary v Gillot [1947] 2 All ER 541, [1947] WN 267, 63 TLR 569 .... 18.22
Christchurch Drainage Board v Brown (1987) Times, 26 October, PC 1.05
Clark v MacLennan [1983] 1 All ER 416 .... 15.07
Clark v Woor [1965] 2 All ER 353, [1965] 1 WLR 650, 109 Sol Jo 251 .... 10.14
Clarke v Bruce Lance & Co (a firm) [1988] 1 All ER 364, [1988] 1 WLR 881, 131
  Sol Jo 1698, [1987] NLJ Rep 1064, [1988] 2 LS Gaz R 37, CA 15.18
Clay v A J Crump & Sons Ltd [1964] 1 QB 533, [1963] 3 All ER 687, [1963]
  3 WLR 866, 107 Sol Jo 664, 4 BLR 80, CA 15.24
Clayton v Woodman & Son (Builders) Ltd [1962] 2 QB 533, [1961] 3 All ER 249,
  [1961] 3 WLR 987, 105 Sol Jo 889; revsd [1962] 2 QB 533, [1962] 2 All ER
  33, [1962] 1 WLR 585, 106 Sol Jo 242, 4 BLR 65, CA 5.01, 15.24
Clegg, Parkinson & Co v Earby Gas Co [1896] 1 QB 592, 65 LJQB 339, 44 WR 606,
  12 TLR 241 .... 13.06, 13.08
Clifford v Charles H Challen & Son Ltd [1951] 1 KB 495, [1951] 1 All ER 72,
  [1951] 1 TLR 234, 95 Sol Jo 119, CA 14.05
Clippens Oil Co Ltd v Edinburgh and District Water Trustees [1907] AC 291,
  76 LJPC 79, 1907 SC (HL) 9, 44 SLR 669, 15 SLT 92 .... 3.12
Close v Steel Co of Wales Ltd [1962] AC 367, [1961] 2 All ER 953, [1961] 3 WLR
  319, 105 Sol Jo 586, 59 LGR 439, HL................................... 14.23
Clough v Bussan (West Yorkshire Police Authority, third party) [1990] 1 All ER
  431, [1990] RTR 178 .... 1.05, 1.17, 1.24
Cocks v Thanet District Council [1983] 2 AC 286, [1982] 3 All ER 1135, [1982]
  3 WLR 1121, 126 Sol Jo 820, 81 LGR 81, 6 HLR 15, [1984] RVR 31, HL.... 13.12
Coddington v International Harvesters of Great Britain Ltd (1969) 113 Sol Jo
  265, 6 KIR 146 .... 14.12
Coenen v Payne [1974] 2 All ER 1109, [1974] 1 WLR 984, 118 Sol Jo 499, [1974]
  2 Lloyd's Rep 270, CA 7.12
Colledge v Bass Mitchells & Butlers Ltd [1988] 1 All ER 536, [1988] ICR 125,
  [1988] IRLR 163, CA 8.20
Collier v Anglian Water Authority (1983) Times, 26 March, CA 16.03
Collins v Hertfordshire County Council [1947] KB 598, [1947] 1 All ER 633,
  [1947] LJR 789, 176 LT 456, 111 JP 272, 63 TLR 317, 45 LGR 263 ... 15.05, 15.08
Coltman v Bibby Tankers Ltd, The Derbyshire [1988] AC 276, [1987] 3 All ER
  1068, [1987] 3 WLR 1181, [1988] ICR 67, 131 Sol Jo 1658, [1988] 1 Lloyd's
  Rep 109, 1 S & B AvR I/165, [1987] NLJ Rep 1157, [1988] 3 LS Gaz R 36,
  HL.. 14.13
Colvilles Ltd v Devine [1969] 2 All ER 53, [1969] 1 WLR 475, 113 Sol Jo 287,
  1969 SC (HL) 67 .... 2.16, 2.17
Commercial Banking Co of Sydney v R H Brown & Co [1972] 2 Lloyd's Rep 360
  (Aust HC) 5.01, 5.28
Commerford v Board of School Comrs of Halifax [1950] 2 DLR 207 .... 13.06
Condo v South Australia (1987) 47 SASR 584 .... 14.13
Condon v Basi [1985] 2 All ER 453, [1985] 1 WLR 866, 129 Sol Jo 382, [1985]
  NLJ Rep 485, CA... 2.11, 4.06
Conley v Strain [1988] IR 628 .... 3.23

xxviii *Table of Cases*

Connolly v Camden and Islington Area Health Authority [1981] 3 All ER 250..	8.16
Conry v Simpson [1983] 3 All ER 369, CA	11.18
Conway v George Wimpey & Co Ltd [1951] 2 KB 266, [1951] 1 All ER 363, [1951] 1 TLR 587, 95 Sol Jo 156, CA	18.12
Cook v Consolidated Fisheries Ltd [1977] ICR 635, CA	8.12
Cook v Cook (1986) 162 CLR 376, 68 ALR 353 (Aust HC)	2.01, 4.06
Cook v Square D Ltd [1992] ICR 262, sub nom Square D Ltd v Cook [1992] IRLR 34, CA	14.16
Cooke v Midland Great Western Rly of Ireland [1909] AC 229, [1908-10] All ER Rep 16, 78 LJPC 76, 100 LT 626, 25 TLR 375, 53 Sol Jo 319, HL	16.07
Cookson v Knowles [1977] QB 913, [1977] 2 All ER 820, [1977] 3 WLR 279, 121 Sol Jo 461, CA; affd [1979] AC 556, [1978] 2 All ER 604, [1978] 2 WLR 978, 122 Sol Jo 386, [1978] 2 Lloyd's Rep 315, HL	7.13, 9.09, 9.11, 9.13, 9.14, 9.20
Cooper v Firth Brown Ltd [1963] 2 All ER 31, [1963] 1 WLR 418, 107 Sol Jo 295	8.21
Cooper v Motor Insurers' Bureau [1985] QB 575, [1985] 1 All ER 449, [1985] 2 WLR 248, 129 Sol Jo 32, [1985] RTR 273, [1985] FLR 175, [1985] LS Gaz R 202, CA	19.05, 19.07
Corbett v Barking, Havering and Brentwood Health Authority [1991] 2 QB 408, [1991] 1 All ER 498, [1990] 3 WLR 1037, 134 Sol Jo 1337, [1990] 43 LS Gaz R 32, CA	9.13, 9.15, 9.19, 9.20
Corisand Investments Ltd v Druce & Co (1978) 248 Estates Gazette 315, 407, 504, [1978] EGD 769	15.21
Corvi v Ellis 1969 SLT 350	4.20
Cotic v Gray (1981) 33 OR (2d) 356, 124 DLR (3d) 641	3.10, 3.17
Couch v Steel (1854) 3 E & B 402, 23 LJQB 121, 22 LTOS 271, 18 Jur 515, 2 WR 170, 2 CLR 940	13.02, 13.10, 13.13
County Personnel (Employment Agency) Ltd v Alan R Pulver & Co [1987] 1 All ER 289, [1987] 1 WLR 916, 131 Sol Jo 474, [1986] 2 EGLR 246, [1986] NLJ Rep 1138, [1987] LS Gaz R 1409, CA	10.17, 15.15, 15.16
Cowley v Newmarket Local Board [1892] AC 345, 62 LJQB 65, 67 LT 486, 56 JP 805, 8 TLR 788, 1 R 45, HL	13.02
Cox v H C B Angus Ltd [1981] ICR 683	14.27
Creed v John McGeoch & Sons Ltd [1955] 3 All ER 123, [1955] 1 WLR 1005, 99 Sol Jo 563	16.33
Cresswell v Eaton [1991] 1 All ER 484, [1991] 1 WLR 1113	9.19
Croke (a minor) v Wiseman [1981] 3 All ER 852, [1982] 1 WLR 71, 125 Sol Jo 726, CA	8.05, 8.13, 8.27
Crook v Derbyshire Stone Ltd [1956] 2 All ER 447, [1956] 1 WLR 432, 100 Sol Jo 302	18.11
Crookall v Vickers-Armstrong Ltd [1955] 2 All ER 12, [1955] 1 WLR 659, 99 Sol Jo 401, 53 LGR 407	14.31
Crossan v Ward Bracewell [1986] NLJ Rep 849	15.15
Crossley v Rawlinson [1981] 3 All ER 674, [1982] 1 WLR 369, 125 Sol Jo 865, [1982] RTR 442	3.18
Cuckmere Brick Co Ltd v Mutual Finance Ltd [1971] Ch 949, [1971] 2 All ER 633, [1971] 2 WLR 1207, 115 Sol Jo 288, 22 P & CR 624, [1971] RVR 126, CA	15.23
Cummings (or McWilliams) v Sir William Arrol & Co Ltd [1962] 1 All ER 623, [1962] 1 WLR 295, 106 Sol Jo 218, 1962 SC 70, 1962 SLT 121, HL	14.33
Cunningham v Harrison [1973] QB 942, [1973] 3 All ER 463, [1973] 3 WLR 97, 117 Sol Jo 547, CA	8.17, 8.23, 8.24, 8.27
Curran v Northern Ireland Co-ownership Housing Association Ltd [1987] AC 718, [1987] 2 All ER 13, [1987] 2 WLR 1043, 131 Sol Jo 506, 19 HLR 318, [1987] NLJ Rep 361, [1987] LS Gaz R 1574, HL	1.02, 1.03, 1.05, 12.13
Curwen v James [1963] 2 All ER 619, [1963] 1 WLR 748, 107 Sol Jo 314, CA:	7.10, 9.18
Cusack v Heath [1950] QWN 16, 44 QJP 88	10.08
Cutler v McPhail [1962] 2 QB 292, [1962] 2 All ER 474, [1962] 2 WLR 1135, 106 Sol Jo 391	4.18
Cutler v United Dairies (London) Ltd [1933] 2 KB 297, [1933] All ER Rep 594, 102 LJKB 663, 149 LT 436, CA	3.18
Cutler v Vauxhall Motors Ltd [1971] 1 QB 418, [1970] 2 All ER 56, [1970] 2 WLR 961, 114 Sol Jo 247, CA	7.02

Cutler v Wandsworth Stadium Ltd [1949] AC 398, [1949] 1 All ER 544, [1949]
LJR 824, 65 TLR 170, 93 Sol Jo 163, HL 13.02, 13.11, 13.13, 13.19

D

D & F Estates Ltd v Church Comrs for England [1989] AC 177, [1988] 2 All ER
992, [1988] 3 WLR 368, 132 Sol Jo 1092, 41 BLR 1, 15 Con LR 35, [1988]
2 EGLR 262, [1988] NLJR 210, HL 1.14, 1.22, 6.07, 6.08, 6.10,
6.13, 11.23, 11.25, 17.26
Daily Office Cleaning Contractors v Shefford [1977] RTR 361 .... 10.06
Dairy Farmers Co-operative Ltd v Azar (1990) 95 ALR 1 (Aust HC) 14.23
Daish v Wauton [1972] 2 QB 262, [1972] 1 All ER 25, [1972] 2 WLR 29, 115 Sol
Jo 891, CA 8.25
Dale v British Coal Corpn (No 2) (1992) 136 Sol Jo LB 199, CA 11.19
Daly v General Steam Navigation Co Ltd, The Dragon [1980] 3 All ER 696,
[1981] 1 WLR 120, 125 Sol Jo 100, [1980] 2 Lloyd's Rep 415, CA 7.03
Daniels v Ford Motor Co Ltd [1955] 1 All ER 218, [1955] 1 WLR 76, 99 Sol Jo
74, 53 LGR 171, CA 14.33
Daniels v Vaux [1938] 2 KB 203, [1938] 2 All ER 271, 107 LJKB 494, 159 LT
459, 54 TLR 621, 82 Sol Jo 335 .... 13.05
Daniels and Daniels v R White & Sons Ltd and Tarbard [1938] 4 All ER 258,
160 LT 128, 82 Sol Jo 912 .... 2.17, 17.11
Dann v Hamilton [1939] 1 KB 509, [1939] 1 All ER 59, 108 LJKB 255, 160 LT
433, 55 TLR 297, 83 Sol Jo 155 .... 4.02, 4.04
Darbishire v Warran [1963] 3 All ER 310, [1963] 1 WLR 1067, 107 Sol Jo 631,
[1963] 2 Lloyd's Rep 187, CA 10.02
Darley Main Colliery Co v Mitchell (1886) 11 App Cas 127, [1886-90] All ER Rep
449, 55 LJQB 529, 54 LT 882, 51 JP 148, 2 TLR 301, HL 11.05
David v Toronto Transit Commission (1977) 77 DLR (3d) 717 .... 3.23
Davie v New Merton Board Mills Ltd [1959] AC 604, [1959] 1 All ER 346, [1959]
2 WLR 331, 103 Sol Jo 177, HL 14.01, 14.13, 14.15
Davies v British Insulated Callender's Cables Ltd (1977) 121 Sol Jo 203 .... 11.19
Davies v Powell Duffryn Associated Collieries Ltd [1942] AC 601, [1942] 1 All
ER 657, 111 LJKB 418, 167 LT 74, 58 TLR 240, 86 Sol Jo 294, HL 9.22
Davies v Swan Motor Co (Swansea) Ltd [1949] 2 KB 291, [1949] 1 All ER 620,
65 TLR 278, CA 4.09
Davies v Taylor [1974] AC 207, [1972] 3 All ER 836, [1972] 3 WLR 801, 116 Sol
Jo 864, HL 9.15
Davies v Whiteways Cyder Co Ltd [1975] QB 262, [1974] 3 All ER 168, [1974] 3
WLR 597, 118 Sol Jo 792, [1974] 2 Lloyd's Rep 556, [1974] STC 411, [1974]
TR 177, 53 ATC 180 .... 9.07
Davis v City and Hackney Health Authority [1989] 2 Med LR 366 .... 11.13
Davis v Foots [1940] 1 KB 116, [1939] 4 All ER 4, 109 LJKB 385, 56 TLR 54, 83
Sol Jo 780, CA 1.14
Davis v Radcliffe [1990] 2 All ER 536, [1990] 1 WLR 821, 134 Sol Jo 862, 1078,
[1990] BCLC 647, [1990] 19 LS Gaz R 43, PC 1.17, 12.12, 12.20
Davis v St Mary's Demolition and Excavation Co Ltd [1954] 1 All ER 578, [1954]
1 WLR 592, 98 Sol Jo 217 .... 16.33
Davis v Saltenpar (1983) 133 NLJ 720 .... 11.19
Dawrant v Nutt [1960] 3 All ER 681, [1961] 1 WLR 253, 105 Sol Jo 129 ...... 4.13
Dawson & Co v Bingley UDC [1911] 2 KB 149, [1911-13] All ER Rep 596, 80
LJKB 842, 104 LT 629, 75 JP 289, 27 TLR 308, 55 Sol Jo 346, 9 LGR 502,
CA 13.02
Deerness v John R Keeble & Son (Brantham) Ltd [1983] 2 Lloyd's Rep 260,
[1983] Com LR 221, 133 NLJ 641, HL 11.06
De Meza and Stuart v Apple, Van Straten, Shena and Stone [1974] 1 Lloyd's
Rep 508; affd [1975] 1 Lloyd's Rep 498, CA 4.16
Denham v Midland Employers' Mutual Assurance Ltd [1955] 2 QB 437, [1955]
2 All ER 561, [1955] 3 WLR 84, 99 Sol Jo 417, [1955] 1 Lloyd's Rep 467, CA: 18.06
Dennis v Charnwood Borough Council [1983] QB 409, [1982] 3 All ER 486,
[1982] 3 WLR 1064, 126 Sol Jo 730, 81 LGR 275, 264 Estates Gazette 442,
[1983] LS Gaz R 35, CA 6.04

Denny v Supplies and Transport Co Ltd [1950] 2 KB 374, 66 (pt 1) TLR 1168, 94
Sol Jo 403, CA 17.09
Department of Health and Social Security v Kinnear (1984) 134 NLJ 886: 12.10, 15.08
Department of the Environment v Thomas Bates & Son Ltd [1991] 1 AC 499,
[1990] 2 All ER 943, [1990] 3 WLR 457, 50 BLR 61, 21 Con LR 54, 134 Sol
Jo 1077, [1990] 2 EGLR 154, [1990] 46 EG 115, HL 1.14, 6.07
Department of Transport v Chris Smaller (Transport) Ltd [1989] AC 1197,
[1989] 1 All ER 897, [1989] 2 WLR 578, 133 Sol Jo 361, [1989] NLJR 363,
[1989] 15 LS Gaz R 40, HL 11.06, 11.07
Derbyshire, The. See Coltman v Bibby Tankers Ltd, The Derbyshire
Derry v Peek (1889) 14 App Cas 337, [1886-90] All ER Rep 1, 58 LJ Ch 864, 61
LT 265, 54 JP 148, 38 WR 33, 5 TLR 625, 1 Meg 292, HL 5.01
Dews v National Coal Board [1987] QB 81, [1986] 2 All ER 769, [1986] 3 WLR
227, 130 Sol Jo 553, [1986] LS Gaz R 2084, CA; affd [1988] AC 1, [1987]
2 All ER 545, [1987] 3 WLR 38, [1987] ICR 602, [1987] IRLR 330, 131 Sol
Jo 840, [1987] NLJ Rep 545, [1987] LS Gaz R 2044, HL 8.22
Dexter v Courtaulds Ltd [1984] 1 All ER 70, [1984] 1 WLR 372, 128 Sol Jo 81,
[1984] LS Gaz R 510, CA 7.13
Diamantis Pateras, The [1966] 1 Lloyd's Rep 179 .... 17.09
Dixons (Scholar Green) Ltd v Cooper (1970) 114 Sol Jo 319, [1970] RTR 222,
CA 10.04
Dodd Properties (Kent) v Canterbury City Council [1980] 1 All ER 928, [1980]
1 WLR 433, 124 Sol Jo 84, 253 Estates Gazette 1335, 13 BLR 45, CA . . 3.12, 10.14,
10.15, 10.16
Dodds v Dodds [1978] QB 543, [1978] 2 All ER 539, [1978] 2 WLR 434, 121 Sol
Jo 619 .... 9.05, 9.20, 9.21
Doe d Rochester (Bishop) v Bridges (1831) 1 B & Ad 847, [1924-34] All ER Rep
167, 9 LJOSKB 113 .... 13.09
Dolbey v Goodwin [1955] 2 All ER 166, [1955] 1 WLR 553, 99 Sol Jo 335, [1955]
CLY 733, CA 9.16
Doleman v Deakin (1990) Times, 30 January, CA 9.26
Dominion Mosaics and Tile Co Ltd v Trafalgar Trucking Co Ltd [1990] 2 All ER
246, [1989] 1 EGLR 164, [1989] 16 EG 101, [1989] NLJR 364, CA ... 10.03, 10.09,
10.10, 10.16
Domsalla v Barr (trading as AB Construction) [1969] 3 All ER 487, [1969]
1 WLR 630, 113 Sol Jo 265, CA 7.03
Donaldson v McNiven [1952] 1 All ER 1213; affd [1952] 2 All ER 691, 96 Sol Jo
747, CA 2.02
Donnelly v Joyce [1974] QB 454, [1973] 3 All ER 475, [1973] 3 WLR 514, 117 Sol
Jo 488, [1973] 2 Lloyd's Rep 130, CA 8.26, 8.27
Donoghue (or McAlister) v Stevenson. See M'Alister (or Donoghue) v Stevenson
Donovan v Gwentoys Ltd [1990] 1 All ER 1018, [1990] 1 WLR 472, 134 Sol Jo
910, [1990] 15 LS Gaz R 40, HL 11.17, 11.19
Donovan v Laing, Wharton and Down Construction Syndicate [1893] 1 QB 629,
[1891-4] All ER Rep 216, 63 LJQB 25, 68 LT 512, 57 JP 583, 41 WR 455,
9 TLR 313, 37 Sol Jo 324, 4 R 317, CA 18.06
Dooley v Cammell Laird & Co Ltd [1951] 1 Lloyd's Rep 271 .... 1.25
Dorman Long (Steel) Ltd v Bell [1964] 1 All ER 617, [1964] 1 WLR 333, 108 Sol
Jo 155, 62 LGR 253, HL 14.27
Doughty v Turner Manufacturing Co Ltd [1964] 1 QB 518, [1964] 1 All ER 98,
[1964] 2 WLR 240, 108 Sol Jo 53, CA 3.08, 3.11
Dove v Banhams Patent Locks Ltd [1983] 2 All ER 833, [1983] 1 WLR 1436, 127
Sol Jo 748 .... 11.24
Dragon, The. See Daly v General Steam Navigation Co Ltd, The Dragon
Dransfield v British Insulated Cables Ltd [1937] 4 All ER 382, 54 TLR 11, 82
Sol Jo 95 .... 17.08
Draper v Hodder [1972] 2 QB 556, [1972] 2 All ER 210, [1972] 2 WLR 992, 116
Sol Jo 178, [1972] 2 Lloyd's Rep 93, CA 1.06
Drinkwater v Kimber [1951] 2 All ER 713, [1951] WN 496, [1951] 2 TLR 630, 95
Sol Jo 547, [1951] 2 Lloyd's Rep 255; affd [1952] 2 QB 281, [1952] 1 All ER
701, [1952] 1 TLR 1486, 96 Sol Jo 181, [1952] 1 Lloyd's Rep 159, CA 5.33
Driscoll-Varley v Parkside Health Authority [1991] 2 Med LR 346 .... 11.11
Drive-Yourself Lessey's Pty Ltd v Burnside [1959] SRNSW 390, 76 WN 209 ... 16.14

Table of Cases xxxi

Drummond v British Building Cleaners Ltd [1954] 3 All ER 507, [1954] 1 WLR
  1434, 98 Sol Jo 819, 53 LGR 29, CA 14.05
Dulhunty v J B Young Ltd (1975) 7 ALR 409 (Aust HC) 2.18
Dunlop v Woollahra Municipal Council [1982] AC 158, [1981] 1 All ER 1202,
  [1981] 2 WLR 693, 125 Sol Jo 199, PC 12.15, 12.17
Dunster v Abbott [1953] 2 All ER 1572, [1954] 1 WLR 58, 98 Sol Jo 8, [1953]
  2 Lloyd's Rep 639, CA 16.06
Dutton v Bognor Regis UDC [1972] 1 QB 373, [1972] 1 All ER 462, [1972]
  2 WLR 299, 136 JP 201, 116 Sol Jo 16, 70 LGR 57, 3 BLR 11, [1972]
  1 Lloyd's Rep 227, CA 6.04, 6.05, 12.04

E

East Suffolk Rivers Catchment Board v Kent [1941] AC 74, [1940] 4 All ER 527,
  110 LJKB 252, 16 LT 65, 105 JP 129, 57 TLR 199, 85 Sol Jo 164, 39 LGR 79,
  HL 12.02, 12.08, 12.11, 12.20
Eastman v South West Thames Health Authority [1991] RTR 389, [1991] 2 Med
  LR 297, CA 4.12
Eaves v Morris Motors Ltd [1961] 2 QB 385, [1961] 3 All ER 233, [1961] 3 WLR
  657, 105 Sol Jo 610, 59 LGR 466, CA 14.23
Ebbs v James Whitson & Co Ltd [1952] 2 QB 877, [1952] 2 All ER 192, [1952]
  1 TLR 1428, 96 Sol Jo 375, 50 LGR 563, CA........................... 14.29
Edwards v West Herts Group Hospital Management Committee [1957] 1 All ER
  541, [1957] 1 WLR 415, 121 JP 212, 101 Sol Jo 190, CA 16.14
Eifert v Holt's Transport Co Ltd [1951] 2 All ER 655n, [1951] WN 467, 95 Sol
  Jo 561, CA 9.21
Elderkin v Merrill Lynch Royal Securities Ltd (1977) 80 DLR (3d) 313 ... 5.05, 15.27
Electrochrome Ltd v Welsh Plastics Ltd [1968] 2 All ER 205 .... 6.12
Eley v Bedford [1972] 1 QB 155, [1971] 3 All ER 285, [1971] 3 WLR 563, 115 Sol
  Jo 369 .... 7.06
Ellis v Scruttons Maltby Ltd and Cunard Steam-Ship Co Ltd [1975] 1 Lloyd's
  Rep 564 .... 16.01
Ellis v Wallsend District Hospital (1989) 17 NSWLR 553, [1990] 2 Med LR 103: 15.12
Emeh v Kensington and Chelsea and Westminster Area Health Authority
  [1985] QB 1012, [1984] 3 All ER 1044, [1985] 2 WLR 233, 128 Sol Jo 705,
  CA 1.19, 10.17
Epp v Ridgetop Builders Ltd (1978) 94 DLR (3d) 505 .... 16.08
Esso Petroleum Co Ltd v Hall Russell & Co Ltd and Shetland Islands Council,
  The Esso Bernicia [1989] AC 643, [1989] 1 All ER 37, [1988] 3 WLR 730,
  132 Sol Jo 1459, [1989] 1 Lloyd's Rep 8, HL 6.04, 6.12, 6.15, 6.17
Esso Petroleum Co Ltd v Mardon [1976] QB 801, [1976] 2 All ER 5, [1976]
  2 WLR 583, 120 Sol Jo 131, 2 BLR 85, [1976] 2 Lloyd's Rep 305, CA .. 5.02, 5.05,
                                                                     5.25, 11.29
Eurymedon, The. See New Zealand Shipping Co Ltd v A M Satterthwaite & Co
  Ltd
Evangelical United Brethren v State 407 P 2d 440 (1965) 12.10
Evans v London Hospital Medical College [1981] 1 All ER 715, [1981] 1 WLR
  184, 125 Sol Jo 48 .... 5.12
Evans v Triplex Safety Glass Co Ltd [1936] 1 All ER 283 .... 17.10
Eyre v Measday [1986] 1 All ER 488, [1986] NLJ Rep 91, CA 15.13

F

F, Re [1990] 2 AC 1, [1989] 2 WLR 1025, [1989] 2 FLR 376, [1989] Fam Law
  390, 133 Sol Jo 785, [1989] NLJR 789, sub nom F v West Berkshire Health
  Authority (Mental Health Act Commission intervening) [1989] 2 All ER 545,
  HL.. 15.07
Fardon v Harcourt-Rivington (1932) 146 LT 391, [1932] All ER Rep 81, 48 TLR
  215, 76 Sol Jo 81, HL 2.04
Farmer v Rash [1969] 1 All ER 705, [1969] 1 WLR 160, 113 Sol Jo 57 .... 3.17

xxxii *Table of Cases*

Farr v Butters Bros & Co [1932] 2 KB 606, [1932] All ER Rep 339, 101 LJKB
  768, 147 LT 427, CA 17.09
Fazlic v Milingimbi Community Inc (1981) 38 ALR 424 (Aust HC) 7.07
Fellowes v Rother District Council [1983] 1 All ER 513 .... 12.20
Ferguson v John Dawson & Partners (Contractors) Ltd [1976] 3 All ER 817,
  [1976] 1 WLR 1213, [1976] IRLR 346, 120 Sol Jo 603, 8 BLR 38, [1976]
  2 Lloyd's Rep 669, CA 18.05
Ferguson v Welsh [1987] 3 All ER 777, [1987] 1 WLR 1553, [1988] IRLR 112,
  131 Sol Jo 1552, 86 LGR 153, [1987] NLJ Rep 1037, [1987] LS Gaz R 3581,
  HL 16.02, 16.06, 16.13
Finch v Telegraph Construction and Maintenance Co Ltd [1949] 1 All ER 452,
  65 TLR 153, 93 Sol Jo 219, 47 LGR 710 .... 14.33
Fine's Flowers Ltd v General Accident Assurance Co of Canada (1977) 81 DLR
  (3d) 139 ....   5.24
Firman v Ellis [1978] QB 886, [1978] 2 All ER 851, [1978] 3 WLR 1, 122 Sol Jo
  147, CA 11.01, 11.17
Fish v Kelly (1864) 17 CBNS 194 ....   5.15
Fisher v CHT Ltd [1965] 2 All ER 601, [1965] 1 WLR 1093, 109 Sol Jo 612 ... 16.02
Fisher v Ruislip-Northwood UDC and Middlesex County Council [1945] KB 584,
  [1945] 2 All ER 458, 115 LJKB 9, 173 LT 261, 110 JP 1, 62 TLR 1, 89 Sol Jo
  434, 43 LGR 224, CA 12.02
Fitzgerald v Lane [1987] QB 781, [1987] 2 All ER 455, [1987] 3 WLR 249, 131
  Sol Jo 976, [1987] NLJ Rep 316, [1987] LS Gaz R 1334, CA; affd [1989] AC
  328, [1988] 2 All ER 961, [1988] 3 WLR 356, 132 Sol Jo 1064, [1990] RTR
  133, [1988] NLJR 209, HL 4.09, 4.10, 4.11, 4.17
Fleming v M'Gillivray 1945 SLT 301 .... 13.05
Fletcher v Autocar and Transporters Ltd [1968] 2 QB 322, [1968] 1 All ER 726,
  [1968] 2 WLR 743, 112 Sol Jo 96, [1968] 1 Lloyd's Rep 317, CA ... 7.04, 7.05, 8.10
Floyd v Bowers (1978) 21 OR (2d) 204, 89 DLR (3d) 559; affd (1979) 106 DLR
  (3d) 702 ....   2.02
Fookes v Slaytor [1979] 1 All ER 137, [1978] 1 WLR 1293, 122 Sol Jo 489,
  [1979] RTR 40, CA 4.07
Ford v White & Co [1964] 2 All ER 755, [1964] 1 WLR 885, 108 Sol Jo 542 .... 15.15
Forsikringsaktieselskapet Vesta v Butcher [1986] 2 All ER 488, [1986] 2 Lloyd's
  Rep 179; on appeal sub nom Forsikringsaktieselskapet Vesta v Butcher,
  Bain Dawles Ltd and Aquacultural Insurance Services Ltd [1989] AC 852,
  [1988] 2 All ER 43, [1988] 3 WLR 565, 132 Sol Jo 1181, [1988] 1 Lloyd's
  Rep 19, CA; affd [1989] AC 852, [1989] 1 All ER 402, [1989] 2 WLR 290,
  133 Sol Jo 184, [1989] 1 Lloyd's Rep 331, [1989] 11 LS Gaz R 42, HL 4.16
Forster v Outred & Co (a firm) [1982] 2 All ER 753, [1982] 1 WLR 86, 125 Sol
  Jo 309, CA 11.05, 11.24, 15.16, 15.18
Fortunity, The, Motor Cruiser Four of Hearts (Owners) v Fortunity (Owners)
  [1960] 2 All ER 64, [1961] 1 WLR 351, 105 Sol Jo 159, [1960] 1 Lloyd's Rep
  252 .... 10.01, 10.04
Foskett v Mistry [1984] RTR 1, [1984] LS Gaz R 2683, CA 4.15
Foster v Tyne and Wear County Council [1986] 1 All ER 567, CA 8.12
Fox v Everingham (1983) 50 ALR 337 .... 15.16
Franklin v Gramophone Co Ltd [1948] 1 KB 542, [1948] 1 All ER 353, [1948]
  LJR 870, 64 TLR 186, 92 Sol Jo 124, CA 14.39
French Knit Sales Pty Ltd v Gold & Sons Pty Ltd [1972] 2 NSWLR 132 ......   6.16
Froom v Butcher [1976] QB 286, [1975] 3 All ER 520, [1975] 3 WLR 379, 119 Sol
  Jo 613, [1975] 2 Lloyd's Rep 478, [1975] RTR 518, CA 4.08, 4.12

G

Gala v Preston (1991) 172 CLR 243 ....   1.20
Gallagher v N McDowell Ltd [1961] NI 26 ....   1.14
Gammell v Wilson [1982] AC 27, [1980] 2 All ER 557, [1980] 3 WLR 591, 124
  Sol Jo 329, CA; affd [1982] AC 27, [1981] 1 All ER 578, [1981] 2 WLR 248,
  125 Sol Jo 116, HL 8.02, 8.14, 8.16, 9.02, 9.27, 9.30
Gardiner v Moore [1969] 1 QB 55, [1966] 1 All ER 365, [1966] 3 WLR 786, 110
  Sol Jo 34, [1965] CLY 2267 ....   4.18

Gardner v Moore [1984] AC 548, [1984] 1 All ER 1100, [1984] 2 WLR 714, 128
  Sol Jo 282, [1984] 2 Lloyd's Rep 135, [1984] RTR 209, [1984] LS Gaz R 1444,
  HL 19.07
Garland v Ralph Pay & Ransom (1984) 271 Estates Gazette 106, 197, [1984]
  EGD 867... 15.23
Garrard v A E Southey & Co and Standard Telephones and Cables Ltd [1952]
  2 QB 174, [1952] 1 All ER 597, [1952] 1 TLR 630, 96 Sol Jo 166 .... 18.07
Gartside v Sheffield, Young and Ellis [1983] NZLR 37 (NZCA) 5.17, 6.23, 15.18
Gaskill v Preston [1981] 3 All ER 427................................... 8.20
Gaynor v Allen [1959] 2 QB 403, [1959] 2 All ER 644, [1959] 3 WLR 221, 123 JP
  413, 103 Sol Jo 677 .... 2.06
Geddis v Bann Reservoir (Proprietors) (1878) 3 App Cas 430, HL........... 12.01
General Cleaning Contractors Ltd v Christmas [1953] AC 180, [1952] 2 All ER
  1110, [1953] 2 WLR 6, 97 Sol Jo 7, 51 LGR 109, HL 14.05
General Engineering Services Ltd v Kingston and St Andrew Corpn [1988] 3 All
  ER 867, [1989] 1 WLR 69, [1989] ICR 88, [1989] IRLR 35, 133 Sol Jo 20,
  [1989] 4 LS Gaz R 44, PC 18.09
George v Pinnock [1973] 1 All ER 926, [1973] 1 WLR 118, 117 Sol Jo 73, CA... 7.04,
                                                                          8.23
Gerrard (Thomas) & Son Ltd, Re [1968] Ch 455, [1967] 2 All ER 525, [1967]
  3 WLR 84, 111 Sol Jo 329... 15.26
Gibb v United Steel Companies Ltd [1957] 2 All ER 110, [1957] 1 WLR 668, 101
  Sol Jo 393 .... 18.07
Ginty v Belmont Building Supplies Ltd [1959] 1 All ER 414 ..... 13.17, 14.33, 14.37
Girard v Royal Columbian Hospital (1976) 66 DLR (3d) 676 .... 15.05
Gitsham v C H Pearce & Sons plc (1991) Times, 11 February, CA 14.27
Glasgow Corpn v Muir [1943] AC 448, [1943] 2 All ER 44, 112 LJPC 1, 169 LT
  53, 107 JP 140, 59 TLR 266, 87 Sol Jo 182, 41 LGR 173, HL 2.01, 2.10
Glasgow Corpn v Taylor [1922] 1 AC 44, [1921] All ER Rep 1, 91 LJPC 49,
  126 LT 262, 86 JP 89, 38 TLR 102, 20 LGR 205, HL 2.08
Glossop v Heston and Isleworth Local Board (1879) 12 Ch D 102, [1874-80] All
  ER Rep 836, 49 LJ Ch 89, 40 LT 736, 44 JP 36, 28 WR 111, CA 13.08
Gold v Haringey Health Authority [1988] QB 481, [1987] 2 All ER 888, [1987]
  3 WLR 649, [1988] 1 FLR 55, [1987] Fam Law 417, 131 Sol Jo 843, [1987]
  NLJ Rep 541, [1987] LS Gaz R 1812, CA 15.10
Goldstein v Salvation Army Assurance Society [1917] 2 KB 291, 86 LJKB 793,
  117 LT 63 .... 9.30
Good Luck, The. See Bank of Nova Scotia v Hellenic Mutual War Risks Associ-
  ation (Bermuda) Ltd, The Good Luck
Goodchild v Greatness Timber Co Ltd [1968] 2 QB 372, [1968] 2 All ER 255,
  [1968] 2 WLR 1283, 112 Sol Jo 192, CA 11.10, 11.11
Goody v Baring [1956] 2 All ER 11, [1956] 1 WLR 448, 100 Sol Jo 320 .... 15.15
Gore v Van der Lann [1967] 2 QB 31, [1967] 1 All ER 360, [1967] 2 WLR 358,
  110 Sol Jo 928, 65 LGR 94, [1967] 1 Lloyd's Rep 145, CA................ 4.27
Gorely v Codd [1966] 3 All ER 891, [1967] 1 WLR 19, 110 Sol Jo 965 .... 2.02
Gorris v Scott (1874) LR 9 Exch 125, 43 LJ Ex 92, 30 LT 431, 22 WR 575, 2 Asp
  MLC 282 .... 13.07, 13.13, 13.20
Gough v Thorne [1966] 3 All ER 398, [1966] 1 WLR 1387, 110 Sol Jo 529, CA .. 4.14
Gouriet v Union of Post Office Workers [1978] AC 435, [1977] 3 All ER 70,
  [1977] 3 WLR 300, 141 JP 552, 121 Sol Jo 543, HL 13.02
Gracie (Owners) v Argentino (Owners), The Argentino (1889) 14 App Cas 519, 59
  LJP 17, 61 LT 706, 6 Asp MLC 433, HL 10.04
Graham v Co-operative Wholesale Society Ltd [1957] 1 All ER 654, [1957]
  1 WLR 511, 101 Sol Jo 267, 55 LGR 137 .... 14.29
Graham v Dodds [1983] 2 All ER 953, [1983] 1 WLR 808, 127 Sol Jo 478, HL .. 9.13
Gran Gelato Ltd v Richcliff (Group) Ltd [1992] Ch 560, [1992] 1 All ER 865,
  [1992] 2 WLR 867, [1992] NLJR 51, [1992] 18 LS Gaz R 36 ..... 4.16, 5.33, 15.18
Grant v Australian Knitting Mills Ltd [1936] AC 85, [1935] All ER Rep 209, 105
  LJPC 6, 154 LT 18, 52 TLR 38, 79 Sol Jo 815 .... 17.04, 17.08, 17.11
Gray v Barr [1970] 2 QB 626, [1970] 2 All ER 702, [1970] 3 WLR 108, 114 Sol Jo
  413, [1970] 2 Lloyd's Rep 69; on appeal [1971] 2 QB 554, [1971] 2 All ER
  949, [1971] 2 WLR 1334, 115 Sol Jo 364, [1971] 2 Lloyd's Rep 1, CA 19.07

xxxiv *Table of Cases*

Greater Nottingham Co-operative Society Ltd v Cementation Piling and
  Foundations Ltd [1989] QB 71, [1988] 2 All ER 971, [1988] 3 WLR 396, 132
  Sol Jo 754, 41 BLR 43, 17 Con LR 43, [1988] NLJR 112, [1988] 16 LS Gaz R
  41, CA 5.25, 6.10
Greaves & Co (Contractors) Ltd v Baynham, Meikle & Partners [1974] 3 All ER
  666, [1974] 1 WLR 1261, 118 Sol Jo 595, [1975] 1 Lloyd's Rep 31; affd [1975]
  3 All ER 99, [1975] 1 WLR 1095, 119 Sol Jo 372, 4 BLR 56, [1975] 2 Lloyd's
  Rep 325, CA 2.09, 15.19
Greene v Chelsea Borough Council [1954] 2 QB 127, [1954] 2 All ER 318, [1954]
  3 WLR 12, 118 JP 346, 98 Sol Jo 389, 52 LGR 352, CA 1.14
Greenhalgh v British Railways Board [1969] 2 QB 286, [1969] 2 All ER 114,
  [1969] 2 WLR 892, 113 Sol Jo 108, CA 16.04, 16.35
Gregson v Hick Hargreaves & Co Ltd [1955] 3 All ER 507, [1955] 1 WLR 1252,
  99 Sol Jo 833, CA 14.30
Greta Holme, The. See No 7 Steam Sand Pump Dredger (Owners) v Greta
  Holme (Owners), The Greta Holme
Griffiths v Dawson & Co (1993) Times, 5 April 15.15
Griffiths v Evans [1953] 2 All ER 1364, [1953] 1 WLR 1424, 97 Sol Jo 812, CA : 15.19
Groom v Crocker [1939] 1 KB 194, [1938] 2 All ER 394, 108 LJKB 296, 158 LT
  477, 54 TLR 861, 82 Sol Jo 374, 60 Ll L Rep 393, CA 15.17
Groves v Lord Wimborne [1898] 2 QB 402, [1895-9] All ER Rep 147, 67 LJQB
  862, 79 LT 284, 47 WR 87, 14 TLR 493, 42 Sol Jo 633, CA 13.06, 13.07, 13.10
Gurtner v Circuit [1968] 2 QB 587, [1968] 1 All ER 328, [1968] 2 WLR 668, 112
  Sol Jo 73, [1968] 1 Lloyd's Rep 171, CA 19.07
Gypsum Carrier Inc v R (1977) 78 DLR (3d) 175 .... 6.13

H

H v Ministry of Defence [1991] 2 QB 103, [1991] 2 All ER 834, [1991] 2 WLR
  1192, [1991] NLJR 420, CA 8.04
HL Motor Works (Willesden) Ltd v Alwahbi [1977] RTR 276, CA 10.06
Haggar v de Placido [1972] 2 All ER 1029, [1972] 1 WLR 716, 116 Sol Jo 396 .. 8.26
Hague v Deputy Governor of Parkhurst Prison. See R v Deputy Governor of
  Parkhurst Prison, ex p Hague
Hahn v Conley (1971) 45 ALJR 631, [1972] ALR 247 (Aust HC) 2.03
Haig v Bamford [1976] 3 WWR 331, 72 DLR (3d) 68 .... 5.21
Haigh v Charles W Ireland Ltd [1973] 3 All ER 1137, [1974] 1 WLR 43, 117 Sol
  Jo 939, [1973] RA 449, HL 13.08
Haley v London Electricity Board [1964] 2 QB 121, [1963] 3 All ER 1003, [1964]
  2 WLR 444, 128 JP 162, 107 Sol Jo 1001, CA; revsd [1965] AC 778, [1964] 3
  All ER 185, [1964] 3 WLR 479, 129 JP 14, 108 Sol Jo 637, 63 LGR 1, HL .. 2.08
Halford v Brookes [1991] 3 All ER 559, [1991] 1 WLR 428, CA 11.14, 11.18
Halifax Building Society v Edell [1992] Ch 436, [1992] 3 All ER 389, [1992] 3
  WLR 136, [1992] 18 EG 151, [1992] 31 LS Gaz R 34 .... 5.17
Hall v Meyrick [1957] 2 QB 455, [1957] 2 All ER 722, [1957] 3 WLR 273, 101 Sol
  Jo 574, CA 15.19
Ham v Los Angeles County 189 P 462 (1920) 12.19
Hambrook v Stokes Bros [1925] 1 KB 141, [1924] All ER Rep 110, 94 LJKB 435,
  132 LT 707, 41 TLR 125, CA 1.25
Harbutt's Plasticine Ltd v Wayne Tank and Pump Co Ltd [1970] 1 QB 447,
  [1970] 1 All ER 225, [1970] 2 WLR 198, 114 Sol Jo 29, [1970] 1 Lloyd's Rep
  15, CA 10.08, 10.10
Hardy v Motor Insurers' Bureau [1964] 2 QB 745, [1964] 2 All ER 742, [1964] 3
  WLR 433, 108 Sol Jo 422, [1964] 1 Lloyd's Rep 397, CA 19.07
Harris v Birkenhead Corpn [1976] 1 All ER 341, [1976] 1 WLR 279, 120 Sol Jo
  200, 74 LGR 229, CA 16.01, 16.03, 16.17
Harris v Bright's Asphalt Contractors Ltd [1953] 1 QB 617, [1953] 1 All ER
  395, [1953] 1 WLR 341, 97 Sol Jo 115, 51 LGR 296 .... 8.24
Harris v Empress Motors Ltd [1983] 3 All ER 561, [1984] 1 WLR 212, 127 Sol
  Jo 647, CA 8.15, 9.12
Harris (infant) v Harris (1972) 116 Sol Jo 904, [1973] 1 Lloyd's Rep 445, CA ... 8.09

Harris v Wyre Forest District Council [1988] QB 835, [1988] 1 All ER 691, [1988] 2 WLR 1173, 132 Sol Jo 91, 87 LGR 19, 20 HLR 278, [1988] 1 EGLR 132, [1988] 05 EG 57, [1988] NLJR 15, [1988] 7 LS Gaz R 40, CA; revsd [1990] 1 AC 831, [1989] 2 All ER 514, [1989] 2 WLR 790, 133 Sol Jo 597, 87 LGR 685, 21 HLR 424, 17 Con LR 1, [1989] 1 EGLR 169, [1989] 17 EG 68, 18 EG 99, [1989] NLJR 576, HL 5.17, 5.31
Harrison v British Railways Board [1981] 3 All ER 679 .... 3.18
Harrison v Michelin Tyre Co Ltd [1985] 1 All ER 918, [1985] ICR 696 ... 14.12, 18.11
Harrison v National Coal Board [1950] 1 KB 466, [1950] 1 All ER 171, 114 JP 86, 66 (pt 1) TLR 300, 94 Sol Jo 145, 48 LGR 203, CA; affd [1951] AC 639, [1951] 1 All ER 1102, 115 JP 413, [1951] 1 TLR 1079, 50 LGR 1, HL 13.18
Hart v Hall and Pickles Ltd, Geoffrey Reyner & Co Ltd (third party) [1969] 1 QB 405, [1968] 3 All ER 291, [1968] 3 WLR 744, 112 Sol Jo 786, CA 4.19
Hartley v Birmingham City District Council [1992] 2 All ER 213, [1992] 1 WLR 968, CA 11.18, 11.19
Hartley v Mayoh & Co [1954] 1 QB 383, [1954] 1 All ER 375, [1954] 1 WLR 355, 118 JP 178, 98 Sol Jo 107, 52 LGR 165, CA 13.06, 17.07
Hartley v Sandholme Iron Co Ltd [1975] QB 600, [1974] 3 All ER 475, [1974] 3 WLR 445, 118 Sol Jo 702, [1974] STC 434, 17 KIR 205 .... 8.21
Harvey v R G O'Dell Ltd [1958] 2 QB 78, [1958] 1 All ER 657, [1958] 2 WLR 473, 102 Sol Jo 196, [1958] 1 Lloyd's Rep 273 .... 18.11, 18.14
Haseldine v C A Daw & Son Ltd [1941] 2 KB 343, [1941] 3 All ER 156, 111 LJKB 45, 165 LT 185, 58 TLR 1, CA 17.04, 17.08
Hawkins v Ian Ross (Castings) Ltd [1970] 1 All ER 180 .... 4.08
Hawkins v New Mendip Engineering Ltd [1966] 3 All ER 228, [1966] 1 WLR 1341, 110 Sol Jo 633, 1 KIR 226, CA 7.11
Hay v Dowty Mining Equipment Ltd [1971] 3 All ER 1136 .... 14.33
Hay v Hughes [1975] QB 790, [1975] 1 All ER 257, [1975] 2 WLR 34, 118 Sol Jo 883, [1975] 1 Lloyd's Rep 12, CA.................................. 9.19, 9.22
Hay (or Bourhill) v Young [1943] AC 92, [1942] 2 All ER 396, 111 LJPC 97, 167 LT 261, 86 Sol Jo 349, HL.. 1.25
Hayden v Hayden [1992] 4 All ER 681, [1992] 1 WLR 986, CA 9.19, 9.23
Hebridean Coast, The. See Lord Citrine, The (Owners) v Hebridean Coast (Owners), The Hebridean Coast
Hedley Byrne & Co Ltd v Heller & Partners Ltd [1964] AC 465, [1963] 2 All ER 575, [1963] 3 WLR 101, 107 Sol Jo 454, [1963] 1 Lloyd's Rep 485, HL ... 1.12, 4.27, 5.01, 5.07, 5.16, 5.22, 5.27, 6.02, 6.03, 12.20, 15.18
Hemmings v Stoke Poges Golf Club [1920] 1 KB 720, [1918-19] All ER Rep 798, 89 LJKB 744, 122 LT 479, 36 TLR 77, 64 Sol Jo 131, CA................ 13.02
Henderson v Henry E Jenkins & Sons and Evans [1970] AC 282, [1969] 3 All ER 756, [1969] 3 WLR 732, 113 Sol Jo 856, [1969] 2 Lloyd's Rep 603, [1970] RTR 70, HL 2.18, 17.12
Hendy v Milton Keynes Health Authority (No 2) [1992] 3 Med LR 114 .... 11.18
Herdman v Walker (Tooting) Ltd [1956] 1 All ER 429, [1956] 1 WLR 209, 100 Sol Jo 150 .... 18.08
Heron II, The. See Koufos v C Czarnikow Ltd, The Heron II
Herschtal (or Herschthal) v Stewart and Ardern Ltd [1940] 1 KB 155, [1939] 4 All ER 123, 109 LJKB 328, 161 LT 331, 56 TLR 48, 84 Sol Jo 79, 45 Com Cas 63 .... 17.08
Hevican v Ruane [1991] 3 All ER 65, [1991] NLJR 235 .... 1.25
Hewitt v Bonvin [1940] 1 KB 188, 109 LJKB 223, 161 LT 360, 56 TLR 43, 83 Sol Jo 869, CA 18.25
Hewson v Downs [1970] 1 QB 73, [1969] 3 All ER 193, [1969] 2 WLR 1169, 113 Sol Jo 309, 6 KIR 343 .... 8.20
Hicks v Chief Constable of the South Yorkshire Police [1992] 2 All ER 65, 8 BMLR 70, HL 9.01, 9.27
Higgs v Drinkwater [1956] CA Transcript 129A 9.17
Hilder v Associated Portland Cement Manufacturers Ltd [1961] 3 All ER 709, [1961] 1 WLR 1434, 105 Sol Jo 725 .... 4.12

Hill v Chief Constable for West Yorkshire [1988] QB 60, [1987] 1 All ER 1173,
 [1987] 2 WLR 1126, 131 Sol Jo 626, [1987] NLJ Rep 222, [1987] LS Gaz R
 982, CA; affd [1989] AC 53, [1988] 2 All ER 238, [1988] 2 WLR 1049, 132 Sol
 Jo 700, [1988] NLJR 126, HL 1.06, 1.18, 1.23, 3.19, 12.10
Hill v Harris [1965] 2 QB 601, [1965] 2 All ER 358, [1965] 2 WLR 1331, 109 Sol
 Jo 333, CA 15.15
Hill v James Crowe (Cases) Ltd [1978] 1 All ER 812, [1978] ICR 298, [1977]
 2 Lloyd's Rep 450 .... 2.17, 17.11
Hills v Potter [1983] 3 All ER 716, [1984] 1 WLR 641n, 128 Sol Jo 224 .... 15.10
Hillyer v St Bartholomew's Hospital (Governors) [1909] 2 KB 820, 78 LJKB
 958, 101 LT 368, 73 JP 501, 25 TLR 762, 53 Sol Jo 714, CA 18.03, 18.19
Hilton v Thomas Burton (Rhodes) Ltd [1961] 1 All ER 74, [1961] 1 WLR 705,
 105 Sol Jo 322 .... 18.11
Hindustan Steam Shipping Co Ltd v Siemens Bros & Co Ltd [1955] 1 Lloyd's
 Rep 167... 5.03
Hoare v M & W Grazebrook Ltd [1957] 1 All ER 470, [1957] 1 WLR 638, 101 Sol
 Jo 373, 55 LGR 149 .... 14.23
Hobbs v Marlowe [1978] AC 16, [1977] 2 All ER 241, [1977] 2 WLR 777, 120 Sol
 Jo 838, CA; affd [1978] AC 16, [1977] 2 All ER 241, [1977] 2 WLR 777, 121
 Sol Jo 272, [1977] RTR 253, HL 19.03
Hodges v Frost (1984) 53 ALR 373 .... 8.27
Hodges v Harland and Wolff Ltd [1965] 1 All ER 1086, [1965] 1 WLR 523, 109
 Sol Jo 178, [1965] 1 Lloyd's Rep 181, CA 8.04
Hodgson v General Electricity Co Ltd [1978] 2 Lloyd's Rep 210 .... 7.10
Hodgson v Trapp [1989] AC 807, [1988] 3 All ER 870, [1988] 3 WLR 1281,
 [1989] 2 LS Gaz R 36, HL 8.11, 8.20, 9.13
Hodkinson v Henry Wallwork & Co Ltd [1955] 3 All ER 236, [1955] 1 WLR
 1195, 99 Sol Jo 778, 53 LGR 656, CA 14.21
Hoffmann-La Roche & Co AG v Secretary of State for Trade and Industry [1975]
 AC 295, [1974] 2 All ER 1128, [1974] 3 WLR 104, 118 Sol Jo 500, HL 12.17
Hogan v Bentinck West Hartley Collieries (Owners) Ltd [1949] 1 All ER 588,
 [1949] LJR 865, [1949] WN 109, HL 3.23
Holden v White [1982] QB 679, [1982] 2 All ER 328, [1982] 2 WLR 1030, 126 Sol
 Jo 230, CA 16.19, 16.35
Hole and Son (Sayers Common) Ltd v Harrisons of Thurnscoe Ltd (1972) 116
 Sol Jo 922, [1973] 1 Lloyd's Rep 345 .... 10.10
Hollebone v Midhurst and Fernhurst Builders Ltd and Eastman and White of
 Midhurst Ltd [1968] 1 Lloyd's Rep 38 .... 10.10
Holliday v National Telephone Co [1899] 2 QB 392, [1895-99] All ER Rep 359,
 68 LJQB 1016, 81 LT 252, 47 WR 658, 15 TLR 483, CA 18.16
Holmes v Ashford [1950] 2 All ER 76, 94 Sol Jo 337, CA 17.06, 17.07
Home Office v Dorset Yacht Co Ltd [1970] AC 1004, [1970] 2 All ER 294, [1970]
 2 WLR 1140, 114 Sol Jo 375, [1970] 1 Lloyd's Rep 453, HL 1.01, 1.06, 1.09,
  1.22, 3.19, 12.03,
  12.05, 12.10, 12.11,
  12.15, 13.08
Honeywill and Stein Ltd v Larkin Bros (London's Commercial Photographers)
 Ltd [1934] 1 KB 191, [1933] All ER Rep 77, 103 LJKB 74, 150 LT 71, 50
 TLR 56, CA 18.17
Horne v Lec Refrigeration Ltd [1965] 2 All ER 898 .... 14.25
Horton v Colwyn Bay and Colwyn UDC [1908] 1 KB 327, 77 LJKB 215, 98 LT
 547, 72 JP 57, 24 TLR 220, 52 Sol Jo 158, 6 LGR 211, CA 6.12
Hotson v East Berkshire Area Health Authority [1987] AC 750, [1987] 2 All ER
 909, [1987] 3 WLR 232, 131 Sol Jo 975, [1987] NLJ Rep 638, [1987] LS Gaz
 R 2365, HL 2.12
Housecroft v Burnett [1986] 1 All ER 332, CA 8.05, 8.09, 8.26, 8.27
Houston v Buchanan. See McLeod (or Houston) v Buchanan
Howard (R P) Ltd v Woodman Matthews & Co [1983] BCLC 117, 133 NLJ 598,
 [1983] Com LR 100 .... 15.16, 15.18
Howard Marine and Dredging Co Ltd v A Ogden & Sons (Excavations) Ltd
 [1978] QB 574, [1978] 2 All ER 1134, [1978] 2 WLR 515, 122 Sol Jo 48,
 9 BLR 34, [1978] 1 Lloyd's Rep 334, CA 5.02, 5.07

Table of Cases xxxvii

Howe v David Brown Tractors (Retail) Ltd (Rustons Engineering Co Ltd, third
  party) [1991] 4 All ER 30, CA 11.08
Hudson v Ridge Manufacturing Co Ltd [1957] 2 QB 348, [1957] 2 All ER 229,
  [1957] 2 WLR 948, 101 Sol Jo 409 .... 14.12
Hughes v Lord Advocate [1963] AC 837, [1963] 1 All ER 705, [1963] 2 WLR
  779, 107 Sol Jo 232, 1963 SC 31, 1963 SLT 150, HL 3.07, 3.18
Hughes v McKeown [1985] 3 All ER 284, [1985] 1 WLR 963, 129 Sol Jo 543 ... 8.09
Hughes v National Union of Mineworkers [1991] 4 All ER 278, [1991] ICR 669: 1.18
Hughes v Waltham Forest Health Authority [1991] 2 Med LR 155, CA 15.09
Hunt v Severs (1993) Times, 13 May, CA 8.26
Hunter v Chief Constable of West Midlands Police [1982] AC 529, [1981] 3 All
  ER 727, [1981] 3 WLR 906, 125 Sol Jo 829, HL 5.11
Hurditch v Sheffield Health Authority [1989] QB 562, [1989] 2 All ER 869,
  [1989] 2 WLR 827, 133 Sol Jo 630, CA 7.11
Hussain v New Taplow Paper Mills Ltd [1987] 1 All ER 417, [1987] 1 WLR 336,
  [1987] ICR 28, 131 Sol Jo 358, [1987] LS Gaz R 1242, CA; affd [1988] AC
  514, [1988] 1 All ER 541, [1988] 2 WLR 266, [1988] ICR 259, [1988] IRLR
  167, 132 Sol Jo 226, [1988] NLJR 45, [1988] 10 LS Gaz R 45, HL 8.17, 8.18
Hussey v Eels [1990] 2 QB 227, [1990] 1 All ER 449, [1990] 2 WLR 234, [1990]
  1 EGLR 215, [1990] 19 EG 77, [1990] NLJR 53, CA 10.11
Hutchinson v Harris (1978) 10 BLR 19, CA 10.16
Hyde v Tameside Area Health Authority (1986) 2 PN 26, [1981] CLY 1854, CA: 1.21
Hyett v Great Western Rly Co [1948] 1 KB 345, [1947] 2 All ER 264, [1947] LJR
  1243, 177 LT 178, 63 TLR 411, 91 Sol Jo 434, CA 3.18

I

ICI Ltd v Shatwell [1965] AC 656, [1964] 2 All ER 999, [1964] 3 WLR 329, 108
  Sol Jo 578, HL 4.02, 4.03, 4.29, 13.17,
                                                        4.36, 18.01, 18.02
Ibaraki Maru, The. See Candlewood Navigation Corpn Ltd v Mitsui OSK Lines
  Ltd, The Mineral Transporter, The Ibaraki Maru
Ichard v Frangoulis [1977] 2 All ER 461, [1977] 1 WLR 556, 121 Sol Jo 287 ... 7.03
Ilkiw v Samuels [1963] 2 All ER 879, [1963] 1 WLR 991, 107 Sol Jo 680, CA .. 18.11
Independent Broadcasting Authority v BICC Construction Ltd (1978) 11 BLR
  38, CA; affd (1980) 14 BLR 9, 130 NLJ 603, HL 15.25
Indian Towing Co v United States 350 US 61, 76 S Ct 122 (1955) 12.11
IRC v Hambrook [1956] 2 QB 641, [1956] 1 All ER 807; affd [1956] 2 QB 641,
  [1956] 3 All ER 338, [1956] 3 WLR 643, 100 Sol Jo 632, CA 6.27
IRC v Hoogstraten [1985] QB 1077, [1984] 3 All ER 25, [1984] 3 WLR 933, 128
  Sol Jo 484, CA 5.13
Iqbal v London Transport Executive (1973) 16 KIR 329, CA 18.10, 18.12
Irene's Success, The. See Schiffahrt und Kohlen GmbH v Chelsea Maritime Ltd,
  The Irene's Success
Iron Trade Mutual Insurance Co Ltd v J K Buckenham Ltd [1990] 1 All ER 808,
  [1989] 2 Lloyd's Rep 85 .... 11.26
Ironfield v Eastern Gas Board [1964] 1 All ER 544n, [1964] 1 WLR 1125n, 108
  Sol Jo 691 .... 10.07
Irwin v White, Tomkins and Courage Ltd [1964] 1 All ER 545, [1964] 1 WLR
  387, 108 Sol Jo 154, 62 LGR 256, [1964] NI 22, HL 14.25
Island Records Ltd, ex p [1978] Ch 122, [1978] 3 All ER 824, [1978] 3 WLR 23,
  122 Sol Jo 298, [1978] FSR 505, CA 13.01, 13.02
Islander Trucking (in liquidation) v Hogg Robinson & Gardner Mountain
  (Marine) Ltd [1990] 1 All ER 826 .... 11.29

J

JEB Fasteners Ltd v Marks, Bloom & Co (a firm) [1981] 3 All ER 289, [1982]
  Com LR 226; on appeal [1983] 1 All ER 583, CA 5.20, 5.33
Jackson v Harrison (1978) 138 CLR 438, 52 ALJR 474, 19 ALR 129 (Aust HC) : 1.20

Table of Cases

Jackson v Horizon Holidays Ltd [1975] 3 All ER 92, [1975] 1 WLR 1468, 119 Sol Jo 759, CA 10.16
Jaenesch v Coffey (1984) 54 ALR 417 (Aust HC) 1.25
James v Hepworth and Grandage Ltd [1968] 1 QB 94, [1967] 2 All ER 829, [1967] 3 WLR 178, 111 Sol Jo 232, CA 14.06
James v Woodall Duckham Construction Co Ltd [1969] 2 All ER 794, [1969] 1 WLR 903, 113 Sol Jo 225, CA 7.02
James Pty Ltd v Duncan [1970] VR 705 .... 4.16
Jamil bin Harun v Yang Kamsiah Bte Meor Rasdi [1984] AC 529, [1984] 2 WLR 668, 128 Sol Jo 281, PC 7.04, 8.13
Janiak v Ippolito (1985) 16 DLR (4th) 1 .... 7.07, 7.08
Jarvis v Swans Tours Ltd [1973] QB 233, [1973] 1 All ER 71, [1972] 3 WLR 954, 116 Sol Jo 822, CA 10.16
Jayes v IMI (Kynoch) Ltd [1985] ICR 155, [1984] LS Gaz R 3180, CA 14.35
Jefford v Gee [1970] 2 QB 130, [1970] 1 All ER 1202, [1970] 2 WLR 702, 114 Sol Jo 206, [1970] 1 Lloyd's Rep 107, CA 7.04, 7.13, 9.20
Jenkins v Allied Ironfounders Ltd [1969] 3 All ER 1609, [1970] 1 WLR 304, 114 Sol Jo 71, HL 14.28
Jenner v Allen West & Co Ltd [1959] 2 All ER 115, [1959] 1 WLR 554, 103 Sol Jo 371, CA 14.37
Jens v Mannix Co [1978] 5 WWR 486 .... 10.10
Jobling v Associated Dairies Ltd [1982] AC 794, [1981] 2 All ER 752, [1981] 3 WLR 155, 125 Sol Jo 481, HL 7.09, 7.10, 9.03
Johnson v State of California 447 P 2d 352 (1968) 12.11, 12.19
Johnston v Caddies Wainwright [1983] ICR 407, CA 14.28
Johnstone v Bloomsbury Health Authority [1992] 1 QB 333, [1991] 2 All ER 293, [1991] 2 WLR 1362, [1991] ICR 269, [1991] IRLR 118, CA 14.02, 14.10
Jones v Department of Employment [1989] QB 1, [1988] 1 All ER 725, [1988] 2 WLR 493, 132 Sol Jo 128, [1987] NLJ Rep 1182, [1988] 4 LS Gaz R 35, CA : 5.13
Jones v G D Searle & Co Ltd [1978] 3 All ER 654, [1979] 1 WLR 101, 122 Sol Jo 435, CA 11.16
Jones v Gooday (1841) 8 M & W 146, 11 Dowl NS 50, 10 LJ Ex 275 .... 10.09
Jones v Griffith [1969] 2 All ER 1015, [1969] 1 WLR 795, 113 Sol Jo 30, CA .. 7.11
Jones v Jones [1985] QB 704, [1984] 3 All ER 1003, [1984] 3 WLR 862, [1985] Fam Law 23, 128 Sol Jo 470, [1984] LS Gaz R 2293, CA 7.03
Jones v Lawrence [1969] 3 All ER 267 .... 4.14
Jones v Lionite Specialities (Cardiff) Ltd (1961) 105 Sol Jo 1082, CA 14.11
Jones v Livox Quarries Ltd [1952] 2 QB 608, [1952] 1 TLR 1377, 96 Sol Jo 344, CA 4.09
Jones v Manchester Corpn [1952] 2 QB 852, [1952] 2 All ER 125, 116 JP 412, [1952] 1 TLR 1589, CA 15.08
Jones v Port of London Authority [1954] 1 Lloyd's Rep 489 .... 10.05
Jordan v Achara (1988) 20 HLR 607, CA 16.03
Joyce v Yeomans [1981] 2 All ER 21, [1981] 1 WLR 549, 125 Sol Jo 34, CA 8.13
Junior Books Ltd v Veitchi Co Ltd [1983] 1 AC 520, [1982] 3 All ER 201, [1982] 3 WLR 477, 126 Sol Jo 538, 21 BLR 66, [1982] Com LR 221, [1982] LS Gaz R 1413, 1982 SLT 492, HL 1.02, 1.09, 4.27, 6.04, 6.09, 6.10, 6.11, 11.23, 17.13

K

K v JMP Co Ltd [1976] QB 85, [1975] 1 All ER 1030, [1975] 2 WLR 457, 5 Fam Law 83, 119 Sol Jo 188, CA 9.06, 9.21
Kamloops v Nielsen, Hughes and Hughes [1984] 5 WWR 1, 10 DLR (4th) 641 .. 12.18
Kandalla v British Airways Board [1981] QB 158, [1980] 1 All ER 341, [1980] 2 WLR 730 .... 9.15
Kapetan Georgis, The. See Virgo SS Co SA v Skaarup Shipping Corpn, The Kapetan Georgis
Karabotsos v Plastex Industries Pty Ltd [1981] VR 675 .... 7.07
Kate, The [1899] P 165, 68 LJP 41, 80 LT 423, 47 WR 669, 15 TLR 309, 8 Asp MLC 539 .... 10.04

Table of Cases xxxix

Kay v ITW Ltd [1968] 1 QB 140, [1967] 3 All ER 22, [1967] 3 WLR 695, 111 Sol
  Jo 351, CA 18.10
Kay's Tutor v Ayrshire and Arran Health Board [1987] 2 All ER 417, 1987 SLT
  577, HL... 2.14, 15.05
Kearney v Eric Waller Ltd [1967] 1 QB 29, [1965] 3 All ER 352, [1966] 2 WLR
  208, 110 Sol Jo 13 .... 16.01
Kecskemeti v Rubens Rabin & Co (1992) Times, 31 December 5.17, 15.18
Kelly v City of Edinburgh District Council 1983 SLT 593 .... 15.24
Kelly v Dawes (1990) Times, 27 September 8.28
Kelly v John Dale Ltd [1965] 1 QB 185, [1964] 2 All ER 497, [1964] 3 WLR 41,
  108 Sol Jo 218, 62 LGR 331..................................... 14.25
Kelly v London Transport Executive [1982] 2 All ER 842, [1982] 1 WLR 1055,
  126 Sol Jo 262, CA 5.08
Kennedy v Bowater Containers Ltd [1990] 2 QB 391, [1990] 1 All ER 669, [1990]
  2 WLR 84, 133 Sol Jo 1606 .... 7.11
Kennett v Brown [1988] 2 All ER 600, [1988] 1 WLR 582, 132 Sol Jo 752, CA .. 11.04
Kenney v Hall, Pain and Foster (1976) 239 Estates Gazette 355, [1976] EGD
  629 .... 15.21
Keppel Bus Co Ltd v Sa'ad bin Ahmad [1974] 2 All ER 700, [1974] 1 WLR 1082,
  17 KIR 90, [1974] RTR 504, PC 18.13
Ketteman v Hansel Properties Ltd [1985] 1 All ER 352, [1984] 1 WLR 1274, 128
  Sol Jo 800, 83 LGR 257, 27 BLR 1, 12 Con LR 16, 271 Estates Gazette 1099,
  [1984] CILL 109, [1984] LS Gaz R 3018, CA; on appeal [1987] AC 189, [1988]
  1 All ER 38, [1987] 2 WLR 312, 131 Sol Jo 134, 85 LGR 409, 36 BLR 1, 12
  Con LR 16, [1987] 1 EGLR 237, [1987] NLJ Rep 100, [1987] LS Gaz R 657,
  HL.. 11.04, 11.24
Kimpton v Steel Co of Wales Ltd [1960] 2 All ER 274, [1960] 1 WLR 527, 104
  Sol Jo 387, CA 14.39
King v Liverpool City Council [1986] 3 All ER 544, [1986] 1 WLR 890, 130 Sol
  Jo 505, 84 LGR 871, 18 HLR 307, [1986] 1 EGLR 181, 278 Estates Gazette
  516, [1986] NLJ Rep 334, [1986] LS Gaz R 2492, CA 1.05
King v Phillips [1953] 1 QB 429, [1953] 1 All ER 617, [1953] 2 WLR 526, 97 Sol
  Jo 171, CA 1.25
King v Victor Parsons & Co [1973] 1 All ER 206, [1973] 1 WLR 29, 116 Sol Jo
  901, [1973] 1 Lloyd's Rep 189, 225 Estates Gazette 611, CA 11.22
Kingston Cotton Mill Co (No 2), Re [1896] 2 Ch 279, 65 LJ Ch 673, 74 LT 568,
  12 TLR 430, 40 Sol Jo 531, 3 Mans 171, CA 15.26
Kirby v Leather [1965] 2 QB 367, [1965] 2 All ER 441, [1965] 2 WLR 1318, 109
  Sol Jo 357, CA 11.03
Kirkham v Chief Constable of the Greater Manchester Police [1990] 2 QB 283,
  [1990] 3 All ER 246, [1990] 2 WLR 987, 134 Sol Jo 758, [1990] NLJR 209,
  [1990] 13 LS Gaz R 47, CA 1.21, 3.17
Kitchen v RAF Association [1958] 2 All ER 241, [1958] 1 WLR 563, 102 Sol Jo
  363, CA 11.22
Klein v Caluori [1971] 2 All ER 701, [1971] 1 WLR 619, 115 Sol Jo 228, [1971]
  1 Lloyd's Rep 421, [1971] RTR 354 .... 18.25
Knapp v Railway Executive [1949] 2 All ER 508, CA 13.07
Knight v Home Office [1990] 3 All ER 237, [1990] NLJR 210 .... 1.21, 1.23, 2.09,
                                                               15.06, 15.08
Knight v Leamington Spa Courier Ltd [1961] 2 QB 253, [1961] 2 All ER 666,
  [1961] 3 WLR 79, 105 Sol Jo 465, 59 LGR 374, CA 14.25
Knightley v Johns [1982] 1 All ER 851, [1982] 1 WLR 349, 126 Sol Jo 101,
  [1982] RTR 182, CA... 3.22
Kondis v State Transport Authority (1984) 154 CLR 672, 55 ALR 225, 58 ALJR
  531 (Aust HC).. 14.15
Kooragang Investments Pty Ltd v Richardson and Wrench Ltd [1982] AC 462,
  [1981] 3 All ER 65, [1981] 3 WLR 493, 125 Sol Jo 641, PC 18.09, 18.13
Kossinski v Chrysler United Kingdom Ltd (1973) 15 KIR 225 .... 14.11
Koufos v C Czarnikow Ltd, The Heron II [1969] 1 AC 350, [1967] 3 All ER 686,
  [1967] 3 WLR 1491, 111 Sol Jo 848, [1967] 2 Lloyd's Rep 457, HL 2.04
Kralj v McGrath [1986] 1 All ER 54, [1985] NLJ Rep 913 .... 7.03, 15.05
Kubach v Hollands [1937] 3 All ER 907, 53 TLR 1024, 81 Sol Jo 766 .... 17.06, 17.07

L

Ladenbau (G & K) (UK) Ltd v Crawley and de Reya (a firm) [1978] 1 All ER
    682, [1978] 1 WLR 266, 121 Sol Jo 356 .... 15.15
Lai Wee Lian v Singapore Bus Service (1978) Ltd [1984] AC 729, [1984] 3 WLR
    63, 128 Sol Jo 432, [1984] LS Gaz R 1597, PC 7.04
Lamb v Camden London Borough Council [1981] QB 625, [1981] 2 All ER 408,
    [1981] 2 WLR 1038, 125 Sol Jo 356, CA 1.05, 1.06, 3.06, 3.20, 19.03
Lampert v Eastern National Omnibus Co Ltd [1954] 2 All ER 719n, [1954]
    1 WLR 1047, 98 Sol Jo 493... 7.03
Lampitt v Poole Borough Council (Taylor, third parties) [1991] 2 QB 545, [1990]
    2 All ER 887, [1990] 3 WLR 179, 49 BLR 82, CA 4.18
Larner v British Steel plc (1993) Times, 19 February, CA 14.28, 14.39
Latimer v AEC Ltd [1953] AC 643, [1953] 2 All ER 449, 117 JP 387, 97 Sol Jo
    486, 51 LGR 457, HL 2.07, 12.08, 14.09, 14.27
Launchbury v Morgans [1971] 2 QB 245, [1971] 1 All ER 642, [1971] 2 WLR
    602, 115 Sol Jo 96, [1971] 1 Lloyd's Rep 197, CA; revsd sub nom Morgans v
    Launchbury [1973] AC 127, [1972] 2 All ER 606, [1972] 2 WLR 1217, 116
    Sol Jo 396, [1972] 1 Lloyd's Rep 483, [1972] RTR 406, HL: 1.09, 1.22, 18.24, 18.26,
                                                                               18.27, 19.03, 19.04
Lawton v BOC Transhield Ltd [1987] 2 All ER 608, [1987] ICR 7, [1987] IRLR
    404 .... 5.19
Leach v Standard Telephones and Cables Ltd [1966] 2 All ER 523, [1966]
    1 WLR 1392, 110 Sol Jo 465 .... 14.37
Le Bagge v Buses Ltd [1958] NZLR 630 .... 9.24, 9.25
Lee v South West Thames Regional Health Authority [1985] 2 All ER 385,
    [1985] 1 WLR 845, 128 Sol Jo 333, [1985] NLJ Rep 438, [1985] LS Gaz R
    2015, CA 15.11
Leicester Wholesale Fruit Market v Grundy (t/a Grundy Harmer) (formerly
    Bedingfield and Grundy) (No 2) (1990) 53 BLR 6, CA 11.22
Leigh and Sillivan Ltd v Aliakmon Shipping Co Ltd, The Aliakmon [1985]
    QB 350, [1985] 2 All ER 44, [1985] 2 WLR 289, 129 Sol Jo 69, [1985]
    1 Lloyd's Rep 199, [1985] NLJ Rep 285, [1985] LS Gaz R 203, CA; affd [1986]
    AC 785, [1986] 2 All ER 145, [1986] 2 WLR 902, 130 Sol Jo 357, [1986] 2
    Lloyd's Rep 1, [1986] NLJ Rep 415, [1986] LS Gaz R 1810, HL ... 1.03, 6.11, 6.12,
                                                                                 6.15, 6.17, 6.19
Levesley v Thomas Firth and John Brown Ltd [1953] 2 All ER 866, [1953]
    1 WLR 1206, 97 Sol Jo 606, 51 LGR 571, CA......................... 14.27
Lewys v Burnett and Dunbar [1945] 2 All ER 555, 173 LT 307, 109 JP 253, 61
    TLR 527, 89 Sol Jo 415, 43 LGR 186 .... 16.01
Lexmead (Basingstoke) Ltd v Lewis [1982] AC 225, sub nom Lambert v Lewis
    [1980] 1 All ER 978, [1980] 2 WLR 299, 124 Sol Jo 50, [1980] RTR 152,
    [1980] 1 Lloyd's Rep 311, CA; revsd sub nom Lexmead (Basingstoke) Ltd
    v Lewis [1982] AC 225, 268, [1981] 2 WLR 713, 125 Sol Jo 310, [1981] RTR
    346, [1981] 2 Lloyd's Rep 17, sub nom Lambert v Lewis [1981] 1 All ER
    1185, HL.. 5.03, 17.13
Liesbosch, Dredger (Owners) v SS Edison (Owners) [1933] AC 449, 102 LJP
    73, 77 Sol Jo 176, sub nom The Edison [1933] All ER Rep 144, 149 LT 49,
    49 TLR 289, 18 Asp MLC 380, 38 Com Cas 267, 45 Ll L Rep 123, HL : 3.12, 10.01
Liff v Peasley [1980] 1 All ER 623, [1980] 1 WLR 781, 124 Sol Jo 360, CA: 11.04, 11.19
Lim Poh Choo v Camden and Islington Area Health Authority [1979] QB 196,
    [1979] 1 All ER 332, [1978] 3 WLR 895, 122 Sol Jo 508, CA; affd [1980] AC
    174, [1979] 2 All ER 910, [1979] 3 WLR 44, 123 Sol Jo 457, HL ... 7.01, 7.04, 7.05,
                                                                             8.01, 8.05, 8.06, 8.11,
                                                                             8.23, 8.24, 8.25, 8.31
Lincoln v Hayman [1982] 2 All ER 819, [1982] 1 WLR 488, 126 Sol Jo 174,
    [1982] RTR 336, CA 8.20
Lister v Romford Ice and Cold Storage Co Ltd [1957] AC 555, [1957] 1 All ER
    125, [1957] 2 WLR 158, 121 JP 98, 101 Sol Jo 106, [1956] 2 Lloyd's Rep 505,
    HL 4.24, 18.14, 19.03
Liston v Liston and Sleep (1983) 31 SASR 245 .... 3.23
Lloyd v Grace, Smith & Co [1912] AC 716, [1911-13] All ER Rep 51, 81 LJKB
    1140, 107 LT 531, 28 TLR 547, 56 Sol Jo 723, HL 18.12, 18.13, 18.24

Table of Cases xli

Lloyde v West Midlands Gas Board [1971] 2 All ER 1240, [1971] 1 WLR 749,
 115 Sol Jo 227, CA... 2.15
Logan v Uttlesford District Council and Hammond [1986] NLJ Rep 541, CA .. 4.19
London and South of England Building Society v Stone [1983] 3 All ER 105,
 [1983] 1 WLR 1242, 127 Sol Jo 446, 267 Estates Gazette 69, [1983] LS Gaz
 R 3048, CA 15.22
LCC v Cattermoles (Garages) Ltd [1953] 2 All ER 582, [1953] 1 WLR 977, 97
 Sol Jo 505, CA 18.10, 18.12
London Graving Dock Co Ltd v Horton [1951] AC 737, [1951] 2 All ER 1, [1951]
 1 TLR 949, 95 Sol Jo 465, [1951] 1 Lloyd's Rep 389, HL 16.10
London Passenger Transport Board v Upson [1949] AC 155, [1949] 1 All ER 60,
 [1949] LJR 238, 65 TLR 9, 93 Sol Jo 40, 47 LGR 333, HL 13.04
Longmeid v Holliday (1851) 6 Exch 761, 20 LJ Ex 430, 17 LTOS 243 .... 17.02
Lonrho Ltd v Shell Petroleum Co Ltd (No 2) [1982] AC 173, [1981] 2 All ER 456,
 [1981] 3 WLR 33, 125 Sol Jo 429, HL 13.01, 13.02
Lonrho plc v Tebbit [1991] 4 All ER 973; affd [1992] 4 All ER 280, CA 6.24, 12.04,
 12.07, 12.10,
 12.12, 12.14
Lord v Pacific Steam Navigation Co Ltd, The Oropesa [1943] P 32, [1943] 1 All
 ER 211, 112 LJP 91, 168 LT 364, 59 TLR 103, CA 3.16, 3.22
Lord Citrine, The (Owners) v Hebridean Coast (Owners), The Hebridean Coast
 [1961] AC 545, [1961] 1 All ER 82, [1961] 2 WLR 48, 105 Sol Jo 37, [1960]
 2 Lloyd's Rep 423, HL 10.04
Losner v Michael Cohen & Co (1975) 119 Sol Jo 340, CA 5.10
Loveday v Renton [1990] 1 Med LR 117............................... 19.14
Luxmoore-May v Messenger May Baverstock (a firm) [1990] 1 All ER 1067,
 [1990] 1 WLR 1009, [1990] 1 EGLR 21, [1990] 07 EG 61, [1990] NLJR 89,
 CA 15.09

M

M'Alister (or Donoghue) v Stevenson [1932] AC 562, 101 LJPC 119, 48 TLR 494,
 37 Com Cas 350, 1932 SC (HL) 31, sub nom McAlister (or Donoghue) v
 Stevenson 147 LT 281, 76 Sol Jo 396, sub nom Donoghue (or McAlister) v
 Stevenson [1932] All ER Rep 1, 1932 SLT 317 ...... 1.01, 1.05, 5.01, 6.04, 16.05,
 17.02, 17.03, 17.08, 17.11
McAlpine (Sir Robert) & Sons Ltd v Minimax Ltd (1970) 114 Sol Jo 206, [1970]
 1 Lloyd's Rep 397 .... 2.10
McAuley v Bristol City Council [1992] 1 QB 134, [1992] 1 All ER 749, [1991]
 3 WLR 968, 89 LGR 931, 23 HLR 586, [1991] 2 EGLR 64, [1991] 46 EG 155,
 CA 16.38, 16.39
McAuley v London Transport Executive [1957] 2 Lloyd's Rep 500, CA 7.07
McCafferty v Metropolitan Police District Receiver [1977] 2 All ER 756, [1977]
 1 WLR 1073, [1977] ICR 799, 121 Sol Jo 678, CA 11.10, 11.11, 11.18
McCall v Abelesz [1976] QB 585, [1976] 1 All ER 727, [1976] 2 WLR 151, 120 Sol
 Jo 81, 31 P & CR 256, 238 Estates Gazette 335, CA 13.06, 13.13, 13.19
McCallion v Dodd [1966] NZLR 710 .... 2.03
McCamley v Cammell Laird Shipbuilders Ltd [1990] 1 All ER 854, [1990]
 1 WLR 963, CA 8.17, 8.18
McCann v Sheppard [1973] 2 All ER 881, [1973] 1 WLR 540, 117 Sol Jo 323,
 [1973] 1 Lloyd's Rep 561, CA 7.03, 8.01
McCormick v National Motor and Accident Insurance Union Ltd (1934) 50 TLR
 528, 78 Sol Jo 633, 40 Com Cas 76, 49 Ll L Rep 361, CA 19.10
McDermid v Nash Dredging and Reclamation Co Ltd [1986] QB 965, [1986]
 2 All ER 676, [1986] 3 WLR 45, [1986] ICR 525, [1986] IRLR 308, 130 Sol
 Jo 372, [1986] 2 Lloyd's Rep 24, [1986] LS Gaz R 1559, CA; affd [1987] AC
 906, [1987] 2 All ER 878, [1987] 3 WLR 212, [1987] ICR 917, [1987] IRLR
 334, 131 Sol Jo 973, [1987] 2 Lloyd's Rep 201, [1987] LS Gaz R 2458, HL .. 14.04,
 14.10, 14.15, 18.07, 18.21
McGhee v National Coal Board [1972] 3 All ER 1008, [1973] 1 WLR 1, 116 Sol
 Jo 967, 13 KIR 471, HL 2.13, 2.14
McHale v Watson [1966] ALR 513 (Aust HC) 2.02

Table of Cases

Machray v Stewarts and Lloyds Ltd [1964] 3 All ER 716, [1965] 1 WLR 602, 109 Sol Jo 270 .... 4.08
McInerny v Lloyds Bank Ltd [1973] 2 Lloyd's Rep 389; affd [1974] 1 Lloyd's Rep 246, CA 5.18
Mackay v Borthwick 1982 SLT 265 .... 4.12
McKay v Essex Area Health Authority [1982] QB 1166, [1982] 2 All ER 771, [1982] 2 WLR 890, 126 Sol Jo 261, CA 1.19
McKew v Holland and Hannen and Cubitts (Scotland) Ltd [1969] 3 All ER 1621 1970 SC (HL) 20, 1970 SLT 68 .... 3.14, 4.07
McLean v Weir and Goff [1980] 4 WWR 330 .... 15.02
McLellan v Fletcher [1987] NLJ Rep 593 .... 15.15
McLeod (or Houston) v Buchanan [1940] 2 All ER 179, 84 Sol Jo 452, 1940 SC (HL) 17, 1940 SN 20, 1940 SLT 232 .... 13.05
McLoughlin v O'Brian [1983] 1 AC 410, [1982] 2 All ER 298, [1982] 2 WLR 982, 126 Sol Jo 347, [1982] RTR 209, [1982] LS Gaz R 922, HL 1.09, 1.25, 6.04
McNamara v Martin Mears & Co (1982) 127 Sol Jo 69 .... 5.10
McNealy v Pennine Insurance Co Ltd (1978) 122 Sol Jo 229, [1978] 2 Lloyd's Rep 18, [1978] RTR 285, CA 5.24
McSherry v British Telecommunications plc [1992] 3 Med LR 129 .... 14.08
Madden v Quirk [1989] 1 WLR 702, 133 Sol Jo 752, [1989] RTR 304, [1989] 26 LS Gaz R 36 .... 4.12, 4.24
Mailer v Austin Rover Group plc. See Austin Rover Group Ltd v HM Inspector of Factories
Malcolm v Broadhurst [1970] 3 All ER 508 .... 3.10
Mallett v McMonagle [1970] AC 166, [1969] 2 All ER 178, [1969] 2 WLR 767, 113 Sol Jo 207, [1969] 1 Lloyd's Rep 127, [1969] NI 91, HL 9.13
Maloco v Littlewoods Ltd [1987] AC 241, [1987] 2 WLR 480, 131 Sol Jo 226, 1987 SLT 425, [1987] LS Gaz R 905, sub nom Smith v Littlewoods Organisation Ltd [1987] 1 All ER 710, [1987] NLJ Rep 149, HL 1.01, 1.03, 1.05, 3.19
Malone v Rowan [1984] 3 All ER 402 .... 9.17
Malyon v Plummer [1964] 1 QB 330, [1963] 2 All ER 344, [1963] 2 WLR 1213, 107 Sol Jo 270, CA 9.07
Man-Waring v Billington [1952] 2 All ER 747, [1952] 2 TLR 689, 96 Sol Jo 747, 51 LGR 22, CA 13.17, 14.37
Mangan v F C Pilgram & Co 336 NE 2d 374 (1975) 13.07
March v E & M H Stramare Pty Ltd (1991) 171 CLR 506 (Aust HC) 4.09
Marcroft v Scruttons Ltd [1954] 1 Lloyd's Rep 395, CA 7.07
Marintrans AB v Comet Shipping Co Ltd, The Shinjitsu Maru No 5 [1985] 3 All ER 442, [1985] 1 WLR 1270, 129 Sol Jo 828, [1985] 1 Lloyd's Rep 568, [1986] LS Gaz R 43 .... 4.16
Market Investigations Ltd v Minister of Social Security [1969] 2 QB 173, [1968] 3 All ER 732, [1969] 2 WLR 1, 112 Sol Jo 905 .... 18.03
Marpessa, The. See Mersey Docks and Harbour Board v Marpessa (Owners)
Marren v Dawson Bentley & Co Ltd [1961] 2 QB 135, [1961] 2 All ER 270, [1961] 2 WLR 679, 105 Sol Jo 383 .... 11.02
Marriott v Carson's Construction Ltd (1983) 146 DLR (3d) 126 .... 10.15
Marshall v Osmond [1983] QB 1034, [1983] 2 All ER 225, [1983] 3 WLR 13, 127 Sol Jo 309, [1983] RTR 475, CA 2.06
Marston v British Railways Board [1976] ICR 124 .... 11.13, 11.18
Martin v Dean [1971] 2 QB 208, [1971] 3 All ER 279, [1971] 2 WLR 1159, 115 Sol Jo 369, [1971] RTR 280 .... 13.05
Martindale v Duncan [1973] 2 All ER 355, [1973] 1 WLR 574, 117 Sol Jo 168, [1973] 1 Lloyd's Rep 558, [1973] RTR 532, CA 3.12
Massey v Crown Life Insurance Co [1978] 2 All ER 576, [1978] 1 WLR 676, [1978] ICR 590, [1978] IRLR 31, 13 ITR 5, 121 Sol Jo 791, CA 18.05
Matania v National Provincial Bank Ltd and Elevenist Syndicate Ltd [1936] 2 All ER 633, 106 LJKB 113, 155 LT 74, 80 Sol Jo 532, CA 18.18
Mathew v Maughold Life Assurance Co Ltd (1987) 3 PN 98, (1987) Times, 19 February, CA 15.16
Maynard v West Midlands Regional Health Authority [1985] 1 All ER 635, [1984] 1 WLR 634, 128 Sol Jo 317, 133 NLJ 641, [1984] LS Gaz R 1926, HL 2.09, 15.05, 15.09

Meah v McCreamer [1985] 1 All ER 367, [1985] NLJ Rep 80 .... 1.20, 3.17, 7.03
Meah v McCreamer (No 2) [1986] 1 All ER 943, [1986] NLJ Rep 235 : 1.20, 9.25, 19.07
Mediana (Owners) v Comet (Owners, Master and Crew of the Lightship), The
   Mediana [1900] AC 113, [1900-3] All ER Rep 126, 69 LJP 35, 82 LT 95, 48
   WR 398, 16 TLR 194, 44 Sol Jo 259, 9 Asp MLC 41, HL 10.04
Mehmet v Perry [1977] 2 All ER 529 .... 9.19
Merrill Lynch Futures Inc v York House Trading Ltd [1984] LS Gaz R 2544,
   CA 15.27
Mersey Docks and Harbour Board v Coggins and Griffiths (Liverpool) Ltd
   [1947] AC 1, [1946] 2 All ER 345, 115 LJKB 465, 175 LT 270, 62 TLR 533,
   90 Sol J 466, HL 18.06
Mersey Docks and Harbour Board v Marpessa (Owners) [1907] AC 241, [1904-7]
   All ER Rep 855, 97 LT 1, 23 TLR 572, 51 Sol Jo 530, 10 Asp MLC 464, sub
   nom The Marpessa 76 LJP 128, HL 10.04
Mersey Docks and Harbour Board Trustees v Gibbs (1866) LR 1 HL 93, 11 HL
   Cas 686, [1861-73] All ER Rep 397, 35 LJ Ex 225, 14 LT 677, 30 JP 467, 12
   Jur NS 571, 14 WR 872, 2 Mar LC 353, 11 ER 1500 .... 12.01
Midland and Low Moor Iron and Steel Co Ltd v Cross [1965] AC 343, [1964]
   3 All ER 752, [1964] 3 WLR 1180, 108 Sol Jo 938, 63 LGR 81, HL 14.23
Midland Bank Trust Co Ltd v Hett, Stubbs and Kemp (a firm) [1979] Ch 384,
   [1978] 3 All ER 571, [1978] 3 WLR 167, 121 Sol Jo 830 .... 4.16, 5.25, 6.23, 11.05,
                                                         11.29, 15.15, 15.17, 15.19
Millard v Serck Tubes Ltd [1969] 1 All ER 598, [1969] 1 WLR 211, 112 Sol Jo
   924, 5 KIR 389, CA 14.24
Miller v Jackson [1977] QB 966, [1977] 3 All ER 338, [1977] 3 WLR 20, 121 Sol
   Jo 287, CA 2.04
Miller v London Electrical Manufacturing Co Ltd (1976) 120 Sol Jo 80, [1976]
   2 Lloyd's Rep 284, CA 11.10
Miller v William Boothman & Sons Ltd [1944] KB 337, [1944] 1 All ER 333, 113
   LJKB 206, 170 LT 187, 60 TLR 218, CA 14.22
Mineral Transporter, The. See Candlewood Navigation Corpn Ltd v Mitsui
   OSK Lines Ltd, The Mineral Transporter, The Ibaraki Maru
Ministry of Housing and Local Government v Sharp [1970] 2 QB 223, [1970]
   1 All ER 1009, [1970] 2 WLR 802, 134 JP 358, 114 Sol Jo 109, 68 LGR 187,
   21 P & CR 166, 213 Estates Gazette 1145, CA 5.01, 5.22, 5.27,
                                                                  6.23, 13.15
Minories Finance Ltd v Arthur Young (a firm) (Bank of England, third party)
   [1989] 2 All ER 105 .... 12.12
Mint v Good [1951] 1 KB 517, [1950] 2 All ER 1159, 66 (pt 2) TLR 1110, 94 Sol
   Jo 822, 49 LGR 495, CA 6.11
Minter v D and H Contractors (Cambridge) Ltd (1983) Times, 30 June 4.15
Miraflores (Owners) v George Livanos (Owners) [1967] 1 AC 826, [1967] 1 All
   ER 672, [1967] 2 WLR 806, 111 Sol Jo 211, [1967] 1 Lloyd's Rep 191, HL: 4.09, 4.10
Misterek v Washington Mineral Products 531 P 2d 805 (1975) 13.07
Mitchell v Liverpool Area Health Authority (1985) Times, 17 June, CA 8.13
Mitchell v Mulholland (No 2) [1972] 1 QB 65, [1971] 2 All ER 1205, [1971]
   2 WLR 1271, 115 Sol Jo 227, [1971] 1 Lloyd's Rep 462, CA 8.10
Mitchell v W S Westin Ltd [1965] 1 All ER 657, [1965] 1 WLR 297, 109 Sol Jo
   49, 63 LGR 219, CA 14.25
Moeliker v A Reyrolle & Co Ltd [1977] 1 All ER 9, [1977] 1 WLR 132, [1976]
   ICR 253, [1976] IRLR 120, 120 Sol Jo 165, CA 8.12
Monk v Warbey [1935] 1 KB 75, [1934] All ER Rep 373, 104 LJKB 153, 152 LT
   194, 51 TLR 77, 78 Sol Jo 783, 50 Ll L Rep 33, CA 13.05, 13.06, 13.13
Montreal v Montreal Locomotive Works Ltd [1947] 1 DLR 161 .... 18.04
Moore v Canadian Pacific SS Co [1945] 1 All ER 128 .... 13.05
Moore v DER Ltd [1971] 3 All ER 517, [1971] 1 WLR 1476, 115 Sol Jo 528,
   [1971] 2 Lloyd's Rep 359, [1972] RTR 97, CA 10.06
Moore v R Fox & Sons [1956] 1 QB 596, [1956] 1 All ER 182, [1956] 2 WLR 342,
   100 Sol Jo 90, [1956] 1 Lloyd's Rep 129, CA 2.16, 2.17
Moore (D W) & Co Ltd v Ferrier [1988] 1 All ER 400, [1988] 1 WLR 267, 132 Sol
   Jo 227, [1987] NLJ Rep 1013, [1988] 10 LS Gaz R 45, CA 11.24

Table of Cases

Moorgate Mercantile Co Ltd v Twitchings [1976] QB 225, [1975] 3 All ER 314, [1975] 3 WLR 286, 119 Sol Jo 559, [1975] RTR 528, CA; revsd [1977] AC 890, [1976] 2 All ER 641, [1976] 3 WLR 66, 120 Sol Jo 470, [1976] RTR 437, HL 5.26
Morales v Eccleston [1991] RTR 151, CA 4.15
Morash v Lockhart & Ritchie Ltd (1978) 95 DLR (3d) 647 .... 5.24, 5.32
Morgan v Perry (1973) 229 Estates Gazette 1737 .... 15.22
Morgan v T Wallis Ltd [1974] 1 Lloyd's Rep 165 .... 7.07, 7.08
Morgan Crucible Co plc v Hill Samuel & Co Ltd [1991] Ch 295, [1991] 2 WLR 655, [1990] BCC 686, [1990] NLJR 1271, sub nom Morgan Crucible Co plc v Hill Samuel Bank Ltd [1990] 3 All ER 330, [1991] BCLC 18; revsd sub nom Morgan Crucible Co plc v Hill Samuel & Co Ltd [1991] Ch 295, [1991] 2 WLR 655, [1991] BCC 82, [1990] NLJR 1605, sub nom Morgan Crucible Co plc v Hill Samuel Bank Ltd [1991] 1 All ER 148, [1991] BCLC 178, CA : 5.23
Morgans v Launchbury. See Launchbury v Morgans
Moriarty v McCarthy [1978] 2 All ER 213, [1978] 1 WLR 155, 121 Sol Jo 745: 8.09
Morris v Breaveglen Ltd (t/a Anzac Construction Co) (1992) 137 Sol Jo LB 13, CA 14.15, 18.07
Morris v C W Martin & Sons Ltd [1966] 1 QB 716, [1965] 2 All ER 725, [1965] 3 WLR 276, 109 Sol Jo 451, [1965] 2 Lloyd's Rep 63, CA 18.13, 18.22
Morris v Ford Motor Co Ltd [1973] QB 792, [1973] 2 All ER 1084, [1973] 2 WLR 843, 117 Sol Jo 393, [1973] 2 Lloyd's Rep 27, CA 18.14
Morris v Murray [1991] 2 QB 6, [1990] 3 All ER 801, [1991] 2 WLR 195, 134 Sol Jo 1300, [1990] NLJR 1459, [1990] 42 LS Gaz R 36, CA 4.02, 4.04, 4.06, 4.13
Morris v West Hartlepool Steam Navigation Co Ltd [1956] AC 552, [1956] 1 All ER 385, [1956] 1 WLR 177, 100 Sol Jo 129, [1956] 1 Lloyd's Rep 76, HL ... 2.09, 14.07, 15.07
Morrison SS Co Ltd v SS Greystoke Castle (Owners of Cargo lately laden on) [1947] AC 265, [1946] 2 All ER 696, [1947] LJR 297, 176 LT 66, 63 TLR 11, HL 6.02, 6.16
Moss v Christchurch RDC [1925] 2 KB 750, 23 LGR 331, 95 LJKB 81, DC 10.09
Muirhead v Industrial Tank Specialities Ltd [1986] QB 507, [1985] 3 All ER 705, [1985] 3 WLR 993, 129 Sol Jo 855, [1986] LS Gaz R 116, CA 6.10, 17.13
Mulholland v McCrea [1961] NI 135 .... 9.05
Mulholland v Mitchell [1971] AC 666, [1971] 1 All ER 307, [1971] 2 WLR 93, 115 Sol Jo 15, HL 7.03
Mullard v Ben Line Steamers Ltd [1971] 2 All ER 424, [1970] 1 WLR 1414, 114 Sol Jo 570, [1970] 2 Lloyd's Rep 121, CA 4.08, 14.34
Munnelly v Calcon Ltd, John Sisk & Sons (Dublin) Ltd and Doyle [1978] IR 387 .... 10.09, 10.10
Murphy v Brentwood District Council [1991] 1 AC 398, [1990] 2 All ER 908, [1990] 3 WLR 414, 134 Sol Jo 1076, 89 LGR 24, 22 HLR 502, 50 BLR 1, 21 Con LR 1, [1990] 2 Lloyd's Rep 467, [1990] NLJR 1111, HL: 1.01, 1.02, 1.03, 1.04, 1.12, 1.14, 1.22, 3.12, 5.17, 6.05, 6.06, 6.07, 6.08, 6.10, 6.13, 6.22, 11.23, 11.24, 11.25, 12.04, 12.13, 17.13, 17.26
Murphy v Culhane [1977] QB 94, [1976] 3 All ER 533, [1976] 3 WLR 458, 120 Sol Jo 506, CA 9.24
Murphy v Stone-Wallwork (Charlton) Ltd [1969] 2 All ER 949, [1969] 1 WLR 1023, 113 Sol Jo 546, HL 7.03
Murray v Harringay Arena Ltd [1951] 2 KB 529, [1951] 2 All ER 320n, 95 Sol Jo 529, CA 4.06
Murray v Lloyd [1990] 2 All ER 92, [1989] 1 WLR 1060, 21 HLR 525, [1990] 1 EGLR 274, [1989] NLJR 938... 10.17
Mutual Life and Citizens' Assurance Co Ltd v Evatt [1971] AC 793, [1971] 1 All ER 150, [1971] 2 WLR 23, 114 Sol Jo 932, [1970] 2 Lloyd's Rep 441, [1971] ALR 235, PC 5.01, 5.02, 5.06
Myers v Peel County Board of Education (1981) 123 DLR (3d) 1 .... 4.15

N

Nabi v British Leyland (UK) Ltd [1980] 1 All ER 667, [1980] 1 WLR 529, 124
Sol Jo 83, CA 8.20
Nash v Eli Lilly & Co [1991] 2 Med LR 169; on appeal (1992) Times, 7 October,
CA 11.09
Naylor v Preston Area Health Authority [1987] 2 All ER 353, [1987] 1 WLR 958,
131 Sol Jo 596, [1987] NLJ Rep 474, [1987] LS Gaz R 1494, CA 15.11
Nettleship v Weston [1971] 2 QB 691, [1971] 3 All ER 581, [1971] 3 WLR 370,
115 Sol Jo 624, [1971] RTR 425, CA 2.01, 4.02, 4.06, 12.19, 19.03, 20.06
New Zealand Shipping Co Ltd v A M Satterthwaite & Co Ltd [1975] AC 154,
[1974] 1 All ER 1015, [1974] 2 WLR 865, 118 Sol Jo 387, sub nom The
Eurymedon [1974] 1 Lloyd's Rep 534, PC 6.11
Ng Chun Pui v Lee Chuen Tat (1988) 132 Sol Jo 1244, [1988] RTR 298, PC ... 2.15
Nicholls v Austin (Leyton) Ltd [1946] AC 493, [1946] 2 All ER 92, 115 LJKB
329, 175 LT 5, 62 TLR 320, 90 Sol Jo 628, 44 LGR 287, HL 14.23
Nicholls v National Coal Board [1976] ICR 266, CA 8.12
Nicholson v Atlas Steel Foundry and Engineering Co Ltd [1957] 1 All ER 776,
[1957] 1 WLR 613, 101 Sol Jo 355, 55 LGR 297, HL 14.29
Nickerson (H B) & Sons Ltd v Wooldridge (1980) 115 DLR (3d) 97 .... 5.32
Nicol v Allyacht Spars Pty Ltd (1987) 163 CLR 611 (Aust HC) 14.37
Nimmo v Alexander Cowan & Sons Ltd [1968] AC 107, [1967] 3 All ER 187,
[1967] 3 WLR 1169, 111 Sol Jo 668, 1967 SC (HL) 79, 1967 SLT 277 ...... 14.28
Nitrigin Eireann Teoranta v Inco Alloys Ltd [1992] 1 All ER 854, [1992] 1 WLR
498, [1992] 3 LS Gaz R 34 .... 11.23
No 7 Steam Sand Pump Dredger (Owners) v Greta Holme (Owners), The Greta
Holme [1897] AC 596, [1895-9] All ER Rep 127, 66 LJP 166, 77 LT 231, 13
TLR 552, 8 Asp MLC 317, HL 10.04
Nocton v Lord Ashburton [1914] AC 932, [1914-15] All ER Rep 45, 83 LJ Ch
784, 111 LT 641, HL 5.01
Nolan v Dental Manufacturing Co Ltd [1958] 2 All ER 449, [1958] 1 WLR 936,
102 Sol Jo 619 .... 14.33
Norton v Canadian Pacific Steamships Ltd [1961] 2 All ER 785, [1961] 1 WLR
1057, 105 Sol Jo 442, [1961] 1 Lloyd's Rep 569, CA 18.27
Norwich City Council v Harvey [1989] 1 All ER 1180, [1989] 1 WLR 828, 133
Sol Jo 694, 45 BLR 14, [1989] NLJR 40, [1989] 25 LS Gaz R 45, CA 4.28, 6.11
Norwood v Navan [1981] RTR 457, CA 18.26
Nottingham v Aldridge [1971] 2 QB 739, [1971] 2 All ER 751, [1971] 3 WLR 1,
115 Sol Jo 328, [1971] 1 Lloyd's Rep 424, [1971] RTR 242 .... 18.24, 18.27
Nottingham Health Authority v Nottingham City Council [1988] 1 WLR 903,
132 Sol Jo 899, CA 4.19

O

Ocean Frost, The. See Armagas Ltd v Mundogas SA, The Ocean Frost
O'Connell v Jackson [1972] 1 QB 270, [1971] 3 All ER 129, [1971] 3 WLR 463,
115 Sol Jo 742, [1971] 2 Lloyd's Rep 354, [1972] RTR 51, CA 4.12
O'Connor v S P Bray (1937) 56 CLR 464 .... 13.03
O'Grady v Westminster Scaffolding Ltd [1962] 2 Lloyd's Rep 238 ...... 10.02, 10.05
Ogwo v Taylor [1988] AC 431, [1987] 3 All ER 961, [1987] 3 WLR 1145, 131 Sol
Jo 1628, [1987] NLJ Rep 1110, [1988] 4 LS Gaz R 35, HL 3.18, 16.08
Oldschool v Gleeson (Contractors) Ltd (1976) 4 BLR 103 .... 15.24
Oliver v Ashman [1962] 2 QB 210, [1961] 3 All ER 323, [1961] 3 WLR 669, 105
Sol Jo 608, CA 8.14, 9.02
Olley v Marlborough Court Ltd [1949] 1 KB 532, [1949] 1 All ER 127, [1949]
LJR 360, 65 TLR 95, 93 Sol Jo 40, CA 4.26
Orchard v South Eastern Electricity Board [1987] QB 565, [1987] 1 All ER 95,
[1987] 2 WLR 102, 130 Sol Jo 956, [1986] NLJ Rep 1112, [1986] LS Gaz R
412, CA 5.08
O'Reilly v C [1978] 3 WWR 145 .... 1.06, 3.19
O'Reilly v ICI Ltd [1955] 3 All ER 382, [1955] 1 WLR 1155, 99 Sol Jo 778, CA: 18.07
O'Reilly v National Rail and Tramway Appliances Ltd [1966] 1 All ER 499 ... 18.11

xlvi *Table of Cases*

Ormindale Holdings Ltd v Ray, Wolfe, Connel, Lightbody & Reynolds (1980) 116 DLR (3d) 346; affd (1982) 135 DLR (3d) 577 .... 5.05, 15.15
Ormrod v Crosville Motor Services Ltd [1953] 2 All ER 753, [1953] 1 WLR 1120, 97 Sol Jo 570, CA 18.25, 18.26
Oropesa, The. See Lord v Pacific Steam Navigation Co Ltd, The Oropesa
Otto v Bolton and Norris [1936] 2 KB 46, [1936] 1 All ER 960, 105 LJKB 602, 154 LT 717, 52 TLR 438, 80 Sol Jo 306 .... 1.14
Overbrooke Estates Ltd v Glencombe Properties Ltd [1974] 3 All ER 511, [1974] 1 WLR 1335, 118 Sol Jo 775 .... 5.31
Overseas Tankship (UK) Ltd v Miller SS Co Pty, The Wagon Mound (No 2) [1967] 1 AC 617, [1966] 2 All ER 709, [1966] 3 WLR 498, 110 Sol Jo 447, [1966] 1 Lloyd's Rep 657, [1966] 1 NSWR 411, [1967] ALR 97, PC 2.06, 3.07
Overseas Tankship (UK) Ltd v Morts Dock and Engineering Co Ltd, The Wagon Mound [1961] AC 388, [1961] 1 All ER 404, [1961] 2 WLR 126, 105 Sol Jo 85, [1961] 1 Lloyd's Rep 1, [1961] ALR 569, PC 3.04, 3.06, 3.10, 3.15, 3.20, 9.25, 13.07
Owens v Brimmell [1977] QB 859, [1976] 3 All ER 765, [1977] 2 WLR 943, 121 Sol Jo 338, [1977] RTR 82 .... 4.03, 4.12, 4.13
Owens v Liverpool Corpn [1939] 1 KB 394, [1938] 4 All ER 727, 108 LJKB 155, 160 LT 8, 55 TLR 246, 82 Sol Jo 1010, CA 1.25

P

Pacific Associates Inc v Baxter [1990] 1 QB 993, [1989] 2 All ER 159, [1989] 3 WLR 1150, 133 Sol Jo 123, 44 BLR 33, 16 Con LR 90, [1989] NLJR 41, [1989] 6 LS Gaz R 44, CA 4.28
Pacific Colcotronis, The. See UBAF Ltd v European American Banking Corpn, The Pacific Colcotronis
Pacific Concord, The, SS or Vessel Georgidore (Owners) v Pacific Concord (Owners), ex Calumet [1961] 1 All ER 106, [1961] 1 WLR 873, 105 Sol Jo 492, [1960] 2 Lloyd's Rep 270 .... 10.04, 10.05
Pactolus, The (1856) Sw 173, 28 LTOS 220, 5 WR 167 .... 10.08
Padbury v Holliday and Greenwood Ltd (1912) 28 TLR 494, CA 18.23
Paine v Colne Valley Electricity Supply Co Ltd and British Insulated Cables Ltd [1938] 4 All ER 803, 160 LT 124, 55 TLR 181, 83 Sol Jo 115, 37 LGR 200 .... 17.08
Palmer v Durnford Ford (a firm) [1992] 1 QB 483, [1992] 2 All ER 122, [1992] 2 WLR 407 .... 5.11, 5.12
Pannett v P McGuinness & Co Ltd [1972] 2 QB 599, [1972] 3 All ER 137, [1972] 3 WLR 386, 116 Sol Jo 335, CA 16.17, 16.21
Pape v Cumbria County Council [1992] 3 All ER 211, [1992] ICR 132, [1991] IRLR 463 .... 14.06
Paris v Stepney Borough Council [1951] AC 367, [1951] 1 All ER 42, 115 JP 22, [1951] 1 TLR 25, 94 Sol Jo 837, 49 LGR 293, 84 Ll L Rep 525, HL 2.05, 14.10
Parry v Cleaver [1970] AC 1, [1969] 1 All ER 555, [1969] 2 WLR 821, 113 Sol Jo 147, [1969] 1 Lloyd's Rep 183, HL 8.17
Parsons (H) (Livestock) Ltd v Uttley Ingham & Co Ltd [1978] QB 791, [1978] 1 All ER 525, [1977] 3 WLR 990, 121 Sol Jo 811, [1977] 2 Lloyd's Rep 522, CA 15.19
Pasmore v Oswaldtwistle UDC [1898] AC 387, [1895-9] All ER Rep 191, 67 LJQB 635, 78 LT 569, 62 JP 628, 14 TLR 368, HL 13.08, 13.11, 13.12
Pass of Ballater, The [1942] P 112, 111 LJP 61, 167 LT 290, 8 TLR 221, sub nom Pass of Ballater, SS (Owners) v Cardiff Channel Dry Docks and Pontoon Co Ltd [1942] 2 All ER 79 .... 18.17
Patel v London Transport Executive [1981] RTR 29, CA 10.07
Paterson Zochonis & Co Ltd v Merfarken Packaging Ltd [1986] 3 All ER 522, [1983] FSR 273, [1982] Com LR 260, CA 1.03, 3.19, 5.24
Paul v Rendell (1981) 55 ALJR 371, 34 ALR 569, PC 7.04, 7.09
Payne v Weldless Steel Tube Co Ltd [1956] 1 QB 196, [1955] 3 All ER 612, [1955] 3 WLR 771, 99 Sol Jo 814, 54 LGR 19, CA 14.26
Payne-Collins v Taylor Woodrow Construction Ltd [1975] QB 300, [1975] 1 All ER 898, [1975] 2 WLR 386, 119 Sol Jo 49 .... 9.06

Table of Cases xlvii

Payton v Brooks [1974] RTR 169, [1974] 1 Lloyd's Rep 241, CA 10.07
Peabody Donation Fund (Governors) v Sir Lindsay Parkinson & Co Ltd [1985]
  AC 210, [1984] 3 All ER 529, [1984] 3 WLR 953, 128 Sol Jo 753, 83 LGR 1,
  28 BLR 1, [1984] CILL 128, [1984] LS Gaz R 3179, HL 1.02, 1.03, 1.10, 12.13
Pearce v Round Oak Steel Works Ltd [1969] 3 All ER 680, [1969] 1 WLR 595,
  113 Sol Jo 163, 6 KIR 339, CA 14.13, 17.12
Pearce v Stanley Bridges Ltd [1965] 2 All ER 594, [1965] 1 WLR 931, 109 Sol Jo
  472, CA 14.23
Peat v N J Muschamp & Co Ltd (1969) 7 KIR 469, CA 14.32
Penner v Mitchell [1978] 5 WWR 328 .... 7.10
Penny v Wimbledon UDC and Iles [1899] 2 QB 72, 68 LJQB 704, 80 LT 615, 63
  JP 406, 47 WR 565, 15 TLR 348, 43 Sol Jo 476, CA..................... 18.23
Performance Cars Ltd v Abraham [1962] 1 QB 33, [1961] 3 All ER 413, [1961]
  3 WLR 749, 105 Sol Jo 748, CA 4.17, 7.10
Perl (P) (Exporters) Ltd v Camden London Borough Council [1984] QB 342,
  [1983] 3 All ER 161, [1983] 3 WLR 769, 127 Sol Jo 581, CA 1.05, 3.19
Perry v Sidney Phillips & Son (a firm) [1982] 1 All ER 1005, 260 Estates
  Gazette 389; on appeal [1982] 3 All ER 705, [1982] 1 WLR 1297, 126 Sol
  Jo 626, 22 BLR 120, 263 Estates Gazette 888, CA .. 3.12, 3.13, 10.12, 10.16, 15.22
Perry v Tendring District Council (1984) 30 BLR 118, 3 Con LR 74, [1985]
  1 EGLR 260, 1 Const LJ 152, [1985] CILL 145......................... 5.34
Perry v Thomas Wrigley Ltd [1955] 3 All ER 243n, [1955] 1 WLR 1164, 99 Sol
  Jo 781 .... 16.33
Petch v Customs and Excise Comrs (1993) Times, 4 March, CA 5.19
Philips v Ward [1956] 1 All ER 874, [1956] 1 WLR 471, 100 Sol Jo 317, 4 BLR
  142, CA 10.12, 10.14, 15.22
Phillips v Britannia Hygienic Laundry Co [1923] 2 KB 832, [1923] All ER Rep
  127, 93 LJKB 5, 129 LT 777, 39 TLR 530, 68 Sol Jo 102, 21 LGR 709, CA .. 13.02,
    13.06, 13.13, 13.15
Phillips v London and South Western Rly Co (1879) 5 CPD 280, [1874-80] All
  ER Rep 1176, 49 LJQB 223, 42 LT 6, 44 JP 217, CA 9.14
Philpott v British Railways Board [1968] 2 Lloyd's Rep 495; on appeal [1969]
  2 Lloyd's Rep 190, CA 2.10
Phipps v Rochester Corpn [1955] 1 QB 450, [1955] 1 All ER 129, [1955] 2 WLR
  23, 119 JP 92, 99 Sol Jo 45, 53 LGR 80 .... 16.07
Photo Production Ltd v Securicor Transport Ltd [1980] AC 827, [1980] 1 All ER
  556, [1980] 2 WLR 283, 124 Sol Jo 147, [1980] 1 Lloyd's Rep 545, 130 NLJ
  188, HL.. 4.26, 10.10
Pickett v British Rail Engineering Ltd [1980] AC 136, [1979] 1 All ER 774,
  [1978] 3 WLR 955, 122 Sol Jo 778, [1979] 1 Lloyd's Rep 519, HL 7.13, 8.14,
    9.02, 9.05
Pickles v National Coal Board (intended action) [1968] 2 All ER 598, [1968]
  1 WLR 997, 112 Sol Jo 354, CA... 11.13
Pidduck v Eastern Scottish Omnibuses Ltd [1990] 2 All ER 69, [1990] 1 WLR
  993, 134 Sol Jo 637, [1990] 22 LS Gaz R 34, CA 9.22
Pigney v Pointers Transport Services Ltd [1957] 2 All ER 807, [1957] 1 WLR
  1121, 101 Sol Jo 851 .... 1.21, 3.17, 9.25
Pirelli General Cable Works Ltd v Oscar Faber & Partners [1983] 2 AC 1,
  [1983] 1 All ER 65, [1983] 2 WLR 6, 127 Sol Jo 16, 21 BLR 99, 265 Estates
  Gazette 979, HL 11.23, 11.24
Pitts v Hunt [1991] 1 QB 24, [1990] 3 All ER 344, [1990] 3 WLR 542, 134 Sol Jo
  834, [1990] RTR 290, [1990] 27 LS Gaz R 43, CA 1.20, 4.04, 4.07, 4.13, 14.35
Poland v John Parr & Sons [1927] 1 KB 236, [1926] All ER Rep 177, 96 LJKB
  152, 136 LT 271, CA 18.13
Polemis and Furness Withy & Co, Re [1921] 3 KB 560, [1921] All ER Rep 40,
  90 LJKB 1353, 126 LT 154, 37 TLR 940, 15 Asp MLC 398, 27 Com Cas 25,
  CA 3.04,
    3.11, 3.20
Pomphrey v James A Cuthbertson Ltd 1951 SC 147, 1951 SLT 191 .... 10.02
Porter v Barking and Dagenham London Borough Council (1990) Times,
  9 April 2.03
Posser (A) & Son Ltd v Levy [1955] 3 All ER 577, [1955] 1 WLR 1224, 99 Sol Jo
  815, CA 3.19

Post Office v Mears Construction Ltd [1979] 2 All ER 813 .... 5.03
Post Office v Norwich Union Fire Insurance Society Ltd [1967] 2 QB 363, [1967]
   1 All ER 577, [1967] 2 WLR 709, 111 Sol Jo 71, [1967] 1 Lloyd's Rep 216, CA   19.10
Potts (or Riddell) v Reid [1943] AC 1, [1942] 2 All ER 161, 111 LJPC 65, 167
   LT 301, 58 TLR 335, HL 13.18
Powell v Phillips [1972] 3 All ER 864, 137 JP 31, 116 Sol Jo 713, [1973] RTR
   19, CA 8.01
Practice Direction [1992] 1 All ER 862, sub nom Practice Note [1992] 1 WLR
   328 .... 8.28
Practice Note [1985] 2 All ER 895, 129 Sol Jo 508, sub nom Practice Direction
   [1985] 1 WLR 961 .... 7.11
Pratt v Patrick [1924] 1 KB 488, [1923] All ER Rep 512, 93 LJKB 174, 130 LT
   735, 40 TLR 227, 68 Sol Jo 387, 22 LGR 185 .... 18.24
Prendergast v Sam & Dee (1989) Times, 14 March, CA 15.05
Pride of Derby and Derbyshire Angling Association Ltd v British Celanese Ltd
   [1953] Ch 149, [1953] 1 All ER 179, [1953] 2 WLR 58, 117 JP 52, 97 Sol Jo
   28, 51 LGR 121, CA 13.08
Pritam Kaur v S Russell & Sons Ltd [1973] QB 336, [1973] 1 All ER 617, [1973]
   2 WLR 147, 117 Sol Jo 91, CA 11.02
Pritchard v J H Cobden Ltd [1988] Fam 22, [1987] 1 All ER 300, [1987] 2 WLR
   627, [1987] 2 FLR 30, [1987] Fam Law 53, 130 Sol Jo 715, [1986] LS Gaz R
   2919, CA 7.03, 8.08, 9.13
Prokop v Department of Health and Social Security [1985] CLY 1037, CA 7.13
Punjab National Bank v de Boinville [1992] 3 All ER 104, [1992] 1 WLR 1138,
   [1992] 1 Lloyd's Rep 7, [1991] NLJR 856, CA 5.18, 5.25
Pyne v Wilkenfeld (1981) 26 SASR 441 .... 3.15

Q

Qualcast (Wolverhampton) Ltd v Haynes [1959] AC 743, [1959] 2 All ER 38,
   [1959] 2 WLR 510, 103 Sol Jo 310, HL 14.04, 14.06, 14.10
Queen (The) in Right of Canada v Saskatchewan Wheat Pool (1983) 143 DLR
   (3d) 9 (Can SC) 13.04
Quinn (or Quin) v Burch Bros (Builders) Ltd [1966] 2 QB 370, [1965] 3 All ER
   801, [1966] 2 WLR 430, 109 Sol Jo 921; affd [1966] 2 QB 370, [1966] 2 All
   ER 283, [1966] 2 WLR 1017, 110 Sol Jo 214, CA 4.16, 16.09
Quinn v Horsfall and Bickham Ltd [1956] 2 All ER 467, [1956] 1 WLR 652, 54
   LGR 400, 100 Sol Jo 435, CA 14.22
Quintas v National Smelting Co Ltd [1961] 1 All ER 630, [1961] 1 WLR 401,
   105 Sol Jo 152, CA 14.39

R

R v Criminal Injuries Compensation Board, ex p Lain [1967] 2 QB 864, [1967]
   2 All ER 770, [1967] 3 WLR 348, 111 Sol Jo 331 .... 1.24, 19.15
R v Deputy Governor of Parkhurst Prison, ex p Hague [1992] 1 AC 58, [1991]
   3 WLR 340, sub nom Hague v Deputy Governor of Parkhurst Prison [1991]
   3 All ER 733, HL 13.12
R v Industrial Injuries Comr, ex p Amalgamated Engineering Union (No 2)
   [1966] 2 QB 31, [1966] 1 All ER 97, [1966] 2 WLR 97, 109 Sol Jo 934, CA .. 18.11,
                                                                          19.12
R v National Insurance Comr, ex p Michael [1977] 2 All ER 420, [1977] 1 WLR
   109, [1977] ICR 121, 120 Sol Jo 856, CA 19.12
RCA Corpn v Pollard [1983] Ch 135, [1982] 3 All ER 771, [1982] 3 WLR 1007,
   126 Sol Jo 672, [1983] FSR 9, CA 13.01
Racine, The [1906] P 273, 75 LJP 83, 95 LT 597, 22 TLR 575, 10 Asp MLC 300,
   CA 10.04
Radford v De Froberville [1978] 1 All ER 33, [1977] 1 WLR 1262, 121 Sol Jo
   319, 35 P & CR 316, 7 BLR 35.. 3.12
Railways Comr v Halley (1978) 20 ALR 409 (Aust HC) 4.08
Railways Comr v McDermott [1967] AC 169, [1966] 2 All ER 162, [1966] 3 WLR

Table of Cases xlix

267, 110 Sol Jo 288, [1966] ALJ 897, [1966] 1 NSWR 420, PC	16.06
Rambarran v Gurrucharran [1970] 1 All ER 749, [1970] 1 WLR 556, 114 Sol Jo 244, [1970] RTR 195, 15 WIR 212, PC	18.25
Ramsden v Lee [1992] 2 All ER 204, CA	11.18, 11.19
Randall v Motor Insurers' Bureau [1969] 1 All ER 21, [1968] 1 WLR 1900, 112 Sol Jo 883, [1968] 2 Lloyd's Rep 553	19.07
Rath v C S Lawrence & Partners (a firm) (P J Crook & Co (a firm), third party) [1991] 3 All ER 679, [1991] 1 WLR 399, CA	11.07
Ravenscroft v Rederiaktiebolaget Transatlantic [1991] 3 All ER 73; revsd [1992] 2 All ER 470n, CA	1.25
Rawlinson v Babcock & Wilcox Ltd [1966] 3 All ER 882, [1967] 1 WLR 481, 111 Sol Jo 76	9.21
Read v Croydon Corpn [1938] 4 All ER 631, 108 LJKB 72, 160 LT 176, 103 JP 25, 55 TLR 212, 82 Sol Jo 991, 37 LGR 53	13.06, 13.16
Read v J Lyons & Co Ltd [1947] AC 156, [1946] 2 All ER 471, [1947] LJR 39, 175 LT 413, 62 TLR 646, 91 Sol Jo 54, HL	18.17
Ready Mixed Concrete (South East) Ltd v Minister of Pensions and National Insurance [1968] 2 QB 497, [1968] 1 All ER 433, [1968] 2 WLR 775, 112 Sol Jo 14	18.04
Reardon v Kings Mutual Insurance Co (1981) 120 DLR (3d) 196	5.24, 5.32
Redpath v Belfast and County Down Rly [1947] NI 167	8.17
Rees v Sinclair [1974] 1 NZLR 180	5.08
Reffell v Surrey County Council [1964] 1 All ER 743, [1964] 1 WLR 358, 128 JP 261, 108 Sol Jo 119, 62 LGR 186	13.11, 13.15
Regan v Williamson [1976] 2 All ER 241, [1976] 1 WLR 305, 120 Sol Jo 217: 9.18, 9.19	
Reibl v Hughes (1980) 114 DLR (3d) 1 (Can SC)	15.10, 15.11, 15.12
Reid v Rush & Tompkins Group plc [1989] 3 All ER 228, [1990] 1 WLR 212, [1990] ICR 61, [1989] IRLR 265, [1990] RTR 144, [1989] 2 Lloyd's Rep 167, CA	1.22, 6.25, 14.03
Reincke v Gray [1964] 2 All ER 687, [1964] 1 WLR 832, 108 Sol Jo 461, CA	9.18
Repton School Governors v Repton RDC [1918] 2 KB 133, 87 LJKB 897, 119 LT 176, 82 JP 257, 34 TLR 407, 16 LGR 569, CA	12.16
Rialas v Mitchell (1984) 128 Sol Jo 704, (1984) Times, 17 July, CA	8.24
Richards v Highway Ironfounders (West Bromwich) Ltd [1955] 3 All ER 205, [1955] 1 WLR 1049, 99 Sol Jo 580, 53 LGR 641, CA	14.30, 14.31
Ricketts v Erith Borough Council [1943] 2 All ER 629, 113 LJKB 269, 169 LT 396, 108 JP 22, 42 LGR 71	17.02
Rickless v United Artists Corpn [1988] QB 40, [1987] 1 All ER 679, [1987] 2 WLR 945, 131 Sol Jo 362, [1987] LS Gaz R 654, CA	13.01
Riddick v Thames Board Mills Ltd [1977] QB 881, [1977] 3 All ER 677, [1977] 3 WLR 63, 121 Sol Jo 274, CA	18.01
Rimmer v Liverpool City Council [1985] QB 1, [1984] 1 All ER 930, [1984] 2 WLR 426, 128 Sol Jo 225, 82 LGR 424, 47 P & CR 516, 12 HLR 23, 269 Estates Gazette 319, [1984] LS Gaz R 664, CA	1.13, 5.03, 15.24, 17.09
Rivtow Marine Ltd v Washington Ironworks [1974] SCR 1189, [1973] 6 WWR 692, 40 DLR (3d) 530	5.03, 17.06
Robbins v Jones (1863) 15 CBNS 221, 3 New Rep 85, [1861-73] All ER Rep 544, 33 LJCP 1, 9 LT 523, 10 Jur NS 239, 12 WR 248, 143 ER 768	1.14
Roberts v J Hampson & Co [1989] 2 All ER 504, [1990] 1 WLR 94, 20 HLR 615, [1988] 2 EGLR 181, [1988] 37 EG 110, [1988] NLJR 166	15.22
Roberts v Johnstone [1989] QB 878, [1988] 3 WLR 1247, [1989] 5 LS Gaz R 44, CA	8.23
Roberts v Ramsbottom [1980] 1 All ER 7, [1980] 1 WLR 823, 124 Sol Jo 313, [1980] RTR 261	2.01, 19.03, 20.06
Robertson v Lestrange [1985] 1 All ER 950	9.11, 9.13
Robinson v Post Office [1974] 2 All ER 737, [1974] 1 WLR 1176, 117 Sol Jo 915, CA	3.09, 3.10, 3.23
Robinson v Workington Corpn [1897] 1 QB 619, 66 LJQB 388, 75 LT 674, 61 JP 164, 45 WR 453, 13 TLR 148, CA	13.08
Rodgers v George Blair & Co Ltd (1971) 116 Sol Jo 77, 11 KIR 391, CA	14.33
Roe v Minister of Health [1954] 2 QB 66, [1954] 2 All ER 131, [1954] 2 WLR 915, 98 Sol Jo 319, CA	2.10, 15.02, 18.19

l *Table of Cases*

Roles v Nathan [1963] 2 All ER 908, [1963] 1 WLR 1117, 107 Sol Jo 680, CA: 16.08, 16.10
Rondel v Worsley [1969] 1 AC 191, [1967] 3 All ER 993, [1967] 3 WLR 1666, 111 Sol Jo 927, HL 1.09, 1.12, 1.16, 5.08, 5.09, 15.14
Ronex Properties Ltd v John Laing Construction Ltd [1983] QB 398, [1982] 3 All ER 961, [1982] 3 WLR 875, 126 Sol Jo 727, CA 11.04
Rootes v Shelton (1967) 116 CLR 383, [1968] ALR 33, 41 ALJR 172 (Aust HC) : 4.06
Rose v Ford [1937] AC 826, [1937] 3 All ER 359, 106 LJKB 576, 157 LT 174, 53 TLR 873, 81 Sol Jo 683, 58 Ll L Rep 213, HL 8.02, 9.27
Rose v Plenty [1976] 1 All ER 97, [1976] 1 WLR 141, [1975] ICR 430, [1976] IRLR 60, 119 Sol Jo 592, [1976] 1 Lloyd's Rep 263, CA 18.12
Ross v Associated Portland Cement Manufacturers Ltd [1964] 2 All ER 452, [1964] 1 WLR 768, 108 Sol Jo 460, 62 LGR 513, HL 13.17, 14.37
Ross v Caunters [1980] Ch 297, [1979] 3 All ER 580, [1979] 3 WLR 605, 123 Sol Jo 605 .... 1.17, 5.01, 5.17, 5.23, 5.27, 6.23, 10.17, 12.05, 15.18
Rouse v Squires [1973] QB 889, [1973] 2 All ER 903, [1973] 2 WLR 925, 117 Sol Jo 431, [1973] RTR 550, CA 4.09
Rowe v Turner, Hopkins & Partners [1980] 2 NZLR 550; revsd [1982] 1 NZLR 178 (NZCA) 4.16
Rowlands (Mark) Ltd v Berni Inns Ltd [1986] QB 211, [1985] 3 All ER 473, [1985] 3 WLR 964, 129 Sol Jo 811, [1985] 2 Lloyd's Rep 437, 276 Estates Gazette 191, [1985] NLJ Rep 962, [1986] LS Gaz R 35, CA 19.03
Rowling v Takaro Properties Ltd [1988] AC 473, [1988] 1 All ER 163, [1988] 2 WLR 418, 132 Sol Jo 126, [1988] 4 LS Gaz R 35, PC 1.02, 1.03, 1.17, 12.04, 12.06, 12.07, 12.15, 12.17, 12.20, 13.08
Royal Bank Trust Co (Trinidad) Ltd v Pampellonne [1987] 1 Lloyd's Rep 218, PC 5.01
Rushton v Turner Bros Asbestos Co Ltd [1959] 3 All ER 517, [1960] 1 WLR 96, 104 Sol Jo 128 .... 14.35
Rylands v Fletcher (1868) LR 3 HL 330, [1861-73] All ER Rep 1, 37 LJ Ex 161, 19 LT 220, 33 JP 70, 14 WR 799 .... 18.15

S

S v Distillers Co (Biochemicals) Ltd [1969] 3 All ER 1412, [1970] 1 WLR 114, 113 Sol Jo 672 .... 8.10, 8.13
SCM (UK) Ltd v W J Whittall & Son Ltd [1971] 1 QB 337, [1970] 3 All ER 245, [1970] 3 WLR 694, 114 Sol Jo 706, CA 3.02, 6.12, 6.16
Saif Ali v Sydney Mitchell & Co (a firm) [1980] AC 198, [1978] 3 All ER 1033, [1978] 3 WLR 849, 122 Sol Jo 761, HL 1.13, 1.17, 5.10, 15.14, 15.15
Salih v Enfield Health Authority [1991] 3 All ER 400, CA 1.19, 7.01, 10.17
Salmon v Seafarer Restaurants Ltd [1983] 3 All ER 729, [1983] 1 WLR 1264, 127 Sol Jo 581, 80 LS Gaz R 2523 .... 16.08
Salsbury v Woodland [1970] 1 QB 324, [1969] 3 All ER 863, [1969] 3 WLR 29, 113 Sol Jo 327, CA 18.15, 18.16, 18.23
Samson v Aitchison [1912] AC 844, [1911-13] All ER Rep Ext 1195, 82 LJPC 1, 107 LT 106, 28 TLR 559 .... 18.24
Samuels v Davis [1943] KB 526, [1943] 2 All ER 3, 112 LJKB 561, 168 LT 296, CA 15.25
Saunders v Edwards [1987] 2 All ER 651, [1987] 1 WLR 1116, 131 Sol Jo 1039, [1987] NLJ Rep 389, [1987] LS Gaz R 2193, 2535, CA 1.20
Saunders v Holborn District Board of Works [1895] 1 QB 64, 64 LJQB 101, 71 LT 519, 59 JP 453, 43 WR 26, 11 TLR 5, 39 Sol Jo 11, 15 R 25, DC 13.02
Savory v Holland Hannen and Cubitts (Southern) Ltd [1964] 3 All ER 18, [1964] 1 WLR 1158, 108 Sol Jo 479, CA 18.06, 18.07
Sayers v Harlow UDC [1958] 2 All ER 342, [1958] 1 WLR 623, 122 JP 351, 102 Sol Jo 419, CA 3.16, 4.16
Scarsbrook v Mason [1961] 3 All ER 767, 105 Sol Jo 889 .... 18.27
Schiffahrt und Kohlen GmbH v Chelsea Maritime Ltd, The Irene's Success [1982] QB 481, [1982] 1 All ER 218, [1982] 2 WLR 422, 126 Sol Jo 101, [1981] 2 Lloyd's Rep 635, [1981] Com LR 219 .... 6.19

Table of Cases li

Scott v London and St Katherine Docks Co (1865) 3 H & C 596, 5 New Rep 420, [1861-73] All ER Rep 246, 34 LJ Ex 220, 13 LT 148, 11 Jur NS 204, 13 WR 410, 159 ER 665, Ex Ch 2.15
Scott Group Ltd v McFarlane [1978] 1 NZLR 553 .... 5.16
Seale v Perry [1982] VR 193 .... 5.17
Selfe v Ilford and District Hospital Management Committee (1970) 114 Sol Jo 935, (1970) Times, 26 November 1.21
Sellars v Best [1954] 2 All ER 389, [1954] 1 WLR 913, 118 JP 326, 98 Sol Jo 424 .... 17.07
Selvanayagam v University of the West Indies [1983] 1 All ER 824, [1983] 1 WLR 585, 127 Sol Jo 288, PC 7.07, 7.08
Semtex Ltd v Gladstone [1954] 2 All ER 206, [1954] 1 WLR 945, 98 Sol Jo 438 .... 4.24, 18.14
Sephton v Lancashire River Board [1962] 1 All ER 183, [1962] 1 WLR 623, 126 JP 112, 106 Sol Jo 353, [1962] RVR 489 .... 13.05, 13.11
Setchell v Snowdon [1974] RTR 389, CA 3.19
Shaddock (L) & Associates Pty Ltd v Parramatta City Council [1979] 1 NSWLR 566; revsd (1981) 55 ALJR 713, 36 ALR 385 .... 5.02
Sharpe v E T Sweeting & Son Ltd [1963] 2 All ER 455, [1963] 1 WLR 665, 107 Sol Jo 666 .... 1.14
Shaw v Groom [1970] 2 QB 504, [1970] 1 All ER 702, [1970] 2 WLR 299, 114 Sol Jo 14, 21 P & CR 137, CA 13.03
Shearman v Folland [1950] 2 KB 43, [1950] 1 All ER 976, 66 (pt 1) TLR 853, 94 Sol Jo 336, CA 8.25
Sheppard v Glossop Corpn [1921] 3 KB 132, [1921] All ER Rep 61, 90 LJKB 994, 125 LT 520, 85 JP 205, 37 TLR 604, 65 Sol Jo 472, 19 LGR 357, CA .. 12.02, 12.08
Shinjitsu Maru No 5. See Marintrans AB v Comet Shipping Co Ltd, The Shinjitsu Maru No 5
Sidaway v Board of Governors of the Bethlem Royal Hospital and the Maudsley Hospital [1985] AC 871, [1985] 1 All ER 643, [1985] 2 WLR 480, 129 Sol Jo 154, [1985] LS Gaz R 1256, HL 15.07, 15.10, 15.11, 15.12
Simaan General Contracting Co v Pilkington Glass Ltd (No 2) [1988] QB 758, [1988] 1 All ER 791, [1988] 2 WLR 761, 132 Sol Jo 463, 40 BLR 28, [1988] NLJR 53, [1988] 11 LS Gaz R 44, CA 6.10
Simkiss v Rhondda Borough Council (1982) 81 LGR 460, CA 16.07
Simmonds v Newport Abercarn Black Vein Steam Coal Co [1921] 1 KB 616, 90 LJKB 609, 124 LT 557, 85 JP 109, 37 TLR 165, 65 Sol Jo 114, CA ... 13.02, 13.05, 13.13
Simmons v Pennington & Son (a firm) [1955] 1 All ER 240, [1955] 1 WLR 183, 99 Sol Jo 146, CA 15.15
Simms v Leigh Rugby Football Club Ltd [1969] 2 All ER 923 .... 4.06
Simpson v Norwest Holst Southern Ltd [1980] 2 All ER 471, [1980] 1 WLR 968, 124 Sol Jo 313, CA 11.12
Singer and Friedlander Ltd v John D Wood & Co (1977) 243 Estates Gazette 212, [1977] EGD 569 .... 5.05, 15.21
Sirros v Moore [1975] QB 118, [1974] 3 All ER 776, [1974] 3 WLR 459, 139 JP 29, 118 Sol Jo 661, CA 5.13
Skeen v British Railways Board [1976] RTR 281 .... 16.19
Skelton v Collins (1966) 115 CLR 94, 39 ALJR 480, [1966] ALR 449 .... 8.06
Slade v Battersea and Putney Group Hospital Management Committee [1955] 1 All ER 429, [1955] 1 WLR 207, 119 JP 212, 99 Sol Jo 169 .... 16.06
Slater v Clay Cross Co Ltd [1956] 2 QB 264, [1956] 2 All ER 625, [1956] 3 WLR 232, 100 Sol Jo 450, CA 4.13, 16.06
Smeaton v Ilford Corpn [1954] Ch 450, [1954] 1 All ER 923, [1954] 2 WLR 668, 118 JP 290, 98 Sol Jo 251, 52 LGR 253 .... 13.08
Smith v Austin Lifts Ltd [1959] 1 All ER 81, [1959] 1 WLR 100, 103 Sol Jo 73, [1958] 2 Lloyd's Rep 583, HL 16.10
Smith v Baveystock & Co Ltd [1945] 1 All ER 531, CA 14.37
Smith v Bradford Metropolitan Council (1982) 126 Sol Jo 624, 80 LGR 713, 44 P & CR 171, 4 HLR 86, [1982] LS Gaz R 1176, CA 16.39
Smith v Cammell Laird & Co Ltd [1940] AC 242, [1939] 4 All ER 381, 109 LJKB 134, 163 LT 9, 104 JP 51, 56 TLR 164, 84 Sol Jo 149, 38 LGR 1, HL 13.14

Table of Cases

Smith v Central Asbestos Co Ltd [1972] 1 QB 244, [1971] 3 All ER 204, [1971]
3 WLR 206, 115 Sol Jo 443, [1971] 2 Lloyd's Rep 151, CA; affd sub nom
Central Asbestos Co Ltd v Dodd [1973] AC 518, [1972] 2 All ER 1135, [1972]
3 WLR 333, 116 Sol Jo 584, [1972] 2 Lloyd's Rep 413, HL 7.05, 11.09
Smith v Chesterfield and District Co-operative Society Ltd [1953] 1 All ER
447, [1953] 1 WLR 370, 97 Sol Jo 132, 51 LGR 194, CA 14.24
Smith v Claremont Haynes & Co (1991) Times, 3 September 15.18
Smith v Crossley Bros Ltd (1951) 95 Sol Jo 655, CA 14.12
Smith v Eric S Bush [1988] QB 743, [1987] 3 All ER 179, [1987] 3 WLR 889,
131 Sol Jo 1423, 19 HLR 287, [1987] BTLC 242, [1987] 1 EGLR 157, 282
Estates Gazette 326, [1987] NLJ Rep 362, [1987] LS Gaz R 3260, CA; affd
[1990] 1 AC 831, [1989] 2 All ER 514, [1989] 2 WLR 790, 133 Sol Jo 597, 87
LGR 685, 21 HLR 424, 17 Con LR 1, [1989] 1 EGLR 169, [1989] 17 EG 68,
18 EG 99, [1989] NLJR 576, HL 1.05, 4.31, 5.17, 5.22,
5.29, 5.30, 5.31, 15.23
Smith v Jenkins (1969) 119 CLR 397, 44 ALJR 78, [1970] ALR 519 (Aust HC): 1.19
Smith v Leech Brain & Co Ltd [1962] 2 QB 405, [1961] 3 All ER 1159, [1962] 2
WLR 148, 106 Sol Jo 77 .... 3.10
Smith v Leurs (1945) 70 CLR 256 .... 3.19
Smith v Littlewoods Organisation Ltd. See Maloco v Littlewoods Ltd
Smith v Manchester City Council (or Manchester Corpn) (1974) 118 Sol Jo 597,
17 KIR 1, CA 8.12
Smith (formerly Westwood) v National Coal Board [1967] 2 All ER 593, [1967]
1 WLR 871, 111 Sol Jo 455, HL 14.39
Smith v Scott [1973] Ch 314, [1972] 3 All ER 645, [1972] 3 WLR 783, 116 Sol Jo
785 .... 1.06, 1.22
Smith v Stages [1989] AC 928, [1989] 1 All ER 833, [1989] 2 WLR 529, [1989]
ICR 272, [1989] IRLR 177, 133 Sol Jo 324, [1989] NLJR 291, [1989] 15 LS
Gaz R 42, HL 18.11
Smoker v London Fire and Civil Defence Authority [1991] 2 AC 502, [1991]
2 All ER 449, [1991] 2 WLR 1052, [1991] ICR 449, [1991] IRLR 271, HL... 8.17
Société Anonyme de Remorquage à Hélice v Bennetts [1911] 1 KB 243, 80
LJKB 228, 27 TLR 77, 16 Com Cas 24 .... 6.01
Société Commerciale de Réassurance v ERAS (International) Ltd, Re ERAS
EIL appeals [1992] 2 All ER 82n, [1992] 1 Lloyd's Rep 570, CA 11.26, 11.29
Sole v W J Hallt Ltd [1973] QB 574, [1973] 1 All ER 1032, [1973] 2 WLR 171,
117 Sol Jo 110 .... 16.09, 16.12
Solomons v R Gertzenstein Ltd [1954] 2 QB 243, [1954] 2 All ER 625, [1954]
3 WLR 317, 98 Sol Jo 539, 52 LGR 433, 164 Estates Gazette 32, CA....... 13.06
Somasundaram v M Julius Melchior & Co (a firm) [1989] 1 All ER 129, [1988]
1 WLR 1394, [1988] NLJR 253, [1989] 4 LS Gaz R 43, CA 1.13, 5.11, 15.14
Southern Water Authority v Carey [1985] 2 All ER 1077 .... 6.11
Southwark London Borough Council v Williams [1971] Ch 734, [1971] 2 All ER
175, [1971] 2 WLR 467, 69 LGR 145, CA 13.11
Sparrow v Fairey Aviation Co Ltd [1964] AC 1019, [1962] 3 All ER 706, [1962]
3 WLR 1210, 106 Sol Jo 875, 62 LGR 379, HL 14.23
Spartan Steel and Alloys Ltd v Martin & Co (Contractors) Ltd [1973] QB 27,
[1972] 3 All ER 557, [1972] 3 WLR 502, 116 Sol Jo 648, CA 6.02, 6.12
Speirs v Gorman [1966] NZLR 897 .... 4.15
Spicer v Smee [1946] 1 All ER 489, 175 LT 163 .... 18.18
Spiers v Halliday (1984) Times, 30 June 8.10
Spittle v Bunney [1988] 3 All ER 1031, [1988] 1 WLR 847, [1988] Fam Law 433,
132 Sol Jo 754, [1988] NLJR 56, CA 9.19, 9.20
Spring v Guardian Assurance plc (1992) 137 Sol Jo LB 47, CA 5.19
Stafford v Conti Commodity Services Ltd [1981] 1 All ER 691, [1981] 1 Lloyd's
Rep 466, [1981] Com LR 10 .... 2.15, 5.05, 15.04, 15.27
Staley v Suffolk County Council and Dean Mason (26 November 1985,
unreported) 2.02
Stanbrook v Waterlow & Sons Ltd [1964] 2 All ER 506, [1964] 1 WLR 825, 108
Sol Jo 334, 62 LGR 613, CA 14.25
Stanley v Saddique [1992] 1 QB 1, [1991] 1 All ER 529, [1991] 2 WLR 459,
CA 9.19, 9.23

Stansbie v Troman [1948] 2 KB 48, [1948] 1 All ER 599, [1948] LJR 1206, 64
  TLR 226, 92 Sol Jo 167, 46 LGR 349, CA 1.05, 3.21
Stanton v Ewart F Youlden Ltd [1960] 1 All ER 429, [1960] 1 WLR 543, 104 Sol
  Jo 368 .... 9.30
Staton v National Coal Board [1957] 2 All ER 667, [1957] 1 WLR 893, 101 Sol Jo
  592 .... 18.11
Staveley Iron and Chemical Co Ltd v Jones [1956] AC 627, [1956] 1 All ER 403,
  [1956] 2 WLR 479, 100 Sol Jo 130, [1956] 1 Lloyd's Rep 65, HL: 14.34, 18.01, 18.02
Steele v Robert George & Co (1937) Ltd [1942] AC 497, [1942] 1 All ER 447, 111
  LJPC 9, 167 LT 1, 58 TLR 181, 35 BWCC 38, HL 7.07, 7.08
Stennett v Hancock and Peters [1939] 2 All ER 578, 83 Sol Jo 379 .... 17.04
Stephens v Anglian Water Authority [1987] 3 All ER 379, [1987] 1 WLR 1381,
  131 Sol Jo 1214, 86 LGR 48, 55 P & CR 348, [1987] NLJ Rep 829, [1987] LS
  Gaz R 2693, CA 1.22
Stevens v Broadribb Sawmilling Co (1985-86) 160 CLR 16 .... 18.17
Stevenson v Nationwide Building Society (1984) 128 Sol Jo 875, 272 Estates
  Gazette 663 .... 5.29
Stevenson (or Stephenson) Jordan and Harrison Ltd v MacDonald and Evans
  [1952] 1 TLR 101, 69 RPC 10, CA 18.03
Stocker v Norprint Ltd (1970) 115 Sol Jo 58, 10 KIR 10, CA 4.08
Stokes v Guest, Keen and Nettlefold (Bolts and Nuts) Ltd [1968] 1 WLR 1776,
  112 Sol Jo 821, 5 KIR 401 .... 14.07
Stone v Taffe [1974] 3 All ER 1016, [1974] 1 WLR 1575, 118 Sol Jo 863, CA ... 16.04,
                                                                16.12, 18.12
Storey v Ashton (1869) LR 4 QB 476, 10 B & S 337, 38 LJQB 223, 33 JP 676, 17
  WR 727 .... 18.09
Stott v West Yorkshire Road Car Co Ltd [1971] 2 QB 651, [1971] 3 All ER 534,
  [1971] 3 WLR 282, 115 Sol Jo 568, CA 4.20
Strangways-Lesmere v Clayton [1936] 2 KB 11, [1936] 1 All ER 484, 105 LJKB
  385, 154 LT 463, 52 TLR 374, 80 Sol Jo 306 .... 15.05
Summers (John) & Sons Ltd v Frost [1955] AC 740, [1955] 1 All ER 870, [1955]
  2 WLR 825, 99 Sol Jo 257, 53 LGR 329, HL 13.14, 14.22
Sumner v William Henderson & Sons Ltd [1964] 1 QB 450, [1963] 1 All ER 408,
  [1963] 2 WLR 330, 107 Sol Jo 74, 61 LGR 233; revsd [1963] 2 All ER 712n,
  [1963] 1 WLR 823, 107 Sol Jo 436, [1963] 1 Lloyd's Rep 537, CA 14.15
Surtees v Kingston-upon-Thames Borough Council [1991] 2 FLR 559, [1991]
  Fam Law 426, CA 2.03
Sutcliffe v Sayer [1987] 1 EGLR 155, 281 Estates Gazette 1452, CA 15.22
Sutcliffe v Thackrah [1974] AC 727, [1974] 1 All ER 859, [1974] 2 WLR 295, 118
  Sol Jo 148, 4 BLR 16, [1974] 1 Lloyd's Rep 318, HL 1.13, 1.17, 5.10, 5.13
Sutherland Shire Council v Heyman (1985) 60 ALR 1, 59 ALJR 564 ..... 1.07, 12.10
Swinfen v Lord Chelmsford (1860) 5 H & N 890, 29 LJ Ex 382, 2 LT 406, 6 Jur
  NS 1035, 8 WR 545 .... 5.08
Swingcastle Ltd v Alastair Gibson (a firm) [1990] 3 All ER 463, [1990] 1 WLR
  1223, [1990] 2 EGLR 149, [1990] 34 EG 49, [1990] NLJR 818, CA; revsd
  [1991] 2 AC 223, [1991] 2 All ER 353, [1991] 2 WLR 1091, 135 Sol Jo 542,
  [1991] 1 EGLR 157, [1991] 17 EG 83, [1991] NLJR 563, [1991] 21 LS Gaz
  R 34, HL 10.13, 15.22
Sykes v Midland Bank Executor and Trustee Co Ltd [1971] 1 QB 113, [1970]
  2 All ER 471, [1970] 3 WLR 273, CA 15.15, 15.16

T

Taff Vale Rly Co v Jenkins [1913] AC 1, [1911-13] All ER Rep 160, 82 LJKB 49,
  107 LT 564, 29 TLR 19, 57 Sol Jo 27, HL 9.15
Tai Hing Cotton Mill Ltd v Liu Chong Hing Bank Ltd [1986] AC 80, [1985] 2 All
  ER 947, [1985] 3 WLR 317, 129 Sol Jo 503, [1985] 2 Lloyd's Rep 313, [1985]
  NLJ Rep 680, [1985] LS Gaz R 2995, PC 4.16, 5.25, 6.25, 11.29, 15.17
Tan Chye Choo v Chong Kew Moi [1970] 1 All ER 266, [1970] 1 WLR 147, 113
  Sol Jo 1000, PC 13.02, 17.12
Targett v Torfaen Borough Council [1992] 3 All ER 27, 24 HLR 164, [1991]
  NLJR 1698, CA 1.14

Table of Cases

Tarry v Ashton (1876) 1 QBD 314, [1874-80] All ER Rep 738, 45 LJQB 260, 34 LT 97, 40 JP 439, 24 WR 581 .... 18.16
Tate and Lyle Industries Ltd v Greater London Council [1983] 2 AC 509, [1983] 1 All ER 1159, [1983] 2 WLR 649, 127 Sol Jo 257, 81 LGR 433, 46 P & CR 243, [1983] 2 Lloyd's Rep 117, HL 6.26
Taylor v Bristol Omnibus Co Ltd [1975] 2 All ER 1107, [1975] 1 WLR 1054, 119 Sol Jo 476, CA 7.05, 8.13, 8.24, 8.27
Taylor v O'Connor [1971] AC 115, [1970] 1 All ER 365, [1970] 2 WLR 472, 114 Sol Jo 132, [1970] TR 37, 49 ATC 37, HL 8.11, 9.10, 9.13
Taylor v Rover Co Ltd [1966] 2 All ER 181, [1966] 1 WLR 1491 .... 14.13
Taylor v Taylor (1984) Times, 14 April, CA 11.16
Taylor (C R) (Wholesale) Ltd v Hepworths Ltd [1977] 2 All ER 784, [1977] 1 WLR 659, 121 Sol Jo 15, 242 Estates Gazette 631 .... 10.09, 10.10
Tennant Radiant Heat Ltd v Warrington Development Corpn [1988] 1 EGLR 41, [1988] 11 EG 71, CA 4.16
Thackwell v Barclays Bank plc [1986] 1 All ER 676 .... 1.20
Thake v Maurice [1986] QB 644, [1984] 2 All ER 513, [1985] 2 WLR 215, 129 Sol Jo 86, [1985] LS Gaz R 871; on appeal [1986] QB 644, [1986] 1 All ER 497, [1986] 2 WLR 337, 129 Sol Jo 894, [1986] NLJ Rep 92, [1986] LS Gaz R 123, CA 1.19, 10.17, 15.13
Thatcher v Littlejohn [1978] RTR 369, CA 10.03
Thomas v Bristol Aeroplane Co Ltd [1954] 2 All ER 1, [1954] 1 WLR 694, 98 Sol Jo 302, 52 LGR 292, CA 14.27, 14.39
Thomas v British Railways Board [1976] QB 912, [1976] 3 All ER 15, [1976] 2 WLR 761, 120 Sol Jo 334, CA 16.19, 16.36
Thomas v Bunn [1991] 1 AC 362, [1991] 1 All ER 193, [1991] 2 WLR 27, 135 Sol Jo 16, [1990] NLJR 1789, HL 7.12
Thomas v Wignall [1987] QB 1098, [1987] 1 All ER 1185, [1987] 2 WLR 930, 131 Sol Jo 362, [1987] LS Gaz R 417, CA 8.11
Thomas (Richard) and Baldwins Ltd v Cummings [1955] AC 321, [1955] 1 All ER 285, 99 Sol Jo 94, 53 LGR 121, HL 14.25
Thompson v Brown Construction (Ebbw Vale) Ltd [1981] 2 All ER 296, [1981] 1 WLR 744, 125 Sol Jo 377, HL 11.06, 11.17, 11.19
Thompson v Price [1973] QB 838, [1973] 2 All ER 846, [1973] 2 WLR 1037, 117 Sol Jo 468, [1973] 1 Lloyd's Rep 591 .... 9.18
Thompson v Smiths Shiprepairers (North Shields) Ltd [1984] QB 405, [1984] 1 All ER 881, [1984] 2 WLR 522, [1984] ICR 236, 128 Sol Jo 225 .. 2.09, 14.07, 14.08
Thompson v Toorenburgh (1973) 29 DLR (3d) 608; affd (1975) 50 DLR (3d) 717: 3.23
Thomson v Cremin (1941) [1953] 2 All ER 1185, [1956] 1 WLR 103n, 100 Sol Jo 73, 71 Ll L R 1, 1956 SLT 357, HL 16.13
Thorne v University of London [1966] 2 QB 237, [1966] 2 All ER 338, [1966] 2 WLR 1080, 110 Sol Jo 231, CA 1.17
Thornton v Kirklees Metropolitan Borough Council [1979] QB 626, [1979] 2 All ER 349, [1979] 3 WLR 1, 144 JP 15, 123 Sol Jo 285, 77 LGR 417, CA 13.01, 13.11, 13.12
Tinsley v Dudley [1951] 2 KB 18, [1951] 1 All ER 252, [1951] 1 TLR 315, 95 Sol Jo 106, CA 16.14
Titchener v British Railways Board [1983] 3 All ER 770, 127 Sol Jo 825, 1984 SLT 192, sub nom McGinlay (or Titchener) v British Railways Board [1983] 1 WLR 1427, HL 4.03
Todd (by his next friend Thompson) v Davison [1972] AC 392, [1971] 1 All ER 994, [1971] 2 WLR 898, 115 Sol Jo 223, HL 11.03
Tolley v Morris [1979] 2 All ER 561, [1979] 1 WLR 592, 123 Sol Jo 353, HL 11.03, 11.06
Topp v London Country Bus (South West) Ltd [1992] RTR 254; affd (1993) Times, 15 February, CA 3.19
Trans Trust SPRL v Danubian Trading Co Ltd [1952] 2 QB 297, [1952] 1 All ER 970, [1952] 1 TLR 1066, 96 Sol Jo 312, [1952] 1 Lloyd's Rep 348, CA 3.12
Travers v Gloucester Corpn [1947] KB 71, [1946] 2 All ER 506, 115 LJKB 517, 175 LT 360, 110 JP 364, 62 TLR 723, 90 Sol Jo 556, 44 LGR 333 ..... 1.01, 1.14
Tremain v Pike [1969] 3 All ER 1303, [1969] 1 WLR 1556, 113 Sol Jo 812, 67 LGR 703, 7 KIR 318 .... 3.09, 3.11

Treml v Ernest W Gibson & Partners (1984) 272 Estates Gazette 68, [1984]
  EGD 922 .... 10.12, 10.16
Tse Kwong Lam v Wong Chit Sen [1983] 3 All ER 54, [1983] 1 WLR 1349, 127
  Sol Jo 632, [1983] BCLC 88, PC 15.23
Turner v Malcolm (1992) 136 Sol Jo LB 236, [1992] 33 LS Gaz R 41, CA: 11.03, 11.06
Twine v Bean's Express Ltd [1946] 1 All ER 202, 62 TLR 155; affd 175 LT 131,
  62 TLR 458, CA 18.01, 18.12

U

UBAF Ltd v European American Banking Corpn, The Pacific Colcotronis
  [1984] QB 713, [1984] 2 All ER 226, [1984] 2 WLR 508, 128 Sol Jo 243,
  [1984] BCLC 112, [1984] 1 Lloyd's Rep 258, [1984] LS Gaz R 429, CA 11.22
Udale v Bloomsbury Area Health Authority [1983] 2 All ER 522, [1983] 1 WLR
  1098, 127 Sol Jo 510 .... 1.19
Uddin v Associated Portland Cement Manufacturers Ltd [1965] 2 QB 582,
  [1965] 2 All ER 213, [1965] 2 WLR 1183, 109 Sol Jo 313, 63 LGR 241, CA : 14.24
Ultramares Corpn v Touche 255 NY 170, 174 NE 441 (1931) 5.16
United Africa Co Ltd v Saka Owoade [1955] AC 130, [1957] 3 All ER 216, [1955]
  2 WLR 13, 99 Sol Jo 26, [1954] 2 Lloyd's Rep 607, PC 18.13
Unitramp SA v Jenson & Nicholson (S) Pte Ltd, The Baiona [1992] 1 All ER 346,
  [1992] 1 WLR 862, [1991] 2 Lloyd's Rep 121 .... 11.19

V

Vacwell Engineering Co Ltd v BDH Chemicals Ltd [1971] 1 QB 88, [1969] 3 All
  ER 1681, [1969] 3 WLR 927, 113 Sol Jo 639, 7 KIR 286; revsd [1971] 1 QB
  111n, [1970] 3 All ER 553n, [1970] 3 WLR 67n, 114 Sol Jo 472, CA ... 3.09,15.03,
                                                                        17.06, 17.23
Vandyke v Fender (Sun Insurance Office Ltd, Third party) [1970] 2 QB 292,
  [1970] 2 All ER 335, [1970] 2 WLR 929, 134 JP 487, 114 Sol Jo 205, [1970]
  1 Lloyd's Rep 320, [1970] RTR 236, CA 18.11
Van Oppen v Clerk to the Bedford Charity Trustees [1989] 1 All ER 273; affd
  [1989] 3 All ER 389, [1990] 1 WLR 235, [1989] NLJR 900, [1990] 16 LS Gaz
  R 42, CA... 6.25
Vicar of Writtle v Essex County Council (1979) 77 LGR 656 .... 1.06, 3.19, 12.11
Videan v British Transport Commission [1963] 2 QB 650, [1963] 2 All ER 860,
  [1963] 3 WLR 374, 107 Sol Jo 458, CA 16.06, 16.30
Videto v Kennedy (1981) 125 DLR (3d) 127 .... 15.12
Virgo SS Co SA v Skaarup Shipping Corpn, The Kapetan Georgis [1988]
  1 Lloyd's Rep 352 .... 17.13
Voli v Inglewood Shire Council (1963) 110 CLR 74, 37 ALJR 25, [1963] Qd R
  256, 57 QJPR 97, [1963] ALR 657, 9 LGRA 1 .... 6.11
Vyner v Waldenberg Bros Ltd [1946] KB 50, [1945] 2 All ER 547, 115 LJKB 119,
  173 LT 330, 110 JP 76, 61 TLR 545, 44 LGR 155, CA 14.35

W

W v Meah [1986] 1 All ER 935, [1986] NLJ Rep 165 .... 1.20
Wadsworth v Lydall [1981] 2 All ER 401, [1981] 1 WLR 598, 125 Sol Jo 309, CA: 3.12
Wagon Mound, The. See Overseas Tankship (UK) Ltd v Morts Dock and Engin-
  eering Co Ltd, The Wagon Mound
Wagon Mound, The (No 2). See Overseas Tankship (UK) Ltd v Miller SS Co Pty,
  The Wagon Mound (No 2)
Wah Tat Bank Ltd v Chan Cheng Kum [1975] AC 507, [1975] 2 All ER 257,
  [1975] 2 WLR 475, 119 Sol Jo 151, [1975] 2 Lloyd's Rep 62, PC 4.18
Walker v Bletchley Flettons Ltd [1937] 1 All ER 170 .... 14.22
Walker v John McLean & Sons Ltd [1979] 2 All ER 965, [1979] 1 WLR 760, 123
  Sol Jo 354, 374, CA 8.07
Walkley v Precision Forgings Ltd [1979] 2 All ER 548, [1979] 1 WLR 606, 123
  Sol Jo 354, HL 11.06

lvi   *Table of Cases*

Wallhead v Ruston & Hornsby Ltd (1973) 14 KIR 285 .... 14.29, 14.30
Walsh v Holst & Co Ltd [1958] 3 All ER 33, [1958] 1 WLR 800, 102 Sol Jo 545,
   CA 18.23
Walton v British Leyland UK Ltd (2 July 1978, unreported) 17.06
Ward v Cannock Chase District Council [1986] Ch 546, [1985] 3 All ER 537,
   [1986] 2 WLR 660, 130 Sol Jo 316, 84 LGR 898, [1986] LS Gaz R 1553 . . 1.05, 3.21,
                                                                                                                                                                                    10.10, 10.15
Ward v James [1966] 1 QB 273, [1965] 1 All ER 563, [1965] 2 WLR 455, 109 Sol
   Jo 111, [1965] 1 Lloyd's Rep 145, CA 8.04
Ward v Tesco Stores Ltd [1976] 1 All ER 219, [1976] 1 WLR 810, [1976] IRLR
   92, 120 Sol Jo 555, CA 2.18
Wardell-Yerburgh v Surrey County Council [1973] RTR 462 .... 2.06
Warren v Henlys Ltd [1948] 2 All ER 935, 92 Sol Jo 706 .... 18.13
Warren v Scruttons Ltd [1962] 1 Lloyd's Rep 497 .... 3.10
Watson v Buckley Osborne Garrett & Co Ltd and Wyrovoys Products Ltd [1940]
   1 All ER 174 .... 17.04
Watson v Powles [1968] 1 QB 596, [1967] 3 All ER 721, [1967] 3 WLR 1364, 111
   Sol Jo 562, CA 7.04, 8.10
Watson (Administrators of) v Willmott [1991] 1 QB 140, [1991] 1 All ER 473,
   [1990] 3 WLR 1103 .... 9.19
Watson-Norie Ltd v Shaw (1967) 111 Sol Jo 117, [1967] 1 Lloyd's Rep 515, CA : 10.06
Watt v Hertfordshire County Council [1954] 2 All ER 368, [1954] 1 WLR 835,
   118 JP 377, 98 Sol Jo 372, 52 LGR 383, CA 2.06, 12.08
Watt v Kesteven County Council [1954] 3 All ER 441, [1954] 3 WLR 729, 119 JP
   37, 98 Sol Jo 806, 52 LGR 539; affd [1955] 1 QB 408, [1955] 1 All ER 473,
   [1955] 2 WLR 499, 119 JP 220, 99 Sol Jo 149, 53 LGR 254, CA 13.08, 13.11
Watts v Rake (1960) 108 CLR 158 .... 7.08
Wearing v Pirelli Ltd [1977] 1 All ER 339, [1977] 1 WLR 48, 121 Sol Jo 11,
   [1977] ICR 90, [1977] IRLR 36, HL 14.23
Weedon v Hindwood, Clarke and Esplin (1974) 234 Estates Gazette 121, [1975]
   EGD 750 .... 15.22
Weiss v Fote 167 NE 2d 63 (1960) 12.10
Weld-Blundell v Stephens [1920] AC 956, [1920] All ER Rep 32, 89 LJKB 705,
   123 LT 593, 36 TLR 640, 64 Sol Jo 529, HL 3.20
Weller & Co v Foot and Mouth Disease Research Institute [1966] 1 QB 569,
   [1965] 3 All ER 560, [1965] 3 WLR 1082, 109 Sol Jo 702, [1965] 2 Lloyd's
   Rep 414 .... 6.03, 6.12, 6.13
Wells v Cooper [1958] 2 QB 265, [1958] 2 All ER 527, [1958] 3 WLR 128, 102
   Sol Jo 508, CA 2.01
Welsh v Chief Constable of the Merseyside Police [1993] 1 All ER 692 ... 15.14, 15.18
Wentworth v Wiltshire County Council [1993] 2 All ER 256, [1993] 2 WLR 175,
   136 Sol Jo LB 198, 90 LGR 625, [1992] NLJR 1377, [1992] 27 LS Gaz R 36,
   CA 13.05
West v Buckinghamshire County Council (1984) 83 LGR 449, [1985] RTR 306 : 12.10
West (H) & Son v Shepherd [1964] AC 326, [1963] 2 All ER 625, [1963] 2 WLR
   1359, 107 Sol Jo 454, HL 8.01, 8.03, 8.06
West Wiltshire District Council v Garland (Cond, third party) (1993) Times,
   4 March 13.02
West Wiltshire District Council v Pugh [1993] NLJR 546 .... 5.23
Westwood v Post Office [1974] AC 1, [1973] 3 All ER 184, [1973] 3 WLR 287,
   117 Sol Jo 600, HL 14.34
Wheat v E Lacon & Co Ltd [1966] AC 552, [1966] 1 All ER 582, [1966] 2 WLR
   581, 110 Sol Jo 149, [1966] RA 193, [1966] RVR 223, HL 16.02
Wheeler v Copas [1981] 3 All ER 405 .... 16.01
Wheeler v New Merton Board Mills Ltd [1933] 2 KB 669, [1933] All ER Rep 28,
   103 LJKB 17, 149 LT 587, 49 TLR 574, 26 BWCC 231n, CA 13.17
White v Blackmore [1972] 2 QB 651, [1972] 3 All ER 158, [1972] 3 WLR 296,
   116 Sol Jo 547, CA 16.10, 16.11, 16.24, 16.27, 16.31
White v Glass (1989) Times, 18 February, CA 11.06
White v Holbrook Precision Castings [1985] IRLR 215, CA 14.11
White v John Warrick & Co Ltd [1953] 2 All ER 1021, [1953] 1 WLR 1285, 97
   Sol Jo 740, CA 4.26
White v Jones [1993] NLJR 473, CA 5.17, 6.23, 10.17, 12.05, 15.18

White v London Transport Executive [1971] 2 QB 721, [1971] 3 All ER 1, [1971] 3 WLR 169, 115 Sol Jo 368, [1971] RTR 326, CA	19.07
White (Arthur) (Contractors) Ltd v Tarmac Civil Engineering Ltd [1967] 3 All ER 586, [1967] 1 WLR 1508, 111 Sol Jo 831, HL	18.08
Whitehouse v Jordan [1980] 1 All ER 650, CA; affd [1981] 1 All ER 267, [1981] 1 WLR 246, 125 Sol Jo 167, HL	2.11, 15.04, 15.05
Whitfield v H & R Johnson (Tiles) Ltd [1990] 3 All ER 426, [1991] ICR 109, [1990] IRLR 525, CA	14.32
Whittingham v Crease & Co [1978] 5 WWR 45, 88 DLR (3d) 353	5.17
Wieland v Cyril Lord Carpets Ltd [1969] 3 All ER 1006	3.09, 3.10, 3.15
Wigg v British Railways Board [1986] NLJ Rep 446n	1.24
Wigley v British Vinegars Ltd [1964] AC 307, [1962] 3 All ER 161, [1962] 3 WLR 731, 106 Sol Jo 609, 61 LGR 1, HL	14.33
Wilkie v London Passenger Transport Board [1947] 1 All ER 258, [1947] LJR 864, 177 LT 71, 111 JP 98, 63 TLR 115, 45 LGR 170, CA	4.27
Wilkinson v Ancliff (BLT) Ltd [1986] 3 All ER 427, [1986] 1 WLR 1352, 130 Sol Jo 766, [1986] LS Gaz R 3248, CA	11.09
Williams v Painter Bros Ltd (1968) 5 KIR 487, CA	14.28
Willson v Ministry of Defence [1991] 1 All ER 638, [1991] ICR 595	7.11
Wilsher v Essex Area Health Authority [1987] QB 730, [1986] 3 All ER 801, [1987] 2 WLR 425, 130 Sol Jo 749, [1986] NLJ Rep 1061, [1986] LS Gaz R 2661, CA; revsd [1988] AC 1074, [1988] 1 All ER 871, [1988] 2 WLR 557, 132 Sol Jo 418, [1988] NLJR 78, [1988] 15 LS Gaz R 37, HL	2.14, 15.05, 15.06, 15.07, 15.08, 18.20
Wilson v Banner Scaffolding Ltd (1982) Times, 22 June	11.06
Wilson v National Coal Board 1981 SLT 67, HL	8.20
Wilson v Tyneside Window Cleaning Co [1958] 2 QB 110, [1958] 2 All ER 265, [1958] 2 WLR 900, 102 Sol Jo 380, CA	14.04, 14.05
Wilsons and Clyde Coal Co Ltd v English [1938] AC 57, [1937] 3 All ER 628, 106 LJPC 117, 157 LT 406, 53 TLR 944, 81 Sol Jo 700, HL	14.04, 14.15, 18.01
Wimpey (George) & Co Ltd v BOAC [1955] AC 169, [1954] 3 All ER 661, [1954] 3 WLR 932, 98 Sol Jo 868, HL	4.19
Wimpey Construction UK Ltd v Poole (1984) 128 Sol Jo 969, [1984] 2 Lloyd's Rep 499, 27 BLR 58	2.10, 15.01, 15.19
Wingfield v Ellerman's Wilson Line [1960] 2 Lloyd's Rep 16, CA	14.04, 14.15
Wipfli v Britten (1983) 145 DLR (3d) 80	8.24
Wise v Kaye [1962] 1 QB 638, [1962] 1 All ER 257, [1962] 2 WLR 96, 106 Sol Jo 14, CA	8.01, 8.03, 8.06
Withers v Perry Chain Co Ltd [1961] 3 All ER 676, [1961] 1 WLR 1314, 105 Sol Jo 648, 59 LGR 496, CA	14.11
Wollington v State Electricity Commission of Victoria (No 2) [1980] VR 91	10.08
Wolverhampton New Waterworks Co v Hawkesford (1859) 6 CBNS 336, 28 LJCP 242, 33 LTOS 366, 5 Jur NS 1104, 7 WR 464	13.09
Wong (Edward) Finance Co Ltd v Johnson, Stokes and Master [1984] AC 296, [1984] 2 WLR 1, 127 Sol Jo 784, PC	15.15
Wood v Bentall Simplex Ltd (1992) Times, 3 March, CA	9.22
Wood v British Coal Corpn (1990) Times, 10 October, CA	8.17
Woods v Durable Suites Ltd [1953] 2 All ER 391, [1953] 1 WLR 857, 97 Sol Jo 454, 51 LGR 424, CA	14.05
Woods v Winskill [1913] 2 Ch 303, [1911-13] All ER Rep 318, 82 LJ Ch 447, 109 LT 399, 20 Mans 261, 57 Sol Jo 740, 6 BWCC 934	13.05
Woodward v Renold Ltd [1980] ICR 387	14.27
Wooldridge v Sumner [1963] 2 QB 43, [1962] 2 All ER 978, [1962] 3 WLR 616, 106 Sol Jo 489, CA	2.11, 4.02, 4.06
Woolfall v Knowsley Borough Council (1992) Times, 26 June, CA	12.05
Workvale Ltd (No 2), Re [1992] 2 All ER 627, [1991] BCLC 531, CA	11.06
World Beauty, The. See Andros Springs (Owners) v Owners of World Beauty, The World Beauty	
Worlock v Saws (1981) 20 BLR 94, 260 Estates Gazette 920; on appeal (1983) 22 BLR 26, 265 Estates Gazette 774, CA	2.10
Worsley v Hollins [1991] RTR 252, CA	2.18
Wright v British Railways Board [1983] 2 AC 773, [1983] 2 All ER 698, [1983] 3 WLR 211, 127 Sol Jo 478, HL	7.13, 8.04, 8.07

Wright v Lodge and Shepherd [1992] NLJR 1269, CA 4.09
Wringe v Cohen [1940] 1 KB 229, [1939] 4 All ER 241, 109 LJKB 227, 161 LT
  366, 56 TLR 101, 83 Sol Jo 923, CA 18.16

Y

Yachuk v Oliver Blais Co Ltd [1949] AC 386, [1949] 2 All ER 150, 65 TLR 300,
  39 Sol Jo 356, [1949] 3 DLR 1, [1949] 2 WWR 764, PC 2.02, 4.14
Yepremian v Scarborough General Hospital (1980) 28 OR (2d) 494, 110 DLR
  (3d) 513, CA 18.19
Yianni v Edwin Evans & Sons [1982] QB 438, [1981] 3 All ER 592, [1981]
  3 WLR 843, 125 Sol Jo 694, 259 Estates Gazette 969 ..... 5.17, 5.34, 15.22, 15.23
York, The [1929] P 178, 98 LJP 147, 141 LT 215, 17 Asp MLC 600, CA 10.05
Young v Percival [1974] 3 All ER 677, [1975] 1 WLR 17, 119 Sol Jo 33, [1975]
  1 Lloyd's Rep 130, CA 8.11, 9.11
Young and Marten Ltd v McManus Childs Ltd [1969] 1 AC 454, [1968] 2 All ER
  1169, [1968] 3 WLR 630, 112 Sol Jo 744, 67 LGR 1, 9 BLR 77, 207 Estates
  Gazette 797, HL 15.25
Young and Woods Ltd v West [1980] IRLR 201, CA 18.05
Yuen Kun Yeu v A-G of Hong Kong [1988] AC 175, [1987] 2 All ER 705, [1987]
  3 WLR 776, 131 Sol Jo 1185, [1987] NLJ Rep 566, [1987] LS Gaz R 2049,
  PC 1.02, 1.0C, 1.07, 1.08, 1.17, 12.12

Part one

The structure of the modern law

Chapter 1

Liability for carelessness

The changing fortunes of foreseeability

Generalisation: its rise and fall

[**1.01**] In the 1987 case of *Smith v Littlewoods Organisation*,[1] Lord Goff of Chieveley said in the House of Lords:

> 'It is very tempting to try to solve all problems of negligence by reference to an all-embracing criterion of foreseeability, thereby effectively reducing all decisions in this field to questions of fact. But this comfortable solution is, alas, not open to us. The law has to accommodate all the untidy complexity of life; and there are circumstances where considerations of practical justice impel us to reject a general imposition of liability for foreseeable damage.'

Ten or more years before this statement was made it seemed as though the courts *were* leaning in favour of an approach which could potentially have elevated foreseeability into an all-embracing test for negligence liability. It is true that if one goes back even further, to the years immediately following the decision in *Donoghue v Stevenson*,[2] Lord Atkin's famous attempt in that case to state the law of negligence in general terms by reference to the concept of foreseeability[3] long met with a rather cautious response. It was rarely allowed to displace established rules of law which were inconsistent with it,[4] and in some cases the courts continued to approach claims in a manner fundamentally at variance with the underlying logic of the principles propounded in it.[5] But in 1970 it seemed as though a turning point in favour of a more far-reaching application of the foreseeability principle might have been reached. In that year Lord Reid, in *Home*

---

1 [1987] AC 241 at 280, [1987] 1 All ER 710 at 736.
2 [1932] AC 562.
3 [1932] AC 562 at 580: 'You must take reasonable care to avoid acts or omissions which you can reasonably foresee should be likely to injure your neighbour.'
4 See, eg *Travers v Gloucester Corpn* [1947] KB 71, [1946] 2 All ER 506 (builder's immunity).
5 See, eg *Ball v LCC* [1949] 2 KB 159, [1949] 1 All ER 1056, CA ('dangerous things').

4 Liability for carelessness

Office v Dorset Yacht Co Ltd,[1] said in reference to Lord Atkin's speech in *Donoghue v Stevenson* that: 'the time has come when we can and should say that it ought to apply unless there is some justification or valid explanation for its exclusion'. Lord Reid's approach was subsequently given greater emphasis in the very well-known case of *Anns v Merton London Borough Council*.[2] The speech of Lord Wilberforce contained a famous passage which initially became highly influential in the development of the law of negligence, but which began subsequently to incur judicial disapproval as being too wide. Finally, in a series of cases decided by the House of Lords and the Judicial Committee of the Privy Council, it was rejected as an acceptable test for the imposition of negligence liability; and the actual decision of the House of Lords in the *Anns* case was itself overruled by a seven-member House in the 1990 case of *Murphy v Brentwood District Council*.[3] Nevertheless, the approach which the more recent cases have preferred can only be understood against the background of the swift rise and dramatic fall of the Wilberforce doctrine, which his Lordship had propounded as follows:[4]

> '... the position has now been reached that in order to establish that a duty of care arises in a particular situation, it is not necessary to bring the facts of that situation within those of previous situations in which a duty of care has been held to exist. Rather the question has to be approached in two stages. First one has to ask whether, as between the alleged wrongdoer and the person who has suffered damage there is a sufficient relationship of proximity or neighbourhood such that, in the reasonable contemplation of the former, carelessness on his part may be likely to cause damage to the latter, in which case a prima facie duty of care arises. Secondly, if the first question is answered affirmatively, it is necessary to consider whether there are any considerations which ought to negative, or to reduce or limit the scope of the duty or the class of person to whom it is owed or the damages to which a breach of it may give rise...'

Rejection of the Wilberforce approach

[**1.02**] In *Peabody Donation Fund (Governors) v Sir Lindsay Parkinson & Co Ltd*,[5] Lord Keith of Kinkel quoted Lord Wilberforce's formula and said: 'There has been a tendency in some recent cases to treat these passages as being themselves of a definitive character. This is a temptation which should be resisted.'

Lord Keith's implied criticism of the *Anns* approach was subsequently echoed by Lord Fraser in the Judicial Committee of the

---

1 [1970] AC 1004 at 1027, [1970] 2 All ER 294 at 297, HL. In *Anns v Merton London Borough Council* (below) Lord Wilberforce observed that '... it may well be that full recognition of the impact of *Donoghue v Stevenson* ... only came with the decision of this house in *Home Office v Dorset Yacht Co*.'
2 [1978] AC 728, [1977] 2 All ER 492, HL.
3 [1991] 1 AC 398, [1990] 2 All ER 908, HL. See David Howarth 'Negligence after *Murphy*: Time to Re-think' [1991] 50 CLJ 58.
4 [1978] AC 728 at 751-752, [1977] 2 All ER 492 at 498, HL.
5 [1985] AC 210 at 240, [1984] 3 All ER 529 at 534.

Privy Council,¹ and by Lord Bridge in the House of Lords.² In 1987 Lord Keith himself, this time delivering a unanimous judgment of the Judicial Committee of the Privy Council, reiterated his criticisms as follows:³ 'Their Lordships venture to think that the two-stage test formulated by Lord Wilberforce for determining the existence of a duty of care in negligence has been elevated to a degree of importance greater than it merits, and greater perhaps than its author intended.' Other Law Lords were content to follow the lead thus given and to reject the Wilberforce approach,⁴ including those who had once been among its supporters.⁵

Need to see criticisms in context

[**1.03**] The cases⁶ in which members of the House of Lords, or of the Judicial Committee of the Privy Council, chose to criticise Lord Wilberforce's formulation concerned the difficult questions either of the scope of recovery for economic loss, or the basing of a negligence claim upon a statutory power, or both. Both of these issues lay at the heart of the controversial decision in *Anns v Merton London Borough Council*⁷ itself, and both are dealt with at length separately in subsequent chapters of this book. Much of the hostility directed at Lord Wilberforce's attempt to generalise negligence liability has to be seen in the context of denunciation of the ill-fated decision in the case in which it was propounded. The strength of the Wilberforce formula was unfortunately obscured by the unusual nature of the *Anns* case. Outside that special area its value was apt to be more apparent. Indeed Lord Goff of Chieveley, an extract from whose speech was quoted at the beginning of this chapter, had in an earlier case⁸ welcomed the Wilberforce statement as 'the coming of age of the law of

1 See *Candlewood Navigation Corpn Ltd v Mitsui OSK Lines Ltd* [1986] AC 1 at 21, [1985] 2 All ER 935 at 945.
2 See *Curran v Northern Ireland Co-ownership Housing Association* [1987] AC 718 at 724-726, [1987] 2 All ER 13 at 17-18.
3 See *Yuen Kun Yeu v A-G of Hong Kong* [1988] AC 175 at 191, [1987] 2 All ER 705 at 710. See also *Rowling v Takaro Properties Ltd* [1988] AC 473, [1988] 1 All ER 163, PC.
4 See, eg Lord Oliver in *Murphy v Brentwood District Council* [1991] 1 AC 398 at 487-488, [1990] 2 All ER 908 at 934-935, HL.
5 Compare, for example, the observations of Lord Roskill in *Caparo Industries v Dickman* [1990] 2 AC 605 at 628, [1990] 1 All ER 568 at 582 with those of the same Law Lord in the earlier case of *Junior Books Ltd v Veitchi Co Ltd* [1993] 1 AC 520 at 541-542, [1982] 3 All ER 201 at 210-211.
6 Ie *Peabody Donation Fund (Governors) v Sir Lindsay Parkinson & Co Ltd* [1985] AC 210, [1984] 3 All ER 529, HL; *Candlewood Navigation Corpn Ltd v Mitsui OSK Lines* [1986] AC 1, [1985] 2 All ER 935; *Leigh & Sillivan v Aliakmon Shipping Co Ltd* [1986] AC 785, [1986] 2 All ER 145; *Curran v Northern Ireland Co-ownership Housing Association* [1987] AC 718, [1987] 2 All ER 13, HL; *Yuen Kun Yeu v A-G of Hong Kong* [1988] AC 175, [1987] 2 All ER 705, PC; *Rowling v Takaro Properties* [1988] AC 473, [1988] 1 All ER 163, PC; *Caparo Industries v Dickman* [1990] 2 AC 605, [1990] 1 All ER 568, HL; *Murphy v Brentwood District Council* [1991] 1 AC 398, [1990] 2 All ER 908, HL.
7 [1978] AC 728, [1977] 2 All ER 492, HL.
8 See *Paterson Zochonis & Co v Merfarken Packaging* [1986] 3 All ER 522 at 539, CA (the case was decided in 1982).

negligence'. Moreover, in his speech in the *Littlewoods* case Lord Goff again referred with approval to the Wilberforce formula and said:[1] '. . . we have nowadays to appreciate that the broad general principle of liability for foreseeable damage is so widely applicable that the function of the duty of care is not so much to identify cases where liability is imposed as to identify those where it is not.'

Two problems with Anns

[**1.04**] The second limb of Lord Wilberforce's proposition itself made clear that foreseeability is not a sufficient condition of liability, and that policy factors can negate it. Moreover, his Lordship actually referred to 'economic loss' as a possible example of this.[2] Nevertheless, many of the critics of his approach apparently consider the distinction between pure economic loss and physical damage (including financial loss consequential upon that damage) to be so fundamental that it cannot appropriately be relegated to the second stage of an attempt to generalise negligence around a general presumption in favour of liability for carelessness.[3] Thus, in *Murphy v Brentwood District Council*[4] Lord Oliver said that: 'The infliction of physical injury to the person or property of another universally requires to be justified. The causing of economic loss does not.' His Lordship considered that it was 'one of the unfortunate features of *Anns* that it resulted in this essential distinction being lost sight of'. The proposition that economic loss should be regarded as a unique category is not beyond question. It is true that important policy arguments exist relating to very large numbers of potential claims, and even to the need not indirectly to subvert the inherent characteristics of a market economy by imposing liability for negligence where the intentional infliction of loss is in fact accepted. But these could have been given full weight at the second stage of the negligence enquiry as envisaged by Lord Wilberforce. Moreover, the proposition that the distinction between economic loss and physical damage is so fundamental as to require elevation outside the general presumption is weakened by the arbitrariness of that distinction: all physical damage to property can be seen in reality as constituting mere financial loss. Nevertheless, the perception that economic loss issues merit special prominence for classification purposes served fatally to undermine the Wilberforce approach when combined with another, more fundamental, flaw in *Anns*. This was the failure to investigate the significance, in the circumstances of the case itself, of the fact that the harm suffered by the plaintiff did not result from any positive action attributable to the defendants.

---

1 See [1987] AC 241 at 280, [1987] 1 All ER 710 at 736.
2 See [1978] AC 728 at 752, [1977] 2 All ER 492 at 499.
3 See J C Smith *Liability in Negligence* (1984) chs 4 to 6 inclusive.
4 [1991] 1 AC 398 at 487, [1990] 2 All ER 908 at 934, HL.

Omissions

[**1.05**] 'For better or worse', observed Slade LJ in *Banque Financière de la Cité v Westgate Insurance*,[1] 'our law of tort draws a fundamental distinction between the legal effects of acts on the one hand and omissions on the other'. Although in borderline cases the distinction may obviously be difficult to draw,[2] that does not derogate from its crucial importance to any system of civil liability based upon intuitive notions of responsibility or, indeed, upon any conception of human action which is geared to the notion of freedom to make choices.[3] It has been powerfully demonstrated, in an influential article,[4] that many of the apparent difficulties in the contemporary law of negligence can be attributed to a tendency to lose sight of the distinction, and to treat foreseeability as a sufficient justification for imposing liability even in cases of nonfeasance.[5] Of course, the circumstances may be such as to give rise to liability, even in situations involving apparent omissions.[6] One example is where the defendant has expressly or impliedly *assumed responsibility* to take positive measures for the plaintiff's benefit.[7] But the existence and scope of any such supposed undertaking needs to be carefully scrutinised if the appropriate limits on the extent of liability are not to be overstepped.[8] In *Anns v Merton London Borough Council*,[9] the House of Lords held that liability could exist where the defendant local authority had allegedly failed to exercise powers of housing inspection which might, if an inspection had actually taken place, have prevented a careless builder from inflicting loss on the plaintiffs. In effect the existence of the statutory

1 [1990] 1 QB 665 at 797, [1989] 2 All ER 952 at 1009.
2 Cf Atiyah *Accidents, Compensation and the Law* (4th edn) at p 102: 'The truth appears to be that there is no really satisfactory way of, or reason for, distinguishing between misfeasance and nonfeasance.' See also per Kennedy J in *Clough v Bussan* [1990] 1 All ER 431 at 433: 'One must not attach too much significance to the distinction between activity and inactivity . . .'
3 See Tony Honoré 'Are Omissions Less Culpable?' in *Essays for Patrick Atiyah* Cane and Stapleton (eds) (1991). See also A J E Jaffey *The Duty of Care* (1992), chs 4 and 6.
4 See Smith and Burns, '*Donoghue v Stevenson*: the Not So Golden Anniversary' (1983) 46 MLR 147 (cited by Lord Bridge in *Curran v Northern Ireland Co-ownership Housing Association* [1987] AC 718 at 724, [1987] 2 All ER 13 at 17, HL).
5 Lord Atkin's speech in *Donoghue v Stevenson* may itself be partly responsible for the confusion since the expression 'acts or omissions' is used in it without clear differentiation between the two: see [1932] AC 562 at 580.
6 See B S Markesinis 'Negligence, Nuisance and Affirmative Duties of Action' (1989) 105 LQR 104, who argues that the common law should relax its hostility to liability for omissions. See also James G Logie 'Affirmative Action in the Law of Tort: the Case of the Duty to Warn' [1989] 48 CLJ 115.
7 See, eg *Christchurch Drainage Board v Brown* (1987) Times, 26 October, PC.
8 Conversely, the approach has also been criticised on the ground that its application might result in an undue *narrowing* of liability if used as a device to circumvent statutory restrictions on the use of exclusion clauses. For this reason Lord Griffiths in *Smith v Eric S Bush* expressed the 'view that the voluntary assumption of responsibility is unlikely to be a helpful or realistic test in most cases': [1990] 1 AC 831 at 864, [1989] 2 All ER 514 at 536, HL. For further discussion see below, ch 5.
9 [1978] AC 728, [1977] 2 All ER 492, HL.

8 Liability for carelessness

power to inspect, contained in the Public Health Act 1936, was held to create a relationship between the plaintiffs and the defendant local authority, whereby the latter were exceptionally under a positive duty to take measures to protect the former from harm inflicted by third parties. In view, however, of the great emphasis placed in the case on foreseeability as a criterion of liability, the legitimacy of using the legislation in question as a basis for creating an exception to the general principle of no liability for mere omissions did not receive the attention which it might have done. This in turn may have led to the making, albeit unsuccessfully, of claims which would more readily have been perceived to be doomed if foreseeability had not been wrongly regarded as a universal panacea which had obliterated the distinction between acts and omissions. In *P Perl (Exporters) v Camden London Borough Council*,[1] the plaintiffs and defendants owned adjoining basement flats. The plaintiffs ran a clothing business and used their flat for the purpose of storage. The defendants' flat was unoccupied and despite the fact that they received complaints about lack of security, and were aware that their premises were accessible to vagrants, the defendants took no action even to ensure that their flat was adequately locked. One day thieves broke onto the defendants' premises, drilled a hole through the wall which separated the two flats, and stole a substantial number of the plaintiffs' garments. The plaintiffs sued the defendants for negligence, and although they succeeded at first instance, they failed before a unanimous Court of Appeal.[2] Waller LJ observed that 'It is not sought here to make the appellants liable for any act, it is sought to make the appellants liable for an omission to act'.[3] His Lordship went on to conclude that, despite the 'very considerable carelessness on the part of the appellants', he was satisfied that there was 'no breach of duty by the appellants to the respondents'.[4] This decision was clearly correct. To have upheld the trial judge would have had far-reaching and unacceptably harsh potential consequences for very many occupiers.[5] The decision in *Perl* was subsequently followed, by the Court of Appeal itself, in *King v Liverpool City Council*.[6] In this case a

---

1   [1984] QB 342, [1983] 3 All ER 161, CA. For discussion see Michael A Jones (1984) 47 MLR 223.
2   See also *Lamb v Camden London Borough Council* [1981] QB 625, [1981] 2 All ER 408, CA but cf *Ward v Cannock Chase District Council* [1986] Ch 546, [1985] 3 All ER 537 (a special case in which the defendants had assumed responsibility to take measures to protect the plaintiff).
3   [1984] QB at 352. See also per Oliver LJ at 352: '. . . the case is one, not of an act, but of an omission'.
4   [1984] QB at 352. A duty in not dissimilar circumstances might, however, be impliedly created by a contract between the parties: see, eg *Stansbie v Troman* [1948] 2 KB 48, [1948] 1 All ER 599, CA.
5   'Is every occupier of a terraced house under a duty to his neighbours to shut his windows or lock his door when he goes out, or to keep access to his cellars secure, or even to remove his fire escape, at the risk of being held liable in damages if thieves thereby obtain access to his own house and thence to his neighbours house? I cannot think that the law imposes any such duty': per Robert Goff LJ, [1984] QB 342 at 360. See also per Oliver LJ at 357-358.
6   [1986] 3 All ER 544, [1986] 1 WLR 890, CA.

local authority's failure to prevent vandals from so damaging an empty council flat, that water flooded from it into the plaintiff's flat, was held not to give rise to liability. More recently the whole matter received the attention of the House of Lords in *Smith v Littlewood's Organisation*,[1] in which vandals set fire to an empty cinema owned by the defendants. The fire spread to the plaintiff's adjoining property. Again the claim failed. Although the decision was unanimous, it is interesting that their Lordships revealed differing approaches to the solution of the problem. Two members of the House delivered full speeches. Lord Mackay of Clashfern insisted that foreseeability should be the determining factor even in cases involving omissions to prevent harm being caused by third parties; but the difficulty of predicting the activities of such parties would mean that liability would rarely be imposed. Lord Goff of Chieveley, on the other hand, consistently with his earlier judgment in *P Perl (Exporters) v Camden London Borough Council*, rejected this view. 'I wish to emphasise', he said, 'that I do not think that the problem in these cases can be solved simply through the mechanism of foreseeability'. Earlier in his speech he stated simply: 'Why does the law not recognise a general duty to prevent others from suffering loss or damage caused by the deliberate wrongdoing of third parties? The fundamental reason is that the common law does not impose liability for what are called pure omissions.' It is respectfully submitted that the approach of Lord Goff is the correct one. It was applied by the Court of Appeal in *Banque Financière de la Cité v Westgate Insurance*[2] to deny liability where one of the parties to a negotiation omitted to pass on to the other party information, of which it had happened to become aware, to the effect that that party had been defrauded by one of its own agents.

Failure to exercise control

[**1.06**] One situation in which an exception is made to the general proposition that failure to prevent third parties from causing harm does not give rise to liability is where the defendant is in a position actually to control their activities. Thus in the leading case of *Home Office v Dorset Yacht Co*,[3] the House of Lords held that borstal officers, and hence the Home Office as their employer, could in principle be liable for negligence if, owing to neglect of their duties, inmates of a borstal institution escaped and did damage.[4] Even here, however, it is significant that the foreseeability test is not applied simpliciter. Lord Reid observed that:

---

1 [1987] AC 241, [1987] 1 All ER 710, HL. See B S Markesinis 'Negligence, Nuisance and Affirmative Duties of Action' (1989) 105 LQR 104.
2 [1990] 1 QB 665, [1989] 2 All ER 952, CA; affd on other grounds in [1991] 2 AC 249, [1990] 2 All ER 947, HL. See also *Bank of Nova Scotia v Hellenic Mutual Ltd* [1990] 1 QB 818, [1989] 3 All ER 628, CA.
3 [1970] AC 1004, [1970] 2 All ER 294. See also *Vicar of Writtle v Essex County Council* (1979) 77 L G R 656. Cf *Smith v Scott* [1973] Ch 314, [1972] 3 All ER 645.
4 If there is a substantial gap in terms of time and space between the initial escape, and the damage done by the escapee, the claim is likely to fail on general grounds of remoteness: see *O'Reilly v C* [1978] 3 WWR 145 (Can).

> 'Where human action forms one of the links between the original wrongdoing of the defendant and the loss suffered by the plaintiff, that action must at least have been something very likely to happen if it is not to be regarded as novus actus interveniens breaking the chain of causation. I do not think that a mere foreseeable possibility is or should be sufficient ...'[1]

The ordinary test of foreseeability is, however likely to be appropriate where failure to control animals[2] or young children[3] is the basis of complaint. But where intentional adult activity is concerned, and the degree of control over that activity enjoyed by the defendant is either non-existent or very low, the plaintiff will fail even if the likelihood of harm occurring is very high. This is because the case will fall within the general rule of non-liability for mere omissions. *Home Office v Dorset Yacht Co* was, therefore, distinguished by the House of Lords itself in *Hill v Chief Constable for West Yorkshire*.[4] In this case it was held that, even assuming that the police had been at fault in failing to apprehend a murderer as quickly as they should have done, making it very probable that he would strike again, this was not sufficient to render them liable in negligence in respect of the murderer's activities.

Generalisation gives way to 'pragmatism'

[1.07] In *Caparo Industries v Dickman*[5] Lord Roskill said:

> 'Phrases such as "foreseeability", "proximity", "neighbourhood", "just and reasonable", "fairness", "voluntary acceptance of risk" or "voluntary assumption of responsibility" will be found used from to time in the different cases. But ... such phrases are not precise definitions. At best they are but labels or phrases descriptive of the very different factual situations which can exist in particular cases and which must be carefully examined in each case before it can be pragmatically determined whether a duty of care exists and, if so, what is the scope and extent of this duty. If this conclusion involves a return to the traditional categorisation of cases as pointing to the existence and scope of any duty of care ... I think this is infinitely preferable to recourse to somewhat wide generalisations which leave their practical application matters of difficulty and uncertainty.'

This statement encapsulates the approach which has found favour with the higher judiciary in preference to Lord Wilberforce's formula

---

1 [1970] AC 1004 at 1030, [1970] 2 All ER 294 at 300. It is noteworthy that in a subsequent case Lord Reid's dictum was actually criticised on the ground that *it did not go far enough* in emphasising the need for an exceptionally high degree of probability where intervening human acts are concerned: see *Lamb v Camden London Borough Council* [1981] QB 625 at 635, [1981] 2 All ER 408 at 412-413, per Lord Denning MR. See also per Oliver LJ at 642-643. This was, however, a case in which the defendants were strangers over whom the defendants had no control.
2 *Draper v Hodder* [1972] 2 QB 556, [1972] 2 All ER 210, CA.
3 See *Camarthenshire County Council v Lewis* [1955] AC 549, [1955] 1 All ER 565, HL.
4 [1989] AC 53, [1988] 2 All ER 238, HL; affg [1988] QB 60, [1987] 1 All ER 1173, CA.
5 [1990] 2 AC 605 at 628, [1990] 1 All ER 568 at 581-582, HL.

in *Anns v Merton London Borough Council*. The degree of hostility shown to that formula in recent cases means that it has unfortunately lost its utility in practice as a basis for development and exposition of the law. In *Yuen Kun Yeu v A-G of Hong Kong*,[1] Lord Keith of Kinkel quoted with approval the following statement of Brennan J in the High Court of Australia in *Sutherland Shire Council v Heyman*:[2] 'It is preferable, in my view, that the law should develop novel categories of negligence incrementally and by analogy with established categories, rather than by a massive extension of a prima facie duty of care ...' Later in his own speech in the *Yuen Kun Yeu* case Lord Keith expressed himself as follows:

> 'In view of the direction in which the law has since been developing, their Lordships consider that for the future it should be recognised that the two-stage test in *Anns* is not to be regarded as in all circumstances a suitable guide to the existence of a duty of care.'[3]

Both *Sutherland Shire Council v Heyman* and *Yuen Kun Yeu v A-G of Hong Kong* involved, however, like *Anns v Merton London Borough Council* itself, attempts to use the existence of a statutory power to argue in favour of an exception to the general rule of non-liability for mere omissions. It is regrettable that the strictures on the Wilberforce formula contained in the two cases were not confined to that context, within which the *Anns* approach is admittedly flawed, so that the generalising tendency of the formula could continue to have been regarded as useful elsewhere.[4] Although the notion of carelessness inevitably becomes highly artificial in its practical application as a test for liability it nevertheless inescapably remains the foundation of negligence as a tort. Since a high degree of uncertainty as to the *facts* is unavoidable in cases in this area a robust presumption in favour of liability for loss or damage caused by careless acts, which can be rebutted if cogent reasons exist for not applying it, would be more likely to produce consistency and clarity than a confused and unstructured combination of reliance upon precedent in the form of 'traditional categorisation' and emphasis ad hoc upon the wide differences in 'factual situations'.

'Proximity' and 'policy'

[**1.08**] The word 'proximity' had been used by Lord Wilberforce himself in his formula in the *Anns* case,[5] but without overmuch significance

---

1 [1988] AC 175 at 191, [1987] 2 All ER 705 at 710, PC.
2 (1985) 60 ALR 1 at 43-44.
3 [1988] AC 175 at 194, [1987] 2 All ER 705 at 710, PC.
4 It is significant that in *Yuen Kun Yeu v A-G of Hong Kong* Lord Keith sought to reinforce his argument for reducing the emphasis upon foreseeability which the *Anns* formula had promoted by observing that '. . . otherwise there would be liability in negligence on the part of one who sees another about to walk over a cliff with his head in the air and forbears to shout a warning'. But this is an example of an *omission* and is therefore beside the point as far as liability for misfeasance is concerned.
5 See [1.01] above.

seemingly being attached to it. The approach which has been adopted in preference to that of Lord Wilberforce, however, seeks to place increased emphasis upon the notion of 'proximity' on the ground that his test, with its apparent readiness to elevate 'foreseeability' above the status of a mere background precondition to a rebuttable presumption in favour of the imposition of liability, would have an unacceptably wide expansive effect.[1] But unlike 'foreseeability' which, whatever the difficulties in its practical application, at least has a clearly understood meaning as a defining characteristic of 'carelessness' itself, 'proximity' is simply an empty metaphor which only begs the question.[2] Nevertheless it is clear from the judgment of the Judicial Committee of the Privy Council in *Yuen Kun Yeu v A-G of Hong Kong*, delivered by Lord Keith, that the purpose which the concept is now intended to play is to import most of the considerations of 'policy', which were formerly incorporated in the second limb of the Wilberforce test, into the initial primary determination of whether the situation in question is one apt to create liability.[3] As a result, in the words of the judgment of the Board: 'The second stage of Lord Wilberforce's test is one which will rarely have to be applied. It can arise only in a limited category of cases where, notwithstanding that a case of negligence is made out on the proximity basis, public policy requires that there should be no liability.'[4] It is difficult to see this as anything other than a step backwards to an earlier age of judicial reticence, a fertile breeding ground for artificiality and legal fiction. The restrictions on the application of the foreseeability principle, and the valid reasons for them in some cases, should be considered openly rather than be obscured by the use of opaque language.

'The limits of the forensic process'

[**1.09**] An even more extreme view than that which favours the shielding of what are loosely termed 'policy' factors behind expressions such as 'proximity' is the thesis that such factors are not justiciable at all. In *McLoughlin v O'Brian*,[5] in which the House of Lords had to

---

1   See *Yuen Kun Yeu v A-G of Hong Kong* [1988] AC 175 at 193, [1987] 2 All ER 705 at 710 per Lord Keith. See also Richard Kidner 'Resiling from the *Anns* principle: the variable nature of proximity in negligence' (1987) 7 LS 319. It is true that Lord Atkin used the expression 'proximate' at several points in his speech in *Donoghue v Stevenson* itself, but the better view is that he was not thereby intending to invest the term with any special significance: see Julius Stone *Precedent and Law*, (1985) pp 265-266.
2   Cf per Lord Oliver in *Caparo Industries v Dickman*: ' "Proximity" is, no doubt, a convenient expression so long as it is realised that it is no more than a label which embraces not a definable concept but merely a description of circumstances from which, pragmatically, the courts conclude that a duty of care exists.' [1990] 2 AC 605 at 633, [1990] 1 All ER 568 at 585, HL.
3   [1988] 1 AC 175 at 191, [1987] 2 All ER 705 at 710: '(T)he expression "proximity or neighbourhood" [is] a composite one, importing the whole necessary relationship between plaintiff and defendant . . . '
4   [1988] 1 AC at 193, [1987] 2 All ER 705 at 712. The Board provides the immunity of advocates (see below, ch 5) as an example of its 'limited category'.
5   [1983] 1 AC 410, [1982] 2 All ER 298, HL.

consider the extent of liability for nervous shock, Lord Scarman expressed the view that consideration of the well-known 'floodgates' argument, the fear of uncontrollably large numbers of plaintiffs in certain situations, was outside the proper scope of the judicial function. He said: '... the policy issue where to draw the line is not justiciable. The considerations relevant to a decision are not such as to be capable of being handled within the limits of the forensic process.'[1]

This statement provoked a sharp response from Lord Edmund-Davies in the same case, who referred to explicit judicial statements to the contrary.[2] 'My Lords', he asserted, 'in accordance with such a line of authorities I hold that public policy issues *are* "justiciable"'.[3] Part of the difficulty here is perhaps an ambiguity in the notion of 'policy' itself. Lord Scarman was apparently concerned, on constitutional grounds, that the courts should not interfere in areas properly belonging solely to the legislature.[4] Clearly the courts should not attempt to involve themselves in broad social and political questions such as, for example, the delineation of the boundaries of the welfare state or the desirability of retaining nuclear weapons.[5] There are also situations in which the judges appropriately defer to Parliament, not for constitutional reasons, but simply because the higher degree of generality which legislation can achieve makes it a more appropriate form of law-making for the particular area in question.[6] Again, special principles apply to cases involving negligence claims based upon alleged carelessness in the exercise of statutory powers, in order to ensure that the various activities of public bodies are not unduly fettered.[7] But it is simply not accurate to categorise *any* judicial concern for the likely *consequences* of deciding a particular case one way or the other, for example whether it will give rise to many more claims or generate anomaly in analogous situations, as raising constitutional or other issues of this kind. Indeed, consideration of such matters seems to be inherent in the common law process itself. The decision whether to extend or limit the

---

1 [1983] 1 AC 410 at 431, [1982] 2 All ER 298 at 311. See also per Lord Roskill in *Junior Books v Veitchi* [1983] 1 AC 520 at 539, [1982] 3 All ER 201 at 209: 'My Lords, although it cannot be denied that policy considerations have from time to time been allowed to play their part in the last century and the present either in limiting or in extending the scope of the tort of negligence since it first developed as it were in its own right in the course of the last century, yet today I think its scope is best determined by considerations of principle rather than of policy.'
2 *Rondel v Worsley* [1969] 1 AC 191 at 228 (Lord Reid); *Home Office v Dorset Yacht Co* [1970] AC 1004 at 1058 (Lord Diplock); *British Railways Board v Herrington* [1972] AC 877 at 897 (Lord Reid).
3 [1983] 1 AC 410 at 428, [1982] 2 All ER 298 at 309 (emphasis is that of Lord Edmund-Davies).
4 Ie '... the court's function is to adjudicate according to principle, leaving policy curtailment to the judgment of Parliament... If principle leads to results which are thought to be socially unacceptable Parliament can legislate to draw a line or map out a new path': [1983] 1 AC 410 at 430, [1982] 2 All ER 298 at 310.
5 Cf *Chandler v DPP* [1964] AC 814, [1962] 3 All ER 142.
6 See, eg *Morgans v Launchbury* [1973] AC 127, [1972] 2 All ER 606, HL.
7 See, generally, ch 12, below.

applicability of principles laid down in previous cases cannot be made in a total vacuum. It is therefore submitted that the objections of Lord Scarman were misconceived and that the views of Lord Edmund-Davies are to be preferred.

'Just and reasonable'

[**1.10**] In *Peabody Donation Fund (Governors) v Sir Lindsay Parkinson & Co Ltd*[1] Lord Keith said that 'in determining whether or not a duty of care of particular scope was incumbent on a defendant it is material to take into consideration whether it is just and reasonable that it should be so'. The expression 'just and reasonable' has, along with 'proximity', been adopted in later cases[2] and become part of the familiar vocabulary of the contemporary law of negligence. Like 'proximity', however, it is conspicuous for its vagueness. Of course there is an irreducible element of intuition in the judicial process, and on one level the expression could be read simply as a frank admission of this. But while an all-embracing formula for the imposition of negligence liability will always be elusive, a failure to identify factors which *are* capable of being made explicit, by means of careful analysis, is to be regretted. It is therefore important to note that the string of recent decisions, in which the courts seem almost to have sought refuge in imprecision as a means of escape from what they appear to regard as the claustrophobic constraints of earlier formulations with their emphasis upon foreseeability, were exceptional in nature. It has been pointed out above that they involved some or all of the following factors: nonfeasance, economic loss, or statutory powers. The phrase 'just and reasonable' has proved particularly popular where statutory powers are concerned, especially *Peabody Donation Fund (Governors) v Sir Lindsay Parkinson & Co Ltd*[3] and *Caparo Industries v Dickman*,[4] essentially as a somewhat loose method of making the valid point that the *purpose* of the statutory provision in question will always be an important factor in such cases.[5] If the contexts of the recent decisions are fully understood their apparently drastic revision of the conceptual machinery of the law of negligence is more likely to be seen in perspective.[6]

---

1 [1985] 1 AC 210 at 241, [1984] 3 All ER 529 at 534.
2 See, eg the passage quoted above from the speech of Lord Roskill in *Caparo Industries v Dickman* [1990] 2 AC 605 at 628, [1990] 1 All ER 568 at 581-582 and the observations of Lord Bridge in the same case: [1990] 2 AC 605 at 618, [1990] 1 All ER 568 at 574.
3 [1985] AC 210, [1984] 3 All ER 529.
4 [1990] 2 AC 605, [1990] 1 All ER 568, HL.
5 For further discussion see below, ch 12.
6 Cf per Potts J in *B v Islington Health Authority* [1991] 1 All ER 825 at 830: '. . . I proceed on the basis that the nature of the duty of care in cases involving physical injury and consequential loss remains as it was before the decisions of the House of Lords in *Caparo Industries v Dickman* and *Murphy v Brentwood District Council.*' (The judgment of Potts J was subsequently affd sub nom *Burton v Islington Heath Authority*: see [1993] QB 204, [1992] 3 All ER 833, CA.)

The erosion of traditional immunities

[1.11] An important reason for not exaggerating the significance of the restrictive approach adopted in recent cases is to ensure that a marked feature of the expansion of the tort of negligence, which immediately preceded them, is not put in jeopardy. This was the progressive erosion of a number of earlier immunities from such liability which had managed to survive the decision in *Donoghue v Stevenson* itself.

Negligent misstatement and economic loss

[1.12] The effect of the current judicial hostility to the recovery of pure economic loss,[1] particularly when caused by deed rather than word, has been to narrow rather than widen the field of liability established by the decision of the House of Lords in *Hedley Byrne & Co v Heller & Partners Ltd*.[2] Nevertheless, that decision of course remains a landmark which shattered the assumption that the tort of negligence did not extend in any circumstances to the protection of purely economic interests. This branch of the law is dealt with in subsequent chapters.[3]

Lawyers

[1.13] The House of Lords in *Rondel v Worsley*[4] declared that members of the Bar could be liable for non-litigious work; a proposition which had formerly been much doubted. A degree of immunity based upon public policy still remains where litigation itself is concerned,[5] but it has subsequently been emphasised that this will be narrowly confined.[6]

Buildings

[1.14] It has long been the law that the vendor or lessor of real property owes no duty of care in negligence to purchasers or lessees, or to third parties,[7] with respect to the state of the premises.[8] This is

---

1 See especially *Murphy v Brentwood District Council* [1991] 1 AC 398, [1990] 2 All ER 908, HL.
2 [1964] AC 465, [1963] 2 All ER 575, HL.
3 Chapters 5 and 6 below.
4 [1969] 1 AC 191, [1967] 3 All ER 993.
5 See *Somasundaram v M Julius Melchior & Co* [1989] 1 All ER 129, [1988] 1 WLR 1394, CA.
6 See *Saif Ali v Sydney Mitchell & Co* [1980] AC 198, [1978] 3 All ER 1033, HL. Cf *Arenson v Casson Beckman Rutley & Co* [1977] AC 405, [1975] 3 All ER 901, HL; *Sutcliffe v Thackrah* [1974] AC 727, [1974] 1 All ER 859, HL. For discussion, see ch 5 below.
7 There may, however, be liability to third parties in nuisance: see, eg *Brew Bros v Snax (Ross) Ltd* [1970] 1 QB 612, [1970] 1 All ER 587, CA. See also Buckley *Law of Nuisance* (1981) pp 77-78.
8 'Fraud apart, there is no law against letting a tumble-down house': *Robbins v Jones* (1863) 15 CBNS 221 at 240. There may, of course, be contractual liability as far as parties to the contract are concerned.

16 Liability for carelessness

so even if the vendor or lessor is actually aware that the premises are in a dangerous or dilapidated condition.[1] In *Bottomley v Bannister*,[2] the Court of Appeal held that this so-called owner's immunity even protected *builders* from a negligence action when they had built on their own land, and subsequently sold, a house so defectively constructed as to cause the deaths of two inhabitants. This case was decided shortly before *Donoghue v Stevenson*, but in a subsequent case it was expressly held that the immunity of builder-owners had survived the decision of the House of Lords in that case.[3] More recently, however, the expansion of the tort of negligence resulted in this immunity being regarded with judicial hostility. It was first made clear that the immunity did not extend automatically to all situations involving realty, so that builders who had not also been owners of the land were unable to invoke it.[4] Finally, in *Anns v Merton London Borough Council*,[5] *Bottomley v Bannister* was overruled. The overruling of *Anns* itself in order to disallow the recovery of pure economic loss,[6] has not had the effect of reinstating *Bottomley v Bannister* as far as physical injury or damage is concerned.[7] Thus although two recent decisions of the House of Lords have held expressly that pure economic losses, such as the cost of repair, cannot be recovered in negligence actions against builders with whom the plaintiffs were not in contractual relationships,[8] both builders and builder-owners whose carelessness causes physical injury or damage to subsequent owners or occupiers will remain liable in tort.[9] Nevertheless the immunity of a 'bare' landlord or vendor (ie one who was not also the builder) still survives. 'It may be', said Stephenson LJ in *Rimmer v Liverpool City Council*,[10] 'that to impose a duty on all landowners who let or sell their land and dwellings, whether or not they are their own designers or builders, would be so great a change in the law as to require legislation'. But it should not be overlooked that

---

1 See *Cavalier v Pope* [1906] AC 428, HL: A case which 'must be kept in close confinement', per Stephenson LJ in *Rimmer v Liverpool City Council* [1985] QB 1 at 9, [1984] 1 All ER 930 at 935, CA, echoing Denning LJ in *Greene v Chelsea Borough Council* [1954] 2 QB 127 at 138, [1954] 2 All ER 318 at 324, CA.
2 [1932] 1 KB 458, CA.
3 See *Otto v Bolton & Norris* [1936] 2 KB 46, [1936] 1 All ER 960. See also *Davis v Foots* [1940] 1 KB 116, [1939] 4 All ER 4, CA; *Travers v Gloucester Corpn* [1947] KB 71, [1946] 2 All ER 506.
4 See *Sharpe v Sweeting & Son Ltd* [1963] 2 All ER 455, [1963] 1 WLR 665; *Gallagher v McDowell Ltd* [1961] N I 26. Cf *Greene v Chelsea Borough Council* [1954] 2 QB 127, [1954] 2 All ER 318, CA. See also the Defective Premises Act 1972, s 1.
5 [1978] AC 728, [1977] 2 All ER 492, HL. See also *Batty v Metropolitan Property Realisations Ltd* [1978] QB 554, [1978] 2 All ER 445, CA.
6 See *Murphy v Brentwood District Council* [1991] 1 AC 398, [1990] 2 All ER 908, HL.
7 See *Targett v Torfaen Borough Council* [1992] 3 All ER 27, CA.
8 See *D & F Estates Ltd v Church Comrs For England* [1989] AC 177, [1988] 2 All ER 992, HL and *Department of the Environment v Thomas Bates & Son* [1991] 1 AC 499, [1990] 2 All ER 943, HL. For further discussion see ch 6, below.
9 See *Rimmer v Liverpool City Council* [1985] QB 1, [1984] 1 All ER 930, CA See also *Targett v Torfaen Borough Council* [1992] 3 All ER 27, CA.
10 [1985] QB 1 at 16, [1984] 1 All ER 930 at 939.

lessors may be liable in public nuisance to third parties not actually on the premises, and that such liability extends to damages for personal injury.[1] Moreover a limited statutory liability for failure to repair is imposed upon landlords by the Defective Premises Act 1972, s 4.[2]

Factors which can limit liability

[1.15] In view of the rejection of Lord Wilberforce's generalised approach, a court faced with a negligence claim in a novel situation is now obliged to consider whether liability should be extended incrementally by analogy with previous decisions. Whether the court chooses to make its reasoning explicit, or instead to adopt the regrettably fashionable reticence on 'policy' issues, several factors can be identified as being among those which may be relevant to resolution of the issue for or against expansion.[3]

'Floodgates' argument

[1.16] Probably the most familiar 'policy' argument is that it would be wrong to allow the plaintiff to succeed because so many other people have suffered, or could suffer, loss or damage in similar situations, in a manner indistinguishable in principle from that of the plaintiff, that the field of liability thus opened up could be uncontrollable and potentially oppressive on defendants. This argument still exerts a powerful influence in restricting liability for economic loss, a matter which is considered at length in a later chapter.[4]

Conflicting interests

[1.17] An argument which sometimes prevailed in the past is that the imposition of liability for negligence would be inappropriate because the defendant filled a role which obliged him to be conscious of other, and potentially conflicting, interests in addition to those of the plaintiff. Thus one of the reasons given for the so-called advocates' immunity was that the advocate owes a duty to the court which may conflict with that owed to his client.[5] Outside the area of litigation or analogous situations, however, it is apparent that this kind of argument will seldom meet with favour today. It has been advanced both by architects, seeking to avoid liability for negligence in evaluating and certifying work done by builders under a building contract,[6] and by accountants attempting to do so for carelessness in

1 See Buckley *Law of Nuisance* (1981) ch 4.
2 See ch 16, below.
3 For discussion see Bell *Policy Arguments in Judicial Decisions* (1983) ch 3.
4 Chapter 6.
5 See *Rondel v Worsley* [1969] 1 AC 191, [1967] 3 All ER 993, HL.
6 See *Sutcliffe v Thackrah* [1974] AC 727, [1974] 1 All ER 859, HL.

18 *Liability for carelessness*

valuing shares at the request of vendor and purchaser.[1] In both cases the House of Lords unanimously rejected the argument and imposed liability. The fundamental proposition that victims of carelessness should normally be allowed to seek reparation from those responsible, with inroads into that principle for reasons of public policy being kept to a minimum, was robustly reasserted. Indeed the underlying logic of the proposition that liability should be negated because of the involvement of conflicting interests is not attractive. If the defendant's role requires him to exercise difficult functions with regard to the balancing of such interests, then negligence may be very difficult actually to *prove*.[2] But the suggestion that sheer carelessness as such should go unremedied for a priori reasons is one which must always be treated with caution.[3] Nevertheless it is regarded with favour by the courts in cases involving public servants, who may be faced with situations of particular complexity when balancing a variety of conflicting interests in the exercise of statutory discretions,[4] and whose judgment may supposedly be affected adversely by the possibility of litigation.[5]

Police activity[6]

[**1.18**] A specific area of public service in which the notion of conflicting and overriding interests of public policy has recently been invoked to justify the negation of negligence liability is that of police activity. This argument was adopted by the House of Lords, as a subordinate ground of decision, in *Hill v Chief Constable for West Yorkshire*,[7] considered above, in which it was alleged that the police had been culpable in failing to catch a murderer. Lord Templeman observed:[8]

> '. . . if this action lies, every citizen will be able . . . to investigate the performance of every policeman. If the policeman concentrates on one crime, he may be accused of neglecting others. If the policeman does not arrest on suspicion a suspect with previous convictions, the police force may be held liable for subsequent crimes. The threat of litigation against a police force would not make a policeman more efficient. The necessity for defending proceedings, successfully or unsuccessfully, would distract the policeman from his duties.'

---

1 See *Arenson v Casson Beckman Rutley & Co* [1977] AC 405, [1975] 3 All ER 901, HL. For further discussion see ch 5 below.
2 Cf per Lord Diplock in *Saif Ali v Sydney Mitchell & Co* [1980] AC 198 at 220, HL. In *Thorne v University of London* [1966] 2 QB 237, [1966] 2 All ER 338, CA, it was held that university examiners owe no duty of care: sed quaere.
3 In *Ross v Caunters* [1980] Ch 297 at 321-322, Sir Robert Megarry V-C rejected a submission that a firm of solicitors should not be liable to a third party for losses arising out of negligent advice given to one of their clients, merely because of hypothetical conflicts of interest which might arise in future cases.
4 See *Yuen Kun Yeu v A-G of Hong Kong* [1988] AC 175, [1987] 2 All ER 705, PC; *Davis v Radcliffe* [1990] 2 All ER 536, [1990] 1 WLR 821, PC.
5 See *Rowling v Takaro Properties* [1988] AC 473, [1988] 1 All ER 163, PC. On negligence and the exercise of statutory powers, see generally ch 12 below.
6 See, generally, R Clayton and H Tomlinson *Civil Actions Against the Police* (2nd edn, 1992).
7 [1989] AC 53, [1988] 2 All ER 238, HL.
8 [1989] AC 53 at 65, [1988] 2 All ER 238 at 245.

In three subsequent reported decisions police authorities have successfully relied on *Hill*'s case to get personal injury actions against them dismissed as disclosing no reasonable cause of action. In *Clough v Bussan*,[1] Kennedy J struck out a claim based upon alleged failure to respond sufficiently quickly when traffic lights became defective, and in *Hughes v National Union of Mineworkers*,[2] May J struck out one based upon alleged negligence during a riot control operation. In *Ancell v McDermott*,[3] the Court of Appeal struck out a claim based upon alleged failure by the police to deal adequately with a traffic hazard resulting from a spillage of diesel oil, which led to a fatal accident when a vehicle skidded on the oil. It appears, therefore, that the courts are disposed to put a wide interpretation on the principle in *Hill*'s case and not to limit it to the context in which it was enunciated, which concerned the detection of crime.[4] Decisions such as that in *Ancell*'s case indicate a readiness to extend the principle to protect what might be described as 'routine' carelessness in the discharge of duties such as traffic control. The desirability of this extension seems open to question.[5]

Public policy and the sanctity of life

[**1.19**] In *McKay v Essex Area Health Authority*,[6] the plaintiff's mother contracted german measles during pregnancy. The defendant doctor negligently failed to diagnose or treat the illness, and consequently failed to advise the mother of the desirability of considering an abortion in such circumstances. The plaintiff was born disabled and claimed damages from the defendant for 'entry into a life in which her injuries are highly debilitating'. The Court of Appeal struck out the claim as disclosing no cause of action. The Court held that while a doctor might in such cases owe a duty to the mother to afford an opportunity for termination of the pregnancy, 'to impose such a duty towards the child would . . . make [an] . . . inroad on the sanctity of human life which would be contrary to public policy'.[7] Although decided in 1982, the birth in this case occurred before the coming into effect of the Congenital Disabilities (Civil Liability) Act 1976 in which the legislature itself ruled out such claims in future. The Act provides that a child may have a cause of action where the defendant's negligent breach of duty to his mother during pregnancy caused him to be born disabled.[8] It is, however, 'so worded as to import the

1   [1990] 1 All ER 431.
2   [1991] 4 All ER 278.
3   (1992) 137 Sol Jo LB 36.
4   Cf *Alexandrou v Oxford* (1990) Times, 19 February, CA.
5   Cf Carol Brennan 'Police negligence defined' (1992) NLJ 1118.
6   [1982] QB 1166, [1982] 2 All ER 771, CA.
7   [1982] QB 1166 at 1180, [1982] 2 All ER 771 at 781, per Stephenson LJ.
8   See s 1. The Act resolved uncertainty which existed at common law as to whether such a cause of action existed (see now *Burton v Islington Health Authority* [1993] QB 204, [1992] 3 All ER 833, CA, holding in respect of a pre-Act birth that it did). The mother herself cannot be liable to her child except in cases arising out of her own negligent driving (when the claim will in effect be against an insurance company): see s 2 of the Act.

assumption that, but for the occurrence giving rise to a disabled birth, the child would have been born normal and healthy, not that it would not have been born at all'.[1] This reflected the view of the Law Commission, which originally drafted the Act, that there should be no so-called right of action for 'wrongful life'.[2] But on the whole the courts seem anxious not to extend such policy reasons for negating liability further than appears strictly necessary. In *Emeh v Kensington and Chelsea and Westminster Area Health Authority*[3] the Court of Appeal held that where pregnancy occurred after a negligently unsuccessful sterilisation operation the parents could recover damages from the surgeon to compensate for the cost of bringing up and looking after the child.[4] The argument that such a claim should be ruled out as contrary to public policy was expressly rejected.[5] Damages are recoverable whether the child is born normal or disabled, but in the former case the sum awarded may be mitigated.[6] Damages may also be reduced where the child is born disabled if the parents would otherwise have *chosen* to embark on another pregnancy but decided not to do so as a result of the birth of the handicapped child. In *Salih v Enfield Health Authority*[7] the Court of Appeal held that the saving produced by not having to bring up another child had to be set against the damages awarded in respect of the birth of the disabled one.

Illegal or anti-social conduct by the plaintiff

[**1.20**] In *Pitts v Hunt*,[8] the 18-year-old plaintiff was a passenger on a motor cycle owned and driven by a 16-year-old friend who, to the plaintiff's knowledge, was unlicensed and uninsured. After both had been on a heavy drinking session the owner, aided and abetted by the plaintiff, drove his motor cycle at high speed in, as Beldam LJ put it, a 'reckless, irresponsible and idiotic way'. The two 'were clearly showing no concern for other users of the road' and it appeared that they were deliberately riding in a way calculated to frighten others'.[9]

---

1 Per Ackner LJ in *McKay v Essex Area Health Authority* [1982] QB 1166 at 1186-1187, [1982] 2 All ER 771 at 786 referring to ss 1(2)(b) and 4(5) of the Act.
2 See the Law Commission's *Report on Injuries to Unborn Children* (Law Com No 60, Cmnd 5709) para 89. See also the *Report of the Royal Commission on Civil Liability and Compensation for Personal Injury (Pearson)* vol 1 (Cmnd 7054-I) para 1485.
3 [1985] QB 1012, [1984] 3 All ER 1044, CA
4 See also *Thake v Maurice* [1986] QB 644, [1986] 1 All ER 497, CA.
5 'In my judgment the court should not be too ready to lay down lines of public policy' per Waller LJ: [1985] QB at 1022, [1984] 3 All ER 1044 at 1051. The Court declined to follow the decision of Jupp J in *Udale v Bloomsbury Area Health Authority* [1983] 2 All ER 522, [1983] 1 WLR 1098 who had held that to award damages for the upkeep of a child in such circumstances would be contrary to public policy. For discussion see C R Symmons, 'Policy Factors in Actions for Wrongful Birth' (1987) 50 MLR 269.
6 See *Emeh v Kensington and Chelsea and Westminster Area Health Authority* [1985] QB 1012 at 1028, [1984] 3 All ER 1044 at 1056 per Purchas LJ. In the *Emeh* case itself the child was actually born congenitally abnormal, but in *Thake v Maurice* [1986] QB 644, [1986] 1 All ER 497, CA, damages were awarded for the upkeep of a healthy child.
7 [1991] 3 All ER 400.
8 [1991] 1 QB 24, [1990] 3 All ER 344, CA.
9 [1991] 1 QB 24 at 36, [1990] 3 All ER 344 at 347.

They were involved in a collision in which the driver was killed. The plaintiff sued his estate for the serious injuries which he suffered in the accident but the Court of Appeal, upholding the decision of the trial judge, rejected his claim. Beldam LJ held that it would be contrary to public policy, as reflected in Acts of Parliament, to allow it to succeed: 'The public conscience is ever-increasingly being focused not only on those who commit the offence but, in the words of recent publicity, those who ask the driver to drink and drive.'[1] Balcombe and Dillon LJJ, although agreeing as to the result, preferred to base their conclusion on the proposition that, as it was put in an Australian case, 'the plaintiff must fail when the character of the enterprise in which the parties are engaged is such that it is impossible for the court to determine the standard of care which is appropriate to be observed'.[2] Dillon LJ considered that 'a test that depends on what would or would not be an affront to the public conscience [would be] very difficult to apply' since it 'would be likely to lead to a graph of illegalities according to moral turpitude'.[3] Nevertheless, it is submitted that the approach of Beldam LJ is to be preferred. Indeed, as he pointed out, the 'duty of care approach' seemed itself to be based upon public policy and would therefore appear to be question-begging. Moreover, his Lordship persuasively observed that he was 'not convinced of the wisdom of a policy which might encourage a belief that the duty to behave responsibly in driving motor vehicles is diminished even to the limited extent that they may in some circumstances not owe a duty to each other, particularly when those circumstances involve conduct which is highly dangerous to others'.[4] In truth a degree of uncertainty in the law is unavoidable in situations involving illegality, as the more numerous cases on the topic in the law of contract[5] amply demonstrate. Precise tests for the operation of public policy are illusory and the adoption of a pragmatic approach based on the gravity of the case is inevitable.[6] Questions arising out of deliberate criminal activity involving violence or dishonesty will be relatively easy to answer. Thus, in *Ashton v Turner*,[7] Ewbank J denied recovery where the plaintiff suffered serious personal injuries when involved in a collision while passenger in a get-away car. The vehicle was being driven by the defendant to escape at speed from the scene of a burglary in which both parties had participated. In so holding his Lordship followed an earlier decision of the High Court of Australia.[8] In *Meah v McCreamer*

1 [1991] 1 QB 24 at 46, [1990] 3 All ER at 355. For the 'conscience test' see also *Thackwell v Barclays Bank* [1986] 1 All ER 676 and *Saunders v Edwards* [1987] 2 All ER 651, [1987] 1 WLR 1116, CA.
2 *Jackson v Harrison* (1978) 138 CLR 438 at 455, quoted by Balcombe LJ in [1991] 1 QB 24 at 49-50, [1990] 3 All ER 344 at 358.
3 [1991] 1 QB 24 at 56, [1990] 3 All ER at 362-363.
4 [1991] 1 QB 24 at 46-47, [1990] 3 All ER at 355-356.
5 See Cheshire, Fifoot and Furmston *Law of Contract* 12th edn, (1991) chs 11 and 12.
6 See per Bingham LJ in *Saunders v Edwards* [1987] 2 All ER 651 at 666.
7 [1981] QB 137, [1980] 3 All ER 870.
8 See *Smith v Jenkins* (1969) 119 CLR 397, 44 ALJR 78 (Aust HC) (Barwick LJ, Kitto, Windeyer, Owen and Walsh JJ). See also *Gala v Preston* (1991) 172 CLR 243. Cf *Burns v Edman* [1970] 2 QB 541, [1970] 1 All ER 886 (widow of burglar unable to recover damages under the Fatal Accidents Acts).

Liability for carelessness

(No 2)[1] the plaintiff became a rapist as a result of personality changes which he underwent due to injuries received in a road accident caused by the defendant's negligence. Although he received damages from the defendant for his injuries, which included compensation for the fact that the behavioural changes had led to his imprisonment,[2] a claim that the award should also include an indemnity against sums which the plaintiff himself had been ordered to pay[3] to the victims of his rape attacks was disallowed. Woolf J held that these losses were too remote from the road accident to be recovered, but also indicated that illegality could have provided an alternative ground for the decision observing that 'to allow the plaintiff to succeed would certainly [have been] distasteful'.[4]

Suicide and public policy[5]

[**1.21**] The adoption of such an approach seems appropriate where serious criminal offences are concerned. But the principles of public policy are not necessarily confined to such cases. It appears that in a suitable case they may also negate liability even where no criminal liability is involved at all. But care needs to be taken to ensure that illegality does not degenerate into a wider defence; thereby causing claims to fail for reasons not related directly to the defendant's carelessness and the loss to which it gave rise. In one case Lord Denning MR expressed the view, obiter, that public policy should operate to prevent persons who injured themselves in unsuccessful suicide attempts, or their personal representatives if the attempt was successful, from suing hospital authorities for negligence in failing to prevent what occurred.[6] In the later case of *Kirkham v Chief Constable of the Greater Manchester Police*,[7] however, the Court of Appeal disapproved of the dictum of Lord Denning MR in so far as it applied to suicide attempts by persons suffering from mental illness even though Lloyd LJ accepted 'that the ex turpi causa defence is not confined to criminal conduct' and that a court faced with an issue in this area has to ask itself 'whether to afford relief . . . would affront the public conscience, or . . . shock the ordinary citizen'.[8] While on the facts of the *Kirkham* case the defence failed, and the personal representatives of the deceased succeeded in obtaining damages for the negligent failure of the prison authorities to follow correctly their own procedures for handling known potential suicides,[9] it will rarely

1 [1986] 1 All ER 943.
2 See *Meah v McCreamer* [1985] 1 All ER 367.
3 See *W v Meah* [1986] 1 All ER 935.
4 [1986] 1 All ER 943 at 950.
5 See Michael Jones 'Saving the patient from himself' (1990) 6 PN 107.
6 'By his act, in self-inflicting this serious injury, [the plaintiff] has made himself a burden on the whole community . . . The policy of [the] law should be to discourage these actions': *Hyde v Tameside Area Health Authority* [1981] CLY 1854, [1981] CA Transcript 130, quoted in *Kirkham v Chief Constable of the Greater Manchester Police* [1990] 2 QB 283 at 292, [1990] 3 All ER 246 at 252.
7 [1990] 2 QB 283, [1990] 3 All ER 246.
8 [1990] 2 QB 283 at 291, [1990] 3 All ER 246 at 251.
9 See also *Selfe v Ilford and District Hospital Management Committee* (1970) 114 Sol Jo 935.

be easy to establish carelessness in such cases. In *Knight v Home Office*,[1] which also concerned the suicide in prison of a person known to be at risk, Pill J examined exhaustively the procedures which had been adopted to monitor the deceased; before dismissing on the facts the allegation that the medical staff had been negligent. But the acceptance in principle of the possibility of such claims, and the disapproval of the dictum of Lord Denning MR, is surely to be welcomed. His view that public policy alone should limit or negate the existence of a duty of care towards patients foreseeably prone to depressive suicidal tendencies seems unacceptable.[2]

Existing law

[**1.22**] In *Home Office v Dorset Yacht Co Ltd*[3] Lord Reid observed that a 'justification or valid explanation' for exclusion of the ordinary principles of negligence might be found in 'cases . . . where the law was settled long ago and neither Parliament nor the House sitting judicially has made any move to alter it'. Accordingly, one of the more difficult questions which arose when the law of negligence was going through a period of relative expansion, concerned those situations in which detailed rules of law already existed, having developed before the full ripening of negligence concepts. Rules which could readily be perceived as being anomalous and out-dated have yielded relatively easily to the advancing tide.[4] Elsewhere the position was often more difficult, and in a number of cases traditional formulations of doctrine remained resistant to change.[5] In the more conservative mood now prevailing arguments based upon the undesirability of disturbing existing patterns of liability and its absence, regardless of their underlying irrationality or lack of it, are unfortunately even more likely to receive a sympathetic reception. Two such arguments, both of which arguably combine excessive caution with an undue concern for symmetry, have gained prominence in recent cases. The first concerns the distinction between contract and tort and includes a strong presumption that the doctrines of the former should enjoy priority in situations in which the parties *could* in theory have provided contractually for the situation which occurred but did not in fact do so, especially where economic loss is involved.[6] The second concerns the relationship between the common law and the legislature and amounts to a presumption against expanding the former if the latter has by its enactments intervened in a particular area, but done

1 [1990] 3 All ER 237.
2 Although suicide was formerly a crime, it ceased so to be with the Suicide Act 1961, s 1. If the deceased committed suicide as a result of depression directly induced by injuries caused by the negligence of the defendants, his dependants can recover under the Fatal Accidents Acts: *Pigney v Pointers Transport Services* [1957] 2 All ER 807, [1957] 1 WLR 1121.
3 [1970] AC 1004 at 1027, [1970] 2 All ER 294 at 297, HL.
4 See above, 'Erosion of traditional immunities'.
5 See, eg *Smith v Scott* [1973] Ch 314, [1972] 3 All ER 645; *Stephens v Anglian Water Authority* [1987] 3 All ER 379, [1987] 1 WLR 1381, CA.
6 See generally chs 5 (negligent misstatement) and 6 (financial loss) below.

24 Liability for carelessness

so in a limited fashion: the highly questionable assumption being that Parliament must thereby have intended to ossify the law and discourage further development. Thus the limited existing scope of statutory protection for employees has been invoked as a justification for not expanding the duties resting at common law upon employers,[1] and legislation regarding defective premises[2] has been similarly treated as a justification for not increasing the tortious liability of builders.[3] Clearly in some areas the overriding need for certainty, and the need not to upset long-term transactions entered into on the basis of the existing law, will make the resolution of the matter in favour of the status quo relatively straightforward. It is nevertheless submitted that the courts should not be too eager to rule on a priori grounds against the entry of negligence into unfamiliar areas. The fear that merely contemplating putting old rules to the test of relevance to contemporary circumstances will cause de-stabilising uncertainty is probably exaggerated.

Legislative or administrative solution more suitable?

[**1.23**] In some cases the imposition of liability may have such far-reaching consequences that legislation, or administrative action initiated by local or national government, may be perceived as more likely to provide an acceptable framework for the delineation of rights and duties in the particular sphere.[4] For example, a suggestion that a particular method of road planning or construction was negligent, and the cause of an accident, might involve a wide-ranging inquiry with substantial resource implications. As Atiyah has written:

> 'If a local authority is condemned as negligent for failing to install traffic lights at a dangerous junction, they may feel obliged to install them in future at that and hundreds of other dangerous junctions. This may involve either raising large extra revenues from the public, or forgoing other expenditure which may actually be more desirable than the installation of traffic lights.'[5]

---

1 *Reid v Rush & Tomkins Group plc* [1989] 3 All ER 228, [1990] 1 WLR 212, CA. On employers' liability to their employees, see generally ch 14 below.
2 Ie the Defective Premises Act 1972.
3 See *D & F Estates v Church Comrs For England* [1989] AC 177, [1988] 2 All ER 992, HL. See also *Murphy v Brentwood District Council* [1991] 1 AC 398, [1990] 2 All ER 908, HL.
4 In *Morgans v Launchbury* [1973] AC 127, [1972] 2 All ER 606, the House of Lords refused to extend the scope of vicarious liability on the ground that only the legislature could consider adequately the far-reaching implications for the insurance market.
5 Atiyah *Accidents, Compensation and the Law* (3rd edn) 62 (The wording on p 58 of the 4th edn differs slightly). See also *Knight v Home Office* [1990] 3 All ER 237 at 243 per Pill J: '. . . the court must . . . bear in mind as one factor that resources available for the public service are limited and that the allocation of resources is a matter for Parliament.'

Nor is the problem confined to the governmental sphere. In *Budden v BP Oil Ltd*[1] it was alleged that the defendants had been negligent in marketing petrol which contained dangerously high levels of lead, but the Court of Appeal struck the claim out. The lead levels had not exceeded the maximum laid down in regulations made by the Secretary of State, and any change in the permitted level, which would necessarily apply to all manufacturers and suppliers of petrol throughout the country, should be made by Parliament and not by the courts.[2] In some cases, especially those involving government, the existence of statutory powers may be relevant to a potential negligence claim; in which event special factors apply and the need not to fetter administrative discretion has to be taken into account.[3] But to allow foreseeably harm-causing activities to continue unremedied in other contexts for, in effect, economic or political reasons or considerations of administrative convenience, is a course which should surely only be adopted in rare cases. An important part of the function of tort, along with law generally in a free society, is to ensure that powerful bodies, public or private, are subject to its constraints.[4] Of course many activities, of which transport is the prime example, necessarily involve risk and will predictably continue to result in death and injury. An irreducible degree of evaluation will therefore be involved in determining whether, say, certain methods of road-building, or the construction techniques of particular car-manufacturers, have appreciably *added* unnecessarily to risks which we all accept as part of day to day life. But the courts should not be too eager to invoke the existence of this need for evaluation as an excuse for wholly abrogating the application, on its own common-sense basis, of the law of negligence.

Alternative remedy more appropriate?

[**1.24**] At the Court of Appeal stage in *Hill v Chief Constable for West Yorkshire*,[5] in which the mother of a murder victim sought unsuccessfully to sue the police for failing to apprehend the mass-murderer involved soon enough to prevent her daughter's death, Fox LJ referred to the existence of the Criminal Injuries Compensation Scheme and said:[6]

---

1 (1980) 124 Sol Jo 376, [1980] JPL 586, CA
2 See [1980] JPL 586 at 587, per Megaw LJ.
3 See, generally, ch 12 below.
4 '... lack of funds would not excuse a public body which operated its vehicles on the public roads without any system of maintenance for the vehicles if an accident occurred because of lack of maintenance. The law would require a higher standard of care towards other road users': per Pill J in *Knight v Home Office* [1990] 3 All ER 237 at 243.
5 [1988] QB 60, [1987] 1 All ER 1173, CA; affd [1989] AC 53, [1988] 2 All ER 238, HL. For comment on the decision of the Court of Appeal, see Richard Clayton and Hugh Tomlinson, 'Suing for Negligent Police Investigations' [1987] Law Soc Gaz 1798. See also Suzanne Bailey 'Beyond the Call of Duty' (1987) 50 MLR 956; B S Markesinis 'Liability of the Police to an Ordinary Citizen for Failing to Arrest a Dangerous Murderer' [1987] 46 CLJ 387.
6 [1988] QB 60 at 73, [1987] 1 All ER 1173 at 1182.

26 Liability for carelessness

> 'The scheme ... make[s] quite wide provision for compensation for such persons as are likely to suffer financial loss as a result of a crime of violence. It is not desirable that inequalities should be produced by providing additional remedies for negligence. Either such remedies will merely duplicate the scheme, or they may give rise to inequalities which may be offensive to the families of other victims of crimes of violence in cases where no negligence by the police was involved ... I think that the problems of compensation for injury from crimes of violence are best dealt with in the framework of the scheme ...'

Similar remarks were made by Lord Denning MR in an earlier case[1] in which a plaintiff unsuccessfully sought to sue his employer for failing adequately to protect him from the risk of robbery when collecting the firm's wages, a risk which materialised resulting in his incurring serious personal injuries.[2] Like the previous general argument based on the feasibility of administrative solutions, however, the existence of the Criminal Injuries Compensation Scheme, or similar arrangements, should not be allowed to become an automatic justification for denying a negligence remedy in appropriate cases.[3] Whatever arguments may be advanced about the efficient administration of such special funds, public or private, as exist to compensate the victims of misfortune,[4] reliance upon the existence of those funds as a reason *in itself* for denying recovery would be likely to undermine the structure and coherence of the common law in this area. This is not to deny, however, that there may occasionally be situations in which judicial review might be a more appropriate method by which to challenge the decisions of a public authority, than a negligence action, if the essence of the complaint is the misallocation of resources.[5]

Nervous shock

[1.25] The question of whether, and in what circumstances, plaintiffs who suffer nervous shock[6] as a result of witnessing, or otherwise

---

1 *Charlton v Forrest Printing Ink* [1980] IRLR 331, CA.
2 'I hope that the compensation board for the victims of crime will realise the plight which [the plaintiff] has been left in by these robbers, and will award him full and adequate compensation for the distressing injury he has received. So I would leave it to the compensation board - and not to the employers.' [1980] IRLR 331 at 333 per Lord Denning MR.
3 This is notwithstanding the fact that the Criminal Injuries Compensation Board, and similar bodies, are subject to judicial review: *R v Criminal Injuries Compensation Board, ex p Lain* [1967] 2 QB 864, [1967] 2 All ER 770. On the Criminal Injuries Compensation Scheme see ch 19 below.
4 See generally, Part six below.
5 See *Clough v Bussan* [1990] 1 All ER 431 at 433 per Kennedy J (referring to the argument of counsel). See, generally, ch 12 below.
6 In *Attia v British Gas* [1988] QB 304 at 317, [1987] 3 All ER 455 at 462, CA. Bingham LJ said: '[The] claim is ... one for what have in the authorities and the literature been called damages for nervous shock. Judges have in recent years become increasingly restive at the use of this misleading and inaccurate expression, and I shall use the general expression "psychiatric damage", intending to comprehend within it all relevant forms of mental illness, neurosis and personality change.'

becoming aware of, horrific situations caused by the defendant's carelessness has traditionally been seen as raising a problem on the frontiers of liability in negligence.[1] It was for long unclear whether the ordinary test of reasonable foreseeability applied to such cases, or whether some narrower principle was applied out of a fear of opening up what might prove to be an unduly wide area of liability.[2] The cases usually involved the infliction of death or serious injury upon a third party, and it was certainly possible to discern a pattern in the actual decisions: the courts would rarely impose liability where the victim who suffered injury was a stranger, unknown to the plaintiff,[3] or where the plaintiff merely learnt of the injury second-hand and was not present at the scene.[4] This tended to suggest that control devices to limit liability were being applied and that foreseeability was merely a necessary, and not a sufficient, condition. On the other hand the judges tended obstinately, if somewhat implausibly, to stick to the ordinary language of foreseeability in such cases; implying that what might have appeared to be policy limitations on liability in fact simply reflected the situations in which nervous shock happened to be foreseeable.[5] All earlier cases now have to be read in the light of two decisions of the House of Lords in recent years, the second of which concerned the 1989 Hillsborough football stadium disaster in Sheffield. In the first case, *McLoughlin v O'Brian*,[6] the plaintiff was at home, two miles from the scene, when her husband and their three children were involved in a road accident caused by the negligence of the defendant. One of the children was killed, and the other children and the husband were seriously injured. Very shortly after the accident the plaintiff visited the hospital, to which the victims had been taken, and witnessed their condition for herself. Her claim for nervous shock failed at first instance and in the Court of Appeal, but succeeded in the House of Lords. Lords Edmund-Davies, Russell, Scarman and Bridge all found for the plaintiff by applying the reasonable foreseeability test. Only Lord Wilberforce expressly

---

1 For academic discussion see Trindade 'The Principles Governing the Recovery of Damages for Negligently Caused Nervous Shock' [1986] 45 CLJ 476; Teff 'Liability for Negligently Inflicted Nervous Shock' (1983) 99 LQR 100; Heffey, 'The Negligent Infliction of Nervous Shock in Road and Industrial Accidents' (1974) 48 ALJ 196, 240. For a rather older, but still valuable, article, see Havard, 'Reasonable Foresight of Nervous Shock' (1956) 19 MLR 478. The recent cases are considered in A J E Jaffey *The Duty of Care* (1992) ch 8.
2 See eg Che*ster v Waverley Municipal Council* (1939) 62 CLR 1 at 7-8 per Latham CJ.
3 See eg *Bourhill v Young* [1943] AC 92, [1942] 2 All ER 396, HL. For an exception see *Chadwick v British Transport Commission* [1967] 2 All ER 945, [1967] 1 WLR 912 (rescuer). Cf *Dooley v Cammell Laird* [1951] 1 Lloyd's Rep 271. For a recent example of a successful claim where the victim of the accident had been a stranger to the plaintiff, see *Wigg v British Railways Board* [1986] NLJ Rep 446n (death of train passenger: claim by driver).
4 See per Bankes LJ *Hambrook* v *Stokes Bros* [1925] 1 KB 141 at 152, CA.
5 See, especially, *Bourhill v Young* [1943] AC 92, [1942] 2 All ER 396, HL and *King v Phillips* [1953] 1 QB 429, [1953] 1 All ER 617, CA.
6 [1983] AC 410, [1982] 2 All ER 298, HL. See also the decision of the High Court of Australia in *Jaenesch v Coffey* (1984) 54 ALR 417, noted by F A Trindade in (1985) 5 OJLS 305.

admitted that the traditional limitations on the extent of recovery for nervous shock did in fact reflect policy considerations. He also made clear his sympathy for those considerations and decided the case on the narrow ground that, although the plaintiff's claim was 'upon the margin', her attendance at the hospital meant that her situation was not different in principle from what it would have been if she had actually been at the scene of the accident herself.[1] The fact that the situation in *McLoughlin v O'Brian* could thus be seen as justifying recovery even on the traditional criteria makes the significance of the wide-ranging views expressed in the other speeches difficult to assess. The speeches in the case arising out of the Hillsborough disaster, *Alcock v Chief Constable of South Yorkshire Police*,[2] were also expressed in rather general terms. But their basic tenor is in contrast with the approach in *McLoughlin*'s case in that they indicate reluctance to contemplate any general expansion of liability in this area: the attitude of their Lordships in the earlier case being, if anything, more liberal. Of the four Law Lords who delivered speeches Lord Keith and Lord Jauncey seemed to prefer the language of 'foreseeability' and 'proximity', while Lord Ackner and Lord Oliver seemed to favour a more overtly policy based approach. But all reached the same result and indicated that since nervous shock cases would depend largely on their own circumstances it was vain to seek clear guidelines. In *Alcock*'s case itself 95 lives were lost in a football stadium when a failure of crowd control by the police caused large numbers of people to be crushed together. Of the particular plaintiffs with whose claims for nervous shock the House of Lords was concerned, one who was actually at the ground himself lost two brothers while another lost his brother-in-law whose body he subsequently identified in the mortuary. Other plaintiffs were not present at the ground but watched the event, a televised cup semi-final, on live television, including one woman who lost her fiancée and a couple who lost their son. All the claims were rejected. In brief, those who had been present at the ground were not proved to have had a sufficiently close relationship with the particular victim in question, whereas those who would have succeeded on this basis were disqualified by their absence from the scene of the tragedy: the television broadcasts not being regarded in the circumstances as equivalent to actual presence. Their Lordships held that a close relationship would normally be necessary for a successful claim (although the possibility of bystanders recovering in exceptionally horrific circumstances was not altogether ruled out,[3]) and that the existence of such a relationship would have to be proved to have existed on the facts of each case, albeit effectively being presumed in cases such as loss of a child. But the relationship remains only a

1 See [1983] 1 AC 410 at 419, [1982] 2 All ER 298 at 302.
2 [1992] 1 AC 310, [1991] 4 All ER 907, HL. See Harvey Teff 'Liability for Psychiatric Illness after Hillsborough' (1992) 12 OJLS 440; K J Nasir 'Nervous Shock; and *Alcock*: The Judicial Buck Stops Here' (1992) 55 MLR 705.
3 Eg if a petrol tanker were to career out of control into a school in session and burst into flames: [1992] 1 AC 310 at 403, [1991] 4 All ER 907 at 919 (Lord Ackner).

necessary condition: 'proximity to the accident must be close both in time and space'.[1] The television pictures in the present case did not satisfy this requirement not least because, as broadcasting guidelines required, they had not involved transmission of images of identifiable individual victims.[2] Their Lordships indicated that merely being told of the death, or identifying the body, would not satisfy the time and space requirement from which it followed that two decisions at first instance, shortly before the Hillsborough case, appeared insupportable.[3] The likely outcome of *Alcock v Chief Constable of South Yorkshire Police* is therefore that the judicial intuition as to the proper limits of liability for nervous shock will change, if at all, marginally in the direction of greater scrutiny and caution before admitting claims.[4] But it is noteworthy that in a 1987 case, which was not considered by the House of Lords in *Hillsborough*, the Court of Appeal held, on trial of a preliminary issue, that a claim for nervous shock might be sustainable where the plaintiff had witnessed her house and its contents being damaged by a fire caused by the defendants' negligence, even though there was no threat to anyone's personal safety.[5] This attractive decision illustrates the protean variety of potential nervous shock situations which makes generalisation about them difficult. Nevertheless, the proposition, albeit negative, that this is a sphere in which the foreseeability test is subject to some degree of qualification is, it is submitted, established. It is both more convincing and, in so far as tenuous guidelines can be formulated, more likely in this unusual area to achieve a measure of predictability than insistence that the foreseeability test alone is the criterion underlying the decisions.

1 [1992] 1 AC 310 at 404, [1991] 4 All ER 907 at 920 (Lord Ackner).
2 But cf per Nolan LJ in the Court of Appeal, sub nom *Jones v Wright* [1991] 3 All ER 88 at 122, [1992] 1 AC 310 at 386-387: 'I would not exclude the possibility in principle of a duty of care extending to the watchers of a television programme. For example, if a publicity-seeking organisation made arrangements for a party of children to go up in a balloon, and for the event to be televised so that their parents could watch, it would be hard to deny that the organisers were under a duty to avoid mental injury to the parents as well as physical injury to the children, and that there would be a breach of that duty if through some careless act or omission the balloon crashed. But that would be a very different case.' Lord Ackner in the House of Lords agreed with this dictum: see [1991] 4 All ER 907 at 921.
3 See *Hevican v Ruane* [1991] 3 All ER 65 and *Ravenscroft v Rederiaktiebolaget Transatlantic* [1991] 3 All ER 73. In the light of the observations of the House of Lords in the Hillsborough case the Court of Appeal subsequently reversed the decision in *Ravenscroft*, finding in favour of the defendants without finding it necessary to hear argument on their behalf: see [1992] 2 All ER 470n.
4 But cf per Bingham LJ in *Attia v British Gas* [1988] QB 304 at 320, [1987] 3 All ER 455 at 464: 'It is submitted, I think rightly, that this claim breaks new ground. No analogous claim has ever, to my knowledge, been upheld or even advanced. If, therefore, it were proper to erect a doctrinal boundary stone at the point which the onward march of recorded decisions has so far reached, we should answer the question of principle in the negative and dismiss the plaintiff's action, as the deputy judge did. But I should for my part erect the boundary stone with a strong presentiment that it would not be long before a case would arise so compelling on its facts as to cause the stone to be moved to a new and more distant resting place.'
5 See *Attia v British Gas* [1988] QB 304, [1987] 3 All ER 455, CA. Cf *Owens v Liverpool Corpn* [1939] 1 KB 394, [1938] 4 All ER 727, CA.

Chapter 2

Evaluation of conduct

Foreseeability and objectivity

Incapacity normally disregarded

[**2.01**] The concept of negligence in the law of tort represents an uneasy compromise between, on the one hand, the supposed principle of 'no liability without fault' and, on the other, the desire to see those who have suffered injury compensated. The former principle has retarded the development of strict liability in this branch of the law; while the latter has prevented a subjective or 'genuine' concept of blameworthiness being adopted since that would inevitably reduce the number of defendants who would succeed in recovering damages. The law therefore adopts the artificial objective standard of the 'reasonable man', which involves ignoring the realities of the defendant's situation in so far as his capacities differ from that standard.[1] This requirement of a reasonable level of competence applies to skills which can only be acquired by training and effort, as well as to basic attributes which most people can be expected to possess.[2] Thus drivers of motor cars owe the same duty to drive with the degree of skill and care to be expected of a competent and experienced driver. The fact that the defendant was incapable of attaining that standard because he was a learner,[3] or had suffered a stroke minutes before the accident,[4] is irrelevant. This insistence upon an objective test, to the benefit of the plaintiff, is not confined to situations in which liability insurance is compulsory or usual, such as those involving motor cars. Thus, in a case involving ordinary domestic repairs to his property carried out by a householder, it was held that:

1   'The standard of foresight of the reasonable man is . . . an impersonal one. It eliminates the personal equation and is independent of the idiosyncrasies of the particular person whose conduct is in question': per Lord Macmillan in *Glasgow Corpn v Muir* [1943] AC 448 at 457, [1943] 2 All ER 44 at 48, HL.
2   For the negligence of professional people see ch 15 below.
3   *Nettleship v Weston* [1971] 2 QB 691, [1971] 3 All ER 581, CA. But cf *Cook v Cook* (1986) 68 ALR 353 (also involving a learner driver) in which the High Court of Australia recently rejected the reasoning in *Nettleship*'s case.
4   *Roberts v Ramsbottom* [1980] 1 All ER 7, [1980] 1 WLR 823.

'the degree of care and skill required of him must be measured not by reference to the degree of competence in such matters which he personally happened to possess, but by reference to the degree of care and skill which a reasonably competent carpenter might be expected to apply to the work in question'.[1]

Duty owed by children

[**2.02**] The general rule of a uniform standard of care is modified in cases involving injuries caused by children. In *McHale v Watson*,[2] a Full Court[3] of the High Court of Australia, after extensive consideration of the matter, held that if the defendant is a child the duty of care is limited to what is normally to be expected of a child of the defendant's age and experience.[4] In this case a 12-year-old boy escaped liability when a piece of steel rod thrown by him accidentally hit another child and caused serious injury to one of her eyes. This accords with the approach adopted in cases in which it is alleged that an infant plaintiff has been contributorily negligent;[5] even though the underlying issue in such cases, in which the courts are understandably reluctant to deprive a child of damages on this ground, is rather different. Nevertheless, *McHale v Watson* would probably be followed in England.[6] Despite what might be seen as unfairness to the plaintiff, the courts are likely to be reluctant to stigmatise a child as a tortfeasor as long as the fault principle still retains a foothold in this branch of the law.[7]

Parental duty owed to children

[**2.03**] '[T]he court should be wary', observed Sir Nicolas Browne-Wilkinson V-C in *Surtees v Kingston-upon-Thames Borough Council*,[8]

---

1 *Wells v Cooper* [1958] 2 QB 265 at 271, [1958] 2 All ER 527 at 530, CA per Jenkins LJ (no liability on the facts).
2 [1966] ALR 513.
3 McTiernan ACJ, Kitto and Owen JJ (Menzies J dissenting).
4 See also the American Law Institute's *Restatement of the Law of Torts* (2nd) para 238A: 'If the actor is a child, the standard of conduct to which he must conform to avoid being negligent is that of a reasonable person of like age, intelligence, and experience under like circumstances.'
5 See, eg *Yachuk v Oliver Blais Co Ltd* [1949] AC 386, [1949] 2 All ER 150, PC.
6 There are isolated English cases in which persons below full age have been held liable in negligence (see eg *Gorely v Codd* [1966] 3 All ER 891, [1967] 1 WLR 19: mentally-retarded 16-year-old) but the question of the nature of liability has never been fully explored. For discussion see Rowe, 'Negligent Children' (1976) 126 NLJ 354. In the unreported case of *Staley v Suffolk County Council and Dean Mason*, Staughton J, sitting at Norwich on 26 November 1985, held a 12-year-old boy liable for injuries caused when a tennis ball hurled by him, with the intention of hitting another boy, hit and injured a member of the school's catering staff: see *Clerk and Lindsell on Torts* (16th edn) para 10-60.
7 In practice claims of this kind are rare since a child is rarely worth suing; it is more common to go primarily against the parent or guardian alleging negligently inadequate supervision: see, eg *Donaldson v McNiven* [1952] 1 All ER 1213; affd [1952] 2 All ER 691, CA (claim failed on the facts); *Floyd v Bowers* (1978) 21 OR (2d) 204; affd (1979) 106 DLR (3d) 702 (parent held liable along with child).
8 [1991] 2 FLR 559 at 583-584, CA.

32 Evaluation of conduct

'in its approach to holding parents in breach of a duty of care owed to their children'. It is clear that in appropriate cases liability may be imposed[1] but, as Sir Nicolas Browne-Wilkinson V-C continued:

> 'There are very real policy considerations to take into account if the conflicts inherent in legal proceedings are to be brought into family relationships. Moreover, the responsibilities of a parent (which in contemporary society normally means the mother) looking after one or more children, in addition to the myriad other duties which fall on the parent at home, far exceed those of other members of society. The studied calm of the Royal Courts of Justice, concentrating on one point at a time, is light years away from the circumstances prevailing in the average home. The mother is looking after a fast-moving toddler at the same time as cooking the meal, doing the housework, looking after the other children and doing all the other things that the average mother has to cope with simultaneously, or in quick succession, in the normal household. We should be slow to characterise as negligent the care which ordinary loving and careful mothers are able to give to individual children, given the rough-and-tumble of home life.'

Thus in the *Surtees* case itself a majority[2] of the Court of Appeal dismissed a claim in respect of a scalding injury which occurred to a two-year-old girl, while in the care of a foster-parent. As children get older other factors also become relevant. In *Porter v Barking and Dagenham London Borough Council* [3] the defendant father allowed his own son, who was 14, and the plaintiff, another boy of the same age, to practise putting the shot. An accident occurred injuring the plaintiff, but Simon Brown J dismissed a claim against the defendant. It was desirable to encourage initiative and independence in children of the plaintiff's age and not to be over-protective of them. With that in mind the defendant's conduct had not fallen short of the standard to be expected of a reasonably prudent parent.

The measurement of risk

Degree of probability

[**2.04**] The concept of reasonable foreseeability does not mean that liability will be imposed whenever it might conceivably have crossed the mind of a normal person that the occurrence of damage was a possibility.[4] The law also takes into account the degree of *probability*[5]

---

1   See *McCallion v Dodd* [1966] NZLR 710 (New Zealand Court of Appeal). Cf *Hahn v Conley* (1971) 45 ALJR 631 (High Court of Australia).
2   Sir Nicolas Browne-Wilkinson V-C and Stocker LJ. Beldam LJ dissenting.
3   (1990) Times, 9 April.
4   '... people must guard against reasonable probabilities, but they are not bound to guard against fantastic possibilities' per Lord Dundedin in *Fardon v Harcourt-Rivington* (1932) 146 LT 391, HL.
5   This does not, of course, mean that the occurrence itself has to have been 'probable' in order to give rise to liability. Obviously there will very frequently be a duty to take precautions even though the odds in favour of an accident are a very long way below an evens chance. Cf *Koufos v Czarnikow, The Heron II* [1969] 1 AC 350, [1967] 3 All ER 686, HL.

of its doing so.[1] Thus, in the well-known case of *Bolton v Stone*[2] the defendant cricket club was exonerated from liability when a cricket ball was hit out of the ground on to the highway, where it injured the plaintiff. The possibility of such an event occurring was clearly foreseeable, because balls had escaped from the ground before. But the fact that they had done so only on some six occasions over a period of 30 years meant that the risk, in the circumstances, was one which the reasonable man could legitimately choose not to guard against.[3] The actual degree of probability required is not fixed but necessarily varies from case to case. This is because three other factors are taken into account in assessing the overall risk. These are the seriousness of the harm if it does actually occur, the overall utility or value of the activity upon which the defendant is engaged, and the extent and cost of effective precautions.

Gravity of harm

[2.05] If the harm, should it take place, would be particularly serious it may be necessary to take precautions to prevent it even if the possibility of its occurring is very low. Thus an employer may be negligent in failing to supply goggles to a workman with one good eye, when injury to that eye could deprive him of sight altogether, even where the risk of any injury occurring is sufficiently small to justify ignoring it where fully-sighted workmen are concerned.[4] The good sense of this is apparent: the precautions needed when, say, handling explosives are of a different order of magnitude from those required when playing cricket.

---

1 'The standard of care in the law of negligence is the standard of an ordinarily careful man, but, in my opinion, an ordinarily careful man does not take precautions against every foreseeable risk. He can, of course, foresee the possibility of many risks, but life would be almost impossible if he were to attempt to take precautions against every risk which he can foresee. He takes precautions against risks which are reasonably likely to happen. Many foreseeable risks are extremely unlikely to happen and cannot be guarded against except by almost complete isolation': *Bolton v Stone* [1951] AC 850 at 863, [1951] 1 All ER 1078 at 1083, HL per Lord Oaksey.
2 [1951] AC 850, [1951] 1 All ER 1078, HL.
3 But note the warning of Lord Reid: 'I think . . . that this case is not far from the border-line. If this appeal is allowed, that does not, in my judgment, mean that in every case where cricket has been played on a ground for a number of years without accident or complaint those who organise matches there are safe to go on in reliance on past immunity. I would have reached a different conclusion if I had thought that the risk here had been other than extremely small because I do not think that a reasonable man, considering the matter from the point of view of safety, would or should disregard any risk unless it is extremely small . . . ' [1951] AC 850 at 867-868, [1951] 1 All ER 1078 at 1086. Cf *Miller v Jackson* [1977] QB 966, [1977] 3 All ER 338, CA.
4 *Paris v Stepney Borough Council* [1951] AC 367, [1951] 1 All ER 42, HL. See also *Buchan v Ortho Pharmaceutical (Canada) Ltd* (1984) 46 OR (2d) 113 (duty to warn unusually susceptible users of contraceptive pill of danger of stroke occurring even though risk small).

Utility of the defendant's conduct

[**2.06**] In *Watt v Hertfordshire County Council*[1] the defendants' fire station received a call to an emergency which could only be dealt with by transporting a heavy jack to the scene of a road accident, in which someone was trapped under a bus. Unfortunately, the only vehicle equipped to carry the jack was out dealing with another matter. The jack was therefore loaded on to a different vehicle upon which it could not, in fact, be properly secured. During the journey to the scene of the accident the jack moved, and in so doing it trapped the plaintiff fire officer and injured him. The Court of Appeal held that the defendants had not been negligent. Denning LJ observed:

> '... you must balance the risk against the end to be achieved. If this accident had occurred in a commercial enterprise without any emergency, there could be no doubt that the servant would succeed. But the commercial end to make profit is very different from the human end to save life or limb. The saving of life justifies taking considerable risk ...'[2]

In effect, therefore, the law operates a kind of sliding-scale. At one extreme are positively laudable activities such as that involved in *Watt v Hertfordshire County Council*. In the middle are acts such as playing cricket which are legitimate or even desirable. At the other extreme are activities which are undesirable or even unlawful. The degree of probability, necessary to create a duty to take precautions, falls as the latter end of the spectrum is approached.[3]

Extent of the precautions necessary for protection

[**2.07**] Once it is established that the degree of risk was such that the defendant should in principle have taken precautions, the next step in determining whether the imposition of liability for negligence would be appropriate is to measure the precautions in fact taken (if any) against those which might reasonably have been expected. The defendant may succeed in avoiding liability at this stage of the inquiry, even in the face of an established risk. In *Latimer v AEC Ltd*,[4] the defendants' factory was badly affected by a flood, during which rain-water became mixed with an oily liquid used in the manufacturing process. After the water had drained away the floor of the factory remained slippery. Although the defendants spread sawdust on the floor, the amount available was insufficient to cover

---

1 [1954] 2 All ER 368, [1954] 1 WLR 835.
2 [1954] 2 All ER 368 at 371, [1954] 1 WLR 835 at 838. In cases where negligent driving is alleged, however, the courts are not prepared to sanction the adoption of lower standards of care by police or other emergency vehicles: *Gaynor v Allen* [1959] 2 QB 403, [1959] 2 All ER 644; *Wardell-Yerburgh v Surrey County Council* [1973] RTR 462. Cf *Marshall v Osmond* [1983] QB 1034, [1983] 2 All ER 225, CA.
3 'If the activity which caused the injury to Miss Stone had been an unlawful activity there can be little doubt but that *Bolton v Stone* would have been decided differently': *Overseas Tankship (UK) v Miller SS Co Pty, The Wagon Mound (No 2)* [1967] 1 AC 617 at 242, PC per Lord Reid.
4 [1953] AC 643, [1953] 2 All ER 449, HL.

the total area. The plaintiff workman subsequently slipped on the floor and injured himself. The trial judge held the defendants liable on the ground that, in the circumstances, they ought to have closed the factory, but this view was rejected by both the Court of Appeal and the House of Lords. Lord Porter considered that it had not been established 'that a reasonably careful employer . . . ought to have taken the drastic step of closing the factory'.[1] It should be noted that the question of probability still remains relevant at this stage of the inquiry.[2]

Care and its quality

Protection of minorities

[**2.08**] Although the basic test for the existence of a duty of care is the foreseeability of a reasonable or average person, it does not of course at all follow that only such persons are themselves foreseeable as persons to whom the duty of care is *owed*. Depending upon the circumstances minorities, or people in relatively unusual categories, may well be foreseeable and a duty of care may be owed to them.[3] Thus in *Haley v London Electricity Board*,[4] the House of Lords held that the plaintiff, who was blind, could recover damages from the defendants when he fell into a trench created by the defendants' road excavations. Although the precautions the defendants had taken were adequate to protect sighted pedestrians they were not sufficient to protect the blind. The evidence in the case was that about one in 500 members of the population was blind, and that many of them habitually went out alone. Lord Reid observed that it was therefore 'quite impossible to say that it is not reasonably foreseeable that a blind person may pass along a particular pavement on a particular day'. His Lordship concluded that since, on the facts, there was 'no question . . . of any great difficulty in affording adequate protection for the blind' liability would be imposed.[5] It is to be noted that, in so holding, the House of Lords unanimously reversed both the trial judge[6] and a unanimous Court of Appeal.[7]

1 [1953] AC 643 at 653, [1953] 2 All ER 449 at 451, HL.
2 '. . . the degree of risk was too small to justify, let alone require closing down': [1953] AC 643 at 662, [1953] 2 All ER 449 at 457 per Lord Asquith.
3 '. . . a measure of care appropriate to the inability or disability of those who are immature or feeble in mind or body is due from others who know of, or ought to anticipate, the presence of such persons within the scope and hazard of their own operations': *Glasgow Corpn v Taylor* [1922] 1 AC 44 at 67, HL per Lord Sumner.
4 [1965] AC 778, [1964] 3 All ER 185.
5 [1965] AC 778 at 791, [1964] 3 All ER 185 at 188. Cf the Disabled Persons Act 1981, s 1.
6 Marshall J.
7 Lord Denning MR, Donovan and Danckwerts LJJ: see [1964] 2 QB 121, [1963] 3 All ER 1030.

Relevance of common practice[1]

[2.09] The defendant may sometimes be able to show that the practices or methods of working he followed, at the time when the incident occurred, accorded with what was common or usual in the particular activity or profession.[2] Such evidence may be of value to the defendant in tending to negative or limit liability.[3] Nevertheless, it will not be conclusive since the court may be prepared to infer that the usual practice was itself negligent.[4] On the whole, however, the cases suggest that the courts are rather more reluctant to draw this conclusion where the activity in question is a highly skilled profession, such as medicine, than where it is not.[5]

Carelessness not to be inferred from subsequent adoption of protective measures

[2.10] It has often been judicially emphasised that the defendant's conduct should be considered in the light of knowledge reasonably to have been expected of him at the time of the incident itself.[6] In *Glasgow Corpn v Muir*[7] Lord Thankerton said:

> 'The court must be careful to place itself in the position of the person charged with the duty and to consider what he or she should have reasonably anticipated as a natural and probable consequence of neglect, and not to give undue weight to the fact that a distressing accident has happened, or that witnesses, in the witness box, are prone to express regret, ex post facto, that they did not take some step, which it is now realised would definitely have prevented the accident.'

It follows that the fact that changes in practice have been introduced since the incident, possibly as a direct result of it, should not be taken into account.[8]

---

1 See Jon Holyoak 'Raising the standard of care' (1990) 10 LS 201.
2 See, eg *Bolam v Friern Hospital Management Committee* [1957] 2 All ER 118, [1957] 1 WLR 582; *Maynard v West Midlands Regional Health Authority* [1985] 1 All ER 635, [1984] 1 WLR 634, HL; *Knight v Home Office* [1990] 3 All ER 237.
3 See, eg *Thompson v Smiths Shiprepairers (North Shields) Ltd* [1984] QB 405, [1984] 1 All ER 881.
4 See *Morris v West Hartlepool Steam Navigation Co Ltd* [1956] AC 552, [1956] 1 All ER 385, HL; *Cavanagh v Ulster Weaving Co* [1960] AC 145, [1959] 2 All ER 745, HL.
5 But cf *Greaves & Co (Contractors) Ltd v Baynham, Meikle & Partners* [1974] 3 All ER 666, [1974] 1 WLR 1261 (engineer). See, generally, ch 15 below for discussion of negligence in situations involving special skill.
6 See, eg per Thesiger J in *Philpott v British Railways Board* [1968] 2 Lloyd's Rep 495 at 502 and in *McAlpine & Sons Ltd v Minimax Ltd* [1970] 1 Lloyd's Rep 397 at 416. See also per Webster J in W*impey Construction UK Ltd v Poole* [1984] 2 Lloyd's Rep 499 at 507.
7 [1943] AC 448 at 454-455, [1943] 2 All ER 44 at 47, HL.
8 See, eg *Roe v Minister of Health* [1954] 2 QB 66 at 86, [1954] 2 All ER 131 at 139, CA per Denning LJ: 'If the hospitals were to continue the practice after this warning, they could not complain if they were found guilty of negligence. Indeed, it was the extraordinary accident to these two men which first disclosed the danger. Nowadays it would be negligence not to realise the danger, but it was not then.' See also *Worlock v Saws* (1981) 20 BLR 94 at 116 per Woolf J.

'Errors of judgment'

[**2.11**] A mere error of judgment, especially in a situation in which rapid action or decision-making is required, does not necessarily constitute actionable negligence. In *Wooldrige v Sumner*,[1] the defendant, who was competing in a horse show, misjudged a bend. As a result he fell off his horse which, out of control, left the track and collided with the plaintiff spectator, severely injuring him. The Court of Appeal, finding for the defendant, held that 'he was guilty of an error or errors of judgment or a lapse of skill' but that that was 'not enough to constitute a breach of the duty of reasonable care which a participant owes to a spectator'.[2] The *principle* reflected in this decision is evidently applicable beyond the special situation of sporting events. Nevertheless, it should be noted that use of the terminology of 'error of judgment', by way of deliberate contrast with the concept of actionable negligence, has been criticised by the House of Lords as question-begging and as being unlikely, at least in medical negligence cases, to be of assistance.[3]

Proof of negligence

Causation

Burden of proof

[**2.12**] The plaintiff must show, on the balance of probabilities, not only that the defendant was careless, but also that that carelessness caused, or helped to cause, the injury or damage for which he claims. In *Barnett v Chelsea and Kensington Hospital Management Committee*[4] a doctor for whom the defendants were responsible negligently failed to treat the deceased, who subsequently died from arsenic poisoning. The defendants escaped liability on the ground that even if the doctor had not been negligent, and treatment had been given to the deceased, the probability was that he would have died anyway. Nor are the courts prepared in cases of this kind to assess the matter on the basis of degrees of probability, and to award the plaintiff a percentage of his loss on the basis that the defendant's negligence had deprived the plaintiff of some chance of recovery. In *Hotson v East Berkshire Area Health Authority*[5] the plaintiff injured

---

1 [1963] 2 QB 43, [1962] 2 All ER 978.
2 [1963] 2 QB at 43 at 72, [1962] 2 All ER 978 at 989-990 per Diplock LJ. Cf *Condon v Basi* [1985] 2 All ER 453, [1985] 1 WLR 866.
3 See *Whitehouse v Jordan* [1981] 1 All ER 267 at 281, [1981] 1 WLR 246 at 263 per Lord Fraser (quoted below, para 15.04). See also per Lord Edmund-Davies at 257-258 and Lord Russell at 268.
4 [1969] 1 QB 428, [1968] 1 All ER 1068.
5 [1987] AC 750, [1987] 2 All ER 909, HL. See Timothy Hill 'A Lost Chance for Compensation in the Tort of Negligence by the House of Lords' (1991) 54 MLR 511 Cf Walter Scott 'Causation in Medico-Legal Practice: a Doctor's Approach to the "Lost Opportunity" Cases' (1992) 55 MLR 521.

Evaluation of conduct

his hip in a fall from a tree. Unfortunately, the medical treatment which he received included a negligent delay in the proper diagnosis of the extent of his injuries. He subsequently developed a permanent disability which he argued that prompt treatment would have averted. The defendants, however, contended that the disability had been inevitable from the moment of the fall. The trial judge, who was upheld by the Court of Appeal, awarded the plaintiff 25% of his loss on the ground that although the risk of his developing the disability after the fall had been as high as 75%, there had been a chance, albeit a relatively small one, that prompt treatment would have brought about a complete recovery. The House of Lords, reversing the courts below, held that the plaintiff failed altogether. It was implicit in the trial judge's finding of fact that, on the balance of probabilities, the fall and not the negligent treatment had caused the disability. Generally speaking, therefore, it would appear that the question of whether a defendant's carelessness had had any causative effect at all must be determined one way or the other as a matter of historical fact.[1]

Where causative factor impossible to isolate

[**2.13**] If the situation was such that more than one cause *materially contributed* thereto, the plaintiff does not have to prove that the cause for which the defendant was responsible would have been sufficient to produce injury *by itself*.[2] Moreover, the House of Lords once held that a broad view of causation should be taken for the purpose of this principle. In the difficult case of *McGhee v National Coal Board*,[3] the plaintiff contracted dermatitis through contact with brick dust at his place of work. It was not alleged that this exposure in itself constituted negligence on the part of his employers, but that their failure to provide shower facilities did so since it obliged him to keep the dust on his skin until he arrived home. As it happened, however, it was impossible for the plaintiff to prove scientifically that the absence of washing facilities had contributed to his contraction of dermatitis; the initial non-negligent contact during his work might have caused it in any event. The House of Lords nevertheless allowed him to recover, asserting that where a defendant's negligence could be taken, in the existing state of knowledge, to have materially increased the *risk* of the plaintiff's developing a certain disease this was sufficient to justify the imposition of liability; even though medical science was simply too uncertain to explain how the particular disease

---

1 For criticism of the approach of the House of Lords see Stapleton 'The Gist of Negligence' (1988) 104 LQR 213 and 389, who argues that it side-steps the question as to the nature of the 'damage' which the defendant needs to be shown to have caused. If that damage were to be perceived as the *loss of the chance itself*, rather than the actual disability, the not unattractive solution reached by the courts below would be seen to be justified. 'It cannot be over-emphasised that the formulation of the "damage" forming the gist of the action *defines* the causation question. Logically one can only deal with causation after one knows what the damage forming the gist of the action is': Stapleton, op cit at 393.
2 See *Bonnington Castings Ltd v Wardlaw* [1956] AC 613, [1956] 1 All ER 615, HL.
3 [1972] 3 All ER 1008, [1973] 1 WLR 1, HL.

came to develop.¹ Thus employers who neglect straightforward and common-sense precautions should not expect the courts to be over-zealous either in investigating the minutiae of scientific research at its frontiers, or in speculating philosophically on the nature of causation, in order to avoid the imposition of liability.

No alteration to burden of proof

[**2.14**] In *Wilsher v Essex Area Health Authority*,² the House of Lords itself emphasised that *McGhee v National Coal Board* had not modified the principle that the burden of proving negligence lies on the plaintiff, rather that it had in fact applied that principle but in a particularly 'robust and pragmatic'³ way. In *Wilsher*'s case a premature baby developed a disorder which *might* have been caused by a slip for which the defendants were responsible. But the disorder could have had *several* other causes *unrelated* to the slip, and was one to which premature babies are prone in any event. The trial judge, relying on what was subsequently held to have been a misreading of *McGhee v National Coal Board,* nevertheless imposed liability on the ground that, given that the slip had been a *possible* cause, the burden of proving that it had not been an *actual* one lay on the defendants. Although a majority of the Court of Appeal felt able to uphold his decision,⁴ the House of Lords ordered a retrial on the causation issue. 'Whether we like it or not', observed Lord Bridge,⁵ 'the law, which only Parliament can change, requires proof of fault causing damage as the basis of liability in tort.' The proposition that the case of *McGhee v National Coal Board* ⁶ is to be treated as a decision on its own facts, and not as developing 'some esoteric principle which in some way modifies, as a matter of law, the nature of the burden of proof of causation',⁷ is also supported by yet another decision of the House of Lords involving an unsuccessful medical negligence claim. In *Kay's Tutor v Ayrshire and Arran Health Board*⁸ the House refused to regard *McGhee* as relevant in a case in which the plaintiff was found to be deaf after an attack of meningitis, in the course of the treatment for which he had received a massive overdose of penicillin. Since deafness is a common after-effect of meningitis, but there is no recorded case of

1 Stapleton 'The Gist of Negligence' (1988) 104 LQR 213 and 389 argues (at 401ff) that in holding the defendants liable for the *entire* loss the result in this case was too harsh, and that a more sophisticated definition of the plaintiff's 'damage' in such situations (ie in terms of the increased *chance* of contracting the disease rather than in terms of the disease itself) could lead to a more satisfactory outcome.
2 [1988] AC 1074, [1988] 1 All ER 871.
3 Per Lord Bridge in *Wilsher v Essex Area Health Authority* [1988] AC 1074 at 1090, [1988] 1 All ER 871 at 881.
4 See [1987] QB 730, [1986] 3 All ER 801.
5 [1988] AC 1074 at 1092, [1988] 1 All ER 871 at 883.
6 [1972] 3 All ER 1008, [1973] 1 WLR 1, HL.
7 Per Lord Bridge in *Wilsher v Essex Area Health Authority* [1988] AC 1074 at 1090, [1988] 1 All ER 871 at 882.
8 [1987] 2 All ER 417, HL.

a penicillin overdose having caused deafness, the House of Lords held that there was simply no factual basis for the contention that the overdose had materially increased the risk that the plaintiff would suffer from this particular after-effect.

Res ipsa loquitur

The initial presumption

[**2.15**] If the plaintiff suffers injury or damage through contact with some mechanical or other agency, he may experience difficulty in gathering evidence to prove negligence if that agency was throughout under the control or management of the defendant. The presumption embodied in the maxim res ipsa loquitur may assist the plaintiff in such a situation. If, but only if,[1] what occurred was something which would not normally be expected to occur in the absence of carelessness on the part of those who have control or management of the operation, then a presumption of negligence will be raised in the plaintiff's favour.[2] It follows that in such a case the defendant cannot succeed on a submission of no case to answer. The defendant must offer evidence if he is to succeed in defeating the plaintiff's claim.[3] If the defendant is able to explain fully and in detail how the accident occurred it will be for the court to decide, applying in the usual way the ordinary principles relating to the evaluation of conduct, whether or not negligence liability should be imposed.[4] The initial presumption in the plaintiff's favour will have no part to play at this conclusive stage of the inquiry in such a relatively straightforward case. Difficult questions arise, however, if even the *defendant* is unable to explain the full sequence of events leading up to the accident. Logically, all that a defendant can do in such a case, in an attempt to rebut the presumption of negligence, is to show two things. Firstly, that his system of working complied with what was usual in the particular activity, and secondly that a reasonably plausible hypothesis exists as to how the accident *might* have been caused which would be consistent with him or his servants not having been careless on the particular occasion.

---

1 Cf *Stafford v Conti Commodity Services* [1981] 1 All ER 691.
2 The classic statement is to be found in the judgment of Erle CJ in *Scott v The London and St Katherine Docks Co* (1865) 3 H&C 596 at 601: '... where the thing is shewn to be under the management of the defendant or his servants, and the accident is such as in the ordinary course of things does not happen if those who have the management use proper care, it affords reasonable evidence, in the absence of explanation by the defendants that the accident arose from want of care'.
3 See *Lloyde v West Midlands Gas Board* [1971] 2 All ER 1240, [1971] 1 WLR 749, CA at 755 per Megaw LJ.
4 See *Barkway v South Wales Transport Co* [1950] AC 185, [1950] 1 All ER 392, HL. See also *Ng Chun Pui v Lee Chuen Tat* [1988] RTR 298, PC.

Covert strict liability?

[**2.16**] In two cases in which causation remained a mystery, *Moore v Fox & Sons*[1] and *Colvilles Ltd v Devine*[2] the defendants failed, despite advancing causation hypotheses consistent with the absence of fault. At first glance these decisions might be taken to suggest that res ipsa loquitur had been converted from a mere rule of evidence into a rule of law covertly imposing strict liability. This is because evidence of the kind indicated towards the end of the last paragraph is the only kind which a defendant unable to explain the cause of the accident *can* give. Accordingly, if such evidence were to be denied any probative value simply on a priori grounds that would effectively turn res ipsa loquitur into an *irrebuttable* presumption. If strict liability is indeed being imposed in this way it would be objectionable. Although it can forcefully be argued that a general regime of strict liability would be preferable, at least in personal injury cases, to the operation of the law of negligence, it would hardly be appropriate to introduce it arbitrarily depending upon whether or not the facts happened to entitle the plaintiff to reply on the maxim res ipsa loquitur. Nevertheless, it has indeed been suggested that the courts *are* using the presumption in this way so as to expand the scope of strict liability.[3]

Better view is that fault principle survives

[**2.17**] It is submitted that the strict liability thesis is not correct. It is important to remember that in order to rebut the presumption the defendant must show *both* that his system was the usual one adopted *and* that a causation hypothesis consistent with the absence of fault existed. Merely to prove one without the other clearly cannot be enough.[4] Thus a defendant who shows that his system is the usual and accepted one cannot, if the case is one to which the presumption applies, succeed on proof of this *alone* (ie without advancing a hypothetical cause for the accident consistent with the absence of fault). The court would still be entitled to conclude that it was more likely than not that the system broke down on the particular occasion, eg because of an isolated act of carelessness on the part of his servants for which he would be vicariously liable.[5] Equally, a defendant who does not even attempt to show that the usual precautions were taken obviously cannot expect to succeed, given the initial presumption, however many hypotheses consistent with the absence of fault he is able to devise. The failure of the defendants in both *Moore v Fox &*

---

1 [1956] 1 QB 596, [1956] 1 All ER 182, CA.
2 [1969] 2 All ER 53, [1969] 1 WLR 475, HL.
3 See Atiyah 'Res Ipsa Loquitur in England and Australia' (1972) 35 MLR 337; Fleming *The Law of Torts* (7th edn, 1987) pp 300-301; Millner *Negligence in Modern Law* (1967) pp 89ff. See also Colin Manchester in (1977) 93 LQR 13.
4 *Colvilles Ltd v Devine* [1969] 2 All ER 53 at 57, [1969] 1 WLR 475 at 477-478 per Lord Guest.
5 See *Hill v James Crowe (Cases) Ltd* [1978] 1 All ER 812 (not following *Daniels and Daniels v R White & Sons* [1938] 4 All ER 258).

Sons[1] and *Colvilles Ltd v Devine*,[2] despite advancing causation hypotheses consistent with the absence of fault, is explicable simply because they had not shown in addition that the usual precautions were taken.[3]

Defendant's evidence must not be avoidably incomplete or inadequate

[**2.18**] Even if the defendant *does* furnish evidence relating both to hypothetical causation and the taking of the usual precautions, the court might still legitimately conclude, without in effect imposing strict liability, that his evidence overall was not satisfactory. There might, for example, be good grounds for supposing that the evidence included significant gaps which the defendants could have filled had they chosen to do so. In *Henderson v Jenkins & Sons*,[4] the brakes on the defendants' lorry suddenly failed, and a fatal accident resulted. The defendants showed that the generally accepted procedures for inspection and servicing of the lorry had been adopted, and postulated that the failure, which had occurred when a hole developed in a pipe carrying brake fluid, might have been due to a latent defect causing the pipe to corrode much more rapidly than was usual. But it was also possible that the corrosion might have been the result of the lorry being put to an unusual use, perhaps involving contact with acid or salt-water, in which case more elaborate procedures for inspection and servicing, than those used generally, would have been appropriate. The defendants did not disclose, however, the uses to which the lorry had been put. They might perhaps, in the words of Lord Pearson:

> 'have been able to show by evidence that the lorry had not been used in any way, or involved in any accident, that would cause abnormal corrosion or require special inspection or treatment, or at any rate that they neither knew nor ought to have known of any such use or incident. But they did not call any such evidence. Their answer was incomplete.'[5]

Another case in which the evidence taken as a whole, combined with the operation of the presumption, justified the imposition of liability for negligence notwithstanding the efforts of the defence, was *Ward v*

---

1 [1956] 1 QB 596, [1956] 1 All ER 182, CA.
2 [1969] 2 All ER 53, [1969] 1 WLR 475.
3 '. . . it was the duty of the maintenance man to inspect the apparatus weekly and the duty of the foreman to supervise the deceased . . . There was, however, no evidence that either of these duties had been performed. There was, therefore, no evidence of conduct which, whatever the actual cause of the accident, was in accordance with a proper performance of the duty of care': per Evershed MR in *Moore v R Fox & Sons* [1956] 1 QB 596 at 609, [1956] 1 All ER 182 at 187. Similarly, in *Colvilles v Devine* 'No evidence was forthcoming from the appellants as to any inspection of the filters being made by them . . . They led no evidence to suggest that any inspection of the filters was ever made to see if they were working properly': [1969] 1 WLR 475 at 478 per Lord Guest. See also per Lord Donovan at 479.
4 [1970] AC 282, [1969] 3 All ER 756, HL.
5 [1970] AC 282 at 303, [1969] 3 All ER 756 at 768. See also per Lord Reid at 291 and per Lord Donovan at 299. Cf *Worsley v Hollins* [1991] RTR 252, CA.

Tesco Stores.[1] The plaintiff slipped on a pool of yoghurt which had been spilt on the floor of the defendants' supermarket. The defendants stated that they had a system for dealing with spillages, which involved each member of staff being instructed to watch out for them and take immediate action when one was noticed; that was in addition to periodical brushing of the floor throughout the day. Moreover, it was possible that the particular spillage had been caused by a customer only seconds before the plaintiff slipped on it, in which case the defendants could not have been regarded as careless. Neither the plaintiff nor the defendants were in fact able, however, to prove how long the spillage had been on the floor and therefore whether it had, in fact, occurred very recently or not. The Court of Appeal held, by a majority,[2] that the maxim res ipsa loquitur applied, and upheld the decision of the county court judge in favour of the plaintiff. The judge had found as a fact that the defendants had not taken reasonable care. This might have been because he felt that although they had a system for spotting and dealing with the spillages, it was simply not quite rigorous enough. Alternatively, he might have considered that the defendants' servants had not been as zealous as they should have been in putting an otherwise sound system into effect, a proposition for which there was some evidential support.[3] Accordingly, although the presumption embodied in the maxim res ipsa loquitur is capable of giving genuine assistance to plaintiffs, it is probably not true to say that it amounts to a rule of law covertly imposing strict liability in an unprincipled fashion. A defendant who can show that all the usual precautions were taken, and can also adduce an explanation for the incident consistent with the absence of fault, should still succeed in rebutting the presumption provided his evidence is perceived to be frank, thorough and plausible.

1 [1976] 1 All ER 219, [1976] 1 WLR 810, CA. Cf *Dulhunty v J B Young* (1975) 7 ALR 409 (High Court of Australia), noted in (1977) 93 LQR 486.
2 Lawton and Megaw LJJ, Ormrod LJ dissenting.
3 On a subsequent visit to the same supermarket the plaintiff herself noticed that some orange juice which had been spilt was left on the floor for about a quarter of an hour with no one coming to clear it up: see [1976] 1 WLR at 812.

Chapter 3

Remoteness of damage

Related issues distinguished

Remoteness and causation

[**3.01**] It is important to distinguish the concept of remoteness of damage, which is one of those concerned with the ascription or non-ascription of legal responsibility, from that of causation, which is concerned with what might be called the 'scientific' perception of the relationship between separate events. But the drawing of this distinction, and the delineation of the scope of the remoteness concept itself, is far from being easy or self-evident. There are three reasons for this. Firstly, for legal purposes the relevant 'causal' relationships will more usually be those perceived on a practical, or day-to-day, basis than those identified by the application of some kind of rigorous scientific analysis. Secondly, it is sometimes argued that these supposed 'practical' assumptions are themselves evaluative and are influenced by the content of the existing rules for the ascription of legal responsibility, or views as to what such rules ought to contain.[1] Thirdly, since the ascription of responsibility is the objective of law in general, it is perfectly possible for different views to be adopted, purely on the basis of convenience, as to the range of problems which it is appropriate to include under the particular umbrella of 'remoteness'.[2]

Scope of the chapter

[**3.02**] It would not be appropriate in a book of this kind to attempt an investigation of the philosophical issues relating to causation. As a result, rather than collect together in this chapter all the cases which touch upon problems of a causal nature, reference is made to some of them elsewhere according to the overall context in which they arose.[3]

---

1 But for the better view see Hart and Honoré *Causation in the Law* (2nd edn 1985).
2 For a particularly wide interpretation see Fleming *The Law of Torts* (6th edn, 1983) ch 9. Cf 7th edn, 1987, chs 9-10 for modified treatment.
3 See, especially, chs 2, 4 and 7.

On the question of the proper scope of remoteness of damage, it is submitted that the concept should be kept relatively narrow and that it should be confined to situations involving 'freakish' concatenations of circumstances.[1] Of course, what situations fall within this category is not self-evident either. But the wider the remoteness umbrella is extended, so as to cover situations which are not in themselves factually uncommon but which happen for *other* reasons to raise controversial questions relating to the ascription of legal responsibility,[2] the greater will be the temptation to evade substantive issues of principle by pretending that they are largely questions of fact. Strictly speaking, the adoption of the narrow approach thus contended for should perhaps lead to the exclusion, from the chapter on remoteness of damage, of some of the cases on intervening human action; especially those on 'rescue' since those normally raise general policy questions rather than illustrate freakish events. Nevertheless it is convenient to refer to those cases in this chapter, notwithstanding their overlap with volenti non fit injuria and contributory negligence.

Remoteness of damage and measure of damages

[**3.03**] It is also important to distinguish the concept of remoteness of damage from that of measure of damages, even though the criteria underlying the drawing of this distinction too can sometimes be a source of difficulty.[3] Questions relating to the assessment, in pecuniary terms, of a plaintiff's loss are not subject to the logically prior rules, including those on remoteness, which identify what types of damage are remediable. Thus although 'foreseeability' is the fashionable criterion for determining remoteness,[4] a motorist who runs over an apparent vagrant remains liable for his victim's loss of earnings even when the latter turns out, unforeseeably, to be a prosperous member of the Bar Theatrical Society on the way to a performance of some avant-garde drama. The law relating to the measure of damages in negligence is dealt with in Part three of this book.

The foreseeability test

Background

[**3.04**] In the famous case of *Overseas Tankship (UK) Ltd v Morts Dock and Engineering Co Ltd, The Wagon Mound*,[5] the Judicial Committee

1 See also Michael A Jones *Textbook on Torts* (3rd edn, 1991) p 143: '... it ... seems sensible to maintain a distinction between cases of multiple cause, where the question is which cause is to be treated as having legal significance, and cases where on any view the defendant's negligence was *the* cause of the harm, but it is thought to be unfair to hold him responsible because it occurred in some unusual or bizarre fashion.'
2 For an example of such unfortunate usage see *SCM (UK) Ltd v Whittall & Son Ltd* [1971] 1 QB 337 at 344-346, CA per Lord Denning MR (economic loss).
3 See, eg the problem of a plaintiff's impecuniosity, discussed below.
4 See below.
5 [1961] AC 388, [1961] 1 All ER 404.

46 *Remoteness of damage*

of the Privy Council held that the concept of 'foreseeability' should be used to determine the extent of the ensuing harm for which a defendant, who had been careless, should be held liable. The Board accordingly refused to impose liability on the defendant shipowners when oil, carelessly discharged from one of their ships, was ignited in a manner taken to be unforeseeable and a conflagration in which the plaintiffs suffered damage resulted. In so holding the Board disapproved the well-known decision of the Court of Appeal, 40 years earlier, in *Re Polemis and Furness Withy & Co.*[1] In that case the careless dropping of a plank led, due to an accumulation of petrol vapour, to a fire which, like that in *The Wagon Mound*, was on the facts unforeseeable. But liability was imposed on the ground that, once the damage was 'directly traceable to the negligent act', the fact that the precise outcome 'was not foreseen [was] immaterial'.[2] In *The Wagon Mound*, however, the proposition that 'for an act of negligence which results in some trivial foreseeable damage, the actor should be liable for all consequences, however unforeseeable and however grave, so long as they can be said to be "direct" ', was castigated as not 'consonant with current ideas of justice or morality'.[3]

Foreseeability not a universal panacea

[**3.05**] Although the Privy Council decision has been accepted by the courts, in subsequent cases, as being the governing authority for the purposes of English law, theoretical controversy still takes place as to whether the earlier decision of the Court of Appeal did not, in fact, embody the better approach. Those who favour *The Wagon Mound* test believe that its use follows logically from the fact that foreseeability is used to determine whether the defendant's act was negligent in the first place, and that it would be inconsistent and unfair to hold the defendant liable for harm which was not part of the reason for stigmatising his act as culpable initially.[4] But it is submitted that this argument is misleading in that the concept of 'foreseeability' is really being used in a different sense, when remoteness of damage is in issue, from when the earlier question of duty of care is being addressed.[5] Using it to determine the normative question of how the defendant ought to have behaved before the event is different from using it to determine how far the consequences of an accident might normally be expected to extend after it has occurred.[6] Moreover, given that some damage to the plaintiff must have been foreseen (and *Re Polemis* is no authority for the proposition that a wholly unforeseeable plaintiff can recover[7]), it is not obvious that

1 [1921] 3 KB 560, CA.
2 [1921] 3 KB 560 at 577 per Scrutton LJ.
3 [1961] AC 388 at 422 per Lord Simonds delivering the judgment of the Board.
4 See, eg Glanville Williams 'The Risk Principle' (1961) 77 LQR 179.
5 See Richard Kidner 'Remoteness of damage: the duty-interest theory and the re-interpretation of *The Wagon Mound*' (1989) 9 LS 1.
6 For discussion see, generally, Hart and Honoré, *Causation in the Law*, (2nd edn, 1985) ch 9.
7 See *Clerk and Lindsell on Torts*, (16th edn) pp. 584-586 (R W M Dias and A Tettenborn).

justice requires the innocent plaintiff rather than the negligent defendant to bear the loss.[1]

[3.06] It is not without significance that, even on the practical level, decisions since 1961 have shown that the principle in *The Wagon Mound*, despite the Privy Council's criticism of the *Polemis* rule as supposedly leading 'to nowhere but the never-ending and insoluble problems of causation',[2] has itself proved to be a source of considerable uncertainty. A line of cases difficult to reconcile, some of which seem to be closer in spirit to the earlier approach, has been handed down in the last three decades. The problem of loss which was clearly foreseeable but which arose indirectly through, for example, intervening human acts, is one of the situations which has given rise to difficulty.[3] Paradoxically, this is an area in which unqualified application of the foreseeability test yields results which seem intuitively too *generous* to plaintiffs rather than the reverse. More generally, however, the vagueness inherent in the concept of foreseeability itself, and the covert discretion which *The Wagon Mound* test consequently confers on the court, has been a marked feature of the subsequent decisions.

The present state of the law

[3.07] In *Hughes v Lord Advocate*,[4] decided two years after *The Wagon Mound* by the House of Lords, the House proceeded on the basis that the general principle enunciated by the Privy Council represented the law. Their Lordships went on to interpret that principle, however, in a manner which extended the scope of liability beyond that which might have been considered appropriate if the *Wagon Mound* test had been adhered to closely or literally. Thus Lord Pearce observed that when 'an accident is of a different type and kind from anything that [a defendant] could have foreseen he is not liable for it', but his Lordship added that 'to demand too great precision in the test of foreseeability would be unfair to [plaintiffs] since the facets of misadventure are innumerable'.[5] In *Hughes*'s case employees of the Post Office negligently left some paraffin lamps unattended near an open manhole. An eight-year-old boy began to play on the deserted site. He tripped over one of the lamps, which then dropped into the manhole; an escape of paraffin vapour was ignited by the flame of the lamp causing an explosion which threw the boy himself into the manhole, where he suffered severe burns. The House of Lords accepted that this precise concatenation of circumstances, and in particular an explosion, could not have been foreseen. Liability was nevertheless imposed on the ground that some injury by burning to children at play

1 See Jolowicz [1961] CLJ 30.
2 [1961] AC 388 at 423.
3 See, eg *Lamb v Camden London Borough Council* [1981] QB 625, [1981] 2 All ER 408, CA, discussed below.
4 [1963] AC 837, [1963] 1 All ER 705, HL.
5 [1963] AC 837 at 853, [1963] 1 All ER 705 at 715, HL.

could have been foreseen from leaving the lamps unattended, and the fact that this foreseeable type of harm came about in an unforeseeable manner was immaterial.[1] In a later case Lord Reid, who had been a party to both of them, summed up the effect of the decisions of the Privy Council and the House of Lords as follows:

> 'It has now been established by *The Wagon Mound* and by *Hughes v Lord Advocate* that . . . damages can only be recovered if the injury complained of not only was caused by the alleged negligence but also was an injury of a class or character foreseeable as a possible result of it.'[2]

[**3.08**] Unfortunately, the even greater than usual degree of artificiality and hindsight in the foreseeability principle caused by using it in the post-accident situation as a test for remoteness, combined with the vagueness inherent in the concept of 'class or character' itself, has had the effect of making the attitudes of the courts to particular situations far from easy to predict. Indeed shortly after it was decided *Hughes v Lord Advocate* itself was narrowly distinguished in the Court of Appeal. In *Doughty v Turner Manufacturing Co Ltd*,[3] the defendants carelessly dropped an asbestos cement cover into a cauldron of molten liquid. It was accepted that if the plaintiff workman, who was nearby, had been splashed by the molten liquid, and burnt as a result, this would have been a foreseeable consequence of the accident for which the defendants would have been liable. As it happened, however, no such splash apparently occurred but a violent chemical reaction, unknown to science at that time, happened instead. This caused the molten liquid to erupt from the cauldron with the result that the plaintiff suffered injury by burning. His claim failed. Harman LJ said that 'the damage . . . was of an entirely different kind from the foreseeable splash', and added that it would have been 'wrong on these facts to make another inroad on the doctrine of foreseeability'.[4] But the nature of the injuries was the same as those which could have been foreseen from a splash, and the act which the defendants ought to have prevented in order to protect the plaintiff from splashing (ie the dropping of the asbestos into the cauldron) was the same as that which occurred and caused the explosion. These facts do, to say the least, render the decision in sharp contrast with that in the *Hughes* case. *Doughty* seems to require precise foresight of causation; whereas the House of Lords in *Hughes* might be taken to have held that providing normal precautions had been carelessly neglected, and harm similar to that which could have been foreseen had occurred as a result, the plaintiff should still

---

1 'This accident was caused by a known source of danger, but caused in a way which could not have been foreseen, and in my judgment that affords no defence': per Lord Reid in [1963] AC 837 at 847, [1963] 1 All ER 705 at 708.
2 See *Overseas Tankship (UK) Ltd v Miller SS Co Pty, The Wagon Mound (No 2)* [1967] 1 AC 617 at 636. (This case arose out of the same fire as *The Wagon Mound* and the conclusion was reached that it had been foreseeable after all! But a different plaintiff was involved and different considerations applied.)
3 [1964] 1 QB 518, [1964] 1 All ER 98, CA.
4 [1964] 1 QB 518 at 529, [1964] 1 All ER 98 at 102, CA.

The foreseeability test 49

recover even if the method of causation itself could not have been foreseen.

Spectrum of liability

[**3.09**] In the aftermath of *Hughes* and *Doughty* a series of cases were reported which seem to indicate that those two decisions represent opposite ends of a spectrum, within which courts have considerable room to manoeuvre to determine whether or not a particular claim can be regarded as fulfilling the requirements of the foreseeability test. Thus injury from frost-bite, so rare in England as to be in itself unforeseeable, was nevertheless held in one case to be within the general class of injury to health from severe cold, to the risk of which the defendant had carelessly exposed the plaintiff, and liability was imposed accordingly.[1] But in another case the court chose to draw a fine distinction between different types of illness caused by rats. On the assumption that the defendant farmer had carelessly exposed one of his employees to the risk of illness, by allowing the farm to become infested with rats, the employee's claim still failed on the ground that the particular illness in fact contracted was extremely rare, and therefore to be distinguished from the foreseeable risk of injury by biting or by food-poisoning.[2] It is difficult to resist the conclusion that the attempt, in *The Wagon Mound*, elegantly to unify virtually the entire law of negligence around the concept of foreseeability has led to greater uncertainty than the supposedly more theoretically vulnerable approach of *Re Polemis*. The older test seems to have been capable of producing more satisfying and consistent results, when applied intuitively, than its successor.

Effect of extraneous circumstances

The 'egg-shell skull' rule

[**3.10**] The operation of the foreseeability principle as a test for remoteness of damage is subject to an important modification or exception in a certain special type of personal injury case. The situation in question is that in which the plaintiff suffers from some unusual, and unforeseeable, latent disease or disability. An accident, arising out of the defendant's negligence and for which he is responsible, foreseeably causes some injury to the plaintiff. As a result of his latent condition, however, the plaintiff suffers harmful consequences which, although in a sense triggered by the defendant's negligence, are far more serious or extensive than could have been foreseen as a result of it. In such cases the defendant remains liable for the full extent of the plaintiff's injuries. In *Smith v Leech Brain &*

---

1 *Bradford v Robinson Rentals* [1967] 1 All ER 267, [1967] 1 WLR 337. See also *Robinson v Post Office* [1974] 2 All ER 737, [1974] 1 WLR 1176, CA; *Wieland v Cyril Lord Carpets Ltd* [1969] 3 All ER 1006; *Vacwell Engineering Co Ltd v BDH Chemicals Ltd* [1971] 1 QB 88, [1969] 3 All ER 1681; varied [1971] 1 QB 111n, [1970] 3 All ER 553n, CA.
2 *Tremain v Pike* [1969] 3 All ER 1303, [1969] 1 WLR 1556.

Co Ltd,[1] which was decided very shortly after *The Wagon Mound*,[2] it was declared that this long-established rule, often known as the 'egg-shell skull' principle, had survived the decision of the Privy Council. The plaintiff suffered burns to his lip when, due to his employer's negligence, molten liquid was spattered upon it. The burn unfortunately activated a pre-malignant condition and the plaintiff subsequently died of cancer. Lord Parker CJ held the defendant employers liable for his death, observing that it had 'always been the law of this country that a tortfeasor takes his victim as he finds him'.[3] In a later case the Court of Appeal even applied the principle in circumstances involving a longer and more complicated chain of causation. In *Robinson v Post Office*[4] the defendants were held fully liable when the medical treatment which the plaintiff received for a minor injury, caused by their negligence, reacted with a pre-existing allergy to cause brain damage, which could not have been foreseen. The principle has also been applied to situations in which the unforeseeable severity of the plaintiff's suffering takes the form of exacerbation of pre-existing nervous or neurotic conditions, as well as those involving physical disabilities in the narrow sense. 'There is no difference in principle', Geoffrey Lane J observed in one case, 'between an egg-shell skull and an egg-shell personality.'[5]

[**3.11**] Notwithstanding the importance of the rule that the defendant takes the plaintiff as he finds him, it is important not to lose sight of its limitations. It appears to be confined to personal injury cases, presumably on grounds of policy,[6] and does not extend to cases of damage to property.[7] Thus it is generally accepted that if the facts of *Re Polemis*[8] were now to recur the decision would, after *The Wagon Mound*, be different and the defendants would escape liability on the ground that the damage had been unforeseeable. But if a principle analogous to the 'egg-shell skull' rule applied the accumulation of petrol-vapour in the hold of the ship could plausibly be seen as a pre-existing condition, and the same decision reached as in the case itself. Moreover, even within the personal injuries field, the rule does not in itself constitute a general abrogation of the foreseeability principle, but only an exception applicable in special circumstances. Thus, if no part *at all* of the plaintiff's injuries are held to have been foreseeable his claim will fail, notwithstanding that he may have suffered very seriously as a consequence of the defendant's carelessness.[9] But it is

1 [1962] 2 QB 405, [1961] 3 All ER 1159.
2 [1961] AC 388, [1961] 1 All ER 404.
3 [1962] 2 QB at 414. See also *Warren v Scruttons Ltd* [1962] 1 Lloyd's Rep 497.
4 [1974] 2 All ER 737, [1974] 1 WLR 1176, CA. See also *Wieland v Cyril Lord Carpets Ltd* [1969] 3 All ER 1006.
5 *Malcolm v Broadhurst* [1970] 3 All ER 508 at 511. See also *Cotic v Gray* (1981) 33 OR (2d) 356; *Brice v Brown* [1984] 1 All ER 997.
6 But for criticism of the rule, even in personal injury cases, see Atiyah *Accidents, Compensation and the Law* (4th edn) pp 114-115.
7 But see *Clerk and Lindsell on Torts* (16th edn) p 592 where it is argued that 'to distinguish between personal and property damage in respect of hypersensitivity is unacceptable' (R W M Dias and A Tettenborn).
8 [1921] 3 KB 560, CA.
9 See, eg *Doughty v Turner Manufacturing Co* [1964] 1 QB 518, [1964] 1 All ER 98, CA; *Tremain v Pike* [1969] 3 All ER 1303, [1969] 1 WLR 1556.

arguable that the courts are becoming discernibly more ready, in personal injury cases, to define the *kind* of injury, which ought to have been foreseen, very broadly in the plaintiff's favour.[1] To the extent that this is true the 'egg-shell skull' principle should become progressively less significant; and personal injury litigation generally perceived as attracting a distinctive approach as far as remoteness of damage is concerned.[2]

Impecuniosity of the plaintiff

[**3.12**] In *Liesbosch Dredger v SS Edison*[3] the House of Lords refused to extend the 'egg-shell skull' rule, by analogy, to a situation in which the plaintiffs' losses, when their ship was negligently sunk by the defendants, were more extensive than they might have been due to their own impecuniosity. Lack of funds prevented the plaintiffs from purchasing a replacement straight away, and they had to incur hiring charges instead. This additional loss was held to be too remote to be recoverable. Lord Wright observed that the plaintiffs' 'financial disability' was not 'to be compared with that physical delicacy or weakness which may aggravate the damage in the case of personal injuries'.[4] More recently, however, the rule in *The Edison* came in for criticism as being too harsh on plaintiffs.[5] It was also suggested, before the trend in question was put into reverse,[6] that developments in the law generally, relating to economic losses and the relationship between contract and tort,[7] may have rendered it out of date:[8] financial losses of the type in question being recoverable in contract if the defendant knew of the plaintiff's impecuniosity.[9] Moreover it was said in *Clippens Oil Co Ltd v Edinburgh & District Water Trustees*,[10] which was decided by the House of Lords more than 20 years before *The Edison* itself, that a defendant could not argue that the plaintiff had failed to take sufficient steps to *mitigate* his loss if impecuniosity had prevented him from doing so. The relevant passage was referred to by Lord Wright, who delivered the only speech in *The Edison*, but dismissed on the ground that as it dealt with 'the victim's duty to minimise damage' it was irrelevant to questions relating to the

---

1 See above, p 47, n1 and cases there cited. Cf Smith *Liability in Negligence* (1984) ch 8.
2 See P J Rowe 'The Demise of the Thin Skull Rule?' (1977) 40 MLR 377.
3 [1933] AC 449.
4 [1933] AC 449 at 461.
5 See, eg R G Lawson 'The Status of *The Edison*' (1974) 124 NLJ 240. See also *Perry v Sidney Phillips & Son* [1982] 3 All ER 705, [1982] 1 WLR 1297, CA discussed below.
6 Ie by cases such as *Murphy v Brentwood District Council* [1991] 1 AC 378, [1990] 2 All ER 908, HL.
7 For discussion of the effect of this relationship in the context of remoteness of damage see Dias and Markesinis, *Tort Law* (2nd edn, 1989) pp 141-143; and Burrows *Remedies for Torts and Breach of Contract* (1987, London) pp 42-45.
8 See Tomkin and Pearce 'The Sinking of *The Edison*: a Voyage in Contract and Tort' (1982) 132 NLJ 1012.
9 See, *Trans Trust SPRL v Danubian Trading Co* [1952] 2 QB 297, [1952] 1 All ER 970, CA; *Wadsworth v Lydall* [1981] 2 All ER 401, [1981] 1 WLR 598, CA.
10 [1907] AC 291 at 303 per Lord Collins.

'measure of damages' which were 'quite a different matter'.[1] But recent Court of Appeal decisions have shown an inclination to construe the rule in the case narrowly,[2] and it appears unlikely that it will be extended. In *Dodd Properties (Kent) v Canterbury City Council*,[3] the plaintiffs' building was damaged by the defendants' building activities. The plaintiffs nevertheless chose not to repair their building straight away. They happened to be going through a period of financial stringency but considered in any event that it would have been commercially imprudent to repair the building in the absence of acceptance of liability for the damage, and the cost of making it good, from the defendants - which was not forthcoming. As a result several years went by, during which the cost of the repairs increased substantially and the defendants ultimately contended, relying on *The Edison*, that only the much smaller sum which the repairs would have cost if they had been carried out earlier could be recovered. The Court of Appeal rejected this contention. In all the circumstances it had been reasonable for the repairs to be postponed.[4] The plaintiffs were not, in the words of Donaldson LJ 'impecunious in the *Liesbosch* sense of one who could not go out into the market'. His Lordship continued as follows:[5]

> '... they were commercially prudent in not incurring the cash flow deficiency which would have resulted from their undertaking the work in the autumn of 1970 and waiting for reimbursement until after the hearing, particularly when the defendants were denying liability and there was a dispute as to what works could and should be done by way of reinstatement. In my judgment, the decision in the *Liesbosch* case has no application to such a situation, which is distinguishable.'

[3.13] In the later case of *Perry v Sidney Phillips & Son*,[6] a plaintiff again failed to repair at the outset a defective building, one which he would not have acquired but for the negligence of the defendant surveyors. The plaintiff lacked the means to carry out the repairs but was nevertheless able to recover damages for the vexation and distress caused to him by having to live in a defective house. Reliance by the defendants on *The Edison* was again to no avail. Oliver LJ observed that the 'real question' was 'was it reasonable in all the circumstances for the plaintiff not to mitigate his damage by carrying out the repairs which were required?'[7] Noting that, as in the *Dodd*

---

1 [1935] AC at 461. But cf Lawson op cit. Cf per Oliver J in *Radford v De Froberville* [1978] 1 All ER 33 at 44, [1977] 1 WLR 1262 at 1272: 'No doubt the measure of damages and the plaintiff's duty and ability to mitigate are logically distinct concepts ... But to some extent, at least, they are mirror images ...' (cited with approval by Megaw and Browne LJJ in *Dodd Properties (Kent) v Canterbury City Council* [1980] 1 All ER 928 at 935, 938, [1980] 1 WLR 433 at 453, 456).
2 See also *Burns v MAN Automotive* (1987) 61 ALJR 81.
3 [1980] 1 All ER 928, [1980] 1 WLR 433.
4 See also *Martindale v Duncan* [1973] 2 All ER 355, [1973] 1 WLR 574, CA.
5 [1980] 1 All ER 928 at 941, [1980] 1 WLR 433 at 459. See also per Megaw LJ (at 451-452).
6 [1982] 3 All ER 705, [1982] 1 WLR 1297, CA.
7 [1982] 3 All ER 705 at 711, [1982] 1 WLR 297 at 1305.

case, the defendants refusal to accept liability had contributed to the plaintiff's financial difficulties, his Lordship answered the question in the latter's favour. The current tendency therefore appears to be to treat *The Edison* as a decision on its own facts,[1] and to emphasise that future cases will be decided by applying the general concepts of foreseeability and reasonableness to the particular circumstances. In *Perry v Sidney Phillips & Son* Kerr LJ expressed the situation as follows:[2]

> 'If it is reasonably foreseeable that the plaintiff may be unable to mitigate or remedy the consequence of the other party's breach as soon as he would have done if he had been provided with the necessary means to do so from the other party, then it seems to me that the principle of the *Liesbosch* case no longer applies in its full rigour. In the *Liesbosch* case, as I see it, it was not reasonably foreseeable that the plaintiff would be put into the difficulties in which he was put by the other party's breach of duty.'

Intervening act by the plaintiff

Remoteness occasionally relevant

[3.14] In some cases the acts of persons other than the defendant, which have become interposed between the original negligence and the injury suffered by the plaintiff, may be treated by the court as rendering that injury too remote from the negligence and hence as absolving the defendant from liability. If the act in question is one of the plaintiff's own the matter will usually be treated, if it is regarded as affecting the outcome at all, as one merely of contributory negligence or, occasionally, as giving rise to the defence volenti non fit injuria; the concept of remoteness of damage will seldom be invoked. Indeed in view of the flexible apportionment machinery available when a case is held to fall within the Law Reform (Contributory Negligence) Act 1945 the use of that machinery, as distinct from the 'all or nothing' concept of remoteness, would seem to be the preferable approach.[3] Nevertheless, in one case decided by the House of Lords in relatively recent years, *McKew v Holland and Hannen and Cubitts (Scotland) Ltd*,[4] their Lordships wholly rejected the plaintiff's claim by holding, in effect, that his own act rendered his injury too remote from the defendant's negligence. That negligence had caused an accident at his place of work as a result of which the plaintiff suffered injuries which included a tendency, on occasions, for his left leg to go numb. Some days later, when visiting a block of flats, he chose to descend by himself, without waiting for assistance which was

---

1 See *Perry v Sidney Phillips & Son* [1982] 3 All ER 705 at 712-713, [1982] 1 WLR 1297 at 1302.
2 [1982] 3 All ER 705 at 712-713, [1982] 1 WLR 297 at 1307.
3 See Millner 'Novus Actus Interveniens: the Present Effect of *Wagon Mound*' (1971) 22 NILQ 168.
4 [1969] 3 All ER 1621, HL.

available, a steep flight of stairs which had no handrail. His leg suddenly went numb and he fell, suffering much more serious injuries. The House of Lords held that the plaintiff's conduct in attempting to descend the stairs was so unreasonable that it constituted a novus actus interveniens rendering the defendants immune from liability for the injuries caused by the fall, even though it would not have occurred but for their initial negligence. The speech of Lord Reid is particularly striking for its refusal to treat the foreseeability test as the sole determinant of liability. His Lordship was prepared to accept that what had happened to the plaintiff may well have been foreseeable as a result of the defendants' original negligence, but that did not of itself mean that his claim should succeed:

> 'A defender is not liable for a consequence of a kind which is not foreseeable. But it does not follow that he is liable for every consequence which a reasonable man could foresee. What can be foreseen depends almost entirely on the facts of the case, and it is often easy to foresee unreasonable conduct or some other novus actus interveniens as being quite likely. But that does not mean that the defender must pay for damage caused by the novus actus . . . For it is not at all unlikely or unforeseeable that an active man who has suffered such a disability will take some quite unreasonable risk. But if he does he cannot hold the defender liable for the consequences.'[1]

[**3.15**] Notwithstanding dicta apparently to the contrary by Lord Simonds in *The Wagon Mound*[2] itself, this statement by Lord Reid clearly affirms that foreseeability is merely a necessary test for recovery and not a sufficient one. It is submitted that this affirmation is in itself welcome, even if the actual decision in *McKew*'s case seems rather harsh on its facts. But it is perhaps significant that three weeks elapsed between the dates of the two accidents. The narrower the interval between the initial negligence and the subsequent injury, the less likely it is that the plaintiff's claim will fail altogether on grounds of remoteness. In *Wieland v Cyril Lord Carpets Ltd*,[3] the plaintiff had to have a surgical collar fitted to her neck due to injuries received in a motor accident caused by the defendants' negligence. This device made it more difficult for her to move her neck, and hence adjust her sight in the manner required by the bi-focal spectacles which she had worn for many years. As a result, later in the same day on which the collar was fitted, she fell down stairs and suffered further injuries. Eveleigh J held the defendant fully liable for these as well as for those suffered in the original accident.[4]

'Dilemma' situations

[**3.16**] If the act by the plaintiff, which is alleged to have broken the chain of causation, actually occurred in the immediate aftermath of

---

1 [1969] 3 All ER 1621 at 1623.
2 See [1961] AC 388 at 426.
3 [1969] 3 All ER 1006.
4 See also *Pyne v Wilkenfeld* (1981) 26 SASR 441.

the defendant's negligence the court is particularly unlikely to be sympathetic towards the latter.¹ A plaintiff whose actions in an emergency might, with hindsight, be subjected to criticism will therefore rarely wholly fail on causal grounds, although a reduction in the damages might sometimes be made for contributory negligence.²

Suicide cases

[**3.17**] In *Pigney v Pointer's Transport Services Ltd*,³ the deceased committed suicide as a result of depression brought about by head injuries caused by the defendants' negligence. His widow was able to recover damages from them under the Fatal Accidents Acts. Although *Re Polemis* was referred to in the judgment in this case, which was decided before *The Wagon Mound*, it is submitted that it would be decided the same way today.⁴ Suicidal depression can presumably be taken to be a foreseeable consequence of serious personal injuries.⁵ Nevertheless, the task of proving the causal link by medical evidence may sometimes be difficult.⁶ But if the deceased had a history of depression the 'egg-shell skull' principle may be prayed in aid; as in a successful claim in Canada, on facts similar to *Pigney*, in which the problem received extensive consideration in the Ontario Court of Appeal.⁷

Rescue

[**3.18**] It is well known that the law is naturally reluctant to deny claims brought by plaintiffs who have suffered injury while engaged in rescue activities necessitated by the negligence of defendants. Nor is this reluctance confined to situations in which the lives and safety of human beings are at risk; in appropriate circumstances it may extend to cases merely involving damage to property.⁸ It will only very rarely, therefore, be possible for the maxim volenti non fit injuria to be invoked successfully against a rescuer.⁹ Nor will remoteness defences usually fare any better: rescue being regarded as pre-eminently likely to occur if an emergency is created.¹⁰ Occasionally,

---

1 Cf *The Oropesa* [1943] P 32, [1943] 1 All ER 211, CA, especially per Lord Wright at 39: 'The question is not whether there was new negligence, but whether there was a new cause.'
2 See, eg *Sayers v Harlow UDC* [1958] 2 All ER 342, [1958] 1 WLR 623, CA.
3 [1957] 2 All ER 807, [1957] 1 WLR 1121.
4 Cf *Kirkham v Chief Constable of the Greater Manchester Police* [1990] 2 QB 283, [1990] 3 All ER 246, CA (discussed above, ch 1) in which the Court of Appeal held that there is now no public policy objection to the recovery of damages in respect of the suicide of persons of unsound mind.
5 Cf *Meah v McCreamer* [1985] 1 All ER 367.
6 Cf *Farmer v Rash* [1969] 1 All ER 705, [1969] 1 WLR 160.
7 See *Cotic v Gray* (1981) 33 OR (2d) 356.
8 See *Hyett v Great Western Rly Co* [1948] 1 KB 345, [1947] 2 All ER 264, CA.
9 For a case in which the defence succeeded see *Cutler v United Dairies (London) Ltd* [1933] 2 KB 297, CA.
10 See, generally, *Baker v TE Hopkins & Son Ltd* [1959] 3 All ER 225, [1959] 1 WLR 966, CA.

however, plaintiffs in rescue situations might find themselves defeated by remoteness arguments. In *Crossley v Rawlinson*,[1] the plaintiff tripped and fell while running with a fire extinguisher towards the scene of a fire caused by the defendant's negligence. His claim for the injury he suffered in the fall was unsuccessful, even though the defendant abandoned volenti non fit injuria as a defence in the course of the trial. The judge held that what had occurred was not reasonably foreseeable and was therefore too remote.[2] Such cases are, however, likely to be rare. The high regard in which the law rightly holds rescuers is further illustrated by resolution in their favour of the question of whether they can sue in cases where the victim carelessly placed *himself* in the situation of danger requiring rescue;[3] a point formerly sometimes doubted on largely unfounded conceptual grounds. Recovery is therefore not limited to the more usual type of case in which the peril has been created by the negligence of a third party. It is also important to note that the House of Lords has recently confirmed that 'professional' rescuers are not in principle to be treated differently from others. Thus, unlike the position apparently prevailing in some American jurisdictions, firemen injured in the course of their duties can sue those whose negligence started the fire.[4]

Intervention by third parties

'Deliberate and mischievous' acts[5]

[**3.19**] 'It is tempting to conclude', observed Robert Goff LJ in *Paterson Zochonis & Co Ltd v Merfarken Packaging Ltd*,[6] 'that, in the absence of some special relationship, there can be no liability for damage caused to the plaintiff by the deliberate wrongdoing of a third party'.[7] It is true that he went on to point out that this proposition was too wide as it stood; not least because liability in tort would presumably be imposed on a defendant who had himself committed a deliberate act, for example by handing the third party a gun knowing that the latter intended to shoot the plaintiff.[8] Nevertheless it remains true that where the defendant has merely been careless the deliberate and

---

1   [1981] 3 All ER 674, [1981] 1 WLR 369.
2   Quaere whether this decision is consistent with *Hughes v Lord Advocate* [1963] AC 837, [1963] 1 All ER 705, HL. See criticism of *Crossley v Rawlinson* by Michael A Jones in (1982) 45 MLR 342.
3   See *Harrison v British Railways Board* [1981] 3 All ER 679 (Boreham J).
4   See *Ogwo v Taylor* [1988] AC 431, [1987] 3 All ER 961, HL.
5   The phrase is taken from *Prosser & Son Ltd v Levy* [1955] 1 WLR 1224 at 1230, CA.
6   [1986] 3 All ER 522, CA.
7   See also the same judge, as Lord Goff of Chieveley, in *Smith v Littlewoods Organisation Ltd* [1987] AC 241 at 271ff, HL.
8   Cf *Setchell v Snowdon* [1974] RTR 389, CA.

wrongful acts of third parties will only exceptionally, in so far as the issue is seen as one of remoteness, give rise to liability.[1] The picture is rather different if the underlying issue in the case is perceived, not as one of remoteness, but as one concerning the criteria for predicating that the plaintiff's carelessness was capable of constituting negligence in law in the first place. Thus those in charge of children may sometimes be liable if, through their failure to keep them under proper control, injury is inflicted on the plaintiff.[2] Similarly, in the well-known case of *Home Office v Dorset Yacht Co*,[3] the House of Lords held that those entrusted with the custody of offenders could in principle be liable for failing to prevent them from escaping and causing damage. These are situations in which the defendants conduct is evaluated in terms of a foreseeable risk of injury to the plaintiffs through the medium of deliberate human action by others.[4] But the courts do not readily evaluate conduct in terms of this particular risk.[5] Indeed, this is an area in which, despite the difficulties sometimes associated with it, the distinction between acts and omissions remains important.[6]

High degree of probability required

[3.20] The question whether the defendant ought to be held liable for loss caused by the independent acts of others therefore becomes one of remoteness in situations where the defendant has admittedly been careless, but not in a way usually associated with a risk of damage through the medium of third parties. Nevertheless, as a consequence of that carelessness harm is occasioned to the plaintiff, the immediate cause of which is intervening human action. This is an area in which the foreseeability approach propounded in *The Wagon Mound*[7] has proved to be particularly unsatisfactory.[8] The judicial intuition that losses suffered in this way will normally be too remote seems to be unchanged as a result of that decision. But it has made giving effect to that intuition unnecessarily difficult and complicated, simply because

---

1 Thus owners of stolen motor cars, who had left their vehicles unlocked, have been held not liable for death or damage caused by the driving of the thieves: see *Topp v London Country Bus (South West) Ltd* (1993) Times, 15 February, CA. See also *Bohdal v Streets* [1984] Tas R 82 (Tasmania).
2 See, eg *Carmarthenshire County Council v Lewis* [1955] AC 549, [1955] 1 All ER 565; *Vicar of Writtle v Essex County Council* (1979) 77 LGR 656.
3 [1970] AC 1004, [1970] 2 All ER 294, HL. See also ch 1 above.
4 Of course such situations may themselves give rise to questions of remoteness: see, eg *O'Reilly v C* [1978] 3 WWR 145 (Can).
5 'The general rule is that one man is under no duty of controlling another man to prevent his doing damage to a third': *Smith v Leurs* (1945) 70 CLR 256 at 262 per Dixon J : cited with approval in *Home Office v Dorset Yacht Co Ltd* [1970] AC 1004, [1970] 2 All ER 294, HL. See also *Hill v Chief Constable of West Yorkshire* [1989] AC 53, [1988] 2 All ER 238, HL.
6 See, eg *P Perl Exporters Ltd v Camden London Borough Council* [1984] QB 342, [1983] 3 All ER 161, CA (especially per Waller LJ at 352).
7 [1961] AC 388, [1961] 1 All ER 404, PC.
8 Cf Michael A Jones 'Paying for the Crimes of Others' (1984) 47 MLR 223.

it may often be unrealistic to deny that the intervening events were foreseeable. Under the *Re Polemis and Furness Withy & Co*[1] test, however, claims of the type in question could plausibly have been dismissed simply as being for losses suffered in a manner too 'indirect'[2] to be recoverable. The difficulties are well illustrated by *Lamb v London Borough of Camden*.[3] The defendant council, while replacing a sewer, carelessly broke a water main. The escaping water undermined the foundations of the plaintiff's house and made it dangerous to live in. In consequence the house was left empty, but squatters moved in and caused considerable further damage for which the plaintiff sought to hold the defendant council liable. The Court of Appeal were unanimous that the claim should fail. At first instance, however, it had been found as a fact that at that time, in that part of London, the entry of squatters was a clearly foreseeable consequence of a property being left vacant for any length of time; nor was the Court of Appeal itself really disposed to disagree with that finding. In resolving the issue of liability in favour of the defendants the members of the Court of Appeal adopted different reasoning. Lord Denning MR said that the question of remoteness was ultimately one of policy, and that the plaintiff should have protected herself against the losses which had occurred by taking out insurance rather than by looking to the defendants. Watkins LJ held expressly that foreseeability was merely a necessary and not a sufficient condition for damage not being too remote, and that policy and judicial intuition had a part to play. Oliver LJ held that, where intervening human action was concerned, a very high degree of probability was required if the loss was not to be held to be too remote, and that that requirement was not satisfied in the instant case. He attempted to reconcile his approach with the foreseeability test by putting special emphasis upon the adjective 'reasonable' in the phrase 'reasonably foreseeable'. Although this attempted reconciliation seems strained, the reasoning of Oliver LJ perhaps gets closest to the heart of the problem of deliberate intervening human action. His Lordship suggested that:[4] 'There may ... be circumstances in which the court would require a degree of likelihood amounting almost to inevitability before it fixes a defendant with responsibility for the act of a third party over whom he has and can have no control.'

[**3.21**] Accordingly, it is submitted that it can be taken as established that foreseeability alone, at any rate in the sense in which that concept is normally used, will be insufficient to prevent damage caused by the deliberate acts of third parties from being too remote, and that a high degree of probability will usually be required in addition if liability is to be imposed. Just how probable the intervention was will obviously be a question of fact in each case. The precise degree of probability that will need to be established may also

---

1 [1921] 3 KB 560, CA.
2 Cf *Weld-Blundell v Stephens* [1920] AC 956 at 986, HL per Lord Sumner.
3 [1981] QB 625, [1981] 2 All ER 408, CA.
4 [1981] QB 625 at 644, [1981] 2 All ER 408 at 419.

vary according to the circumstances of each case, including the nature of the defendant's carelessness or other breach of duty. In *Ward v Cannock Chase District Council*,[1] the defendants expressly undertook to repair the plaintiff's house, which had been rendered uninhabitable by their own earlier negligence. They failed to honour their undertaking and, in consequence, vandals entered the empty house and caused further damage. Scott J imposed liability on the defendants and distinguished *Lamb v London Borough of Camden*. He held, in effect, that a duty actually to repair an empty house warranted requiring a lower degree of probability of illegal entry, for the purposes of remoteness of damage, than did a duty not carelessly to burst a water main.[2] His Lordship also held that, in any event, 'the likelihood of unoccupied property receiving the attention of vandals was very much higher'[3] in the locality in question in the case before him, even than it had been in the *Lamb* case.

Negligence

[3.22] If the intervening act was merely careless or negligent, as distinct from deliberate and mischievous, it is less likely to render the damage ultimately suffered by the plaintiff too remote from the defendant's own initial negligence. It is particularly unlikely to do so if the intervening act was itself a reaction, albeit perhaps with hindsight an unfortunate one, to the situation which the defendant had created. Theoretically questionable decisions taken in a dangerous and uncertain situation produced by a collision at sea, for example, will not readily be treated as depriving of causal force the carelessness responsible for the initial collision.[4] Nevertheless, each case necessarily depends upon its own facts, and in *Knightley v Johns*,[5] in which the whole subject was considered at length by the Court of Appeal, an intervening act of negligence *was* held to have broken the chain of causation. The defendant's negligence caused a serious accident near the exit of a tunnel carrying one-way traffic. Unfortunately, the police inspector who arrived at the scene forgot to close the tunnel to traffic and subsequently ordered the plaintiff, one of his subordinates, to do so belatedly by riding his motor cycle through the tunnel against the oncoming traffic. In so doing the plaintiff met with an accident for which the trial judge held the defendant liable. The Court of Appeal, however, reversed this decision holding that 'the inspector's negligence was not a concurrent cause running with [the defendant's] negligence, but a new cause disturbing the sequence of events'.[6] But Stephenson LJ, who delivered the judgment of the Court, emphasised, that the test was one of

---

1 [1986] Ch 546, [1985] 3 All ER 537.
2 Cf *Stansbie v Troman* [1948] 2 KB 48, [1948] 1 All ER 599, CA.
3 [1986] Ch 546 at 570, [1985] 3 All ER 537 at 553.
4 See *The Oropesa* [1943] P 32, [1943] 1 All ER 211, CA.
5 [1982] 1 All ER 851, [1982] 1 WLR 349, CA.
6 [1982] 1 All ER 851 at 866, [1982] 1 WLR 349 at 367, CA.

reasonable foreseeability in all the circumstances.[1] Accordingly, in the case of negligent intervening acts, as distinct from those actually intended to do harm, an unusually high degree of probability will not be required before the defendant can be held liable for all that occurred. On the contrary, only relatively *unexpected* acts of subsequent negligence will suffice to *discharge* the defendant in such cases.

Inadequate medical treatment

[**3.23**] A particular context in which the defendant is apt to contend that the chain of causation has been broken is where the victim of an accident, for which his negligence was responsible, subsequently receives medical treatment which is alleged to have been inadequate or negligent. While the courts are, on the whole, reluctant to absolve defendants in such cases there is no clear English decision to the effect that negligent medical treatment will *not* sever the chain of causation.[2] On the contrary, in *Hogan v Bentinck West Hartley Collieries*,[3] the House of Lords apparently held, albeit by a bare majority in a case decided under the old Workmen's Compensation Act, that it *would* do so.[4] But in practice plaintiffs usually succeed in full against those responsible for the initial accident, because the courts appear reluctant to hold that intervening medical treatment was actually negligent. The usual technique is to hold that it involved a mere error of judgment, falling short of negligence,[5] or that in any event it ultimately had no causative effect on the outcome.[6] It is submitted, however, that there is much to be said for holding overtly that the possibility of negligently induced misadventure can be foreseen as a result of emergency hospital treatment, for example, and that those whose carelessness creates a need for such treatment should therefore as a general rule be liable for its consequences notwithstanding inadequacies in its administration.[7]

---

1 See [1982] 1 All ER 851 at 866, [1981] 1 WLR 349 at 366.
2 But see *Thompson v Toorenburgh* (1973) 29 DLR (3d) 608; affd (1975) 50 DLR (3d) 717 (Can).
3 [1949] 1 All ER 588.
4 See also *David v Toronto Transit Commission* (1977) 77 DLR (3d) 717 (Can). Sed quaere.
5 See, eg. *Liston v Liston and Sleep* (1983) 31 SASR 245 (Aus). See also per Lord Reid (dissenting) in *Hogan v Bentinck Collieries* [1949] 1 All ER 588 at 607-608.
6 See, eg *Robinson v Post Office* [1974] 2 All ER 737, [1974] 1 WLR 1176, CA; *Conley v Strain* [1988] IR 628. Cf *Barnett v Chelsea and Kensington Hospital Management Committee* [1969] 1 QB 428, [1968] 1 All ER 1068.
7 See Smith *Liability in Negligence* (1984) pp 151-153.

Chapter 4

Assumption of risk, contribution and exclusion

Scope of the chapter

[**4.01**] This chapter deals with four separate matters: the defences of assumption of risk and contributory negligence, contribution between wrongdoers, and the problem of exclusion of liability. Although logically distinct, various overlapping concepts provide the topics with a sufficient degree of similarity for it to be convenient to consider them together. Assumption of risk and contributory negligence are closely related in any event. The issue of apportionment makes for a degree of resemblance between contributory negligence and contribution between wrongdoers. Finally, exclusion of liability involves questions which touch upon the ground dealt with by the defence of assumption of risk.

Assumption of risk

Knowledge not enough

[**4.02**] In *Morris v Murray*[1] Stocker LJ said:

'. . . in order to defeat an otherwise valid claim on the basis that the plaintiff was volens the defendant must establish that the plaintiff at the material time knew the nature and extent of the risk and voluntarily agreed to absolve the defendant from the consequences of it by consenting to the lack of reasonable care that might produce the risk. It is common ground and long established that knowledge of the risk is not sufficient but there must also be consent to bear the consequences of it.'[2]

1 [1991] 2 QB 6 at 18, [1990] 3 All ER 801 at 809, CA.
2 See also *Nettleship v Weston* [1971] 2 QB 691 at 701, [1971] 3 All ER 581 at 587, CA, per Lord Denning MR: 'Knowledge of the risk of injury is not enough. Nor is a willingness to take the risk of injury. Nothing will suffice short of an agreement to waive any claim for negligence. The plaintiff must agree, expressly or impliedly, to waive any claim for any injury that may befall him due to the lack of reasonable care by the defendant.'

Thus merely taking a risk, with full knowledge of the hazards involved, will not in itself be enough to bring the maxim into effect so as to absolve the defendant from all liability.[1] There must also be evidence of some understanding, even if only tacit and falling short of an actual contract,[2] that the plaintiff was prepared to abandon any right of legal redress which he might otherwise have enjoyed against the defendant, if loss or injury eventually occurred. In extreme cases, however, the very deliberate taking of a known risk can, if the plaintiff had a free choice and was not constrained,[3] be enough to constitute the necessary evidence. The recent decision of the Court of Appeal in *Morris v Murray*[4] provides a rare example. The plaintiff went for a joyride in a light aircraft piloted by the deceased after he and the deceased had engaged in a heavy drinking session during which the latter consumed the equivalent of seventeen whiskies. In a crash caused by the pilot's inability properly to control the aircraft he was killed and the plaintiff was seriously injured. An action by the plaintiff against the deceased's estate was, however, defeated by the defence of volenti. Sir George Waller said:[5]

> 'To fly with a pilot who has consumed a large quantity of alcohol is very dangerous indeed. In this case ... the plaintiff was taking a very active part in the arrangements. He drove to the airfield; he had flown twice before with Mr Murray; he helped to start the aircraft; he helped to fill it with petrol; and he had been drinking with the pilot all the afternoon. In my judgment, having engaged himself to take part from the beginning, he not only knew the risks but the only implication is that he agreed to take them.'

Relationship with other defences

[**4.03**] It is submitted that the decision in *Morris v Murray* was correct, but it is important that its exceptional nature is borne in mind so as to prevent it from having the effect of blurring, in less unusual cases, the distinction between the defence of volenti on the one hand and the concepts of contributory negligence and of supervening events breaking the chain of causation on the other.[6] Since a finding of contributory negligence enables a flexible apportionment technique to be applied as between plaintiff and defendant it would seem, in most cases, to be preferable to the application of the 'all or nothing' concept of volenti non fit injuria.[7] Most academic opinion supports this

---

1 Cf per Diplock LJ in *Wooldridge v Sumner* [1963] 2 QB 43 at 69, [1962] 2 All ER 978 at 990, CA.
2 'The defendant must prove on the balance of probabilities that the plaintiff did assent ... to exempt the defendant from liability for the negligence which caused this accident. There is no requirement for a contract': per Ackner J in *Bennett v Tugwell* [1971] 2 QB 267 at 274, [1971] 2 All ER 248 at 253. See also *ICI Ltd v Shatwell* [1965] AC 656 at 681, HL, per Lord Hodson.
3 Cf *Burnett v British Waterways Board* [1973] 2 All ER 631, [1973] 1 WLR 700, CA.
4 [1991] 2 QB 6, [1990] 3 All ER 801, CA. Cf *Dann v Hamilton* [1939] 1 KB 509, [1939] 1 All ER 59.
5 [1991] 2 QB 6 at 32, [1990] 3 All ER 801 at 820.
6 See Jaffey 'Volenti Non Fit Injuria' [1985] CLJ 87.
7 See, eg *Owens v Brimmell* [1977] QB 859, [1976] 3 All ER 765.

view.¹ On balance most of the modern case law also does so.² Support for the proposition that something in the nature of a tacit understanding is necessary can also be found in the decision of the House of Lords in *ICI v Shatwell*, ³ in which the defence was actually applied. In this case two shot-firers in a quarry together decided quite deliberately to test an electrical shot-firing circuit in a manner which they knew to be dangerous and contrary to safety regulations. An explosion resulted in which both were injured. One of them subsequently attempted to recover damages from their employer for his injuries, claiming that the company was vicariously liable for the negligence of each of them in their disastrous joint enterprise. The House of Lords held that the maxim volenti non fit injuria would have prevented the men from suing each other, and that there was therefore no basis for the imposition of vicarious liability on their employer. Lord Pearce even invoked the concept of the implied term, from the law of contract, in support of the applicability of volenti, contending that both men would have ridiculed the idea that they would be able to sue each other if the 'officious bystander' had raised it before the accident.⁴ Lord Hodson, similarly, expressly stated that 'the maxim is based on agreement'.⁵ The decision in this case was striking, not least because it applied the defence in the master and servant situation; a context in which many thought that it had in practice long been obsolete. The special facts of the case, however, made it unusually easy to imply the existence of an actual agreement not to sue.⁶ The workmen had deliberately and consciously embarked together on the specific dangerous act which led to the disaster.

Road Traffic Act 1988, s 149(2)

[**4.04**] It is difficult to infer an agreement in a situation where the plaintiff has suffered as the result of a continuing activity, carelessly carried out by the defendant across a period of time.⁷ It did prove possible to make such an implication in a number of cases in which passengers in motor-cars were confronted with explicit disclaimers of liability for accidents,⁸ but these are no longer applicable in their own

---

1   See Jaffey, *op cit*; Glanville Williams, *Joint Torts and Contributory Negligence*, (1951), pp 308ff. For the contrary view see Gordon (1966) 82 LQR 62.
2   But cf the decision of the House of Lords in *Titchener v British Railways Board* [1983] 3 All ER 770, [1983] 1 WLR 1427 where, however, volenti only represented a subordinate ground of decision and the question of the nature of the defence was not really addressed by the House.
3   [1965] AC 656, [1964] 2 All ER 999, HL.
4   See [1965] AC 656 at 688, [1964] 2 All ER 999 at 1013.
5   [1965] AC 656 at 681, [1964] 2 All ER 999 at 1009.
6   See Atiyah 'Causation, Contributory Negligence and Volenti Non Fit Injuria' (1965) 43 Can Bar Rev 609 at 630-631.
7   See, eg *Dann v Hamilton* [1939] 1 KB 509, [1939] 1 All ER 59. But cf *Morris v Murray* [1991] 2 QB 6, [1990] 3 All ER 801, CA.
8   See *Buckpitt v Oates* [1968] 1 All ER 1145; *Bennett v Tugwell* [1971] 2 QB 267, [1971] 2 All ER 248.

context since such disclaimers were nullified by the same legislation which made it compulsory for drivers to carry insurance against the risk of injury to passengers.[1] Regardless of whether volenti is in truth to be seen as based on implied agreement or not, the effect of the provision in question, s 149(2) of the Road Traffic Act 1988, is to strike generally at the applicability of the defence in the context with which it deals, ie it is not confined to explicit disclaimers.[2] The words of the section—

> 'clearly mean that it is no longer open to the driver of a motor vehicle to say that the fact of his passenger travelling in a vehicle in circumstances in which for one reason or another it could be said that he had willingly accepted a risk of negligence on the driver's part relieves him of liability for such negligence'.[3]

Objective test

[4.05] It is obviously not necessary, in order to prove the existence of an 'agreement', to show that there was a complete meeting of minds between the parties in a subjective sense. In one of the motoring cases, *Bennett v Tugwell*,[4] Ackner J put it as follows: 'What is required is an objective approach. Legal inquiry into a person being *volens* is not into what he feels or inwardly consents to, but into what his conduct or words evidence that he is consenting to.' Nevertheless, given the difficulties which, even on this basis, defendants in most situations will have in proving the existence of an agreement, the number of cases in which volenti non fit injuria can be successfully invoked is likely to be very small. It is submitted, moreover, that this is as it should be.

Relationship with the duty of care[5]

[4.06] A question sometimes debated is whether volenti non fit injuria is not really a 'defence' as such but rather a denial that a duty of care was owed, or had been broken: the plaintiff having in the circumstances absolved the defendant from the need to take the usual precautions as far as he was concerned.[6] In fact the issue would appear to be semantic since nothing of substance seems to turn on it,[7] even as

---

1   See now the Road Traffic Act 1988, ss 143 and 149(2).
2   See *Pitts v Hunt* [1991] 1 QB 24, [1990] 3 All ER 344, CA. See also Kevin Williams 'Defences for Drunken Drivers: Public Policy on the Roads and in the Air' (1991) 54 MLR 745.
3   [1991] 1 QB 24 at 48, [1990] 3 All ER 344 at 356 per Beldam L J. See also per Balcombe LJ at 359: '. . . the effect of [the section] is to exclude any defence of volenti which might otherwise be available.'
4   [1971] 2 QB 267 at 273, [1971] 2 All ER 248 at 252.
5   See Richard Kidner 'The variable standard of care, contributory negligence and *volenti*' (1991) 11 LS 1.
6   For discussion of this issue see Jaffey 'Volenti Non Fit Injuria' [1985] CLJ 87 at 104-109.
7   See *Condon v Basi* [1985] 2 All ER 453 at 454, [1985] 1 WLR 866 at 868, CA, per Sir John Donaldson MR: 'I do not think it makes the slightest difference'.

far as pleading is concerned.[1] But for what it is worth, it is submitted that the cause of clarity is likely to be better served by treating volenti as a specific defence in its own right.[2] This approach is less likely to cause confusion in cases in which differing plaintiffs are all adversely affected by the same act of the defendant; but some of them are unable to recover damages by virtue of their having earlier agreed with the defendant that they would not be able to do so. The concept of a defence seems more straightforward in these situations than the notion of differing duties, or standards, of care.[3] Conversely, in situations where questions about the nature of the duty, and standard of care are properly to be regarded as the central issue, analysis in terms of volenti non fit injuria may be unhelpful and misleading. Thus in situations in which participants, or spectators, have been injured at sporting events what will sometimes be called for is an attempt to fashion criteria enabling conduct and behaviour in these rather special circumstances to be appropriately evaluated.[4] The question-begging dismissal of claims on the basis of assumption of risk is hardly likely to be conducive to this.[5]

Contributory negligence

Background

[4.07] The Law Reform (Contributory Negligence) Act 1945, s 1(1) provides as follows:

> 'Where any person suffers damage as the result partly of his own fault and partly of the fault of any other person or persons, a claim in respect of that damage shall not be defeated by reason of the fault of the person suffering the damage, but the damages recoverable in respect thereof shall be reduced to such extent as the court thinks just and equitable having regard to the claimant's share in the responsibility for the damage.'

This provision replaced the old common law rule that contributory negligence was a complete defence. Prior to its abolition that rule led

---

1 '. . . it seems improbable that a court would refuse to allow a defendant who had clearly pleaded the maxim to raise the defence notwithstanding that he may have admitted negligence': Atiyah 'Causation, Contributory Negligence and Volenti non Fit Injuria' (1965) 43 Can Bar Rev 609 at 628.
2 Cf per Fox LJ in *Morris v Murray* [1991] 2 QB 6 at 15, [1990] 3 All ER 801 at 807: 'You may say that [a plaintiff] is volens, or that he has impliedly waived the right to claim or that the [defendant] is impliedly discharged from the normal duty of care. In general, I think that the volenti doctrine can apply to the tort of negligence.'
3 See *Nettleship v Weston* [1971] 2 QB 691, [1971] 3 All ER 581, CA. In *Cook v Cook* (1986) 162 CLR 376 the High Court of Australia adopted the opposite approach and chose not to follow *Nettleship*'s case: sed quaere. For criticism of *Cook v Cook* see Stephen Todd 'The Reasonable Incompetent Driver' (1989) 105 LQR 24.
4 See *Condon v Basi* [1985] 2 All ER 453, [1985] 1 WLR 866, CA; *Wooldridge v Sumner* [1963] 2 QB 43, [1962] 2 All ER 978, CA. See also *Rootes v Shelton* [1968] ALR 33.
5 Cf *Simms v Leigh Rugby Football Club* [1969] 2 All ER 923; *Murray v Harringay Arena Ltd* [1951] 2 KB 529, [1951] 2 All ER 320n, CA.

to the development of an elaborate body of doctrine relating to causation; the objective of much of it being to circumvent the rule and enable plaintiffs to succeed notwithstanding that they had themselves been careless. The possibility of apportionment introduced by the Act rendered the more far-fetched of these refinements in effect obsolete. It remains true, however, that a plaintiff may still wholly fail, and do so on causal grounds, if the court is satisfied that antecedent carelessness by the defendant had lost all its causative potency by the time of the accident so that the plaintiff was in reality the author of his own misfortune.[1] But in practice the availability of apportionment means that the court will normally lean against such a result except in extreme cases. Moreover, a practice whereby the same result was reached indirectly by making a finding of 100% contributory negligence has now been declared impermissible by the Court of Appeal. In *Pitts v Hunt*[2] Beldam LJ said:

> 'Section 1 of the Law Reform (Contributory Negligence) Act 1945 . . . begins with the premise that the person suffers damage as a result partly of his own fault and partly of the fault of any other person or persons. Thus before the section comes into operation, the court must be satisfied that there is fault on the part of both parties which has caused damage. It is expressly provided that the claim shall not be defeated by reason of the fault of the person suffering the damage. To hold that he is himself entirely responsible for the damage effectively defeats his claim. It is then provided that the damages recoverable in respect thereof (that is the damage suffered partly as a result of his own fault and partly the fault of any other person) shall be reduced. It therefore presupposes that the person suffering the damage will receive some damage. Finally reduction is to be to such extent as the court thinks just and equitable, having regard to the claimant's share in the responsibility for the damage. To hold that the claimant is 100% responsible is not to hold that he shared in the responsibility for the damage.'

The court cannot raise the question of contributory negligence by its own motion: the defence has to be specifically pleaded.[3]

[**4.08**] A defendant who alleges contributory negligence does not have to show that the plaintiff owed him a duty of care in the sense in which that expression is used in the context of negligence as a cause of action. In *Froom v Butcher*,[4] Lord Denning MR put it as follows:

> 'Negligence depends on a breach of duty, whereas contributory negligence does not. Negligence is a man's carelessness in breach of duty to *others*. Contributory negligence is a man's carelessness in looking after *his own* safety. He is guilty of *contributory* negligence if he ought reasonably to have foreseen that, if he did not act as a reasonable prudent man, he might hurt himself.'

---

1 See, eg *McKew v Holland and Hannen and Cubitts (Scotland) Ltd* [1969] 3 All ER 1621, HL.
2 [1991] 1 QB 24 at 48, [1990] 3 All ER 344 at 357. See also per Balcombe LJ at 51 and 359 and Dillon LJ at 52 and 359.
3 See *Fookes v Slaytor* [1979] 1 All ER 137, [1978] 1 WLR 1293, CA.
4 [1976] QB 286 at 291 (The italics are those of Lord Denning).

Whether the plaintiff failed to take such care is to be judged in the light of all the circumstances. The court will, for example, be reluctant to hold contributorily negligent a plaintiff who is criticised merely for his actions in the heat of the moment following an emergency created solely by the defendant's carelessness.[1] Similarly, although in clear cases people injured at their places of work may be held to have been contributorily negligent, the court will rarely be prepared to scrutinise in every last detail, in order to detect contributory negligence at the behest of a negligent employer, the conduct of conscientious employees.[2] In two cases it was even suggested that the phrase 'just and equitable' in s 1(1) enabled the court to refuse to make any reduction in the damages even where contributory negligence had been made out.[3] But in the subsequent case of *Boothman v British Northrop*[4] a unanimous Court of Appeal rejected this view.

Basis of apportionment

[4.09] Lord Pearce, in a case decided by the House of Lords in 1967, expressed himself as follows in relation to contributory negligence:[5]
'. . . the investigation is concerned with "fault" which includes blameworthiness as well as causation. And no true apportionment can be reached unless both those factors are borne in mind.'[6]

Causation and blameworthiness are distinct, if sometimes interrelated,[7] concepts. A person may, for example, have been grossly careless and yet his carelessness may have been irrelevant, in the causal sense, to the injuries which he received. A hypothetical instance was given by Singleton L J in *Jones v Livox Quarries Ltd*:[8]

> '... someone ... negligently and improperly sits upon an unsafe wall, and the driver of a motor car not keeping a proper look-out runs into the wall and knocks it down; is the person sitting on the wall, who is injured, guilty of negligence which contributed to the accident? In those circumstances it might well be said he would not be ...'

---

1 Cf *British School of Motoring Ltd v Simms* [1971] 1 All ER 317 at 320-321.
2 See *Machray v Stewarts and Lloyds Ltd* [1964] 3 All ER 716, [1965] 1 WLR 602. See also *Railways Comr v Halley* (1978) 20 ALR 409 (High Court of Australia). Cf *Mullard v Ben Line Steamers Ltd* [1971] 2 All ER 424, [1970] 1 WLR 1414, CA.
3 See *Hawkins v Ian Ross (Castings) Ltd* [1970] 1 All ER 180 at 188 (Fisher J) and *Stocker v Norprint Ltd* (1970) 10 KIR 10 at 14, CA (Phillimore LJ).
4 (1972) 13 KIR 112: see, especially, per Stephenson LJ at 121-122. See also Ian Fagelson 'The Last Bastion of Fault? Contributory Negligence in Actions for Employers' Liability' (1979) 42 MLR 646 at 662-663.
5 *Miraflores (Owners) v George Livanos (Owners)* [1967] 1 AC 826 at 845. Criticism of Lord Pearce's speech in this case on other grounds by Lord Ackner in *Fitzgerald v Lane* [1989] AC 328 at 343-344, [1988] 2 All ER 961 at 969 does not affect this point.
6 See also *Davies v Swan Motor Co (Swansea) Ltd* [1949] 2 KB 291 at 326, CA per Denning LJ. Cf The American Law Institute's *Restatement of the Law of Torts* (2nd edn) para 463: 'Contributory negligence is conduct on the part of the plaintiff which falls below the standard to which he should conform for his own protection, and which is a legally contributing cause co-operating with the negligence of the defendant in bringing about the plaintiff's harm.'
7 See Hart and Honoré *Causation in the Law* (2nd edn) p 234.
8 [1952] 2 QB 608 at 612, CA.

Clearly, the need for the defendant to show that the plaintiff's conduct contributed causally to the accident is logically prior to consideration of the latter's blameworthiness. But causal arguments designed to show that the plaintiff's act had no causal potency at all, or alternatively that the plaintiff was the sole author of his own misfortune, will in practice now seldom find favour with the courts in borderline cases given the existence of the Law Reform (Contributory Negligence) Act 1945. Broadly speaking, if such arguments need to be at all complex or elaborate they will usually be out of place. In *Rouse v Squires*,[1] the defendant negligently caused his lorry to jack-knife and block a motorway. Five to ten minutes later, and after several other vehicles had successfully navigated round the obstruction, a collision occurred when another vehicle came on to the scene at excessive speed and failed to stop in time. Despite strenuous attempts to persuade the Court of Appeal that the original jack-knifing had become causally irrelevant by the time of the collision that court reversed the trial judge, before whom the attempts had been successful, and found the defendant 25% responsible for the accident.[2] If, however, the situation is broadly similar to that which occurred in *Rouse v Squires* except that the later driver who crashed into the wreckage of the earlier accident had actually been driving *recklessly*, and would have avoided causing the second collision if he had *merely* been negligent, then the later driver may be held solely responsible for the second collision.[3]

[4.10] In reaching their figures for apportionment in individual cases the courts rarely separate out causation from blameworthiness. The concepts are interwoven in the largely intuitive process which is involved. It has sometimes been contended by commentators that, once the initial causation requirement is satisfied, blameworthiness should be the only factor used to determine apportionment;[4] on the ground that attempts to evaluate in percentage terms the relative strengths of causal factors which had contributed to an accident would be both artificial and hopelessly complicated.[5] But the better view appears to be that it is possible, on a common sense basis, coherently to assess degrees of causation.[6] In truth, the extent to which causation or blameworthiness predominate in the judicial assessment will vary depending on the facts of each case. If several defendants are involved, for example, the recent insistence by the House of Lords on a rigid separation between the issues of the

---

1   [1973] QB 889, [1973] 2 All ER 903, CA.
2   See also *March v E & M H Stramare Pty Ltd* (1991) 171 CLR 506 (High Court of Australia).
3   See *Wright v Lodge and Shepherd* [1992] NLJR 1269, CA. But cf the decision of the High Court of Australia in *March v E & M H Stramare Pty Ltd* (cited in previous note).
4   See, eg Glanville Williams, *Joint Torts and Contributory Negligence*, (1951) para 98. Cf Fagelson 'The Last Bastion of Fault?' (1979) 42 MLR 646.
5   'Causation itself is difficult enough; degrees of causation really would be a nightmare': S Chapman in (1948) 64 LQR 26 at 28. See also Payne 'Reduction of Damages for Contributory Negligence' (1955) 18 MLR 344 at 353-354.
6   See, eg Hart and Honoré *Causation in the Law*, (2nd edn) p 233. See also Gravells 'Three Heads of Contributory Negligence' (1977) 93 LQR 581 at 595-596.

plaintiff's own contributory negligence on the one hand and the apportionment of the damages as between the defendants themselves on the other,[1] could in practice increase the emphasis upon the plaintiff's blameworthiness in such cases. In less complicated situations, however, it is suggested that causation will often take pride of place where the activities of plaintiff and defendant are very similar, drivers of moving vehicles which collide on the road being the most obvious example. Assuming that both drivers have been careless (without which the question of contributory negligence obviously does not arise) an analysis of the accident in terms of causative potency will perhaps more often be fruitful than one which attempts precisely to categorise on a scale of iniquity the lack of driving skill shown by each party. This will certainly be true if, as in the majority of such cases, both drivers were guilty merely of momentary inattention.[2] On the other hand, blameworthiness is more likely to prove appropriate as the major factor in situations where the activities carried on by plaintiff and defendant were markedly different in nature. An example is provided by the differing roles of employer and employee in a factory. The desirability of treating blameworthiness as the primary criterion in situations of that kind was once clearly expressed by Lord Pearce who said:[3]

> 'A dangerous machine is unfenced and a workman gets his hand caught in it. So far as causation alone is concerned it may be fair to say that at least half the cause of the accident is the fact that the workman put his hand into the danger. But so far as 'fault' (and therefore liability) is concerned the answer may be very different. Suppose that the workman was a normally careful person who, by a pardonable but foolish reaction, wanted to save an obstruction from blocking the machine and so put his hand within the danger area. Suppose further that the factory owner had known that the machine was dangerous and ought to be fenced, that he had been previously warned on several occasions but through dilatoriness or on the grounds of economy failed to rectify the fault and preferred to take a chance. In such a case the judge, weighing the fault of one party against the other, the deliberate negligence against the foolish reaction, would not assess the workman's fault at anything approaching the proportion which causation alone would indicate.'

If there is more than one defendant

[**4.11**] In *Fitzgerald v Lane*,[4] the plaintiff was seriously injured when struck by two cars while attempting to cross a pelican pedestrian crossing when the lights were red for pedestrians. The trial judge, having held that the plaintiff was equally to blame with the two motorists, proceeded to award the plaintiff two-thirds of his damages.

---

1   See *Fitzgerald v Lane* [1989] AC 328, [1988] 2 All ER 961, HL, discussed below.
2   Clearly if one of them was drunk, for example, the position would be different.
3   See *Miraflores (Owners) v George Livanos (Owners)* [1967] 1 AC 826 at 845, [1967] 1 All ER 672 at 678, HL.
4   [1989] AC 328, [1988] 2 All ER 961, HL; affg (on other grounds) [1987] QB 781, [1987] 2 All ER 455, CA.

The Court of Appeal allowed an appeal against his decision, and the House of Lords confirmed the result reached by the Court of Appeal. The judge had confused the extent of the plaintiff's contribution to his own loss with the separate issue of the apportionment of the damages between the defendants. Given his finding that the plaintiff had been equally to blame with the motorists for the accident the judge should only have awarded the plaintiff one-half of his loss and not two-thirds of it. Lord Ackner said:[1]

> 'Apportionment of liability in a case of contributory negligence between plaintiff and defendants must be kept separate from *apportionment of contribution between the defendants inter se*. Although the defendants are each liable to the plaintiff for the whole amount for which he has obtained judgment, the proportions in which, as between themselves, the defendants must meet the plaintiff's claim do not have any direct relationship to the extent to which the total damages have been reduced by the contributory negligence.'

The judge in the present case had erred in—

> 'allowing his judgment on the issue of contributory negligence to be coloured by his decision as to the proper apportionment of blame between the defendants. While stating in substance on the one hand that the plaintiff's responsibility was no more and no less than that of either of the defendants, his ultimate conclusion, as mirrored in his order, was that each of the defendants was twice as much to blame as the plaintiff. This could not be right on the facts'.[2]

In effect, therefore

> 'where the plaintiff successfully sues more than one defendant for damages for personal injuries and there is a claim between co-defendants for contribution, there are two distinct and different stages in the decision-making process, the one in the main action and the other in the contribution proceedings.'[3]

Where the plaintiff contributes to the severity of his damage

[**4.12**] In certain circumstances the damages awarded to a plaintiff may be reduced for contributory negligence even though his carelessness did not contribute to the causing of the accident itself, which would have occurred anyway. The situations in which some reduction will nevertheless be made include those in which the plaintiff's failure to take reasonable safety precautions had the effect of causing him to suffer injuries in an accident from which he would otherwise have escaped without injury, or to suffer injuries more severe than he need have done. The most common instances are failure by motor cyclists to wear crash-helmets, and failure by drivers and passengers in motor cars to wear seat-belts. After some initial judicial disagreement in the lower courts it was established by the

---

1 [1989] AC 328 at 339, [1988] 2 All ER 961 at 965 (the italics are in the original).
2 [1989] AC 328 at 341, [1988] 2 All ER 961 at 966 per Lord Ackner.
3 [1989] AC 328 at 339, [1988] 2 All ER 961 at 966.

Court of Appeal, even before Parliament made the wearing of crash-helmets and seat-belts compulsory, that it was appropriate to reduce damages on the ground of failure in these respects. In *O'Connell v Jackson*,[1] the Court of Appeal reduced by 15% the damages awarded to a motor cyclist who had suffered head injuries in an accident, caused solely by the defendant's negligence, which would have been less severe if he had worn a crash-helmet. In *Froom v Butcher*,[2] the Court of Appeal reduced by 20% the damages awarded to the driver of a motor car in circumstances in which his injuries would have been less severe had he worn his seat-belt. The court in this case also took the opportunity to issue guidelines to promote uniformity in future decisions. Thus if the injuries would have been prevented altogether if a seat-belt had been worn the reduction will be 25%. If the plaintiff would probably have suffered considerable injuries in any event, but their severity would have been reduced, the appropriate reduction will usually be in the region of 15%. Of course if the evidence shows that the wearing of a seat-belt would have made no difference at all, and that the same injuries would have occurred anyway, the defendant will not have made out a case of contributory negligence of the relevant type and no reduction at all will be made.[3] In *Capps v Miller*[4] the Court of Appeal had to consider a case in which a motor-cyclist had been wearing his crash helmet but had carelessly omitted to secure it correctly so that, when he was involved in an accident, it came off before his head hit the ground. 'It seems to me', said Glidewell LJ, 'that in the altered circumstances where a crash helmet is worn but not properly fastened, the whole scale of reduction, because of the lesser blameworthiness, should to an extent be less'.[5] By a majority[6] the court reduced the damages by 10%. Exceptions may also be made to the general rule of deduction itself in special circumstances. Thus, as Lord Denning MR put it in *Froom v Butcher,* 'a man who is unduly fat or a woman who is pregnant may rightly be excused because, if there is an accident, the strap across the abdomen may do more harm than good'.[7] It should finally be noted that claims by passengers that their drivers had been at fault in failing to encourage the wearing of seat-belts will rarely succeed.[8] '(A)dult passengers possessed of their faculties', observed Lord Denning MR in *Froom v Butcher*,[9] 'should not need telling what to do'.

1 [1972] 1 QB 270, [1971] 3 All ER 129, CA. Cf *Hilder v Associated Portland Cement Manufacturers Ltd* [1961] 3 All ER 709, [1961] 1 WLR 1434.
2 [1976] QB 286, [1975] 3 All ER 520, CA.
3 See *Owens v Brimmell* [1977] QB 859, [1976] 3 All ER 765.
4 [1989] 2 All ER 333, [1989] 1 WLR 839, CA.
5 [1989] 3 All ER 333 at 343.
6 Ie Glidewell and May LJJ. Croom-Johnson LJ, dissenting, would have made a 15% reduction.
7 [1976] QB 286 at 295, [1975] 3 All ER 520 at 527. See also *MacKay v Borthwick* 1982 SLT 265.
8 See *Eastman v South West Thames Health Authority* [1991] RTR 389, CA.
9 [1976] QB 286 at 296. See also *Madden v Quirk* [1989] 1 WLR 702 at 708 per Simon Brown J.

General exposure to risk by the plaintiff

[4.13] Another type of case in which a plaintiff may have his damages reduced for contributory negligence, despite his not having contributed in an immediate sense to the causing of the accident itself, occurs where he has knowingly placed himself in an avoidable situation of potential danger.[1] The most typical situation of this kind again involves passengers in motor-vehicles.[2] In *Owens v Brimmell*[3] the plaintiff passenger accompanied the defendant driver on a visit to a series of public houses during which they each consumed at least eight pints of beer. The car subsequently hit a lamp-post due to the defendant's greatly impaired driving, and the plaintiff suffered serious injuries. Tasker Watkins J did, however, reduce the damages awarded by 20% for contributory negligence. Following a review of the relevant Commonwealth authorities his Lordship set out the relevant principles as follows:[4]

> '. . . a passenger may be guilty of contributory negligence if he rides with the driver of a car whom he knows has consumed alcohol in such quantity as is likely to impair to a dangerous degree that driver's capacity to drive properly and safely. So, also, may a passenger be guilty of contributory negligence if he, knowing that he is going to be driven in a car by his companion later, accompanies him on a bout of drinking which has the effect, eventually, of robbing the passenger of clear thought and perception and diminishes the driver's capacity to drive properly and carefully.'

It is to be noted that, as the first part of the quotation makes clear, the principle can apply where the passenger himself, unlike the plaintiff in *Owens v Brimmell*, is in fact sober, and only the driver is drunk, as well as to situations in which both have been drinking. The principle has also been applied in a situation in which the plaintiff passenger knew that the vehicle in which she was travelling was mechanically defective. In *Dawrant v Nutt*[5] the plaintiff rode in the side-car attached to her husband's motor-cycle when she knew that the lights had failed. The damages for the injuries she received in an accident were reduced by 25% for contributory negligence.

Contributory negligence by children

[4.14] In *Gough v Thorne*[6] Lord Denning MR said:

> 'A very young child cannot be guilty of contributory negligence. An older child may be; but it depends on the circumstances. A judge should

---

1 For valuable discussion of this topic, and of contributory negligence generally, see Gravells 'Three Heads of Contributory Negligence' (1977) 93 LQR 581.
2 For a different type of case see *Slater v Clay Cross Co Ltd* [1956] 2 QB 264, [1956] 2 All ER 625, CA.
3 [1977] QB 859, [1976] 3 All ER 765. Cf *Morris v Murray* [1991] 2 QB 6, [1990] 3 All ER 801, CA. See also *Pitts v Hunt* [1991] 1 QB 24, [1990] 3 All ER 344, CA.
4 [1977] QB 859 at 866-867, [1976] 3 All ER 765 at 771.
5 [1960] 3 All ER 681, [1961] 1 WLR 253 (Stable J).
6 [1966] 3 All ER 398 at 399, [1966] 1 WLR 1387 at 1390.

only find a child guilty of contributory negligence if he or she is of such an age as reasonably to be expected to take precautions for his or her own safety: and then he or she is only to be found guilty if blame should be attached to him or her.'

In the case from which this quotation is taken the Court of Appeal, reversing the trial judge, acquitted a 13½-year-old girl from contributory negligence for crossing a busy road in reliance on an indication from a lorry driver, who had waved her across in front of him and signalled following traffic to stop. The plaintiff was hit by an overtaking vehicle, being negligently driven by the defendant, which failed to stop in time. The court rejected as unreasonable the trial judge's view that the plaintiff had been contributorily negligent in relying wholly on the lorry driver's signal, and not making an independent check of her own that the following traffic had stopped. While such prudence and caution 'might reasonably be expected of a grown-up person with a fully developed road sense',[1] it was not to be expected of someone the plaintiff's age. In an earlier case[2] a boy of nine, who told a deliberate lie to buy petrol with which he subsequently caused serious burns to himself while playing 'Red Indians', was acquitted of all contributory negligence by the Judicial Committee of the Privy Council in an action for negligence against the defendant petrol station for having allowed him to have the petrol. The Board considered that the boy's behaviour was only such as could have been expected from a nine year old; but there is some indication in the judgment that a subjective test is appropriate in such cases. Their Lordships indicated that they might have taken a different view if it had been shown, which it had not, that the boy had been specially instructed by his parents about the dangers of petrol.[3]

[4.15] Obviously the older the child is the more ready the court is likely to be, depending upon the circumstances, to make a finding of contributory negligence. The Canadian Supreme Court upheld a finding that a 15-year-old-boy had been 20% contributorily negligent in an accident in a school gymnasium in which he had been seriously injured.[4] In a road accident case involving a 16 and a half year old plaintiff the Court of Appeal, while holding that the trial judge had been wrong to equate the plaintiff with an adult and dismiss his claim altogether, nevertheless assessed damages on the basis of 75% contributory negligence.[5] Findings of contributory negligence towards the lower end of the age range are not, however, unknown. In the case of *Minter v D & H Contractors (Cambridge) Ltd*[6] Tudor Evans J, emphasising that such cases depended purely on their own facts, held

---

1   [1966] 3 All ER 398 at 399, [1966] 1 WLR 1387 at 1391 per Lord Denning MR. See also *Jones v Lawrence* [1969] 3 All ER 267.
2   *Yachuk v Oliver Blais Co Ltd* [1949] AC 386, [1949] 2 All ER 150, PC.
3   See [1949] AC 386 at 396 per Lord Du Parcq delivering the judgment of the Board ('A careful examination of the evidence has satisfied their Lordships that the boy had no knowledge of the peculiarly dangerous quality of gasoline').
4   See *Myers v Peel County Board of Education* (1981) 123 DLR (3d) 1.
5   See *Foskett v Mistry* [1984] RTR 1.
6   (1983) Times 30 June. See also *Speirs v Gorman* [1966] NZLR 897.

74 Assumption of risk, contribution and exclusion

that a nine year old boy, who had suffered injuries while riding his bicycle, was contributorily negligent to the extent of 20%. No other vehicle had been involved in the accident, in which the child had ridden his bicycle into a pile of hardcore left on the road. In *Morales v Eccleston*,[1] an 11-year-old boy was held by the Court of Appeal to have been 80% contributorily negligent when he ran into the road without looking while chasing a ball. In the light of this case it is of interest to note that the *Royal Commission on Civil Liability and Compensation for Personal Injury (Pearson)*[2] recommended that a statutory change in the law should be made. This would be in order to provide 'that the defence of contributory negligence should not be available in cases of motor vehicle injury where the plaintiff was, at the time of the injury, under the age of 12'. No action has been taken on this recommendation.

Contributory negligence and contract

[4.16] The recent decision of the Court of Appeal in *Forsikringsaktieselskapet Vesta v Butcher*[3] has removed much of the uncertainty which formerly surrounded the question of whether a defendant sued for breach of contract could seek apportionment under the provisions of the Law Reform (Contributory Negligence) Act 1945. Prior to the *Butcher* case differing approaches to the problem had been adopted. Some judges of first instance considered that the Act could apply to contract cases,[4] a view which had academic support.[5] Other judges took the opposite view.[6] But the need to consider various *types* of contract claim, as well as the statutory wording itself, militated against the emergence of a general solution.[7] Indeed in a previous case the Court of Appeal treated the question as an open one,[8] notwithstanding that in an earlier decision, albeit one in which the point had not really been argued, that court had itself actually applied the Act in a contractual context.[9] But it can probably now be taken as settled, as a result of the *Butcher* case, that if the defendant's liability in contract depended on his having failed to take reasonable care, and that failure also constituted negligence actionable as such in

---

1 [1991] RTR 151.
2 Cmnd 7054-I, para 1077.
3 [1989] AC 852, [1988] 2 All ER 43, CA; affg [1986] 2 All ER 488 (Hobhouse J).
4 See, eg *Quinn v Burch Bros (Builders) Ltd* [1966] 2 QB 370, [1965] 3 All ER 283, CA (Paull J) and *De Meza and Stuart v Apple, Van Straten, Shena and Stone* [1974] 1 Lloyd's Rep 508 (Brabin J).
5 See Glanville Williams *Joint Torts and Contributory Negligence* (1951), pp 328-329. Cf Jane Swanton, 'Contributory Negligence as a Defence to Actions for Breach of Contract' (1981) 55 ALJ 278.
6 See, especially, *AB Marintrans v Comet Shipping Co Ltd* [1985] 3 All ER 442, [1985] 1 WLR 1270 (Neill LJ sitting as a judge of first instance).
7 See *Basildon District Council v JE Lesser (Properties) Ltd* [1985] QB 839, [1985] 1 All ER 20; *Rowe v Turner, Hopkins & Partners* [1980] 2 NZLR 550; *James Pty Ltd v Duncan* [1970] VR 705.
8 See *De Meza v Apple* [1975] 1 Lloyd's Rep 498, CA.
9 See *Sayers v Harlow UDC* [1958] 2 All ER 342, [1958] 1 WLR 623, CA.

tort, then the Act will apply and apportionment can be sought. This result appears to be sensible. A rigid demarcation between tort and contract would seem mechanistic and outdated today,[1] not least in the expanding field of professional negligence where allegations, amounting in substance to claims that defendants failed to take reasonable care, are often advanced in a contractual context. Thus in *Gran Gelato Ltd v Richcliff (Group) Ltd* [2] Sir Donald Nicholls V-C held that the Law Reform (Contributory Negligence) Act and its apportionment provisions apply to a claim under s 2(1) of the Misrepresentation Act 1967, which is predicated upon the misrepresentor's failure to show that he took reasonable care.[3] If, however, the liability in contract is strict, so that negligence is not a prerequisite, it would seem to be equally clear that the 1945 Act will be inapplicable.[4] Some uncertainty still remains with respect to an intermediate type of case, in which the contractual liability is fault-based but where the situation would, for some reason or other, fall outside the scope of the tort of negligence itself. The balance of existing authority is probably against applicability in such circumstances. But the expansion of tort in recent times, which current more conservative trends have not succeeded wholly in reversing,[5] combined with acceptance of the possibility of concurrent liability in contract and tort,[6] is likely to render the size of the intermediate category relatively small. On the other hand, if the courts were eventually to attempt to undo the move in favour of concurrent liability[7] the whole issue of the applicability of the apportionment legislation in contract cases would once again become prominent.

Contribution between wrongdoers

Where more than one is liable

[**4.17**] As the case of *Fitzgerald v Lane*,[8] discussed above, illustrates, situations sometimes arise in which more than one person is liable to the plaintiff for the loss which he has suffered. Special rules exist to govern the liability of such persons among themselves. In former times it was sometimes important to distinguish 'joint' tortfeasors,

---

1   Nevertheless in the context of the recovery of economic loss the courts unfortunately seem currently to favour differentiation of liability along conceptual lines: see, generally, ch 6 below.
2   [1992] Ch 560, [1992] 1 All ER 865.
3   For comment see Peter Cane 'Negligent Solicitor Escapes Liability' (1992) 108 LQR 539 at 544.
4   Cf *Tennant Radiant Heat Ltd v Warrington Development Corpn* [1988] 1 EGLR 41, CA.
5   See, generally, ch 1 above.
6   See, especially, *Midland Bank Trust Co Ltd v Hett, Stubbs & Kemp* [1979] Ch 384, [1978] 3 All ER 571.
7   See *Tai Hing Cotton Mill Ltd v Liu Chong Hing Bank Ltd* [1986] AC 80 at 107, PC (Lord Scarman delivering the judgment of the Board).
8   [1989] AC 328, [1988] 2 All ER 961, HL.

strictly so-called, from 'several' tortfeasors. The former inflicted damage on the plaintiff in pursuit of a common design, co-conspirators for example, whereas the latter acted separately even though the combined effect of their actions was to inflict on the plaintiff the loss of which he complained.[1] It will be apparent that in negligence cases the latter type of situation is much more common than the former, such as where a passenger is injured in a collision between two careless motorists. In cases of vicarious liability, however, master and servant are regarded as joint tortfeasors. But although this distinction between joint and several tortfeasors had certain consequences at common law,[2] these have largely ceased, mainly through statutory intervention, to be of practical significance in negligence cases. In *either* type of situation every individual tortfeasor is potentially liable in full to the plaintiff for the loss incurred, and they can also all be joined in one action. The statutory rules now to be considered provide for the recovery of contribution towards that liability as between the persons responsible for infliction of the loss.

When contribution can be claimed

[**4.18**] The Civil Liability (Contribution) Act 1978 now governs the circumstances in which a defendant who is liable to a plaintiff, whether in negligence or otherwise, can by statute recover contribution from someone else whom he claims is also responsible, as well as himself, for the loss which the plaintiff has suffered. The statute law on this subject was previously to be found in the Law Reform (Married Women and Tortfeasors) Act 1935 s 6 which originally abrogated the old common law rule whereby contribution between tortfeasors was, in general, forbidden on the ground that a person should not be able to make a cause of action out of his own wrong. The 1978 Act, which followed an investigation of the subject by the Law Commission,[3] replaced the 1935 Act in this regard and also significantly increased the scope of the relevant provisions. The most important change is that contribution can now be sought from someone else who is responsible for the same damage even though the legal basis of that other person's liability is different.[4] The 1935 Act only provided that tortfeasors could claim contribution from other tortfeasors, but it can now be sought as between eg a tortfeasor and someone liable to the plaintiff in contract.[5] Alongside this change the

---

1 Clearly, if the loss inflicted by one defendant is itself separate from that inflicted by another, the tortfeasors will be neither joint nor several and each one will simply be liable for the loss which he inflicted: see, eg *Performance Cars Ltd v Abraham* [1962] 1 QB 33, [1961] 3 All ER 413, CA.
2 For a concise account see *Winfield on Tort*, (13th edn) pp 591-592.
3 See Law Commission Report No 79 (1977).
4 The 1978 Act clearly has no retrospective effect: see s 7(2). This section fell to be construed by the Court of Appeal in *Lampitt v Poole Borough Council* [1991] 2 QB 545, [1990] 2 All ER 887 where the court was able to reject an ingenious argument that it had inadvertently had a further and unintended consequence of *removing* rights to contribution which would otherwise have existed.
5 See ss 1(1) and 6(1) of the 1978 Act.

1978 Act makes of general application the removal, made originally by the 1935 Act itself but confined by that Act to situations involving joint tortfeasors, of the old common law doctrine whereby even an unsatisfied judgment was a bar to recovery against another person jointly liable for the same loss. In thus broadening the scope of the abrogation of that harsh rule the new Act also took the opportunity to make clear that the removal of the bar extended to situations in which judgment is obtained against one of a number of defendants sued in a single action, as well as to those in which the plaintiff brought successive actions:[1] a point which the wording of the 1935 Act had left somewhat unclear.[2] On the other hand if the plaintiff actually reaches an agreement with one joint tortfeasor, and that agreement is construed as a 'release' of the plaintiff's cause of action as distinct from a mere covenant not to sue the particular defendant, then the common law rule that such an agreement releases all the tortfeasors jointly liable remains intact and is unaffected by the Act. The Law Commission decided against recommending the abolition of this rule even though the technical distinction to which it gives rise, between releases[3] and covenants not to sue,[4] can lead to decisions being reached which turn on fine points of construction and which may have unintended consequences.[5] Since, however, a release of one 'several', as distinct from 'joint' tortfeasor does not, even at common law, release the other several tortfeasors[6] the point will rarely be material in negligence cases apart from those involving vicarious liability.

Claim for contribution against a defendant no longer liable to the plaintiff

[**4.19**] Section 1(3) of the 1978 Act provides that a wrongdoer who has ceased to be liable to the plaintiff himself, eg because of the expiry of the limitation period[7] or dismissal of an action for want of prosecution,[8] can nevertheless be called upon to make contribution by another wrongdoer who is actually liable to the plaintiff.[9] The other wrongdoer's claim for contribution will only fail in such circumstances

---

1 'Judgment recovered against any person liable in respect of any debt or damage shall not be a bar to an action, or to the continuance of an action, against any other person who is (apart from any such bar) jointly liable with him in respect of the same debt or damage': s 3.
2 Cf *Bryanston Finance Ltd v de Vries* [1975] QB 703 at 722 per Lord Denning MR; *Wah Tat Bank Ltd v Chan Cheng Kum* [1975] AC 507, [1975] 2 All ER 257, PC.
3 See, eg *Cutler v McPhail* [1962] 2 QB 292, [1962] 2 All ER 474.
4 See, eg *Gardiner v Moore* [1969] 1 QB 55, [1966] 1 All ER 365.
5 See Law Commission Report No 79 (1977), paras 42-43. See also Morgan, 'Civil Liability (Contribution) Act 1978' (1978) NLJ 1042.
6 The reason for this is that there is a separate cause of action against each 'several' tortfeasor, but only one cause of action against joint tortfeasors.
7 Cf *George Wimpey & Co Ltd v BOAC* [1955] AC 169, [1954] 3 All ER 661, HL; *Nottingham Health Authority v Nottingham City Council* [1988] 1 WLR 903, CA.
8 Cf *Hart v Hall and Pickles Ltd* [1969] 1 QB 405, [1968] 3 All ER 291, CA.
9 'A person shall be liable to make contribution . . . notwithstanding that he has ceased to be liable in respect of the damage in question since the time when the damage occurred . . .'

if that claim is itself barred by limitation.[1] It follows that a defendant who has previously reached a settlement (but not a 'release'[2]) with the plaintiff whereby the latter promised not to sue him, may nevertheless be called upon to make contribution by another defendant against whom the plaintiff has proceeded.[3]

Claim for contribution by a defendant who has settled

[**4.20**] Section 1(4) of the Act of 1978 provides as follows:

> 'A person who has made or agreed to make any payment in bona fide settlement or compromise of any claim made against him in respect of any damage (including a payment into court which has been accepted) shall be entitled to recover contribution . . . without regard to whether or not he himself is or ever was liable in respect of the damage, provided, however, that he would have been liable assuming that the factual basis of the claim against him could be established.'

This subsection encourages settlements by making it unnecessary for one defendant to fight a claim against him to the finish in order to ensure that his rights to contribution against other wrongdoers are not prejudiced. The position as between joint tortfeasors before the passing of the 1978 Act was that a defendant who had compromised the plaintiff's claim could seek contribution from another party, but would fail in his attempt unless he was able, in the contribution proceedings, to achieve the paradoxical task of proving that he had indeed been himself a tortfeasor who could have been sued to judgment.[4] Such proof is no longer required. The reference in the subsection to the need for the settlement to be bona fide should, however, be noted. Collusive or fraudulent agreements between plaintiff and defendant, whereby the latter deliberately settles the claim for more than it is worth in the hope of passing on a major share of the burden to someone else, will obviously not be effective for contribution purposes.[5]

Conclusiveness of judgments

[**4.21**] If the plaintiff himself had earlier brought an action against the defendant from whom contribution is subsequently sought by another party, and that action had proceeded to judgment, then the judgment thus given will be conclusive on any question determined by it in favour of the defendant. Thus someone who has, for example, been acquitted of negligence after trial on the merits cannot be subjected to having that finding reopened in contribution proceedings. This is achieved by s 1(5) of the 1978 Act which provides as follows:

---

1   The relevant period is two years: see the Limitation Act 1980, s 10.
2   See above.
3   See *Logan v Uttlesford District Council* [1986] NLJ Rep 541, CA.
4   See *Stott v West Yorkshire Road Car Co Ltd* [1971] 2 QB 651, [1971] 3 All ER 534, CA.
5   Cf *Corvi v Ellis* 1969 SLT 350.

'A judgment given in any action brought in any part of the United Kingdom by or on behalf of the person who suffered the damage in question against any person from whom contribution is sought... shall be conclusive in the proceedings for contribution as to any issue determined by that judgment in favour of the person from whom the contribution is sought.'

[**4.22**] If the 'judgment' is merely a dismissal on procedural grounds, sub-s (5) will presumably not apply and s 1(3), which preserves rights to contribution, will apply instead. It has been suggested,[1] however, that this is far from self-evident and that there could in fact be a conflict between sub-ss (3) and (5), particularly with respect to limitation. The wide words 'any issue' in the latter subsection could, taken literally, prevent a defendant who secured dismissal of the plaintiff's claim against him on the ground that it was statute-barred, from being held liable in contribution proceedings. Whereas sub-s (3) provides, as explained above, that limitation as against the plaintiff, at any rate where no actual judgment was involved, should not be a bar in such proceedings. But the solution is probably that sub-s (5) should be read subject to sub-s (3), so that a judgment based solely on limitation will not constitute determination of an issue within sub-s (5).

Abolition of the 'sanction in damages'

[**4.23**] Under the provisions of the 1935 Act a plaintiff who chose to bring more than one action in respect of the damage he had suffered (for example because not all the tortfeasors had been traced when he first commenced proceedings so that it was not possible to sue them together) was unable to recover by execution a higher sum than the damages awarded in the first action, even though the amounts actually awarded in the subsequent actions might have been higher. This 'sanction in damages' reflected a fear that multiplicity of proceedings might otherwise be encouraged, particularly at a time when juries normally assessed damages in civil actions so that plaintiffs might have been encouraged to 'shop around' for higher awards. But the rule could operate unfairly if, for example, the first defendant to be sued enjoyed some special limitation on his liability which those sued later did not. The Law Commission concluded that this sanction was no longer appropriate in modern circumstances and it has accordingly been abolished by the 1978 Act.[2] The new Act does retain a 'sanction in costs', which was also included in the 1935 Act. The Law Commission considered that this was an adequate deterrent against the avoidable bringing of a series of actions. Section 4 accordingly provides as follows:

'If more than one action is brought in respect of any damage by or on behalf of the person by whom it was suffered against persons liable in

---

1 See *Clerk and Lindsell on Torts* (16th edn) p 186.
2 This is the effect of the wording of s 4, quoted below, being narrower than the wording of the equivalent provision in the 1935 Act which it replaced.

respect of the damage (whether jointly or otherwise) the plaintiff shall not be entitled to costs in any of those actions, other than that in which judgment is first given, unless the court is of the opinion that there was reasonable ground for bringing the action.'

It should be noted that the abolition of the 'sanction in damages' obviously 'does not . . . mean that the plaintiff should be allowed to enforce judgments twice over for the same damages but simply that the amount for which one defendant may be adjudged liable should not set a limit on the sum for which judgment may be enforced against another'.[1]

Assessment of contribution

[**4.24**] Sections 2(1) and (2) of the 1978 Act in substance reproduce an equivalent provision in the 1935 Act. Subsection (1) provides that the amount recoverable in contribution proceedings 'shall be such as may be found by the court to be just and equitable having regard to the extent of that person's responsibility for the damage in question'. Subsection (2) gives the court power 'to exempt any person from liability to make contribution, or to direct that the contribution to be recovered shall amount to a complete indemnity'.[2] The 'just and equitable' formula is, of course, the same as that used in the Law Reform (Contributory Negligence) Act 1945. The theoretical questions concerning the relationship between causation and blameworthiness, for the purposes of apportionment, are the same in both contexts.[3] At the practical level, however, the Law Commission felt able to conclude that the existing formula 'had given rise to no difficulties or injustices in contribution proceedings between tortfeasors'[4] and it was therefore retained in the new legislation.

Where a contributor's liability to the plaintiff is limited

[**4.25**] Situations may arise in which some of those who have contributed to the plaintiff's damage enjoy a limitation on their liability to him which the other contributors do not.[5] For example, since the 1978 Act enables contribution to be sought as between tortfeasors and contract-breakers, the contract-breaker may point to some special clause in his contract which limits his liability to the plaintiff to a certain sum: and that sum may be less than he would otherwise be required, if the limiting clause were to be disregarded, to

---

1 Law Commission Report No 79 (1977) para 41.
2 See, eg *Semtex Ltd v Gladstone* [1954] 2 All ER 206, [1954] 1 WLR 945. See also *Lister v Romford Ice and Cold Storage* [1955] AC 555 at 579-80, HL, per Lord Simonds.
3 See *Madden v Quirk* [1989] 1 WLR 702, especially at 707 (Simon Brown J).
4 Law Commission Report No 79 (1977) para 69. But cf Hervey ' "Responsibility" under the Civil Liability (Contribution) Act 1978' (1979) 129 NLJ 509 at 510: 'If the courts are presented with a case requiring an apportionment, they will respond by providing a set of percentages. But the process by which these percentages are achieved has never been adequately elucidated.'
5 See Law Commission Report No 79 (1977) paras 70-79.

contribute on apportionment. Conversely, a defendant who was a contract-breaker could sometimes be at a *disadvantage* as against a defendant who was a tortfeasor. This would happen if the plaintiff himself had been contributorily negligent, but the defendant's contractual liability happened to be strict in which event contributory negligence is probably not a defence.[1] The tortfeasor will then be able to rely on the contributory negligence to limit the extent of his liability to the plaintiff, but the contract-breaker will not. The 1978 Act does indeed provide that any such advantages which a defendant could rely on as against the plaintiff will also apply as between himself and the other contributors. A defendant cannot, therefore, be required to contribute on apportionment a greater sum than that for which he could have been held liable to the plaintiff directly. This may seem unfair to the other contributors, who will as a result shoulder a greater share of the overall burden of the liability to the plaintiff than they otherwise would have done. On the other hand it might also have seemed unfair to deny in contribution proceedings the benefits of limitations on liability which otherwise existed; and the Act refuses to do so. Section 2(3) of the Act, which is a new provision, accordingly provides as follows:

> 'Where the amount of the damages which have or might have been awarded in respect of the damage in question in any action brought in England and Wales by or on behalf of the person who suffered it against the person from whom the contribution is sought was or would have been subject to—
> (a) any limit imposed by or under any enactment or by any agreement made before the damage occurred;
> (b) any reduction by virtue of section 1 of the Law Reform (Contributory Negligence) Act 1945 or section 5 of the Fatal Accidents Act 1976; or
> (c) any corresponding limit or reduction under the law of a country outside England and Wales;
> the person from whom the contribution is sought shall not by virtue of any contribution awarded . . . be required to pay in respect of the damage a greater amount than the amount of those damages as so limited or reduced.'

Exclusion of liability

Exclusion by contract

[4.26] The freedom of contracting parties to limit their liability to each other in tort for negligence has, over the years, gradually been restricted by legislative intervention in various fields.[2] The most widespread of such restrictions were imposed by the Unfair Contract Terms Act 1977. The provisions of this Act severely limit the extent to

---

1 See discussion above.
2 See, eg the Road Traffic Act 1960, s 151 and the Transport Act 1962, s 43(7) which prevent public transport operators from contracting out of liability to their passengers for death or bodily injury.

which 'business' defendants can rely on exemption clauses in their contracts to exclude liability. Such defendants cannot exclude liability for 'death or personal injury resulting from negligence'[1] at all, and attempts by them to exclude liability for negligence in other cases are subject to a test of 'reasonableness'.[2] Of course, a plaintiff will not even need to rely on the provisions of the Act if the defendant is unable to show that the clause was incorporated into the contract at all;[3] or if the strict rules of construction applied to exemption clauses by the common law prevent the wording of the clause from being effective to exclude negligence liability in the first place.[4] Moreover, the common law learning on exemption clauses remains of general importance in cases which fall outside the terms of the Unfair Contract Terms Act because the defendant relying on the clause is not a 'business'.[5]

Non-contractual disclaimers[6]

[4.27] It is well-established at common law that, in certain situations, a defendant can exclude his liability in tort for negligence by a mere notice or disclaimer to that effect, even though it does not form part of an actual contract. The best-known situations are those involving the liability for negligent misstatement established by *Hedley Byrne & Co Ltd v Heller & Partners Ltd*,[7] and the liability of an occupier to his visitors.[8] No general principle underlying these instances, capable of application throughout the law of negligence, has ever been clearly enunciated. They do, however, in themselves possess a strong 'contractual flavour', even if the technical requirements such as offer and acceptance are not satisfied. Thus if a defendant attempts gratuitously to assist the plaintiff by making a statement intended for the latter's benefit, or by permitting him to enter the defendant's property when he could be kept out, it is perhaps not unreasonable that the generosity should be accompanied by conditions limiting the defendant's liability for misfortune. Such situations represent an area on the borderline between contract and tort, in which the very distinction between these two concepts is itself under strain.[9] It is therefore submitted that a mere exclusion notice should not be effective to exclude liability for negligence unless the situation is, in fact, closely analogous to contract in that the disclaimer is accompanied by some benefit conferred upon the plaintiff which the

---

1 See s 2(1).
2 See ss 2(2) and 11(1).
3 Cf *Olley v Marlborough Court Ltd* [1949] 1 KB 532, [1949] 1 All ER 127, CA.
4 See, eg *White v John Warrick & Co Ltd* [1953] 2 All ER 1021, [1953] 1 WLR 1285, CA. Cf *Photo Production Ltd v Securicor Transport* [1980] AC 827, [1980] 1 All ER 556, HL.
5 See ss 1 and 14.
6 See also ch 5, below, for further discussion of disclaimers in the context of negligent misstatement.
7 [1964] AC 465, [1963] 2 All ER 575, HL. See, generally, below, ch 5.
8 See below, ch 16.
9 Cf *Junior Books Ltd v Veitchi Co Ltd* [1983] 1 AC 520, [1982] 3 All ER 201, HL (especially at 546, 214 per Lord Roskill).

latter has a choice whether or not to accept.[1] To hold otherwise would surely be contrary to principle: the law of tort exists for the benefit of society in general, and it cannot be right to allow defendants of their own motion unilaterally to declare themselves independent of it.[2]

Disclaimers and privity of contract

[4.28] The fact that issues involving disclaimers frequently arise in territory surrounding the border between tort and contract is also illustrated by two recent decisions of the Court of Appeal. In both cases plaintiffs who had suffered damage while engaged in activities arising out of their contractual relationships sought unsuccessfully to sue in tort defendants who were not parties to the contracts in question. In *Norwich City Council v Harvey*[3] the Court of Appeal in effect permitted a defendant sub-contractor, whose negligence had caused a fire, to invoke an exemption clause in the plaintiff's agreement with the main contractor, for the erection of a building, which would clearly have protected the latter if the damage had been caused by him. May LJ said[4] that the question had to be approached 'on the basis of what [was] just and reasonable' and he did 'not think that the mere fact that there [was] no strict privity between the employer and the sub-contractor should prevent the latter from relying on the clear basis on which all the parties contracted in relation to damage to the employer's building caused by fire, even when due to the negligence of the contractors or sub-contractors'. Similarly, in *Pacific Associates Inc v Baxter*[5] the question whether the defendant owed a duty of care to the plaintiff in a claim for negligent misstatement was said only to be answerable 'in the context of the factual matrix, including especially the contractual structure against which such duty [was] said to arise'.[6] That that structure included a disclaimer intended to protect the defendant was one of the reasons which led the Court of Appeal to find in his favour even though he was not himself a party to the contract.

Relationship with volenti non fit injuria

[4.29] It was suggested at the beginning of this chapter that the maxim volenti non fit injuria will only take effect when there was at least a tacit or implied agreement between plaintiff and defendant, whereby the former agreed to release the latter from liability. If this contention is correct it will be apparent that there is a close connection between that defence and exclusion of liability by disclaimer,

---

1 See, eg *Wilkie v London Passenger Transport Board* [1947] 1 All ER 258, CA. Cf *Gore v Van der Lann* [1967] 2 QB 31, [1967] 1 All ER 360, CA.
2 Cf LCB Gower 'A Tortfeasor's Charter?' (1956) 19 MLR 532 and 'Tortfeasor's Charter Upheld' (1957) 20 MLR 181.
3 [1989] 1 All ER 1180, [1989] 1 WLR 828, CA.
4 [1989] 1 All ER 1180 at 1187.
5 [1989] 2 All ER 159, CA.
6 [1989] 2 All ER 159 at 171, per Purchas LJ.

particularly if the analysis of the latter suggested above[1] is also correct. Indeed, it may well be that in many cases in which the defendant is treated as having succeeded specifically by virtue of a disclaimer the same result could have been reached by analysing the situation, including the disclaimer, as one in which the plaintiff was volens. Nevertheless, it is probably still useful to regard the two defences as conceptually distinct, for two reasons. Firstly, if the disclaimer merely took the form of a notice issued to persons generally the court may be reluctant to give effect to it unless its position had been very prominent and its wording had been clear and precise. By contrast, if the plaintiff and defendant dealt personally with each other the court may be prepared, as some of the volenti decisions show,[2] to infer the existence of an agreement which was never even made explicit. In this sense the paradigm volenti case involves that defence being easier to establish than disclaimer, when the latter defence is based merely on a general notice. Secondly and more importantly, however, if it is true that some element of 'benefit to the plaintiff' is necessary to make a disclaimer as such effective, then this also constitutes a distinguishing factor. Perhaps, indeed, the relationship between these two factors, and in truth the defences themselves, is a reciprocal one. The more general the disclaimer the more specific and tangible the benefit to the plaintiff will need to be before it can be effective. Conversely, as the degree of specific (even if implied) agreement between plaintiff and defendant increases, so the need for any 'benefit' to the former is reduced until, in what might be termed 'pure' volenti cases such as *ICI Ltd v Shatwell*,[3] it reaches vanishing point.

Non-contractual disclaimers and the Unfair Contract Terms Act

[**4.30**] It is submitted that the analysis in the previous paragraph, of the relationship between disclaimers and the defence of volenti, helps to explain a somewhat obscure sub-section of the Unfair Contract Terms Act 1977. Section 2(3) of that Act provides, where relevant, as follows: 'Where a ... notice purports to exclude or restrict liability for negligence a person's agreement to or awareness of it is not of itself to be taken as indicating his voluntary acceptance of any risk.' The provision may be taken to mean that if the disclaimer is merely a general notice, then it will not be effective to exclude liability for negligence (if the defendant is a 'business') unless specifically accompanied by some recognisable quid pro quo to the plaintiff.[4]

1 Ie in para [**4.27**].
2 See, eg *ICI Ltd v Shatwell* [1965] AC 656, [1964] 2 All ER 999, HL. See also *Bennett v Tugwell* [1971] 2 QB 267, [1971] 2 All ER 248.
3 See previous note.
4 An admitted difficulty with the suggested interpretation is that the subsection also refers to 'contract terms', whereas a case in which the technical requirements of the doctrine of consideration are satisfied, would seem a fortiori to come within the proposed 'benefit to plaintiff' doctrine. But perhaps in the contract field the legislature was simply concerned to prevent a defendant from invoking the volenti doctrine merely by pointing to some obscure exclusion clause buried in a standard form contract.

Applicability of the Act

[**4.31**] More generally, as s 2(3) itself indeed illustrates, it is of course important to remember that, despite its name, the provisions of the Unfair Contract Terms Act are not confined to the law of contract. Non-contractual disclaimers also fall within its scope. Thus businesses cannot by 'a notice given to persons generally or to particular persons exclude or restrict' their 'liability for death or personal injury resulting from negligence'.[1] In the case of 'other loss or damage'[2] the non-contractual notice has to satisfy the reasonableness test if the defendant is a 'business'. It is in effect left to the courts themselves to fashion the criteria for the application of that test in this context. The relevant provision of the Act, s 11(3), merely provides as follows:

> 'In relation to a notice (not being a notice having contractual effect), the requirement of reasonableness under this Act is that it should be fair and reasonable to allow reliance on it, having regard to all the circumstances obtaining when the liability arose or (but for the notice) would have arisen.'

In *Smith v Eric S Bush*[3] the House of Lords applied the Unfair Contract Terms Act and invalidated a disclaimer contained in a survey report which had been produced by a building society's surveyor and relied upon by the plaintiff house purchaser.[4]

---

1 See s 2(1).
2 Section 2(2).
3 [1990] 1 AC 831, [1989] 2 All ER 514.
4 See further, ch 5 below.

Part two

Negligence and economic interests

Chapter 5

Liability for negligent misstatement

The impact of *Hedley Byrne*[1]

The concept of the 'special relationship'

[**5.01**] Prior to the decision in *Hedley Byrne & Co Ltd v Heller & Partners Ltd*,[2] the law of tort did not impose liability for careless words which had caused the plaintiff to suffer financial loss, unless there was a fiduciary relationship between the parties,[3] or unless fraud was proved.[4] Liability for careless words causing physical injury was, however, recognised.[5] In *Hedley Byrne* itself, the House of Lords held that bankers who carelessly gave a favourable reference, about one of their customers, to another bank could in principle be liable in negligence to a customer of the inquiring bank for losses thereby suffered.[6] The defendant bank in fact escaped liability, however, because they had issued a disclaimer with their advice declaring it to be given 'without responsibility'. The precise effect of the change in the law brought about by this decision was a source of considerable uncertainty, much of which still remains 30 years later. This uncertainty was caused partly by the fact that the members of the House interwove in their speeches the two separate questions of the legal principles relating to a certain type of *conduct*, ie the making of negligent statements, with those relating to liability for a certain kind

---

1 See, generally, Peter Cane *Tort Law and Economic Interests* (1991). See also AJE Jaffey *The Duty of Care* (1992), Part III.
2 [1964] AC 465, [1963] 2 All ER 575, HL.
3 *Nocton v Lord Ashburton* [1914] AC 932, HL.
4 *Derry v Peek* (1889) 14 App Cas 337, HL. Cf *Commercial Banking Co of Sydney v Brown & Co* [1972] 2 Lloyd's Rep 360 (High Court of Australia).
5 See, eg *Clayton v Woodman & Son (Builders) Ltd* [1962] 2 QB 533, [1961] 3 All ER 249: advice by an architect (claim failed on the facts).
6 For a recent decision of the Privy Council, concerning a situation closely resembling that in *Hedley Byrne v Heller*, see *Royal Bank Trust Co (Trinidad) Ltd v Pampellonne* [1987] 1 Lloyd's Rep 218. The claim against the defendant bank failed on the facts, but the decision was by a bare majority (Lords Bridge, Oliver and Goff) of the Judicial Committee. The dissentients (Lord Templeman and Sir Robin Cooke) asserted that: 'The opinion of the majority of the Board ... seems to depart in spirit, if not in express words, from the approach in leading cases of recent times, such as *Hedley Byrne*.' [1987] 1 Lloyd's Rep at 229.

90 Liability for negligent misstatement

of *harm* ie pure economic loss (as distinct from physical injury and losses consequent thereupon).[1] It so happened in *Hedley Byrne* itself that both questions arose, but in other situations they can obviously arise independently (ie a negligent misstatement may give rise to physical injury and negligent action may give rise to economic loss). One thing which did emerge clearly from the speeches, however, was that the House of Lords was anxious to limit the extent of the newly created liability for misstatement by requiring a 'special relationship' between the parties before it could arise.[2] This would involve 'reliance' upon the defendant by the plaintiff, with the former being aware that that reliance existed.[3] This was, of course, a narrower approach than that adopted to the problem of careless acts in *Donoghue v Stevenson*,[4] where, in general, the objective concept of the foreseeability of the reasonable man is usually sufficient to give rise to liability. The nature of the 'special relationship' concept has been a source of controversy in subsequent cases. In one case the requirement was used as a device sharply to limit the scope of liability for negligent misstatement.[5] But the effect of other decisions has been to extend liability to situations in which the plaintiff cannot meaningfully be said to have 'relied' on the defendant.[6] All previous cases in this area now have to be considered in the light of the decision of the House of Lords in *Caparo Industries plc v Dickman*,[7] which is discussed later in this chapter.

Is there a need for special skills?

[5.02] In *Mutual Life and Citizens' Assurance Co Ltd v Evatt*[8] the plaintiff sought advice from the defendant company about the safety of investments in another company, which was a subsidiary company of the same organisation as that to which the defendant company itself belonged. By a bare majority[9] the Judicial Committee of the Privy Council held that the plaintiff would fail since the defendant company did not hold itself out as having any special skill and competence in giving advice on investments, and that possession by the defendant of a special skill was a general, though not exclusive,[10]

---

1 See, eg [1964] AC 465 at 509 (Lord Hodson); 517 (Lord Devlin); 538 (Lord Pearce).
2 See [1964] AC 465 at 483, 486 (Lord Reid); 502-503 (Lord Morris); 511 (Lord Hodson); 528-529 (Lord Devlin: 'circumstances in which, but for the absence of consideration, there would be a contract'); 539 (Lord Pearce).
3 See [1964] AC 465 at 486 (Lord Reid); 497 (Lord Morris); 514 (Lord Hodson).
4 [1932] AC 562.
5 See *Mutual Life and Citizens' Assurance Co Ltd v Evatt* [1971] AC 793, [1971] 1 All ER 150, PC (discussed below).
6 See *Ministry of Housing and Local Goverment v Sharp* [1970] 2 QB 223, [1970] 1 All ER 1009, CA; *Ross v Caunters* [1980] Ch 297, [1979] 3 All ER 580.
7 [1990] 2 AC 605, [1990] 1 All ER 568.
8 [1971] AC 793, [1971] 1 All ER 150.
9 Lord Hodson, Guest and Diplock (Lords Reid and Morris dissenting).
10 See the treatment, discussed below, by the majority (in [1971] AC 793 at 809, [1971] 1 All ER 150 at 161) of the case of *WB Anderson & Sons Ltd v Rhodes (Liverpool) Ltd* [1967] 2 All ER 850.

condition for the existence of a 'special relationship'.[1] If it had been followed, the decision would have severely limited the impact of *Hedley Byrne*. Significantly, however, two of the three members of the Board in *Evatt* who had also been members of the House of Lords which decided *Hedley Byrne* itself,[2] dissented, asserting that a limitation of the new liability to persons possessing special skills had not been envisaged when the earlier case was decided. Subsequently there were judicial expressions of dislike in the Court of Appeal for the principle in *Evatt*'s case[3] and the better view would therefore seem to be that the case does not now represent English law. But in view of the prevailing conservative mood among the judiciary a return to the restrictive approach in *Evatt* cannot be entirely ruled out.[4]

Types of misstatement

[5.03] Negligent misstatement can take many different forms. The most obvious type of case is a careless response to a request for a specific piece of information, as in *Hedley Byrne* itself. But it also includes careless advice and evaluation in situations requiring special skill, and extends to professional activities of a more positive nature such as the carrying out of an audit on a company[5] or the preparation of maps[6] and charts[7] and the like. It might also be taken to include cases of negligent design, eg of buildings,[8] or of cranes[9] and other complex pieces of machinery.[10]

---

1 'The carrying on of a business or profession which involves the giving of advice of a kind which calls for special skill and competence is the normal way in which a person lets it be known to the recipient of the advice that he claims to possess that degree of skill and competence and is willing to exercise that degree of diligence which is generally possessed and exercised by persons who carry on the business or profession of giving advice of the kind sought': [1971] AC 793 at 805, per Lord Diplock delivering the judgment of the majority.
2 Ie Lord Reid and Lord Morris.
3 See *Esso Petroleum Co Ltd v Mardon* [1976] QB 801 at 827, [1976] 2 All ER 5 at 22 per Ormrod LJ; *Howard Marine and Dredging Co Ltd v Ogden & Sons (Excavations) Ltd* [1978] QB 574 at 591 (Lord Denning MR) and 600 (Shaw LJ). See also *L. Shaddock & Associates v Parramatta City Council* [1979] 1 NSWLR 566 566 at 586 per Hutley J A: 'The judgment of the majority has given almost universal dissatisfaction both to courts and to the learned.'
4 In *Caparo Industries plc v Dickman* [1990] 2 AC 605 at 637, [1990] 1 All ER 568 at 588 Lord Oliver observed that it was unnecessary in that case to express a view as to the correctness of *Mutual Life v Evatt* since *Caparo* involved something done in the ordinary course of the defendants' business (ie the certification of accounts by auditors).
5 See, eg *Caparo Industries plc v Dickman* [1990] 2 AC 605, [1990] 1 All ER 568, HL.
6 Cf *Post Office v Mears Construction Ltd* [1979] 2 All ER 813.
7 See, eg *Caltex Oil (Australia) Pty Ltd v Dredge Willemstad* (1976) 136 CLR 529.
8 See *Rimmer v Liverpool City Council* [1985] QB 1, [1984] 1 All ER 930, CA.
9 See, eg *Rivtow Marine Ltd v Washington Ironworks* (1973) 40 DLR (3d) 530.
10 See *Hindustan Steam Shipping Co Ltd v Siemens Bros & Co* [1955] 1 Lloyd's Rep 167 at 177, per Willmer J (design of ship's engine-room telegraph). Cf *Lexmead (Basingstoke) Ltd v Lewis* [1982] AC 225 (defective coupling mechanism for towing vehicles on the road).

Difficulties which can arise

[5.04] The difficulties which arise in this branch of the law stem essentially from the fear that the ease with which words can be disseminated could lead to the imposition of liability in a manner absurd as well as oppressive if 'foreseeability' alone was the relevant criterion. Thus the extent to which third parties, to whom the defendant did not actually address his statement, may sue in respect of it, is a particularly sensitive area and one which raises fundamental questions as to the nature of the underlying principles involved. Questions have also been raised as to the potential liability of professional people for casual remarks made on social occasions. Establishing the liability of such people even in more formal contexts may be difficult where the defendant has had to apply his mind to a complex situation and balance various conflicting factors.

Proving breach of duty

Where delicate professional judgments are involved[1]

[5.05] Where the alleged misstatement takes the form of professional advice[2] a distinctive feature is that the giving of such advice will frequently have involved the exercise of judgment and evaluation. For this reason claims based upon it may give rise to special difficulties of proof. Advice which eventually turns out to have been 'wrong' was not necessarily given negligently. In *Stafford v Conti Commodity Services Ltd*[3] an investor who had incurred large losses on the commodities market unsuccessfully sought to sue his broker for negligent advice. It was held that 'a broker cannot always be right in the advice that he gives in relation to so wayward and rapidly changing a market'.[4] Where advice takes the form of prediction (as it often does) much will therefore depend in practice upon the degree of accuracy generally to be expected in the particular field.[5] The clearest example of liability being imposed in such a case is *Esso Petroleum Co*

---

1 See also ch 15, below.
2 In such cases the parties will obviously frequently be in a contractual relationship, but (except in very rare cases where the defendant expressly undertakes otherwise) it is well established that even the contractual duty is not absolute but is limited to the taking of reasonable care.
3 [1981] 1 All ER 691. Cf *Elderkin v Merrill Lynch Royal Securities Ltd* (1977) 80 DLR (3d) 313 (liability imposed upon stockbroker for negligent investment advice).
4 [1981] 1 All ER 691 at 697, per Mocatta J.
5 See, eg, *Ormindale Holdings Ltd v Ray, Wolfe, Connel, Lightbody & Reynolds* (1980) 116 DLR (3d) 346 (lawyer's advice not necessarily negligent merely because his opinion as to the law is ultimately rejected by the court). The narrowness of the line which may separate negligence from a view subsequently rejected is, however, illustrated by cases involving the valuation of property in which liability has been imposed: see, eg *Singer and Friedlander Ltd v John D Wood & Co* (1977) 243 Estates Gazette 212. For discussion see Brazier, 'Surveyor's Negligence: A Survey' (1981) Conv 96. See also ch 15, below.

Ltd v Mardon.[1] An employee of the defendant[2] oil company told a tenant of one of the company's new garages that his throughput of petrol would be in the order of 200,000 to 250,000 gallons per year. In fact the garage subsequently turned out to be capable of little more than a quarter of this figure. The Court of Appeal held the company liable. They had great experience in judging the capacity of retail outlets for their product, which the plaintiff did not have. In the words of Lord Denning MR:[3]

> 'It seems to me that *Hedley Byrne*, properly understood, covers this particular proposition: if a man, who has or professes to have special knowledge or skill, makes a representation by virtue thereof to another - be it advice, information or opinion - with the intention of inducing him to enter into a contract with him, he is under a duty to use reasonable care to see that the representation is correct, and that the information or opinion is reliable. If he negligently gives unsound advice or misleading information or expresses an erroneous opinion, and thereby induces the other side into a contract with him, he is liable in damages.'

Knowledge or skill

[**5.06**] It is to be noted that in this passage Lord Denning refers to *'knowledge or skill'* (italics supplied). Clearly one can exist without the other. Indeed, *Esso Petroleum v Mardon* was one of those cases in which the opportunity was taken to make clear that the restrictive approach favoured by the Privy Council in *Mutual Life and Citizens' Assurance Co Ltd v Evatt*,[4] which would have required the possession of skill of a professional nature as a prerequisite to liability in most cases, would not be adopted. In the pre-*Evatt* case of *Anderson & Sons Ltd v Rhodes (Liverpool) Ltd*,[5] Cairns J, sitting at Liverpool Assizes, held expressly that the duty of care under *Hedley Byrne* was not limited to professional people. In *Anderson*'s case fruit and vegetables dealers, who sometimes also acted as commission agents, were held liable to other traders for a negligent misstatement as to the creditworthiness of certain potato merchants with whom they had had business dealings. In *Mutual Life and Citizens' Assurance Co Ltd v Evatt* Lord Diplock apparently suggested that the decision in *Anderson v Rhodes* should be regarded as correct, and distinguishable from *Evatt*, on the narrow basis that, in the absence of a professional skill, liability would only be imposed when the 'advisor has a financial interest in the transaction on which he gives his advice'.[6] However,

---

1 [1976] QB 801, [1976] 2 All ER 5, CA.
2 Ie on a counter-claim: the oil company had itself brought the action which their tenant (as plaintiff in the counter-claim) resisted.
3 [1976] QB 801 at 820B-D, [1976] 2 All ER 5 at 16.
4 [1971] AC 793, [1971] 1 All ER 150.
5 [1967] 2 All ER 850.
6 [1971] AC 793 at 809. Quaere, however, whether such a financial interest did not exist in *Evatt's* case itself, since the advice led the plaintiff to invest in a company belonging to the same group as the defendants: cf per Lord Reid, delivering the judgment of the minority [1971] AC 793 at 811.

this limited interpretation of the case, of which there is no suggestion in the actual judgment, can probably be regarded as incorrect in view of the predominantly hostile reception which the decision in *Evatt* itself received.[1]

Standard of care

[5.07] In any type of misstatement case difficult questions may arise as to the precise degree of care which a defendant ought to have shown. An interesting example is provided by *Howard Marine and Dredging Co Ltd v Ogden & Sons (Excavations) Ltd*.[2] In this case, which concerned pre-contractual negotiations, the defendant[3] was asked to give the carrying capacity of certain of his firm's barges, which the plaintiffs were thinking of hiring. He gave an immediate answer in reliance on the figure given in Lloyd's Register, which unfortunately turned out to be inaccurate, instead of taking the trouble to consult the ships's documents which would have given the true figure. The plaintiffs took the barges in reliance on the statement, but the error as to carrying capacity rendered them useless for the purpose for which they had been hired. The trial judge, Bristow J, exonerated the defendant on the ground that it was reasonable for him to have relied on Lloyd's Register, an error in that publication being most unusual. By a majority, Lord Denning MR dissenting, the Court of Appeal reversed that decision. The case turned mainly on the Misrepresentation Act 1967, s 2, but the position as to liability under the principle in *Hedley Byrne v Heller* was also considered. Lord Denning MR felt that the statement was an 'impromptu opinion given offhand'[4] and that the plaintiffs had been aware of that. In those circumstances the defendants' only duty was to be 'honest', which he had been. Bridge LJ, who based his decision in favour of the plaintiffs solely on the 1967 Act, was sympathetic to Lord Denning's approach on the common law point. Shaw LJ, however, expressed a clear view in favour of liability under *Hedley Byrne*. The fact that the only reliable source of knowledge, ie the ships' documents, were exclusively in the defendant's possession, and that the question of carrying capacity was crucial to the outcome of the negotiations, was sufficient to enable the plaintiffs to succeed. Shaw LJ said[5] that, in those circumstances, the fact that the defendant 'chose to answer and important question from mere recollection "off the cuff" does not in my view diminish, if I may adopt the language of Lord Pearce,[6] the "gravity of the inquiry or the importance and influence attached to the answer" '. The judgment of

1 See above, p 89, n 3, and cases there cited.
2 [1978] QB 574, [1978] 2 All ER 1134, CA.
3 Ie on a counter-claim. The parties referred to in the text as plaintiff and defendant, for the sake of convenience, in fact had their roles reversed in the main action.
4 [1978] QB 574 at 591H, [1978] 2 All ER 1134 at 1141.
5 [1978] QB 574 at 601C, [1978] 2 All ER 1134 at 1148.
6 Ie in *Hedley Byrne & Co Ltd v Heller & Partners Ltd* [1964] AC 465 at 539, HL.

Shaw LJ is perhaps a salutary warning to those who make statements which are obviously central to the matter under consideration, and of which the maker of the statement is in a particularly strong position, by contrast with the person to whom it is made, to know whether it is true or false. In these circumstances the perhaps relatively informal manner, in which the inquiry might happen to be made, should not mislead the person giving the answer into skimping his inspection of the relevant sources.

Public policy

Advocate's immunity

[**5.08**] A special type of question which may arise, in certain types of case involving negligent advice, is whether the defendant should be immune from liability on grounds of public policy. In the well-known case of *Rondel v Worsley*[1] the House of Lords held that counsel could not be sued for alleged negligence in the conduct of litigation itself or in work preparatory to it.[2] This confirmed that the understanding of the law on this point prior to *Hedley Byrne* had not been overturned by that case.[3] The reasons for the immunity included recognition of the fact that counsel owes a duty to the court as well as to his client, and a desire to prevent unsuccessful litigants from indirectly seeking retrials by taking proceedings against their legal advisors.[4] Advocates would not be protected from suit, however, for negligence in drafting documents or other work unconnected with litigation.[5] But if the situation *is* one involving litigation it appears to follow a fortiori from *Rondel v Worsley*, notwithstanding an apparent obiter dictum to the contrary by Lord Denning MR in one case,[6] that the advocate is equally immune from liability to the opposing litigant.[7]

1 [1969] 1 AC 191, [1967] 3 All ER 993, HL.
2 'The same [immunity] applies when drawing pleadings or conducting subsequent stages in a case as applies to counsel's conduct during the trial. And there will be cases where the same will apply at a stage when litigation is impending': per Lord Reid in [1969] 1 AC 191 at 213G-232A. See also per Lord Upjohn at 285G-286A: 'As a practical matter, I do no more than suggest that the immunity of counsel in relation to litigation should start at the letter before action where, if my recollection is correct, taxation of party and party costs starts.'
3 See *Swinfen v Lord Chelmsford* (1860) 5 H & N 890.
4 The fact that counsel cannot sue for his fees is not a basis for the immunity: see [1969] 1 AC at 232B-C (Lord Reid); 261A: '. . . the hypothesis that the immunity stems from the inability to sue for fees is unsound' (Lord Pearce); 281B-C (Lord Upjohn). See also *Rees v Sinclair* [1974] 1 NZLR 180. Cf the Courts and Legal Services Act 1990, s 62(2) (immunity unaffected even where suing for fees is possible).
5 Lord Pearce dissented on this point and would have allowed immunity to extend to such work: see [1969] 1 AC 191 at 276-277.
6 *Kelly v London Transport Executive* [1982] 1 WLR 1055 at 1065, CA.
7 'I can find no basis in logic or authority for holding that the essential public interest immunity affirmed in *Rondel v Worsley* protects the Bar only in relation to claims by their own lay clients, leaving them unprotected in respect of the far greater risk of claims by disgruntled litigants on the other side.': per Sir John Donaldson MR in *Orchard v South Eastern Electricity Board* [1987] QB 565 at 571, [1987] 1 All ER 95 at 99, CA.

Immunity not confined to the Bar

[5.09] The Courts and Legal Services Act 1990, s 62(1) provides that:

> 'A person –
> (a) who is not a barrister; but
> (b) who lawfully provides any legal services in relation to any proceedings,
> shall have the same immunity from liability for negligence in respect of his acts or omissions as he would have if he were a barrister lawfully providing those services.'

The main value of this provision is that it puts beyond doubt that, if the circumstances are such as to attract it, there is no difference between solicitors and barristers with respect to the applicability of the immunity.[1]

Rondel v Worsley narrowly interpreted

[5.10] In retrospect *Rondel v Worsley* appears to have represented, as far as the post-*Hedley Byrne* period is concerned, the high-water mark of the doctrine of advocates' immunity. In the later case of *Saif Ali v Sydney Mitchell & Co Ltd*[2] the House of Lords, albeit by a bare majority,[3] put a narrow interpretation upon the scope of the immunity and indicated that decisions subsequent to *Rondel v Worsley*, which had expanded the duty of care owed by professional people in analogous situations,[4] required that decision to be restrictively construed. In the *Saif Ali* case a barrister was instruct to settle proceedings on behalf of a person injured in a motor car accident. Unfortunately he sued only the owner of the vehicle involved, on the basis that the driver had been acting as his agent, and omitted to advise that a claim should also be made against the driver herself. When the allegation of agency collapsed proceedings against the driver were barred by limitation, and the plaintiff sought to sue his legal advisers for professional negligence. Reversing the Court of Appeal, which had held that proceedings against the barrister should be struck out on the ground that the advice in question was connected with pending litigation in sufficient degree to bring it within the advocates' immunity, the House of Lords held that this claim could go forward to trial.[5] Lord Salmon observed that much of what had been

---

1 This was generally understood to be the position after *Rondel v Worsley* itself: see [1969] 1 AC 191 at 232 (Lord Reid) and 267 (Lord Pearce). But cf the relatively cautious approach on this point of Lord Upjohn (at 284) and Lord Pearson (at 294).
2 [1980] AC 198, [1978] 3 All ER 1033, HL.
3 Lords Wilberforce, Diplock and Salmon (Lords Russell and Keith dissenting).
4 See, especially, *Sutcliffe v Thackrah* [1974] AC 727, [1974] 1 All ER 859, HL; *Arenson v Casson Beckman Rutley & Co* [1977] AC 405, [1975] 3 All ER 901 discussed below.
5 See also the earlier case of *Losner v Michael Cohen & Co* (1975) 119 Sol Jo 340, in which the Court of Appeal held a solicitor liable for negligently bringing proceedings against the wrong defendant.

said in *Rondel v Worsley* had been obiter and added that, in the years since it had been decided, there had been a 'strong tendency' for the House of Lords 'to cut down the immunity enjoyed by professional men from being sued in actions for negligence'.¹ Lord Diplock similarly felt that the policy arguments for immunity relied upon by the House in the earlier case lost much of their 'cogency when the scene . . . is shifted from the hurly-burly of the trial to the relative tranquillity of the barrister's chambers'.² The outcome seems to be that the immunity will stretch as far as public policy requires but no further. In particular, the mere fact that the giving of legal advice will often involve the exercise of 'finely balanced judgments'³ is not in itself a reason for totally excluding claims for negligence, since similar skills have to be deployed by members of other professions all of whom can be sued.⁴ The outcome would seem to be that it is dangerous to assume that the immunity extends to any advice given, or statements made, other then during the actual period of a trial itself.⁵

Abuse of process

[**5.11**] In *Somasundaram v Melchior & Co*⁶ the plaintiff sued his solicitors for negligence alleging that he had been wrongly pressurised to plead guilty to an offence in criminal proceedings. The Court of Appeal struck out the claim as an abuse of process on the ground that it involved a collateral attack on a court of competent jurisdiction. The court rejected the argument that to strike out the claim on this ground would be inconsistent with the narrow scope of the advocate's immunity as laid down in *Saif Ali v Sydney Mitchell & Co (a firm)*. The argument was based on the submission that advice unprotected by that principle might nevertheless subsequently lead directly to a decision of a court of competent jurisdiction and hence effectively become protected under the abuse of process approach. The court was not convinced that any inconsistency existed but apparently took the view that, even if it did, the need to protect the decisions of at least criminal courts from collateral attack would be the paramount principle.⁷

---

1 [1980] AC 198 at 229E.
2 Ibid at 220.
3 Per Lord Diplock, ibid.
4 'I recognise that it is most unpleasant for a barrister to have to fight an allegation that he has been negligent, but such an experience is no more unpleasant for a barrister than it is for a physician or a surgeon, an architect or an accountant. I cannot understand how there can be any justification for the law affording a blanket immunity to a barrister in respect of all work done out of court when it affords none to the members of any other profession; nor do I believe that the Bar would wish to claim such an immunity': [1980] AC 198 at 229-229 per Lord Salmon.
5 In *McNamara v Martin Mears & Co* (1982) 127 Sol Jo 69 a solicitor was held liable for negligently advising a client to accept a lower settlement of her financial claim in relation to a divorce than could have been achieved.
6 [1989] 1 All ER 129, [1988] 1 WLR 1934, CA.
7 See also *Hunter v Chief Constable of West Midlands Police* [1982] AC 529, [1981] 3 All ER 727, HL; *Palmer v Durnford Ford (a firm)* [1992] 1 QB 483, [1992] 2 All ER 122.

Witnesses

[5.12] The immunity from liability relating to litigation, based on public policy, is not confined to those professionally involved as advocates or judges. In *Evans v London Hospital Medical College*,[1] the defendants were pathologists whose alleged negligence in carrying out a post-mortem investigation, and producing a report containing their findings, led to the plaintiff being charged with murder (she was subsequently acquitted when the prosecution offered no evidence). The plaintiff conceded that the defendants would have been immune from liability for anything said in court, but contended that there was no immunity in respect of negligent acts or omissions prior to the prosecution even being commenced. Drake J held that this argument would fail and that the action would be struck out. It is to be noted that the witnesses' immunity is wider that that enjoyed by advocates. His Lordship observed that in so far as it was 'possible to compare the position of a barrister to that of the defendants in this case I think it clear that the barrister would not be immune from being sued for negligence'.[2] The police frequently collected statements from large numbers of witnesses, sometimes even before it was known whether any criminal offence had been committed at all. Public policy required that these should be protected from liability, otherwise 'the immunity attaching to the giving of evidence in court . . . could easily be outflanked and rendered of little use'.[3] On the other hand, the immunity given to expert witnesses, especially in civil litigation, is far from being unlimited. In *Palmer v Durnford Ford (a firm)*[4] it was held that since 'the immunity should only be given where to deny it would mean that expert witnesses would be inhibited from giving truthful and fair evidence in court' there was 'no good reason why an expert should not be liable for the advice which he gives to his client as to the merits of the claim, particularly if proceedings have not been started, and a fortiori as to whether he is qualified to advise at all'.[5]

Arbitrators and Mutual Valuers

[5.13] Two decisions of the House of Lords handed down in the years which separated *Rondel v Worsley* and *Saif Ali v Sydney Mitchell*, and were regarded as significant in the latter case, concern another area in which liability for negligent misstatement has prevailed over a suggested immunity based upon public policy. In *Sutcliffe v Thackrah*,[6] the House held that the issuing of interim certificates by an architect, which create an obligation upon his client to pay the builder involved in the construction, is not a function which attracts an immunity from liability for negligence, analogous to that enjoyed

---

1 [1981] 1 All ER 715, [1981] 1 WLR 184.
2 [1981] 1 WLR 184 at 191C.
3 [1981] 1 All ER 715 at 721, [1981] 1 WLR 184 at 191H.
4 [1992] 1 QB 483, [1992] 2 All ER 122.
5 [1992] 1 QB 483 at 488, [1992] 2 All ER 122 at 127 per Simon Tuckey QC sitting as a deputy judge of the High Court.
6 [1974] AC 727, [1974] 1 All ER 859, HL.

by judges, merely because the architect is under a duty to act fairly and impartially as between the two parties involved. In so holding their Lordships overruled a decision of the Court of Appeal which had stood for over 70 years.[1] Lord Salmon suspected that the contrary argument rested 'on the fallacy that since all judges and arbitrators must be impartial and fair, anyone who has to be impartial and fair must be treated as a judge or an arbitrator'.[2] In *Arenson v Casson Beckman Rutley & Co*,[3] a case which came soon after *Sutcliffe v Thackrah*, the hostility to the existence of immunity from liability, beyond the narrowest conception of necessity dictated by policy, was again demonstrated, if not increased. The defendant was the auditor of a private company who was asked to value a parcel of shares in the company when one member decided to sell them to another member. Shortly afterwards the company went public and the purchaser sold the shares for six times the valuation price at which he had purchased them from the plaintiff. The latter claimed that the valuation had been negligent, but the auditors claimed that in valuing the shares they had been acting in a quasi-arbitral capacity which rendered them immune from suit. This argument, which was supported by earlier authority, prevailed in the Court of Appeal. The House of Lords reversed that decision, however, on the ground that an arbitrator was someone called upon to resolve a specific dispute, and that a mutual valuer was not in this position. Moreover two members of the House, Lord Kilbrandon and Lord Fraser, cast doubt upon the proposition that even an actual arbitrator, formally appointed to settle a dispute, would enjoy immunity while a third, Lord Salmon, also admitted that this question may have to be examined in the future. Lord Kilbrandon considered that immunity should be limited to judges,[4] tribunal chairmen and the like, appointed by the State as distinct from persons appointed by parties to a dispute: 'Immunity is judged by the origin and character of the appointment, not by the duties which the appointee has to perform, or his methods of performing them.'[5] It would thus appear that attempts to defend claims for negligent misstatement by seeking to invoke an immunity based upon public policy will nowadays rarely succeed.[6] Of course this is not to say that plaintiffs will find actions alleging negligent advice easy to win. Where difficult questions of judgment are involved there is no indication that courts are any more prepared that heretofore to infer that a prognosis invalidated by hindsight was careless when it was made.

1   Ie *Chambers v Goldthorpe* [1901] 1 KB 624, CA.
2   [1974] AC 727 at 759G-H, [1974] 1 All ER 859 at 882. See also per Lord Reid at 737G.
3   [1977] AC 405, [1975] 3 All ER 901, HL.
4   See *Sirros v Mocre* [1975] QB 118, [1974] 3 All ER 776, CA. Cf *Jones v Department of Employment* [1989] QB 1, [1988] 1 All ER 725,CA (no private law duty of care owed by adjudicating officer considering claims for unemployment benefit).
5   [1977] AC 405 at 432B-C, [1975] 3 All ER 901 at 919.
6   In *IRC v Hoogstraten* [1985] QB 1077, [1984] 3 All ER 25 the Court of Appeal rejected a suggestion that the public interest in the administration of justice required that sequestrators appointed by the court should be immune from actions for negligence.

Social occasions

Liability only in very exceptional cases

[**5.14**] In *Chaudhry v Prabhakar*[1] the defendant acted as unpaid adviser for the plaintiff, a friend of his who was seeking to buy a second-hand motor car. When the car turned out to be unroadworthy and quite valueless the plaintiff sued him for negligent misstatement and the Court of Appeal, albeit with some reluctance on the part of one member of the court who felt that the imposition of liability in such cases could 'make social regulations and responsibilities between friends unnecessarily hazardous',[2] held him liable. The case is complicated by the fact that counsel for the defendant had *conceded* the existence of a duty of care[3] and fought the case on the basis of what standard of care that admitted duty imposed. The decision is therefore a somewhat uncertain guide for future cases. Indeed Stocker LJ emphasised that 'in the absence of other factors giving rise to such a duty, the giving of advice sought in the context of family, domestic or social relationships will not in itself give rise to any duty in respect of such advice'.[4] If one single factor can be identified as having tipped the scales against the defendant, it is probably that his advice was sought in a very specific situation leading to the actual purchase of the vehicle which he sought out and recommended. Thus Stuart-Smith LJ said:

> '... where, as in this case, the relationship of principal and agent exists, such that a contract comes into existence between the principal and the third party, it seems to me that, at the very least, this relationship is powerful evidence that the occasion is not a purely social one, but ... is in a business connection.'[5]

[**5.15**] Professional people who happen casually to express opinions on matters within their sphere at social gatherings are therefore probably safe in assuming that they are at no greater risk of incurring *Hedley Byrne* liability after *Chaudhry v Prabhakar* than they were before. This risk would still seem to be minimal. Apart from *Chaudhry v Prabhakar* the only decision which touches on the point is the old case of *Fish v Kelly*.[6] The defendant was a solicitor who had drawn up, and who kept in his possession, a deed relating to the terms of employment for workers at a company for which he acted. When he happened to be on the company's premises, one of the employees took the opportunity to ask him whether the deed provided for certain money to be paid to him if he left the company's service. The

---

1 [1988] 3 All ER 718, [1989] 1 WLR 29, CA.
2 [1988] 3 All ER 718 at 725 per May LJ.
3 May LJ doubted whether this concession had been rightly made: see [1988] 3 All ER 718 at 725.
4 [1988] 3 All ER 718 at 723.
5 [1988] 3 All ER 718 at 722.
6 (1864) 17 CBNS 194.

defendant honestly replied in the affirmative, having unfortunately forgotten that the detailed provisions of the deed meant that the money would only be payable to the plaintiff's executor after his death. The plaintiff left the company in consequence of the answer which he received, and subsequently sued the solicitor. The action failed. Erle CJ was 'unable to perceive any duty arising out of the casual conversation here',[1] and Byles J said that 'If this sort of action could be maintained, it would be extremely hazardous for an attorney to venture to give an opinion upon any point of law in the course of a journey by railway'.[2] Of course this case was decided long before *Hedley Byrne* and was based in part (though not, interestingly enough, wholly) on the absence of a contract between plaintiff and defendant. On its facts the decision seems rather harsh. The defendant was the person best qualified to answer the plaintiff's query, and to expect the latter to cross-examine the company's solicitor to ensure that the advice given had been fully considered, or to request confirmation from him in writing, was surely expecting rather a lot of an ordinary employee. Perhaps, however, this criticism would be less valid today, when employees are better educated and informed, than in the middle of the nineteenth century when the case was actually decided. Nevertheless, *Fish v Kelly* would still seem to be a decision very close to the borderline, and the specific context of the question posed to the defendant might possibly have led to liability if the approach subsequently adopted in *Chaudhry v Prabhakar* had been applied. There can be little doubt, however, that the courts will remain reluctant to hold liable those who are, in a sense, generous in choosing to respond to chance inquiries made in informal circumstances.[3]

Claims by third parties

Fear of indeterminate liability

[**5.16**] The development of liability for negligent misstatement has long been influenced by a belief which was encapsulated in a famous dictum of Cardozo CJ in *Ultramares Corpn v Touche*,[4] in which he expressed fear of the danger of 'liability in an indeterminate amount for an indeterminate time to an indeterminate class'. In the *Ultramares* case itself the Court of Appeals of New York refused to hold accountants, who had carelessly audited the accounts of a

---

1 Ibid, at 206.
2 (1864) 17 CBNS 194 at 207.
3 Cf The American Law Institute's *Second Restatement of the Law of Torts* (1977) p 130 (comment on para 552), denying liability 'when an attorney gives a casual and offhand opinion on a point of law to a friend whom he meets on the street'.
4 174 NE 441 at 450 (1931). But see also the reference to this dictum by Woodhouse J in *Scott Group Ltd v McFarlane* [1978] 1 NZLR 553 at 571-572: 'those . . . words have been repeated in some judgments almost as though they reveal a self-evident truth; and not unnaturally they were referred to by counsel for the auditors in the present case. But the attraction and force of the language ought not to lead to uncritical acceptance of that sort of argument.'

Liability for negligent misstatement

company, liable to an investor who lost heavily in reliance on the bill of health given to the company by the defendants. This was despite the fact that they had been fully aware that the balance sheet, when certified by them, would be exhibited to 'banks, creditors, stockholders, purchasers, or sellers, according to the needs of the occasion'.[1] The same result was reached, on similar facts, in the case of *Candler v Crane Christmas & Co*,[2] which provoked the famous dissenting judgment of Denning LJ later to be vindicated in *Hedley Byrne v Heller*. Indeed, although it was not a major point in the case, it is worth noting that in *Hedley Byrne v Heller* itself the defendants did not know the identity of the plaintiffs (Hedley Byrne), the request for advice having come from the plaintiffs' bankers (National Provincial). Nevertheless, this was not regarded as an obstacle to liability. Lord Morris expressly stated that this fact was not material since the defendants 'must have known that the inquiry was being made by someone who was contemplating doing business with Easipower Ltd and that their answer or the substance of it would in fact be passed on to such person'.[3]

Surveyors and solicitors

[**5.17**] In *Smith v Eric S Bush*[4] the defendant firm of surveyors prepared a survey report for a building society, on the basis of which the plaintiff was able to obtain a mortgage advance from the society in order to buy the property surveyed. Unfortunately, the defendants failed to exercise reasonable care and skill and defects, which should have been detected, materialised subsequently causing considerable damage. The House of Lords held the surveyor, whose only contract had been with the building society, liable to the plaintiff. In so holding, the House approved a first instance decision some years earlier,[5] and confirmed a significant stage in the development of liability to third parties for negligent misstatement.[6] 'The valuer', said Lord Templeman, 'is liable in tort if he receives instructions from and is paid by the mortgagor but knows that the valuation is for the purpose of a mortgage and will be relied on by the mortgagee'.[7] The House emphasised, in the words of Lord Griffiths,[8] that the case before it concerned 'a dwelling house of modest value in which it is widely recognised by surveyors that purchasers are in fact relying on their

---

1   174 NE 441 at 442 (1931).
2   [1951] 2 KB 164, [1951] 1 All ER 426, CA.
3   [1964] AC 465 at 493-494. See also per Lord Reid at 482 ('It seems to me quite immaterial that they did not know who these contractors were . . .').
4   [1990] 1 AC 831, [1989] 2 All ER 514; affg [1988] QB 743, [1987] 3 All ER 179, CA. The case was decided jointly with another appeal which raised the same point: *Harris v Wyre Forest District Council* [1988] QB 835, [1988] 1 All ER 691, CA; revsd [1990] 1 AC 831, [1989] 2 All ER 514.
5   *Yianni v Edwin Evans & Sons* [1982] QB 438, [1981] 3 All ER 592.
6   '. . . no decision of this House has gone further than *Smith v Eric S Bush*': per Lord Oliver in *Caparo Industries plc v Dickman* [1990] 2 AC 605 at 642, [1990] 1 All ER 568 at 592.
7   [1990] 1 AC 831 at 844, [1989] 2 All ER 514 at 520.
8   [1990] 1 AC 831 at 859, [1989] 2 All ER 514 at 532.

care and skill'.¹ While the decision would 'obviously be of general application in broadly similar circumstances' it could not be taken to apply 'in respect of valuations of quite different types of property for mortgage purposes, such as industrial property, large blocks of flats or very expensive houses'. Purchasers of such properties would normally be expected to obtain their own survey rather than rely on that commissioned by the mortgagor. A decade before the decision of the House of Lords in *Smith v Eric S Bush* an even more striking decision in favour of a third party was reached by Sir Robert Megarry V-C. In *Ross v Caunters*² a solicitor who negligently failed to advise a client that his will should not be witnessed by a potential beneficiary was held liable to that beneficiary, after the client's death, for the consequent failure of the bequest³ even though it was evident that the plaintiff, as distinct from the deceased testator, could not plausibly be said to have 'relied' on the defendant in any meaningful sense. Notwithstanding criticism of this decision, and the expression of doubt in some circles as to whether it had survived the recent narrowing by the House of Lords in the scope of recovery for pure economic loss,⁴ *Ross v Caunters* was followed in a 1992 case on the same facts⁵ and its correctness affirmed by the Court of Appeal in 1993 in a case involving failure to draw up a will at the request of the deceased testator.⁶ The liability of surveyors and solicitors is considered further in a subsequent chapter devoted to professional negligence.⁷

Third party in negotiation with recipient of advice

[**5.18**] An interesting situation, in which a plaintiff who claimed to have relied to his detriment on advice which had been specifically addressed to another person, attempted to sue for negligent misstatement occurred in *McInerny v Lloyds Bank*.⁸ A manager of the defendant bank wrote to a customer of his about certain guarantees to be given to the plaintiff, McInerny, in connection with a complex transaction involving him and the customer using the words 'I think ... Mr McInerny ought to be satisfied with this'. As was intended by all the parties, this letter was copied to McInerny himself who, on the

---

1   In *Halifax Building Society v Edell* [1992] Ch 436, [1992] 3 All ER 389 Morritt J held that the Building Societies Ombudsman Scheme gave jurisdiction to the ombudsman to investigate claims by house-buyers that surveys carried out on behalf of the societies had been negligent, rejecting the argument by the societies that such claims fell outside the scope of the scheme.
2   [1980] Ch 297, [1979] 3 All ER 580.
3   The same result has been reached in decisions in Canada (see *Whittingham v Crease & Co* [1978] 5 WWR 45) and New Zealand: see *Gartside v Sheffield, Young & Ellis* [1983] NZLR 37. On the other hand in Australia the Full Court of the Supreme Court of Victoria (see *Seale v Perry* [1982] VR 193) took the opposite view and refused to follow *Ross v Caunters* (see Harold Luntz in (1983) 3 OJLS 284).
4   Ie in the line of cases culminating in *Murphy v Brentwood District Council* [1991] 1 AC 398, [1990] 2 All ER 908, HL. See below, ch 6 and above, ch 1.
5   *Kecskemeti v Rubens Rabin & Co* (1992) Times, 31 December.
6   *White v Jones* (1993) Times, 9 March, CA.
7   Ie ch 15.
8   [1973] 2 Lloyd's Rep 389; affd [1974] 1 Lloyd's Rep 246, CA.

strength of it, went ahead with the transaction. When things subsequently went wrong he attempted to sue the bank for negligent misstatement. His claim failed, both before Kerr J at first instance and in the Court of Appeal. On the facts all the judges who heard the case were unanimous that the plaintiff had misinterpreted the letter and, by choosing to rely upon it, had attached a degree of importance to its contents which they did not warrant. There is, however, a significant difference between the way in which Lord Denning MR analysed the case, in the Court of Appeal, and the way in which Kerr J, along with the other two members of the Court of Appeal, Megaw and James LJJ did so. The majority of the judges felt that the bank manager did not even owe the plaintiff a duty of care in the first place. Kerr J felt that it was not appropriate to impose a duty in favour of a third party 'where the statement has been addressed to a particular person concerning his affairs, so that it was made with that person's interests primarily in mind', and that this was so 'even if it was liable to be shown by him to another person for information or confirmation of its contents'.[1] Lord Denning, however, took a different view:

> 'When [the defendant] sent his reply to the customer, he knew that it was likely that the customer would show it to the other party ... He must have known that both would study his reply, and, if it was satisfactory, would sign the contract on the faith of it. Such conduct seems to me to put him in a position such that he must be regarded as accepting responsibility for what he said - *not only to the customer to whom he said it - but also to the other party to whom it was to be passed.*'[2]

It is submitted that Lord Denning's view is to be preferred. Advice is normally given in circumstances in which it is confidential to the recipient, and the person giving it will have no reason to suppose that the latter, even though he is free to do so, will disclose it to a third party. In such cases there can be no question of liability. But if the adviser is aware that the advice is to be shown to a third party, particularly if to his knowledge it is actually sought with this in mind, there seems no reason why he should escape liability for negligence merely because of the relationship between himself and the original recipient of his advice.[3] For example, persons who have formed differing views on the application of the law to a particular situation about which they are negotiating, not infrequently agree that counsel's opinion should be sought by one of them and that they will both accept the result. If counsel is aware of this, and the situation is not one which attracts immunity on grounds of public policy, there seems to be no reason why he should not owe to both parties a duty to take care in giving his advice.

---

1 [1973] 2 Lloyd's Rep 389 at 401.
2 [1974] 1 Lloyd's Rep 246 at 254 (italics supplied).
3 Cf *Punjab National Bank v de Boinville* [1992] 3 All ER 104 at 118 per Staughton LJ: '. . . an insurance broker owes a duty of care to the specific person who he knows is to become an assignee of the policy, at all events if . . . that person actively participates in giving instructions for the insurance to the broker's knowledge.'

References

[5.19] A familiar situation in which a statement addressed by one person to another may cause loss to a third party is that of the giving of references, for employment or for other purposes. This situation has, however, long been governed by the complex principles of the tort of defamation which provide in particular that such references will normally be protected by qualified privilege, so that a referee will not be liable for errors in his reference provided only that he was not malicious. But in a 1987 decision at first instance it was held that referees could in principle be liable for negligent misstatement, thereby outflanking the malice requirement and the protection afforded by the privilege.[1] In the 1992 case of *Spring v Guardian Assurance plc*,[2] however, the Court of Appeal held that this was incorrect and that misstatement claims would not be permitted so as to circumvent defamation principles in this way.[3] It is not obvious, however, that these principles are more in accord, than is the law of negligence, with modern views as to the appropriate balance to be struck between the need to compensate victims of carelessness and the need to encourage the writing of uninhibited references.[4] The matter awaits authoritative resolution by the House of Lords.[5]

Auditors and the extent of liability

[5.20] In *Caparo Industries plc v Dickman*[6] the plaintiff shareholders in a public company, having received the company's audited accounts, purchased further shares. When the shares underwent a dramatic fall in value, due to profits being well below their predicted level, the plaintiffs sued the company's auditors alleging that they had been negligent in auditing the accounts. The action ultimately failed in the House of Lords, having also failed at first instance but having succeeded by a majority in the Court of Appeal. The House considered that to hold auditors liable to the investing public generally, notwithstanding the foreseeable possibility of their reliance on the accounts, 'would be to create a liability wholly indefinite in area, duration and amount and would open up a limitless vista of

---

1 See *Lawton v BOC Transhield Ltd* [1987] 2 All ER 608, [1987] ICR 7 (Tudor Evans J). For criticism see Tettenborn, 'Negligence v Defamation: a Little Awkwardness' [1987] 46 CLJ 390.
2 [1993] 2 All ER 273, CA (Glidewell and Rose LJJ and Sir Christopher Slade).
3 See also the decision of the New Zealand Court of Appeal in *Bell-Booth Group Ltd v A-G* [1989] 3 NZLR 148.
4 In *Petch v Customs and Excise Comrs* (1993) Times, 4 March another division of the Court of Appeal (Dillon, Beldam and Roch LJJ) followed the decision in *Spring v Guardian Assurance* but the reservations of one member of the Court, Roch LJ, should be noted. While concurring in the result he effectively dissented from the reasoning of the majority and would have been prepared to distinguish *Spring*'s case very narrowly.
5 Leave to appeal was granted in *Spring*'s case.
6 [1990] 2 AC 605, [1990] 1 All ER 568; revsg [1989] QB 653, [1989] 1 All ER 798.

uninsurable risk for the professional man'.[1] The mere fact that the plaintiffs were existing shareholders did not distinguish them from investors generally, at least as far as the purchase of additional shares was concerned.[2] Their Lordships focused upon the legislative policy underlying the requirement for annual audited accounts, which was considered to be to enable shareholders to exercise their powers of control over the company.[3] 'In my judgment', said Lord Oliver, 'the purpose for which the auditor's certificate is made and published is that of providing those entitled to receive the report with information to enable them to exercise in conjunction those powers which their respective proprietary interests confer on them and not for the purposes of individual speculation with a view to profit'.[4] In taking a relatively narrow view of the scope of auditors' liability the House disapproved the views of Woolf J to the contrary effect in *JEB Fasteners Ltd v Marks, Bloom & Co*,[5] and adopted instead an approach broadly consistent with the approach of Denning LJ in *Candler v Crane Christmas & Co.*[6]

Notion of a class

[5.21] In the search for a workable test to limit liability to third parties for negligent misstatement a device sometimes invoked is the notion that a duty will be owed only to an 'ascertainable *class*'[7] of potential plaintiffs. Without further amplification, however, this concept appears to be question-begging. In the absence of criteria to determine how the 'class' in question is to be identified, the notion is inherently ambiguous.[8] It could be interpreted merely as encapsulating what a reasonable man, in the position of the defendant, ought in fact to have foreseen: but if so it adds nothing to the foreseeability test itself and hence remains unacceptably wide. Alternatively, and perhaps more probably, it really reflects the opposing narrow view that the defendant needs to have had a

1   [1990] 2 AC 605 at 643, [1990] 1 All ER 568 at 593 per Lord Oliver. See also per Lord Roskill: 'The submission that there is a virtually unlimited and unrestricted duty of care in relation to the performance of an auditor's statutory duty to certify a company's accounts, a duty extending to anyone who may use those accounts for any purpose such as investing in the company or lending the company money, seems to me untenable' [1990] 2 AC 605 at 628, [1990] 1 All ER 568 at 582.
2   The House appears to have left open the question, upon which the Court of Appeal had been divided, of whether shareholders who *sold* their *existing* shares, in reliance upon negligently audited accounts, would be able to claim. Lord Bridge and Lord Oliver do not rule out the possibility of such liability (see [1990] 2 AC 605 at 627 and 653, [1990] 1 All ER 568 at 581 and 601 respectively) but the reasoning of Lord Jauncey (see [1990] 2 AC 605 at 662, [1990] 1 All ER 568 at 607-608: 'no duty to an individual shareholder') would appear to do so.
3   See the Companies Act 1985, Pt VII.
4   [1990] 2 AC 605 at 654, [1990] 1 All ER 568 at 601. See also per Lord Jauncey in [1990] 2 AC 605 at 658ff, [1990] 1 All ER 568 at 605ff.
5   [1981] 3 All ER 289; affd [1983] 1 All ER 583, CA.
6   [1951] 2 KB 164, [1951] 1 All ER 426, CA. See also *Al Saudi Banque v Clark Pixley (a firm)* [1990] Ch 313, [1989] 3 All ER 361 (Millett J).
7   Per Lord Oliver in *Caparo Industries plc v Dickman* [1990] 2 AC 605 at 638, [1990] 1 All ER 568 at 589, italics supplied. Lord Bridge, in the same case, speaks of an 'identifiable class' ([1990] 2 AC 605 at 621, [1989] 1 All ER 568 at 576). See also *Haig v Bamford* [1976] 3 WWR 331.
8   Cf *Candlewood Navigation Corpn Ltd v Mitsui OSK Lines Ltd* [1986] AC 1 at 24, [1985] 2 All ER 935 at 945, PC, per Lord Fraser.

specific type of transaction in mind, and simply emphasises (with a misleading appearance of elegance) that it is nevertheless not a requirement that the defendant should have known the precise *identity* of the particular plaintiff.[1]

'Assumption of responsibility'?

[**5.22**] 'I do not think', said Lord Griffiths in *Smith v Eric S Bush*,[2] 'that voluntary assumption of responsibility is a helpful or realistic test for liability'. He continued that, notwithstanding use of the expression in *Hedley Byrne & Co Ltd v Heller and Partners Ltd*[3] itself, 'the phrase "assumption of responsibility" can only have any real meaning if it is understood as referring to the circumstances *in which the law will deem* the maker of the statement to have assumed responsibility to the person who acts on the advice'.[4] It is submitted that Lord Griffiths' criticisms are justified.[5] The concept clearly has overtones of fiction. This is especially true where, as in *Smith v Eric S Bush* itself, liability is imposed on a defendant who had sought unsuccessfully to disclaim responsibility.[6]

Purpose

[**5.23**] What then is the correct approach? It is clear from *Caparo Industries plc v Dickman*[7] that the *purpose* for which the statement was made is likely to be treated as a factor of great importance. Of course, in that case the statement had been made pursuant to a statutory duty, which itself provided the context in which the statement was made, and the notion was in consequence somewhat easier to apply than it might otherwise have been.[8] But the concept does appear to have wider utility.

1   Cf the American Law Institute's *Restatement (Second) of Torts* (1977) vol 3, para 552, and see the commentary on it which includes the following (at pp 132-133): 'It is enough that the maker of the representation intends it to reach and influence either a particular person or persons, known to him, or a group or class of persons, distinct from the much larger class who might reasonably be expected sooner or later to have access to the information, and foreseeably to take some action in reliance upon it.' See also *Prosser and Keeton on Torts* (4th edn, 1984) pp 746-747.
2   [1990] 1 AC 831 at 862, [1989] 2 All ER 514 at 534.
3   [1964] AC 465, [1963] 2 All ER 575, HL.
4   [1989] 2 All ER 514 at 534.
5   The voluntary assumption of responsbility approach found favour with the Court of Appeal in *Banque Keyser Ullman SA v Skandia (UK) Insurance Co Ltd* [1990] 1 QB 665, sub nom *Banque Financière de la Cité SA v Westgate Insurance Co Ltd* [1989] 2 All ER 952 (see especially [1989] 2 All ER 952 at 1007 per Slade LJ delivering the judgment of the Court). Sed quaere.
6   See also *Ministry of Housing and Local Government v Sharp* [1970] 2 QB 223, [1970] 1 All ER 1009, CA. On disclaimers see, further, below.
7   [1990] 2 AC 605, [1990] 1 All ER 568, HL.
8   See also *West Wiltshire District Council v Pugh* 1993 NLJR 546 (Morritt J). But even against a statutory background the application of the notion will often be far from automatic. The statutory duty upon the defendant mortgagors in *Smith v Eric S Bush* is arguably imposed to protect the investments of building societies and hence analogous to the statutory duty upon companies to provide shareholders with audited annual accounts: reasoning which would seem potentially to bring the recent House of Lords decisions in *Smith's* case and *Caparo Industries plc v Dickman* into conflict. But the fact situations in the two cases were in reality very different: see the observations of Hoffman J in his (reversed) judgment in *Morgan Crucible Co Ltd v Hill Samuel Bank plc* [1990] 3 All ER 330 at 334-335; (revd [1991] Ch 295, [1991] 1 All ER 148.)

108 Liability for negligent misstatement

In *Ross v Caunters*,[1] for example, the *purpose* of the defendant solicitor can plausibly be described as having been to facilitate his client's wish to confer a benefit on the plaintiff. The concept can be seen at work in recent cases in which lower courts have either applied or distinguished the decision of the House of Lords in *Caparo Industries plc v Dickman* itself. Thus in *Al Nakib Investments (Jersey) Ltd v Longcroft*[2] Mervyn Davies J held that alleged misstatements in a prospectus issued to shareholders for the particular purpose of inviting a *subscription* for further shares did not avail a plaintiff shareholder who chose, albeit in reliance on the prospectus, to buy his shares in the stock market instead. On the other hand in *Morgan Crucible plc v Hill Samuel Bank*[3] the Court of Appeal held that directors and financial advisers of a target company in a contested take-over bid situation risk liability if they choose to make express representations for the *purpose* of influencing the conduct of the bidder. Of course no test can be expected to solve all problems, and the 'purpose' approach is no exception: especially where the number of plaintiffs plausibly identified by it is so large as to resemble the effect of foreseeability. The famous hypothetical case of the marine hydographer whose carelessness causes the loss of an ocean liner[4] is perhaps an example. In practice currently fashionable expressions such as 'proximity' and 'just and reasonable' would be likely to be prayed in aid nowadays to negate liability in such circumstances. Their invocation, if unattractive when used to render opaque judicial reasoning in more straightforward situations,[5] is probably unavoidable in dealing with such exceptional cases.

Omissions

Focus upon question of law

[5.24] In many cases the distinction between making a statement and failing to do so, in effect the same as that between misfeasance and nonfeasance, will be artificial. If a statement is made, but owing to carelessness it is incomplete, seldom will anything be gained by attempting to classify the situation in these terms.[6] But if the

---

1 [1980] Ch 297, [1979] 3 All ER 580.
2 [1990] 3 All ER 321, [1990] 1 WLR 1390.
3 [1991] 1 All ER 148.
4 See per Asquith LJ in *Candler v Crane Christmas & Co* [1951] 2 KB 164 at 194-195, [1951] 1 All ER 426 at 442; Winfield was apparently the first to raise this possible fact-situation: see the first edition of his *Textbook of the Law of Tort* (1937) p 414.
5 See generally ch 1 above.
6 Insurance brokers have often been held liable for omissions of this kind: see, eg *Cherry Ltd v Allied Insurance Brokers Ltd* [1978] 1 Lloyd's Rep 274; *Fine's Flowers Ltd v General Accident Assurance Co of Canada* (1977) 81 DLR (3d) 139; *Morash v Lockhart & Ritchie Ltd* (1978) 95 DLR (3d) 647; *Reardon v Kings Mutual Insurance Co* (1981) 120 DLR (3d) 196. Cf *McNealy v Pennine Insurance Co Ltd* [1978] 2 Lloyd's Rep 18, CA (failure to ask a relevant question).

complaint is that the defendant remained wholly silent, or failed to take a specific step which it is alleged he ought to have taken, the distinction does have utility. Just as in the rare cases of *inaction* where it is alleged that the defendant had been under a positive duty, the distinction facilitates clarification of the fundamental issue involved.[1] The investigation is less likely to be a largely factual one as to whether or not the defendant was actually careless, than it is a discussion of whether, as a matter of law, the defendant owed a duty of care to the plaintiff requiring the taking of positive steps.[2] In *Argy Trading Development Co Ltd v Lapid Developments Co Ltd*,[3] landlords of business premises who had previously relieved their tenants of the obligation to insure the premises, by doing so themselves, suddenly decided not to renew the relevant policies but omitted to inform the tenants of this. The tenants were unable to sue for losses incurred when the premises were gutted by fire because it was held, after argument, that the defendants simply owed no duty to notify the plaintiffs of their decision: the responsibility for checking annually that their premises were adequately insured lay with the plaintiffs.[4]

Relevance of contract

[**5.25**] In the important case of *Tai Hing Cotton Mill Ltd v Liu Chong Bank Ltd*[5] the Judicial Committee of the Privy Council had to consider whether, given the existence between them of a contractual relationship, a bank could sue one of its customers in tort for an 'omission'. The bank had paid out on forged cheques, and alleged that the customer should bear the losses since the latter's failure promptly to examine their bank statements had prevented them from discovering what was happening, and hence notifying the bank, as early as they could have done. The contention failed and the bank was liable for the losses. The Privy Council refused to allow the law of negligence to upset long-established principles of banking law. If the bank had wished to impose a positive duty on their customers to examine their bank statements they should have done so expressly by contract. It is submitted that this decision was correct, although certain observations by Lord Scarman, delivering the judgment of the Board, were wider than was necessary for the decision and would seem to be open to question. His Lordship appeared to imply that *whenever* parties are in a contractual relationship that relationship will be exclusive and will always prevent the imposition of a wider tort liability.[6] Such a proposition would clearly be too wide:

1   Cf Smith and Burn, '*Donoghue v Stevenson*: the Not So Golden Anniversary' (1983) 46 MLR 147.
2   See, eg *Paterson Zochonis & Co Ltd v Merfarken Packaging Ltd* [1986] 3 All ER 522, CA (printers under no duty to check that material printed involves breach of copyright).
3   [1977] 3 All ER 785, [1977] 1 WLR 444.
4   [1977] 1 WLR 444 at 461.
5   [1986] AC 80, [1985] 2 All ER 947.
6   'Their Lordships do not believe that there is anything to the advantage of the law's development in searching for a liability in tort where the parties are in a contractual relationship.': [1986] AC at 107. Cf *Greater Nottingham Co-operative Society Ltd v Cementation Piling and Foundations Ltd* [1989] QB 71, [1988] 2 All ER 971, CA.

110 *Liability for negligent misstatement*

concurrent liability in both contract and tort is a well-recognised feature of a number of situations.[1] Nevertheless the present conservative tendency of the courts is undoubtedly to approach situations, in which well-established contractual principles apply to the relationship between the parties, with a presumption against allowing tort doctrines to expand into the area if they have not done so in the past. Thus in *Banque Keyser Ullmann SA v Skandia (UK) Insurance Co Ltd* [2] the Court of Appeal held that liability for misstatement by *omission* [3] in a pre-contractual situation could not be imposed in circumstances in which that liability would upset the rule, long-established in the law of misrepresentation, that there is no general duty of disclosure in such situations.[4]

Tort and property

[5.26] A case in which what was, in effect, an omission to make a statement led to a sharp difference of judicial opinion as to whether on the facts a duty of care existed was *Moorgate Mercantile Co Ltd v Twitchings*.[5] Finance houses set up a voluntary clearing house to receive notice of cars let on hire purchase, so as to provide a register against which any car offered for sale could be checked. Moorgate Mecantile, a finance company, became a member of the clearing house but carelessly omitted to register a car, the letting of which on hire purchase it had financed. Prior to absconding, the person who was purchasing the car offered it for sale to a dealer who, having checked the register, assumed that the title to the vehicle was clear and bought it. Moorgate Mercantile subsequently sought to assert their title against the dealer, who resisted the claim by alleging that they were liable to him under *Hedley Byrne* for the loss caused by their failure to register the car with the clearing house. The Court of Appeal, by a majority[6] found for the dealer but were reversed by a bare majority[7] of the House of Lords which found for Moorgate. The majority felt that since finance houses were not compelled to become members of the clearing house, and even if they did so, were not actually compelled by the rules of the scheme to register their transactions, those which joined should not be put in a worse position with respect to the assertion of their title than those which had not

---

1 Eg employers' liability to their employees. See also *Punjab National Bank v de Boinville* [1992] 3 All ER 104, [1992] 1 WLR 1138, CA; *Midland Bank Trust Co v Hett, Stubbs & Kemp* [1979] Ch 384, [1978] 3 All ER 571.
2 [1990] 1 QB 665, sub nom *Banque Financière de la Cité SA v Westgate Insurance Co Ltd* [1989] 2 All ER 952, CA; affd on other grounds [1991] 2 AC 249, [1990] 2 All ER 947, HL.
3 It was established by the Court of Appeal in *Esso Petroleum Co Ltd v Mardon* [1976] QB 801, [1976] 2 All ER 5, that *Hedley Byrne* liability can attach to *positive statements* made in pre-contractual negotiations.
4 See, especially, [1990] 1 QB 665 at 802, [1989] 2 All ER 952 at 1013 per Slade LJ (delivering the judgment of the court).
5 [1977] AC 890, [1976] 2 All ER 641; rvsg [1976] QB 225, [1975] 3 All ER 314.
6 Lord Denning MR and Browne LJ, Geoffrey Lane LJ dissenting.
7 Lords Edmund Davies, Fraser and Russell; Lords Wilberforce and Salmon dissenting.

bothered to join at all. The dissentients were not impressed by this supposed paradox; they felt that membership of the clearing house was mutually advantageous to its members and that they owed a duty of care to register their transactions once they had joined. It is submitted that the minority view is to be preferred. In the final analysis the case involved a conflict between the concept of title in the law of property, and the more fluid concepts of tort which seek to compensate victims of carelessness. No doubt there are valid grounds for resisting the encroachments of tort into areas where existing rules are clear, and where undesirable uncertainty would be caused by upsetting them, particularly in the real property field where the rules may have formed the background to long-term transactions.[1] But it is not easy to see why justice to the victim of carelessness should have been subordinated in the *Moorgate Mercantile* situation.[2]

Disclaimers of liability[3]

When possible

[5.27] The expansion of liability for negligent misstatement in favour of third parties, and beyond the confines of a narrowly defined 'special relationship', raises a question-mark over a defendant's freedom to avoid liability by stipulating that his statement is given 'without responsibility' (or some similar phrase). The use of such a disclaimer was, of course, the basis of the actual decision in *Hedley Byrne & Co Ltd v Heller & Partners Ltd* itself, in favour of the defendants.[4] But if the way in which the plaintiff suffers as a result of the statement is indirect (especially where the negligence is by omission)[5] it will often be impossible for any disclaimer, even if one had been made, to have been brought to the plaintiff's attention. Of course the mere fact that the situation is one involving a third party will not *necessarily* make it impracticable for liability to be disclaimed. If, as will often be the case, a written document is involved, an appropriate clause can be included in it. But if the situation *is* one in which the third party will normally be unaware of the disclaimer, or be powerless in any event to take any special steps to protect himself in consequence of it, it must surely on general principles be held ineffective. In *Ministry of Housing and Local Goverment v Sharp*[6] the plaintiffs, the Ministry of Housing, were entitled by statute to receive payment, from the

---

1 Cf RJ Smith 'The Economic Torts: Their Impact on Real Property' (1977) 41 Conv (NS) 318.
2 After the facts which gave rise to the litigation had arisen, the rules of the clearing house scheme were themselves amended so as to impose a duty to register upon members: [1977] AC 890 at 910B per Lord Salmon.
3 See also ch 4, above.
4 See [1964] AC 465 at 492-493 (Lord Reid); 504 (Lord Morris); 553 (Lord Devlin); 540 (Lord Pearce).
5 See, eg *Ross v Caunters* [1980] Ch 297, [1979] 3 All ER 580, discussed above.
6 [1970] 2 QB 223, [1970] 1 All ER 1009. (This report contains the reversed judgment of Fisher J at first instance as well as the judgments delivered in the Court of Appeal.)

developer involved, should planning permission to develop a certain piece of land ever be granted by the relevant authority. This was because the ministry had earlier paid compensation to the then owner of the land in respect of a refusal of planning permission. The ministry's entitlement, known as a 'compensation notice', was entered on the local land charges register. Planning permission was subsequently granted and solicitors acting for the new owner sent a requisition for an official search of the register. Unfortunately an employee of the registry carried out the search carelessly and issued the owner with a clear certificate which omitted the compensation notice. As a result the ministry lost their right, and successfully sued the registry for negligent misstatement to recover their loss. In fact the registry's reply to the owner's requisition had contained a disclaimer of legal responsibility in respect of the replies to the inquiries.[1] But it was never suggested, nor could it rationally have been, that this could have any effect on the Ministry's claim since they were not the recipients of the search.[2]

Requirements

[5.28] If the situation is one in which disclaiming liability is possible, it is important that any statement to this effect should be express and unambiguous: the court will not be prepared to identify a disclaimer as a matter of inference.[3] It should also be noted, however, that even an express provision that a statement is made 'without responsibility' will not protect a defendant who is fraudulent.[4]

Effect of the Unfair Contract Terms Act[5]

[5.29] It is important to remember that if the negligent misstatement was made in the course of a business, its enforceability may depend upon its satisfying the 'requirement of reasonableness' under the Unfair Contract Terms Act 1977.[6] Despite the title of the Act its provisions extend to disclaimers of tort liability outside contract. In *Smith v Eric S Bush*,[7] a surveyor who surveyed a house for a building society, but whose report, in accordance with widespread practice, was supplied to the purchaser, sought unsuccessfully to rely on a general disclaimer of responsibility contained in the report when sued by the purchaser for negligence. The House of Lords held that the

---

1 See [1970] 2 QB at 243G per Fisher J.
2 An analogous situation occurred in *Moorgate Mercantile v Twitchings* where the clearing-house disclaimed liability but this was not relevant since they were not the defendants: see [1976] QB at 239G per Lord Denning MR.
3 See *Box v Midland Bank Ltd* [1979] 2 Lloyd's Rep 391 at 399 per Lloyd J.
4 See *Commercial Banking Co of Sydney v RH Brown & Co* [1972] 2 Lloyd's Rep 360 (High Ct of Australia).
5 See also ch 4 above.
6 See ss 1(3), 2(2) and 11(3) of the Act. If the statement actually gave rise to death or personal injury the reasonableness requirement will not be relevant and the disclaimer will automatically be ineffective: s 2(1).
7 [1990] 1 AC 831, [1989] 2 All ER 514.

disclaimer was invalidated by the Act and that the claim would succeed. 'It is not fair and reasonable', said Lord Templeman, 'for building societies and valuers to agree together to impose on purchasers the risk of loss arising as a result of incompetence or carelessness on the part of valuers'.[1]

'Reasonableness'

[**5.30**] The House of Lords was anxious to emphasise in *Smith v Eric S Bush* that nullification of disclaimers by the statutory 'reasonableness' test would necessarily depend on the particular circumstances in question. The instant case concerned domestic purchasers of small houses.[2] Other situations might be very different. Lord Griffiths said:[3]

> 'I would not . . . wish it to be thought that I would consider it unreasonable for professional men in all circumstances to seek to exclude or limit their liability for negligence. Sometimes breathtaking sums of money may turn on professional advice against which it would be impossible for the adviser to obtain adequate insurance cover and which would ruin him if he were to be held personally liable. In these circumstances it may indeed be reasonable to give the advice on a basis of no liability or possibly of liability limited to the extent of the adviser's insurance cover.'

His Lordship outlined some of the factors relevant to determining 'reasonableness'.[4] These included equality of bargaining power, the practicability of obtaining advice from an alternative source, the difficulty of the task being undertaken, and the consequences to the parties of upholding the disclaimer.

Denial of duty?

[**5.31**] In *Harris v Wyre Forest District Council*[5] the House of Lords rejected an argument, which had found favour with the Court of Appeal in that case, that a disclaimer of tort liability for negligent misstatement could be drafted which would escape the provisions of

---

1 [1990] 1 AC 831 at 854, [1989] 2 All ER 514 at 528. In the unusual case of *Stevenson v Nationwide Building Society* (1984) 272 Estates Gazette 663, in which the plaintiff was himself an estate agent, a disclaimer *was* held to be effective to protect against a surveyor's negligence. For criticism see, generally, Harwood 'A Structural Survey of Negligent Reports' (1987) 50 MLR 588.
2 'We are dealing ... with a loss which will be limited to the value of a modest house and against which it can be expected that the surveyor will be insured. Bearing the loss will be unlikely to cause significant hardship if it has to be borne by the surveyor but it is, on the other hand, quite possible that it will be a financial catastrophe for the purchaser who may be left with a valueless house and no money to buy another.': [1990] 1 AC 831 at 859, [1989] 2 All ER 514 at 531 per Lord Griffiths.
3 [1990] 1 AC 831 at 859, [1989] 2 All ER 514 at 531-532.
4 See [1990] 1 AC 831 at 858, [1989] 2 All ER 514 at 531.
5 [1990] 1 AC 831, [1989] 2 All ER 514, HL; rvsg [1988] QB 835, [1988] 1 All ER 691, CA. The appeal was decided by the House simultaneously with that in *Smith v Eric S Bush*.

the Unfair Contract Terms Act by denying the existence of a duty of care in the first place instead of seeking to exclude an admitted existing liability.[1] The House fortunately preferred the view that a provision in the Act which 'also prevents . . . excluding or restricting liability by reference to terms or notices which exclude or restrict the relevant obligation or duty'[2] was, in the words of Lord Jauncey, 'entirely appropriate to cover a disclaimer which prevents a duty coming into existence'.[3]

Contributory negligence[4]

Relevance of the defence

[5.32] The original development of liability for negligent misstatement via such concepts as 'special relationship' and 'reliance' probably accounts for the relative dearth of English authority on the role of contributory negligence in this sphere.[5] There is obviously no intrinsic reason, however, why contributory negligence should not, on the facts of a particular case, be established in this area.[6] A person might legitimately have been heavily influenced by the defendant's misstatement, while also being himself blameworthy for having failed to seek appropriate further advice.

Law Reform (Contributory Negligence) Act 1945

[5.33] Assuming that the defence is applicable in this area, it would seem to be clear that the apportionment provisions of the Law Reform (Contributory Negligence) Act 1945 will also be available to prevent the injustice which occurs if one party – be it plaintiff or defendant –

---

1 See B Coote (1978) 41 MLR 312. Cf *Overbrooke Estates Ltd v Glencombe Properties Ltd* [1974] 3 All ER 511, [1974] 1 WLR 1335.
2 Section 13(1). See Elisabeth McDonald 'Exclusion clauses: the ambit of s 13(1) of the Unfair Contract Terms Act 1977' (1992) 12 LS 277.
3 [1990] 1 AC 831 at 873, [1989] 2 All ER 514 at 543. The proposition that *Hedley Byrne* disclaimers preclude the existence of a duty is premised on the 'voluntary assumption of responsibility' approach to liability for negligent misstatement, which seems to be largely a legal fiction and which was itself repudiated by the House of Lords in its decisions in *Smith v Eric S Bush* and *Harris v Wyre Forest District Council*. For further discussion see earlier in this chapter.
4 See, generally, ch 4 above.
5 Cf Bishop in 'Negligent Misrepresentation through Economists' Eyes' (1980) 96 LQR 360 at 373: 'Reasonable reliance subtracts out contribution before the negligence sums are computed. In effect it functions in exactly the way that contributory negligence did before the enactment of apportionment statutes – it functions as an all-or-nothing bar.'
6 The concept has been applied in several Canadian decisions: see *Morash v Lockhart & Ritchie Ltd* (1978) 95 DLR (3d) 647; *HB Nickerson & Sons Ltd v Wooldridge* (1980) 115 DLR (3d) 97; *Reardon v Kings Mutual Insurance Co* (1981) 120 DLR (3d) 196.

wins outright when both of them have in fact be at fault.¹ Devlin J once suggested a peculiarly narrow construction of the Act which would have led to the opposite conclusion;² but his view was expressly rejected by Woolf J in one case which actually dealt with negligent misstatement,³ and it seems inconsistent with the now generally accepted view of the scope of the Act.⁴

Contributory negligence not to be established easily

[**5.34**] Of course the existence of the possibility of apportionment does not imply that the courts should strain to make findings of contributory negligence against plaintiffs in negligent misstatement cases. In the particular context of house purchasers relying on their building societies' survey reports, for example, it has been forcefully argued that there are cogent policy reasons for refusing to categorise as contributory negligence the purchasers' failure to commission their own separate surveys.⁵ Such an allegation of contributory negligence failed on the facts in one important early case.⁶

---

1 Loss was apportioned under Canadian legislation in all three cases cited in the previous note.
2 See *Drinkwater v Kimber* [1951] 2 All ER 713 at 715 arguing that the word 'damage' in s 1(1) did not extend to financial loss as distinct from loss of life and personal injury.
3 See *JEB Fasteners Ltd v Marks, Bloom & Co* [1981] 3 All ER 289 at 297e (the point was not considered on appeal in [1983] 1 All ER 353, CA).
4 Especially its applicability in certain circumstances to contract cases: see ch 4 above. In *Gran Gelato Ltd v Richcliff (Group) Ltd* [1992] Ch 560, [1992] 1 All ER 865 the availability of the apportionment provisions to common law negligent misstatement claims was assumed to be self-evident.
5 See Michael Harwood, 'A Structural Survey of Negligent Reports' (1987) 50 MLR 588.
6 See *Yianni v Edwin Evans & Sons* [1982] QB 438 at 457D-F per Park J. But cf *Perry v Tendring District Council* (1984) 1 Const LJ 152, where the view was expressed obiter that if liability had been established against the defendants they could have invoked contributory negligence.

Chapter 6

Financial loss caused by careless acts

The background to the modern law

Fear of multiplicity of claims

[**6.01**] In the well-known case of *Cattle v Stockton Waterworks Co*,[1] the Court of Queen's Bench held that economic losses consequential upon damage to property not owned by the plaintiff were not recoverable. The plaintiff was a contractor who had undertaken to do certain work on the land of a third party. It transpired, however, that the defendant's negligence, or other breach of duty, had caused damage to the land such as to render the plaintiff's task more expensive to carry out, with the result that his contract became less profitable. If the plaintiff's claim for this loss were to succeed it would follow, said Blackburn J delivering the judgment of the court, that in, for example, a case where a mine was flooded the person responsible:

> 'would be liable, not only to an action by the owner of the drowned mine, and by such of his workmen as had their tools or clothes destroyed, but also to an action by every workman and person employed in the mine, who in consequence of its stoppage made less wages than he otherwise would have done.'[2]

Infliction of actual physical damage upon the property of a third party is obviously not the only way in which careless deeds may cause pure economic loss.[3] Nevertheless, *Cattle v Stockton Waterworks & Co*, and the fear of very extensive liability which it adumbrated, continues to exert a major influence upon the approach of the common law to the general question of the recovery of such losses. It is important to distinguish 'pure' economic loss from economic loss

---

1 (1875) LR 10 QB 453.
2 Ibid at 457. See also *Société Anonyme de Remorquage à Helice v Bennetts* [1911] 1 KB 243.
3 Cases involving defective products are another type of situation: see below.

consequential upon physical damage to the plaintiff's own person or property. It has, of course, always been clear that a plaintiff who himself suffered personal injury, or whose property was damaged, could recover financial losses consequential upon this injury or damage. The most common example is a claim for lost income by a person incapacitated through the defendant's negligence.

Pragmatic approach

[**6.02**] The distinction thus drawn, for the pragmatic reason of protecting defendants from a possible avalanche of claims, between 'pure' economic loss and financial loss consequential upon injury or damage to the plaintiff or his property, is evidently arbitrary from the point of view of principle.[1] It also has the paradoxical effect of enabling a defendant who has caused havoc, in the form of widespread economic loss, to avoid liability while at the same time holding liable with full rigour a defendant who has merely damaged the property of one plaintiff. Nevertheless, apart from one House of Lords decision in 1947,[2] which was arguably inconsistent with the orthodox view in that it allowed recovery for pure economic loss, but the significance of which was obscured by its somewhat esoteric context,[3] it was not until *Hedley Byrne & Co Ltd v Heller & Partners Ltd*[4] was decided in 1963 that there appeared any serious possibility of the law in this area undergoing any change or modification.

Effect of *Hedley Byrne*[5]

[**6.03**] In *Hedley Byrne*, Lord Hodson observed that it was 'difficult to see why liability as such should depend on the nature of the damage'.[6] Lord Devlin, similarly, could 'find neither logic nor commonsense' in the proposition that it should be crucial 'whether financial loss is caused through physical injury or whether it is caused directly'.[7] Since, however, the primary focus of *Hedley Byrne* was upon financial loss caused by negligent misstatement, which could be regarded as a special case,[8] the precise effect of the decision upon the more general question of liability for pure economic loss consequential upon negligent deeds, rather than words, was equivocal. The first major case on the point to be decided, after *Hedley Byrne*, adopted a

---

1 See the criticisms by Edmund Davies LJ in his dissenting judgment in S*partan Steel and Alloys Ltd v Martin & Co (Contractors) Ltd* [1973] QB 27 at 39ff, CA.
2 See *Morrison SS Co Ltd v SS Greystoke Castle (Cargo Owners)* [1947] AC 265, [1946] 2 All ER 696, HL.
3 Ie the law of general average.
4 [1964] AC 465, [1963] 2 All ER 575, HL.
5 See, generally, Peter Cane *Tort Law and Economic Interests* (1991). See also A J E Jaffey *The Duty of Care* (1992), Pt III.
6 [1964] AC 465 at 509, [1963] 2 All ER 575 at 598.
7 [1964] AC 465 at 517, [1963] 2 All ER 575 at 602.
8 See, generally, Atiyah 'Negligence and Economic Loss' (1967) 83 LQR 248. See also John Dwyer 'Negligence and Economic Loss' in *Essays for Patrick Atiyah*, Cane and Stapleton (eds) (1991) who reviews developments in this area since the publication of Atiyah's influential 1967 paper.

conservative approach. In *Weller & Co v Foot and Mouth Disease Research Institute*,¹ a virus escaped, due to the negligence of the defendants, causing an outbreak of foot and mouth disease among cattle in the vicinity. The plaintiffs were auctioneers who lost business due to the closure of the cattle markets. Widgery J held that they could not recover for their losses; only the owners of the cattle affected could have had a claim against the defendants. *Hedley Byrne* had not altered the rule 'that in an action of negligence founded on failure to take care to avoid damage to the property of another, only those whose property is injured, or is at least indirectly threatened with injury, can recover'.²

A false dawn

[6.04] Although the traditional hostility to allowing recovery for economic loss subsequently came under some strain, and decisions which apparently created exceptions to the general rule were handed down by appellate courts both in England³ and the Commonwealth,⁴ this liberal trend has recently been put into reverse. The older orthodoxy, and authoritative status of the *Cattle* case itself,⁵ have been reasserted at the highest level. This followed a period of about a decade, starting around the middle of the 1970s, when it looked as though two factors were combining to destabilise the long-standing hostility to liability for pecuniary loss. The first was a series of decisions in which plaintiffs recovered in tort for the cost of repairs to buildings which, owing to various kinds of negligence, had been, or would become, unsafe due to defective construction.⁶ The various fact situations involved in these cases served to highlight the narrowness, in practice, of any line purporting to separate a claim based upon the alleged dangerousness of a building from one which simply alleged that it was less valuable than it ought to have been.⁷ The other factor favouring a change in the law was that some judges began to manifest a degree of hostility towards arguments based upon 'policy', particularly the so-called 'floodgates', or avalanche of claims, argument used in *Cattle v Stockton Waterworks* and succeeding

---

1   [1966] 1 QB 569, [1965] 3 All ER 560.
2   [1966] 1 QB 569 at 583C, [1965] 3 All ER 560 at 567.
3   See, especially *Junior Books Ltd v Veitchi Co Ltd* [1983] 1 AC 520, [1983] 3 All ER 201, HL.
4   See, eg *Caltex (Australia) Pty Ltd Oil v Dredge Willemstad* (1976) 136 CLR 529.
5   See *Candlewood Navigation Corpn Ltd v Mitsui OSK Lines Ltd* [1986] AC 1 at 17, [1985] 2 All ER 935 at 944, PC per Lord Fraser. See also *Esso Petroleum Co Ltd v Hall Russell & Co Ltd* [1989] AC 643, [1989] 1 All ER 37, HL.
6   See *Dutton v Bognor Regis UDC* [1972] 1 QB 373, [1972] 1 All ER 462, CA; *Bowen v Paramount Builders (Hamilton) Ltd* [1977] 1 NZLR 394; *Anns v Merton London Borough Council* [1978] AC 728, [1977] 2 All ER 492, HL; *Batty v Metropolitan Property Realisations Ltd* [1978] QB 554, [1978] 2 All ER 445 CA; *Dennis v Charnwood Borough Council* [1983] QB 409, [1982] 3 All ER 486, CA.
7   See, generally, Grubb 'A case for Recognising Economic Loss in Defective Building Cases' [1984] CLJ 111.

economic loss cases.[1] There was, for a time, a degree of judicial awareness that the history of other branches of the law, in which this fear has been used to resist change, has subsequently shown it to have been exaggerated.[2] But the House of Lords and Privy Council have now made clear, in a number of recent decisions, their conceptual preference for according the law of contract a primary role in the recovery of pure economic loss and their belief that this preference, allied with the 'floodgates' argument and renewed emphasis upon the need for certainty in the law, entails a return to the older learning. The main cases fall broadly into two categories: those where the plaintiff complains that his own property, while undamaged, has nevertheless been reduced in value by the defendant's negligence and those in which, as in *Cattle v Stockton Waterworks Co* itself, the plaintiff suffers pure economic loss as a result of damage to someone else's property. Other types of situation also need to be considered in a residual category.

Where the plaintiff's property is reduced in value by the defendant's negligence

Older approach still valid

[6.05] In *Murphy v Brentwood District Council*[3] Lord Bridge said:

> '... if a manufacturer produces and sells a chattel which is merely defective in quality, even to the extent that it is valueless for the purpose for which it is intended, the manufacturer's liability at common law arises only under and by reference to the terms of any contract to which he is a party in relation to the chattel; the common law does not impose on him any liability in tort to persons to whom he owes no duty in contract but who, having acquired the chattel, suffer economic loss because the chattel is defective in quality.'

His Lordship added that if 'a dangerous defect is discovered before it causes any personal injury or damage to property, because the danger is now known and the chattel cannot be safely used unless the defect is repaired, the defect becomes merely a defect in quality'. Moreover, he made clear his belief that 'these principles' are not confined to chattels but 'are equally applicable to buildings'. In *Murphy's* case the House of Lords held that in exercising its statutory powers of building control a local authority owes no duty of care to building owners, to protect them from expenditure on repairs, should the authority carelessly permit defective construction to take place. In so holding the House, which consisted of seven members on this occasion,

---

1   See, especially, per Lord Roskill in *Junior Books Ltd v Veitchi Co Ltd* [1983] 1 AC 520 at 539D-F. See also *Bowen v Paramount Builders (Hamilton) Ltd* [1977] 1 NZLR 394 at 422 per Cooke J ('floodgates' argument described as 'specious'). Cf *McLoughlin v O'Brian* [1983] 1 AC 410, [1982] 2 All ER 298, HL.
2   See, eg the notorious dissenting speech of Lord Buckmaster in *Donoghue v Stevenson* [1932] AC 562 at 566ff.
3   [1991] 1 AC 398 at 475, [1990] 2 All ER 908 at 925.

overruled its own earlier decision in *Anns v Merton London Borough Council*[1] which had held that such a duty did exist if the relevant defect was a source of imminent danger to the health and safety of the occupants of the building. The emphasis in *Anns* upon health and safety reflected three interwoven strands in the reasoning in that case. Firstly, the legislation which formed the basis of the negligence claim against the local authority was itself concerned with public health.[2] Secondly, liability ostensibly based upon safety could seem, in a sense, to be closer to liability for actual personal injury than to the much more doubtful area of pure economic loss.[3] Thirdly, assuming that liability would have been imposed if the building in question had actually collapsed and caused personal injury, it would be illogical to deny recovery for the cost of a pre-emptive strike by an occupier who averted disaster by repairing in advance.[4]

Rejection of Anns

[**6.06**] In *Murphy v Brentwood District Council*[5] the reasoning in *Anns* was comprehensively rejected.[6] The House of Lords in the later case refused to accept that the health and safety idea rendered the situation analogous to one involving actual property damage or personal injury. It was 'incontestable on analysis', said Lord Oliver, 'that what the plaintiffs [ie in *Anns*] suffered was pure pecuniary loss and nothing more'.[7] There was 'equally nothing in the statutory provisions', his Lordship continued, 'which even suggest that the purpose of the statute was to protect owners of buildings from pure economic loss'.[8] The House also undermined the argument in favour of allowing occupiers to recover from allegedly negligent local authorities the cost of repairs in advance of collapse by expressly reserving its opinion on the question of whether a local authority, as distinct from a negligent building owner, could be held liable on the basis of its

---

1 [1978] AC 728, [1977] 2 All ER 492, HL.
2 Ie the Public Health Act 1936.
3 'To allow recovery for ... damage to the house follows, in my opinion, from normal principle. If classification is required, the relevant damage is in my opinion material, physical damage, and what is recoverable is the amount of expenditure necessary to restore the dwelling to a condition in which it is no longer a danger to the health or safety of persons occupying': [1978] AC 728 at 759, [1977] 2 All ER 492 at 505 per Lord Wilberforce.
4 This point was made more emphatically in the earlier Court of Appeal decision of *Dutton v Bognor Regis UDC* [1972] 1 QB 373, [1972] 1 All ER 462 which was upheld in *Anns v Merton London Borough Council* (and subsequently overruled in *Murphy* along with *Anns* itself). See, especially, per Lord Denning MR in *Dutton* [1972] 1 QB 373 at 369D-F.
5 [1991] 1 AC 398, [1990] 2 All ER 908, HL. See Richard O'Dair '*Murphy v Brentwood District Council*: A House With Firm Foundations?' (1991) 54 MLR 561. See also Sir Robin Cooke 'An Impossible Distinction' (1991) 107 LQR 46.
6 See IN Duncan Wallace QC '*Anns* Beyond Repair' (1991) 107 LQR 228. See also BS Markesinis and Simon Deakin 'The Random Element of their Lordships' Infallible Judgment: An Economic and Comparative Analysis of the Tort of Negligence from *Anns* to *Murphy*' (1992) 55 MLR 619.
7 [1991] 1 AC 398 at 484, [1990] 2 All ER 908 at 932.
8 [1991] 1 AC 398 at 490, [1990] 2 All ER 908 at 937.

statutory powers even if a badly constructed building *did* collapse and cause injury.¹ Finally, the House considered that to impose liability in favour of occupiers on the *Anns* basis would outflank the limited scope of the statutory protection afforded to them by the Defective Premises Act 1972.² Lord Keith robustly summarised the views of the House in *Murphy* thus:

> 'In my opinion it is clear that *Anns* did not proceed on any basis of established principle, but introduced a new species of liability governed by a principle indeterminate in character but having the potentiality of covering a wide range of situations, involving chattels as well as real property, in which it had never hitherto been thought that the law of negligence had any proper place.'³

'Complex structures'?

[**6.07**] In the 1988 case of *D & F Estates Ltd v Church Comrs For England*,⁴ decided by the House of Lords two years before its decision in *Murphy*, the House addressed directly the liability in tort for pure economic loss of a *builder*; as distinct from that of a local authority which was the focus of both the *Anns* and *Murphy* cases. In the *D & F Estates* case the plaintiffs, who were the lessees and occupiers of a flat, sought to claim from the defendant builders, with whom they were not in a contractual relationship, the cost of repairing allegedly defective plastering work which had been carried when the block of flats in question had been constructed. The claim failed.⁵ 'It seems to me clear that the cost of replacing the defective plaster', said Lord Bridge,⁶ 'was not an item of damage for which the builder . . . could possibly be made liable in negligence under the principle of *Donoghue v Stevenson* or any legitimate development of that principle. To make him so liable would be to impose on him for the benefit of those with whom he had no contractual relationship the obligation of one who warranted the quality of the plaster as regards materials, workmanship and fitness for purpose'. The House criticised the *Anns* case, which had not then been overruled, but distinguished it by emphasising its focus upon local authority liability and health and safety concepts. Moreover the argument that, since the builder would be liable if his defective structure caused personal injury or damage to property other than the structure itself, he should also be liable in tort

---

1   See [1991] 1 AC 398 at 457, [1990] 2 All ER 908 at 912 (Lord Mackay LC), 463 and 917 (Lord Keith) and 492 and 938 (Lord Jauncey).
2   See [1991] 1 AC 398 at 457, [1990] 2 All ER 908 at 912 (Lord Mackay); 472 and 923 (Lord Keith); 480 and 930 (Lord Bridge); 938 (Lord Oliver) 491 and 498 and 942-3 (Lord Jauncey). On the Defective Premises Act 1972 see ch 16 below.
3   [1991] 1 AC 398 at 471, [1990] 2 All ER 908 at 922.
4   [1989] AC 177, [1988] 2 All ER 992, HL. See I N Duncan Wallace QC 'Negligence and Defective Buildings: Confusion Confounded?' (1989) 105 LQR 46.
5   See also *Department of the Environment v Thomas Bates & Son Ltd* [1991] 1 AC 499, [1990] 2 All ER 943, HL (decided by the House of Lords on the same day as *Murphy v Brentwood District Council.*
6   [1989] AC 177 at 207, [1988] 2 All ER 992 at 1007.

for the cost of repairs made pre-emptively by the owner, was rejected.[1] In the words again of Lord Bridge:[2]

> 'If the defect is discovered before any damage is done, the loss sustained by the owner of the structure, who has to repair or demolish it to avoid a potential source of danger to third parties, would seem to be purely economic. Thus, if I acquire a property with a dangerously defective garden wall which is attributable to the bad workmanship of the original builder, it is difficult to see any basis in principle on which I can sustain an action in tort against the builder for the cost of either repairing or demolishing the wall. No physical damage has been caused. All that has happened is that the defect in the wall has been discovered in time to prevent damage occurring.'

[**6.08**] Unfortunately, in an attempt to limit the scope of his own dictum, Lord Bridge continued in a manner which was to cause a degree of confusion which had to be clarified when *Murphy v Brentwood District Council* was decided. He stated that, while the principle operated to negate liability on the facts of *D & F Estates* itself, he could 'see that it may well be arguable that in the case of complex structures, as indeed possibly in the case of complex chattels, one element of the structure should be regarded for the purpose of the application of the principles under discussion as distinct from another element, so that damage to one part of the structure caused by a hidden defect in another part may qualify to be treated as damage to "other property"' so as to give rise to liability in tort on orthodox general principles.[3] This 'complex structure' theory, motivated in part by a desire to provide a possible rationalisation for the description by Lord Wilberforce in *Anns* of the damage in that case as 'material, physical damage',[4] caused concern to critics who feared that it would lead to much sterile litigation in which plaintiffs would seek to distinguish between the component parts of what were, in essence, single unified buildings or products. Thus in *Murphy v Brentwood District Council* Lord Bridge clarified his earlier judgment as follows:[5]

> 'The reality is that the structural elements in any building form a single indivisible unit of which the different parts are essentially interdependent. To the extent that there is any defect in one part of the

1 Lord Bridge did, however, subsequently suggest in *Murphy v Brentwood District Council* that recovery of pre-emptive costs might be possible in one situation: '... if a building stands so close to the boundary of the building owner's land that after discovery of the dangerous defect it remains a potential source of injury to persons or property on neighbouring land or on the highway, the building owner ought, in principle, to be entitled to recover in tort from the negligent builder the cost of obviating the danger, whether by repair or demolition, so far as that cost is necessarily incurred in order to protect himself from potential liability to third parties.': [1991] 1 AC 398 at 475, [1990] 2 All ER 908 at 926. This suggestion, which perhaps reflects the influence of the law of nuisance was, however, doubted by Lord Oliver in his own speech in *Murphy's* case: see [1991] 1 AC 398 at 489, [1990] 2 All ER 908 at 936.
2 [1989] AC 177 at 206, [1988] 2 All ER 992 at 1006.
3 See also per Lord Oliver in [1989] AC 177 at 212, [1988] 2 All ER 992 at 1010.
4 See [1978] AC 728 at 759, [1977] 2 All ER 492 at 505.
5 [1991] 1 AC 398 at 478, [1990] 2 All ER 908 at 928.

structure it must to a greater or lesser degree necessarily affect all other parts of the structure. Therefore any defect in the structure is a defect in the quality of the whole and it is quite artificial, in order to impose a legal liability which the law would not otherwise impose, to treat a defect in an integral structure, so far as it weakens the structure, as a dangerous defect liable to cause damage to "other property".'

Thus no distinction would be drawn between the foundations of a house and its superstructure. On the other hand, 'if a defective central heating boiler explodes and damages a house or a defective electrical installation malfunctions and sets the house on fire', his Lordship saw 'no reason to doubt that the owner of the house, if he can prove that the damage was due to the negligence of the boiler manufacturer in the one case or the electrical contractor in the other, can recover damages in tort on *Donoghue v Stevenson* principles'.[1] Although, therefore, there may be difficult borderline cases it is now clear that the courts will not encourage the analysis of the components of buildings and chattels into separate parts in order to facilitate liability by concluding that one part had damaged another. Accordingly, as the law now stands the traditional position has been re-established that a plaintiff unable to rely on a contract will normally have no redress for a defect, which reduces the value of any building or chattel acquired by him, unless he is afforded protection by a statute such as the Defective Premises Act 1972.[2]

An exception?

[**6.09**] A possible exception to the general rule of non-liability in tort for defective products is based upon the controversial majority decision of the House of Lords in *Junior Books Ltd v Veitchi Co Ltd*.[3] In this case the plaintiffs contracted with a building company to construct a factory. Specialist sub-contractors were appointed by the building company to carry out flooring work in the factory. Unfortunately this work was done carelessly and the floor was seriously defective: although it posed no threat to persons, or to other property of the plaintiffs', keeping it properly maintained would have been vastly more expensive than if the work had been done properly. For some reason which was never explained the plaintiffs chose not to proceed in contract against the building company, but instead sued the careless sub-contractors, with whom they were not in a contractual relationship, in tort. By a majority the House of Lords held that the claim succeeded. Lord Roskill and Lord Fraser, with whom Lord Russell agreed, asserted that, in the *particular circumstances of the case,* pure economic loss resulting from a product

---

1   Ibid at the same page. See also per Lord Keith in [1991] 1 AC at 470, [1990] 2 All ER 922.
2   See below, ch 16. See also, for discussion of possible reform of this area of the law, John A Hayes 'After Murphy: Building on the Consumer Protection Principle' (1992) 12 OJLS 112.
3   [1983] 1 AC 520, [1982] 3 All ER 201, HL.

being, in effect, less valuable than it ought to have been, was recoverable in tort. Lord Brandon disagreed with this proposition and delivered a dissenting speech. He broadly favoured the traditional view that the proper sphere of such liability was contract. Similarly Lord Keith, although he somehow felt able to agree with the majority as to the actual result,[1] in effect dissented. He felt that it would 'necessarily follow', from the approach of the majority, 'that any manufacturer of products would become liable to the ultimate purchaser if the product, owing to negligence in manufacture, was, without being harmful in any way, useless or worthless or defective in quality so that the purchaser wasted the money he spent on it'.[2] His Lordship expressly associated himself with Lord Brandon in rejecting this proposition.

[**6.10**] Of course if that proposition *had* accurately stated the ratio decidendi of the majority *Junior Books* would clearly now no longer be good law after *D & F Estates v Church Comrs for England* and *Murphy v Brentwood District Council*. But the majority did *not* accept that the wide general proposition, of liability for foreseeable economic loss caused by products defective in quality, was implicit in their reasoning in the way that Lord Brandon and Lord Keith alleged that it was. Such liability was appropriate in the instant case, the majority argued, because of the very close relationship between plaintiffs and defendants; it did not follow that other cases, in which the relationship was not so close, would be decided the same way merely because the loss suffered by the plaintiff was in some sense foreseeable. In the instant case the plaintiffs had actually nominated the defendants as specialist sub-contractors and, in the words of Lord Fraser, the 'proximity' between them was 'extremely close, falling only just short of a direct contractual relationship'.[3] Lord Roskill considered that the language and concepts used in the negligent misstatement cases, particularly *Hedley Byrne v Heller* itself, were applicable to the present context. He said that 'The concept of proximity must always involve, at least in most cases, some degree of reliance'. This requirement 'would not easily be found to exist', he continued, 'as between an ultimate consumer and a manufacturer ... in the ordinary everyday transaction of purchasing chattels when it is obvious that in truth the real reliance was on the immediate vendor and not on the manufacturer'.[4] In both *D & F Estates Ltd v Church Comrs for*

1 His Lordship's reasoning is far from easy to follow and seems to be internally contradictory: it apparently contemplated recovery for pure pecuniary loss on an extraordinarily wide basis where a plaintiff's general economic prospects had been adversely affected while expressly denying it in the much narrower specific situation of a defective product.
2 [1983] 1 AC 520 at 536G-H, [1982] 3 All ER 201 at 207, HL.
3 [1983] 1 AC 520 at 533, [1982] 3 All ER 201 at 204, HL. See also per Lord Roskill at 546C and 214: 'The relationship between the parties was as close as it could be short of actual privity of contract.' *Actual* privity, however, in a situation similar to that in *Junior Books* may paradoxically put the plaintiff at a disadvantage: see *Greater Nottingham Co-operative Society Ltd v Cementation Piling and Foundations Ltd* [1989] QB 71, [1988] 2 All ER 971, CA.
4 See, eg *Muirhead v Industrial Tank Specialities Ltd* [1986] QB 507, [1985] 3 All ER 705, CA; *Simaan General Contracting Co v Pilkington Glass Ltd (No 2)* [1988] QB 758, [1988] 1 All ER 791, CA.

England[1] and *Murphy v Brentwood District Council*[2] the House of Lords appears to have accepted the correctness of the decision in *Junior Books* on the basis that it did indeed concern the application of *Hedley Byrne* principles to a 'uniquely proximate relationship'.[3] Thus when facts similar to those in *Junior Books v Veitchi* occur the decision still stands as an authority for the imposition of liability.

Relevance of the contract

[**6.11**] Although the number of cases in which the *Junior Books* principle will actually be applicable is likely to be few, a difficulty which may arise in them concerns the evaluation of the *allegedly* defective chattel or building. What if, for example, the quality of the product was lower than the contract which provided for its construction intended, but the agreement incorporated a clause which purported to restrict or exclude the manufacturer's contractual liability? In *Junior Books* itself Lord Roskill suggested that, in principle, a contractual provision could be relevant to the particular type of tort claim there in issue, notwithstanding that the plaintiff was not a party to the contract.[4] It is true that in the later case of *Leigh and Sillivan Ltd v Aliakmon Shipping Co Ltd*[5] Lord Brandon reiterated his own opposition to this proposal, and expressed specifically his continued disagreement with Lord Roskill's views in *Junior Books*. The facts of the *Aliakmon* case were, however, far removed from those of *Junior Books* and the relationship between the parties was nowhere near as close. It is submitted that, at least within the peculiarly narrow sphere of a true *Junior Books* type of claim, which presupposes a very high degree of reliance by the plaintiff on the defendant, usually involving knowledge on the part of the former of the terms of the contract, the views of Lord Roskill are to be preferred. Accordingly, even an exemption clause could in principle be effective, 'according to the manner in which it was worded',[6] to limit the defendant's duty of care in tort as well as in contract. Such a disclaimer would not be effective against a third party suing for personal injury,[7] but in appropriate cases it probably should be against a claim for economic loss. The clause might have been incorporated, conceivably even at the suggestion of the original purchaser, in order to relieve the manufacturer of the burden of

---

1   See [1989] AC 177 at 202, [1988] 2 All ER 992 at 1003 per Lord Bridge and 215 and 1013 per Lord Oliver.
2   See [1991] 1 AC 398 at 466, [1990] 2 All ER 908 at 919 per Lord Keith and 481 and 930 per Lord Bridge.
3   Per Lord Bridge in *D & F Estates Ltd v Church Comrs for England* [1989] AC 177 at 202, [1988] 2 All ER 992 at 1003.
4   See [1983] 1 AC 520 at 546, [1982] 3 All ER 201 at 214.
5   [1986] AC 785 at 817.
6   [1983] 1 AC 520 at 546F, [1982] 3 All ER 201 at 214 per Lord Roskill. See also *Southern Water Authority v Carey* [1985] 2 All ER 1077 at 1086 and *Norwich City Council v Harvey* [1989] 1 All ER 1180, [1989] 1 WLR 828, CA. Cf *Voli v Inglewood Shire Council* (1963) 110 CLR 74 at 85.
7   Cf *Mint v Good* [1951] 1 KB 517 at 528, [1950] 2 All ER 1159 at 1166, CA per Denning J. See also the Unfair Contract Terms Act, 1977, s 2(1).

carrying liability insurance and thereby enable a lower price to be charged for the product. In such circumstances it would not be appropriate to impose upon the defendant a liability to which, at the outset, it was not intended he should be subjected.[1]

Where the plaintiff suffers economic loss which is conseqential upon injury or damage to a third party

Traditional approach reasserted

[**6.12**] The House of Lords, in *Leigh and Sillivan Ltd v Aliakmon Shipping Co Ltd*,[2] and the Judicial Committee of the Privy Council, in *Candlewood Navigation Corpn Ltd v Mitsui OSK Lines Ltd*,[3] both reasserted in the 1980s the traditional position, that the law of tort does not provide a remedy for those who suffer financial losses due to the infliction of damage to property in which they do not have an interest. These cases affirmed the authority of the two best-known pre-existing decisions on the point handed down in recent times: the decision of Widgery J in *Weller & Co v Foot and Mouth Disease Research Institute*,[4] which was set out earlier in this chapter, and *Spartan Steel and Alloys Ltd v Martin & Co (Contractors) Ltd*.[5] The latter was a majority decision of the Court of Appeal. It concerned the negligent severing, by the defendants' employees, of an electricity cable while they were doing excavating work on a road near to a factory at which the plaintiffs manufactured stainless steel alloys. The damage to the cable, which was the property of the electricity board, led to the electricity supply to the factory being cut off for many hours. As a result, the plaintiffs suffered physical damage when molten metal began to solidify in their furnaces and also suffered pure economic loss through the cessation of production. The defendants denied liability for the latter, a contention which Lord Denning MR and Lawton LJ accepted.[6] Lawton LJ stressed the authorities, in particular *Cattle v Stockton Waterworks Co*,[7] while Lord Denning MR frankly based the decision upon policy: 'If claims for economic loss were permitted for this particular hazard, there would be no end of claims.'[8] Edmund

---

1 Cf *New Zealand Shipping Co Ltd v Satterthwaite & Co Ltd* [1975] AC 154, [1974] 1 All ER 1015, PC. But note that the Unfair Contract Terms Act, 1977, which applies to common law liability for negligence (ie is not confined to actions in contract) subjects all attempts to exclude liability outside the personal injury sphere (where any exclusion is normally prohibited) to the 'reasonableness' test: see ss 2(2) and s 11. The relevant part of the Act only applies to things 'done or to be done by a person in the course of a business', (s 1(3)(a)) but most defective products cases will obviously fall within this definition.
2 [1986] AC 785, [1986] 2 All ER 145, HL, see below. See also *Esso Petroleum Co Ltd v Hall Russell & Co Ltd* [19849] AC 643, [1989] 1 All ER 37, HL.
3 [1986] AC 1, [1985] 2 All ER 935, PC, see below.
4 [1966] 1 QB 569, [1965] 3 All ER 560.
5 [1973] QB 27, [1972] 3 All ER 557, CA.
6 See also *Electrochrome Ltd v Welsh Plastics Ltd* [1968] 2 All ER 205.
7 (1875) LR 10 QB 453.
8 [1973] QB at 38G.

Davies LJ dissented. He favoured the wide proposition 'that an action lies in negligence for damages in respect of purely economic loss, provided that it was a reasonably foreseeable and direct consequence of failure in the duty of care';[1] and found these conditions satisfied in the instant case. The court was, however, unanimous in rejecting the proposition that the plaintiffs could recover for their lost production simply because they happened fortuitously to have a valid, but independent, claim arising out of the same incident for physical damage. A so-called doctrine of 'parasitic damages', for which some support could be found in the authorities[2] enabling a plaintiff to attach a claim for economic loss to one for physical damage, even if the former was unconnected with the latter, was repudiated. In the result, therefore, although the plaintiffs were in fact awarded a modest sum for economic loss, the calculation of it was strictly limited to losses flowing directly from the physical damage which had occurred in the furnaces.[3]

Avalanche of claims

[**6.13**] The underlying reason for denying liability in cases of this general type remains the fear that some of them could generate a wholly oppressive avalanche of claims against the defendant. The following example was given in an Australian case:[4]

> '... if, through the momentary inattention of an officer, a ship collided with a bridge, and as a result a large suburban area, which included shops and factories, was deprived of its means of access to a city, great loss might be suffered by tens of thousands of persons, but to require the wrongdoer to compensate all those who had suffered pecuniary loss would impose upon him a burden out of all proportion to his wrong'.[5]

It has been argued that this position has validity when subjected to economic analysis.[6] It would be both inefficient and impracticable to expect those whose isolated acts of carelessness in, eg excavating near underground cables, could deprive a whole town of electricity to insure against all economic losses resulting therefrom. It is much more sensible, it is said, for individual businesses to insure against interruption of production from such causes if they wish.[7] This highly

---

1 [1973] QB at 45A.
2 See *Horton v Colwyn Bay and Colwyn UDC* [1908] 1 KB 327 at 341, CA per Buckley LJ, and per counsel, arguendo, in *Spartan Steel:* [1973] QB at 32D.
3 See also *British Celanese Ltd v AH Hunt (Capacitors) Ltd* [1969] 2 All ER 1252, [1969] 1 WLR 959; *SCM (UK) Ltd v Whittall & Son Ltd* [1971] 1 QB 337, [1970] 3 All ER 245, CA.
4 *Caltex Oil (Australia) Pty Ltd v Dredge Willemstad* (1976) 136 CLR 529 at 551-552 per Gibbs J. Cf *Weller & Co v Foot and Mouth Disease Research Institute* [1966] 1 QB 569, [1965] 3 All ER 560.
5 Cf the Canadian case *Gypsum Carrier Inc v R* (1977) 78 DLR (3d) 175 (ship collided with railway bridge owned by third party: railway company unable to claim for cost of re-routing trains). But see also *Canadian National Rly Co v Norsk Pacific SS Co* (1992) 91 DLR (4th) 289 discussed below, in which the Supreme Court of Canada *imposed* liability in similar circumstances to those in the *Gypsum* case.
6 See Bishop 'Economic Loss in Tort' (1982) 2 OJLS 1, especially pp 14-17.
7 See Atiyah *Accidents, Compensation and the Law* (4th edn) p 76.

pragmatic reason for denying liability is often reinforced in the cases by two further ones. Firstly, there is the contention that to make exceptions to the general rule in situations in which, on the facts, there would be no danger of an avalanche of claims would be potentially anomalous and a cause of uncertainty. Secondly, and more fundamentally, there is the conceptual argument that economic losses should, in general, be the prerogative of the law of contract. Such losses are frequently inflicted through the operation of the *market*, which is an intrinsic function of a capitalist society: even *intentional* losses thus inflicted having to be accepted if they were suffered in the ordinary course of business competition.[1] The doctrinal objection to liability has, of course, been powerfully reinforced by the decisions of the House of Lords in *D & F Estates Ltd v Church Comrs for England*[2] and *Murphy v Brentwood District Council*,[3] discussed above. The a priori hostility to the recovery of pure economic loss in tort demonstrated by these cases is not confined to their own context of defective buildings reduced in value by the tortfeasor.

Confirmation of orthodox view

[**6.14**] In *Candlewood Navigation Corpn Ltd v Mitsui OSK Lines Ltd*[4] the plaintiffs, who were time charterers of a vessel which was damaged in a collision caused by the negligent navigation of the defendants' vessel, sought to recover the profits they lost due to the ship being unable to trade while it was undergoing repair. The Privy Council rejected the claim. In their capacity as time charterers the plaintiffs did not own the damaged vessel[5] so that their loss was purely economic. Lord Fraser, delivering the judgment of the Board, referred to the fact that *Cattle v Stockton Waterworks* had 'stood for over a hundred years' and asserted that 'the justification for denying a right of action to a person who has suffered economic damage through injury to the property of another is that for reasons of practical policy it is considered to be inexpedient to admit his claim'.[6] Although the Board had been pressed by counsel for the plaintiffs with the argument that the policy justification for denying liability based upon an avalanche of claims was not applicable on the facts of the case, in that no such avalanche was conceivable, their Lordships remained unimpressed. To distinguish on that factual basis between economic loss cases which in principle were considered to be similar would undermine the certainty important in commercial relationships, nor were attempts to draw more principled distinctions by attempting to

---

1 See Smith *Liability in Negligence* (1984) p 77: 'It would indeed be strange if one were to be held liable for doing negligently that for which there would be no liability if done intentionally.'
2 [1989] AC 177, [1988] 2 All ER 992, HL.
3 [1991] 1 AC 398, [1990] 2 All ER 908, HL.
4 [1986] AC 1, [1985] 2 All ER 935. The case is criticised in (1986) 102 LQR 13 (Michael A Jones), and defended in [1986] 45 CLJ 10 (Andrew Tettenborn).
5 As it happened the plaintiffs *were* the owners of the vessel, but due to the peculiar facts of the case they were unable to sue for the relevant loss in that capacity.
6 [1986] AC at 17.

classify various groups of potential plaintiffs likely to prove successful.[1]

Possibility of exceptions to the general rule rejected

[**6.15**] Towards the end of his judgment in the *Candlewood* case.[2] Lord Fraser conceded that there might be 'exceptional cases', unlike the one before him, in which liability for pure economic loss caused by a negligent act would, contrary to the general rule, be imposed. In the subsequent case of *Leigh and Sillivan Ltd v Aliakmon Shipping Co Ltd*,[3] however, the House of Lords apparently set its face against the possibility of such exceptions, notwithstanding that a persistent and not unpersuasive line of earlier authorities favoured them.

The pre-Aliakmon cases

[**6.16**] In a number of these cases the recovery in tort of pure economic loss, consequential upon physical damage to a third party's property, was either anticipated *obiter* or even actually allowed. The underlying reasoning appears to have been that such a claim should be permitted if the commercial relationship between the plaintiff and the owner of the damaged property was so close that it would be artificial to allow the incidence of liability to depend upon the ownership of that property, especially since such particular facts are unlikely to give rise to the 'floodgates' problem. A hypothetical example of the application of this approach was given by Lord Roche, in the House of Lords, in *Morrison SS Co Ltd v Greystoke Castle (Cargo Owners)*.[4] His Lordship said:[5]

> '... if two lorries A and B are meeting one another on the road, I cannot bring myself to doubt that the driver of lorry A owes a duty to both the owner of lorry B and to the owner of goods then carried in lorry B. Those owners are engaged in a common adventure with or by means of lorry B, and if lorry A is negligently driven and damages lorry B so severely that, while no damage is done to the goods in it, the goods have to be unloaded for the repair of the lorry and then reloaded or carried forward in some other way and the consequent expense is (by reason of his contract or otherwise) the expense of the owner of the goods, then, in my judgment, the owner of the goods has a direct cause of action to recover such expense.'

This dictum was subsequently referred to with approval by Lord Denning MR.[6] A decision of the High Court of Australia in the 1970s which appeared in effect to provide an example of this principle in operation, is *Caltex Oil (Australia) Pty Ltd v Dredge Willemstad*.[7] A

1 See ibid at 24.
2 See ibid at 25.
3 [1986] AC 785, [1986] 2 All ER 145, HL. See also *Esso Petroleum Co Ltd v Hall Russell & Co Ltd* [1989] AC 643, [1989] 1 All ER 37, HL.
4 [1947] AC 265, [1946] 2 All ER 696, HL.
5 [1947] AC 265 at 280.
6 See *SCM (UK) Ltd v Whittall & Son Ltd* [1971] 1 QB 337 at 346A-C, CA.
7 (1976) 136 CLR 529.

pipeline laid across a bay, which belonged to an oil refinery, was fractured when a dredging vessel collided with it due to the negligence of the defendants. The pipeline connected the refinery to an oil terminal, on the opposite shore of the bay, operated by the plaintiffs. There was an arrangement whereby the plaintiffs supplied the oil refinery with crude oil through the pipeline and received back refined oil by the same method. The plaintiffs successfully sued the defendants for the economic loss which they suffered while the pipeline, which they did not own, could not be used. It is not easy to extract a single ratio decidendi from the five judgments delivered.[1] The members of the court do, however, appear to have been in general agreement that policy factors precluded the imposition of liability for pure economic loss on the same general basis as for physical damage.[2] But they were also unanimous that the present case was nevertheless one of those in which recovery could be permitted. The fact that the pipeline served only the plaintiffs and its owners, so that there was no danger of an avalanche of claims, was regarded as relevant. Moreover, it was a case in which 'the plaintiff, and the person whose property was injured, were engaged in a common adventure'.[3]

The Aliakmon case

[6.17] *Leigh and Sillivan Ltd v Aliakmon Shipping Co Ltd*[4] concerned a situation involving the carriage of goods by sea. The plaintiffs had agreed to buy the goods in question but, owing to the peculiar facts of the case, they were not holders of the bill of lading and so did not have title to them at the time when the goods were unfortunately damaged in transit. The question arose whether the plaintiffs could nevertheless sue the defendant shipowners in negligence. A majority of the Court of Appeal, and a unanimous House of Lords, held that they could not. Lord Brandon, who delivered the only speech in the House of Lords, re-asserted the 'floodgates' doctrine as a general proposition, and responded as follows to the suggestion that it was not appropriate to apply that doctrine to the facts of the particular case:[5]

> 'If an exception to the general rule were to be made in the field of carriage by sea, it would no doubt have to be extended to the field of carriage by land, and I do not think that it is possible to say that no

1 For a note on the case see PF Cane in (1977) 93 LQR 333.
2 See, eg the particularly clear statement in (1976) 136 CLR 529 at 555 per Gibbs J: 'In my opinion it is still right to say that as a general rule damages are not recoverable for economic loss which is not consequential upon injury to the plaintiff's person or property. The fact that the loss was foreseeable is not enough to make it recoverable.'
3 (1976) 135 CLR 529 at 555 per Gibbs J. See also per Stephen J at pp 579-580. But cf per Jacobs J at p 602: 'I do not think that Lord Roche's reference [ie in the *Greystoke Castle* case] to "common adventure" was more than a statement of commercial reality. It introduced no special qualification of law.' See also *French Knit Sales Pty Ltd v Gold & Sons Pty Ltd* [1972] 2 NSWLR 132 in which the Court of Appeal in New South Wales refused to accept that *Greystoke Castle* embodied any principle of general application.
4 [1986] AC 785, [1986] 2 All ER 145, HL.
5 [1986] AC 785 at 816-817, [1986] 2 All ER 145 at 154-155. See also *Esso Petroleum Co Ltd v Hall Russell & Co Ltd* [1989] AC 643, [1989] 1 All ER 37, HL.

undue increase in the scope of a person's liability for want of care would follow. In any event, where a general rule, which is simple to understand and easy to apply, has been established by a long line of authority over many years, I do not think that the law should allow special pleading in a particular case within the general rule to detract from its application. If such detraction were to be permitted in one particular case, it would lead to attempts to have it permitted in a variety of other particular cases, and the result would be that the certainty, which the application of the general rule presently provides, would be seriously undermined. Yet certainty of the law is of the utmost importance, especially but by no means only, in commercial matters.'

[6.18] Lord Brandon also denied that the result was inherently unjust, by arguing that with proper advice the plaintiffs could have taken precautions in advance to ensure that they would have had a right to sue in the circumstances which ultimately transpired.[1] The plausibility of this particular point is, however, open to question. Even assuming that such a move had been a realistic and practical,[2] as distinct from theoretical[3] possibility, it is hardly convincing in itself as a justification for shifting responsibility from an actual wrongdoer. A victim's failure to lock his house does not exonerate a burglar.

Goff LJ and the 'principle of transferred loss'

[6.19] When the *Aliakmon* case was before the Court of Appeal Goff LJ (as he then was), found himself in the minority on the point of principle and favoured recovery on the basis of what he described as 'the principle of transferred loss'. He expounded this principle as follows:[4]

'Where A owes a duty of care in tort not to cause physical damage to B's property, and commits a breach of that duty in circumstances in which the loss of or physical damage to the property will ordinarily fall on B but (as is reasonably foreseeable by A) such loss or damage, by reason of a contractual relationship between B and C, falls on C, then C will be entitled, subject to the terms of the contract restricting A's liability to B, to bring an action in tort against A in respect of such loss or damage to the extent that it falls on him, C.'

Lord Brandon flatly rejected this proposition and overruled a recent English decision at first instance which had been consistent with it.[5] In principle, however, the theory of Goff LJ seems to have much to commend it. If, as Lord Brandon asserted, the ultimate reason for the denial of liability is the purely pragmatic 'floodgates' argument that

---

1 See [1986] AC at 818-819.
2 See the doubts expressed in Todd 'Actions by Banks Against Carriers - An update of the Tort Position' (1986) 2 JIBL 127 at 130 (cited in Markesinis, 'An Expanding Tort Law – The Price of a Rigid Contract Law' (1987) 103 LQR 354 at p 386, footnote 92).
3 See the doubts expressed by Malcolm Clarke in 'Buyer Fails to Recover Economic Loss from the Negligent Carrier' [1986] 45 CLJ 382 at 384.
4 [1985] QB 350 at 399.
5 See *Schiffahrt und Kohlen GmbH v Chelsea Maritime Ltd, The Irene's Success* [1982] QB 481, [1982] 1 All ER 218.

argument should surely not be applied outside situations in which a real danger of an avalanche of claims exists: *unless* refusal to do so would indeed lead to the drawing of arbitrary factual distinctions between claims on the basis of hindsight and hence to injustice and uncertainty. The approach of Goff LJ might have facilitated the development of rules which might have succeeded in avoiding these difficulties while at the same time ensuring that the application of the 'floodgates' argument was not needlessly extended.

Priority of contract?

[6.20] The current judicial refusal to make any exceptions to the general rule of non-liability is, however, powered not only by a blend of considerations of pragmatism and justice but also, as has already been emphasised, by a conceptual preference for confining the recovery of pure economic loss to the law of contract as far as possible. This preference would, in a sense, be easier to defend if it were consistently applied. But apart from the fact that completely consistent application is impossible in terms of authority 30 years after *Hedley Byrne*, it is open to question whether the rigid and inflexible distinction between contract and tort, which such an approach implies, is ultimately in tune with the deeply pragmatic nature of the common law as a whole. It remains to be seen whether the stream of recent judicial pronouncements at the highest level will have their apparently intended effect of freezing development of this branch of the law.[1] Ironically their own insistence upon an incremental, rather than generalised, approach to liability in negligence has prevented the higher judiciary from expounding clearly the policy issues which underly their determination to reverse earlier trends in favour of an expansion of liability. Until these questions are addressed openly the law in this area will continue to display a singular lack of coherence.[2]

Liability imposed in Canada

[6.21] In a major case decided after *Murphy v Brentwood District Council,* in which it was considered along with most of the other leading English cases, the Supreme Court of Canada chose by a bare majority not to adopt the exclusionary approach to the recovery of pure economic loss. In *Canadian National Rly Co v Norsk Pacific SS Co,*[3] a barge which was being towed down a river by the defendants' tug collided with a bridge, due to the defendants' negligence, and

---

1 Cf BS Markesinis in 'An Expanding Tort Law - The Price of a Rigid Contract Law' (1987) 103 LQR 354 at 389 who says of the *Aliakmon* case that its 'reasoning, which aims at re-establishing the authority of a rule that has clearly broken down in practice . . . makes [him] doubt the longevity of the judgment.'
2 See Jane Stapleton 'Duty of Care and Economic Loss: a Wider Agenda' (1991) 107 LQR 249.
3 (1992) 91 DLR (4th) 289. See BS Markesinis 'Compensation for Negligently Inflicted Pure Economic Loss: Some Canadian Views' (1993) 109 LQR 5.

caused extensive damage to it. The bridge was owned by a third party but the plaintiffs, who had no legal interest in the bridge itself, had a contractual right to run trains across it and suffered pure economic loss when it was closed for several weeks for repairs. By a four to three majority the Supreme Court held that the plaintiffs could recover their losses from the defendants. The majority[1] considered that there was sufficient 'proximity' between plaintiffs and defendants and, on the facts of the case, no danger of a 'floodgates' situation: the close relationship which in practice existed between the plaintiffs and the actual owners of the bridge being treated as an important factor in this respect. The dissentients[2] considered that the nature of the plaintiffs' loss was in principle indistinguishable from the economic loss suffered by many people in the 'ripple' effect following a major disruption of the kind in question, and that the case therefore did raise the spectre of indeterminate liability. The debate within the common law about the recovery of pure economic loss in tort is therefore a continuing one elsewhere. Perhaps differing socio-economic situations in different countries justify the adoption of different approaches on policy grounds but, if so, those grounds have yet to be clearly articulated. An unfortunate consequence, as far as English law is concerned, of the current hostility of the judges to the overt consideration of policy issues is that such grounds of possible distinction are likely to remain unexplored.

Other cases of economic loss

Recovery still possible in some cases

[6.22] Even in England it would clearly be a major over-simplification to assume that recent decisions have put into reverse all earlier developments in the direction of expanding liability for economic loss. It is significant that even in *Murphy v Brentwood District Council*[3] Lord Oliver had this to say:

> 'It does not . . . follow as a matter of necessity from the mere fact that the only damage suffered by a plaintiff in an action for the tort of negligence is pecuniary or 'economic' that his claim is bound to fail . . . The critical question . . . is not the nature of the damage in itself, whether physical or pecuniary, but whether the scope of the duty of care in the circumstances of the case is such as to embrace damage of the kind which the plaintiff claims to have sustained . . . The infliction of physical injury to the person or property of another universally requires to be justified. The causing of economic loss does not. If it is to be categorised as wrongful it is necessary to find some factor beyond the mere occurrence of the loss and the fact that its occurrence could be foreseen. Thus the categorisation of damage as economic serves at least the useful purpose of indicating that something more is required . . .'

---

1 L'Heureux-Dubé, Cory, McLachlin and Stevenson JJ.
2 La Forest, Sopinka and Iacobucci JJ.
3 [1991] 1 AC 398 at 485-487, [1990] 2 All ER 908 at 933-934.

Acts, statements, and purposes

[6.23] One type of economic loss situation which is apt to give rise to particularly difficult questions concerning the frontiers of liability is that in which the precise classification of the carelessness as an 'act' or a 'statement' is itself open to dispute.[2] In *Ross v Caunters*[3] the defendant solicitor was held liable to the intended beneficiary under a will for carelessly failing to advise the testator, who had been the defendant's client, that witnessing of the will by the spouse of an intended beneficiary would render it invalid, and for carelessly failing to notice that the will had been thus witnessed. It is submitted that this controversial decision[4] was correct.[5] There was no danger of an avalanche of claims or 'opening of the floodgates', and no danger of any conflict of interest between the solicitor's duty to his actual client and the protection of the third party; the conferring of a benefit upon the latter being the former's very purpose.[6] The defendant's *purpose* was to perform a particular service carelessness in the discharge of which would foreseeably injure the plaintiff's interests. While the concept of purpose should not be regarded as a *necessary* condition for the imposition of liability, it is one of those likely to prove useful in delineating the scope of liability for pure economic loss in future cases.[7] The notion may assist in limiting the number of potential plaintiffs so as to avoid any danger of 'opening the floodgates'. It may also prove particularly appropriate in cases such as *Ross v Caunters*, in which classification of what occurred in terms of 'act' or 'statement' is apt to appear particularly arbitrary or unfruitful.

---

1   See above ch 5.
2   See, eg *Ministry of Housing and Local Government v Sharp* [1970] 2 QB 223, [1970] 1 All ER 1009, CA (issue of cerificate by land registry). Cf *Midland Bank Trust Co v Hett, Stubbs & Kemp* [1979] Ch 384, [1978] 3 All ER 571 (failure to register a land charge).
3   [1980] Ch 297, [1979] 3 All ER 580.
4   In *White v Jones* [1993] NLJR 473, the Court of Appeal held that *Ross v Caunters* had been correctly decided. It has also been followed by the New Zealand Court of Appeal: see *Gartside v Sheffield, Young & Ellis* [1983] NZLR 37.
5   It should be noted that a defence suggestion, that the mere fact that the plaintiff had been deprived by the defendant of a prospective advantage (as distinct from actually being made worse off) should prevent recovery, was rejected: 'I do not think that the expression "loss" can be confined to deprivation.' [1980] Ch at 321 per Sir Robert Megarry V-C.
6   See [1980] Ch 297 at 321-315 per Sir Robert Megarry V-C. For further discussion, see ch 15 below.
7   See also ch 5 above.

Statutory powers

[6.24] One factor which may, in the words of Lord Oliver, indicate that 'the scope of the duty of care in the circumstances of the case [was] such as to embrace damage of the kind which the plaintiff claims to have sustained' is the existence of a statute creating the context in which the defendant acted or failed to act. Thus in *Lonrho plc v Tebbit*,[1] the Court of Appeal in 1992 refused to strike out a negligence action against a Secretary of State, in which the plaintiffs alleged that the defendant's supposedly careless failure to release them from a redundant and superseded undertaking had caused them economic loss. This aspect is dealt with in Chapter 12.

Losses due to failure to insure

[6.25] In the absence of a specific undertaking the court will not allow the law of tort to supplement the strictly limited rules governing the implication of terms into contracts.[2] In two recent cases plaintiffs in existing contractual relationships with defendants suffered economic loss due to their being uninsured when they unfortunately suffered serious personal injury. In *Reid v Rush & Tomkins Group*[3] the plaintiff, while working abroad for the defendant employer, was injured by an uninsured driver in a road accident in a country which had no scheme similar to the Motor Insurers' Bureau which compensates victims in Britain in such circumstances.[4] The plaintiff alleged that his employers should have insured him against such injuries themselves or should have advised him to insure himself, but the Court of Appeal rejected his claim. Similarly in *Van Oppen v Bedford Charity Trustees*[5] the Court of Appeal denied that a school owed a duty to pupils to insure them against the risk of injury while playing rugby football or to advise their parents to take out such insurance. 'An existing relationship between the parties', said Balcombe LJ,[6] 'which may give rise to a duty of care by one party for the physical well-being and safety of the other (eg master and servant), does not of itself mean that there is sufficient proximity between the parties to justify finding the existence of a duty of care not to cause economic loss'. The correctness of the decisions reached in neither of these two cases is beyond question. In neither of them would a decision the other way have been likely to open the 'floodgates' or impose onerous duties on employers or schools respectively. The effect of them was to leave seriously injured plaintiffs uncompensated in circumstances in which it was assumed that the defendants could have foreseen such a situation occurring and easily taken appropriate precautions. The justice of such a result, based at least in part upon

---

1 [1992] 4 All ER 280, CA affg [1991] 4 All ER 973.
2 See also *Tai Hing Cotton Mill Ltd v Liu Chong Hing Bank Ltd* [1986] AC 80, [1985] 2 All ER 947, PC.
3 [1989] 3 All ER 228, [1990] 1 WLR 212, CA.
4 See ch 19 below.
5 [1989] 3 All ER 389, [1990] 1 WLR 235 , CA; affg [1989] 1 All ER 273.
6 [1989] 3 All ER 389 at 409.

Financial loss caused by careless acts

doctrinal arguments concerning the relationship between different branches of the law, is not obvious.

Recovery of economic loss in public nuisance

[**6.26**] The law relating to public nuisance is an area of the law of tort which is unusual in that it has long allowed the recovery of pure economic loss.[1] In *Tate and Lyle Industries Ltd v Greater London Council* [2] the plaintiffs sought to recover for foreseeable economic loss caused to them through the defendants' having carelessly allowed a river to become silted up. The House of Lords allowed the claim to succeed in public nuisance, for interference with the right of passage along a public navigable river, but disallowed the claim as framed in negligence.

Abolition of actions for loss of services

[**6.27**] Consistent with the principle that normally disallows the recovery of pure economic loss in negligence the infliction of injury upon one person does not at common law provide another with a cause of action. Formerly, however, there were two ancient exceptions to this rule.[3] These were the master's right to sue for the loss of the services of his servant,[4] and the husband's right to sue for the loss of the services of his wife. As specific actions these were long seen to be anomalous,[5] and they were finally abolished by the Administration of Justice Act 1982, s 2.

---

1   See Buckley *Law of Nuisance* (1981) p 63, and cases there cited.
2   [1983] 2 AC 509, [1983] 1 All ER 1159, HL.
3   See *Salmond and Heuston on Torts* (18th edn, 1981) pp 326-336.
4   The person injured had to be a 'menial' servant, eg injury to an established civil servant did not give rise to the action: *IRC v Hambrook* [1956] 2 QB 641, [1956] 1 All ER 807.
5   Eg the wife enjoyed no corresponding right to the services of her husband: *Best v Samuel Fox & Co Ltd* [1952] AC 716, [1952] 2 All ER 394, HL.

Part three

Damages and their assessment

Chapter 7

The making of awards in personal injury cases

Heads of damage

[7.01] 'The practice is now established', said Lord Denning MR when *Lim Poh Choo v Camden and Islington Area Health Authority* was in the Court of Appeal,[1] 'that, in personal injury cases, the award of damages is assessed under four main heads. First, special damages in the shape of money actually expended. Second, cost of future nursing and attendance and medical expenses. Third, pain and suffering and loss of amenities. Fourth, loss of future earnings'. The latter three headings are collectively referred to as 'general damages'.

Special damages

[7.02] These consist of 'accrued and ascertained financial loss'[2] which the plaintiff has incurred by the date of the trial. They have to be expressly pleaded and, in practice, are usually agreed by the parties prior to the hearing. Although they relate to specific pecuniary losses which the plaintiff claims to have already incurred, they are governed by the same principles which apply to damages generally and, in particular, future probabilities can be taken into account in calculating them. In *Cutler v Vauxhall Motors Ltd*[3] the plaintiff grazed one of his ankles at work due to his employers' negligence. Shortly afterwards he was discovered to have a varicose condition in both legs, which must have existed before the accident. The effect of the injury, against the background of that condition, was to cause an ulcer to develop at the site of the graze. This necessitated surgery for the varicose condition itself. The operation was properly carried out,

---

1   [1979] QB 196 at 217-218 , [1979] 1 All ER 332 at 342.
2   Per Edmund Davies LJ in *Cutler v Vauxhall Motors* [1971] 1 QB 418 at 426, [1970] 2 All ER 56 at 61.
3   [1971] 1 QB 418, [1970] 2 All ER 56. Cf *Salih v Enfield Health Authority* [1991] 3 All ER 400, CA.

but in consequence the plaintiff lost £173 in wages due to time off work. The Court of Appeal held by a majority,[1] however, that this sum was was not recoverable as special damages since the probability was that, because of the pre-existing condition, he would have had to have had the same operation in a few years' time anyway. Special damages for pre-trial lost earnings may also be reduced if a plaintiff disabled by a neurotic condition, which can be expected to clear up after the trial, prolongs his disability by unjustifiably delaying the trial.[2]

General damages

[**7.03**] These consist of all post-trial pecuniary losses along with all non-pecuniary loss. They familiarly include the three items listed in the above quotation by Lord Denning MR, but those headings, although often convenient, are not exclusive in the sense that losses which cannot easily be categorised within them are thereby excluded. For example the *distress* caused by enstrangement[3] or divorce,[4] or even imprisonment,[5] if a foreseeable consequence of the plaintiff's injuries, can be taken into account in calculating general damages. Distress caused by potential difficulties in starting or completing a family has been the subject of awards in medical negligence cases.[6] Successful claims have also included awards for inability to carry out unpaid services, such as housework,[7] and even loss of enjoyment of a holiday.[8] Although general damages as such do not have to be pleaded, a plaintiff who alleges that he will sustain losses in the future of a kind not normally to be expected must nevertheless ensure that the basis for such a claim appears on the pleadings, and that appropriate evidence is adduced in support.[9] Particular items of loss might, of course, be too remote,[10] or irrecoverable on grounds of public policy.[11] If a plaintiff's situation changes dramatically between the date of the trial and the hearing of an appeal, the otherwise rarely exercised discretion to admit fresh evidence may be exercised in relation to the assessment of general damages.[12] Even the House of Lords may be prepared in such a case to take into account events which have occurred since the hearing in the Court of Appeal.[13]

1 Edmund Davies and Karminski LJJ; Russell LJ dissenting.
2 *James v Woodall Duckham Construction Co Ltd* [1969] 2 All ER 794, [1969] 1 WLR 903, CA.
3 See *Lampert v Eastern National Omnibus Co* [1954] 2 All ER 719n, [1954] 1 WLR 1047.
4 The *financial* consequences of divorce, however, apparently *cannot* be taken into account: see *Pritchard v J H Cobden Ltd* [1988] Fam 22, [1987] 1 All ER 300, CA, not following *Jones v Jones* [1985] QB 704, [1984] 3 All ER 1003, CA.
5 See *Meah v McCreamer* [1985] 1 All ER 367.
6 See, eg *Kralj v McGrath* [1986] 1 All ER 54.
7 *Daly v General Steam Navigation Co* [1980] 3 All ER 696, [1981] 1 WLR 120, CA.
8 *Ichard v Frangoulis* [1977] 2 All ER 461, [1977] 1 WLR 556.
9 See *Domsalla v Barr* [1969] 3 All ER 487, [1969] 1 WLR 630, CA.
10 See ch 3 above.
11 Cf *Burns v Edman* [1970] 2 QB 541, [1970] 1 All ER 886.
12 *Mulholland v Mitchell* [1971] AC 666, [1971] 1 All ER 307, HL; *McCann v Sheppard* [1973] 2 All ER 881, [1973] 1 WLR 540, CA.
13 *Murphy v Stone-Wallwork (Chorlton) Ltd* [1969] 2 All ER 949, [1969] 1 WLR 1023, HL.

Itemisation and the overall sum

[7.04] The practice of assessing the various components of general damages separately, referred to by Lord Denning MR in the *Lim* case, is of relatively recent origin. Lord Denning himself once apparently favoured the view that one global sum should be awarded comprising both the pecuniary and non-pecuniary losses, and that trial judges should not perceive themselves as being under a duty expressly to itemise in their judgments the sums awarded under the various heads.[1] The main justification advanced in support of this view was the belief that itemisation would tend to produce larger awards, and that this would be undesirable.[2] The adoption of itemisation fortuitously became necessary, however, as a result of a change in the statute law quite unrelated to the underlying issues of principle or policy involved. In 1969, the Administration of Justice Act, s 22 made it obligatory for the courts to award interest on damages in personal injury cases. In *Jefford v Gee*[3] the Court of Appeal held that it would be appropriate for the different components of an award to carry interest at differing rates, and for differing periods, and that in consequence itemisation of awards would henceforth become necessary. Since 1970 the practice of itemisation has accordingly become general.[4] As a result it is now possible for awards to be appealed on the basis that individual components thereof have been wrongly assessed;[5] and if an error of principle is disclosed which would make a substantial difference to the total figure the appeal will succeed.[6] Nevertheless it remains the case that, in the words of Lord Scarman, '. . . the separate items, which constitute a total award of damages, are interrelated. They are parts of a whole, which must be fair and reasonable'.[7] It is also important to bear in mind that the inevitably uncertain premises, upon which awards in personal injury cases are nearly always based, make intricate arithmetical arguments inappropriate. In delivering the judgment of the Board on an appeal to the Privy Council from South Australia, Lord Diplock said:[8]

> 'To undertake detailed mathematical calculations in which nearly every factor is so speculative or unreliable in order to assess the capital sum to represent what is only one of several components in a total award of

---

1 See *Watson v Powles* [1968] 1 QB 596, [1967] 3 All ER 721, CA.
2 See *Fletcher v Autocar & Transporters* [1968] 2 QB 322 at 335-336 per Lord Denning MR.
3 [1970] 2 QB 130, [1970] 1 All ER 1202.
4 Cf *Jamil bin Harun v Yang Kamsiah Bte Meor Rasdi* [1984] AC 529, [1984] 2 WLR 668, PC; see also *Lai Wee Lian v Singapore Bus Service (1978) Ltd* [1984] AC 729, [1984] 3 WLR 63, PC.
5 See *George v Pinnock* [1973] 1 All ER 926, [1973] 1 WLR 118, CA.
6 See *Lai Wee Lian v Singapore Bus Service (1978) Ltd* [1984] AC 729, [1984] 3 WLR 63, PC.
7 In *Lim Poh Choo v Camden and Islington Area Health Authority* [1980] AC 174 at 191, [1979] 2 All ER 910 at 921, HL.
8 (1981) 34 ALR 569 at 580. The *Royal Commission on Civil Liability and Compensation for Personal Injury (Pearson)* recommended that 'an award of damages, however itemised, should not be interfered with on appeal unless it is inordinately high or inordinately low as a whole'. (Cmnd 7054-I, para 763).

compensation for personal injuries, is, in their Lordships' view, not only not worthwhile but, worse than this, it has a tendency to mislead . . . The reality is that as a result of the judgment the plaintiff will have at his disposal a single capital sum to compensate him for all the loss, economic and non-economic, past and future, that he has sustained or will sustain. That is the figure that matters to the plaintiff.'

Overlap

[**7.05**] 'In most cases', said Lord Scarman in *Lim Poh Choo v Camden and Islington Area Health Authority*, 'the risk of overlap is not great, nor, where it occurs, is it substantial'.[1] Nevertheless, the danger of 'over-compensation', by duplication of losses under different heads, is one to which the courts have been alive.[2] Clearly, the expenses involved in earning the income which has been lost have to be taken into account in calculating the award for lost earnings. Similarly, where a plaintiff is totally incapacitated, and requires permanent care, the damages awarded under this head must not overlap with the award for lost earnings in so far as the actual expenses of living itself are concerned.[3] In addition, however, it has sometimes been judicially suggested that the courts should also take into account a supposed possible overlap between damages for lost earnings on the one hand, and damages for pain and suffering and loss of amenities on the other. One basis for the suggestion was that enjoyment of the amenities, if the plaintiff had not been injured, would have involved expenditure of part of the earnings.[4] Another was simply that, particularly where the figure for lost earnings is very substantial, this in itself should to some extent reduce the plaintiff's distress and could therefore be allowed to count towards compensation for pain and suffering and loss of amenities.[5] On the other hand both the Law Commission,[6] and the Pearson Commission,[7] were opposed to any alteration in the size of awards, for pecuniary and non-pecuniary loss respectively, by reference to the size of the other. In *Lim v Camden Health Authority* Lord Scarman expressed no final opinion on the point, but he noted the view of the Pearson Commission and stated that he, too, doubted the possibility of overlap between these two heads.[8]

---

1 [1980] AC 174 at 191, [1979] 2 All ER 910 at 921, HL.
2 See, eg *Taylor v Bristol Omnibus Ltd* per Lord Denning MR, [1975] 2 All ER 1107 at 1113, [1975] 1 WLR 1054 at 1057, CA.
3 See *Lim v Camden Health Authority* [1980] AC 174 at 191, [1979] 2 All ER 910 at 921.
4 See *Fletcher v Autocar & Transporters* [1968] 2 QB 322 at 351 per Diplock LJ, CA.
5 See *Smith v Central Asbestos Co Ltd* [1972] 1 QB 244 at 262, [1971] 3 All ER 204 at 213, per Lord Denning MR (not considered in [1973] AC 518).
6 See Law Commission Report No 56 (*Report on Personal Injury Litigation – Assessment of Damages*) 1973.
7 See the Report of the *Royal Commission on Civil Liability and Compensation for Personal Injury (Pearson)* (Cmnd 7054-I) para 759.
8 [1980] AC 174 at 192, [1979] 2 All ER 910 at 922.

Mitigation

Plaintiff's state of knowledge

[7.06] The general law relating to a plaintiff's duty to mitigate his loss applies to damages for personal injury. In one case[1] it was unsuccessfully contended that the plaintiff had failed in this duty by omitting to claim, until it was too late to do so, certain social security benefits which, had they been obtained, would have been partially deducted from the damages under the Law Reform (Personal Injuries) Act 1948, s 2(1). The reason for the plaintiff's failure to claim was ignorance on her part of her entitlement to do so. In resolving the point in the plaintiff's favour MacKenna J observed that:

> 'a plaintiff must always do what is reasonable to mitigate his loss, but in deciding what was reasonable for him to do, one must have regard to his actual knowledge whether of law or of fact. A plaintiff who does not know that he has a right does not act unreasonably in failing to exercise it.'[2]

Refusal of medical treatment

[7.07] Questions involving the duty to mitigate often arise where the plaintiff refuses to undergo surgery, or other medical treatment, which the defendant claims would remove or ameliorate the condition brought about by the latter's negligence.[3] Here also the matter is to be resolved in the light of the plaintiff's state of knowledge having regard to the medical or other advice actually received by him. A plaintiff may therefore be reasonable, for the purposes of the rule, in refusing treatment even if it can be shown that if better informed, or better presented, advice had been given to him the same decision would have been unreasonable.[4] The question of reasonableness itself, however, is usually resolved objectively: 'would a reasonable man in all the circumstances, receiving the advice which the plaintiff did receive, have refused the operation'.[5] Thus overwhelming fear of surgical treatment, however bona fide and deep-seated, will not apparently be enough in itself to justify refusal.[6] This objective

---

1 *Eley v Bedford* [1972] 1 QB 155, [1971] 3 All ER 285.
2 [1972] 1 QB at 158. On the deductibility of social security benefits generally, and the effect of the Social Security Administration Act 1992, see below.
3 See AH Hudson 'Refusal of Medical Treatment' (1983) 3 LS 50.
4 See *Fazlic v Milingimbi Community Inc* (1981) 38 ALR 424 (Full Court of the High Court of Australia), referred to with approval by the Privy Council in *Selvanayagam v University of the West Indies* [1983] 1 All ER 824, [1983] 1 WLR 585, PC. See also *Karabotsos v Plastex Industries Pty Ltd* [1981] VR 675.
5 *Morgan v T Wallis Ltd* [1974] 1 Lloyd's Rep 165 at 170 per Browne J.
6 *Morgan v T Wallis* [1974] 1 Lloyd's Rep 165. See also *Marcroft v Scruttons Ltd* [1954] 1 Lloyd's Rep 395, CA.

approach has recently been adopted by the Supreme Court of Canada.[1] On the other hand there are also indications in the authorities that the objective approach should not be applied with excessive rigour.[2] In a case on the point decided under the old Workmen's Compensation Acts, which reached the House of Lords,[3] Lord Wright observed that 'the workman's own physical or mental idiosyncrasy cannot in general be excluded'. His Lordship favoured the adoption of 'a humane and liberal spirit, realising that the question cannot be decided save on a sympathetic estimate of the workman's personality and the special circumstances of the particular case'.[4] Where the relevant medical opinions given to the plaintiff are at all conflicting it is very unlikely that his decision to refuse treatment will be regarded as unreasonable.[5] If, however, the plaintiff *is* found to have been unreasonable in refusing treatment, the Supreme Court of Canada has held that he may nevertheless be entitled to damages to reflect the chance that even if the treatment had been administered it might not in fact have been successful.[6]

Onus of proof

[7.08] The burden of proving that the plaintiff is in breach of his duty to mitigate is in general on the defendant.[7] In *Selvanayagam v University of the West Indies*,[8] however, the Judicial Committee of the Privy Council held that on the particular question of refusal of treatment in the present context the onus was on the plaintiff to show that his refusal was reasonable, and not on the defendant to show that it was unreasonable.[9] This view is, however, inconsistent with a long line of authorities to the contrary which do not appear to have been cited to the Board.[10] It is therefore submitted that the view expressed in *Selvanayagam* is open to considerable doubt, and it is noteworthy that in *Janiak v Ippolito*[11] the Canadian Supreme Court refused to follow it.

---

1 See *Janiak v Ippolito* (1985) 16 DLR (4th) 1. For a valuable note on the various issues in this case see A H Hudson, 'Mitigation and Refusal of Medical Treatment Again' (1986) 49 MLR 381.
2 See *Karabotsos v Plastex Industries Pty Ltd* [1981] VR 675 in which the cases are reviewed.
3 *Steele v Robert George & Co (1937) Ltd* [1942] AC 497, [1942] 1 All ER 447, HL.
4 Ibid at 503-504, 450.
5 See *Steele v Robert George & Co (1937) Ltd* [1942] AC 497, [1942] 1 All ER 447, HL. See also *McAuley v London Transport Executive* [1957] 2 Lloyd's Rep 500 at 505, CA, per Jenkins LJ.
6 See *Janiak v Ippolito* (1985) 16 DLR (4th) 1.
7 *McGregor on Damages* (15th edn) p 172, para 289.
8 [1983] 1 All ER 824, [1983] 1 WLR 585.
9 [1983] 1 All ER 824 at 827, [1983] 1 WLR 585 at 589 per Lord Scarman delivering the judgment of the Board (burden discharged on the facts).
10 See, eg *Steele v Robert George & Co (1937) Ltd* [1942] AC 497, [1942] 1 All ER 447 HL; *Watts v Rake* (1960) 108 CLR 158 at 159 per Dixon CJ; *Morgan v T Wallis Ltd* [1974] 1 Lloyds' Rep 165 at 170 per Browne J.
11 (1985) 16 DLR (4th) 1.

Subsequent events

Allowance for contingencies

[**7.09**] In assessing damages for personal injury it is, in the words of Lord Wilberforce in *Jobling v Associated Dairies*,[1] 'accepted doctrine' that 'allowance, if necessary some discount, has to be made ... for the normal contingencies of life'. Since damages are awarded as a lump sum whenever the trial is concluded, and usually represent a once and for all payment,[2] it is felt that the plaintiff would be over-compensated if the possibility of contingencies such as illness or unemployment, which might have struck him at some time in the future irrespective of the injury inflicted by the defendant, were to be ignored. The need to allow for them is reflected in the 'multiplier' system used to calculate damages for lost earnings; in that the figure chosen is almost always considerably less than the number of earning years which the plaintiff would have had left to him, if he had completed his working life without interruption to normal retirement age.[3] The practice of assessing damages in this way is well-established, even though it is necessarily speculative.[4]

Occurrence of events before trial

[**7.10**] It is paradoxical that in the case law itself greater uncertainty has in fact been generated by situations in which the need for speculation has been removed. This occurs where a subsequent and unrelated event, which substantially affects the plaintiff, actually materialises before the trial of his claim against the defendant. Where the subsequent event is illness, however, it is now established that the principle that 'the court must not speculate when it knows'[5] will apply and the illness will therefore be taken into account so that, if appropriate, the award of damages will be reduced. In *Jobling v Associated Dairies Ltd*[6] the plaintiff suffered a back injury, due to the negligence of the defendants, which halved his former earning capacity. But before the case came on for trial the plaintiff developed a disease, unrelated to the accident, which rendered him wholly unfit

---

1 [1982] AC 794 at 802, [1981] 2 All ER 752 at 754, HL.
2 But see below for the possibility now of an award of 'provisional damages' in certain circumstances. See also ch 8, below, para [**8.28**], on 'structured settlements'.
3 See ch 8 below.
4 'The assessment of damages in actions for personal injuries is not a science. A judgment as to what constitutes proper compensation in money terms for pain, suffering or deprivation of amenities of life, can only be intuitive, and the assessment of future economic loss involves a double exercise in the art of prophesying not only what the future holds for the injured plaintiff but also what the future would have held for him if he had not been injured.' Per Lord Diplock delivering the judgment of the Privy Council in *Paul v Rendell* (1981) 34 ALR 569 at 571.
5 Per Lord Edmund-Davies in *Jobling v Associated Dairies Ltd* [1982] AC 794 at 807, [1981] 2 All ER 752 at 758, HL. Cf *Curwen v James* [1963] 2 All ER 619, [1963] 1 WLR 748, CA.
6 [1982] AC 794, [1981] 2 All ER 752, HL.

for work. Although the trial judge held that the illness should nevertheless be ignored in calculating the plaintiff's damages for lost earnings, his decision was unanimously reversed by the Court of Appeal and the House of Lords which held that the plaintiff was not entitled from the date of the onset of the illness.[1] The position is less certain, however, if the subsequent event is itself a tort. In *Baker v Willoughby*[2] the plaintiff suffered an injury to his left leg in a road accident. But before his claim, for the injuries which he incurred, was tried he was unfortunately the victim of an attack by armed robbers. He was shot in the left leg and the leg had to be amputated. In these circumstances the House of Lords held that the defendant, the negligent motorist, was liable for all the plaintiff's losses calculated on the assumption that the disability caused by the motor accident had not been superseded by the robbery. Their Lordships were concerned to avoid a situation in which the first defendant in such circumstances could claim that his damages should be reduced by the second incident, while the second defendant could claim that since his victim had already been disabled the extent of his liability should on that account be reduced. If this were to be allowed the plaintiff would obviously be under-compensated even if he succeeded in obtaining judgment against both defendants.[3] In order to avoid the injustice of such a result it is possible that, in its own facts, the decision in *Baker v Willoughby* remains correct.[4] Nevertheless a sharp distinction between tortious and non-tortious supervening events does not in principle seem easy to support in the present context.[5] Moreover, although the case was not overruled, the reasoning in *Baker v Willoughby* was heavily criticised by the House of Lords itself in *Jobling v Associated Dairies*,[6] and will certainly not be extended.[7] It is also somewhat surprising that, as Lord Edmund-Davies pointed out in the latter case,[8] no mention was made in *Baker v Willoughby* of the possibility of the plaintiff's claiming under the Criminal Injuries Scheme in respect of the injuries inflicted by the robbers.

1 See also *Hodgson v General Electricity Co Ltd* [1978] 2 Lloyd's Rep 210; *Penner v Mitchell* [1978] 5 WWR 328.
2 [1970] AC 467. Cf *Performance Cars Ltd v Abraham* [1962] 1 QB 33, [1961] 3 All ER 413, CA.
3 See [1970] AC 467 at 495 per Lord Pearson.
4 See *Jobling v Associated Dairies Ltd* [1982] AC 794 at 810, [1981] 2 All ER 752 at 764 per Lord Russell and 815 per Lord Keith. Cf Borrowdale 'Vicissitudes in the Assessment of Damages' (1983) 32 ICLQ 651.
5 Cf per Lord Keith in *Jobling v Associated Dairies Ltd* [1982] AC 752 at 816, [1981] 2 All ER 752 at 764. See also Alan Davies in (1982) 45 MLR at 332.
6 [1982] AC 794. But for a forceful defence of *Baker v Willoughby* see Michael A Jones *Textbook on Torts* (3rd edn, 1991) pp 139-141. See also Trindade and Cane *The Law of Torts in Australia* (1985, Melbourne) pp 366-368.
7 See especially, per Lord Edmund-Davies; [1982] AC 794 at 804ff and per Lord Bridge at 816ff, [1981] 2 All ER 752 at 757ff and 765ff.
8 See [1982] AC 794 at 807, [1981] 2 All ER 752 at 758.

Provisional damages

[7.11] In certain cases a complicating factor in the assessment of damages is that the full nature and extent of the plaintiff's injuries may not reveal themselves until long after the trial, perhaps not until years have elapsed. The chance that epilepsy[1] may subsequently develop as a result of a blow on the head is a well known example.[2] The best that the court could formerly do in such a case was to award a sum greater than would have been appropriate if development of the disability had not been a possibility, but smaller than would have been appropriate had it been a certainty. Depending upon the eventual outcome, the level of compensation received would of necessity be unfair to either the plaintiff or the defendant. The Administration of Justice Act 1982, s 6, however, sought to tackle this problem by making possible awards of 'provisional damages' in such cases. The section added a new provision, s 32A, to the Supreme Court Act 1981 which, where material, reads as follows:

'... provision may be made by rules of court, in such circumstances as may be prescribed, to award the injured person–
(a) damages assessed on the assumption that the injured person will not develop the disease or suffer the deterioration in his condition; and
(b) further damages at a future date if he develops the disease or suffers the deterioration.'

The provision came into force in 1985 when the relevant rules of court were promulgated.[3] The court therefore now has the power to achieve, in theory at least, accurate awards in situations of the kind in question by certifying that the award at the trial is to be provisional only and that the plaintiff can apply for further damages if the situation so warrants. It should be noted that a claim for provisional damages has to be included in the statement of claim and the court has to be satisfied, if the defendant objects, that the action is of a kind within the scope of s 32A.[4] The section was considered by Scott Baker J in *Willson v Ministry of Defence*[5] who held, inter alia, that 'serious deterioration' had to be distinguished from the ordinary deterioration

---

1 See Malcolm Weller, 'The Statute of Time Limitation in Post-Traumatic Epilepsy' (1986) NLJ 409.
2 See, eg *Hawkins v New Mendip Engineering* [1966] 3 All ER 228, [1966] 1 WLR 1341, CA; *Jones v Griffith* [1969] 2 All ER 1015, [1969] 1 WLR 795, CA.
3 See Ord 37, rr 7-10 and *Hurditch v Sheffield Health Authority* [1989] QB 562, [1989] 2 All ER 869, CA. See also Practice Note [1985] 2 All ER 895, sub nom Practice Direction (provisional damages: procedure) [1985] 1 WLR 961. For discussion see Richard James 'The Provisional Damages Rules – Some Criticisms' (1986) NLJ 231. Provisional damage orders can be made in the county court: see the County Court (Amendment No 4) Rules 1989. Cf *Kennedy v Bowater Containers Ltd* [1990] 2 QB 391, [1990] 1 All ER 669.
4 See Ord 37, r 8(1). The court has a discretion: *Willson v Ministry of Defence* [1991] 1 All ER 638.
5 [1991] 1 All ER 638.

148 *The making of awards in personal injury cases*

to be expected as part of the progression of the particular condition in question.

Other procedures for postponing assessment

[7.12] Other, longer-established, procedures will sometimes be relevant in situations in which the assessment of damages either will, or ought to be, delayed for any reason. One of these is the power, if liability is admitted (or established by interlocutory judgment), to compel certain categories of defendant to make interim payments of damages to the plaintiff prior to the full hearing on quantum.[1] Another is the power of the court to order that the issues of liability and quantum be tried separately.[2]

Interest

[7.13] Since 1969 the courts have been obliged to award interest on damages in cases of personal injury.[3] Special damages normally carry interest at half the 'appropriate rate' from the date of service of the writ to the date of the trial.[4] The 'appropriate rate' is the rate payable on money paid into court which is placed on special investment account.[5] The rate is halved in order to allow, in a rough and ready way, for the fact that not all of the recoverable expenditure will have been incurred at the same time, so that the plaintiff will not have been out of pocket with respect to the whole sum throughout the relevant period. Damages for loss of future earnings, or for loss of earning capacity, do not carry interest since, ex hypothesi, they compensate for losses which have not yet been incurred.[6] For a time there was considerable judicial uncertainty as to the position

---

1 See RSC Ord 29, rr 9-12. See also Emlyn Williams, 'Personal Injuries: Interim Payment and Assessment of Damages' (1979) 129 NLJ 626.
2 See RSC Ord 33, r 4(2) and *Coenen v Payne* [1974] 2 All ER 1109, [1974] 1 WLR 984, CA. Awards in such cases only carry interest from the date of the final judgment on quantum and not from that of the earlier judgment on liability: *Thomas v Bunn* [1991] 1 AC 362, [1991] 1 All ER 193, HL.
3 See now the Supreme Court Act 1981, s 35A and the County Courts Act 1959, s 97A: provisions inserted by the Administration of Justice Act 1982, s 15 to supersede the Administration of Justice Act 1969, s 22.
4 *Jefford v Gee* [1970] 2 QB 130, [1970] 1 All ER 1202, CA. A plaintiff who wishes to claim interest on his special damages at a different rate must make clear the special circumstances on which he relies in so claiming: *Dexter v Courtaulds* [1984] 1 All ER 70, [1984] 1 WLR 372, CA, but cf *Prokop v Department of Health* [1985] CLY 1037, CA, discussed by Roderick L Denyer in (1986) LS Gaz 1293 and Nicholas J Worsley (1986) LS Gaz 2826.
5 Formerly known as the short-term investment account: see now the Court Funds Rules 1987 (SI 87/821). The relevant rates since 1965 are set out in a note to Ord 6, r 2 in the Supreme Court Practice.
6 *Jefford v Gee* [1970] 2 QB 130, [1970] 1 All ER 1202, CA; *Cookson v Knowles* [1979] AC 556, [1978] 2 All ER 604, HL.

regarding damages for non-economic loss, ie pain and suffering and loss of amenities. In one case the Court of Appeal suggested that no interest at all should be awarded under this head,[1] but this was overruled by the House of Lords in *Pickett v British Rail Engineering Ltd*.[2] The House did not indicate, however, in *Pickett's* case what rate of interest should be applied. Subsequently the Court of Appeal, in *Birkett v Hayes*,[3] held that normally 2% would be appropriate, and this was confirmed by the House of Lords in *Wright v British Railways Board*.[4] The underlying reasoning was that in a period of high inflation, such as appertained until relatively recently, it is extremely difficult to increase in real terms the value of sums invested, and the effect of inflation upon the value of money generally should be reflected by appropriate increases in the figures awarded for the non-economic loss itself.[5] Their Lordships accepted that, in the event of greater stabilisation in the value of money, an increase in the 2% figure would be appropriate. But they also emphasised the desirability of having a fixed figure that will remain constant for long periods, in order to facilitate settlement of the great majority of personal injury cases which never come to trial.[6]

1 See *Cookson v Knowles* [1977] QB 913, [1977] 2 All ER 820, CA; not considered in [1979] AC 556, [1978] 2 All ER 604, HL.
2 [1980] AC 136, [1979] 1 All ER 774, HL.
3 [1982] 2 All ER 710, [1982] 1 WLR 816.
4 [1983] 2 AC 773, [1983] 2 All ER 698.
5 See *Wright v British Railways Board* [1983] 2 AC 773 at 785E, [1983] 2 All ER 698 at 706 per Lord Diplock.
6 See [1983] 2 AC 773 at 784H, [1983] 2 All ER 698 at 705 per Lord Diplock. The rate remained at 2% in September 1992: RM Nelson-Jones 'Personal Injury Interest' (1992) LS Gaz, 23 September, p 19.

Chapter 8

Damages recoverable for personal injury

Non-pecuniary loss

Pain and suffering

[**8.01**] Diplock LJ once said:[1]

> ' "Pain and suffering", which . . . I take as comprising both physical and mental anguish, if there be any scientific distinction between the two, cannot be measured in pounds, shillings and pence. Looked at in isolation, there is no logical reason why for one week of pain the right award should be £20 rather than £200. All that can be said is that, once you accept as a premise or convention that £20 is the right award for one week of pain, the right award for two weeks of similar pain is in the region of £40 and not in the region of £400, and that a figure in the same region is the right award for each of two sufferers with similar thresholds of pain.'

In practice the award for pain and suffering is usually lumped together with that for loss of amenities, and is rarely itemised separately. Nevertheless, it is clear from cases involving unconscious accident victims that pain and suffering is a conceptually distinct head of damage, since such victims are awarded damages for loss of amenity[2] but not for pain and suffering. The latter is necessarily a subjective matter and a person who, due to unconsciousness, is unaware of his condition and cannot feel pain, will not receive any award under this head.[3] By contrast, a person in the position of the plaintiff in one case, who was described as having 'painful and prolonged awareness of how much she has lost and what little she has left',[4] will warrant a substantial award. But the presence or absence of awareness can, in some cases of seriously injured victims, itself be a

---

1 See *Wise v Kaye* [1962] 1 QB 638 at 664, [1962] 1 All ER 257 at 271, CA.
2 See below.
3 See *H West & Son v Shepherd* [1964] AC 326, [1963] 2 All ER 625, HL. See also *Wise v Kaye* [1962] 1 QB 638, [1962] 1 All ER 257, CA.
4 *Powell v Phillips* [1972] 3 All ER 864 at 871 per Stephenson LJ, CA.

Non-pecuniary loss 151

matter of uncertainty. In practice, however, it appears that if the plaintiff is not actually comatose he will usually be taken to have some degree of awareness of his condition, and assumed thereby to 'suffer' in consequence of it, even if not in actual physical pain. The plaintiff in *Lim Poh Choo v Camden Health Authority*[1] suffered very extensive brain damage in an anaesthetic accident. In the words of the trial judge, a doctor who examined her 'found her emotional state to be blank and she was completely lacking in volition and spontaneity. Her powers of reasoning were impossible to test'.[2] Nevertheless, in the Court of Appeal Lawton LJ said that he did 'not accept that the plaintiff was in such an insensitive condition that it can be assumed that she does not appreciate what her condition is ... The fact that she cannot express what she feels does not mean she does not feel at all'.[3] Although compensation for pain and suffering necessarily involves quantifying the unquantifiable, actual or probable *duration* of the pain is in principle measurable. As a part of general damages the sum awarded for pain and suffering notionally covers both pre-trial and future 'loss'. But if the plaintiff dies before the trial the finite duration of any pain and suffering will necessarily produce a lower award than would otherwise have been the case.[4]

Reduced life expectancy

[8.02] Until recently plaintiffs whose lives had been shortened as a result of negligence were able to recover a fixed conventional sum[5] (by 1981 it was usually a little over £1,000)[6] in respect of this loss. If they died before trial their estate could similarly recover the same sum under the Law Reform (Miscellaneous Provisions) Act 1934.[7] This award was always distinct from the much more substantial amount payable to living plaintiffs, as part of their damages for pain and suffering, to compensate them for their distress in *knowing* that their expectation of life had been reduced. The conventional award for loss of expectation of life was abolished by the Administration of Justice Act 1982, s 1(1)(*a*), but the same Act also made clear that the recovery as appropriate under the head of pain and suffering is not affected by the abolition. Section 1(1)(*b*) of the Act provides as follows:

> 'If the injured person's expectation of life has been reduced by the injuries, the court, in assisting damages in respect of pain and suffering caused by the injuries, shall take account of any suffering caused or likely to be caused to him by awareness that his expectation of life has been so reduced.'

1 [1980] AC 174, [1979] 2 All ER 910, HL; affg [1979] QB 196, [1979] 1 All ER 332, CA.
2 [1979] QB 196 at 201 (Bristow J).
3 Ibid at 224, CA; see also per Browne LJ at 227. Cf per Lord Scarman in the House of Lords [1980] AC 174 at 189.
4 See *McCann v Sheppard* [1973] 2 All ER 881, [1973] 1 WLR 540, CA.
5 See *Benham v Gambling* [1941] AC 157, [1941] 1 All ER 7, HL.
6 In *Gammell v Wilson* [1982] AC 27, [1981] 1 All ER 578, HL. £1,250 was awarded under this head.
7 See *Rose v Ford* [1937] AC 826, [1937] 3 All ER 359, HL.

Loss of amenity

[8.03] The general principles underlying the award of damages for loss of amenity were set out by Lord Morris in *West & Son v Shepherd*[1] as follows:

> '... money cannot renew a physical frame that has been battered and shattered. All that judges and courts can do is to award sums which must be recognised as giving reasonable compensation. In the process there must be the endeavour to secure some uniformity in the general method of approach. By common assent awards must be reasonable and must be assessed with moderation. Furthermore, it is eminently desirable that so far as possible comparable injuries should be compensated by comparable awards. When all this is said it still must be said that amounts which are awarded are to a considerable extent conventional.'

In trying to decide upon 'reasonable compensation' for personal injury the courts adopt a broadly objective approach. It has sometimes been argued that the extent to which the injury interfered, or must be taken to have interfered, with the plaintiff's 'happiness' should be the basis of the assessment.[2] But this view has been rejected,[3] largely because it is felt that the subjectivity inherent in it would undermine the principle that, in the words of Lord Morris, 'comparable injuries should be compensated by comparable awards'. This principle is desirable in the interests of certainty and the promotion of settlements. It is submitted that it also accords with intuitive notions of justice. As Lord Pearce put it in *West v Shepherd*: 'It would be lamentable if the trial of a personal injury claim put a premium on protestations of misery and if a long face was the safe passport to a large award.'[4] This is not to say that subjective factors are wholly ignored; a keen sportsman will, for example, be awarded more for the loss of a leg than someone whose work and leisure pursuits are largely sedentary.[5] It is a corollary of the objective approach, however, that it is no concern of the court how the money awarded to the plaintiff will ultimately be used.[6]

---

1 [1964] AC 326 at 346, [1963] 2 All ER 625 at 631, HL.
2 See *Wise v Kaye* [1962] 1 QB 638 at 665-666, [1962] 1 All ER 257 at 271, CA per Diplock LJ. Cf Ogus 'Damages for Lost Amenities: For a foot, a feeling or a function?' (1972) 35 MLR 1.
3 Ie by the majorities in *Wise v Kaye* [1962] 1 QB 638, [1962] 1 All ER 257, CA and *H West & Son v Shepherd* [1964] AC 326, [1963] 2 All ER 625, HL.
4 [1964] AC 326 at 368-369, [1963] 2 All ER 625 at 645, Lord Pearce continued as follows: 'Under the present practice there is no call for a parade of personal unhappiness. A plaintiff who cheerfully admits that he is as happy as he was, may yet receive a large award as reasonable compensation for the grave injury and loss of amenity over which he has managed to triumph.'
5 See *H West & Son v Shepherd* [1964] AC 326 at 365, [1963] 2 All ER 625 at 643, per Lord Pearce.
6 'He can spend it well or stupidly; he can enjoy it by gambling or giving it away; he can invest it and accumulate the income and give it by will to his relations or to charity; it is under his entire dominion in every way, and he can deal with it as he pleases...': per Upjohn LJ in *Wise v Kaye* [1962] 1 QB 638 at 658, [1962] 1 All ER 257 at 267, CA.

Relevance of awards in other cases

[**8.04**] The pursuit of moderation and consistency in awards has been facilitated by the fact that virtually all personal injury cases are now tried by judge alone; a practice in effect made general by the decision of a five member Court of Appeal in 1965 in *Ward v James*,[1] and further reinforced by the recent decision of the Court of Appeal in *H v Ministry of Defence*.[2] This made possible the citation in argument of awards in other cases, which had not been permitted when trial was by jury. Such awards are collected systematically in various publications,[3] and this enables as high a degree of predictability to be achieved as can reasonably be expected in this sphere.[4] The House of Lords has held, in *Wright v British Railways Board*,[5] that the Court of Appeal is, in the words of Lord Diplock, 'the tribunal best qualified to set the guidelines' for non-pecuniary loss in personal injury cases and that the House of Lords itself 'should hesitate before deciding to depart from them, particularly if the departure [would] make the guideline less general in its applicability or less simple to apply'. The guidelines thus established are not binding precedents, and can be varied as circumstances require, but 'too frequent alteration deprives them of their usefulness in providing a reasonable degree of predictability in the litigious process and so facilitating settlement of claims without going to trial'. Lord Diplock described the process whereby consistency is sought to be achieved in these cases as follows:[6]

> 'As regards assessment of damages for non-economic loss in personal injury cases the Court of Appeal creates the guidelines as to the appropriate conventional figure by increasing or reducing awards of damages made by judges in individual cases for various common kinds of injuries. Thus so-called 'brackets' are established, broad enough to make allowance for circumstances which make the deprivation suffered by an individual plaintiff in consequence of the particular kind of injury greater or less than in the general run of cases, yet clear enough to reduce the unpredictability of what is likely to be the most important factor in arriving at settlement of claims. 'Brackets' may call for alteration not only to take account of inflation, for which they ought automatically to be raised, but also it may be to take account of

---

1 [1966] 1 QB 273, [1965] 1 All ER 563, CA. Since this case was decided there has apparently been only one reported instance of an order for trial by jury of a personal injury case (being *Hodges v Harland & Wolff Ltd* [1965] 1 All ER 1086, [1965] 1 WLR 523, CA).
2 [1991] 2 QB 103, [1991] 2 All ER 834, CA. See also the Supreme Court Act 1981, s 69(3) which was construed in *H*'s case as 'indicating that, other things being equal, jury trial was to be considered as less preferable than hitherto': per Lord Donaldson MR, delivering the judgment of the court, ibid at 110, 838.
3 See Kemp & Kemp *The Quantum of Damages*; *Current Law*; The *Abridgement* to *Halsbury's Laws of England*, and also LEXIS.
4 The Law Commission and the *Royal Commission on Civil Liability and Compensation for Personal Injury (Pearson)* both rejected the idea that an actual legislative tariff should be laid down (*Pearson*, Cmnd 7054-I, paras, 337-380; *Law Com Report No 56*, paras 32-35).
5 [1983] 2 AC 773, [1983] 2 All ER 698.
6 Ibid at 785, 706.

advances in medical science which may make particular kinds of injuries less disabling or advances in medical knowledge which may disclose hitherto unsuspected long term effects of some kinds of injuries or industrial diseases.'

Catastrophic injury cases

[**8.05**] In recent years increasing numbers of serious accident victims have survived, due to advances in treatment, where formerly many of them might not have done so.[1] The courts have therefore been obliged to assess damages for pain, suffering and loss of amenity in respect of plaintiffs who, though conscious, may be brain-damaged and may also be totally or partially paralysed. The inherent difficulty of placing a money value upon personal injuries is particularly conspicuous in such cases, while at the same time their place at an extreme of the spectrum makes them especially sensitive for the system of 'guidelines' generally. The Pearson Commission was equally divided over a suggestion that the maximum award for pain, suffering and loss of amenity should be set at five times average industrial earnings.[2] Lord Denning MR evidently sympathised with this proposal, however, and referred to it judicially on at least two occasions.[3] Nevertheless, in practice, the highest awards have exceeded this figure. In *Croke v Wiseman*[4] the Court of Appeal approved an award, made in 1979, of £35,000 under this head to a boy aged seven who was blind, paralysed in all four limbs, and unable to speak. Lord Denning MR, dissenting, would have reduced the award to £25,000. Important guidance was provided by *Housecroft v Burnett*.[5] In this case the Court of Appeal indicated that, on April 1985 values, £75,000[6] provided an appropriate guideline figure for what O'Connor LJ referred to as 'a typical middle-of-the-road case of tetraplegia'. His Lordship continued as follows:[7]

> 'These are cases where the injured person is not in physical pain, is fully aware of the disability, has an expectation of life of 25 years or more, powers of speech, sight and hearing are present, and needs help with bodily functions. The factors which operate to make the case one for awarding more than average are physical pain and any diminution in the powers of speech, sight or hearing. The factors which operate to make the case one for awarding less than average are lack of awareness of the condition and a reduction in expectation of life. These factors

---

1 See *Lim Poh Choo v Camden and Islington Area Health Authority* [1979] QB 196 at 216, [1979] 1 All ER 332 at 340, CA, per Lord Denning MR.
2 See the Report of the *Royal Commission on Civil Liability and Compensation for Personal Injury* (Cmnd 7054-I), paras 390-392.
3 See *Lim Poh Choo v Camden and Islington Area Health Authority* [1979] QB 196 at 217, [1979] 1 All ER 332 at 341, and *Croke v Wiseman* [1981] 3 All ER 852 at 858, [1982] 1 WLR 71 at 75.
4 [1981] 3 All ER 852, [1982] 1 WLR 71.
5 [1986] 1 All ER 332, CA.
6 Of course, *overall* sums awarded are very much higher in most cases because such plaintiffs usually recover substantial amounts for lost earnings and for the cost of future care.
7 [1986] 1 All ER 332 at 338.

often cancel each other to a greater or lesser extent, especially where there is severe brain damage.'

Unconscious plaintiffs

[**8.06**] In *H West & Son v Shepherd*[1] the House of Lords upheld the award of substantial damages for loss of amenity in respect of a plaintiff who was permanently unconscious. 'The fact of unconsciousness', said Lord Morris, 'does not . . . eliminate the actuality of the deprivations of the ordinary experiences and amenities of life'.[2] Cases of this kind are unique in that the plaintiff will be unaware that he has been awarded the damages and, since the cost of nursing and care is compensated separately, it will not be possible for them to be put to any use on his behalf. Not surprisingly, the issue has revealed a high degree of judicial disagreement. The decision of the House in *West* was by a bare majority,[3] and upheld an earlier decision of the Court of Appeal, on the same point, which had also been reached by a majority.[4] A subsequent decision of the Court of Appeal, again by a majority, awarded substantial damages under this head in respect of a child aged eight, who lived in an unconscious state for 12 months after a road accident but who had actually died by the date of the trial.[5] On the other hand the High Court of Australia,[6] also by a majority, refused to follow *West v Shepherd*. The view that substantial damages for loss of amenity should be awarded in these cases appears to be based upon two considerations. One is the belief that they are necessary in order to maintain the integrity of the 'objective' approach to such damages generally, and hence the system of 'guidelines' which facilitates predictability in the case of awards to conscious plaintiffs.[7] The other is the belief that it would be undesirable, as a matter of public policy, for courts of law to be perceived as treating unconscious people as being, for practical purposes, already dead.[8] Nevertheless, the award of large sums of money under this head in respect of the permanently unconscious would appear, in the final analysis, to be difficult to justify rationally. The Pearson Commission[9] recommended 'that non-pecuniary damages

1 [1964] AC 326, [1963] 2 All ER 625, HL.
2 Ibid at 349, 633.
3 Lords Tucker, Morris and Pearce; Lords Reid and Devlin dissenting.
4 See *Wise v Kaye* [1962] 1 QB 638, [1962] 1 All ER 257, CA (Sellers and Upjohn LJJ; Diplock LJ dissenting).
5 *Andrews v Freeborough* [1967] 1 QB 1, [1966] 2 All ER 721, CA (Willmer and Davies L JJ; Winn LJ dissenting).
6 See *Skelton v Collins* [1966] ALR 449.
7 See, especially, the speech of Lord Pearce in *H West & Son v Shepherd* [1964] AC 326 at 369, [1963] 2 All ER 625 at 645.
8 See *Wise v Kaye* [1962] 1 QB 638 at 654, [1962] 1 All ER 257 at 265, CA per Sellers LJ. Cf Skegg 'Irreversibly Comatose Individuals: "Alive" or "Dead"' [1974] CLJ 130.
9 *Royal Commission on Civil Liability and Compensation for Personal Injury* (Cmnd 7054-I) paras 393-398. Cf *Lim Poh Choo v Camden and Islington Area Health Authority* [1980] AC 174 at 188-189, [1979] 2 All ER 910 at 918-919, HL, per Lord Scarman.

should no longer be recoverable for permanent unconsciousness', but this recommendation has not been implemented.

Effect of inflation

[**8.07**] Damages for non-pecuniary loss are assessed by reference to the value of money at the date of the trial.[1] Accordingly awards should broadly keep pace with inflation,[2] but the courts will not apply a strict arithmetical approach to achieve formal indexation of them.[3]

Financial loss

Calculation of future lost earnings

[**8.08**] The existing method of calculating damages for future lost earnings is conveniently and concisely summarised in the report of the *Royal Commission on Civil Liability (Pearson)*.[4] 'The starting point', in the words of the Report, 'is the plaintiff's net annual loss. In broad terms, the net annual loss suffered by a living plaintiff is equal to the annual value of his lost 'take home' earnings (that is, his lost earnings net of tax and social security contributions)'. The report continues to describe the present practice as follows:

> 'The traditional method of calculating lump sum damages for future pecuniary loss has been to multiply the plaintiff's net annual loss by an appropriate factor representing a number of "years' purchase". This factor, known as the "multiplier", has always been less than the number of years for which compensation is to be provided, since it is scaled down to take account of the fact that the plaintiff receives his compensation in advance as a lump sum. A reduction is also made for future contingencies, such as the chance that the plaintiff would have died for a reason unconnected with the injury. The method in theory provides a lump sum sufficient, when invested for this purpose, to produce an income equal to the lost income over the relevant period, when the interest is supplemented by withdrawals of capital.'

The multiplier will obviously vary with the age of the plaintiff but in practice 18 is the maximum,[5] even for young adults at the commencement of their working lives. The Pearson Commission itself

---

1 See *Walker v John McLean & Sons* [1979] 2 All ER 965 at 970, [1979] 1 WLR 760 at 765, CA, per Cumming-Bruce LJ.
2 See per Lord Diplock in *Wright v British Railways Board* [1983] 2 AC 773 at 785, [1983] 2 All ER 698 at 706, HL, quoted above.
3 See *Walker v John McLean & Sons* [1979] 2 All ER 965 at 970, [1979] 1 WLR 760 at 765 per Cumming-Bruce LJ.
4 (Cmnd 7054-I) paras 636 and 647.
5 See Pearson, op cit, para 648.

argued that the whole range of multipliers was unrealistically low,[1] but the courts have not seen fit to modify their approach.[2]

Loss of marriage prospects

[**8.09**] Where young female plaintiffs lost marriage prospects as a result of their injuries it was formerly held that, in the calculation of future lost earnings, some discount should be made for the probability that, if uninjured, they would in any event have taken some years out of employment for marriage and child-bearing.[3] It is, however, no longer the practice to do this in most cases, not least in recognition of the forceful argument that the services of a wife and mother represent an economic contribution normally at least as great as that made by persons in paid employment.[4] Some deduction might still be considered appropriate, however, if the woman's earnings and income expectation had, prior to the accident, been at so exceptionally high a level that they could not reasonably be regarded as the economic equivalent of the services of a wife and mother.[5] It must also be remembered that loss of marriage prospects is a recognised factor in awarding damages for pain and suffering and loss of amenity. In assessing the correctness of the overall sum, and in order to avoid overlap, courts have sometimes allowed high sums under this head of non-pecuniary loss to offset awards for loss of future earnings which, taken in isolation, might have been too low because the erroneous concept of marriage and child-bearing as economically negative had been used to reduce them.[6]

Actuarial tables not normally to be used

[**8.10**] The submission of actuarial evidence by plaintiffs in support of claims for future lost earnings is not encouraged by the courts.[7]

---

1 The members of the commission were unanimous on this point even though they were divided as to the detailed method to be adopted for devising fresh multipliers. See, generally, the *Report*, vol 1, paras 651-725. See also Kemp 'The Assessment of Damages for Future Pecuniary Loss in Personal Injury Claims' (1984) 3 CJQ 120.
2 Multipliers used in actual cases are conveniently listed in Kemp & Kemp, *The Quantum of Damages*, vol 1. The appropriate date for determining the multiplier is that of the trial. In *Pritchard v JH Cobden* [1988] Fam 22, [1987] 1 All ER 300, CA, the Court of Appeal rejected a defendant's contention that the date of the accident (by analogy with Fatal Accidents Act cases in which the date of death is taken) would be more appropriate.
3 See *Harris v Harris* [1973] 1 Lloyd's Rep 445, CA; *Moriarty v McCarthy* [1978] 2 All ER 213, [1978] 1 WLR 155.
4 See *Hughes v McKeown* [1985] 3 All ER 284, [1985] 1 WLR 963.
5 See *Housecroft v Burnett* [1986] 1 All ER 332, CA at 345 per O'Connor LJ.
6 See *Harris v Harris* [1973] 1 Lloyd's Rep 445, CA; and *Moriarty v McCarthy* [1978] 2 All ER 213, [1978] 1 WLR 155, as explained in *Hughes v McKeown* [1985] 3 All ER 284, [1985] 1 WLR 963. See also *Housecroft v Burnett* [1986] 1 All ER 332, CA at 345 per O'Connor LJ.
7 See *Watson v Powles* [1968] 1 QB 596, [1967] 3 All ER 721, CA; *Mitchell v Mulholland (No 2)* [1972] 1 QB 65, [1971] 2 All ER 1205, CA; *Auty v National Coal Board* [1985] 1 All ER 930, [1985] 1 WLR 784, CA.

158 Damages recoverable for personal injury

Although oral evidence by actuaries has occasionally been admitted,[1] it cannot be said to have met with a favourable reception. The prevailing judicial view is that to rely closely on actuarial calculations would lend a false aura of certainty to an essentially speculative exercise, and would tend to over-compensate plaintiffs by giving insufficient allowance for the contingencies of life and their possible impact upon the future of the individual claimant.[2] This position has, however, been forcefully criticised.[3] The Law Commission recommended that legislation should be passed to promote and facilitate the use of actuarial evidence, and that actuarial tables should be officially prepared for use in personal injury and Fatal Accident Act cases.[4] The recommendation for a statutory provision has not been acted upon. Nevertheless a working party, with the assistance of the Government Actuary, has compiled a document entitled 'Actuarial Tables with Explanatory Notes for Use in Personal Injury and Fatal Accident Cases', which has been published by Her Majesty's Stationery Office.[5] In *Spiers v Halliday*[6] however, a judge of first instance held that since the tables had not been officially adopted, or proved before any higher court, they would not themselves be admissible in the absence of evidence as to the correctness of their contents. It was also held that the practice continued to be that actuarial evidence would rarely be considered appropriate by the courts in determining economic loss in personal injury cases.[7]

Inflation and higher rates of taxation generally ignored

[**8.11**] 'The law appears to me to be now settled', said Lord Scarman in *Lim Poh Choo v Camden and Islington Area Health Authority*,[8] 'that only in exceptional cases, where justice can be shown to require it, will the risk of future inflation be brought into account in the assessment

---

1   See, eg *Fletcher v Autocar & Transporters* [1968] 2 QB 322, [1968] 1 All ER 726, CA; *S v Distillers Co (Biochemicals) Ltd* [1969] 3 All ER 1412, [1970] 1 WLR 114. See also Prevett: 'Actuarial Assessment of Damages: The Thalidomide Case' (1972) 35 MLR 140, 257.
2   See, eg, per Edmund Davies LJ in *Mitchell v Mulholland (No 2)* [1972] 1 QB 65 at 77, [1971] 2 All ER 1205 at 1212-1213. Cf per Oliver LJ in *Auty v National Coal Board* [1985] 1 All ER 930 at 939, [1985] 1 WLR at 800-801: '. . . as a means of providing a reliable guide to individual behaviour patterns, or to future economic and political events, the predictions of an actuary can be only a little more likely to be accurate (and will almost certainly be less entertaining) than those of an astrologer.'
3   See, eg, Kemp 'The Assessment of Damages for Future Pecuniary Loss in Personal Injury Claims' (1984) 3 CJQ 120.
4   See *Report on Personal Injury Litigation - Assessment of Damages* (Law Commmission No 56, 1973) paras 215-230 (pp 59-63). See also *Structured Settlements and Interim and Provisional Damages* (Law Commission Consultation Paper No 125, 1992) paras 2.16-2.22 (pp 9-13).
5   The Working Party was chaired by Mr Michael Ogden QC. Extracts from the report can be found in (1984) 134 NLJ 454.
6   (1984) Times, 30 June (JP Gorman QC sitting as a High Court Judge in the Queen's Bench Division).
7   *Spiers v Halliday*, ibid.
8   [1980] AC 174 at 193, [1979] 2 All ER 910 at 923, HL.

of damages for future loss'.[1] His Lordship identified several reasons for the reluctance of the courts to consider the impact of inflation when calculating awards. They include the highly speculative nature of any inquiry into future inflation rates;[2] and the assumption that the plaintiff will endeavour to mitigate the effects of inflation by prudent investment in so far as it is possible to do so. Given that the tort system is one of lump sum compensation the view is taken that it is appropriate, in the words of Lord Scarman, to leave 'the recipient in the same position as others, who have to rely on capital for their support to face the future'.[3] In *Hodgson v Trapp*[4] the House of Lords re-iterated its opposition to the taking into account of inflation and decided that, in addition, the fact that the income from a large damages award might attract a high rate of tax should not be taken into account so as to increase the size of the award itself.[5] Lord Oliver said:[6]

> 'That tax will be levied is, no doubt, as Benjamin Franklin observed, one of the two certainties of life, but the extent and manner of its exaction in the future can only be guessed at. It is as much an imponderable as any of the other uncertainties which are embraced in the exercise of making a just assessment of damages for future loss. The system of multipliers and multiplicands conventionally employed in the assessment of loss takes account of a variety of factors, none of which is or, indeed, is capable of being worked out scientifically, but which are catered for by allowing a reasonably generous margin in the assumed rate of interest on which the multiplier is based. There is, in my judgment, no self-evident justification for singling out this particular factor and making for it an allowance which is not to be made for the equally imponderable factor of inflation.'

His Lordship therefore concluded[7] that 'the incidence of taxation in the future should ordinarily be assumed to be satisfactorily taken care of in the conventional assumption of an interest rate applicable to a stable currency and the selection of a multiplier appropriate to that rate'.

Risk of future unemployment due to injury

[**8.12**] An accident victim may incur a permanent degree of disability which is not so severe as to deprive him immediately of his present employment, but which would have an adverse effect upon his chances

---

1 Cf *Taylor v O'Connor* [1971] AC 115, [1970] 1 All ER 365, HL; *Young v Percival* [1974] 3 All ER 677, [1975] 1 WLR 17, CA.
2 For a specific reform proposal which would apparently provide the court with a straightforward method of taking future inflation into account, based upon the rate of return from index-linked securities, see Kemp, 'Discounting Compensation for Future Loss' (1985) 101 LQR 556.
3 *Lim Poh Choo v Camden and Islington Area Health Authority* [1980] AC 174 at 193, [1979] 2 All ER 910 at 923.
4 [1989] AC 807, [1988] 3 All ER 870.
5 Overruling the majority decision of the Court of Appeal in *Thomas v Wignall* [1987] QB 1098, [1987] 1 All ER 1185, CA.
6 [1989] AC 807 at 834, [1988] 3 All ER 870 at 885.
7 [1989] AC 807 at 835, [1988] 3 All ER 870 at 885.

of obtaining another job should his present employment cease for any reason at some future date.[1] It is clear that this handicap, although in a sense only potential in that its financial consequences have yet to materialise, represents an *existing* loss for which, if negligence is proved, the plaintiff is entitled to damages.[2] The calculation of such damages is necessarily highly speculative, however, and the multiplier system, used where the plaintiff is already suffering an immediate loss of earnings, has not been considered appropriate by the courts for adoption in the present context.[3] In *Moeliker v Reyrolle & Co*[4] Browne LJ observed that 'any guidance can only be on very broad lines, because the facts may vary almost infinitely'.[5] His Lordship subsequently continued as follows:[6]

> 'I do not think one can say more by way of principle than this. The consideration of this head of damages should be made in two stages. 1. Is there a 'substantial' or 'real' risk that a plaintiff will lose his present job at some time before the estimated end of his working life? 2. If there is (but not otherwise), the court must assess and quantify the present value of the risk of the financial damage which the plaintiff will suffer if that risk materialises, having regard to the degree of the risk, the time when it may materialise, and the factors, both favourable and unfavourable, which in a particular case will, or may, affect the plaintiff's chances of getting a job at all, or an equally well paid job.'

The plaintiff will therefore normally be required to adduce evidence to establish both the existence of a risk of loss of his present employment, and the extent to which his earning capacity would be adversely affected by the disability were he to do so.[7] There was formerly a dispute as to whether the sums thus awarded for loss of earning capacity represent a head of damage distinct from that for loss of future earnings.[8] The better view, however, is that they do not do so.[9] It follows that they are liable to the same deductions as are required to be made from awards for loss of future earnings.[10]

---

1 See, eg *Smith v Manchester Corpn* (1974) 17 KIR 1, CA. In certain circumstances a claim may arise under this head even if the plaintiff is not actually employed at the time of the trial: *Cook v Consolidated Fisheries* [1977] ICR 635, CA.
2 See *Smith v Manchester Corpn* (1974) 17 KIR 1, CA, at 8 per Scarman LJ.
3 See *Smith v Manchester Corpn* (1974) 17 KIR 1 at 6 per Edmund Davies LJ and at 8 per Scarman LJ. Cf Bankes 'Quantifying Loss of Earning Capacity' (1983) 80 LS Gaz 1150.
4 [1976] ICR 253. See also *Nicholls v National Coal Board* [1976] ICR 266, CA.
5 [1977] 1 All ER 9 at 15, [1976] ICR 253, CA, at 261G.
6 [1977] 1 All ER 9 at 17, [1976] ICR 253 at 263D-E.
7 See *Chan Wai Tong v Li Ping Sum* [1985] AC 446 at 460, [1985] 2 WLR 396 at 404 (per Lord Fraser delivering the judgment of the Privy Council).
8 See *Foster v Tyne and Wear County Council* [1986] 1 All ER 567, CA, at 571-572 and the references there given.
9 See the Law Commission's Report on *Personal Injury Litigation, Assessment of Damages* (Law Com No 56) para 204; the Report of the *Royal Commission on Civil Liability and Compensation for Personal Injury (Pearson)* (Cmnd 7054-I), para 338; *McGregor on Damages* (15th edn, 1988) para 1466.
10 See *Foster v Tyne and Wear County Council* [1986] 1 All ER 567, CA. For the deductions, see below.

Children

[8.13] Children who, through disablement caused by the defendant's negligence, have had their eventual adult employment prospects reduced or destroyed, are also entitled to compensation.[1] The calculation will inevitably vary with the facts of each individual case. In two such cases, in each of which the plaintiff was totally disabled, the Court of Appeal used the multiplier system, apparently taking a figure approximating to the national average wage as the starting point.[2] In two other cases, however, where the plaintiffs were only partially disabled and could be expected to find employment of some kind, the Court of Appeal preferred to approach the matter more broadly and simply stated what it considered to be an appropriate sum.[3]

Damages for the 'lost years'

[8.14] In *Pickett v British Rail Engineering Ltd*[4] the House of Lords held that a plaintiff whose life expectancy has been reduced as a result of the accident can recover damages to compensate for the earnings which would be lost to him as a result of his premature death. In so holding their Lordships overruled the much criticised decision of the Court of Appeal in *Oliver v Ashman*,[5] which had held that lost earnings could only be recovered on the basis of the post-accident expectation of life. A central reason for the decision of the House of Lords was the injustice which occurred where a plaintiff whose life expectancy had been reduced, but who had dependants to support, brought an action during his own lifetime. Since it has always been understood that this debars the dependants from bringing their own action under the Fatal Accidents Act after his death, the rule in *Oliver v Ashman* meant that the dependants would go uncompensated. Although it remedied this anomaly, one effect of the *Pickett* decision was to create another, but this was swiftly corrected by statute. The Administration of Justice Act 1982, s 4(2) modifies the Law Reform (Miscellaneous Provisions) Act 1934, s 1(2)(a) so as to provide that 'any damages for loss of income in respect of any period after [a] person's death' will not survive for the benefit of his estate. This was to prevent defendants being liable to the deceased's estate under the 1934 Act, as well as to his dependants under the Fatal Accidents Act, for future economic loss caused by the death of the victim.[6]

---

1   See eg *S v Distillers Co (Biochemicals) Ltd* [1969] 3 All ER 1412, [1970] 1 WLR 114. See also *Jamil Bin Harun v Yang Kamsiah Bte Meor Rasdi* [1984] AC 529, [1984] 2 WLR 668, PC.
2   See *Taylor v Bristol Omnibus Co* [1975] 2 All ER 1107, [1975] 1 WLR 1054, CA; *Croke v Wiseman* [1981] 3 All ER 852, [1982] 1 WLR 71, CA (Lord Denning MR, dissenting, would have allowed no damages for lost future earnings).
3   See *Joyce v Yeomans* [1981] 2 All ER 21, [1981] 1 WLR 549, CA (but cf per Brandon LJ at 557); *Mitchell v Liverpool Area Health Authority* (1985) Times, 17 June, CA.
4   [1980] AC 136, [1979] 1 All ER 774, HL.
5   [1962] 2 QB 210, [1961] 3 All ER 323, CA.
6   Cf *Gammell v Wilson* [1982] AC 27, [1981] 1 All ER 578, HL.

162 *Damages recoverable for personal injury*

Amount of damages

[8.15] In *Pickett v British Rail Engineering* itself the House of Lords apparently contemplated that damages for lost earnings during the lost years would be calculated in a manner broadly similar to that used in Fatal Accident Act cases. This indeed was consistent with the underlying raison d'être of the decision in *Pickett*. But this method, which while deducting the deceased's own living expenses normally still credits his dependants with a substantial proportion of his earnings, might be considered less appropriate where no dependants are actually involved.[1] The general principles governing the calculation of deductions must, however, presumably be the same regardless of the plaintiff's actual family commitments.[2] Nevertheless it does appear that a method which will tend to reduce awards in this category generally, by taking a more limited view of the amount which the plaintiff would be likely to have had available to him after a realistic proportion of his income had been expended, is likely to be favoured by the courts.[3]

Children unlikely to recover under the Pickett principle

[8.16] Although even small children can theoretically claim for lost earnings during the lost years,[4] in practice such an award would be so speculative that usually none is made.[5] Children can, however, claim for prospective lost earnings during their post-accident life-expectancy.[6]

Relevance of gains

[8.17] Notwithstanding that damages for personal injury are intended to compensate the plaintiff, and should therefore not render him better off financially than he was before the accident, it has long been established that, in calculating them, no account is to be taken of ex gratia or charitable payments made to the plaintiff because of the misfortune which has befallen him.[7] Similarly, benefits accruing,

---

1 See, generally, the valuable discussion by Evans and Stanton, 'Valuing the Lost Years' (1984) 134 NLJ 515 at 553.
2 See *Harris v Empress Motors* [1983] 3 All ER 561, [1984] 1 WLR 212, CA.
3 See *Harris v Empress Motors* (previous note). Although the facts in this case arose before the passing of the Administration of Justice Act 1982, s 4(2) and concerned a deceased plaintiff, the general problem of assessing damages remains relevant after the Act in relation to living plaintiffs.
4 See *Connolly v Camden and Islington Area Health Authority* [1981] 3 All ER 250.
5 See ibid. Cf per Lord Scarman in *Gammell v Wilson* [1982] AC 27 at 78E, [1981] 1 All ER 578 at 593, HL.
6 See above.
7 See *Cunningham v Harrison* [1973] QB 942 at 950-951, [1973] 3 All ER 463 at 468 per Lord Denning MR. See also *Redpath v Belfast and County Down Rly* [1947] NI 167. It has, however, been suggested that ex gratia payments made by the *defendant tortfeasor himself* should be set off against any damages subsequently awarded: see *Hussain v New Taplow Paper Mills* [1987] ICR 28, CA, at 43 per Lloyd LJ. But the Court of Appeal in *McCamley v Cammell Laird Shipbuilders Ltd* [1990] 1 All ER 854, [1990] 1 WLR 963, CA, held that *some* payments by the tortfeasor could still be regarded as non-deductible acts of benevolence.

albeit in consequence of the accident, to the plaintiff as a result of private insurance policies are not to be taken into account.[1] It is generally considered to be inconsistent with intuitive notions of justice that advantages gained by the plaintiff by virtue of his own thrift should be deducted from damages. In *Parry v Cleaver*[2] the House of Lords held that this principle extended to include disablement pensions paid by virtue of the plaintiff's former employment, and to do so regardless of whether the pension scheme had been contributory or non-contributory. Participation in such a scheme should, it was held, be regarded as analogous in principle to a private insurance policy; in choosing a job which had such a scheme the plaintiff had presumably voluntarily accepted lower levels of remuneration while working in order to pay for it. *Parry v Cleaver* was decided by a bare majority,[3] and overruled an earlier majority decision of the Court of Appeal.[4] Nevertheless, that it continues to represent the law has recently been put beyond doubt. In the 1991 case of *Smoker v London Fire and Civil Defence Authority*[5] the House of Lords was invited to invoke the 1966 Practice Statement to depart from it, but chose instead expressly and unanimously to affirm its authority. The point had earlier been considered both by the Law Commission[6] and by the Pearson Commission,[7] but neither had recommended any change in the law.

Entitlements for which plaintiff has not paid

[**8.18**] The underlying rationale of the principle in *Parry v Cleaver*, however, that the plaintiff indirectly paid for the benefits himself, means that the outcome will be different if the benefits were not paid for by him. In *Hussain v New Taplow Paper Mills*[8] a disablement income, which the plaintiff became contractually entitled to receive as a result of an accident at his place of work, was deducted in a negligence action from his damages for loss of earnings.[9] The defendant employers had in fact insured against their liability to pay the sums in question; and it was contended that the payments forthcoming represented in essence the fruits of insurance, *in effect* paid for by the plaintiff himself, through the services he had given to his employer prior to the accident. This contention was rejected. The

---

1 *Bradburn v Great Western Rly Co* (1874) LR 10 Exch 1.
2 [1970] AC 1, [1969] 1 All ER 555, HL. See also *Wood v British Coal Corpn* (1990) Times, 10 October, CA.
3 Lords Reid, Pearce and Wilberforce. (Lords Morris and Pearson dissented).
4 See *Browning v War Office* [1963] 1 QB 750 per Lord Denning M R and Diplock LJ. Donovan LJ dissented.
5 [1991] 2 AC 502, [1991] 2 All ER 449, HL.
6 See Law Commission Report No 56 (1973): *Report on Personal Injury Litigation – Assessment of Damages*, at p 34 et seq.
7 See the Report of the *Royal Commission on Civil Liability and Compensation for Personal Injury*, Cmnd 7054-I (1978), paras 517-520.
8 [1988] AC 514, [1988] 1 All ER 541.
9 For comment on the decision of the Court of Appeal, reported in [1987] ICR 28 and upheld by the House of Lords, see Lesley J Anderson 'Assessment of Loss in Personal Injury Cases' (1987) 50 MLR 963.

164 Damages recoverable for personal injury

House of Lords held that the disablement income was indistinguishable in principle from the wages he would have received if uninjured. Lord Bridge said:[1]

> 'It positively offends my sense of justice that a plaintiff, who has certainly paid no insurance premiums *as such*, should receive full wages during a period of incapacity to work from two separate sources, his employer and the tortfeasor. It would seem to me still more unjust and anomalous where, as here, the employer and the tortfeasor are one and the same.'[2]

Relationship with state benefits: Social Security Administration Act 1992, Part IV

[8.19] The Social Security Act 1989 introduced a new regime regulating the relationship between tort damages and state benefits. This replaced an earlier, more limited, provision in the Law Reform (Personal Injuries) Act 1948 which does, however, continue to apply to a restricted number of cases albeit in an amended form.[3] The new regime is now to be found in Pt IV of the consolidating Social Security Administration Act 1992.

Full deductibilty

[8.20] In a series of decisions culminating in the decision of the House of Lords in *Hodgson v Trapp*,[4] which dealt with attendance and mobility allowances, the courts had moved in the direction of favouring the deductibility from damages of most of the state benefits not expressly made deductible by the 1948 Act.[5] This policy was originally put into statutory form by the Social Security Act 1989, s 22 and Sch 4,[6] with the addition of elaborate machinery to ensure that tortfeasors themselves do not benefit, at the taxpayer's expense, from the deductions so made.[7] For accidents occurring after 1 January

---

1 [1988] 1 All ER 514 at 548 (italics supplied).
2 But the mere fact that the payment comes from the tortfeasor does not, apparently, disqualify it from being construed as an act of benevolence and, as such, not deductable. See the decision of the Court of Appeal in *McCamley v Cammell Laird Shipbuiders Ltd* [1990] 1 All ER 854, [1990] 1 WLR 963 in which *Hussain v New Taplow Paper Mills* was narrowly distinguished on the facts.
3 Section 2(1) of the 1948 Act provided for the deduction from damages of *one half* of the value of certain social security benefits payable for five years after the accident. It remains in force, and has been widened in scope with respect to the benefits deductible and the heads of damages from which the deduction is to be made, but is now confined to cases in which the damages are £2,500 or less: see the Social Security Act 1989, Sch 4 and the Social Security (Consequential Provisions) Act 1992, Sch 2.
4 [1989] AC 807, [1988] 3 All ER 870, HL.
5 See eg *Nabi v British Leyland (UK) Ltd* [1980] 1 All ER 667, [1980] 1 WLR 529, CA (unemployment benefit); *Lincoln v Hayman* [1982] 2 All ER 819, [1982] 1 WLR 488, CA (supplementary benefit); *Gaskill v Preston* [1981] 3 All ER 427 (family income supplement).
6 See now the Social Security Administration Act 1992, Pt IV.
7 See Patrick Green 'The damages lottery-the new recoupment regulations' 1991 NLJ 1009. See also 'Compensation payments: recovering benefits' LS Gaz 12 December 1990, p 32ff.

1989, and for which the damages exceed £2,500, the main benefits[1] paid or to be paid to the victim for five years from the date of the accident are to be deducted *in full* from the damages award (or out-of-court settlement), in order to avoid over-compensation. But in order simultaneously to ensure that the state does not thereby subsidise tortfeasors the latter are obliged to reimburse to the Department of Social Security the value of the benefits so paid or to be paid. The tortfeasor is required to obtain a certificate from the department of the relevant sums and to make the deduction, and reimbursement to the department, accordingly. A major difference between the new regime and the old is that the deduction is now to be made from the total amount of damages, ie both pecuniary and non-pecuniary loss. It is not to be confined to damages for loss of income as was formerly the position under the earlier legislation. Moreover, the deduction is apparently to be made in full from the actual award *even if* that award has already been reduced for contributory negligence.[2] Finally, as far as benefits not coming within the statutory regime are concerned, it should be noted that state retirement pensions have been held not to be deductible.[3] But redundancy payments may constitute a contribution to earnings which will be lost due to injury, and in such cases they will be deducted from damages.[4]

Tax

[8.21] It was established by the well-known decision of the House of Lords in *British Transport Commission v Gourley*,[5] itself a personal injuries case, that the likely incidence of taxation must be taken into account in assessing damages for lost earnings. The plaintiff will therefore only be awarded a sum representing his probable net loss after tax rather than one representing his gross pre-tax income. It follows from *Gourley* that the plaintiff must give credit, in his claim for special damages, for any tax rebate received by him as a result of his absence from work due to the injury.[6] In *Cooper v Firth Brown Ltd*[7] it was held that the *Gourley* principle also applied in respect of

---

1 Ie income support and family credit, attendance allowance, disability benefits and mobility allowance, statutory sick pay and unemployment benefits: Social Security (Recoupment) Regulations 1990 (SI 1990/322) and Social Security (Recoupment) Amendment Regulations (S I 1990/1558). Regulations made under the Social Security Act 1989 remain in force, where appropriate, for the purposes of the Social Security Administration Act 1992: see the Social Security (Consequential Provisions) Act 1992.
2 See Gordon Exall 'Personal Injury Litigation after the Social Security Recoupment Regulations and the Effects of Contributory Negligence' [1990-91] 10 *Litigation* 58.
3 See *Hewson v Downs* [1970] 1 QB 73, [1969] 3 All ER 193.
4 See *Wilson v National Coal Board* 1981 SLT 67, HL, applied in *Colledge v Bass Mitchells & Butlers* [1988] 1 All ER 536, CA.
5 [1956] AC 185, [1955] 3 All ER 796. See William Bishop and John Kay, 'Taxation and Damages: The Rule in Gourley's Case' (1987) 103 LQR 211.
6 See *Hartley v Sandholme Iron Co* [1975] QB 600, [1974] 3 All ER 475.
7 [1963] 2 All ER 31, [1963] 1 WLR 418.

the plaintiff's social security contributions, and that a sum representing these too should be taken into account. If it can be proved to the satisfaction of the court, however, that the plaintiff was in the habit of making certain dispositions, such as covenanted gifts, in order to *reduce* his tax liability, then this factor will also be taken into account in calculating the damages.[1]

Pension contributions not recoverable

[**8.22**] In *Dews v National Coal Board*[2] the plaintiff was injured in an accident for which the defendants were liable. He contended that his award for lost earnings should not be reduced to take account of pension scheme contributions which would have been deducted from his wages if he had not been injured. The House of Lords rejected his contention. The plaintiff had sought to invoke the principle that it is, in general, no concern of the defendant how the plaintiff chooses to spend his own disposable income. Their Lordships held, however, that an exception had to be made to that principle where part of the income is used to provide a pension for retirement. This is because loss of pension rights is itself a recoverable head of loss for which damages can be awarded. Therefore, to allow a plaintiff to recover both a sum in respect of such lost rights, if any,[3] *and* the contributions which would have been necessary to secure them had they not been lost, would be to permit double recovery. It is important to note that the House did *not* decide *Dews*'s case on the ground that the mere fact that the deduction of the pension contributions from the plaintiff's wages would have been *compulsory* was itself sufficient to defeat his contention. This reasoning had been adopted by Sir John Donaldson MR in the Court of Appeal,[4] which had decided the case the same way as the House of Lords. However, the other two members of the Court of Appeal, Parker and Woolf LJJ, had pointed out that this approach could be a source of anomaly in other situations. For example those in which a plaintiff contractually agrees with his employer that the latter may deduct trade union dues, or charitable donations, at source.

Cost of care

General calculation

[**8.23**] Plaintiffs who are seriously and permanently disabled often require constant nursing attendance and medical care for the rest of their lives. The cost of this is recoverable as a recognised head of general damages. Adaptations to the plaintiff's house or even, in

---

1 See *Beach v Reed Corrugated Cases Ltd* [1956] 2 All ER 652, [1956] 1 WLR 807.
2 [1988] AC 1, [1987] 2 All ER 545, HL. For comment see Lesley J Anderson, 'Assessment of Loss in Personal Injury Cases' (1987) 50 MLR 963.
3 On the facts of *Dews v National Coal Board* itself the plaintiff had not, in fact, suffered any diminution in his pension entitlement.
4 See [1987] QB 81, [1986] 2 All ER 769, CA.

some cases, the purchase of new accommodation may be necessary.[1] The calculation of the cost of future care is usually made by working out the likely annual cost and then multiplying it to yield the appropriate lump sum. 'The true principle', said Lord Scarman in *Lim Poh Choo v Camden and Islington Area Health Authority*,[2] 'is that the estimate of damages under this head must proceed on the basis that resort will be had to capital as well as income to meet the expenditure; in other words, the cost of care, having been assessed, must be met by an award calculated on an annuity basis'.

Use of National Health Service facilities

[**8.24**] The Law Reform (Personal Injuries) Act 1948, s 2(4) provides as follows:

> 'In an action for damages for personal injuries . . . there shall be disregarded, in determining the reasonableness of any expenses, the possibility of avoiding those expenses or part of them by taking advantage of facilities available under the National Health Service . . .'

Accordingly, if the plaintiff chooses to be treated within the private medical sector, the defendant cannot argue that the expenditure incurred should be disallowed as unreasonable merely because the equivalent facilities could have been obtained free of charge in the state sector. The Pearson Commission in fact recommended that this provision should be repealed: 'If a plaintiff decides to seek private treatment for injuries when the same treatment would have been equally available under the National Health Service, we do not think that the defendant can reasonably be expected to meet the cost.'[3] This recommendation has not, however, been implemented. But if the expenditure incurred in caring for the plaintiff at his own home is substantially greater than that of caring for him in an institution, the burden of proving that it is reasonable for him to remain at home lies on the plaintiff.[4] It is also important to note that the 1948 Act does not require that a plaintiff should be allowed to recover expenses which he will never, in fact, incur.[5] It is, of course, true that a plaintiff who obtains damages assessed on the basis of private medical care can subsequently use National Health Service facilities and spend the award on something else, since the court cannot interfere with the use to which the plaintiff ultimately puts his own money. Nevertheless, if it is clear that the plaintiff will in fact be treated under the National

---

1   See eg *George v Pinnock* [1973] 1 All ER 926, [1973] 1 WLR 118, CA (purchase of bungalow). Cf *Cunningham v Harrison* [1973] QB 942, [1973] 3 All ER 463, CA. On the approach to be adopted in calculating the appropriate sum to be awarded in respect of the purchase of special accommodation see *Roberts v Johnstone* [1989] QB 878, CA.
2   [1980] AC 174 at 193, [1979] 2 All ER 910 at 922, HL.
3   Report of the *Royal Commission of Civil Liability and Compensation for Personal Injury* (1978) Cmnd 7054-I, para 341.
4   See *Rialas v Mitchell* (1984) 128 Sol Jo 704, CA (burden discharged on the facts).
5   See *Harris v Bright's Asphalt Contractors Ltd* [1953] 1 QB 617 at 635, [1953] 1 All ER 395 at 402.

Health Service, he cannot claim damages assessed on the basis of private treatment. Moreover, in some situations the plaintiff is regarded as having no real choice, because it is shown that suitable accommodation or treatment, for his condition or disability, can only be found within the state sector.[1] In such cases, however, the court must not assume that all the services which the plaintiff will receive from the state will necessarily be completely free of charge to him. Although medical treatment under the National Health Service is (except for prescriptions) free of charge to the user, local authorities are entitled to charge disabled people for certain welfare services which they may provide for them.[2]

Living expenses sometimes deductible

[8.25] A plaintiff who is disabled both from working and from looking after himself will normally recover damages both for the cost of care and for lost earnings. If the care is residential in, for example, a hospital or nursing home, it will usually be appropriate to make a deduction from the award for the cost of care to allow for the 'domestic element' of board and lodging etc.[3] Since the plaintiff would have used part of his earnings to feed and house himself, if he had not been injured, there would be an element of over-compensation in such a case if the plaintiff recovered all his lost earnings along with the full cost of care, where the latter includes food and basic necessities.[4] Similarly, when the plaintiff obtains board and lodging either subsidised, or free of charge, in a state institution it is now the law that a reduction may be made in any award for lost earnings to allow for this. The Court of Appeal had held in *Daish v Wauton*[5] that no such reduction should be made, but the Pearson Commission recommended that this decision should be reversed,[6] and s 5 of the Administration of Justice Act 1982 accordingly provides as follows: 'In an action . . . for personal injuries . . . any saving to the injured person which is attributable to his maintenance wholly or partly at public expense in a hospital, nursing home or other institution shall be set off against any income lost by him as a result of his injuries.'

---

1 See *Cunningham v Harrison* [1973] QB 942, [1973] 3 All ER 463, CA. See also *Lim Poh Choo v Camden and Islington Area Health Authority* [1980] AC 174 at 188, [1979] 2 All ER 910 at 918, HL, per Lord Scarman.
2 See the National Assistance Act 1948, s 29(5) referred to in *Taylor v Bristol Omnibus Co* [1975] 2 All ER 1107 at 1112 and 1116, [1975] 1 WLR 1054 at 1058 and 1063, CA. Cf *Wipfli v Britten* (1983) 145 DLR (3d) 80.
3 See *Lim Poh Choo v Camden and Islington Area Health Authority* [1980] AC 174 at 191, [1979] 2 All ER 910 at 921 per Lord Scarman. The deduction should not be reflected in the choice of multiplier but should, instead, be made from the starting-point (or 'multiplicand'): see per Lord Scarman ibid (at 196, 925). See also per Browne LJ in the Court of Appeal [1979] QB 196 at 234-235.
4 Cf *Shearman v Folland* [1950] 2 KB 43, [1950] 1 All ER 976, CA.
5 [1972] 2 QB 262, [1972] 1 All ER 25, CA.
6 See the Report of the *Royal Commission on Civil Liability and Compensation for Personal Injury* (1978) Cmnd 7054-I, paras 508-512.

Care by relatives

[8.26] Often an injured plaintiff will be cared for at home by a parent or spouse in circumstances in which, had this help not been forthcoming, professional nursing assistance, or an increase in the existing level of such assistance, would have been necessary. It has been clear since the decision of the Court of Appeal in *Donnelly v Joyce*,[1] which resolved earlier uncertainty, that the plaintiff can recover in his damages a sum enabling him to pay for the services so provided. It is not necessary for any formal agreement to be drawn up obliging the plaintiff to pay for the care he receives.[2] The plaintiff claims in his own right and not, in theory at least, on behalf of the relative or relatives in question. In *Donnelly v Joyce* Megaw LJ put it as follows:[3]

> 'The question from what source the plaintiff's needs have been met, the question who has . . . given the services, the question whether or not the plaintiff is or is not under a legal or moral liability to repay, are, so far as the defendant and his liability are concerned, all irrelevant. The plaintiff's loss . . . is the existence of the need for . . . nursing services, the value of which for purposes of damages – for the purpose of the ascertainment of the amount of his loss – is the proper and reasonable cost of supplying those needs.'[4]

Calculation

[8.27] It follows from the reasoning of Megaw LJ that an award can be made under his head even though the relative in question has not given up paid employment to look after the plaintiff.[5] If such employment has been given up the value of the income lost will be relevant in calculating the award; provided that it does not exceed the full commercial rate for the services received by the plaintiff, which is the ceiling for such an award.[6] This ceiling figure will not necessarily be awarded in every case since, as it was put in an Australian case, the–

> 'calculation of compensation with reference to charges made for the supply of services on a commercial basis may not always be appropriate . . . Services provided by relatives and friends may not be exactly the same as those provided by commercial agencies. The latter will also necessarily have an element of profit in their charges.'[7]

1   [1974] QB 454, [1973] 3 All ER 475, CA.
2   Cf *Haggar v de Placido* [1972] 2 All ER 1029, [1972] 1 WLR 716. Any such agreement drawn up, for the purpose of increasing the award, will now be regarded as a sham: see *Housecroft v Burnett* [1986] 1 All ER 332, CA at 343 per O'Connor LJ.
3   [1974] QB 454 at 462, [1973] 3 All ER 475 at 480 (judgment of the Court).
4   See also the striking decision in *Hunt v Severs* (1993) Times, 13 May, CA, in which the plaintiff's husband, who supplied the care, was also the defendant tortfeasor. The plaintiff was held able to recover from the defendant (ie in practice from his insurers) the value of his *own* services.
5   See *Cunningham v Harrison* [1973] QB 942, [1973] 3 All ER 463, CA; *Taylor v Bristol Omnibus Co* [1975] 2 All ER 1107, [1975] 1 WLR 1054, CA.
6   *Housecroft v Burnett* [1986] 1 All ER 332, CA at 343. On the calculation of compensation under this head see, generally, *Hodges v Frost* (1984) 53 ALR 373 (Federal Court of Australia).
7   Per Kirby J in *Hodges v Frost* (1984) 53 ALR 373 at 381.

170 *Damages recoverable for personal injury*

In *Donnelly v Joyce* the damages were calculated by reference to the wages in fact lost by the plaintiff's mother, it being clear that the cost of professional help, if she had been unavailable, would have been greater.[1] In *Croke v Wiseman*[2] the plaintiff's mother gave up her job as a teacher to look after him, and the claim for nursing care included a sum in respect of the pension rights which she had thereby forfeited. By a majority,[3] the Court of Appeal allowed this claim on the ground that the overall sum thereby awarded for care was not excessive given the high quality of the nursing care which the mother provided and that the 'parents [would] in fact be on duty for longer hours every week than ... professional nurses, and they [would] have the whole of the weekends to cope with'.[4]

Structured settlements[5]

[**8.28**] One of the most striking and significant developments relating to personal injuries compensation in the last few years has been the development of 'structured settlements'. The effect of these is to provide a plaintiff with periodic payments, instead of a lump sum, for the remainder of his or her life.[6] The payments are usually funded by the purchase of a series of annuities enabling the achievement, inter alia, of indexation. This fact, coupled with a favourable tax regime, can make such settlements very attractive to plaintiffs.[7] As the law stands at present such settlements cannot be imposed by the court itself but only agreed as a result of negotiation between the parties. Nevertheless, the potential advantages to accident victims of this method of compensation are such that no practitioner can afford to overlook its importance. Any plaintiff's adviser who failed to consider the possibility of seeking such a settlement for his client, instead of the conventional lump sum, would arguably now be guilty of professional negligence. In 1992 the Law Commission embarked on a major review of structured settlements and related issues which could well lead to legislative developments in this important field.[8]

---

1   See [1974] QB 454, CA at 459-460, [1973] 3 All ER 475 at 478 per Megaw LJ delivering the judgment of the court.
2   [1981] 3 All ER 852, [1982] 1 WLR 71, CA.
3   Griffiths and Shaw LJJ, Lord Denning MR dissenting.
4   [1981] 3 All ER 852 at 860, [1982] 1 WLR at 81 per Griffiths LJ.
5   See Iain S Goldrein and Margaret de Haas (eds) *Structured Settlements - A Practical Guide* (1st edn, 1993).
6   See *Kelly v Dawes* (1990) Times, 27 September. See also *Practice Direction* [1992] 1 All ER 862, sub nom *Practice Note* [1992] 1 WLR 328.
7   See David Allen 'Structured Settlements' (1988) 104 LQR 448.
8   See *Structured Settlements and Interim and Provisional Damages* Law Commission Consultation Paper No 125 (HMSO, 1992).

Scope for reform

Future of tort as a compensation system[1]

[8.29] The very acceptability of the law of negligence, as a means of compensating sufferers from misfortune, has come under increasing scrutiny in recent years.[2] Three basic but related criticisms can be identified. Firstly, the 'fault' principle is capricious, and in practice arbitrary, in the way that it selects successful plaintiffs in accident cases, because so much depends on the availability of witnesses and their recollection of incidents which often occurred very quickly. Secondly, tort does not extend compensation to victims of organic illness and disease, the sufferers from which often experience handicaps at least as severe as many of those injured in accidents.[3] Thirdly, negligence is apt to be extraordinarily wasteful: nearly as much money is spent on administering the tort system in personal injury cases as is actually awarded in damages.[4] Various reform proposals have been made in the light of these criticisms. The most radical would eliminate tort from this area altogether, and expand the welfare state in its place. A scheme on these lines exists in New Zealand, but sufferers from organic illness and disease are still excluded.[5] Proposals for a somewhat similar scheme were put forward in Britain by the Pearson Commission, but the law of negligence would have been permitted to continue in existence alongside the scheme albeit with financial disincentives to the use of it by certain potential plaintiffs.[6] A flaw in the Pearson proposals, however, in the opinion of some commentators, was that the Commission's suggested no-fault compensation scheme would have applied only to persons injured on the roads or at work.[7] Although it is the great increase in road accidents which, over the course of the present century, has put the adequacy of the law of negligence and its accompanying forensic processes under strain, to build an expanded state compensation system around a particular cause of harm would, it has been argued, only add to the supposed anomalousness of the present position.[8]

---

1 See also ch 20 below, where the issues outlined in the text at this point are considered at greater length.
2 See, generally, Atiyah *Accidents, Compensation and the Law* (4th edn, 1987) (ed Cane).
3 Cf Stapleton *Disease and the Compensation Debate* (1986).
4 See the Report of the *Royal Commission on Civil Liability and Compensation for Personal Injury* (1978) Cmnd 7054-I at para 83, quoted below, para 20.02.
5 See, generally, ch 20, below.
6 See, generally, the Report of the *Royal Commission on Civil Liability and Compensation for Personal Injury* (Cmnd 7054-I) (1978).
7 In fairness, it should be said that the special focus of the Pearson Commission upon road accidents was, at least in part, a reflection of their terms of reference.
8 See Atiyah *Accidents, Compensation and the Law* (3rd edn) pp 623ff (Cf 4th edn, 1987, at pp 571ff). For general discussion of the Pearson proposals see the papers collected in Allen, Bourn and Holyoak (eds) *Accident Compensation after Pearson* (1979).

Computation of damages

[8.30] The operation of the law relating to damages for injuries and disabilities necessarily reflects the underlying values or priorities of the legal system of which it forms a part. If causation were to cease entirely to be relevant to the award of compensation, and victims of disease were to be compensated on the same basis as those accidentally injured by others, it is clear that, since resources are limited, the amounts which all beneficiaries would receive would necessarily be substantially smaller than those currently awarded to successful tort plaintiffs.[1] Whether this consequence of the total abrogation of the 'fault' principle, with all its undoubted clumsiness and artificiality, would itself be found to accord with intuitive notions of justice is at least open to question.

Specific reforms

[8.31] Whatever the philosophical implications of far-reaching reform or abolition of the law of tort, however, few would deny that the law of damages, even within its existing general framework, is in need of reform. For example the award of massive sums for both loss of amenities and lost earnings to unconscious or barely sentient plaintiffs, in addition to the full cost of caring for them, is not easy to justify. Lord Denning MR strongly criticised this practice in his dissenting judgment in the Court of Appeal in *Lim Poh Choo v Camden and Islington Area Health Authority*.[2] Lord Scarman, in the House of Lords, agreed that 'a radical reappraisal of the law' was needed, but added that 'such a reappraisal calls for social, financial, economic and administrative decisions which only the legislature can take'.[3] Lord Scarman also observed, in reference to the *Lim* case itself, that it 'illustrate[d], with devastating clarity, the insuperable problems implicit in a system of compensation for personal injuries which ... can yield only a lump sum assessed by the Court at the time of judgment'.[4] The power to award provisional damages in a certain type of personal injury case,[5] introduced by the Administration of Justice Act 1982, s 6, has made only a relatively modest qualification to the lump sum principle. Perhaps the most far-reaching reform which could be effected in the law of damages, without seriously calling into question the whole framework of negligence itself, would be the introduction of a periodic payments system which would eliminate much of the artificiality and guesswork at present inherent in the award of damages for future pecuniary loss. Although the Law Commission decided against such a system[6] the Pearson Commission,

---

1 Illness is still a much more common cause of disability than accidents are: 'It is probable that only about 10% of the permanently disabled and handicapped owe their disabilities to accidental injury' (Atiyah, op cit, (4th edn) at p 18).
2 See [1979] QB 196 at 214ff, [1979] 1 All ER 332 at 341ff.
3 See [1980] AC 174 at 182, [1979] 2 All ER 910 at 914.
4 Ibid at 182 and 914.
5 See ch 7 above.
6 See Law Commission Report No 56: *Report on Personal Injury Litigation - Assessment of Damages* (1973) paras 26-30, (pp 9-10).

Scope for reform 173

in its subsequent and more wide-ranging inquiry, recommended in favour.[1] Fortunately it is now possible that developments in the field of structured settlements, provisionally favoured by the Law Commission,[2] may have the effect, albeit by a rather indirect route, of making periodic payments widely available.

---

1 See the report of the *Royal Commission on Civil Liability and Compensation for Personal Injury* (Cmnd 7054-I) (1978) ch 14.
2 See Consultation Paper 125, cited above.

Chapter 9

Cases involving death

Survival of causes of action

Law Reform (Miscellaneous Provisions) Act 1934

[**9.01**] At common law the death of a person automatically terminated all causes of action against or in favour of that person. This inconvenient rule was largely abrogated by the Law Reform (Miscellaneous Provisions) Act 1934, s 1(1), which provides that, with the exception of claims for defamation, 'on the death of any person . . . all causes of action subsisting against or vested in him shall survive against, or, as the case may be, for the benefit of, his estate'. Thus, if the plaintiff is seriously injured by the negligence of the defendant, and subsequently dies from his injuries, his estate can bring or continue an action for the losses, both pecuniary or non-pecuniary, incurred by him up to the date of his death. In *Hicks v Chief Constable of the South Yorkshire Police*,[1] which was the second case arising out of the 1989 Hillsborough football stadium disaster to reach the House of Lords,[2] an attempt by the estates of victims to recover damages on this basis failed on the facts: it being found that the deaths had, in effect, been instantaneous so that no actionable pre-death pain and suffering had occurred.

'Lost years' loss of income does not survive

[**9.02**] An important provision was added to the Law Reform (Miscellaneous Provisions) Act 1934 by the Administration of Justice Act 1982, s 4. As a result s 1(2) of the 1934 Act now reads, where relevant, as follows:

> 'Where a cause of action survives . . . for the benefit of the estate of a deceased person, the damages recoverable for the benefit of the estate of that person shall not include . . . any damages for loss of income in respect of any period after that person's death.'

---

1   [1992] 2 All ER 65, HL.
2   For the first one see ch 1 above.

This provision became necessary as a consequence of the decision of the House of Lords in *Pickett v British Rail Engineering*[1] which was reflected in the later decision of the House in *Gammell v Wilson*.[2] In the former case the House of Lords held that a living plaintiff whose life had been shortened by the negligence of the defendant could recover damages for the lost earnings which he would never receive due to his likely premature death.[3] This decision enabled justice to be achieved in the case of a living plaintiff not least because it enabled such a person, if he wished, to ensure that any dependants of his would be appropriately catered for after his death; his own action during his lifetime in respect of his injury having destroyed any claims they might themselves have subsequently brought under the Fatal Accidents Act.[4] The decision of the House in *Gammell v Wilson* made clear, however, that the effect of the Law Reform (Miscellaneous Provisions) Act 1934, s 1, when combined with the *Pickett* decision, was to enable the estates of already deceased persons to claim lost earnings for the 'lost years'. Such claims would necessarily be irrespective of whether or not the deceased had left any dependants and, if he had done so, would be additional to any claim by those dependants under the Fatal Accidents Act. Defendants could thus even have found themselves liable twice over for the same economic loss: once to the deceased's estate under the 1934 Act and once to his dependants under the Fatal Accidents Act. The new statutory provision rectifies this situation by preventing claims for lost income during the lost years from surviving for the benefit of the estate.

Where injured person dies from another cause

[9.03] It is to be noted that the wording of the new provision which prevents the deceased's estate from claiming for future lost earnings does not distinguish between victims who die from their injuries and injured persons who die from other causes. A person's life expectancy may be shortened by an accident caused by the defendant's negligence, but he may die from some unrelated non-tortious cause before he has brought an action in respect of his injuries. In such an eventuality his dependants will necessarily have no claim under the Fatal Accidents Act, and yet the blanket wording of the new provision will prevent his estate from recovering the lost earnings which, in the majority of cases, would actually have passed to the dependants and so protected them indirectly. Dependants in such circumstances will therefore be in the same position in which they would have been before *Pickett v British Rail Engineering* was decided, when lost earnings during the 'lost years' could not be recovered at all. It has been suggested that this result is anomalous.[5] But the criticism seems misplaced since the

---

1 [1980] AC 136, [1979] 1 All ER 774.
2 [1982] AC 27, [1981] 1 All ER 578.
3 This overruled the decision of the Court of Appeal in *Oliver v Ashman* [1962] 2 QB 210, [1961] 3 All ER 323. For further discussion, see ch 8 below.
4 See below.
5 See Cane and Harris (1983) 46 MLR 478.

dependants are only in the same position as those of persons generally who die from causes, such as disease, for which there is no legal redress.[1]

Claims by dependants

Background

[**9.04**] The long-standing hostility of the common law to the recovery of pure economic loss meant that a family whose breadwinner was killed by the defendant's negligence was remediless. Statutory intervention, to ameliorate this situation, came as early as 1846 with the passing in that year of the Fatal Accidents Act. The relevant statute law is now contained in the consolidating Fatal Accidents Act 1976. It is important to note, however, that the first four sections of this Act are now to be found in the Administration of Justice Act 1982, s 3 which substituted new provisions for those originally contained in the 1976 Act when it was passed.

Who can claim

[**9.05**] The Fatal Accidents Act only applies if the victim of the accident would himself have been able to obtain judgment, usually for negligence, in respect of it had he lived.[2] If, however, he does obtain judgment in his lifetime, or settles the claim, then the dependants cannot subsequently sue the defendant under the Fatal Accidents Act.[3] Consistent with its general approach, the Act provides that the damages recoverable under it may be reduced by virtue of the Law Reform (Contributory Negligence) Act 1945 if the victim of the accident had himself been contributorily negligent.[4] If the person whose negligence caused the death of the deceased was himself one of the dependants he obviously cannot bring a Fatal Accidents Act claim but will, on the contrary, be himself liable under the Act to the other dependants.[5] Any claim under the Act has to be brought by the executor or administrator of the deceased; but may be brought by the dependants themselves six months after the death, if no action has been brought by then.[6]

---

1 Cf *Jobling v Associated Dairies* [1982] AC 794, [1981] 2 All ER 752, HL. See also Burrows *Remedies for Torts and Breach of Contract* (1987) p 182, note 17.
2 'If death is caused by any wrongful act, neglect or default which is such as would (if death had not ensued) have entitled the person injured to maintain an action and recover damages in respect thereof, the person who would have been liable if death had not ensued shall be liable to an action for damages, notwithstanding the death of the person injured.': Fatal Accidents Act 1976, s 1(1).
3 Cf *Pickett v British Rail Engineering* [1980] AC 136, [1979] 1 All ER 774, HL.
4 See Fatal Accidents Act 1976, s 5.
5 See *Dodds v Dodds* [1978] QB 543, [1978] 2 All ER 539 (husband killed by wife's driving; action on behalf of children). A dependant whose negligence *contributed* to the death will be able to recover but the damages will be reduced proportionately: *Mulholland v McCrea* [1961] NI 135.
6 Fatal Accidents Act 1976, s 2.

The dependants

[**9.06**] The dependants of the deceased, who are entitled to claim under the Fatal Accidents Act, are listed in s 1 of the Act. The relevant subsections read as follows:

'(3) In this Act 'dependant' means—
(a) the wife or husband or former wife or husband of the deceased;
(b) any person who—
  (i) was living with the deceased in the same household immediately before the date of the death; and
  (ii) had been living with the deceased in the same household for at least two years before that date; and
(c) any parent or other ascendant of the deceased;
(d) any person who was treated by the deceased as his parent;
(e) any child or other descendant of the deceased;
(f) any person (not being a child of the deceased) who, in the case of any marriage to which the deceased was at any time a party, was treated by the deceased as a child of the family in relation to that marriage;
(g) any person who is, or is the issue of, a brother, sister, uncle or aunt of the deceased.

(4) The reference to the former wife or husband of the deceased in subsection (3)(a) above includes a reference to a person whose marriage to the deceased has been annulled or declared void as well as a person whose marriage to the deceased has been dissolved.

(5) In deducing any relationship for the purposes of subsection (3) above—
(a) any relationship by affinity shall be treated as a relationship by consanguinity, any relationship of the half blood as a relationship of the whole blood, and the stepchild of any person as his child, and
(b) an illegitimate person shall be treated as the legitimate child of his mother and reputed father.'

In its new form this provision considerably expands the list of possible dependants beyond that originally contained in the 1976 Act itself and earlier legislation. For example, divorced spouses can now claim for the first time,[1] as can persons unrelated to the deceased but who were treated by him, in respect of his marriage, as children of the family. Perhaps the most significant change, however, is the addition to the list of unmarried cohabitees[2] of deceased persons, provided that the partners had been living together for at least two years.[3]

Loss must flow from the defined relationship

[**9.07**] In *Burgess v Florence Nightingale Hospital*[4] the plaintiff and his wife had been professional dancing partners. After his wife had been

---

1 Cf *Payne-Collins v Taylor Woodrow Construction Ltd* [1975] QB 300, [1975] 1 All ER 898.
2 Cf *K v JMP Co Ltd* [1976] QB 85, [1975] 1 All ER 1030, CA.
3 See s 1(3)(b) above. For criticism of the somewhat ambiguous way in which this provision is worded, with its use of the phrase 'as the husband or wife of the deceased', see Borkowski and Stanton (1983) 46 MLR 191 at 195.
4 [1955] 1 QB 349, [1955] 1 All ER 511.

killed by the negligence of the defendants the plaintiff claimed under
the Fatal Accidents Act for earnings lost due to his inability to perform
professionally without his partner. His claim failed. It was clear on
the evidence that not all professional dancing partners were married,
and Devlin J held that the earnings lost had not been derived from the
marital relationship itself as such.[1] On the other hand, in determining
whether losses did in truth flow from the relationship within the Act
the court will look at the reality of the situation rather than its form.
In *Malyon v Plummer*[2] the plaintiff and her deceased husband had
been co-directors of a family company. The plaintiff had been paid a
salary by the company which was considerably in excess of the market
value of her services. This had apparently been for tax reasons and
was accepted by the court as having been legitimate. The defendants
claimed, however, that the full value of the salary actually paid to the
plaintiff should be taken into account in calculating the extent of her
dependency on her husband. This argument failed. The Court of
Appeal held that only a sum representing the market value of her
services should be taken into account. In reality the plaintiff was
substantially dependent upon her husband whose activity in running
an essentially one-man company generated the family income. The
book-keeping transaction whereby the wife was nominally a well paid
employee of the company would not be allowed to obscure the true
situation. Another defence attempt to claim that losses incurred
should be treated as outside the scope of the relationship defined by
the Act failed in *Davies v Whiteways Cyder Co Ltd*.[3] During his
lifetime the deceased had made substantial capital payments to his
wife and son in order to avoid the fiscal disadvantages of disposing of
the sums in his will. Since he was, however, killed by the negligence
of the defendants less than seven years after making the gifts the tax
advantages were lost. The deceased's widow successfully claimed
under the Fatal Accidents Act a sum representing the amount which
had had to be paid to the revenue to discharge the tax liability. A
suggestion that the loss flowed from the relationship of donor to
donee, as distinct from the family relationship within the Act, was
rejected.

Shared expenses

[9.08] If the person claiming under the Act, and the deceased, had in
fact both been earners, and had shared the expenses of the household,
a sum reflecting the increased expense to the claimant of living alone
can properly be awarded as damages. In *Burgess v Florence
Nightingale Hospital* Devlin J said:[4]

> 'It seems to me that when a husband and wife, either with separate
> incomes or with a joint income to which they are both beneficially

1 Cf *Behrens v Bertram Mills Circus* [1957] 2 QB 1, [1957] 1 All ER 583 in which
   Devlin J distinguished his own earlier decision in *Burgess v Florence Nightingale
   Hospital* and reached a different conclusion on very special facts.
2 [1964] 1 QB 330, [1963] 2 All ER 344.
3 [1975] QB 262, [1974] 3 All ER 168 (O'Connor J).
4 [1955] 1 QB 349 at 362, [1955] 1 All ER 511 at 519.

entitled, are living together and sharing their expenses, and in consequence of that fact their joint living expenses are less than twice the expenses of each one living separately, then each, by the fact of the sharing, is conferring a benefit on the other, and I think that mutual benefits clearly arise from the relationship by virtue of which they are living together, namely, the relationship of husband and wife, and, accordingly, that comes within the Fatal Accidents Act.'

Joint operations

[**9.09**] A somewhat unusual situation was considered in *Cookson v Knowles*.[1] The deceased husband and his wife had separate jobs, but the former's help was partly necessary for the full discharge of the latter's duties. The wife worked as a cleaner at a school but attending to certain high windows, and dealing with the boiler, was not physically possible for her unaided. Accordingly, she lost her own job when her husband was killed due to the negligence of the defendants. On the other hand her earning capacity as such had not been lost, as she would be able to do other work in the future. On the facts of the case the Court of Appeal held that, for the purpose of calculating the Fatal Accidents Act award, the lost earnings of the deceased husband would be regarded as his own income plus one third of his wife's.

How damages are assessed

[**9.10**] It is the practice to divide awards made under the Fatal Accidents Act into two parts: the first consisting of the actual loss between the date of the death and the date of the trial, and the second the future pecuniary loss.[2] In *Taylor v O'Connor*[3] Lord Pearson described the process followed in making the award under the second head as follows:

'There are three stages in the normal calculation, namely: (i) to estimate the lost earnings, ie the sums which the deceased probably would have earned but for the fatal accident; (ii) to estimate the lost benefit, ie the pecuniary benefit which the dependants probably would have derived from the lost earnings, and to express the lost benefit as an annual sum over the period of the lost earnings; and (iii) to chose the appropriate multiplier which, when applied to the lost benefit expressed as an annual sum, gives the amount of the damages which is a lump sum.'

Lost earnings

[**9.11**] The starting point for the estimation of future pecuniary loss is the deceased's net income as it would have been at the date of the trial.[4] The dependants are also entitled, however, to have taken into account possible future increases in his earnings which the defendant

1 [1977] QB 913, [1977] 2 All ER 820 (not considered in [1979] AC 556, [1978] 2 All ER 604).
2 *Cookson v Knowles* [1979] AC 556, [1978] 2 All ER 604.
3 [1971] AC 115 at 140, [1970] 1 All ER 365 at 377, HL.
4 See *Cookson v Knowles* [1979] AC 556 at 575, [1978] 2 All ER 604 at 614 per Lord Fraser.

180 Cases involving death

might have received had he lived. But only real increases due to such factors as promotion are relevant: increases due merely to inflation are ignored.[1] Where the likelihood of some such real increase is sufficient to justify its being reflected in the final award, but the evidence is imprecise as to what the increases might have been, the court may simply choose a higher multiplier than it would otherwise have done. If, however, there is a clear promotion ladder, or evidence of a similarly specific kind is available, the approach which is apparently preferred by the courts is to take this factor into account at the initial stage of the calculation by reaching a figure for the deceased's likely average future earnings over the dependency period.[2]

Lost benefit: the 'dependency'

[9.12] Obviously not all the deceased's net income would have been spent on his dependants; apart from anything else part of it would have been necessary for his own food and clothing. The pecuniary benefit which the dependants have lost must therefore be calculated by subtracting from the deceased's earnings his own keep and any other relevant disbursements such as, for example, the cost of any expensive hobbies of his or regular payments to his favourite charities. Although the calculation has necessarily to be made on the facts of each case the task is usually simplified by the adoption of a standardised approach, unless the context otherwise requires. In *Harris v Empress Motors Ltd* O'Connor LJ said:[3]

> 'In the course of time the courts have worked out a simple solution to the . . . problem of calculating the net dependency under the Fatal Accidents Acts in cases where the dependants are wife and children. In times past the calculation called for a tedious inquiry into how much housekeeping money was paid to the wife, who paid how much for the children's shoes, etc. This has all been swept away and the modern practice is to deduct a percentage from the net income figure to represent what the deceased would have spent exclusively on himself. The percentages have become conventional in the sense that they are used unless there is striking evidence to make the conventional figure inappropriate because there is no departure from the principle that each case must be decided upon its own facts. Where the family unit was husband and wife the conventional figure is 33 per cent and the rationale of this is that broadly speaking the net income was spent as to one-third for the benefit of each and one-third for their joint benefit . . . No deduction is made in respect of the joint portion because one cannot buy or drive half a motor car . . . Where there are children the deduction falls to 25 per cent.'

---

1 See *Young v Percival* [1974] 3 All ER 677, [1975] 1 WLR 17, CA.
2 See, eg *Young v Percival* [1974] 3 All ER 677, [1975] 1 WLR 17, CA; *Robertson v Lestrange* [1985] 1 All ER 950.
3 [1983] 3 All ER 561 at 565, [1984] 1 WLR 212 at 216-217, CA.

The multiplier and the capital sum

[**9.13**] A multiplier is applied to the figure representing the annual dependency in order to produce a lump sum which in principle is intended to provide, by the use of both capital and income, replacement for the financial support lost by the dependants until it becomes exhausted at the expiry of the likely period of dependency.[1] The date for the selection of the appropriate multiplier is the date of the death, not that of the trial.[2] The number of years which have elapsed since the death, for which a separate award of pre-trial loss is made, is then simply deducted from the multiplier.[3] A figure of 16 years purchase is usually taken to be the highest multiplier,[4] but 18 has occasionally been awarded.[5] Although the range of multipliers became established at a time when the level of real return on capital was higher than was generally achievable during the periods of high inflation seen in the recent past, the courts were not been willing to sanction any significant increase in the range on account of inflation.[6] And although it has been judicially suggested that the multiplier might be increased in exceptional cases to take into account the impact of taxation,[7] this too has been doubted.[8]

Contingencies

[**9.14**] It is evident that the calculation which has to be made is highly conjectural; not least because the choice of the multiplier has to take into account what were once described as the 'ordinary accidents and vicissitudes of life'.[9] As Lord Diplock pointed out in *Cookson v Knowles*,[10] guesswork has to take place on two levels. The judge has to allow for what the future might hold in store for the family without

---

1 See per Lord Pearson in *Taylor v O'Connor* [1971] AC 115 at 143, [1970] 1 All ER 365 at 379, HL.
2 See *Graham v Dodds* [1983] 2 All ER 953, [1983] 1 WLR 809, HL . Cf *Pritchard v J H Cobden Ltd* [1988] Fam 22, [1987] 1 All ER 300, CA (confirming that date of trial remains appropriate in personal injury cases).
3 See, eg *Corbett v Barking, Havering and Brentwood Health Authority* [1991] 2 QB 408, [1991] 1 All ER 498 CA in which the majority of the Court of Appeal (Purchas and Farquaharson LJJ) did, however, adjust the multiplier upwards to avoid hardship which this rule would have caused to the plaintiff on the facts of the case. Ralph Gibson LJ dissented on the ground that the course adopted by the majority was 'in effect, to calculate the multiplier as at the date of trial' ([1991] 2 QB 408 at 440, [1991] 1 All ER 498 at 524) which was impermissible.
4 See per Lord Diplock in *Mallett v McMonagle* [1970] AC 166 at 177, [1969] 2 All ER 178 at 191, HL. Cf per Lord Bridge in *Graham v Dodds* [1983] 2 All ER 953 at 969, [1983] 1 WLR 809 at 816.
5 See the table of awards in Kemp and Kemp *The Quantum of Damages*.
6 See *Cookson v Knowles* [1979] AC 556, [1978] 2 All ER 604, HL; see also *Robertson v Lestrange* [1985] 1 All ER 950
7 See per Lord Fraser in *Cookson v Knowles* [1979] AC 556 at 577-578, [1978] 2 All ER 604 at 616 See also *Attree v Baker* (1983) Times, 18 November, Kenneth Jones J.
8 See *Hodgson v Trapp* [1988] 3 All ER 870, HL (a personal injuries case) per Lord Oliver at 886.
9 Per Brett LJ in *Phillips v London and South Western Rly Co (1879)* 5 CPD 280 at 291, CA.
10 [1979] AC 556 at 568, HL.

the deceased, and for what it might have held in store for them if he had not been killed. His Lordship said:

> 'This kind of assessment, artificial though it may be, nevertheless calls for consideration of a number of highly speculative factors, since it requires the assessor to make assumptions not only as to the degree of likelihood that something may actually happen in the future, such as the widow's death, but also as to the hypothetical degree of likelihood that all sorts of things might happen in an imaginary future in which the deceased lived on and did not die when in actual fact he did. What in that event would have been the likelihood of his continuing in work until the usual retiring age? Would his earnings have been terminated by death or disability before the usual retiring age or interrupted by unemployment or ill-health?'

Degree of likelihood and its effect on quantum

[9.15] In making its assessment of what the future might hold, or have held, in store for the purpose of calculating damages under the Fatal Accidents Act the court does not confine itself to probabilities. Mere possibilities may also be relevant. It is clear that a plaintiff can qualify for an award even in respect of a dependency which had not existed at the time of the death, but which might have possibly have developed at some future time. Thus, if the circumstances warrant it, parents may recover under the Act in respect of a deceased son or daughter even though the deceased may still have been in education or training at the time of the death and had not yet begun to earn.[1] Especially if the parents are infirm or elderly they might have had a reasonable expectation that the deceased would eventually have provided them with some financial support.[2] In cases of this type, and those involving similar situations, the court should estimate the degree of likelihood that a dependency would have occurred, or that some change in the level of an existing dependency might have developed, and the damages awarded should be proportionate to that assessment[3] (even if in straightforward cases this process of reasoning is rarely made explicit). The leading case on the approach to be adopted in the face of uncertainties of this kind is the decision of the House of Lords in *Davies v Taylor*.[4] The plaintiff and her deceased husband had separated prior to his death but the plaintiff brought an action under the Fatal Accidents Act contending that, if he had lived, a reconciliation might have taken place resulting in her becoming dependent upon him. The trial judge, Bridge J, held that the plaintiff would fail because she had not established on the balance of probabilities that a reconciliation would have occurred. The House of Lords held, however, that this approach, based on the burden of proof used to determine questions of existing fact, was not correct where the issue turned upon the chances of possible events occurring in the

---

1 See *Taff Vale Rly Co v Jenkins* [1913] AC 1, HL (16-year-old daughter). Cf *Barnett v Cohen* [1921] 2 KB 461 (deceased a child aged 4: no award).
2 See, eg *Kandalla v British Airways Board* [1981] QB 158, [1980] 1 All ER 341.
3 See *Davies v Taylor,* below.
4 [1974] AC 207, [1972] 3 All ER 836.

future.¹ Lord Cross observed that 'so long as the chance of future support which the plaintiff has lost was substantial or fairly capable of valuation the court ought ... to set a value on it even though it was less-and possibly much less-than a 50 per cent chance'.² If the balance of probabilities were the test the anomalous result would follow that where the chances of reconciliation were just below evens the plaintiff would receive no damages at all whereas full damages, with no discount, would be awarded if the chances were just above evens.³ In neither case would the result be satisfactory. Instead 'the damages would', in the words of Lord Simon, 'be scaled down from those payable to a dependent spouse of a stable union, according as the possibility [of reconciliation] became progressively more remote. But she would still be entitled to some damages up to the point where the possibility was so fanciful and remote as to be de minimis'.⁴ On the facts of *Davies v Taylor* itself the House of Lords held that the possibility of reconciliation fell within the 'fanciful and remote' category, so that the actual decision rejecting the plaintiff's claim altogether was ultimately affirmed.⁵

Allowance for possible discontinuance where existing support had not been legally enforceable

[**9.16**] The general principle of calculating the damages for future loss with respect to the estimated degree of likelihood of particular events occurring is also applicable where the plaintiff was already enjoying financial support from the deceased at the time of his death, but not by virtue of any actual legal obligation. In *Dolbey v Goodwin*,⁶ the deceased was a 29-year-old bachelor who lived with, and helped to maintain, his widowed mother. The award by the trial judge, which had apparently been as high as might have been expected if the deceased had been the plaintiff's husband, was substantially reduced by the Court of Appeal. Not only had there been no legal liability on the deceased to maintain the plaintiff, but allowance also had to be made for the possibility that the deceased might have married at some point in the future with a consequent reduction in his capacity to assist his mother. The possible discounting of damages to allow for the degree of likelihood of discontinuance, where support existing at the time of the death had not been legally enforceable, is also

---

1 See ibid at 212H-213B and 838-839 per Lord Reid.
2 Ibid at 223C and 847. See also *Corbett v Barking Havering and Brentwood Health Authority* [1991] 2 QB 408, [1991] 1 All ER 498, CA (dependent child entitled to have his chances of proceeding to higher education assessed and valued in percentage terms).
3 See [1974] AC at 213D-E, [1972] 3 All ER at 847 per Lord Reid; see also per Lord Cross at 223B and 847.
4 [1974] AC at 220D, [1972] 3 All ER at 845.
5 See also *Burns v Edman* [1970] 2 QB 541, [1970] 1 All ER 886: possibility that deceased, who had been a criminal, would have reformed and earned an honest living described as 'entirely speculative and unproven to the point of impossibility' (Crichton J).
6 [1955] 2 All ER 166, [1955] 1 WLR 553.

184 Cases involving death

contemplated by the new provision enabling unmarried cohabitees to establish dependencies. The Fatal Accidents Act 1976, s 3(4) (inserted by the Administration of Justice Act 1982, s 3(1)) reads as follows:

> 'In an action under this Act where there fall to be assessed damages payable to a person who is a dependant ... in respect of the death of the person with whom the dependant was living as husband or wife there shall be taken into account (together with any other matter that appears to the court to be relevant to the action) the fact that the dependant had no enforceable right to financial support by the deceased as a result of their living together.'

No increase in dependency to allow for possibility that plaintiff and deceased might have started a family

[9.17] Of course, some of the contingencies which might have occurred if the deceased had not been killed might have increased his financial support of the plaintiff rather than reduced it. Hence the well-established practice of taking into account the deceased's promotion prospects.[1] Nevertheless, one contingency which will not be allowed to increase the dependency is the possibility that, had he not been killed, a deceased husband and his widow might have started a family, causing the latter to give up work and become wholly supported by the former whose support had previously only been partial. This was affirmed by the decision of Russell J in *Malone v Rowan*,[2] following an unreported decision of the Court of Appeal[3] which had held that since the death had deprived the plaintiff of the chance of starting a family it had also negated the possibility of a consequent increase in the dependency. This decision has been criticised,[4] and Russell J followed it with reluctance. But the Court of Appeal appears to have based its decision, at least in part, on the proposition that to increase the dependency in such circumstances would indirectly constitute damages for the non-financial loss of 'the joys of motherhood',[5] which cannot be compensated for under the Act.

Remarriage and prospects of re-marriage by widow ignored

[9.18] The Fatal Accidents Act 1976, s 3(3) (as enacted in the Administration of Justice Act 1982, s 3(1)) provides as follows:

> 'In an action under this Act where there fall to be assessed damages payable to a widow in respect of the death of her husband there shall not be taken account the re-marriage of the widow or her prospects of re-marriage.'

---

1 See above.
2 [1984] 3 All ER 402.
3 *Higgs v Drinkwater* [1956], CA Transcript 129A.
4 See Kemp and Kemp on the *Quantum of Damages*, vol 1 para 25-003. For a different view, supporting the outcome, see Burrows *Remedies for Torts and Breach of Contract*, (1987 London) p 187.
5 Per Denning LJ in *Higgs v Drinkwater* (quoted in *Malone v Rowan* [1984] 3 All ER at 405).

This provision, which dates back to 1971,[1] had its origin in judicial distaste for the task of evaluating the marriage prospects, and hence attractiveness, of widows.[2] It constitutes an exception not only to the general principle that contingencies should be taken into account in assessing future loss, but also to the principle that facts existing at the date of the trial should not be ignored;[3] since it applies to actual re-marriage as well as to prospects of re-marriage. The provision has been heavily criticised,[4] particularly on the ground that it leads to over-compensation where remarriage has actually taken place. The Royal Commission on Civil Liability and Compensation for Personal Injury recommended that such remarriage before trial should be taken into account,[5] but the recommendation has not been implemented. Two other aspects of the provision have also rendered it vulnerable to criticism. Firstly, it applies only to widows and not to widowers: an anomalous distinction which both the Law Commission and the Royal Commission considered should be removed to make the law the same for both sexes.[6] Secondly, it follows from the wording, which confines the provision to damages 'payable to a widow', that re-marriage or the prospects thereof will still be relevant in the case of any children of the widow and her deceased husband. That this is so was confirmed by the decision of Boreham J in *Thompson v Price*.[7] Thus, if the children acquire, or are likely to acquire, a stepfather who becomes under a legal obligation to maintain them, their damages under the Fatal Accidents Act will still fall to be reduced correspondingly.[8] The Law Commission recommended that the provision ought to be amended 'so that the remarriage of the widow or her prospects of remarriage should not be taken into account in assessing the damages payable to the children'.[9] No action has been taken on this recommendation.

Loss of services of mother

[9.19] 'Where a very young child is orphaned', said Croom-Johnson LJ in *Spittle v Bunney*,[10] 'there is a practice of valuing the lost services of

---

1 See the Law Reform (Miscellaneous Provisions) Act 1971, s 4.
2 See eg *Buckley v John Allen & Ford (Oxford) Ltd* [1967] 2 QB 637 at 644-645, [1967] 1 All ER 539 at 542 per Phillimore J.
3 Cf *Curwen v James* [1963] 2 All ER 619, [1963] 1 WLR 748, CA.
4 See, eg Atiyah, *Accidents, Compensation and the Law*, (4th edn, 1987) p 157 ('. . . one of the most irrational pieces of law 'reform' ever passed by Parliament').
5 See Cmnd 7054-1 (1978), paras 409-412 (referring to 'the manifest absurdity of awarding damages for a loss which is known to have ceased').
6 See Law Commission Report No 56 (1973) para 252; Royal Commission (see previous note) para 414. Cf *Regan v Williamson* [1976] 2 All ER 241 at 245, [1976] 1 WLR 350 at pp 309-310 per Watkins J: '. . . widowers must still, by reason of a distinction which I am unable to comprehend, go through the embarrassing process of being asked questions in the witness box about the possibility of remarrying.'
7 [1973] QB 838, [1973] 2 All ER 846.
8 See *Reincke v Gray* [1964] 2 All ER 687, [1964] 1 WLR 832, CA.
9 Law Commission Report No 56 (1973) para 252.
10 [1988] 3 All ER 1031 at 1037, [1988] 1 WLR 847 at 854, CA.

the mother by having regard to the cost of hiring a nanny'. But his Lordship emphasised that the calculations thus made have to be on a flexible common-sense basis which takes into account 'that as children get older they may also get more independent of their parents and less in need of being looked after'. He continued:[1]

> 'In the early years the services rendered by her mother to her small child may be valued by the cost of a hired nanny. The requirements are to some degree comparable. As the child grows older, and reaches school age, the valuation by commercial standards becomes less and less appropriate, and to use them is . . . not comparing like with like. Once the child has begun school, at least by the age of six, the extent of the services decreases in amount. She needs, for a time, to be taken to and from school. Later on, she may go there by herself. Not only is the yardstick of a nanny's wage less appropriate, but the services rendered by the mother change in nature.'[2]

The circumstances of the particular case, as Sir David Croom-Johnson himself observed on another occasion, may also serve to displace the cost of employing a nanny even as a starting-point.[3] In *Mehmet v Perry*[4] the plaintiff widower was left with five young children, two of whom suffered from a rare disease which required treatment on a daily basis. The plaintiff gave up his own employment to look after the children. The court took the view that this was a reasonable thing for the father to have done, and held that damages for loss of his wife's housekeeping services should be assessed by reference to his own loss of wages rather than by reference to the cost of employing a housekeeper.[5] In the similar case of *Bailey v Barking and Havering Area Health Authority*[6] the same result was reached, even though the plaintiff widower there sought to have the calculation based on the cost of employing a housekeeper in preference to his own loss of wages since the former would have produced a higher figure. Peter Pain J observed that it would be repugnant to allow a husband to make a profit from his wife's death, and confined the award to the value of the plaintiff's actual lost wages. In the more usual type of case, where the court has to evaluate the loss of the wife's housekeeping services as such, there is some authority for the adoption of a rather broader approach than one based narrowly on the cost of obtaining housekeeping assistance in the open market. In *Regan v Williamson*[7] Watkins J, in awarding a higher figure than this latter test would have provided, expressed himself as follows:

1 [1988] 3 All ER 1031 at 1040, [1988] 1 WLR 847 at 858.
2 But cf per Purchas LJ in *Corbett v Barking Havering and Brentwood Health Authority* [1991] 2 QB 408 at 421, [1991] 1 All ER 498 at 526, CA.
3 'On the facts of this case the whole concept of valuing the lost services by reference to a "notional nanny" is inappropriate. Whether this expedient is useful in other cases is another matter, but there is no room for using it when on the facts a nanny would never have been employed. Mr Hayden was not going to use one, and never did': *Hayden v Hayden* [1992] 4 All ER 681 at 693, CA, per Sir David Croom-Johnson.
4 [1977] 2 All ER 529.
5 See also *Cresswell v Eaton* [1991] 1 All ER 484, [1991] 1 WLR 1113.
6 (1977) Times 22 July QBD.
7 [1976] 2 All ER 241 at 244, [1976] 1 WLR 305 at 309.

'I am . . . of the view that the word 'services' has been too narrowly construed. It should, at least, include an acknowledgement that a wife and mother does not work to set hours and, still less, to rule. She is in constant attendance, save for those hours when she is, if that is the fact, at work. During some of those hours she may well give the children instruction on essential matters to do with their upbringing and, possibly, with such things as their homework. This sort of attention seems to me to be as much of a service, and probably more valuable to them, than the other kinds of service conventionally so regarded.'[1]

Even in *Mehmet v Perry,* in which the children of the deceased had the full-time attention of their father, the judge awarded a 'modest' additional sum to reflect 'the fact that the children have lost the personal attention of their mother and that they now have only one parent to look after them instead of two'.[2] On the other hand if the deceased had been a somewhat inadequate parent this will be reflected in the award of a lower sum.[3] And if the child is adopted after her mother's death the adoptive mother becomes legally obliged to look after the child and the non-pecuniary dependency on the deceased mother is accordingly extinguished from the date of the adoption.[4]

Interest

[9.20] In *Cookson v Knowles*[5] the House of Lords held, as mentioned above, that awards under the Fatal Accidents Act should be divided into two parts. The first consisting of the loss actually sustained up to the date of the trial, and the second the sum in respect of future loss. Only the pre-trial loss would carry interest, and the rate would be one-half of that payable over the relevant period on money in court placed in a special investment account.[6] If the court considers the plaintiff to have been guilty of serious delay some of the interest may be forfeited.[7]

Apportionment

[9.21] The Fatal Accidents Act 1976, s 3(1) (as enacted by the Administration of Justice Act 1982, s 3(1)) provides that: 'In the action such damages . . . may be awarded as are proportioned to the injury resulting from the death to the dependants respectively.'

---

1 See also *Hay v Hughes* [1975] QB 790 at 802-803, [1975] 1 All ER 257 at 261 per Lord Edmund-Davies, and *McGregor on Damages* (15th edn) para 1588.
2 [1977] 2 All ER 529 at 537. Cf *Hayden v Hayden* [1992] 4 All ER 681, CA.
3 See *Stanley v Saddique* [1992] 1 QB 1, [1991] 1 All ER 529, CA.
4 *Watson v Willmott* [1991] 1 QB 140, [1991] 1 All ER 473.
5 [1979] AC 556, [1978] 2 All ER 604.
6 See *Jefford v Gee* [1970] 2 QB 130, [1970] 1 All ER 1202, CA. See also *Dodds v Dodds* [1978] QB 543 at 553, [1978] 2 All ER 539 at 548.
7 See, eg *Spittle v Bunney* [1988] 3 All ER 1031, [1988] 1 WLR 847, CA, and *Corbett v Barking Havering and Brentwood Health Authority* [1991] 2 QB 408, [1991] 1 All ER 498, CA ('The power to deprive a tardy litigant of interest when he is guilty of unjustifiable delay is an essential discipline': per Farquaharson LJ, ibid, at 446 and 528).

In *K v JMP Co Ltd*[1] Stephenson LJ observed that 'what has to be ascertained is the net loss of the family and the apportionment between widow and children is comparatively unimportant, [and] is often a matter of agreement'. If, however, the defendant in fact disagrees with the apportionment made by the court this will not give him any right to challenge the award on appeal if the overall sum is correct.[2] In the most common type of case, where the deceased breadwinner leaves a widow and children, the largest sum is usually apportioned to the widow. In *Rawlinson v Babcock & Wilcox*[3] Chapman J expressed himself as follows:

> 'Frequently in making an assessment under the Fatal Accidents Acts the courts have taken the total dependency figure for the whole family and, after fixing an appropriate multiplier by referring to the expectation of life of the deceased and his widow, have arrived at an equitable sum to cover all the claims, comparatively modest sums being then allocated to the children. The basis for this is that their support through infancy and school days and until able to earn their own living is the legal obligation of the widow and that she can be trusted to fulfil this obligation out of the money allocated to her.'

His Lordship went on to observe, however, that this method was not always 'appropriate or justifiable' and that a 'separate assessment should be made . . . whenever doubts may arise as to the continued ability and willingness of the widow to safeguard the child adequately'. Indeed some judges are inclined to place even greater emphasis on the need to ensure as far as is possible that the interests of a dependant child cannot be adversely affected by future events. Thus in *Benson v Briggs Wall & Co Ltd*[4] Peter Pain J said:

> 'Certainly it is my experience in a large number of these cases, both at the Bar and on the Bench, that one looked at the child's genuine dependency and not merely at what I might call a "pocket money" dependency. That seems to be right in principle, because the function of the court is to safeguard the child. Even with a mother who is a model one could not effectively safeguard the child if one treated the child's dependency as being partly included in the mother's figure. The point being this, that if one leaves the cost of maintaining the child as being included in the mother's figure that money becomes hers; she may well spend it on the child, look after it beautifully, but decide after a short while that it would be to the child's advantage as well as to her own if she remarries, then unhappily in a year or two she meets with an accident or something and dies without having taken the precaution of making a will. Then so far as the Fatal Accidents Act money is concerned which has gone to her, if that has been saved it will pass to the stepfather so far as the first £25,000 is concerned plus a life interest in half the remainder. The stepfather, one would hope, would give effect to the moral claim of the child, but law is not content to rely on a moral claim.'

---

1 [1976] QB 85 at 95-96, [1975] 1 All ER 1030 at 1037, CA.
2 See *Eifert v Holt's Transport Co* [1951] 2 All ER 655n, CA.
3 [1966] 3 All ER 882 at 884, [1967] 1 WLR 481 at 483.
4 [1982] 3 All ER 300 at 303, [1983] 1 WLR 72n at 74.

Moreover, the 'global sum' approach should in any event not be allowed to obscure the fact that, although only one Fatal Accidents Act action can be brought in respect of the death,[1] each dependant is nevertheless individually entitled to his own damages. Thus if one dependant is himself the tortfeasor, and hence unable to claim, he will still be liable to the other dependants under the Act.[2] Time may also begin to run against different dependants at different times for limitation purposes.[3] If individual assessments are made where several children of differing ages are involved, separate multipliers will normally be chosen for each child according to when he or she could be expected to achieve independence.[4]

Disregard of benefits

[9.22] The Administration of Justice Act 1982 effected a radical simplification of the law by enacting a new provision in place of the existing version of the Fatal Accidents Act 1976, s 4. It reads as follows:

> 'In assessing damages in respect of a person's death in an action under this Act, benefits which have accrued or will or may accrue to any person from his estate or otherwise as a result of his death shall be disregarded.'

Although it had long been the case that the proceeds of insurance policies, gratuitous payments and the like, would not be deducted from a Fatal Accidents Act award 'the general rule' was nevertheless that 'any benefit accruing to a dependant by reason of the relevant death must be taken into account'.[5] A complex body of law developed to determine whether particular benefits fell within the general rule,[6] or whether one of the established exceptions to it applied. The elaborate refinements thereby created have now been swept away by the legislature in response to a recommendation by the Law Commission that the general rule, which gave rise to them, should itself be abrogated.[7] That the principle, that benefits are to be disregarded,[8] is in sharp contrast with the position applying to common law actions for personal injury[9] was emphasised by the Court of Appeal in *Pidduck v Eastern Scottish Omnibuses*.[10] In this case a

---

1 'One action alone can be brought, and the persons who stand out stand out for ever': *Avery v London and North Eastern Rly Co* [1938] AC 606 at 613, [1938] 2 All ER 592 at 595, HL per Lord Atkin.
2 See *Dodds v Dodds* [1978] QB 543, [1978] 2 All ER 539.
3 See the Limitation Act 1980, s 13.
4 See, eg *K v JMP Co Ltd* [1976] QB 85, [1975] 1 All ER 1030.
5 *Davies v Powell Duffryn Associated Collieries Ltd* [1942] AC 601 at 606, [1942] 1 All ER 657 at 658, HL per Lord Russell of Killowen.
6 Cf *Hay v Hughes* [1975] QB 790, [1975] 1 All ER 257.
7 See Law Commission Report No 56 *Personal Injury Litigation – Assessment of Damages* 1973, paras 255 and 256.
8 See, eg *Wood v Bentall Simplex Ltd* (1992) Times, 3 March, CA.
9 See ch 8 above.
10 [1990] 2 All ER 69, CA.

190 *Cases involving death*

defendant's attempt to circumvent the section, by arguing that the recipient of a widow's pension had not suffered any loss as a result of her husband's death since the same pension fund had indirectly supported her via her husband during his life, was rejected. Sir Roger Ormrod said:[1]

> 'This argument goes too far. If it is right, it would pre-empt the express provisions of s 4 of the 1976 Act and emasculate it in many cases because it would apply to all pension fund cases where the deceased was living on a pension and the scheme included a widow's benefit. In my judgment, the "injury" suffered by the widow is the loss of her dependency on her deceased husband. The value of this loss is to be quantified in accordance with the provisions of s 4. The widow's allowance is, therefore, to be disregarded in the calculation.'

Non-material benefits

[**9.23**] The Court of Appeal has also held that the section is not confined to the disregard of material benefits. In *Stanley v Saddique*[2] the court held that a child who lost his mother's services was not disentitled to recover damages when, as a result of her death, he benefited by acquiring a stepmother who in fact provided him with a much higher standard of care than the deceased whose services would have been, according to the trial judge, 'of an indifferent quality and lacking in continuity'. This decision was, however, narrowly distinguished by the Court of Appeal itself in *Hayden v Hayden*[3] where care provided in substitution for the services of the deceased mother by the plaintiff's father (who was also the tortfeasor, having caused his wife's death by his own negligent driving) was taken into account in reduction of the damages on the ground that such care was not a 'benefit' resulting from the death and could legitimately be taken into account at the earlier stage in calculating the level of the plaintiff's *loss*.

Public policy

[**9.24**] In certain circumstances a claim under the Fatal Accidents Act may fail on grounds of public policy. Although trivial illegalities will normally be ignored,[4] if the deceased met his death in the course of the commission of a serious criminal act his widow may well be found not to have a cause of action. Thus in *Murphy v Culhane*[5] the Court of Appeal held that the defendant, who had himself been convicted of the manslaughter of the deceased, was nevertheless entitled to plead illegality as a defence to his widow's claim on the basis that her

---

1   [1990] 2 All ER 69 at 76-77.
2   [1992] 1 QB 1, [1991] 1 All ER 529.
3   [1992] 4 All ER 681, [1992] 1 WLR 986, Parker LJ and Sir David Croom-Johnson, McCowan LJ dissenting.
4   Cf *Le Bagge v Buses Ltd* [1958] NZLR 630.
5   [1977] QB 94, [1976] 3 All ER 533.

husband had died in a criminal affray in which he had been a deliberate participant. Lord Denning MR observed:[1]

> '... suppose that a burglar breaks into a house and the householder, finding him there, picks up a gun and shoots him, using more force maybe than is reasonably necessary. The householder may be guilty of manslaughter and liable to be brought before the criminal courts. But I doubt very much whether the burglar's widow could have an action for damages. The householder might well have a defence ... of *ex turpi causa non oritur actio.*'

[**9.25**] Even if the widow has a cause of action under the Act she may still fail to recover substantial damages if the earnings of the deceased, out of which she had been maintained during his lifetime, were to her knowledge themselves the proceeds of a life of crime.[2] In *Burns v Edman*[3] the claim of the widow of an apparently full-time professional criminal, whose record included a conviction for robbery with violence, failed on this ground despite the fact that he had been killed by the defendant's negligence in an ordinary motor-accident. On the other hand if the deceased had not earned his living unlawfully, the mere fact that his own criminal act was the immediate cause of his death will not defeat his widow's claim, if there remains an unbroken chain of causation back to the earlier tortious infliction of injuries upon him by the defendant. In *Pigney v Pointers Transport Services*[4] the deceased took his own life as a direct result of depression brought on by injuries for which the defendants were responsible. Although suicide was at that time still a crime,[5] his widow succeeded in obtaining damages under the Act.

Damages for bereavement

Fixed sum to be awarded to spouses or parents

[**9.26**] The Administration of Justice Act 1982, s 3 added an entirely new provision to the Fatal Accidents Act 1976, which takes effect as s 1A of that Act. It reads as follows:

> '(1) An action under this Act may consist of or include a claim for damages for bereavement.
> (2) A claim for damages for bereavement shall only be for the benefit–

---

1 [1976] 3 All ER 533 at 536.
2 Quaere what her position would be if she were ignorant of the facts. Cf per Crichton J in *Burns v Edman* [1970] 2 QB 541 at 544, [1970] 1 All ER 886 at 887: 'I have already found as a fact that she did know, or that she did not succeed in establishing that she did not know ...'
3 [1970] 2 QB 541, [1970] 1 All ER 886. Cf *Le Bagge v Buses Ltd* [1958] NZLR 630.
4 [1957] 2 All ER 807, [1957] 1 WLR 1121. Quaere whether the suicide was a foreseeable consequence of the the defendant's negligence (cf *Meah v McCreamer (No 2)* [1986] 1 All ER 943). It should be noted that *Pigney*'s case was decided before *Overseas Tankship (UK) Ltd v Morts Dock and Engineering Co, The Wagon Mound)* [1961] AC 388, [1961] 1 All ER 404, PC.
5 See now the Suicide Act 1961, s 1.

(a) of the wife or husband of the deceased: and
(b) where the deceased was a minor who was never married-
   (i) of his parents, if he was legitimate; and
   (ii) of his mother, if he was illegitimate.
(3) Subject to subsection (5) below, the sum to be awarded as damages under this section shall be £3,500.
(4) Where there is a claim for damages under this section for the benefit of both of the parents of the deceased, the sum awarded shall be divided equally between them (subject to any deduction falling to be made in respect of costs not recovered from the defendant).
(5) The Lord Chancellor may by order made by statutory instrument, subject to annulment in pursuance of a resolution of either House of Parliament, amend this section by varying the sum for the time being specified in subsection (3) above.'

In introducing the new concept of damages for bereavement the section implements a recommendation of the Law Commission[1] which believed 'that an award of damages, albeit small, can have some slight consoling effect where parents lose an infant child or where a spouse loses husband or wife'. The Commission considered that 'if money can, even minimally, compensate for such bereavement . . . it should be recoverable'.[2] Where an infant dies after attaining the age of 18 his parents will be unable to claim bereavement damages even if the injuries which led to his death were suffered before he was 18.[3]

The law prior to the 1982 Act

[9.27] Until the head of damages for loss of expectation of life was abolished by the Administration of Justice Act 1982 itself, it had been possible for the parents of children to recover what amounted to compensation for bereavement by an indirect and artificial route. As a result of the Law Reform (Miscellaneous Provisions) Act 1934 the estate of a deceased person could recover damages for loss of expectation of life even if death had been instantaneous, or had occurred soon after the accident.[4] By what was, in effect, judicial legislation[5] this award became a conventional sum which in 1979 was around £1,250.[6] If the estate passed to persons also able to claim for lost dependency under the Fatal Accidents Act the conventional sum was simply deducted from their damages under that Act, so that if the bereaved parent or spouse had actually been dependent upon the deceased they did not benefit from damages under the 1934 Act. Moreover, the whole concept of damages for non-pecuniary loss in respect of shortened life expectancy (as distinct from damages for

---

1 See Report No 56 *Personal Injury Litigation – Assessment of Damages* (1973) paras 172-180, pp 48-49.
2 Ibid, para 174.
3 *Doleman v Deakin* (1990) Times, 30 January, CA.
4 See *Rose v Ford* [1937] AC 826, [1937] 3 All ER 359, HL. Cf *Hicks v Chief Constable of the South Yorkshire Police* [1992] 2 All ER 65, HL.
5 See *Benham v Gambling* [1941] AC 157, [1941] 1 All ER 7, HL.
6 See *Gammell v Wilson* [1982] AC 27, [1981] 1 All ER 578, HL.

awareness of that shortening) was in any event much criticised.¹ The 1982 Act therefore replaces that anomalous head of damage and provides overtly and more fully for compensation for bereavement, which the earlier law merely permitted covertly in a fortuitous and partial fashion. The *Royal Commission on Civil Liability and Compensation for Personal Injury* would have preferred an even more far-reaching proposal than that favoured by the Law Commission. The Royal Commission recommended that damages for non-pecuniary loss arising out of the death of a close relative should not be confined to parents and spouses, and that an unmarried minor child should also be able to recover such damages in respect of the loss of a parent.² This proposal has not, however, been implemented.

Nature of award

[9.28] By providing for a fixed sum, currently of £7,500, which the court cannot vary, and which is subject only to alteration by statutory instrument,³ the Act is intended to ensure that, in the words of the Law Commission,⁴ there will 'be no judicial enquiry at all into the consequences of bereavement'. The fact that the new head of damage takes effect under the Fatal Accidents Act, however, necessarily means that the award will only be recoverable if the deceased would have had a cause of action for negligence had he lived; and also that the sum will in fact fall to be reduced if the deceased had been contributorily negligent.⁵

Funeral expenses

[9.29] Damages in respect of the funeral expenses of a person negligently killed may be recovered by his estate from the defendant.⁶ Alternatively such damages can be recovered under the Fatal Accidents Act by his dependants if they have incurred them.⁷

Scope

[9.30] Questions may sometimes arise as to what is properly included in funeral expenses.⁸ In *Stanton v Ewart F Youlden*,⁹ for example, McNair J said the following:

1 See, eg per Lord Diplock in *Gammell v Wilson* [1982] AC 27 at 62-63, [1981] 1 All ER 578 at 581-582.
2 See Cmnd 7054-1 (1978) paras 418-431, pp 96-99.
3 See The Damages for Bereavement (Variation of Sum) (England and Wales) Order 1990 (SI 1990/2575) which substituted £7,500 for the original figure of £3,500.
4 Report No 56, para 175.
5 Report No 56, para 175.
6 See the Law Reform (Miscellaneous Provisions) Act 1934, s 1(2)(c).
7 See Fatal Accidents Act 1976, s 3(5) (as re-enacted by the Administration of Justice Act 1982, s 3(1)). Damages in respect of funeral expenses may be recovered by the dependants even if they are not able to recover any other damages under the Act: see, eg *Burns v Edman* [1970] 2 QB 541, [1970] 1 All ER 886.
8 Cf *Goldstein v Salvation Army Assurance Society* [1917] 2 KB 291.
9 [1960] 1 All ER 429 at 432, [1960] 1 WLR 543 at 545-546.

'The legal position is that a stone over a grave may properly be considered as part of the funeral expenses if it is a reasonable expenditure for the persons in the position of the deceased and of the relatives who are responsible for the actual ordering of the stone; but in so far as it is merely a memorial set up as a sign of love and affection, then it should not be included.'

In *Gammell v Wilson* the Court of Appeal[1] upheld, albeit with some hesitation, a trial judge's award of £595 for a headstone in respect of a funeral which had taken place in 1976. One member of the court observed that the 'the tombstone . . . in this case was very near the boundary between a headstone and a memorial'.[2]

---

1 Reported in [1982] AC 27, [1980] 2 All ER 557. The point was not considered in the House of Lords.
2 [1982] AC 27 at 55, [1980] 2 All ER 557 at 578 per Sir David Cairns. See also per Megaw LJ at 43 and 569.

Chapter 10

Property damage and other losses

Chattels

'Restitutio in integrum'

[**10.01**] A plaintiff whose chattel has been negligently damaged by the defendant is entitled to damages calculated according to 'the principle of restitutio in integrum'.[1] In the present context the application of this principle will normally involve the award of *either* the market value of the chattel in question, *or* the cost of repairing it. Determining which of these two approaches is appropriate on the facts of the particular case can sometimes be a source of difficulty. In addition it may be possible to seek damages for loss of use.

Repair or difference in value?

[**10.02**] In *Darbishire v Warran*[2] Harman LJ said:

'It has come to be settled that in general the measure of damage is the cost of repairing the damaged article; but there is an exception if it can be proved that the cost of repairs greatly exceeds the value in the market of the damaged article . . . In the latter cases the measure is the value of the article in the market and this, of course, supposes that there is a market in which the article can be bought. If there is none the cost of repairs may still be claimed.'

The question whether, in the particular circumstances, the appropriate course was to repair, or to seek the market value, is determined on the basis of reasonableness. In one Scottish case[3] the claimant's dilemma was put as follows:

'The owner of a damaged article must . . . decide whether the article is capable of being economically repaired or is to be treated as a

---

1 Per Hewson J in *The Fortunity* [1960] 2 All ER 64 at 68, [1961] 1 WLR 351 at 356. See also per Lord Wright in *Liesbosch Dredger v SS Edison (Owners)* [1933] AC 449 at 459, HL.
2 [1963] 3 All ER 310 at 312, [1963] 1 WLR 1067 at 1071, CA.
3 *Pomphrey v James A Cuthbertson Ltd* 1951 SC 147 at 161 per Lord Jamieson.

constructive total loss. If he makes a wrong decision, he may lay himself open to the charge by the wrongdoer that he has failed in his duty to minimise the damage. The test is: What would a prudent owner, who had himself to bear the loss, do in the circumstances?'

In *Darbishire v Warren* itself the plaintiff owned an eleven year old second-hand car which was damaged in a collision caused by the defendant's negligence. He chose to have the car repaired even though the cost of the repairs was more than twice the cost in the market of a second-hand car of the same age and make. The plaintiff sought to justify his decision on the ground that the vehicle was in an unusually good condition for its age since, being a mechanical engineer, he had maintained it himself with great care. The Court of Appeal rejected his contention, however, and limited the damages to the market value of the car before the accident.[1] In so doing the court distinguished the earlier case of *O'Grady v Westminster Scaffolding*,[2] which was decided the other way on the facts. The owner of an MG motor car, which was over 20 years old, had the car repaired after it had been negligently damaged. Defence evidence at the trial, however, estimated the car's pre-accident market value as lower than the cost of the repairs. But Edmund Davies J took into account the excellent condition of the vehicle prior to the accident: it had been impeccably maintained and had recently had a new engine fitted and its coachwork renewed. His Lordship emphasised 'that the pre-accident market value of chattels affords a guide to the measure of compensation when, and only when, a similar chattel can be obtained on the open market'[3] and concluded that the plaintiff had 'acted reasonably'.

Assessment of value

[**10.03**] If the case is one of total, or constructive total, loss the court, in estimating the value of the article before it was damaged, must reach its decision on the evidence before it and not on some kind of judicial intuition. In *Thatcher v Littlejohn*[4] the plaintiff led expert evidence as to the pre-accident value of a motor car. Even though this evidence went unchallenged the judge awarded a lower figure. The Court of Appeal allowed an appeal by the plaintiff. Sir David Cairns said of the judge's figure that there 'was no evidence to support that assessment at all'. His Lordship continued:[5]

'It is said . . . that the valuation of second-hand motor cars is not an exact science and that the judge is entitled to take his own view of the probable value even if that does not accord with the evidence. I am afraid I do not accept that proposition where the whole of the evidence

1 But see dicta per Pearson LJ on the desirability of avoiding an excessively rigid approach to the assessment of the market value, and on the need for 'an element of flexibility in the assessment of damages to achieve a result which is fair and just as between the parties in the particular case': [1963] 1 WLR at 1077.
2 [1962] 2 Lloyd's Rep 238.
3 Ibid at 240.
4 [1978] RTR 369, CA.
5 Ibid at 371-372.

points in one direction. There is no indication that the judge regarded either of the two witnesses as being in any way untrustworthy, and it seems to me that it is upon that evidence that the assessment must be based.'[1]

Loss of use

[10.04] If his chattel is damaged or destroyed due to the defendant's negligence the plaintiff is entitled to damages for loss of its use until it is repaired or replaced.[2] These will be additional to the cost of repair or replacement itself.[3] If the chattel was used for trading purposes the measure of damages will be such a sum as can reasonably be taken to reflect the profits which would have been earned during the relevant period.[4] Moreover, it has long been established that damages for loss of use can also be recovered even if the chattel was not used to earn profit,[5] and that such damages will be substantial and not nominal.[6] Broadly speaking, two methods of estimating the damages for lost use in such cases have been developed, mainly in a series of decisions reached in collision actions involving ships. The first method is to award a figure representing interest on the capital value of the chattel.[7] The second is to make a calculation based on the normal cost to the plaintiff of maintaining the chattel in service, on the assumption that this expenditure represents its value.[8] In *Birmingham Corpn v Sowsbery*[9] Geoffrey Lane J, in a useful judgment which outlines the basic principles involved, applied the latter method to a claim by a non-profit making municipal bus company for loss of the use of one of its vehicles. If the plaintiff in fact bases his claim on lost profits he cannot seek to obtain additional damages for lost use based on one of the other methods of calculation.[10]

[10.05] A plaintiff clearly cannot claim damages for lost use if, for reasons unconnected with the defendant's negligence, he would not in fact have enjoyed the use of the chattel during the relevant period anyway.[11] But a plaintiff is not prevented from claiming merely because he takes advantage of an inevitable period of detention for

---

1   See also *Dominion Mosaics & Tile Co Ltd v Trafalgar Trucking Co* [1990] 2 All ER 246 at 254-255 per Taylor LJ. In this case the Court of Appeal awarded the plaintiffs the reinstatement value of certain machines, reversing the trial judge who had awarded a lesser figure on an incorrect basis unsupported by evidence.
2   *The Argentino* (1889) 14 App Cas 519, HL.
3   See *The Racine* [1906] P 273, CA, approving *The Kate* [1899] P 165.
4   See *The Fortunity* [1960] 2 All ER 64, [1961] 1 WLR 351; see also *Dixons (Scholar Green) Ltd v Cooper* [1970] RTR 222, CA
5   *The Greta Holme* [1897] AC 596, HL
6   See *The Mediana* [1900] AC 113, HL. See also *Berrill v Road Haulage Executive* [1952] 2 Lloyd's Rep 490 (though quaere whether the £2 awarded in that case was consistent with the spirit of the principle that damages should not be nominal).
7   See *Admiralty Comrs v SS Chekiang* [1926] AC 637, HL; *The Hebridean Coast* [1961] AC 545, [1961] 1 All ER 82, HL.
8   See *The Marpessa* [1907] AC 241, HL.
9   [1970] RTR 84.
10 *The Pacific Concord* [1961] 1 All ER 106, [1961] 1 WLR 873.
11 See *Carslogie SS Co Ltd v Royal Norwegian Government* [1952] AC 292, [1952] 1 All ER 20, HL. See also *The York* [1929] P 178, CA.

Property damage and other losses

repairs, caused by the defendant's negligence, to do other work on the damaged chattel in addition.[1] In deciding when and how to do repairs the plaintiff must act reasonably and not eg needlessly prolong the period during which he is deprived of the use of his chattel.[2]

Hire of substitute

[10.06] In certain circumstances, commonly where motor accidents are involved, the plaintiff may simply hire a substitute until the damaged chattel is repaired or replaced. In such a case the damages for lost use will be the cost of the hire. The plaintiff must, however, act reasonably. Where hire of a motor car is involved, for example, the full cost may not be awarded if the court takes the view that the plaintiff could have obtained more cheaply a vehicle still broadly similar to, if less prestigious than, the one damaged.[3] But each case depends on its own facts, and in one case in which a defence attempt was made on these lines to reduce the award it was judicially rejected as follows: 'I see no reason why the plaintiffs should have been required to shop around in order to hire for a lesser sum a car of a lower standard from some concern with whom they did not normally deal'.[4] In *Moore v DER Ltd*[5] the plaintiff was entitled to the pre-accident second-hand value of his car, after the defendant's negligence had caused it to become a constructive total loss, but chose to buy a new car instead, of course paying the difference himself. But this involved him in a wait of 18 weeks whereas a second-hand model, comparable in age and make to the damaged one, could have been acquired in three weeks or less. The Court of Appeal nevertheless held that he was entitled to the full cost of the hire of a substitute until the arrival of the new car: he was a busy professional man and his insistence on the need for the reliability of a new car was considered to be not unreasonable. It has also been held that if the plaintiff was only a bailee of the damaged car it may be reasonable for him to reimburse the owner for the full cost of hiring an exactly equivalent vehicle during repairs, and to recover that full cost from the negligent defendants, even if such a course could possibly have been considered extravagant if taken directly by the owner himself.[6]

Other losses

[10.07] The proposition that the plaintiff is entitled to recover the repair cost or pre-accident value of the chattel, combined with compensation for loss of use, is only a general guide appropriate in the

---

1 *Admiralty Comrs v SS Chekiang* [1926] AC 637, HL.
2 See, eg *The Pacific Concord* [1961] 1 All ER 106, [1961] 1 WLR 873; *O'Grady v Westminster Scaffolding* [1962] 2 Lloyd's Rep 238. Cf *Jones v Port of London Authority* [1954] 1 Lloyd's Rep 489.
3 See *Watson-Norie Ltd v Shaw* (1967) 111 Sol Jo 117, CA.
4 *Daily Office Cleaning Contractors v Shefford* [1977] RTR 361 at 364 per Judge William Stabb QC (sitting as a deputy Judge of the Queen's Bench Division).
5 [1971] 3 All ER 517, [1971] 1 WLR 1476, CA.
6 See *HL Motorworks (Willesden) Ltd v Alwahbi* [1977] RTR 276, CA.

majority of cases. Since the overriding principle is that of restitutio in integrum all losses flowing from the defendant's negligence are recoverable, provided only that they are not too remote[1] and that the plaintiff acted reasonably in mitigating his damage. For example in *Ironfield v Eastern Gas Board*[2] the plaintiff, who had been compensated by his own insurers after his car had been damaged by the defendants' negligence, was able to recover compensation for the loss of his 'no-claims' bonus. This decision was approved by the Court of Appeal in the later case of *Patel v London Transport Executive*,[3] in which a plaintiff in similar circumstances was able to recover from the defendants the unexpired premium on his motor insurance, since that was forfeited under the terms of the policy. Moreover in *Payton v Brooks*[4] the Court of Appeal held that even where it had been appropriate to repair a damaged chattel the plaintiff might, providing adequate proof was forthcoming, recover compensation for diminution in its market value *in addition* to the cost of repairs. Roskill LJ put it as follows:[5]

'... the cost of repairs is a prima facie method of ascertaining the diminution in value. But it is not the only method of measuring the loss. In a case where the evidence justifies a finding that there has been, on top of the cost of repairs, some diminution in market value – or, to put the point another way, justifies the conclusion that the loss to the plaintiff has not been fully compensated by the receipt of the cost of complete and adequate repairs, because of a resultant diminution in market value – I can see no reason why the plaintiff should be deprived of recovery under that head of damage also.'

Gains by the plaintiff

[**10.08**] The plaintiff may sometimes experience a gain as a result of the defendant's negligence.[6] For example, the damage inflicted upon it may free a profit-earning chattel from a losing contract and its repairs may be completed, or its replacement become available, at a time when the plaintiff is fortuitously able to take advantage of better market conditions. In those circumstances the plaintiff must give credit to the defendants for the value of the benefit thus obtained.[7] But where a chattel which has been repaired becomes more valuable than it was before it was damaged, because of the addition of new parts or materials, it is not normally considered appropriate to require the plaintiff to give credit for 'betterment'.[8] The plaintiff will usually

---

1 On remoteness of damage see, generally, ch 3 above.
2 [1964] 1 All ER 544n, [1964] 1 WLR 1125n.
3 [1981] RTR 29, CA.
4 [1974] RTR 169, [1974] 2 Lloyd's Rep 241, CA.
5 Ibid at 245.
6 But ex gratia payments to the plaintiff from charitable and similar sources will be disregarded: see *Wollington v State Electricity Commission of Victoria (No 2)* [1980] VR 91; *Cusack v Heath* [1950] QWN 16.
7 See *The World Beauty* [1969] P 12, [1968] 2 All ER 673 (varied in [1970] P 144, [1968] 3 All ER 158, CA).
8 See *The Pactolus* (1856) Sw 173 at 174. See also *Bacon v Cooper (Metals) Ltd* [1982] 1 All ER 397 at 401-402.

have had no choice but to repair, and it would not be appropriate to assume that he would have chosen to invest his resources in improvement of his existing equipment had the damage not occurred.[1]

Land and buildings

Reinstatement or difference in value

[**10.09**] In *Dominion Mosaics & Tile Co Ltd v Trafalgar Trucking Co*[2] Taylor LJ said:

> 'The basic principle governing the measure of damages where the defendant's tort has caused damage to the plaintiff's land or building is restitutio in integrum. The damages should be such as will, so far as money can, put the plaintiff in the same position as he would have held had the tort not occurred. In applying that principle to particular cases, the problem has been whether restitutio is to be achieved by assessing the diminution in value of the damaged premises or the cost of reinstatement or possibly on some other basis.'

The appropriateness or reasonableness of claiming the cost of restoration may be a source of dispute, since in the majority of cases involving buildings that cost is likely to exceed the diminution in value caused by the damage. In earlier times the view adopted appears to have been that restoration cost would hardly ever be awarded and that plaintiffs would have to be content with the difference in value.[3] More recently, however, there have been signs of greater flexibility. The usefulness of attempting to amplify, with more precise guidelines as to the measure of damages in postulated situations, the general principle that the defendant must make restitution subject only to the overriding requirement of reasonableness, has also been questioned.[4] The issue is one to be determined on the facts of each case. In the *Dominion Mosaics* case the plaintiffs' business premises were severely damaged by fire due to the negligence of the defendants. The plaintiffs decided that rebuilding would be too expensive and impracticable and that it would be cheaper to acquire new premises, which they did. They claimed the cost of so doing from the defendants who asserted that their liability should be limited to the mere diminution in value of the existing premises. The Court of Appeal found in favour of the plaintiffs. If they had not sought new premises quickly they would, as a commercial concern, have suffered heavy consequential loss of profits which might have exceeded the cost of acquiring the new premises and which they could have looked to the defendants to reimburse. Awarding the cost of the

---

1 See *Harbutt's Plasticine Ltd v Wayne Tank and Pump Co Ltd* [1970] 1 QB 447 at 472-473, [1970] 1 All ER 225 at 240 per Widgery LJ, CA.
2 [1990] 2 All ER 246 at 249, CA.
3 See *Jones v Gooday* (1841) 8 M & W 146. See also *Moss v Christchurch RDC* [1925] 2 KB 750.
4 See per May J in *CR Taylor (Wholesale) Ltd v Hepworths Ltd* [1977] 2 All ER 784 at 791-793, [1977] 1 WLR 659 at 667-669.

new premises was therefore favourable, in a sense, to the defendants who might indeed have argued that the plaintiffs had been in breach of their duty to mitigate had they not swiftly sought the means to continue trading. Notwithstanding the admitted presumption in favour of the diminution in value approach,[1] its displacement in favour of 'reinstatement or its equivalent' would, in the words of Stocker LJ,[2] sometimes be appropriate in the case of commercial premises as 'the only reasonable method of compensating a plaintiff for future loss of profits derived from the asset destroyed'.

[**10.10**] Nevertheless, there will often be cases in which the application of the presumption in favour of diminution in value will remain appropriate notwithstanding the presence of a commercial element. In *CR Taylor (Wholesale) Ltd v Hepworths Ltd*[3] the plaintiffs owned a disused billiard hall which they had continued to own only for the potential development value of the site. Their attempt to recover on the basis of restoration cost, when the building was destroyed by a fire for which the defendants were responsible, was understandably rejected. Reinstatement of the unwanted building would have cost some ten times the site value. 'In these circumstances', observed May J, 'it would in my opinion not only be totally unrealistic, but also unreasonable as between the plaintiffs and the defendants, to award the former the notional cost of reinstating the premises'.[4] On the other hand in *Hollebone v Midhurst and Fernhurst Builders Ltd*[5] the owner-occupier of a distinctive dwelling-house with unique characteristics was awarded restoration cost, rather than the lower figure for diminution in value, when it was damaged by fire due to the negligence of the defendants.[6] Nor did the judge consider it appropriate to make any allowance in favour of the defendants for 'betterment' as a result of the restoration. Indeed the reluctance of the court to make such an allowance, in cases where restoration cost is considered to be the appropriate award, is also illustrated by *Harbutt's Plasticine Ltd v Wayne Tank and Pump Co*:[7] a case which shows in

1 'The true principle is that the owner of a building is entitled to the diminution in value between the building as it was before the wrong and after it, unless he establishes that he intends to or has reasonably rebuilt the structure damaged or destroyed *and* that his is an exceptional case in which justice requires that he should be paid the cost of restoration': per Kenny J in *Munnelly v Calcon Ltd* [1978] IR 387 at 407 (the italics are those of Kenny J).
2 [1990] 2 All ER 246 at 256.
3 [1977] 2 All ER 784, [1977] 1 WLR 659.
4 Ibid at 794 and 670. See also *Munnelly v Calcon Ltd* [1978] IR 387 and *Hole & Son (Sayers Common) Ltd v Harrisons of Thurnscoe Ltd* [1973] 1 Lloyd's Rep 345.
5 [1968] 1 Lloyd's Rep 38. See also *Jens v Mannix Co* [1978] 5 WWR 486 (Can).
6 See also *Ward v Cannock Chase District Council* [1986] Ch 546 at 577, [1985] 3 All ER 537 at 558 ('. . . an exceptional case in which justice requires . . . the cost of reinstatement').
7 [1970] 1 QB 447, [1970] 1 All ER 225, CA. This was a case of breach of contract but on the facts the relevant principles as to measure of damages were the same as those in tort : see per May J (who had been counsel for the successful plaintiffs in the *Harbutt's Plasticine* case) in *CR Taylor (Wholesale) Ltd v Hepworths Ltd* [1977] 2 All ER 784 at 791, [1977] 1 WLR 659 at 666E.

addition that reinstatement can be legitimate in a commercial context and is not confined to the residential. The plaintiff's factory was burnt down in circumstances for which the defendants were responsible.[1] Lord Denning MR expressed himself as follows:[2]

> '... when this mill was destroyed, the plasticine company had no choice. They were bound to replace it as soon as they could, not only to keep their business going, but also to mitigate the loss of profit (for which they would be able to charge the defendants). They replaced it in the only possible way, without adding any extras. I think they should be allowed the cost of replacement. True it is that they got new for old; but I do not think the wrongdoer can diminish the claim on that account. If they had added extra accommodation or made extra improvements, they would have to give credit. But that is not this case.'[3]

Gains

[**10.11**] In *Hussey v Eels*[4] the plaintiffs were induced to buy a bungalow from the defendants due to a negligent misrepresentation by the latter that it had not been subject to subsidence when in fact it had. After living in the property for some time the plaintiffs decided that, in view of the subsidence, their best course was to demolish the bungalow and seek planning permission for the erection of two new bungalows on the same ground. Before the plaintiffs' action against the defendants for negligent misrepresentation came on for trial the plaintiffs had in fact sold the property to a developer, with the benefit of the planning permission, for substantially more than they had paid for it. The defendants claimed that this profit extinguished the loss which the plaintiffs had suffered in paying, as a result of the misrepresentation, more for the bungalow than it had been worth. The Court of Appeal rejected this argument and allowed the plaintiffs to recover a sum representing the difference in value at the time of the original sale. It could not be said that the plaintiffs had been under any duty to mitigate their loss by taking the elaborate steps with respect to planning permission and eventual sale which they in fact took. Moreover, although circumstances can clearly occur to prevent a plaintiff from suffering any loss without these circumstances having arisen as a result of mitigation by him, that overriding principle did not avail the defendants in the present case. The plaintiffs were not property speculators; and their subsequent sale of the bungalow with planning permission could not plausibly be regarded as an event so intertwined with the original purchase, induced by the defendants' negligent misrepresentation, that the latter could rely upon it as having given rise to a gain inseparable from the loss which their wrong had caused.

---

1   The overruling of the *Harbutt's Plasticine* case in *Photo Production Ltd v Securicor Transport Ltd* [1980] AC 827, [1980] 1 All ER 556, HL, does not affect the point in the text.
2   [1970] 1 QB 447 at 468, [1970] 1 All ER 225 at 236.
3   See also *Dominion Mosaics & Tile Co Ltd v Trafalgar Trucking Co Ltd* [1990] 2 All ER 246 at 252, CA per Taylor LJ.
4   [1990] 2 QB 227, [1990] 1 All ER 449, CA.

Negligent surveys

[10.12] In *Perry v Sidney Phillips & Son*[1] Lord Denning MR said:

> '[where a] surveyor agrees to survey a house and make a report on it - and he makes it negligently - and the client buys the house on the faith of the report, then the damages are to be assessed . . . according to the difference in price which the buyer would have given if the report had been carefully made from that which he in fact gave owing to the negligence of the surveyor . . . The buyer is not entitled to remedy the defects and charge the cost to the surveyor.'

There is no doubt that these observations, although obiter on the facts of *Perry v Sidney Phillips & Son* itself since the house which had been negligently surveyed in that case was actually sold by the plaintiff instead of repaired by him, accurately reflect the usual position which the courts will adopt in the case of negligence by privately appointed surveyors. Oliver LJ expressly agreed[2] with Lord Denning's view which followed the earlier decision of the Court of Appeal in *Philips v Ward*.[3] Nevertheless, the possibility that, if justice requires it in exceptional circumstances, a surveyor might be held liable for repair costs should not be entirely discounted.[4] In *Perry v Sidney Phillips & Son* the judge at first instance, who heard the case before the house was sold and when the possibility of repair was still a live issue, made his award of damages on this basis.[5] And in the Court of Appeal, the third judge, Kerr LJ, chose to reserve his view on the question[6] rather than associate himself with the explicit rejection, by Lord Denning MR and Oliver LJ, of the trial judge's approach.

Liability to lenders

[10.13] In *Swingcastle Ltd v Alastair Gibson (a firm)*[7] the House of Lords considered the liability of a surveyor for negligent valuation not to a purchaser but to a mortgagee. Due to the defendant's overvaluation the plaintiff lenders advanced money, which they would not otherwise have done, at a high rate of interest. When the borrowers defaulted the plaintiffs sought to recover, as part of their damages, the outstanding interest which the borrowers had contracted to pay but which was now irrecoverable. The claim was rejected by the House, which reversed the Court of Appeal[8] and overruled an earlier decision of that court.[9] Lord Lowry said:[10]

---

1 [1982] 3 All ER 705 at 708, [1982] 1 WLR 1297 at 1302A, CA.
2 See [1982] 1 WLR at 1304.
3 [1956] 1 All ER 874, [1956] 1 WLR 471, CA. See also *Treml v Ernest W Gibson & Partners* (1984) 272 Estates Gazette 68. Cf *Bolton v Puley* (1982) 2647 Estates Gazette 1160.
4 See PA Chandler 'Negligent Surveys: An Expanding Liability?' (1990) 106 LQR 196.
5 The case is reported at first instance in [1982] 1 All ER 1005 (Patrick Bennett QC sitting as a Deputy Judge of the High Court).
6 See [1982] 1 WLR at 1306A.
7 [1991] 2 AC 223, [1991] 2 All ER 353, HL.
8 Reported at [1990] 3 All ER 463, [1990] 1 WLR 1223.
9 Ie *Baxter v F W Gapp & Co Ltd* [1939] 2 KB 271, [1939] 2 All ER 752, CA.
10 [1991] 2 AC 223 at 238, [1991] 2 All ER 353 at 365.

'My Lords, it is clear that the lenders ought to have presented their claim on the basis that, if the valuer had advised properly, they would not have lent the money. Where they went wrong was to claim, not only correctly that they had to spend all the money which they did, but incorrectly that the valuer by his negligence deprived them of the interest which they would have received from the borrowers if the borrowers had paid up. The security for the loan was the property but the lenders did not have a further security consisting of a guarantee by the valuer that the borrowers would pay everything, or indeed anything, that was due from them to the lenders at the date, whenever it occurred, on which the loan transaction terminated. The fallacy of the lenders' case is that they have been trying to obtain from the valuer compensation for the borrowers' failure and not the proper damages for the valuer's negligence.'

Date of assessment

[**10.14**] When rates of inflation are high the date at which damages are to be assessed can be very significant. It is notorious that in such periods interest rates do not in practice provide full protection against the fall in the value of money. So unless a case involves unusual facts in which values and costs have not increased at the full inflationary rate, even the inclusion of interest in the judgment would still leave the plaintiff out of pocket if the award was based upon the date at which the damage occurred.[1] Nevertheless that was long understood to be the position in cases of damage to property.[2] In *Dodd Properties (Kent) v Canterbury City Council*,[3] however, the Court of Appeal emphasised that this was not an inflexible rule but was indeed qualified by the general principle that, subject to overriding considerations of reasonableness, a plaintiff is entitled to full compensation for his loss. In this case the plaintiffs' building was damaged in 1968. The defendants denied liability until just before the trial, which did not occur until ten years later. The parties then agreed that repair costs, rather than difference in value, was the appropriate basis for the award of damages; but they disagreed as to the date for the making of the calculation. The building had not, in fact, been repaired by the time of the trial and the plaintiffs claimed the cost of repair at 1978 values. The Court of Appeal held that it had been commercially reasonable for the plaintiffs to have postponed the repairs until liability was admitted and they could be sure of recouping the cost. The court then went on to hold that in consequence

---

1 See Feldman and Libling, 'Inflation and the Duty to Mitigate' (1979) 95 LQR 270; Duncan Wallace 'Cost of Repair and Inflation' (1980) 96 LQR 101 at 341.
2 See, eg *Philips v Ward* [1956] 1 All ER 874 at 876, [1956] 1 WLR 471, CA, at 474, per Lord Denning MR. See also *Clark v Woor* [1965] 2 All ER 353, [1965] 1 WLR 650. In 'The Date for the Assessment of Damages' (1981) 97 LQR 445, SM Waddams argues that preservation of the traditional rule, combined with the award of interest, is to be preferred on grounds of efficiency to compensating for inflation by choosing a later date.
3 [1980] 1 All ER 928, [1980] 1 WLR 433, CA. See Rogers 'Damages for Injury to a Building' (1980) 124 Sol Jo 383.

the plaintiff's claim as to the appropriate date would be upheld.[1] Megaw LJ said:[2]

'The true rule is that, where there is a material difference between the cost of repair at the date of the wrongful act and the cost of repair when the repairs can, having regard to all relevant circumstances, first reasonably be undertaken, it is the latter time by reference to which the cost of repair is to be taken in assessing damages.'

[10.15] Of course what is a reasonable date will depend upon the facts of each case, in *Dodd*'s case itself it happened to be the year when liability was admitted which itself just happened to be the year of the trial.[3] Moreover Donaldson LJ expressed the view that 'in normal circumstances' the date of the damage would remain the relevant one in cases where difference in value rather than reinstatement was the appropriate measure of damage.[4] Even in reinstatement cases the appropriate date would by no means necessarily be the date of the trial. Donaldson LJ put it as follows:[5]

'... in a case in which a plaintiff has reinstated his property before the hearing, the costs prevailing at the date of that operation which were reasonably incurred by him are prima facie those which are relevant. Equally in a case in which a plaintiff has *not* effected reinstatement by the time of the hearing, there is a prima facie presumption that the costs then prevailing are those which should be adopted in ascertaining the cost of reinstatement. There may indeed be cases in which the court has to estimate costs at some future time as being the reasonable time at which to reinstate... This is, however, only a prima facie approach. It may appear on the evidence that the plaintiff, acting reasonably, should have undertaken the reinstatement at some date earlier than that in fact adopted or, as the case may be, earlier than the hearing. If so, the relevant costs are those ruling at that earlier date.'

Additional losses

[10.16] If a building is damaged it is not unlikely that the plaintiff will suffer losses additional to the difference in the building's value or the cost of reinstating it. Thus, if the building is used for commercial purposes, a sum will frequently be claimable due to interruption of the business caused by the damage itself or by inability to trade normally while repairs are taking place.[6] Recoverable losses arising

---

1 Cf *Birmingham Corpn v West Midland Baptist (Trust) Association Inc* [1970] AC 874, [1969] 3 All ER 172, HL.
2 [1980] 1 WLR 433 at 451.
3 See also *Marriott v Carson's Construction Ltd* (1983) 146 DLR (3d) 126.
4 See [1980] 1 WLR 433 at 457C. Cf *Ward v Cannock Chase District Council* [1985] 3 All ER 537 at 559 per Scott J (continuing wrong leading to eventual demolition: date of demolition appropriate).
5 [1980] 1 WLR 433 at 458.
6 See, eg *Dodd Properties (Kent) v Canterbury City Council* [1980] 1 All ER 928, [1980] 1 WLR 433, CA. Cf *Dominion Mosaics & Tile Co Ltd v Trafalgar Trucking Co* [1990] 2 All ER 246.

out of property damage are not, however, necessarily confined to those which are purely financial. In *Perry v Sidney Phillips & Son*[1] the Court of Appeal upheld an award of damages to the plaintiff for all the 'vexation, distress and worry'[2] which he suffered due to his purchase, brought about by the negligence of his surveyor, of a house in a deplorable condition.[3] Such awards will not be large[4] and are likely, in practice, to be confined to owner-occupiers. In *Hutchinson v Harris*[5] the Court of Appeal refused to make an award under this head to a plaintiff who had purchased the property for letting purposes. Waller LJ emphasised that the plaintiff 'was not concerned with her own home' and therefore had to accept that she had 'to concern herself with this sort of problem as an inevitable incident of being a landlord'.[6] Moreover to qualify for an award the distress and anxiety suffered by the plaintiff must not be due merely to the 'tension or frustration of a person who is involved in a legal dispute',[7] because this is obviously not a recoverable head of damage.

New areas of recovery

[10.17] The expansion of the tort of negligence in recent years has led to successful claims being made in situations unrelated to the traditional fields of property damage and personal injury. The focus of concentration in these cases has inevitably been on the nature of the causes of action rather than specifically upon the measure of damages. Indeed the widely differing nature of the circumstances involved has meant that little has emerged in these areas to provide more detailed amplification of the general principle that damages should, as far as possible, put the plaintiff in the position which he would have been in if the tort had not been committed.[8] But one which should be noted is that, particularly in professional negligence cases, losses themselves

---

1 [1982] 3 All ER 705, [1982] 1 WLR 1297, CA.
2 [1982] 1 WLR 1302H per Lord Denning MR. Cf *Jarvis v Swan Tours* [1973] QB 233, [1973] 1 All ER 71, CA; *Jackson v Horizon Holidays* [1975] 3 All ER 92, [1975] 1 WLR 1468, CA.
3 See generally, Kim Franklin 'Damages for Heartache: The Award of General Damages for Inconvenience and Distress in Building Cases' (1988) 4 Const LR 264.
4 See *Perry v Sidney Phillips & Son* [1982] 3 All ER 705 at 709, [1982] 1 WLR 1297 at 1303 per Lord Denning MR. £500 was awarded in the 1982 case of *Bolton v Puley* (1982) 267 Estates Gazette 1160. But cf the 1984 case of *Treml v Ernest W Gibson & Partners* in which Popplewell J described a sum of £1,250, agreed between the parties, as 'somewhat modest': [1984] EGD 922 at 934.
5 (1978) 10 BLR 19, CA.
6 Ibid at 46. See also per Stephenson LJ at 37.
7 Per Kerr LJ in *Perry v Sidney Phillips & Son* [1982] 3 All ER 705 at 712, [1982] 1 WLR 1297 at 1307.
8 Cf *County Personnel (Employment Agency) Ltd v Alan R Pulver & Co* [1987] 1 All ER 289 at 297, [1987] 1 WLR 916 at 925, CA per Bingham J (need for a 'general assessment' rather than 'an invariable approach . . . mechanically applied' in claims against solicitors for professional negligence).

may be calculated in a fashion formerly more familiar in contract than in tort. Thus if the defendant undertakes to provide a service for the benefit of the plaintiff,[1] the latter may be able to recover the losses he suffers in consequence of the task in question not being correctly performed due to negligence, and such losses could well include compensation for *gains* which the plaintiff has failed to realise.[2] Another kind of loss for which the courts have been prepared to award compensation, in a certain type of medical negligence case, is the cost of bringing up a child conceived as the result of failure in connection with a sterilisation procedure.[3]

---

1   See Burrows *Remedies for Torts and Breach of Contract* (1987) pp 161-163.
2   See, eg *White v Jones* [1993] NLJR 473, CA, applying *Ross v Caunters* [1980] Ch 297, [1979] 3 All ER 580. In *Murray v Lloyd* [1990] 2 All ER 92, [1989] 1 WLR 1060 a plaintiff was awarded substantial damages against her solicitors whose negligent advice had caused her to lose the opportunity of becoming a statutory tenant when the existing lease on her home expired.
3   See *Emeh v Kensington and Chelsea and Westminster Area Health Authority* [1985] QB 1012, [1984] 3 All ER 1044, CA; *Allen v Bloomsbury Health Authority* [1993] 1 All ER 651. Damages may also include compensation for the plaintiffs' distress at the prospect of further parenthood: *Thake v Maurice* [1986] QB 644, [1984] 2 All ER 513. But cf *Salih v Enfield Health Authority* [1991] 3 All ER 400, CA.

Chapter 11

Limitation of actions

General principles

Time limits

[**11.01**] The law on limitation of actions is now contained in the Limitation Act 1980 which consolidates earlier legislation.¹ With the major exception of cases involving personal injuries, negligence actions are governed by s 2 of the Act which provides that: 'An action founded on tort shall not be brought after the expiration of six years from the date on which the cause of action accrued.'

In personal injury and Fatal Accidents Act cases, the basic limitation period is not six years but three.² But by virtue of a provision originally introduced to protect victims of insidious industrial diseases, where the existence of illness may not be immediately apparent, time in personal injury cases may be calculated from the date of knowledge of the person injured if that is later than the date on which the cause of action actually accrued. Moreover, since 1975,³ the court has had a very wide discretion to override the three-year time limit in personal injury cases if 'it would be equitable'⁴ to do so. The special provisions relating to personal injury, and Fatal Accidents Act, cases are dealt with separately below.

Computation of dates

[**11.02**] For the purpose of calculating the limitation period the day on which the cause of action accrued is not included.⁵ Moreover, if the

---

1 See, generally, McGhee *Limitation Periods* (1990). For criticism of the 1980 Act see Davies, 'Limitations on the Law of Limitation' (1982) 98 LQR 249. For a very concise history of the law down to 1978 see *Firman v Ellis* [1978] QB 886, at 903-905, [1978] 2 All ER 851 at 858-859, CA, per Lord Denning.
2 See, s 11(4) of the 1980 Act. The shortening of the period from six years to three in personal injury cases was originally introduced by the Law Reform (Limitation of Actions &c) Act 1954.
3 See, the Limitation Act 1975, s 2D.
4 See the Limitation Act 1980, s 33(1).
5 See *Marren v Dawson Bentley & Co Ltd* [1961] 2 QB 135, [1961] 2 All ER 270.

court offices were closed on the last available day, the period will not expire until the end of the next day on which the offices reopen.[1]

Persons under a disability

[11.03] If a person is under a disability on the date when a cause of action accrues to him, the limitation period is extended so that he is allowed the full period (whether it be six years or three) calculated from the date on which he ceased to be under the disability.[2] A person is under a disability if he is an infant or of unsound mind.[3] In the case of infants there was formerly a rule that time did begin to run against an infant if he was in the custody of a parent when the cause of action accrued.[4] This rule was considered too harsh,[5] however, and was abrogated by the Limitation Act 1975. In consequence a defendant who injures a very young child may find himself sued more than 20 years after the event took place.[6]

Procedure

[11.04] Limitation is technically a matter of procedure. The Act does not extinguish the plaintiff's right but merely bars his remedy. It follows that a defendant who considers that he has a valid defence of limitation cannot have the claim struck out as disclosing no reasonable cause of action.[7] Striking out on the ground of abuse of process might, however, be possible in a very clear case; otherwise the defence has to be pleaded and the matter tried.[8] Complicated procedural issues sometimes arise where an action is commenced within the limitation period, but an attempt is made to add an additional party to it by amendment of the pleadings after the period has expired.[9] In general, the long-established rule of practice is that

---

1 See *Pritam Kaur v S Russell & Sons Ltd* [1973] 1 QB 336, [1973] 1 All ER 617, CA.
2 See the Limitation Act 1980, s 28. It follows that if the plaintiff is under a *permanent* disability there is in effect no limitation period at all: *Turner v Malcolm* (1992) 136 Sol Jo LB 236, CA.
3 Ibid s 38(2). A person is of unsound mind if he 'by reason of mental disorder within the meaning of the Mental Health Act 1959, is incapable of managing and administering his property and affairs': s 38(3). Cf *Kirby v Leather* [1965] 2 QB 367, [1965] 2 All ER 441, CA. See also Limitation Act 1980, s 38(4): (conclusive presumption as to unsoundness of mind in certain cases).
4 See *Todd v Davison* [1972] AC 392, [1971] 1 All ER 994, HL. The rule was introduced by the Law Reform (Limitation of Actions &c) Act 1954.
5 For criticism of the rule see the Twentieth Report of the Law Reform Committee: 'Interim Report on Limitation of Actions in Personal Injury Claims', 1974 Cmnd 5630, pp 35-39.
6 Cf *Tolley v Morris* [1979] 2 All ER 561, [1979] 1 WLR 592, HL.
7 See *Ronex Properties Ltd v John Laing Construction Ltd* [1983] QB 398, [1982] 3 All ER 961, CA.
8 Ibid.
9 For discussion see Scott 'Limitation of Actions and Amendments to Joint Defendants', (1982) 1 CJQ 205. See also *Ketteman v Hansel Properties Ltd* [1985] 1 All ER 352 at 360-362, [1984] 1 WLR 1274 at 1285-1288 per Lawton LJ, and the same case in the House of Lords: [1987] AC 189, [1988] 2 All ER 38.

Limitation of actions

such an amendment will not be permitted if to allow it would deprive the new party of a limitation defence which he would otherwise have enjoyed.[1]

Accrual of the cause of action

[11.05] Since negligence is not actionable without proof of damage the cause of action will not accrue until damage occurs.[2] Nevertheless, damage may occur before the party suffering it is conscious of the fact. In *Bell v Peter Browne & Co*[3] the defendant solicitors acted for the plaintiff on the breakdown of his marriage. The plaintiff transferred ownership of the former matrimonial home to his wife in return for her agreement to provide him with a one-sixth share of the proceeds in the event of sale. Unfortunately, the defendants negligently failed to take the appropriate steps to protect and register the plaintiff's interest, but this only came to light eight years later when the wife sold the house and spent all the proceeds.[4] The Court of Appeal held that the plaintiff's claim against his solicitors ran from a date on or around the making of the agreement between the plaintiff and his wife, when the defendants failed to act as they should have done, and not from the later date when the house was sold. In consequence the claim was statute-barred.[5] Originally, this principle was applied even in personal injury cases, but the hardship which it could cause, especially where insidious industrial diseases were concerned,[6] gave rise to substantial statutory changes in the law in that area. These were eventually followed by legislative reform in the area of latent damage in cases other than personal injury. As a result of these changes cases such as *Bell v Peter Browne & Co* which, although decided in 1990 was in fact governed by the old law, will be decided differently in the future. The rules relating generally to limitation in personal injury cases will be considered below, followed by those relating to latent damage in other types of case.

Limitation and dismissal for want of prosecution

[11.06] The court has an inherent jurisdiction to dismiss actions for want of prosecution. Such dismissal for delay in taking specific

---

1 See *Liff v Peasley* [1980] 1 All ER 623, [1980] 1 WLR 781, CA. See also the Limitation Act 1980, s 35(3) and *Kennett v Brown* [1988] 2 All ER 600, [1988] 1 WLR 582, CA.
2 Cf *Darley Main Colliery Co v Mitchell* (1886) 11 App Cas 127, HL.
3 [1990] 3 All ER 124, CA. See also *Forster v Outred & Co* [1982] 2 All ER 753, [1982] 1 WLR 86, CA; *Baker v Ollard & Bentley* (1982) 126 Sol Jo 593, CA.
4 'Once the solicitors closed their file, it was unlikely that [their] failure would come to the notice of Mr Bell, or the solicitors, until the house was sold and it was too late. That, on the pleaded facts, is exactly what happened.': [1990] 3 All ER 124 at 128 per Nicholls LJ.
5 The court questioned the correctness of the approach of Oliver J in *Midland Bank Trust Co v Hett, Stubbs & Kemp* [1979] Ch 384, [1978] 3 All ER 571, in which he held that where a solicitor negligently fails to register an option as a land charge damage is not suffered until a transaction occurs destroying the option.
6 See *Cartledge v E Jopling & Sons Ltd* [1963] AC 758, [1963] 1 All ER 341, HL.

procedural steps is also expressly authorised by the Rules of Court.[1] After a decision of the Court of Appeal[2] in 1968 this jurisdiction began to be used much more widely than heretofore, in order to discourage protracted delays in litigation. In *Birkett v James*,[3] however, the House of Lords held that the jurisdiction could not normally be exercised *inside* the limitation period, since in such a case the court would have no power to prevent the plaintiff from simply issuing a new writ and starting all over again.[4] Although laying down a general principle, *Birkett v James* itself concerned an action for breach of contract, and uncertainty arose as to its application to personal injury cases in which there is now a very wide discretion to override the time limit. On one view the existence of this discretion, combined with the rule in *Birkett v James,* could have made it impossible ever to dismiss a personal injuries action for want of prosecution since the plaintiff could, in theory, seek the exercise of the discretion in his favour at any time in the future to bring a new action. The House of Lords soon made clear, however, that this is not the case. In *Walkley v Precision Forgings Ltd*[5] the House held that a plaintiff who brings an action within the normal three-year period for a personal injuries claim, but either discontinues it or allows it to become liable to dismissal for want of prosecution, ipso facto becomes disentitled to seek the exercise of the discretion to override the time limit in order to bring a new action. The decision was based on a statutory condition precedent, for the existence of the discretion to override, that the plaintiff would be 'prejudiced' by the normal time limit if that limit were to be insisted upon.[6] Their Lordships held that a plaintiff who did manage to commence proceedings within the time limit cannot be said to have been prejudiced by it, but rather by his own dilatoriness or that of his advisers, if that first action was not properly pursued.[7] The rule in *Walkley v Precision Forgings* is therefore of general application.[8] The only possible exception to it is apparently if the discontinuance of the first action was procured by some misrepresentation or other improper conduct on the part of the defendant.[9] The rule cannot apply, however, if the earlier proceedings were rendered a nullity by

1 See, eg RSC Ord 25, r 1, and the note thereon in the Supreme Court Practice.
2 See *Allen v Sir Alfred McAlpine & Sons Ltd* [1968] 2 QB 229, [1968] 1 All ER 543, CA.
3 [1978] AC 297, [1977] 2 All ER 801, HL. See also *Tolley v Morris* [1979] 2 All ER 561, [1979] 1 WLR 592, HL; *Turner v Malcolm* (1992) 136 Sol Jo LB 236, CA.
4 See also *Department of Transport v Chris Smaller (Transport) Ltd* [1989] AC 1197, [1989] 1 All ER 897, HL.
5 [1979] 2 All ER 548, [1979] 1 WLR 606, HL.
6 See the Limitation Act, 1980 s 33(1).
7 A paradoxical consequence is that a plaintiff whose solicitors are so grossly negligent that they do not issue a writ at all will be better off, in terms of being able subsequently to seek exercise of the discretion to override the time limit, than a plaintiff whose solicitors issue a writ but then, eg omit to serve it: see, eg *Chappell v Cooper* [1980] 2 All ER 463, [1980] 1 WLR 958, CA. Cf *Thompson v Brown Construction (Ebbw Vale) Ltd* [1981] 2 All ER 296 at 303, [1981] 1 WLR 744, HL, at 752 per Lord Diplock.
8 See *Deerness v John R Keeble & Son (Brantham) Ltd* [1983] 2 Lloyd's Rep 260, HL (erroneous belief by plaintiff's solicitor's clerk that an interim payment by the defendants made service of the writ unnecessary was insufficient to take the case outside *Walkley's* case).
9 See per Lord Diplock in *Walkley's* case: [1979] 1 WLR at 619.

statute, and the power to override the time limit therefore survives in such a case.[1]

Pre-limitation delay relevant after expiry

[11.07] Although an action cannot be dismissed for want of prosecution inside the limitation period it does not follow that delay which occurs after the issue of the writ but *during* that period cannot be relied upon by a defendant seeking dismissal of the action for want of prosecution *after* the limitation period has expired.[2] In *Rath v CS Lawrence & Partners*[3] the plaintiffs issued a writ early in the six-year limitation period but then allowed a delay in excess of four years to occur before taking further steps. After the expiry of the limitation period there was hardly any *further* delay, nevertheless the defendants succeeded in getting the action dismissed for want of prosecution. 'The late issue of a writ', said Slade LJ,[4] 'is one thing; by itself it cannot be regarded as culpable. The casual and dilatory conduct of proceedings in breach of the rules, after a writ has been issued is another thing'. Farquaharson LJ expressed himself as follows:[5]

> 'The position of the plaintiff who has delayed the issue of his writ until the last moment of the limitation period is, it is true, in one sense more advantageous than that of the plaintiff who issues his writ without delay. The former has exploited the period given to him by Parliament to the fullest extent, and cannot be criticised unless he is guilty of further delay after the limitation period has expired. The position of the latter is however quite different. Once a plaintiff has issued his writ and set the treadmill of litigation in motion, he is bound to observe the rules of the court. If he flouts them to the extent that the plaintiffs have in the present case I can see no reason why the defendants should not rely upon it, after the limitation period has expired, to support an application to strike out.'

Personal injuries

Special time limit

[11.08] In the case of personal injury claims the basic time limit is only three years.[6] But not only is there a wide discretion to override this time limit,[7] the limit itself can be calculated, if necessary, in a way more favourable to the plaintiff than that available in situations

---

1 See, eg *Re Workvale Ltd (No 2)* [1992] 2 All ER 627, CA (action against a dissolved company). See also *White v Glass* (1989) Times, 18 February, CA and *Wilson v Banner Scaffolding* (1982) Times, 22 June (Milmo J).
2 Cf *Department of Transport v Chris Smaller (Transport) Ltd* [1989] AC 1197, [1989] 1 All ER 897, HL.
3 [1991] 3 All ER 679, [1991] 1 WLR 399, CA.
4 [1991] 3 All ER 679 at 688.
5 [1991] 3 All ER 679 at 684.
6 See Limitation Act 1980, s 11.
7 See below.

Personal injuries 213

not involving personal injury.[1] Thus s 11(4) of the 1980 Act provides that the three years run from:

'(*a*) the date on which the cause of action accrued; or
(*b*) the date of knowledge (if later) of the person injured.'

This provision, expressly allowing calculation to be made from the date of the plaintiff's knowledge, dates back to the Limitation Act 1975. The original concept reflected by the provision first appeared in the Limitation Act 1963, which was passed in the wake of the decision of the House of Lords in *Cartledge v E Jopling & Sons Ltd*;[2] a case involving pneumoconiosis which showed that as the law then stood a claim could become statute-barred before the victim even knew that he had the disease.

Date of knowledge

[**11.09**] Section 14 of the 1980 Act contains elaborate provisions defining the 'date of knowledge'. Section 14(1) is as follows:

'... references to a person's date of knowledge are references to the date on which he first had knowledge of the following facts –
(*a*) that the injury in question was significant; and
(*b*) that the injury was attributable[3] in whole or in part to the act or omission which is alleged to constitute negligence, nuisance of breach of duty; and
(*c*) the identity of the defendant; and
(*d*) if it is alleged that the act or omission was that of a person other than the defendant, the identity of that person and the additional facts supporting the bringing of an action against the defendant;
and knowledge that any acts or omissions did or did not, as a matter of law, involve negligence, nuisance or breach of duty is irrelevant.'

The proviso in the concluding words of the subsection, making knowledge of the law irrelevant, was passed in order to overcome uncertainty on the point reflected in the decision of the House of Lords in *Central Asbestos Co Ltd v Dodd*,[4] based on the construction of the earlier provision in the Limitation Act 1963.

'significant'

[**11.10**] The requirement in s 14(1)(*a*) 'that the injury in question was significant' is expanded by s 14(2) which provides as follows:

'For the purposes of this section an injury is significant if the person whose date of knowledge is in question would reasonably have

---

1   Contractual claims in respect of personal injuries are within the scope of the provision, which is not confined to actions in tort: see *Howe v David Brown Tractors (Retail) Ltd* [1991] 4 All ER 30, CA. Cf *Ackbar v CF Green & Co Ltd* [1975] QB 582, [1975] 2 All ER 65.
2   [1963] AC 758, [1963] 1 All ER 341, HL.
3   On the use of the word 'attributable' in s 14(1)(*b*) see *Wilkinson v Ancliff (BLT) Ltd* [1986] 3 All ER 427, [1986] 1 WLR 1352, CA. See also *Nash v Eli Lilly* [1991] 2 Med LR 169.
4   [1973] AC 518, [1972] 2 All ER 1135, HL.

considered it sufficiently serious to justify his instituting proceedings for damages against a defendant who did not dispute liability and was able to satisfy a judgment.'

Although the case was decided under earlier, and differently worded, legislation, a passage in the judgment of Lord Denning MR in *Goodchild v Greatness Timber Co Ltd*[1] conveniently expresses the underlying purpose of this somewhat curiously-worded provision:

'... I would say this on those words: they are intended to apply to cases where a man has an injury which he reasonably believes is trifling (for example, a knock on the head) and it is not worthwhile to bring an action for it, but then after three years it is found to be far more serious than anyone realised (for instance, to cause a tumour)... His time will be extended. But if the injury was from the beginning fairly serious, or at any rate sufficiently serious to make it worth while to bring an action, then he must bring it within the first three years. The time will not be extended simply because it turns out after three years to be more serious than he at first thought.'

The meaning of what is now s 14(2) was itself expounded by Geoffrey Lane LJ in *McCafferty v Metropolitan Police District Receiver*[2] as follows:

'... it is clear that the test is partly a subjective test, namely: would this plaintiff have considered the injury sufficiently serious? And partly an objective test, namely: would he have been reasonable if he did *not* regard it as sufficiently serious? It seems to me that [s 14(2)] is directed at the nature of the injury as known to the plaintiff, with *that* plaintiff's intelligence, would he have been reasonable in considering the injury not sufficiently serious to justify instituting proceedings for damages?'

[**11.11**] An accident victim who refrains from bringing an action initially merely ' because of the regard he has for the defendants or ... because he is averse to litigation'[3] cannot claim subsequently that his injury was not 'significant' for the purposes of the subsection. Nor can one who failed to make a claim because he did not want to 'sponge',[4] or was simply afraid of losing his job,[5] do so. Such factors may, however, be taken into account when the court is considering the exercise of its general discretion to override the time limit.[6]

---

1 [1968] 2 QB 372 at 380, [1968] 2 All ER 255 at 257, CA. In *Miller v London Electrical Manufacturing Co Ltd* [1976] 2 Lloyd's Rep 284 the Court of Appeal apparently took the view that, by the wording of what is now s 14(2), 'Parliament has in effect given its imprimatur to [*Goodchild's*] case': [1976] 2 Lloyd's Rep 284 at 288 per Bridge LJ.
2 [1977] ICR 799, CA at 807-808 (italics are those of Geoffrey Lane LJ).
3 Per Salmon LJ in *Goodchild v Greatness Timber Co Ltd* [1968] 2 QB 372 at 381, [1968] 2 All ER 255 at 258, CA.
4 *Buck v English Electric Co* [1978] 1 All ER 271, [1977] 1 WLR 806.
5 *McCafferty v Metropolitan Police District Receiver* [1977] 2 All ER 756, [1977] 1 WLR 1073, CA. Cf *Driscoll-Varley v Parkside Health Authority* [1991] 2 Med LR 346.
6 See below.

'the identity of the defendant'

[**11.12**] The working of s 14(1)(c) is illustrated by *Simpson v Norwest Holst Southern Ltd*.[1] The plaintiff injured his leg while working on a building site. He consulted solicitors within weeks of the accident, but confusion then ensued in determining precisely who the plaintiff's employers were. The documents which had been given to him ostensibly containing such particulars, pursuant to the employment legislation, identified them as the 'Norwest Holst Group', and a similar expression appeared on his pay slips. That expression did not, however, identify any legal entity, there being at least four companies forming the 'group', each with registered titles embodying different variations of the 'Norwest' theme. In consequence, some letters from the plaintiff's solicitors went unanswered, other met with long delays. By the time they were in a position to commence proceedings more than three years had elapsed since the date of the accident. Nevertheless, the Court of Appeal held, applying the subsection, that the proceedings were within the time limit because, in the circumstances, it ran from the date on which the plaintiff discovered his employer's identity.

Relevance of expert advice

[**11.13**] Section 14(3) is as follows:

'For the purposes of this section a person's knowledge includes knowledge which he might reasonably have been expected to acquire -
(*a*) from facts observable or ascertainable by him; or
(*b*) from facts ascertainable by him with the help of medical or other appropriate expert advice which it is reasonable for him to seek;
but a person shall not be fixed under this subsection with knowledge of a fact ascertainable only with the help of expert advice so long as he has taken all reasonable steps to obtain (and, where appropriate, to act on) that advice.'

Thus constructive, as well as actual, knowledge will be sufficient to start time running against the plaintiff if he unreasonably fails to obtain expert advice which could have been expected to reveal the true state of facts to him.[2] The proviso incorporated in the closing words of the sub-section was applied in *Marston v British Railways Board*.[3] The plaintiff was injured at work in 1957 when a chip flew off a hammer he was using, and embedded itself in his neck. Shortly after the accident expert advice was taken as to whether the hammer had been defective but the expert's report was not comprehensive and it failed to indicate, as it could have done, that the hammer had in fact been defective in a material respect. In the light of the report the

---

1   [1980] 2 All ER 471, [1980] 1 WLR 968, CA.
2   In *Davis v City and Hackney Health Authority* [1989] 2 Med LR 366 Jowitt J held, in a plaintiff's favour, that in deciding whether he had acted unreasonably for the purposes of this provision such factors as his age, background, intelligence and disabilities could be taken into account.
3   [1976] ICR 124.

216 *Limitation of actions*

plaintiff assumed that he had no cause of action against his employers, and the hammer was subsequently destroyed. It was not until 1969 that the chip itself was removed from the plaintiff's neck (it having been too dangerous to do so earlier) and expert testing of it finally revealed at that stage that the hammer had, in fact, been defective. Croom-Johnson J held, in the plaintiff's favour, that a claim brought after the discovery of the true facts was not time-barred. Since he had acted reasonably in obtaining expert advice initially, it followed from the wording of the the proviso that the inadequacy of that advice did not adversely affect the plaintiff's position.[1]

[**11.14**] It is important to note that the proviso only protects the plaintiff with respect to defective advice on questions of *fact*. It follows from the proviso to s 14(1) that if a plaintiff believes that he has no cause of action merely on account of his having received incorrect advice as to the law, time will still run against him.[2]

Discretion to override the time limit

[**11.15**] Section 33 of the 1980 Act re-enacts a provision originally introduced by the Limitation Act 1975 in the light of a recommendation made by the Law Reform Committee in its Twentieth Report.[3] The section confers a general discretion upon the court, if ' it appears ... that it would be equitable to allow an action to proceed', to direct that the three-year time limit imposed by s 11 ' shall not apply'.[4] The court is enjoined, in deciding whether to exercise the discretion, to balance the 'prejudice [to] the plaintiff' which would occur if the time limit were to be insisted upon against the 'prejudice [to] the defendants' which would occur if it were to be overridden.[5]

Factors of particular relevance

[**11.16**] Section 33(3) provides a list of particular factors to which the court should have regard in coming to its decision. The list is not, however, exhaustive.[6] The factors enumerated are as follows: the length of the plaintiff's delay and the reasons for it,[7] the effect of the delay upon the cogency of the evidence,[8] the conduct of the

---

1 Cf *Pickles v National Coal Board (Intended Action)* [1968] 2 All ER 598, [1968] 1 WLR 997, CA.
2 Cf Davies 'Limitations of the Law of Limitation' (1982) 98 LQR 249 at 255-256. See also *Halford v Brookes* [1991] 3 All ER 559, [1991] 1 WLR 428, CA.
3 See Cmnd 5630: 'Interim Report on Limitation of Actions in Personal Injury Claims' (1974).
4 Section 33(1).
5 Ibid. For discussion see Morgan 'Limitation and Discretion: Procedural Reform and Substantive Effect' (1982) 1 CJQ 109. See also Davies 'Limitations of the Law of Limitation' (1982) 98 LQR 249 at 260-275.
6 '... the court shall have regard to *all* the circumstances': s 33(3) (italics supplied). See also *Taylor v Taylor* (1984) Times, 14 April, CA.
7 Section 33(3)(*a*).
8 Section 33(3)(*b*).

defendant,[1] the duration of any disability affecting the plaintiff,[2] the degree to which the plaintiff in fact acted promptly once he knew the facts,[3] and the steps taken by the plaintiff to obtain expert advice along with the nature of any such advice.[4]

Width of discretion

[11.17] As has already been explained,[5] the discretion will not normally exist if the plaintiff has already issued a writ within the three year time limit provided by s 11, but allowed the proceedings to lapse until after that limit had expired. This appears to be the only situation, however, in which the plaintiff is actually precluded from seeking the exercise of the statutory discretion in his favour. The scope of what is now s 33 was considered by the House of Lords in *Thompson v Brown Construction (Ebbw Vale) Ltd*.[6] In a speech with which his brethren agreed, Lord Diplock observed that the 'onus of showing that in the particular circumstances of the case it would be equitable' to override the limit 'lies on the plaintiff; but, subject to that, the court's discretion to make or refuse an order if it considers it equitable to do so is, in my view, unfettered'.[7] In *Donovan v Gwentoys Ltd*[8] the plaintiff suffered an injury while below the age of majority. She brought an action less than six months after the expiry of the three-year limitation period which commenced with her eighteenth birthday. The House of Lords held, however, that in considering the prejudice to the defendants in the general exercise of its discretion the court was entitled to have regard to the fact that they were unaware of the claim until five years after the accident: ie it was not confined to considering only the delay which occurred *after* the expiry of the limitation period. The House upheld the limitation defence and Lord Oliver expressed himself as follows:[9]

> 'A defendant is always likely to be prejudiced by the dilatoriness of a plaintiff in pursuing his claim. Witnesses' memories may fade, records may be lost or destroyed, opportunities for inspection and report may be lost. The fact that the law permits a plaintiff within prescribed limits to disadvantage a defendant in this way does not mean that the defendant is not prejudiced. It merely means that he is not in a position to

---

1 Section 33(3)(*c*).
2 Section 33(3)(*d*).
3 Section 33(3)(*e*).
4 Section 33(3)(*f*). See also *Jones v GD Searle & Co Ltd* [1978] 3 All ER 654, [1979] 1 WLR 101, CA (statutory wording means that plaintiff can be required to answer an interrogatory on the nature of legal advice received, professional privilege notwithstanding).
5 See 'Limitation and Dismissal for Want of Prosecution', above.
6 [1981] 2 All ER 296, [1981] 1 WLR 744, HL.
7 Ibid at 752. See also *Firman v Ellis* [1978] QB 886, [1978] 2 All ER 851 (a decision of the Court of Appeal no longer correct on its facts, as earlier proceedings had already been commenced within the time limit, but correct on the otherwise unfettered nature of the discretion: see *Chappell v Cooper* [1980] 2 All ER 463, [1980] 1 WLR 958, CA.
8 [1990] 1 All ER 1018, [1990] 1 WLR 472, HL.
9 [1990] 1 All ER 1018 at 1025.

complain of whatever prejudice he suffers. Once a plaintiff allows the permitted time to elapse, the defendant is no longer subject to that disability, and in a situation in which the court is directed to consider all the circumstances of the case and, to balance the prejudice of the parties, the fact that the claim has, as a result of the plaintiff's failure to use the time allowed to him, become a thoroughly stale claim cannot, in my judgment, be irrelevant.'

Not to be fettered by guidelines

[**11.18**] An appellate court will therefore be very reluctant to interfere with the exercise by the trial judge of the discretion entrusted to him.[1] 'I do not consider that', said Parker LJ in *Hartley v Birmingham City District Council*,[2] 'it is either useful or desirable to attempt to lay down guidelines, for circumstances are infinitely variable. The task of the judge is to consider whether in all the circumstances it is equitable, or fair and just, that the action should be allowed to proceed'. In *Ramsden v Lee*[3] the Court of Appeal expressly declined an invitation to introduce a guideline which would in effect have constituted a presumption against exercise of the discretion in a plaintiff's favour if the delay had not been minimal and the defendant had not been at fault with respect to it.[4] It is important to note that the fact that the plaintiff may initially have sought unsuccessfully to bring himself within s 11, by relying on the 'date of knowledge' principle, is no bar to his succeeding under s 33.[5] Moreover, the same evidence which proved insufficient to establish an extended time limit under s 11 may be influential in persuading the court to exercise its discretion in the plaintiff's favour.[6] In several of the cases in which the court has overridden the time limit it had earlier ruled against the plaintiff on s 11.[7]

[**11.19**] Since every case will therefore depend on its own facts the decisions in past cases are merely examples. Clearly the longer the delay the heavier will be the burden on the plaintiff,[8] but his task will be eased if the availability of the evidence has not been substantially

1 *Conry v Simpson* [1983] 3 All ER 369, CA.
2 [1992] 2 All ER 213 at 224-225, CA.
3 [1992] 2 All ER 204, CA.
4 'To my mind there is a considerable danger in laying down guidelines where the need for guidelines has not been made entirely apparent. The risk is that then more and more cases will come which are treated as matters of law on the application not of the statute but of the guidelines': [1992] 2 All ER 204, CA, at 209 per Dillon LJ.
5 *McCafferty v Metropolitan Police District Receiver* [1977] 2 All ER 756, [1977] 1 WLR 1073, CA.
6 See, eg *McCafferty v Metropolitan Police District Receiver* [1977] 2 All ER 756, [1977] 1 WLR 1073, CA; *Buck v English Electric Co* [1978] 1 All ER 271, [1977] 1 WLR 806.
7 See, eg *McCafferty v Metropolitan Police District Receiver* and *Buck v English Electric Co* above. See also *Halford v Brookes* [1991] 3 All ER 559, [1991] 1 WLR 428, CA and *Hendy v Milton Keynes Health Authority (No 2)* [1992] 3 Med LR 114. Cf *Marston v British Railways Board* [1976] ICR 124.
8 See, eg *Davies v British Insulated Callender's Cables* (1977) 121 Sol Jo 203; *Dale v British Coal Corpn (No 2)* (1992) 136 Sol Jo LB 199, CA.

affected.¹ If the plaintiff is likely to have a remedy against his own solicitor for negligence if the normal time limit is insisted upon this will be taken into account as a factor pointing against exercise of the discretion,² but it will by no means be decisive.³ If the defendant is not fully insured this will be relevant as an indication of the degree of prejudice which *he* will suffer if the time limit is overridden.⁴ Conversely, 'it is legitimate to take into account that the defendant *is* insured. If he is deprived of his fortuitous defence he will have a claim on his insurers'.⁵

Where death results

[**11.20**] If the victim dies from his injuries, but fails to bring an action himself within the normal three-year time limit (calculated, if appropriate, from his 'date of knowledge') then it will not be possible for his dependants to bring an action under the Fatal Accidents Act 1976. Moreover the possibility that, had he lived, the court might have exercised its discretion under s 33 is to be discounted for this purpose.⁶ If, however, a claim by the deceased would not have been statute-barred in this way, then his dependants have three years from the date of his death or from 'the date of knowledge of the person for whose benefit the action is brought', whichever is the later, in which to claim.⁷ As a result, the time limit may expire at different times for different dependants depending upon their respective 'dates of knowledge'.⁸ In addition the exercise of the discretion to override the time limit, under s 33, may also be sought by dependants in a Fatal Accidents Act claim.⁹

---

1 See, eg *Buck v English Electric Co* [1978] 1 All ER 271, [1977] 1 WLR 806; *Brooks v J & P Coates (UK) Ltd* [1984] 1 All ER 702, [1984] ICR 158.
2 See *Donovan v Gwentoys Ltd* [1990] 1 All ER 1018, [1990] 1 WLR 472, HL. Cf *Unitramp SA v Jenson & Nicholson (S) Pte Ltd* [1992] 1 All ER 346, [1992] 1 WLR 862.
3 See *Thompson v Brown Construction (Ebbw Vale) Ltd* [1981] 2 All ER 296, [1981] 1 WLR 744, HL; *Ramsden v Lee* [1992] 2 All ER 204, CA. See also *Hartley v Birmingham City District Council* [1992] 2 All ER 213, especially per Parker LJ at 224, CA: '. . . if the plaintiff has to change from an action against a tortfeasor, who may know little or nothing of the weak points of his case, to an action against his solicitor, who will know a great deal about them, the prejudice may well be major rather than minor.'
4 See, eg *Davis v Soltenpar* (1983) 133 NLJ 720. Cf *Liff v Peasley* [1980] 1 WLR 781, CA at 789 per Stephenson LJ ('unrealistic and inequitable to disregard the insurance position').
5 Per Parker LJ in *Hartley v Birmingham City District Council* [1992] 2 All ER 213 at 224, CA (italics supplied).
6 Limitation Act 1980, s 12(1).
7 Ibid s 12(2).
8 Ibid s 13(1).
9 Ibid s 12(3).

Concealment of the cause of action

Start of period postponed

[**11.21**] The Limitation Act 1980, s 32 deals, inter alia, with situations in which the defendant has been guilty of fraud, or analogous misconduct, and provides for postponement of the start of the limitation period in such cases. It re-enacts, as subsequently amended, a similar provision in the Limitation Act 1939. The only provision likely to be of direct relevance in cases where the plaintiff's basic cause of action is merely for negligence is s 32(1)(*b*), which provides as follows:

> '[If] any fact relevant to the plaintiff's right to action has been deliberately concealed from him by the defendant . . . the period of limitation shall not begin to run until the plaintiff has discovered the . . . concealment . . . or could with reasonable diligence have discovered it.'

Requirements

[**11.22**] For the provision to be relevant in a negligence action there must be some factor, giving rise to the concealment, which is distinct from the defendant's initial act of carelessness itself.[1] That is to say, the subsection does not deal with the problem which arises when it is in the nature of the defendant's activity itself that any negligence may not manifest itself for some time.[2]

Nevertheless, the defendant need not have acted positively to conceal his carelessness for the provision to apply.[3] Where he is in fact aware that he has been negligent (or even merely reckless as to whether he has been or not)[4] it may be enough that the defendant simply keeps it secret, if the relationship between the parties is such that non-disclosure would be unconscionable.[5] The equivalent provision in the Limitation Act 1939 was applied in unusual circumstances in *Kitchen v RAF Association*.[6] In 1946 the defendant

---

1 Cf *UBAF Ltd v European American Banking Corpn* [1984] QB 713, [1984] 2 All ER 226, CA.
2 For this, see below, 'Latent Damage in Cases other than Personal Injury'.
3 It is to be noted that the expression 'deliberately concealed' is used in preference to the phrase 'concealed by fraud' in the equivalent provision (s 26(*b*)) of the Limitation Act 1939. This was in order to give effect to court decisions which had construed the earlier wording widely to extend to so-called 'equitable fraud': see the Twenty-first Report of the Law Reform Committee (Final Report on Limitation of Actions) pp 6-16. This legislative history would appear to cast doubt on the apparent acceptance by the Court of Appeal in *Leicester Wholesale Fruit Market v Grundy (No 2)* (1990) 53 BLR 6 at 16 that it is 'not proper to allege concealment, *just as it would not be proper to allege fraud*, unless . . . there was clearly material upon which such an allegation could be based' (italics supplied). See the *Commentary* on the case in (1990) 53 BLR at p 5.
4 Cf *Beaman v ARTS Ltd* [1949] 1 KB 550, [1949] 1 All ER 465, CA.
5 See *King v Victor Parsons & Co* [1973] 1 All ER 206, [1973] 1 WLR 29, CA.
6 [1958] 2 All ER 241, [1958] 1 WLR 563, CA.

solicitors negligently failed to bring an action on behalf of the plaintiff, against a tortfeasor, until it was impossible to do so. The tortfeasor, acting through the solicitors, subsequently made a modest ex gratia payment to the plaintiff on condition that the source of the payment was not disclosed to her. It was found as a fact that the defendants had accepted, and perhaps even themselves suggested, the secrecy requirement as a means of keeping from the plaintiff the fact of their earlier carelessness. The plaintiff did not discover what had happened until 1955, but the Court of Appeal held that the provision enabled her to sue the solicitors for their breach of duty nine years earlier.

Latent damage in cases other than personal injury

Background

[11.23] The situation in which the limitation of actions is most likely to cause hardship is where 'damage' is deemed to have occurred, so as to create a cause of action, but nevertheless fails actually to manifest itself in a discoverable form until after the time limit has expired. Reform by statute to deal with the problem came first in the personal injuries field, in the form of the provisions already discussed. Legislative change to the basic rule outside that sphere came only with the passing of the Latent Damage Act 1986. The provisions of this Act are explained below. Nevertheless, ascertainment of the date on which damage occurred or is deemed to have occurred remains the starting point for the running of time in negligence cases and may therefore necessarily still prove crucial in many situations in which limitation is in issue. Unfortunately, a degree of confusion has crept into the law on this point largely as a result of a 1983 decision of the House of Lords in which questions relating to limitation became interwoven with the principles governing the recovery of economic loss in negligence, which were at that time in a state of flux. Although the economic loss issue has now been clarified the precise effect of that clarification on the status of the case, *Pirelli General Cable Works Ltd v Oscar Faber & Partners*,[1] is not altogether clear. In *Pirelli* the defendant firm of consulting engineers negligently designed a chimney which was built for the plaintiffs. It was found as a fact that damage, in the form of cracks in the chimney, had actually occurred soon after it was built. Nevertheless, the cracks were at the very top of the chimney, and it was also found that they could not reasonably be regarded as having been actually discoverable until significantly later. The House of Lords held that time ran from the date at which the cracks first occurred, notwithstanding that they were then in practice undiscoverable, and in consequence the plaintiff's claim was statute-barred. At the time when *Pirelli* was decided it was a tenable view, which the case itself helped to reinforce, that economic loss caused by a building or chattel being merely defective, and not a

---

1 [1983] 2 AC 1, [1983] 1 All ER 65. See Ewan McKendrick '*Pirelli* re-examined' (1991) 11 LS 326.

source of damage to persons or *other* property, was recoverable in tort[1]. That assumption was, however, exploded by the decisions of the House of Lords itself in *D & F Estates Ltd v Church Comrs for England*[2] and *Murphy v Brentwood District Council*.[3] The impact of these decisions upon the law relating to limitation of actions was considered by May J in *Nitrigin Eireann Teoranta v Inco Alloys Ltd*.[4] The plaintiffs, who operated a chemical production plant, acquired alloy tubing manufactured by the defendants. Less than six years before the issue of the writ the tubing ruptured, causing gases to escape and explode, resulting in damage to the plant. The defendants argued, however, that any claim against them for negligence was statute-barred since although the explosion occurred inside the limitation period the plaintiffs had in fact discovered cracks in the building *more* than six years before the issue of the writ. The plaintiffs had taken reasonable but unsuccessful steps to diagnose the cause of the cracks and had continued to use the tubing. The defendants, relying upon *Pirelli*, contended that time ran from the cracking and not from the explosion. This contention was rejected; May J emphasised the changes which had taken place in the law relating to recovery of pure economic loss, and hence to the background to *Pirelli*, since that case had been decided. He therefore concluded that the cracking, which had merely been a defect in the tubing itself, had not provided the plaintiffs with a cause of action and that time only ran from the date of the subsequent explosion with the consequence that the claim was not out of time.

Negligent design

[11.24] It should be noted that the decision in *Pirelli General Cable Works Ltd v Oscar Faber & Partners*[5] has not actually been overruled. It was referred to by Lord Keith in *Murphy v Brentwood District Council*,[6] who suggested that it could be considered as a *Hedley Byrne* type of negligent misstatement case, rather than simply as one involving pure economic loss resulting from a defective product. On the other hand, if this is the correct interpretation, it is not altogether easy to see why time did not run from the date when the advice was acted upon by the commencement of the construction, rather than from the later date when cracks developed in the completed chimney.[7] Lord Fraser did, however, reject a submission to that effect, albeit obiter and tentatively, in his speech in *Pirelli* itself. He said:[8]

---

1   Cf *Junior Books Ltd v Veitchi Co Ltd* [1983] 1 AC 520, [1982] 3 All ER 201, HL.
2   [1989] AC 177, [1988] 2 All ER 992, HL.
3   [1991] 1 AC 398, [1990] 2 All ER 908, HL. See, generally, ch 6 above.
4   [1992] 1 All ER 854, [1992] 1 WLR 498.
5   [1983] 2 AC 1, [1983] 1 All ER 65, HL.
6   [1991] 1 AC 398 at 466, [1990] 2 All ER 908 at 919, HL.
7   Cf *Forster v Outred & Co* [1982] 2 All ER 753, [1982] 1 WLR 86, CA.
8   [1983] 1 All ER 65 at 72, [1983] 2 AC 1 at 18.

'Counsel for the defendants submitted that the fault of his clients in advising on the design of the chimney was analogous to that of a solicitor who gives negligent advice on law, which results in the client suffering damage and a right of action accruing when the client acts on the advice . . . It is not necessary for the present purpose to decide whether that submission is well founded, but as at present advised, I do not think it is. It seems to me that perhaps where the advice of an architect or consulting engineer leads to the erection of a building which is so defective as to be doomed from the start, the cause of action accrues only when physical damage occurs to the building.'

The phrase 'doomed from the start', which appears in this passage, was also used by Lord Fraser in an earlier and seemingly contradictory part of his speech.[1] The precise significance to be attached to the expression proved a difficult matter of interpretation in subsequent cases.[2] Nevertheless there is no actual presumption that damage occurs when advice is acted upon: it is a question of fact in each case.[3] Accordingly, the actual decision in *Pirelli* may still be correct if seen as one purely on limitation in a special type of negligent design case.[4]

Latent Damage Act 1986

[**11.25**] The limitation problem in cases of latent damage not involving personal injury was in referred to the Law Reform Committee in 1980. The Committee reported in 1984,[5] and its recommendations formed the basis of the Latent Damage Act 1986.[6] The Act inserts two additional sections, ss 14A and 14B, into the Limitation Act 1980. In addition the 1986 Act makes provision[7] to protect purchasers, of property with latent defects, who only acquire their interest after the cause of action has accrued but before the damage manifests itself. This was to overcome the difficulty that, not being owners at the time when the cause of action first accrued, such purchasers arguably had

---

1 'There may perhaps be cases where the defect is so gross that the building is doomed from the start, and where the owner's cause of action will accrue as soon as it is built . . .' [1983] 2 AC 1 at 16, [1983] 1 All ER 65 at 70.
2 See, eg *Ketteman v Hansel Properties* [1987] AC 189, [1988] 1 All ER 38, HL; affg [1985] 1 All ER 352, [1984] 1 WLR 1274, CA.
3 See *D W Moore & Co Ltd v Ferrier* [1988] 1 All ER 400 at 410, [1988] 1 WLR 267 at 278, CA per Neill LJ.
4 Cf *Dove v Banhams Patent Locks Ltd* [1983] 2 All ER 833, [1983] 1 WLR 1436 in which a defective security system was installed in a house 13 years before its inadequacy became apparent when it was easily foiled by a burglar. Hodgson J held that time only ran from the date of the burglary.
5 Twenty-Fourth Report ('Latent Damage') Cmnd 9390. For comment see Michael Jones 'Latent Damage – Squaring the Circle?' (1985) 48 MLR 564. See also Nicholas J Mullany 'Reform of the Law of Latent Damage' (1991) 54 MLR 349, who compares the United Kingdom approach to the problem with that adopted in other Commonwealth jurisdictions.
6 The Act is applicable generally to latent damage claims in tort for negligence and is not confined, as some had apparently suggested when the reform was being considered, to the construction industry: see the Twenty-Fourth Report of the Law Reform Committee (Latent Damage) Cmnd 9390, para 4.22 (p 25).
7 In s 3.

no cause of action at all.[1] Now they are given the same cause of action, *if any*, as if they had in fact had an interest in the property at the time when the original cause of action accrued in favour of their predecessor in title. Since, however, the scope for recovery in negligence of economic loss resulting from latent defects to property has been drastically curtailed by the common law since the Act was passed[2] this particular provision is presumably now unlikely to be invoked with any frequency.

Three year extension

[**11.26**] The new s 14A of the Limitation Act 1980 provides that the basic principle continues to be that a six-year period runs from when damage occurs, but that this is subject to an *extension* of three years, in cases involving latent defects, from the date when the damage was actually discovered or reasonably could have been discovered. Thus a plaintiff in a case where damage only becomes discoverable at the end of the six-year period will be able to claim up to nine years after the damage actually occurred. A plaintiff in a case where the damage only became discoverable *after* the six-year period had already expired would have three years, from the date of discoverability, in which to claim. Section 14A also contains detailed provisions which, broadly speaking, are similar to those already in the 1980 Act for personal injury cases,[3] dealing with the meaning of 'knowledge' for the purposes of awareness of the existence of the damage. It is important to note that the section is confined to actions in tort for negligence and does not extend to situations in which the plaintiff can claim only in contract.[4]

'Long stop'

[**11.27**] The new s 14B of the Limitation Act 1980 contains a very important 'long stop' provision to protect defendants in latent defect cases not involving personal injury. It provides that claims will in any event become statute-barred 15 years after the occurrence of the original act of negligence which gave rise to the damage, regardless of when that damage subsequently manifested itself and even if it only did so after the 15-year period itself had expired. Claims outside the

---

1 See Professor G Robertson, 'Defective Premises and Subsequent Purchasers' (1983) 99 LQR 599 and Michael Jones 'Defective Premises and Subsequent Purchasers – A comment' (1984) 100 LQR 413.
2 Ie in *D & F Estates Ltd v Church Comrs for England* [1989] AC 177, [1988] 2 All ER 992, HL and *Murphy v Brentwood District Council* [1991] 1 AC 398, [1990] 2 All ER 908, HL. See generally ch 6 above.
3 See above.
4 *Société Commerciale de Réassurance v ERAS Ltd* [1992] 2 All ER 82n, CA. See also *Iron Trade Mutual Insurance Co Ltd v JK Buckenham Ltd* [1990] 1 All ER 808.

15-year period will only be possible in the event of fraud, concealment or mistake, or where the plaintiff had been under a disability.

Where causes of action have already accrued

[11.28] The Latent Damage Act 1986, s 4 provides that its provisions will not operate retrospectively so as to resuscitate causes of action already actually statute-barred before it came into force. Accordingly the pre-existing law will continue to be of relevance in some cases. On the other hand s 4 also provides that the new provisions will apply to causes of action which accrued before the coming into force of the Act as well as after it; so plaintiffs in 'pre-Act' cases will also benefit from its provisions provided they were not already out of time on 18 September 1986, when the Act came into force.

Concurrent liability?

[11.29] A series of decisions in the 1970s suggested that, where the defendant's negligence also happened to constitute breach of a contract between himself and the plaintiff, the latter may be free to choose to sue in either contract or tort.[1] But, in contract, time begins to run from the date of the breach, regardless of when damage occurred. Accordingly, a plaintiff able to sue either in tort or contract will potentially be in a more favourable position with respect to limitation than one able only to sue in contract. On the other hand, Lord Scarman, in *Tai Hing Cotton Mill Ltd v Liu Chong Hing Bank Ltd*,[2] appeared to question the very possibility of concurrent liability and to imply that, in any matter to which the contract between them is relevant, the parties will be unable to step outside its confines by suing in tort. His Lordship expressly gave avoidance of possible confusion with respect to limitation as one of his reasons for taking this view.[3] Similarly, in the limitation case of *Bell v Peter Browne & Co*,[4] Mustill LJ thought it 'a pity that English law has elected to recognise concurrent rights of action in contract and tort . . . That precisely the same breach of precisely the same organisation should be capable of generating causes of action which arise at different times is in my judgment an anomaly which our law could well do without'.[5] It is not inconceivable that the House of Lords may decide at some stage that plaintiffs in a contractual relationship with their defendants will be confined to suing in contract if the events which

---

1   See *Midland Bank Trust Co Ltd v Hett, Stubbs and Kemp* [1979] Ch 384, [1978] 3 All ER 571; *Batty v Metropolitan Property Realisations Ltd* [1978] QB 554, [1978] 2 All ER 445, CA. See also *Esso Petroleum Co Ltd v Mardon* [1976] QB 801, [1976] 2 All ER 5, CA.
2   [1986] AC 80 at 107, PC.
3   Cf *Bagot v Stevens, Scanlan & Co Ltd* [1966] 1 QB 197, [1964] 3 All ER 577.
4   [1990] 3 All ER 124 at 134, CA.
5   See also observations by the same judge in *Société Commerciale de Réssurance v ERAS Ltd* [1992] 2 All ER 82n at 85, and by Evans J in *Islander Trucking v Hogg Robinson Ltd* [1990] 1 All ER 826 at 834-835.

caused their loss were originally actionable under the agreement. The scope of the Latent Damage Act would, however, be significantly narrowed if persons in a contractual relationship with the defendant were unable to invoke it. Nor should it be thought that the possibility of concurrent liability in some cases renders the very existence of a different limitation period for contract claims anomalous. In the majority of cases of breach of contract liability is strict and the defendant will therefore not necessarily have been at fault. It is therefore at least arguable that a shorter limitation period in such cases is defensible. But in the case of professional people exercising special skills, whose contractual liability is normally fault-based only, the existence of differing limitation periods for contract and tort does seem difficult to support. Moreover, the work of such people is more than usually apt to give rise to limitation problems if something goes wrong. The fundamental issue, here as elsewhere, is whether preservation of a rigid distinction between tort and contract makes sense in contemporary circumstances.

Part four

Negligence against a statutory background

Chapter 12

Negligence and the exercise of statutory powers

The problem of discretion

The early decisions

[12.01] It was established well over a century ago that bodies which owe their existence and functions to Acts of Parliament can, in appropriate cases, be liable in tort for negligence. In *Mersey Docks and Harbour Board Trustees v Gibbs*[1] the trustees, a statutory body, were held liable for carelessly allowing an accumulation of mud to occur at their dock. Damage was caused to the cargo of a ship when a collision took place between the ship and the bank of mud. The trustees argument that as a non-profit-making statutory body, which raised money solely for the purpose of operating the dock, their funds should not be called upon to pay damages, was rejected. Subject to any contrary indication in the statute creating the particular body in question, the legislature was presumed to have 'intended that the liability of corporations thus substituted for individuals should, to the extent of their corporate funds, be co-extensive with that imposed by the general law on the owners of similar works.'[2] If necessary they would have to use their statutory fund-raising powers to acquire the additional finance necessary to meet any claims. Thus, if the plaintiff has been the victim of straightforward negligence, such as a carelessly caused traffic accident, the status of the defendant, whether it be a statutory body, a limited company, or a private individual, will usually be irrelevant.[3]

1 (1866) LR 1 HL 93, HL.
2 Per Blackburn J in (1866) LR 1 HL at 107 (delivering the opinion of the judges requested by the House of Lords).
3 In theory, and depending upon the construction of the statute, the defence of statutory authority may of course be available to bodies exercising statutory powers. In practice, however, this defence is unlikely ever to avail against a negligence claim. Parliament is presumed to intend that statutory powers be exercised without carelessness (see *Geddis v Proprietors of Bann Reservoir* (1878) 3 App Cas 430 at 455, HL, per Lord Blackburn). But in any event, the infinite variety of forms which carelessness may take would make it impossible for Parliament to authorise it in advance by the use of normal drafting techniques.

Nevertheless, as the range and complexity of statutory powers became greater, with the increased outpouring of legislation in recent times, the courts gradually became aware that not all cases involving alleged carelessness in the exercise of statutory powers could in fact simply be treated as indistinguishable from ordinary negligence claims against individuals or commercial organisations. In some situations the body in question may have been endowed with a very wide discretion, the nature of which implies that reconsideration of its decisions, within the limited framework of a private law claim for damages in negligence, is unlikely to be appropriate.

[**12.02**] In the cases in which this problem was first perceived the effect was to produce decisions which, whether or not they were correct on their facts, were certainly based on reasoning and distinctions which now seem somewhat clumsy and difficult to support. In *Sheppard v Glossop Corp*[1] the defendants had a statutory power to provide street lighting. They exercised it, but from 'motives of economy'[2] switched off the lamps every evening at 9 pm. The plaintiff met with an accident at 11.30 pm, which lighting would probably have prevented. The Court of Appeal dismissed the claim on the short ground that the Act itself did not impose any actual duty on the defendants to light, and that it followed that the plaintiff should fail as there would have been nothing wrongful if the defendants had simply chosen not to exercise their discretion and had provided no lighting at all. The court observed that the result might have been different if the defendants had themselves created the source of danger which had become hazardous due to lack of illumination,[3] but that was not the case. Similarly, in *East Suffolk Rivers Catchment Board v Kent*[4] a board entrusted with statutory powers to deal with flood-damage was held not liable when, in exercising its powers, it adopted very inefficient methods and in consequence allowed flooding to continue for much longer than it otherwise would have done. The board had to strike 'a just balance between the rival claims of efficiency and thrift'[5] and could have chosen not to exercise their powers at all. The House of Lords indicated that liability could have been imposed if the board's activities had actually made matters worse and *added* to the damage which the flooding had caused to the plaintiff,[6] but on the facts they had merely failed to remedy loss caused essentially by natural agencies as swiftly as they might otherwise have done.

---

1 [1921] 3 KB 132, CA.
2 Ibid at 144 per Scrutton LJ.
3 See ibid at 140 (Bankes LJ); 143-144 (Scrutton LJ) and 151 (Atkin LJ). Cf *Fisher v Ruislip-Northwood UDC* [1945] KB 584, [1945] 2 All ER 458, CA.
4 [1941] AC 74, [1940] 4 All ER 527, HL.
5 Per du Parcq LJ *dissenting* in the Court of Appeal (the decision of which was reversed by the House of Lords), and quoted with approval by Viscount Simon LC in [1941] AC at 86, [1940] 4 All ER 527 at 532 and by Lord Romer at 103 and 544.
6 See [1941] AC at 102, [1940] 4 All ER 527 at 542 per Lord Romer and 104 and 545 per Lord Porter.

The policy and operational distinction

[**12.03**] In two decisions of the House of Lords in the 1970s an approach, more sophisticated than that previously adopted, was fashioned to deal with the problem of carelessness in the exercise of statutory powers. In *Home Office v Dorset Yacht Co*[1] the property of the plaintiff yacht company was damaged by borstal boys in the course of their escape from an open borstal, an escape which had allegedly been facilitated by carelessness on the part of prison officers. The House of Lords held that, in principle, the Home Office could be liable for negligence on such facts. The defendants contended that the possibility of such liability would unduly fetter the exercise of statutory powers to run open prisons and borstals, which inevitably involve a greater degree of risk of escapes than other types of prison regime. The House accepted that it would certainly not be appropriate for the courts to seek to evaluate the merits of penal policies as such, but denied that imposition of liability for specific acts of carelessness by prison officers *in carrying out* whatever policy was chosen by the Home Office would have that effect. Lord Diplock, in particular, drew attention to the role of the ultra vires doctrine in limiting the scope and effectiveness of challenges in the courts to administrative decisions. In his Lordship's view it was a condition precedent to a successful negligence action arising out of the exercise of a statutory power that the acts or decisions impugned should have been ultra vires the power in question.[2] Once this was established the court could proceed to consider whether the carelessness allegedly involved did in truth amount to actionable negligence. Although this analysis was beneficial in identifying explicitly the underlying problem involved in cases of negligence against the background of statutory discretion it did not, in itself, constitute a solution to that problem. In particular the precise relationship which had to exist, if liability was to be imposed, between the exercise of the discretion and the act of carelessness remained unclear. The latter may have been far removed from the former both in time and space. In the *Dorset Yacht* case itself penal policy was decided in the Home Office, but the immediate cause of the escape was alleged to be prison officers sleeping on duty on an island off the south coast. To require that this carelessness should be measured against the administrative law criteria used to determine the validity of discretionary decisions, even if only as a preliminary to applying the ordinary tests of the tort of negligence, seemed rather artificial.

[**12.04**] Some degree of clarification was provided by the decision of the House of Lords in *Anns v Merton London Borough Council*,[3] which still retains a measure of influence in this particular area despite being subsequently overruled on another point.[4] In this case the

---

1 [1970] AC 1004, [1970] 2 All ER 294, HL.
2 See ibid at 1064-1069 and 331-335.
3 [1978] AC 728, [1977] 2 All ER 492, HL.
4 Ie the recoverability of economic loss in the circumstances of the case: see *Murphy v Brentwoood District Council* [1991] 1 AC 398, [1990] 2 All ER 908, HL. For discussion see, generally, ch 6 above; see also ch 1.

plaintiffs' flats developed structural damage as a result of having been built on inadequate foundations. They sought to sue, inter alia, the local authority for the area in question which possessed statutory powers, under the Public Health Act 1936 and byelaws made thereunder, to inspect and approve the foundations of new buildings.[1] It was unclear on the facts whether the foundations had been inspected carelessly or not inspected at all. The defendant local authority contended that since it had a statutory discretion it was free to choose not to exercise its powers at all, and that it should be immune from liability for negligence lest that discretion be subverted by its being turned into a *duty* to inspect in all cases. The matter was tried as a preliminary issue and the House of Lords in effect conceded the premise, but denied that the conclusion followed from it. The authority was free to choose to make no inspections, or to adopt a limited system of inspection, provided that in choosing to exercise its discretion in that way, perhaps for reasons of economy, it acted intra vires. This requirement would necessarily include the giving, in reaching its decision, of due and proper consideration to all the relevant factors. But once a system of making inspections had in fact been adopted, liability for negligence could be imposed if due to carelessness in its implementation the task itself was carried out negligently, or inspections which ought to have been made under the system were inadvertently omitted. Lord Wilberforce drew a distinction which was intended both to protect discretions from being improperly fettered, and to delineate the area within which negligence claims could nevertheless be entertained. He said:[2]

> 'Most, indeed probably all, statutes relating to public authorities or public bodies, contain in them a large area of policy. The courts call this "discretion" meaning that the decision is one for the authority or body to make, and not for the courts. Many statutes also prescribe or at least presuppose the practical execution of policy decisions: a convenient description of this is to say that in addition to the area of policy or discretion, there is an operational area. Although this distinction between the policy area and the operational area is convenient, and illuminating, it is probably a distinction of degree; many "operational" powers or duties have in them some element of "discretion". It can safely be said that the more "operational" a power or duty may be, the easier it is to superimpose upon it a common law duty of care.'

The distinction thus drawn between the policy and operational spheres represented an ambitious attempt to reconcile the need to protect discretionary powers from being unduly restricted, with the perceived need to provide a remedy in tort for losses suffered through carelessness.[3] It raised, however, a number of questions and difficulties which have yet to be fully resolved, and in later cases the

---

1 See also *Dutton v Bognor Regis UDC* [1972] 1 QB 373, [1972] 1 All ER 462 (a decision of the Court of Appeal approved by the House of Lords in *Anns* case, but on different grounds). For recent legislation on building control see the Building Act 1984.
2 [1978] AC 728 at 754.
3 The distinction originated in American case-law: see Craig, 'Negligence in the Exercise of a Statutory Power' (1978) 94 LQR 428 at 442-447.

tendency has been to treat it as a somewhat loose presumption rather than as a firmly established doctrine.[1]

The policy 'immunity'

Applicability

[**12.05**] In what might be termed 'ordinary' cases of negligence which nevertheless involve some statutory element in the background, such as a road accident caused by the careless driving of an employee of a statutory body on that body's business, the distinction between policy and operational areas of activity would seem to be neither helpful nor relevant.[2] The case should be decided on the same basis as negligence cases generally, without the added complication of that distinction. A difficulty at the outset, however, is to know precisely which cases fall within the 'ordinary' category and which do not. In *Home Office v Dorset Yacht Co*,[3] Lord Diplock suggested that the test is whether 'the act or omission complained of is not of a kind which would itself give rise to a cause of action at common law if it were not authorised by the statute'. Thus in the *Dorset Yacht* case itself the statutory power to detain the borstal boys was the foundation of the negligence claim in the sense that, without that power, it would have been wrongful to have detained the boys at all; and a complaint about premature release would therefore have been meaningless. Similarly, in *Anns v Merton London Borough Council*,[4] the complaint about careless inspection of the building would have been meaningless without the statutory power to inspect. In the road accident cases, by contrast, the obvious analogy with ordinary litigation between private individuals would place such cases clearly on the other side of the line, even if the accident was caused by someone driving a vehicle in pursuance of a purpose ultimately referable to a statute. The Diplock test does, therefore, have a certain utility as a rough and ready guide to the applicability of the policy and operational dichotomy. Nevertheless, as Harlow pointed out,[5] in strict logic the test is circular and hence cannot ultimately provide a sound basis for distinguishing between cases in which the dichotomy will be relevant and cases in which it will not.[6] This is because carelessness may take an infinite variety of forms, and it is therefore impossible to predicate of a certain act that it could never 'give rise to a cause of action at common law'. Even the fact situations in *Dorset Yacht* and *Anns*, which give the Diplock test

---

1 See, especially, *Rowling v Takaro Properties Ltd* [1988] AC 473, [1988] 1 All ER 163, and *Lonrho plc v Tebbit* [1992] 4 All ER 280, CA; affg [1991] 4 All ER 973, discussed below.
2 Cf *Woolfall v Knowsley Borough Council* (1992) Times, 26 June, CA (no excuse that a local authority failed to remove rubbish which constituted a hazard merely because it wished to avoid aggravating an industrial dispute with its employees).
3 [1970] AC 1004 at 1066, [1970] 2 All ER 294 at 331, HL.
4 [1978] AC 728, [1977] 2 All ER 492, HL.
5 See 'Fault Liability in French and English Public Law' (1976) 39 MLR 516 at 531.
6 See also Bailey and Bowman 'The Policy/Operational Dichotomy – A Cuckoo in the Nest'(1986) 45 CLJ 430 at 432.

an appearance of plausibility, have analogies with other tort cases not involving statutory powers. Thus a private school may release a small child prematurely and hence cause an accident,[1] or a solicitor's carelessness committed against the background of his contractual relationship with his client may cause loss to a third party.[2] In both situations ordinary common law claims for negligence may exist, and yet they are not wholly dissimilar from the situations in *Dorset Yacht* and *Anns* respectively. This does not, of course, in itself indicate that the policy and operational dichotomy was irrelevant even in the cases in which it was developed, but simply that the Diplock test for the applicability of the dichotomy is flawed.

Presumption

[12.06] To assume that every case involving an allegation of negligence against the background of a statutory power had to be subjected at the outset to some test to determine whether it was one to which the policy and operational dichotomy applied and, if so, whether the alleged carelessness fell within one category or the other, would be to adopt an approach both unnecessarily cumbersome and dubious in principle. From a constitutional standpoint the objection in principle is that the approach would notionally place all negligence claims against public bodies in a special category, and hence conflict with the ideal of equality before the law. The approach is unduly cumbersome in that a great many of the cases involving statutory powers which would be 'tested' for the applicability of the dichotomy would result in its being held irrelevant on their facts: the motor accident cases being the prime example. This is not to say, however, that the need to protect bodies exercising statutory discretions from being unduly fettered does not justify some negligence actions against public bodies being treated differently from ordinary tort claims against private individuals. The right approach would appear to be to *presume* that all negligence claims against bodies exercising statutory powers are to be governed by private law principles, *unless* the body in question succeeds in satisfying the court that the facts bring the case within the scope of a 'defence', or objection to judicial scrutiny, based upon public policy.[3] This concept would be intended to ensure that matters not appropriate to determination by the court, at least in the context of a negligence action, are properly kept non-justiciable. Thus in *Rowling v Takaro Properties*[4] Lord Keith, delivering the judgment of the Judicial Committee of the Privy Council, said[5] that the distinction between policy and operational areas 'does not provide a touchstone of liability, but rather is expressive of the need to exclude altogether those cases in which the decision under attack is of such a

---

1 Cf *Carmarthenshire County Council v Lewis* [1955] AC 549, [1955] 1 All ER 565, HL.
2 Eg as in *White v Jones* [1993] NLJR 473, CA, applying *Ross v Caunters* [1980] Ch 297, [1979] 3 All ER 580.
3 Cf the 'public interest immunity' relating to the withholding of documents.
4 [1988] AC 473, [1988] 1 All ER 163.
5 [1988] 1 All ER 163 at 172, [1988] AC 473 at 501.

kind that a question whether it has been made negligently is unsuitable for judicial resolution.'

Justiciability of government decisions

[**12.07**] In the *Rowling* case the plaintiff was refused consent by the Government of New Zealand for a proposed enterprise in that country. This refusal was subsequently held by the courts to have been ultra vires, as having been based upon irrelevant considerations. But by the time the legality of the enterprise had been determined it was too late to proceed with it and the plaintiff thereupon brought a negligence action against the government for economic loss alleging, inter alia, that the minister in question had been careless in failing to take adequate legal advice before improperly refusing the consent. On appeal to the Privy Council it was held that the claim would fail. It is interesting, however, that the board expressly declined to decide that the issue was non-justiciable but held instead that, on the assumption that it *was* justiciable, the situation was one in which, even had carelessness been established which it had not, the imposition of a duty of care would be inappropriate for pragmatic reasons.[1] Lord Keith said:[2]

> '[Their Lordships] recognise that the decision of the minister is capable of being described as having been of a policy rather than an operational character; but, if the function of the policy/operational dichotomy is as they have already described it, the allegation of negligence in the present case is not, they consider, of itself of such a character as to render the case unsuitable for judicial decision. Be that as it may, there are certain considerations which militate against imposition of liability in a case such as the present.'

The possibility of actually imposing liability upon government, for inaction in what could broadly be described as a policy context, was contemplated by the Court of Appeal in *Lonrho plc v Tebbit*[3]. The plaintiff company had given an undertaking to the Secretary of State for Trade and Industry that it would not acquire more than 30% of the shares in a certain company, following a report by the Monopolies and Mergers Commission that it would be against the public interest for it to do so. A subsequent report by the Commission concluded that acquisition of the company by the plaintiffs would not, after all, be against the public interest and the Secretary of State eventually released them from their undertaking. That release did, however, come too late for the plaintiffs to launch a takeover bid for the company in question, which they would otherwise have done, and they alleged that this delay had been avoidable and negligent and had caused them economic loss. The defendant (ie the government) sought to have the claim struck out on the ground that it disclosed no cause of action. Sir Nicolas-Browne Wilkinson V-C, in a judgment upheld by the Court of Appeal, held that the striking out application would fail.

---

1 For which see below.
2 [1988] 1 All ER 163 at 172, [1988] AC 1 at 501.
3 [1992] 4 All ER 280, CA; affg [1991] 4 All ER 973.

Notwithstanding the statutory and governmental context of the negligence action, and the fact that the claim was for economic loss, it was arguable that there were no contervailing considerations of public interest which would necessarily preclude the imposition upon the defendant of a private law duty of care in favour of the defendant.

Could ordinary negligence concepts do the job?

[12.08] It is sometimes argued that distinctions such as that between policy and operational decisions or spheres of activity is unnecessary, and that the normal principles of the law of negligence themselves embody sufficient flexibility to cater for the problems relating to the exercise of statutory discretions.[1] Indeed a measure of support for this view may perhaps be gleaned from the approach adopted in the *Rowling* and *Lonrho* cases themselves. It is certainly the case that determinations in 'ordinary' negligence cases may involve evaluative elements. Thus, foreseeability of a risk does not, of itself, give rise to a duty to obviate it.[2] Furthermore, the concept of reasonable care, as a test for the actual imposition of liability (or 'breach of duty'), allows for the degree of risk to be measured both against the resources necessary to provide protection from it,[3] and against conflicting objectives which may sometimes legitimately be allowed to take priority over safety.[4] It is nevertheless submitted that the framework of the ordinary private law of negligence is still not adequate, at least without very considerable modification, to take the weight of the need for a special approach where wide statutory discretions are concerned. The extent to which evaluative considerations play a part in determining reasonableness is too confined and limited to allow for recognition within itself of the existence of a wide area, where even to begin to bring the machinery of negligence to bear upon the issues involved would be an inappropriate exercise. Of course it may be objected that the difference is merely one of degree and that the debate is ultimately semantic. But the purpose of legal concepts should be to promote clarity and to bring into sharp focus the differing factors relevant to disputes, thereby facilitating their resolution in as satisfactory a manner as possible. The temptation to use Ockham's razor so as to achieve spurious over-simplification, or artificial elegance in exposition of the law, should be resisted.[5] In this branch of the law, after all, the consequences of attempting to grapple with situations involving negligence against the background of statutory

---

1   See Bailey and Bowman 'The Policy/Operational Dichotomy – A Cuckoo in the Nest' (1986) 45 CLJ 430. See also the same writers' 'Negligence in the Realms of Public Law - A Positive Obligation to Rescue?' [1984] PL 277.
2   *Bolton v Stone* [1951] AC 850, [1951] 1 All ER 1078, HL See, generally, ch 2, above.
3   See, eg *Latimer v AEC Ltd* [1953] AC 643, [1953] 2 All ER 449, HL.
4   See, eg *Watt v Hertfordshire County Council* [1954] 2 All ER 368, [1954] 1 WLR 835, CA.
5   Cf the debate over whether the tort of nuisance could be assimilated within that of negligence, considered by the present writer in *The Law of Nuisance* (1981) pp 3-4 and 19-21.

discretions, by using the ordinary negligence framework and without overt recognition of the special problems involved, can readily be seen in the earlier cases. Those consequences included the proliferation of unsatisfactory distinctions such as that between new and existing sources of danger,[1] and mechanistic application of the distinction between misfeasance and nonfeasance.[2] To advocate rejection of the insights provided by cases such as *Dorset Yacht* and *Anns*, in favour of a return to the older approach, therefore seems very difficult to support.

[**12.09**] While the constitutional issues highlighted by justiciability and related concepts should therefore not be lost sight of, the utility of necessarily imprecise distinctions such as that between policy and operational decisions nevertheless appears admittedly to be somewhat limited as a vehicle for exposition of the current law. While the judicial trend in negligence generally towards pragmatism rather than principle may be regretted, the flexibility which it confers in very difficult and developing areas such as the present is not wholly without its advantages. The most constructive approach is therefore to attempt to identify the kinds of situation in which liability will be imposed, or not imposed, upon bodies exercising statutory discretions, and the factors which the courts take into account in reaching their decisions. While some judgments use the language of immunity or justiciability, and others use that of pragmatism and private law negligence, it is not unlikely that they reflect a broadly shared underlying judicial perception as to the proper extent of liability.

Factors which bear upon liability

Competing public interests

[**12.10**] 'In my judgment', said Sir Nicolas Browne-Wilkinson V-C in *Lonrho plc v Tebbitt*,[3] 'it is well established that in cases where the exercise of a statutory discretion involves the weighing of competing public interests, particularly financial or economic interests, no private law duty of care arises because the matter is not justiciable by the courts. It is for the body to whom Parliament has committed that discretion to weigh the competing public interest factors: the courts cannot undertake that task.'[4]

Since so much depends on the circumstances of the particular case the emergence of highly specific criteria is unlikely.[5] The best that can be

---

1 See *Sheppard v Glossop Corpn* [1921] 3 KB 132, CA.
2 See *East Suffolk Rivers Catchment Board v Kent* [1941] AC 74, [1940] 4 All ER 527, HL.
3 [1991] 4 All ER 973 at 981.
4 See also *Sutherland Shire Council v Heyman* (1985) 59 ALJR 564 at 582 per Mason J.
5 For extensive discussion of the case law from a number of common law jurisdictions see Aronson and Whitmore *Public Torts and Contracts*, (1982, Sydney) pp 36-99.

238 *Negligence and the exercise of statutory powers*

done is to provide examples. The reasoning in *Home Office v Dorset Yacht Co*[1] itself indicates that if the escapes in that case had been brought about by the decision to allocate the borstal boys to the particular institution in question, with the relaxed regime the existence of which itself reflected a high-level decision on penal policy, the Home Office would enjoy an immunity from suit which would not apply if prison officers had simply fallen asleep on duty.[2] Similarly if, in *Anns v Merton London Borough Council*,[3] the building site had not been inspected because of a policy decision, perhaps reflecting economic constraints, to reduce inspections generally or to adopt a random system of inspection, the public policy objection to liability would have applied.[4] In two cases reported in the 1980s decisions taken in the exercise of statutory discretions to determine the placing of road-hazard markings on highways,[5] and the extent to which measures should be adopted by a highway authority to control the hazard to road-users posed by stray-dogs,[6] were unsuccessfully challenged with the court in each case emphasising the degree of policy content in the decisions. In *Department of Health and Social Security v Kinnear*[7] the Department succeeded in getting struck out certain allegations in a negligence action arising out of the use of whooping cough vaccine. The policy of promoting immunisation had been taken in pursuance of statutory powers conferred by the National Health Service Act 1946. In *Hill v Chief Constable for West Yorkshire*,[8] which raised analogous issues even though strictly speaking it concerned a common law power, the House of Lords refused to accept that liability could be imposed upon the police in respect of alleged negligence by them in investigating crime. 'The manner of such an investigation', observed Lord Keith,[9] 'must necessarily involve a variety of decisions to be made on matters of policy and discretion, for example as to which particular line of inquiry is most advantageously to be pursued and what is the most advantageous way to deploy the available resources'.[10]

Liability imposed

[**12.11**] If the decision taken pursuant to the statutory power does involve the making of broad choices affecting the allocation of

---

1 [1970] AC 1004, [1970] 2 All ER 294 HL. Cf *Evangelical United Brethren v State* 407 P 2d 440 (1965).
2 See [1970] AC 1004 at 1068-1069, [1970] 2 All ER 294 at 332-333 per Lord Diplock.
3 [1978] AC 728, [1977] 2 All ER 492, HL.
4 See Craig 'Negligence in the Exercise of a Statutory Power' (1978) 94 LQR 428 at 440.
5 *West v Buckinghamshire County Council* (1984) 83 LGR 449. See also *Weiss v Fote* 167 NE 2d 63 (1960) (timing of traffic lights). But cf *Bird v Pearce* [1978] RTR 290; affd [1979] RTR 369, CA.
6 *Allison v Corby District Council* [1980] RTR 111.
7 (1984) 134 NLJ 886.
8 [1989] AC 53, [1988] 2 All ER 238, HL.
9 [1988] 2 All ER 238 at 244, [1989 AC 53 at 63].
10 See also *Ancell v McDermott* (1993) Times, 4 February.

resources it is not unlikely that the court will decline to entertain a negligence claim. In *Anns v Merton London Borough Council* itself Lord Wilberforce, while casting doubt on the overall reasoning in *East Suffolk Rivers Catchment Board v Kent*,[1] referred with approval to one familiar phrase from that case observing that 'public authorities have to strike a balance between the claims of efficiency and thrift: whether they get the balance right can only be decided through the ballot box, not in the courts'.[2] Nevertheless, it is important to bear in mind that the 'resources' point is only one factor that may be relevant in determining where the public interest lies in a particular case. Many decisions which would unquestionably be regarded as justiciable will have resource implications:[3] the level of expenditure necessary to achieve a safe system of work in a government factory for example. Thus in in *Indian Towing Co v United States*[4] the defendant Coast Guard authority, in the exercise of a statutory discretion, erected a lighthouse. Due to carelessness in maintaining it, however, the light was not illuminated when the plaintiff's vessel ran aground in circumstances in which it would probably not have done if the lighthouse had been functioning properly. 'The Coast Guard', said Mr Justice Frankfurter in the US Supreme Court, 'need not undertake the lighthouse service. But once it exercised its discretion to operate a light . . . it was obligated to use due care to make certain that the light was kept in good working order'. Similarly, attempts by local authorities in England to avoid liability for negligence against the background of statutory discretion by seeking to invoke public policy not infrequently fail. The defence was rejected in *Bird v Pearce*[5] in which the claim arose out of an accident partly caused by the defendant local authority's failure to take advantage of its powers to erect a temporary traffic sign at a dangerous road junction, when the permanent markings were obliterated during maintenance work. In *Vicar of Writtle v Essex County Council*[6] liability was imposed in circumstances which recalled *Home Office v Dorset Yacht Co*[7] itself. Inadequate supervision by social workers of a boy with fire-raising propensities, who had been remanded into the care of the defendant local authority, left him with sufficient freedom to enable him to set fire to the plaintiff's church.

Regulatory functions

[**12.12**] In *Davis v Radcliffe*[8] the plaintiffs lost money when a bank, which had been operated under a licence issued by an agency of the Government of the Isle of Man, collapsed. The plaintiffs sued the

1 [1941] AC 74, [1940] 4 All ER 527, HL and see above.
2 [1978] AC 728 at 754, HL.
3 See Peter Cane *An Introduction to Administrative Law*, 2nd edn (1992) pp 245-247.
4 350 US 61, 76 S Ct 122 (1955).
5 [1979] RTR 369 CA; affg [1978] RTR 290.
6 (1979) 77 LGR 656. See also *Johnson v State of California* 447 P 2d 352 (1968).
7 [1970] AC 1004, [1970] 2 All ER 294, HL.
8 [1990] 2 All ER 536, [1990] 1 WLR 821.

defendant agency for negligence in not revoking the licence. But the Privy Council held that the defendants owed no duty of care to the plaintiff and, applying an earlier decision of its own in an appeal from Hong Kong involving similar facts,[1] struck the claim out. Lord Goff said:[2]

> '... it must have been the statutory intention that the licensing system should be operated in the interests of the public as a whole; and, when those charged with its operation are faced with making decisions with regard, for example, to refusing to renew licences or to revoking licences, such decisions can well involve the exercise of judgment of a delicate nature affecting the whole future of the relevant bank in the Isle of Man, and the impact of any consequent cessation of the bank's business in the Isle of Man, not merely on the customers and creditors of the bank, but indeed on the future of financial services in the island. In circumstances such as these, competing interests have to be carefully weighed and balanced in the public interest, and, in some circumstances ... it may for example be more in the public interest to attempt to nurse an ailing bank back to health than to hasten its collapse. The making of decisions such as these is a characteristc task of modern regulatory agencies; and the very nature of the task, with its emphasis on the broader public interest, is one which militates strongly against the imposition of a duty of care being imposed on such an agency in favour of any particular section of the public.'[3]

Thus bodies entrusted with regulatory functions in the public interest are unlikely to be subject to negligence liability in so far as the discharge of wide discretionary functions is concerned. But if the exercise of discretion is not involved it appears that liability may be imposed even if the overall context is one of regulatory governmental activity in the public interest. Thus in *Lonrho plc v Tebbit*[4] Sir Nicolas Browne-Wilkinson V-C, and the Court of Appeal, were prepared to contemplate the possibility of the Secretary of State for Trade and Industry being liable for negligence in failing promptly to release the plaintiffs from an undertaking given by them following a report from the Monopolies and Mergers Commission, once that report had been superseded.[5]

Statutory purpose

[12.13] In *Peabody Donation Fund (Governors) v Sir Lindsay Parkinson & Co Ltd*[6] the House of Lords had occasion to consider the law relating to negligence claims against local authorities, arising out

---

1 See *Yuen Kun Yeu v A-G of Hong Kong* [1988] AC 175, [1987] 2 All ER 705.
2 [1990] 2 All ER 536 at 541.
3 See also *Minories Finance Ltd v Arthur Young (a firm)* [1989] 2 All ER 105.
4 [1991] 4 All ER 973; affd [1992] 4 All ER 280.
5 'For all I know, the reason for the delay in releasing the undertaking was a purely administrative blunder (eg the papers being wrongly filed), involving no considerations of policy at all': [1991] 4 All ER 973 at 985 per Sir Nicolas Browne-Wilkinson V-C.
6 [1985] AC 210, [1984] 3 All ER 529, HL.

of building control, at a time when *Anns v Merton London Borough Council*[1] was still the leading case in the area. The plaintiffs, a charitable body, were building developers of a large-scale housing project. They suffered substantial losses when, due to the negligence of their own architects, a defective drainage system was incorporated in the development and had to be replaced. Lambeth London Borough Council had initially approved plans for an effective drainage system but failed to exercise their powers of building control under the London Government Act 1963[2] to prevent the ultimately harmful departure from those plans, even when that departure was brought to the notice of their building inspector in the course of construction. The plaintiffs accordingly sued the local authority as well as the architects. The latter settled the claim against them but the trial judge held the local authority liable, under the *Anns* principle, for 25% of the loss. His judgment was, however, reversed by a unanimous Court of Appeal, whose denial of any liability at all on the local authority, was in turn affirmed by a unanimous House of Lords. In view of the overruling of the *Anns* case[3] a claim such as that in *Peabody* would obviously now be wholly untenable but as the law then stood that was not the case. The significance of the decision for present purposes is the way in which the House of Lords focused upon the nature of the statutory background against which the claim was made.[4] Lord Keith delivered the only speech, the four other members of the House being content to express their agreement with it. Lord Keith expressed the main reason for the decision as follows:[5]

> 'The purpose for which the powers... have been conferred on Lambeth is not to safeguard building developers against economic loss resulting from their failure to comply with approved plans. It is in my opinion to safeguard the occupiers of houses built in the local authority's area, and also members of the public generally, against dangers to their health which may arise from defective drainage installations. The provisions are public health measures.'

Economic loss

[**12.14**] The approach adopted in the *Peabody* case clearly resembles that adopted in the longer-established context of actions in tort for breach of statutory *duty*, in which the general legislative purpose underlying the statute in question is of paramount importance.[6] In *Peabody* the adoption of this approach led to the conclusion that the imposition of liability would be inappropriate. But this will not always

---

1 [1978] AC 728, [1977] 2 All ER 492, HL.
2 Schedule 9, Pt III paras 13(1) and 15(1) and (2).
3 Ie in *Murphy v Brentwood District Council* [1991] 1 AC 398, [1990] 2 All ER 908: see ch 6 above, see also ch 1.
4 See also *Curran v Northern Ireland Co-ownership Housing Association Ltd* [1987] AC 718, [1987] 2 All ER 13, HL.
5 [1985] AC 210 at 241, [1984] 3 All ER 529 at 534-535.
6 See, generally, Stanton *Breach of Statutory Duty in Tort* (1986); Buckley 'Liability in Tort for Breach of Statutory Duty' (1984) 100 LQR 204. See also ch 13 below.

be the case. In other contexts statutory powers are frequently concerned overtly with financial matters; and in view of the increasing hostility of the common law to the recovery of pure economic loss, outside the narrowly defined area of negligent misstatment, questions may arise as to the legitimacy of permitting the recovery of such loss by virtue of the statute. An answer broadly favourable in principle to such liability was given by Sir Nicolas Browne-Wilkinson V-C at first instance in *Lonrho plc v Tebbit*. He said:[1]

> 'Lonrho's claim is for economic loss only. The defendants contend that English law does not recognise that there can ever be a duty of care owed by someone exercising statutory powers not to cause economic loss to those affected by the exercise of such powers . . . In my judgment the. . . contention is unsustainable. If it is held that the circumstances otherwise justify the imposition of a duty of care in the exercise of these statutory powers, the fact that the damage suffered is purely economic will not, by itself, exclude liability. In most cases involving the negligent exercise of statutory powers the loss suffered by the plaintiff will be purely economic . . . (T)he fact that the damage claimed is purely economic is not, by itself, decisive so as to preclude an action for negligence which would otherwise be appropriate.'

Carelessness and policy

Danger of 'overkill'

[**12.15**] At least in theory it seems to be clear that a body upon which a statutory power has been conferred may lose the protection of the public policy 'defence', and hence become subject to liability in negligence, even if the alleged carelessness related to the exercise or non-exercise of the discretion itself.[2] That is to say a claim in negligence is not a weapon which is inherently limited to the so-called 'operational' sphere. A condition precedent to the establishment of such liability at the 'planning' or 'policy' level is that the body in question should have acted ultra vires the statutory power. This indeed lies at the heart of the reasoning both of Lord Diplock in *Home Office v Dorset Yacht Co*[3] and of Lord Wilberforce in *Anns v Merton London Borough Council*.[4] Even if this condition is satisfied, however, it will be far from easy to make out a valid claim in negligence. The mere fact that a decision was ultra vires certainly does not mean that it was necessarily taken negligently. In *Dunlop v Woollahra Municipal Council*[5] the plaintiff complained that he had suffered loss as a result of certain resolutions of a local planning authority, which had subsequently been judicially determined to have been ultra vires. The authority had, however, passed the resolutions in good faith and

---

1 [1991] 4 All ER 973 at 985-986.
2 See per Lord Wilberforce in *Anns v Merton London Borough Council* [1978] AC 728 at 755 ('Their immunity from attack . . . though great is not absolute').
3 [1970] AC 1004, [1970] 2 All ER 294, HL.
4 [1978] AC 728, [1977] 2 All ER 492, HL.
5 [1982] AC 158, [1981] 1 All ER 1202.

after taking competent legal advice. Moreover until the resolutions were formally pronounced invalid the arguments relating to their invalidity had been 'evenly balanced'.[1] The Judicial Committee of the Privy Council held that the plaintiff's allegation that the authority had been negligent in passing the resolutions failed. Indeed situations in which plaintiffs will succeed in proving that ultra vires decisions were reached negligently are likely to be extremely rare. The formidable difficulties facing those who seek to establish cases on these lines were emphasised by the Judicial Committee of the Privy Council in *Rowling v Takaro Properties*[2] in which such a claim was unsuccessfully advanced. The Board identified what it described as 'overkill' as one of the arguments ab inconvenienti against the imposition of liability. 'Once it became known', said Lord Keith delivering the judgment of the Board,[3] 'that liability in negligence may be imposed on the ground that a minister has misconstrued a statute and so acted ultra vires, the cautious civil servant may go to extreme lengths in ensuring that legal advice, or even the opinion of the court, is obtained before decisions are taken, thereby leading to unnecessary delay in a considerable number of cases'. If a statutory body *deliberately* misuses its powers it may be liable to damages for the tort of misfeasance in public office.[4] But falling short of instances of that kind wrongdoing capable of constituting actionable carelessness will be very difficult to prove. Political compromises and trade-offs, not to mention clashes of personality between individuals involved, are characteristic, and quite legitimately so, of the ways in which committees and similar bodies function when charged with deciding broad policy questions. To attempt to dissect their deliberations, using the delicate apparatus of the law of negligence, will seldom be anything other than a thoroughly unsatisfactory exercise.

Unreasonableness in administrative law

[**12.16**] It is sometimes suggested that the head of ultra vires usually associated with the leading case of *Associated Provincial Picture Houses v Wednesbury Corp*,[5] namely that the decision was so unreasonable that no reasonable body could have reached it, is more likely than some other heads to lead to a finding of negligence.[6] It is submitted, however, that shared use of the terminology of 'reasonableness' does not necessarily imply a particularly close relationship with the tort of negligence. The concept of reasonable care in negligence, used to test conduct for carelessness, is quite different from that of unreasonableness in administrative law. In that context the concept is sometimes used simply to enable the ultra vires doctrine to operate where an enabling Act has conferred powers in

1 Ibid at 172 and 1209 per Lord Diplock delivering the judgment of the Board.
2 [1988] AC 473, [1988] 1 All ER 163.
3 [1988] AC 473 at 502, [1988] 1 All ER 163 at 173.
4 See Craig *Administrative Law* (2nd edn, 1989) pp 462ff and see *Bourgoin SA v Ministry of Agriculture, Fisheries and Food* [1986] QB 716, [1985] 3 All ER 585.
5 [1948] 1 KB 223, [1947] 2 All ER 680, CA.
6 See, eg Craig *Administrative Law* (2nd edn, 1989) p 457.

such general terms that a more familiar determination of vires, by detailed examination of the parent statute itself, is not possible.[1] Admittedly, however, in those cases in which the *Wednesbury* terminology is indeed used to highlight deliberate administrative *perversity* the relationship with the tort of negligence is closer. The possibility of showing that the authority in question acted not merely ultra vires, but also negligently, will be somewhat greater in such situations.[2]

Causation

[12.17] If a plaintiff should ever succeed in proving that an ultra vires decision was reached carelessly he may still experience difficulty in showing that any losses which he suffered were, in the legal sense, caused by the defendant.[3] It is even sometimes suggested that since everyone is entitled to ignore an invalid act someone who relies on one to his detriment is the source of his own loss![4] But this is quite unrealistic. Until a decision has actually been pronounced invalid by a competent court it will seldom be prudent simply to ignore it.[5] It is submitted that this particular causation argument should therefore not constitute an effective obstacle to a plaintiff. A much more formidable objection, however, is that merely because a particular decision is held to have been, in the particular circumstances, ultra vires it does not follow that the body in question could not have reached exactly the same decision and yet have stayed intra vires.[6] This will obviously be particularly so if the basis of invalidity is simply procedural irregularity, such as breach of the rules of natural justice. It will often be perfectly possible for the administrative body to correct the defect and act *validly* against the plaintiff's interest, for example by revoking his licence or whatever. In such circumstances there will clearly be considerable force in the contention that the plaintiff suffered no actionable loss.

City of Kamloops v Nielsen

[12.18] In view of all the attendant difficulties it is not surprising that there appears to be no reported case decided in England in which an allegation of negligence has succeeded, in circumstances in which the

---

1 See, eg cases involving byelaws, in which power to legislate for their area has been delegated to local authorities in general terms, such as *Arlidge v Islington Corpn* [1909] 2 K B 127 and *Repton School Governors v Repton UDC* [1918] 2 KB 133, CA.
2 Cf the tort of misfeasance in public office: *Bourgoin SA v Ministry of Agriculture, Fisheries and Food* [1986] QB 716, [1985] 3 All ER 585.
3 See, generally, Harlow *Compensation and Government Torts* (1982) pp 92-97.
4 See per Lord Diplock delivering the judgment of the Privy Council in *Dunlop v Woollahra Municipal Council* [1982] AC 158 at 172, [1981] 1 All ER 1202 at 1209.
5 In any event, ignoring it may not be possible : see *Hoffman-La Roche & Co Ltd v Secretary of State for Trade* [1975] AC 295, [1974] 2 All ER 1128, HL.
6 Cf per Lord Keith, delivering the judgment of the Judicial Committee of the Privy Council, in *Rowling v Takaro Properties* [1988] AC 473, [1988] 1 All ER 163.

decision in question could plausibly and unambiguously be regarded as having been one of discretion or policy with no 'operational' content. In *City of Kamloops v Nielsen*,[1] however, the Supreme Court of Canada, by a bare majority,[2] actually held a local authority liable in a situation somewhat similar to *Anns v Merton London Borough Council* except that inspection *had* taken place but follow-up action to restrain a clear breach of building regulations was not taken: the authority having, in the words of the majority judgment, 'dropped the matter because one of its aldermen was involved'.[3] The interest of this case is increased by the fact that two members of the court dissented precisely on the ground that the decision had been one of policy upon which a private law duty of care in negligence should not be superimposed.

Public and private law

[**12.19**] It is evident that there can be no rigid criteria for the application of the concept of immunity based upon public policy. It is certainly not the case that the defence applies automatically whenever some element of discretion can be identified in the conduct impugned.[4] But equally it is important that mechanistic application of ordinary negligence concepts should not result in the immunity being outflanked or indirectly subverted. Suppose, for example, that a local authority empowered, but not expressly obliged, to discharge some function of inspection[5] decided to use partly-trained or 'student' inspectors as an economy measure. The objective test of the standard of care in negligence could result in the work of the trainees being assessed in the same way as that of fully experienced inspectors.[6] But the outcome of such an assessment, if it resulted in the imposition of liability, might be to undermine the authority's freedom at the policy level to effect a legitimate reorganisation of its activities in the light of the various constraints upon it. If, however, the situation is one to which the public policy defence is clearly inapplicable, and which can therefore be evaluated by the use of negligence concepts, the question arises as to the relevance, if any, of the ultra vires doctrine at the operational, as distinct from the policy, level. It is sometimes suggested that it remains a necessary condition for the imposition of

---

1 (1984) 10 DLR (4th) 641. This case is among those discussed by Stephen Todd in 'The Negligence Liability of Public Authorities: Divergence in the Common Law' (1986) 102 LQR 370.
2 Wilson, Ritchie and Dickson JJ; McIntyre and Estey JJ dissenting.
3 (1984) 10 DLR (4th) at 673.
4 Cf per Sloane J in *Ham v Los Angeles County* 189 P 462 (1920) at p 468: '... it would be difficult to conceive of any official act ... that did not admit of some discretion, even if it involved only the driving in of a nail' (quoted in *Johnson v State of California* 447 P 2d 352 (1968) at 357).
5 Cf *Anns v Merton London Borough Council* [1978] AC 728, [1977] 2 All ER 492 HL.
6 Cf *Nettleship v Weston* [1971] 2 QB 691, [1971] 3 All ER 581, CA (negligence for learner driver to fail to conform to the standard of a qualified driver).

liability that the operational carelessness should have had the effect of rendering the outcome ultra vires the statutory body. Since, however, those who take this view also contend that at *this* level, in contrast to the planning stage, carelessness can simply be *assumed* to be ultra vires,[1] it would seem to be more appropriate to regard public law principles as being in truth simply irrelevant to the determination of liability. To do otherwise has overtones of legal fiction. It is also constitutionally objectionable because it implies that all governmental activity is subject to a presumption against liability rather than the other way round.[2]

Omissions

[12.20] In many of the situations in which attempts are made to impose liability upon statutory bodies the complaint is essentially that the body in question omitted to act promptly or decisively enough to prevent a third party, such as an insolvent bank, from inflicting loss on the plaintiff. In such circumstances the imposition of liability may potentially be in conflict with common law principles relating to the absence of liability for omissions as distinct from positive acts.[3] On the other hand, there are established common law exceptions to the fundamental principle of non-liability for such omissions,[4] and it is arguable that statutory situations could be brought within the scope of these exceptions on fairly orthodox grounds. Thus the existence of statutory powers might be regarded as creating a 'special relationship',[5] between public bodies and potential plaintiffs, enabling concepts such as those of 'undertaking' or 'reliance' to be invoked. It would certainly be unfortunate if emphasis upon the omissions question had the effect of resuscitating some of the unsatisfactory distinctions drawn in earlier cases involving negligence claims based upon statutory powers. Thus as Robert Goff J observed in *Fellowes v Rother District Council*,[6] there is now 'no rule that, merely because the defendant was acting under a statutory power as opposed to a statutory duty, liability is contingent on the defendant causing the plaintiff fresh or additional damage'.[7] Nevertheless the desirability of imposing wholly novel positive obligations upon public bodies, by grafting common law duties on to statutory powers, remains doubtful in view of the practical consequences of so doing upon administration

---

1 See Craig *Administrative Law* (2nd edn, 1989) pp 457-458.
2 See Peter Cane *Introduction to Administrative Law* (2nd edn 1992) p 243. See also para **[12.06]** above.
3 See Bowman and Bailey 'Negligence in the Realms of Public Law – A Positive Obligation to Rescue?' [1984] PL 277. See also *Davis v Radcliffe* [1990] 2 All ER 536 at 541, PC.
4 For discussion of liability for omissions see, generally Atiyah *Accidents, Compensation and the Law* (4th edn) pp 80ff. See also ch 1 above.
5 Cf *Hedley Byrne & Co Ltd v Heller & Partners Ltd* [1964] AC 465, [1963] 2 All ER 575, HL.
6 [1983] 1 All ER 513 at 522.
7 Cf *East Suffolk Rivers Catchment Board v Kent* [1941] AC 74, [1940] 4 All ER 527, HL.

in general,¹ and the allocation of resources in particular. At its most general what is involved in this area, whether or not the situation is one involving the imposition of liability for failure to prevent the infliction of harm by a third party, is a conflict between the underlying objective of the law of negligence to compensate victims of carelessness, and the role of public law in ensuring that the exercise of statutory discretions by those to whom they are entrusted is not unduly fettered. It can certainly be argued that there is a case for a substantial overhaul of public law and, in particular, of its reluctance to award compensation to victims of administrative failure.² But the award of such compensation by manipulating the law of tort is capable of producing arbitrariness and uncertainty.³

1   Cf per Lord Keith, delivering the judgment of the Judicial Committee of the Privy Council in *Rowling v Takaro Properties* [1988] AC 473, [1988] 1 All ER 163.
2   For discussion see, generally, Harlow, *Compensation and Government Torts* (1982).
3   Cf Tony Weir 'Governmental Liability' [1989] PL 40.

Chapter 13

The action for breach of statutory duty[1]

The nature of liability

Introduction

[13.01] The precise scope of the law relating to actions for damages for breach of statutory duty is notoriously uncertain. Some aspects of the topic, including those which have given rise in recent times to a series of important appellate decisions,[2] concern the extent to which intentional activities of the defendant, which have adversely affected the plaintiff, should attract a legal remedy. Although it is often the case that the tort of negligence can be said to apply to deliberate acts on the basis of a fortiori reasoning, the social issues to which such acts give rise in the statutory duty context are in practice usually rather different from those addressed by the mainstream of the law of negligence. Thus much litigation has involved the relationship between statutory duties and the law of economic torts concerned with unfair trade competition.[3] Such issues fall outside the scope of this book, although the reasoning in some of the recent cases, on the scope of the action for breach of statutory duty in general, is of relevance. In fact, however, the prominent recent reported cases are atypical: most contexts in which the action for breach of statutory duty falls to be considered involve careless rather than deliberate conduct[4] and their relationship with negligence is therefore much

---

1   See K M Stanton, *Breach of Statutory Duty in Tort* (1986); R A Buckley 'Liability in Tort for Breach of Statutory Duty' (1984) 100 LQR 204. (The permission of Stevens & Sons Ltd to reproduce below material which formerly appeared in this article in the *Law Quarterly Review* is gratefully acknowledged.)
2   See *Ex p Island Records* [1978] Ch 122, [1978] 3 All ER 824, CA; *Thornton v Kirklees Metropolitan Borough Council* [1979] QB 626, [1979] 2 All ER 349, CA; *Lonrho Ltd v Shell Petroleum Co Ltd (No 2)* [1982] AC 173, [1981] 2 All ER 456, HL; *RCA Corpn v Pollard* [1983] Ch 135, [1982] 3 All ER 771, CA; *Rickless v United Artists* [1988] QB 40, [1987] 1 All ER 679; *CBS Songs Ltd v Amstrad Consumer Electronics plc* [1988] Ch 1, [1987] 3 All ER 151, CA.
3   See the cases cited in the previous note (except *Kirklees*).
4   See, for example, the numerous cases arising out of accidents at work, some of which are considered in greater detail in ch 14 below.

closer. Allied to, or specific aspects of, the broad question of the relationship between negligence and breach of statutory duty are issues such as the following. Just when will liability for the latter arise? Is such liability 'strict' or fault-based? What defences are available?

Background

[**13.02**] The Statute 7 & 8 Vict c 112, s 18, required ships sailing from the UK to carry medicines on board as prescribed in a list published by the Board of Trade. In *Couch v Steel*[1] the plaintiff sailor became ill while at sea and suffered damage as a result of the defendant shipowner's having failed to comply with this requirement. His claim for damages was successful. Lord Campbell CJ spoke in broad terms of the 'right, by the common law, to maintain an action on the case for special damage sustained by the breach of a public duty'.[2] As is well known, however, the correctness of this wide approach was subsequently doubted in *Atkinson v Newcastle Waterworks*.[3] In this case the Court of Appeal held the defendant statutory undertakers not liable for damages arising out of their failure to maintain the water-pressure in a 'fire-plug', used for fighting fires, at the level required by statute.[4] Lord Cairns LC stated that the availability of a civil action, where a statute had been breached, 'must ... depend on the purview of the legislature in the particular statute, and the language which they have there employed'.[5] Although *Couch v Steel* has never been overruled, and in one twentieth century case was relied on with approval by a strong Court of Appeal,[6] *Atkinson's* case is generally regarded as having marked a sharp change in approach whereby a narrower 'construction' technique replaced the earlier, wider, view as to the scope of tortious liability in this context.[7] Thus in *Phillips v Britannia Hygienic Laundry Co*,[8] the Court of Appeal emphatically adopted the restrictive 'construction' approach when refusing to allow a claim for losses suffered by the plaintiff in a road accident, which had occurred in circumstances in which the Motor Cars (Use and Construction) Order 1904 had been contravened by the defendant.[9] In a later case in the House of Lords[10] Lord Simonds stated

---

1 (1854) 3 E & B 402.
2 Ibid at 415.
3 (1877) 2 Ex D 441.
4 Distinguished in *Dawson & Co v Bingley UDC* [1911] 2 KB 149, CA (liability imposed for incorrect marking, contrary to statute, of the position of a 'fire-plug', which resulted in delay in fighting a fire).
5 (1877) 2 Ex D 441 at 448. See also *Cowley v Newmarket Local Board* [1892] AC 345, HL, at 352 per Lord Herschell; *Saunders v Holborn District Board of Works* [1895] 1 QB 64 at 68 per Mathew J.
6 See *Simmonds v Newport Abercarn Black Vein Steam Coal Co* [1921] 1 KB 616, CA (Bankes, Scrutton and Atkin LJJ).
7 See, eg *Winfield and Jolowicz on Tort* (13th edn, 1989), p 172; *Street on Torts* (8th edn, 1988) p 363, note 3.
8 [1923] 2 KB 832, CA.
9 See also *Tan Chye Choo v Chong Kew Moi* [1970] 1 All ER 266, [1970] 1 WLR 147 PC. Cf *Badham v Lambs Ltd* [1946] KB 45, [1945] 2 All ER 295.
10 *Cutler v Wandsworth Stadium* [1949] AC 398 at 407, [1949] 1 All ER 544 at 548.

expressly that the 'only rule which in all circumstances is valid is that the answer must depend on a consideration of the whole Act and the circumstances, including the pre-existing law, in which it was enacted'. Nevertheless, traces of the older, wider, attitude still sometimes manifest themselves in contemporary judgments. These are apt to reflect the terminology and concepts familiar in the anomalous tort of public nuisance,[1] and to assert that an individual who can show that a criminal act has caused him 'special damage over and above the generality of the public'[2] can bring a civil action. It is conceivable that this approach may still occasionally be of relevance to claims for injunctive relief in cases involving the intentional carrying on of unlawful activities.[3] As far as claims in tort for damages are concerned, however, it is submitted that with the exception of isolated historical survivals, such as public nuisance highway cases,[4] this wider view was finally swept away by the decision of the House of Lords in *Lonrho v Shell Petroleum*.[5] Lord Diplock, with whom the other members of the House agreed, echoed the words of Lord Simonds in *Cutler v Wandsworth Stadium*, and observed that:

> 'the question whether legislation which makes the doing or omitting to do a particular act a criminal offence renders the person guilty of such offence liable also in a civil action for damages at the suit of any person who thereby suffers loss or damage is a question of construction of the legislation.'[6]

The demise of the 'special damage' approach in this area is to be welcomed. It would have made all crimes potentially torts as well. But the reasons for the imposition of criminal liability in a given situation might be quite different from those which normally underlie civil liability for damages,[7] and such an unprincipled extension of the law of tort would therefore be quite inappropriate.

---

1 See Buckley, *Law of Nuisance* (1981) pp 62-64.
2 Per Lord Denning in *Ex p Island Records* [1978] Ch 122 at 135, [1978] 3 All ER 824 at 829, CA. See also per Lord Fraser in *Gouriet v Union of Post Office Workers* [1978] AC 435 at 518E, HL: 'The general rule is that a private person is only entitled to sue in respect of interference with a public right if *either* there is also interference with a private right of his *or the interference with the public right will inflict special damage on him*' (italics supplied).
3 Cf *CBS Songs Ltd v Amstrad Consumer Electronics plc* [1988] Ch 61, [1987] 3 All ER 151, CA.
4 See *Lonrho Ltd v Shell Petroleum Co Ltd (No 2)* [1982] AC 173 at 185, [1981] 2 All ER 456 at 461 per Lord Diplock.
5 [1982] AC 173, [1981] 2 All ER 456, HL.
6 Ibid at 183 and 460. See also *West Wiltshire District Council v Garland* (1993) Times, 4 March.
7 A good example is provided by the now repealed statutes against forcible entry, which could subject a person to criminal liability for re-entering his own property following an illegal dispossession. The courts understandably always refused to allow illegal possessors to recover damages for breach of statutory duty after a forcible re-entry had taken place: see *Beddall v Maitland* (1881) 17 Ch D 174; *Hemmings v Stoke Poges Golf Club* [1920] 1 KB 720, CA.

Fiction of legislative intention as to civil liability

[**13.03**] Rejection of the 'special damage' approach to the imposition of civil liability for damages in this context should not be confused with approval of the proposition that the task of the courts is to determine whether or not the legislature, in passing the Act in question, impliedly *intended* to create a right of action in tort. On the contrary, the notion that liability in this area depends exclusively upon legislative intention, an intention ex hypothesi wholly unexpressed, is a patent fiction.[1] It is high time that it was finally abandoned.[2] The *general* purpose of the statute undoubtedly lies at the heart of the determination of the question, and to that extent the matter is rightly regarded as one of construction, but whether it is appropriate to seek to further that purpose by the addition of civil liability is ultimately a question for the common law itself.[3] As Lord Diplock observed in a case decided by the House of Lords on the Factories Act 1961: 'The statutes say nothing about civil remedies for breaches of their provisions. The judgments of the courts say all.'[4]

Not confined to existing law of negligence

[**13.04**] It is sometimes suggested that civil claims for damages arising out of breaches of statutes should be confined to situations in which the existing common law of negligence already imposes liability for carelessness.[5] The statutory provision is then regarded as determining, either conclusively or persuasively, that failure to take the measures required by it constitutes carelessness thereby rendering it difficult or impossible for the defendant to argue that failure to take the relevant steps was not unreasonable in the circumstances. This approach may be unexceptionable in situations in which the statutory provision does in fact overlap with existing common law liability, but it is submitted that it would have an undesirable limiting effect on the imposition of liability in other types of case. It would, for example, imply that statutes which created positive duties to act could never give rise to civil liability unless the situation was one of those in which the existing common law, atypically, also imposed such a duty. Indeed a refusal to countenance liability outside the existing tort framework could soon lead to paradox; since in any given situation it will be precisely on account of

---

1 A misleading comparison is sometimes drawn between the action in tort for breach of statutory duty and certain specific aspects of the law relating to illegality in contract: see, eg *Shaw v Groom* [1970] 2 QB 504 at 523, [1970] 1 All ER 702 at 711, CA, per Sachs LJ. In the latter context, however, the concept of legislative intent may be meaningful: see Buckley 'Implied Statutory Prohibition of Contracts' (1975) 38 MLR 535.
2 See *O'Connor v SP Bray* (1937) 56 CLR 464 at 477-478 per Dixon J.
3 See Thayer 'Public Wrong and Private Action' (1914) 27 Harv LR 317; Alexander 'Legislation and the Standard of Care in Negligence' (1964) 42 Can B Rev 243.
4 *Boyle v Kodak Ltd* [1969] 2 All 439 at 446, [1969] 1 WLR 661, HL, at 672.
5 See Glanville Williams 'The Effect of Penal Legislation in the Law of Tort' (1960) 23 MLR 223. See also Thayer 'Public Wrong and Private Action' (1914) 27 Harv LR 317.

defects or lacunae in the existing law that the statute will have been enacted. Fortunately, although this 'statutory negligence' doctrine has apparently enjoyed some degree of support in the USA[1] and Canada,[2] English courts have never accepted the invitation to decline to use statutes to develop the law, in favour of the preservation of an existing conceptual straitjacket. In *London Passenger Transport Board v Upson*[3] Lord Wright expressed himself as follows:

> '... a claim for damages for breach of statutory duty intended to protect a person in the position of the particular plaintiff is a specific common law right which is not to be confused in essence with a claim for negligence. The statutory right has its origin in the statute, but the particular remedy of an action for damages is given by the common law in order to make effective, for the benefit of the injured plaintiff, his right to the performance by the defendant of the defendant's statutory duty. It is an effective sanction. It is not a claim in negligence in the strict or ordinary sense . . . it is essential to keep in mind the fundamental differences of the two classes of claim.'

[13.05] Perhaps the most famous example of implicit rejection of the constraints of the 'statutory negligence' doctrine is the decision of the Court of Appeal in *Monk v Warbey*.[4] In this case a defendant who, in breach of statute, permitted an uninsured driver to use his car, was held liable to a victim injured by the driver's negligence when the latter had insufficient funds to satisfy the claim himself. Despite being criticised as an 'improper type of judicial invention'[5] this decision has been followed in subsequent cases[6] and its correctness assumed in the House of Lords.[7] There are also other situations in which liability for breach of statutory duty has been imposed in circumstances in which no common law duty existed.[8] Thus, long before the decision in *Hedley Byrne v Heller,* it seems to have been clear that pure financial loss could be recovered in the action for breach of statutory duty.[9] In the final analysis the highly theoretical emphasis of the 'statutory negligence' doctrine, with its appeal to conceptual neatness, renders it inconsistent with the deeply pragmatic nature of the common law.

---

1   See Thayer, op cit. For discussion of current American approaches see, generally, Harper, James & Gray *The Law of Torts* (2nd edn, 1986) vol 3, pp 613-648; *Prosser and Keeton on Torts* (5th edn, 1984) pp 220-234.
2   See *The Queen in Right of Canada v Saskatchewan Wheat Pool* (1983) 143 DLR (3d) 9. Noted by M H Mathews in (1984) 4 Oxford Journal of Legal Studies 429.
3   [1949] AC 155 at 168, [1949] 1 All ER 60 at 67, HL.
4   [1935] 1 KB 75, CA.
5   See Glanville Williams in 'The Effect of Penal Legislation in the Law of Tort' (1960) 23 MLR 233 at 259.
6   See *Martin v Dean* [1971] 2 QB 208, [1971] 3 All ER 279. Cf *Daniels v Vaux* [1938] 2 KB 203, [1938] 2 All ER 271; *Fleming v M'Gillivray* 1945 SLT 301.
7   See *Houston v Buchanan* [1940] 2 All ER 179, 1940 SC (HL) 17.
8   See, eg *Sephton v Lancashire River Board* [1962] 1 All ER 183, [1962] 1 WLR 623.
9   Such a claim succeeded in *Woods v Winskill* [1913] 2 Ch 303. See also *Simmonds v Newport Abercarn Black Vein Steam Coal Co* [1921] 1 KB 616, CA; *Moore v Canadian Pacific SS Co* [1945] 1 All ER 128. But cf *Wentworth v Wiltshire County Council* [1993] 2 All ER 256, [1993] 2 WLR 175, CA.

The scope of the Act

Protection of a 'class'

[**13.06**] An expression often found in the cases, including modern ones,[1] is that before liability can arise the statute must have been intended for the benefit of a certain 'class' of persons, as distinct from the public at large. The origins of the notion can perhaps be found in *Clegg, Parkinson & Co v Earby Gas Co.*[2] In this case a consumer was refused an action when the defendant company failed to provide him with a supply of gas in the quantity, and of the purity, required by the Gasworks Clauses Act 1871. Wills J observed that 'where there is an obligation created by statute to do something for the benefit of the public generally ... there is no separate right of action to every person injured, by breach of the obligation, in no other manner than the rest of the public'.[3] His Lordship felt that were the law otherwise 'the undertakers might speedily be ruined'. Emphasis specifically upon a 'class' of persons as such, however, probably dates from the famous case of *Groves v Lord Wimborne*,[4] which established that an action would lie in favour of workpeople injured through failure to fence dangerous machinery as required by the Factories Acts. Rigby LJ observed that the legislation was 'intended for the protection from injury of a particular class of persons, who come within the mischief of the Act'.[5] A L Smith and Vaughan Williams LJJ also both used very similar language.[6] Statements to the same effect have often been made in subsequent cases.[7] The notion has, however, also been forcefully criticised, most notably by Atkin LJ in *Phillips v Britannia Hygienic Laundry Co.*[8] Indeed, it is submitted that as a control device to limit liability for breach of statutory duty, the concept of class benefit represents a muddled and inappropriate attempt to achieve two separate objectives. The first of these, which concerns the mischief at which the Act in question was directed, is already effectively

---

1 See below.
2 [1896] 1 QB 592.
3 Ibid at 594-595.
4 [1898] 2 QB 402, CA.
5 Ibid at 414.
6 Ibid at 407 per A L Smith LJ and 415 per Vaughan Williams LJ.
7 See, eg *Read v Croydon Corpn* [1938] 4 All ER 631 at 652 per Stable J; *Hartley v Mayoh & Co* [1954] 1 QB 383 at 391, [1954] 1 All ER 375 at 379, CA per Singleton LJ; *Solomons v R Gertzenstein Ltd* [1954] 2 QB 243 at 261, [1954] 2 All ER 625 at 634-635, CA, per Birkett LJ and at 256 and 637 per Romer LJ; *Canadian Pacific Steamships Ltd v Bryers* [1958] AC 485 at 505, [1957] 3 All ER 572 at 581, HL, per Lord Tucker; *A-G v St Ives RDC* [1960] 1 QB 312 at 324, [1959] 3 All ER 371 at 377 per Salmon J.
8 'It would be strange if a less important duty which is owed to a section of the public may be enforced by an action, while a more important duty which is owed to the public at large cannot': [1923] 2 KB 832 at 841. See also *Monk v Warbey* [1935] 1 KB 75 at 82, CA per Greer LJ and at 85 per Maugham LJ; *Solomons v Gertzenstein Ltd* [1954] 2 QB 243 at 255, [1954] 2 All ER 625 at 630-631, CA, per Somervell LJ (dissenting on this point); *McCall v Abelesz* [1976] QB 585 at 596, [1976] 1 All ER 727 at 732, CA, per Ormrod LJ; *Commerford v Board of School Comrs of Halifax* [1950] 2 DLR 207 at 212 per Ilsey J.

covered by a different device; and to this extent the notion simply produces a confusing and unnecessary duplication of tests to embarrass the court. The second objective, which relates mainly to the special position of public authorities and statutory undertakers, would be better dealt with by explicit examination of the issues involved. These issues tend to be obscured rather than illuminated by the concept of 'benefit of a class'; this criticism of the concept will be amplified in the next two paragraphs.

Need for harm to be within the risk

[**13.07**] The first apparent purpose of the concept of 'benefit of a class' is to ensure that, before damages for breach of statutory duty can be recovered, the plaintiff is obliged to demonstrate that the harm which he has suffered is of a kind which the legislation was intended to prevent. A good example of its use for this purpose is to be found in *Knapp v Railway Executive*.[1] In this case a car collided with the closed gates of a level-crossing. Pursuant to a provision of the relevant private Act,[2] the gates should have been firm enough to stay closed despite the collision, but they were not. As a result they swung open into the path of an oncoming train. The driver of the train was injured and the question arose whether he had a right of action for breach of statutory duty. The Court of Appeal held that he did not.[3] Jenkins LJ[4] stated that the legislation 'define[d] the class of person to whom the company owe[d] a duty', and concluded that the particular duty to provide secure level-crossings was owed only to users of the highway and not to persons travelling on the railway itself.[5] It is submitted that the issue in *Knapp*'s case was similar in principle to that in the well-known case of *Gorris v Scott*.[6] In this case the plaintiff's sheep were washed overboard from the defendant's ship. This would not have occurred if the defendant had not neglected the precaution required by a statutory order to keep the animals in pens. An action for breach of statutory duty nevertheless failed on the ground that the purpose of the relevant legislation[7] had been to prevent the spread of disease and not to prevent what had happened in the case in question, even though the precaution would incidentally have had that effect if it had been taken. Similarly in *Knapp*'s case the legislature obviously contemplated injury occurring to road users rather than train drivers if the statutory precautions were neglected. But had they been taken, the train driver would not have been injured. Clearly, the rule in *Gorris v Scott* operates to delineate the scope of the risk in a statutory

1 [1949] 2 All ER 508, CA.
2 The Brighton and Chichester Railway Act 1844, s 274.
3 Cf *Buxton v North Eastern Rly Co* (1868) LR 3 QB 549.
4 [1949] 2 All ER 508 at 515D. See also per Rigby LJ in *Groves v Lord Wimborne* (quoted in the text above) who expressly linked the notions of 'class' and 'mischief'.
5 Even if a passenger on the train had been injured he or she could not have recovered. Cf dictum, per Kelly CB in *Gorris v Scott* (1874) LR 9 Exch 125 at 128, explained in *Knapp*'s case at 516 per Jenkins LJ.
6 (1874) LR 9 Exch 125.
7 The Contagious Diseases (Animals) Act 1869.

duty case in a manner similar to that of the rules relating to remoteness of damage in other types of tort case.[1] This being so, the rule furnishes a useful encapsulation of a principle which the notion of 'benefit of a class' appears to duplicate. Clarity would therefore be served if this overlap were recognised and the number of concepts with which the courts have to grapple in these cases reduced accordingly.[2]

Protection of statutory undertakers

[**13.08**] The other purpose for which the idea underlying the concept of benefit of a particular class is invoked is rather different from that of remoteness of damage. It is clear from *Clegg, Parkinson & Co v Earby Gas Co*[3] that the denial in that case of a right of action in favour of any member of the general public, who had suffered as a result of breach of statutory duty by the defendant undertakers, was to protect the undertakers from a burden potentially so great as to be capable of overwhelming them or even driving them out of existence. The same idea can be seen at work in the background in other cases, including *Atkinson v Newcastle Waterworks Co*[4] itself. It is also reflected in a series of decisions in the law of nuisance in which private law remedies, such as damages and injunctions, were refused in situations where sewerage systems had overflowed due to failure on the part of the drainage authorities, in breach of statutory requirements, to expand and improve their plant and equipment.[5] Of course, the

---

1   Cf *Overseas Tankship (UK) Ltd v Morts Dock and Engineering Co* [1961] AC 388, [1961] 1 All ER 404, PC. See also Fleming *Law of Torts* (7th edn, 1987) 122, note 15. See, generally, Glanville Williams 'The Risk Principle' (1961) 77 LQR 179.
2   Unfortunately, the overlap is embodied in the American Law Institute's Second *Restatement of Torts*, para 286 as follows:
    '*When Standard of Conduct Defined by Legislation or Regulation Will be Adopted.*
    The court may adopt as the standard of conduct of a reasonable man the requirements of a legislative enactment or an administrative regulation whose purpose is found to be exclusively or in part
    (a) to protect a class of persons which includes the one whose interest is invaded, and
    (b) to protect the particular interest which is invaded, and
    (c) to protect that interest against the kind of harm which has resulted, and
    (d) to protect that interest against the particular hazard from which the harm results.'
    Categories (b), (c) and (d) would seem to make category (a) largely redundant. Indeed the fact-situations involved in the cases in which the *Restatement* has been judicially cited could be seen as supporting the contention that the concepts of 'class benefit' and 'risk' are usually interchangeable: see, eg *Mangan v FC Pilgram & Co* 336 NE 2d 374, 381 (1975); *Misterek v Washington Mineral Products* 531 P 2d 805, 807 (1975).
3   [1896] 1 QB 592.
4   (1877) 2 Ex D 441, CA.
5   See *Glossop v Heston and Isleworth Local Board* (1879) 12 Ch D 102, CA. Cf *Robinson v Workington Corpn* [1897] 1 QB 619, CA; *Pasmore v Oswaldtwistle UDC* [1898] AC 387, HL; *Smeaton v Ilford Corpn* [1954] Ch 450, [1954] 1 All ER 923. Cf *Pride of Derby and Derbyshire Angling Association Ltd v British Celanese Ltd* [1953] Ch 149, [1953] 1 All ER 179, CA.

argument ab inconvenienti based on the large number of potential plaintiffs,[1] which is evidently one aspect of the judicial anxiety in these cases, is one which is often criticised. But it is not the only aspect of the problem. Statutory duty cases often arise out of situations involving some major objective which the legislature wishes to promote. It might still be perfectly be possible to argue in a modern case, depending on the particular facts, that the legislative strategy could be excessively hindered if individual plaintiffs were permitted to polarise debate around their specific grievances.[2] Alternatively, of course, a decision in favour of liability might provide a desirable stimulus to action as well as meet a just claim for compensation. Whether, on balance, an action for breach of statutory duty should be permitted might well call ideally for sophisticated evaluation of these and other policy factors.[3] In the past the courts appear sometimes to have used the concept of a distinction between legislation intended to benefit the 'public', and legislation intended to benefit a 'class', in order to give effect to a decision reached in reliance on factors of this kind but without making their reasoning on the issues explicit. It is respectfully submitted that the judges should discuss the relevant factors openly[4] and not invoke the question-begging 'public benefit' terminology which in effect merely obscures the need to do so.

Relevance of provision in the Act for a penalty

[**13.09**] One of the most confusing questions in this area of the law concerns the relevance of the presence or absence of provision in the statute itself for a sanction, be it criminal penalty or some other kind of remedy. In *Doe d Bishop of Rochester v Bridges*[5] Lord Tenterden CJ observed that:

> 'where an Act creates an obligation, and enforces the performance in a specified manner, we take it to be a general rule that performance cannot be enforced in any other manner. If an obligation is created, but no mode of enforcing its performance is ordained, the common law may, in general, find a mode suited to the particular nature of the case.'[6]

1 Ie the fear of 'opening the floodgates'.
2 Cf *Watt v Kesteven County Council* [1955] 1 QB 408, [1955] 1 All ER 473, CA (education).
3 It is interesting to note that the Robens Committee on *Safety and Health at Work* suggested that the availability of the action for breach of statutory duty in factory accident cases had hindered rather than helped accident prevention: Cmnd 5034, pp 144-147; 185-187. See also Glanville Williams in (1960) 23 MLR 233 at 239, who questioned the need for the action in this context, given the existence of the social security industrial injuries scheme. Cf *Haigh v Charles W Ireland Ltd* [1973] 3 All ER 1137, [1974] 1 WLR 43 at 54-55, HL, per Lord Diplock.
4 Cf the question which has arisen in cases involving negligence against a statutory background of delineating between those issues which are appropriate for judicial resolution and those which are not: see *Home Office v Dorset Yacht Co Ltd* [1970] AC 1004, [1970] 2 All ER 294, HL; *Anns v Merton London Borough Council* [1978] AC 728, [1977] 2 All ER 492, HL; *Rowling v Takaro Properties Ltd* [1988] AC 473, [1988] 1 All ER 163 PC. See also, generally, ch 12, above.
5 (1831) 1 B & Ad 847 at 859.
6 Cf *Wolverhampton New Waterworks Co v Hawkesford* (1859) 6 CBNS 336 at 356 per Willes J.

This dictum, which has frequently been cited in later cases, and can probably fairly be said to represent the orthodox view, thus favoured a presumption *against* liability for breach of statutory duty where the Act provides for a sanction, and a presumption *in favour* of liability where it does not do so. It is submitted, however, that both aspects of the proposition are open to serious criticism, and that a different and preferable interpretation of the authorities is in fact tenable.

Criminal sanction should be irrelevant

[**13.10**] As far as the supposed presumption *against* liability is concerned, it has in fact long been clear that provision for the imposition of a *fine* is not in itself conclusive against the availability of a civil action.[1] This point was occasionally obscured in the older cases by provision for recovery by a common informer[2] (who might himself be the sufferer of the mishap) of all or part of any penalty imposed, or even for payment of it direct to the victim in his capacity as such. Even in these situations, however, the courts would not hesitate to impose liability if they considered it appropriate. This was particularly apparent in the industrial injuries field, where one of the attractions of the action for breach of statutory duty was that it provided an avenue of escape from the consequences of the defence of common employment. The leading example is *Groves v Lord Wimborne*,[3] in which Rigby LJ observed[4] that even if the maximum fine which could have been imposed under the provision in question, £100, were eventually to reach the plaintiff, it would nevertheless seem 'monstrous to suppose that it was intended that in the case of death or severe mutilation arising through a breach of the statutory duty, the compensation to the workman or his family should never exceed' that figure.[5] The level at which a fine is imposed will usually reflect the defendant's culpability (which may be relatively small) as distinct from the plaintiff's loss (which may well be much larger).[6]

---

1 See, eg the numerous cases decided under the Factories Acts.
2 See, eg *Couch v Steel* (1854) 3 E & B 402.
3 [1898] 2 QB 402, CA. See also *Black v Fife Coal Co* [1912] AC 149, HL. Cf *Caswell v Worth* (1856) 5 E & B 849.
4 [1898] 2 QB 402 at 414.
5 Vaughan Williams LJ was more cautious than Rigby LJ. He reserved his opinion on what the position might have been if the victim had been statutorily *entitled* to the money; as it was the Secretary of State had a *discretion* whether to make it over to him: see [1898] 2 QB 402 at 417.
6 See per AL Smith LJ in [1898] 2 QB at 402 at 408. Professor Glanville Williams invoked this point as an argument *against* imposing liability for breach of statutory duty where no pre-existing tort exists. He argued that such liability is unprincipled as not providing the defendant with the protection which the careful limitations on the extent of criminal liability afford him: see (1960) 23 MLR 233 at 256. This argument does, however, prove too much. The courts not infrequently reinforce the criminal law, most prominently in the sphere of illegality in contract where forfeiture of contractual rights can constitute a substantial additional sanction for wrong-doing: see, eg *Ashmore Benson Pease & Co Ltd v AV Dawson Ltd* [1973] 2 All ER 856, [1973] 1 WLR 828, CA. Of course it can be argued that the courts sometimes go too far, but denial a priori of any legitimacy in their adoption of this role would surely be difficult to support.

Even in cases in which the plaintiff was unsuccessful, and one of the reasons given was that the statutorily provided penalty excluded any other remedy, it is likely that the real reason for denying liability was different. The doctrine already discussed, which is concerned to minimise the liability of public utilities, was probably a predominant factor in a number of the relevant decisions.[1] Moreover, although most of the cases on the point in fact concerned fines, since they happened to involve provisions supported by that sanction, similar reasoning would seem to be applicable to other criminal penalties. It is therefore submitted that a bold statement of the law is possible to the effect that a provision in the statute for the imposition of a fine, or any other criminal sanction on the defendant, does not lean at all against the availability of an action for breach of statutory duty.[2]

Where the Act makes no provision for a remedy

[13.11] The second limb of Lord Tenterden's dictum from *Bishop of Rochester v Bridges,* quoted above, dealing with a supposed presumption in favour of liability where no sanction is stipulated by the statute, was echoed in a much more recent obiter dictum by Lord Simonds in his influential speech in *Cutler v Wandsworth Stadium Ltd*.[3] His Lordship stated that 'if a statutory duty is prescribed but no remedy by way of penalty or otherwise for its breach is imposed, it can be assumed that a right of action accrues to the person who is damnified by the breach'. One of the difficulties which has arisen in this context is that it is unclear exactly what counts as a 'remedy' for the purpose of the presumption. Confusion has occurred in situations where the Act provides for alternative machinery, such as mandamus or intervention by a minister after complaint to him, but no criminal sanction. Sometimes provisions of this type have been classified as being equivalent to a criminal penalty for the purposes of the supposed presumption against a civil action,[4] and sometimes as being equivalent to no penalty at all and hence within Lord Simonds' statement in favour of liability.[5] The dilemma was highlighted in one case[6] involving an Act[7] which did provide for criminal proceedings but

---

1 See, eg *Atkinson v Newcastle Waterworks* (1877) 2 Ex D 441, CA.
2 Cf the American Law Institute's Second *Restatement of Torts*, para 287:
    '*Effect of Provision for Penalty*
    A provision for a penalty in a legislative enactment or administrative regulation has no effect upon liability . . . unless the penalty is found to be intended to exclude it.'
3 [1949] AC 398 at 407, [1949] 1 All ER 544 at 548, HL.
4 See, eg *Pasmore v Oswaldtwistle UDC* [1898] AC 387, HL; *Watt v Kesteven County Council* [1955] 1 QB 408 at 415, CA; affg [1954] 3 All ER 441 at 444 per Ormerod J at first instance; *Southwark London Borough Council v Williams* [1971] Ch 734, [1971] 2 All ER 175, CA.
5 See, eg *Reffell v Surrey County Council* [1964] 1 All ER 743 at 746, [1964] 1 WLR 358 at 362 per Veale J; *Thornton v Kirklees Metropolitan Borough Council* [1979] QB 626, [1979] 2 All ER 349, CA; *Sephton v Lancashire River Board* [1962] 1 All ER 183, [1962] 1 WLR 623.
6 *Argyll v Argyll* [1967] Ch 302, [1965] 1 All ER 611.
7 The Judicial Proceedings (Regulation of Reports) Act 1926.

only with the consent of the Attorney General. The judge, Ungoed-Thomas J, observed that:

> 'this might be relied on on the one hand as a factor tending to indicate that persons injured were to have a remedy otherwise than by criminal proceedings, and on the other hand as a factor tending to indicate that there was to be no remedy except with the sanction of the Attorney-General.'[1]

[13.12] If the situation is one in which no formal legal sanction at all, not even an order of mandamus, is available to support the statutory 'duty', Lord Simonds' view that civil liability can be 'assumed' to exist seems highly questionable. Notwithstanding the understandable feeling that an Act of Parliament should be something more than a 'pious aspiration',[2] there is something of a paradox in the notion that such a provision should be capable of giving rise to a tort action. Where mandamus is available,[3] but no criminal sanction, there is, perhaps, less of a paradox in a presumption in favour of civil liability. Nevertheless, the basic objection remains. Prescriptions unsupported by penalties are usually instructions of an essentially administrative nature, often addressed to public bodies. The grafting of civil liability in tort upon such provisions is likely to give rise to considerable practical difficulties and may also involve defiance of the policy factors relating to public utilities, and similar bodies, which have been referred to above.[4] But there is, unfortunately, a relatively recent interlocutory decision of a two-member Court of Appeal in which it was held that an action for breach of statutory duty could be based upon a provision of an administrative nature,[5] even though the Act contemplated the exercise of a considerable degree of discretion on the part of the public body whose activities were at best only controllable by mandamus rather than by any criminal sanction. The decision, *Thornton v Kirklees Metropolitan Borough Council*,[6] does, however, appear to be in conflict with basic principles of public law, relating to the absence of any general right to damages for losses brought about by the exercise of administrative discretions, and its correctness is therefore subject to very considerable doubt.[7] It is accordingly submitted, contrary to the dictum of Lord Simonds in *Cutler v Wandsworth Stadium*, that the absence of any specific penalty in the statute is in fact a powerful indication against the imposition of an

---

1 [1967] Ch 302 at 341, [1965] 1 All ER 611 at 632.
2 [1949] AC 398 at 407.
3 Of course this itself may be a matter of dispute: see, eg *Pasmore v Oswaldtwistle UDC* [1898] AC 387, HL.
4 In *Booth & Co (International) Ltd v National Enterprise Board* [1978] 3 All ER 624 absence of any sanction was held in interlocutory proceedings at first instance to be a factor favouring a prima facie presumption of liability for breach of statutory duty, sed quaere.
5 In the Housing (Homeless Persons) Act 1977.
6 [1979] QB 626, [1979] 2 All ER 349, CA.
7 In addition to criticism by the present writer (to be found in (1984) 100 LQR 204 at 217-220) it has also been criticised by Stanton in his *Liability in Tort for Breach of Statutory Duty* (1986) pp 80-81. Cf per Lord Bridge in *Cocks v Thanet District Council* [1983] 2 AC 286 at 293, [1982] 3 All ER 1135 at 1138, HL.

action for damages for breach of statutory duty rather than a pointer in its favour. This submission derives some support from the recent decision of the House of Lords in *Hague v Deputy Governor of Parkhurst Prison*,[1] in which the House held that breach of a statutory rule dealing with the segregation of inmates in prison was not actionable by a prisoner who was improperly segregated. No specific penalty was provided for breach of the rule, and Lord Jauncey expressed himself as follows:[2]

> 'The Prison Act is designed to deal with the administration of prisons and the management and control of prisoners. It covers such wide-ranging matters as central administration, prison officers, confinement and treatment of prisoners, release of prisoners on licence, provision and maintenance of prisons and offences. Its objects are far removed from those of legislation such as the Factories and Coal Mines Acts whose prime concern is to protect the health and safety of persons who work therein . . . I find nothing in . . . the Act to suggest that Parliament intended thereby to confer on prisoners a cause of action sounding in damages in respect of a breach of those provisions.'

A new presumption suggested

[13.13] If it is correct that provisions unsupported by remedies will not normally provide an appropriate basis for imposition of an action for damages for breach of statutory duty, because they will normally be administrative or discretionary in nature, the *converse* of the proposition does, it is submitted, shed some light on the more general problem of identifying the situations in which such liability *will* properly be imposed. It is suggested that the correct approach is the adoption of a *presumption* to the effect that an action for breach of statutory duty is more likely to lie the more *specific* is the nature of the statutory obligation.[3] Similarly, the less specific the obligation the less likely is it that the action will arise.[4] Of course, some element of judgment is often left to the persons subject to the duty even by quite specific provisions; for example, an obligation to fence dangerous machinery pursuant to the factories legislation may involve the making of choices as to the most appropriate protection in the particular circumstances. Moreover, it must be emphasised that the proposed test is subordinate both to the general question of the desirability of an action in the particular context, which it has already been suggested above the court should consider overtly as a matter of policy, and to determination that the harm suffered was 'within the risk' for the purposes of the rule in *Gorris v Scott*.[5] Nevertheless, the

---

1 [1991] 3 All ER 733, HL.
2 [1991] 3 All ER 733 at 750-751.
3 Cf per Shaw LJ in *McCall v Abelesz* [1976] QB 585 at 600, [1976] 1 All ER 727 at 735, CA: 'the offence must consist of a failure to perform a *defined duty* which the statute imposes on the potential offender' (italics supplied).
4 Cf per Lord Reid in *Cutler v Wandsworth Stadium Ltd* [1949] AC 398 at 417, [1949] 1 All ER 544 at 554, HL: 'If the legislature had intended to create . . . rights I would expect to find them capable of reasonably precise definition.'
5 (1874) LR 9 Exch 125, discussed above.

proposed presumption could, perhaps, provide an aid to clarity in this somewhat confused branch of the law, and it is thought that the proposition which it embodies also explains most of the authorities. Thus the actual decision in *Couch v Steel*[1] can be supported on the ground that a specific list of medicaments had been laid down which the defendant failed to supply.[2] Similarly, in *Monk v Warbey*[3] the duty was simply to refuse to allow an uninsured person to use a motor car. In *Phillips v Britannia Hygienic Laundry Co*,[4] on the other hand, the relevant article of the statutory order there in question simply imposed criminal liability for use of a defective motor-vehicle, it did not specify particular measures or precautions to be taken with respect to the maintenance of such vehicles.[5]

The relevance of fault

[13.14] Focus upon the specific nature of the statutory duty as a factor favouring the imposition of civil liability also casts light upon the question whether a defendant can avoid such liability by showing that he had not been careless, or otherwise blameworthy, in allowing the breach to occur. As Lord Atkin said in *Smith v Cammell Laird & Co Ltd*:[6] 'It is precisely in the absolute obligation imposed by statute to perform or forbear from performing a *specified activity* that a breach of statutory duty differs from the obligation imposed by common law, which is to take reasonable care to avoid injuring another.'

If the legislation sets out in detail what the defendant is meant to do it will rarely be plausible for him to argue that he was not blameworthy in not doing what was required.[7] In effect, therefore, the position in most cases will be one of strict liability.

Two types of provision

[13.15] There will, however, occasionally be situations in which the imposition of liability will be appropriate even though the statute is *not* specific in laying down exactly what has to be done. In such cases the degree of discretion left to the defendant will not be so great as to attract the presumption against civil liability but will simply reflect the impracticability, in the particular context, of laying down very

---

1 (1854) 3 E & B 402.
2 See also *Simmonds v Newport Abercarn Black Vein Steam Coal Co* [1921] 1 KB 616, CA (statutory obligation to provide written statement showing how wages payment was arrived at).
3 [1935] 1 KB 75, CA.
4 [1923] 2 KB 832, CA.
5 See also *Barkway v South Wales Transport Co* [1950] AC 185, [1950] 1 All ER 392, HL and discussion in Linden *Canadian Tort Law* (1977) pp 199-201. See also below for discussion of the position under such general statutory provisions where fault can be proved against the defendant.
6 [1940] AC 242 at 258, [1939] 4 All ER 381 at 390, HL (italics supplied).
7 The mere fact that the taking of the precautions would render the operation not viable economically is no defence: see *John Summers & Sons Ltd v Frost* [1955] AC 740, [1955] 1 All ER 870, HL. The general principle that ignorance of the law is no defence will presumably also apply.

precise requirements in advance. It seems to be clear that in situations of this type liability for breach of statutory duty will normally be fault-based. In consequence there will usually be an overlap in such cases with ordinary negligence liability, especially in view of the tendency of that tort, until recently, to expand.[1] But the existence of the action may still prove valuable in cases for which there is no liability at common law (such as most of those involving omissions), or in which the existence of liability at common law is doubtful.

Read v Croydon Corporation

[13.16] The distinction between the strict and fault-based types of liability for breach of statutory duty was well brought out in the judgment of Stable J in *Read v Croydon Corpn*.[2] In this case the defendant corporation had allowed their water supply to become polluted with typhoid. They were held liable in tort both for negligence, and for breach of their duty under the Waterworks Clauses Act 1847 to provide 'a supply of pure and wholesome water'.[3] Even their liability for breach of statutory duty, however, was based upon a finding that they had been at fault as having failed to take reasonable care. The learned judge drew a distinction between statutory provisions whereby 'certain means are directed to serve a particular end' and those 'where the statute enjoins the end but not the means'. Examples of the former class, which attracted strict liability, were to be found in the detailed provisions of the Factories Acts. In the case before him, however, the legislation did not indicate how the provision of a pure water supply was to be maintained, but only that that was the end to be achieved. Indeed, his Lordship envisaged situations, such as prolonged drought, in which the maintenance of such a supply might become impossible without there being any question of the corporation's having been at fault. It followed that the obligation on the corporation was 'limited to the exercise of all reasonable care and skill to ensure that the water provided accord[ed] with the provisions of the Act'.[4]

---

1 There are a number of cases in which civil liability for breach of general statutory provisions has been imposed and in which the court has indicated that liability in ordinary common law negligence had also been established: see *Ching v Surrey County Council* [1910] 1 KB 736, CA; *Abbott v Isham* (1920) 90 LJKB 309; *Reffell v Surrey County Council* [1964] 1 All ER 743, [1964] 1 WLR 358 (all decided under enactments relating to the safety of premises used for educational purposes). See also *Ministry of Housing and Local Government v Sharp* [1970] 2 QB 223, [1970] 1 All ER 1009, CA. Cf *Phillips v Britannia Hygienic Laundry Co* [1923] 2 KB 832, CA.
2 [1938] 4 All ER 631.
3 The infant plaintiff, who had actually contracted typhoid, succeeded in negligence. Her father succeeded for breach of statutory duty, which was held to have been owed to him qua payer of water rates, for the expenses he had incurred in consequence of his daughter's illness.
4 See [1938] 4 All ER 631 at 650-651.

Defences and relationship with criminal liability

Contributory negligence and volenti non fit injuria

[**13.17**] Even where the defendant's liability is strict, because the statutory duty is specific in nature, it is well established that contributory negligence[1] and even, in very rare cases, volenti non fit injuria,[2] may be available as defences. In particular circumstances it may also be possible to avoid liability on the basis that, as between plaintiff and defendant, responsibility for the actual discharge of a statutory duty which was imposed upon both of them rested wholly with the plaintiff, and that he alone had been at fault.[3] The availability of these defences should not be regarded, however, as amounting to the introduction into this area of general negligence principles. There is not necessarily anything inappropriate in taking the plaintiff's conduct into account even in circumstances in which the liability of the defendant is not itself fault-based.[4] The defences are best seen as a legitimate exercise of the function of the court in coming to its own policy decision as to how best to give effect to the underlying purposes of the legislation in question. Thus the promotion of safety standards would hardly be enhanced if those whom they were intended to protect could be certain that their own disregard of elementary precautions would have no effect on their recovery of damages, if they had the misfortune to suffer an accident.[5]

Where no offence has been committed

[**13.18**] The question may sometimes arise whether civil liability for breach of statutory duty can be imposed even though, in the particular circumstances, the defendant would not have incurred criminal liability. There may have been an absence of mens rea where the relevant provision is not, for the purposes of the criminal law, one of strict liability; or there may be a special defence to criminal

---

1 See *Caswell v Powell Duffryn Collieries Ltd* [1940] AC 152, [1939] 3 All ER 722, HL. The apportionment provisions of the Law Reform (Contributory Negligence) Act 1945 apply: *Cakebread v Hopping Bros (Whetstone) Ltd* [1947] KB 641, [1947] 1 All ER 389, CA. Such apportionment is, of course, a common occurrence in cases decided under the Factories Acts or similar legislation.
2 See *ICI Ltd v Shatwell* [1965] AC 656, [1964] 2 All ER 999, HL. The general rule is probably still that the defence is inapplicable in such cases, at least where employer and employee are concerned: *Wheeler v New Merton Board Mills* [1933] 2 KB 669, CA. On volenti non fit injuria generally see ch 4 above.
3 See *Man-Waring v Billington* [1952] 2 All ER 747, CA; *Ginty v Belmont Building Supplies Ltd* [1959] 1 All ER 414. See also *Ross v Associated Portland Cement Manufacturers Ltd* [1964] 2 All ER 452 at 455, [1964] 1 WLR 768 at 776, HL, per Lord Reid. For discussion generally of employer's liability to their employees see ch 14 below.
4 See Glanville Williams *Joint Torts and Contributory Negligence* (1950) pp 207-210. See also Payne 'Reduction of Damages for Contributory Negligence' (1955) 18 MLR 344.
5 Cf per Lord Diplock in *Boyle v Kodak Ltd* [1969] 2 All ER 439 at 446, [1969] 1 WLR 661 at 673, HL: 'To say "You are liable to me for my own wrongdoing" is neither good morals nor good law.'

proceedings, of 'due diligence' or the like, expressly provided for in the Act.¹ Judicial views have conflicted on the relationship between civil and criminal liability in such circumstances. Some have favoured giving the defendant the benefit of defences to criminal liability in civil proceedings,² while others have taken the opposite view.³ It is submitted that the proposition that such defences will not normally be available to a defendant in a civil action is to be preferred. The policy issues underlying civil and criminal liability are usually different (and the former does not attract the stigma of the latter). Of course, if the statute itself makes the position clear by dealing expressly and separately with both types of liability there is no room for argument. And it is noteworthy that while some statutes do provide that criminal defences are to be available in a civil action,⁴ others emphatically provide the opposite.⁵

Reform?

An express provision?

[13.19] The suggestion is often made that Parliament should state expressly, either in each individual Act or by means of a general statutory presumption, whether or not contravention will give rise to a civil action.⁶ The matter was considered in the 1960s by the Law

1 See, eg the Mineral Workings (Offshore Installations) Act 1971, s 9(3).
2 See the references to earlier cases collected by Tucker LJ in *Harrison v National Coal Board* [1950] 1 KB 466 at 476, [1950] 1 All ER 171 at 178, CA. See also Glanville Williams in (1960) 23 MLR 233 at 243, note 34, who believes that to extend such defences to civil liability would represent 'sounder juristic principle', sed quaere.
3 'Criminal and civil liability are two separate things ... The legislature might well be unwilling to convict an owner who failed to carry out an absolute statutory duty of a crime with which he was not himself directly concerned, but still be ready to leave the civil liability untouched ... The duty is broken though no crime has been committed": per Lord Porter in *Potts v Reid* [1943] AC 1 at 31, HL. See also *Harrison v National Coal Board* [1950] 1 KB 466 at 477, CA, per Tucker LJ and [1951] AC 639 at 664, HL, per Lord Normand.
4 See, eg the Control of Pollution Act 1974, s 88(2).
5 See, eg the Mineral Workings (Offshore Installations) Act 1971, s 11(4). Cf the Health and Safety at Work Act 1974, s 47(3).
6 The best-known expression of this view is by Lord du Parcq in *Cutler v Wandsworth Stadium* [1949] AC 398 at 410, [1949] 1 All ER 544 at 549, HL: 'To a person unversed in the science or art of legislation it may well seem strange that Parliament has not by now made it a rule to state explicitly what its intention is in a matter which is often of no little importance, instead of leaving it to the courts to discover, by a careful examination and analysis of what is expressly said, what that intention may be supposed probably to be. There are no doubt reasons which inhibit the legislature from revealing its intention in plain words. I do not know, and must not speculate, what those reasons may be. I trust, however, that it will not be thought impertinent, in any sense of that word, to suggest respectfully that those who are responsible for framing legislation might consider whether the traditional practice, which obscures, if it does not conceal, the intention which Parliament has, or must be presumed to have, might not safely be abandoned.' See also *McCall v Abelesz* [1976] QB 585 at 597G, [1976] 1 All ER 727 at 733, CA, per Ormrod LJ; Cross *Statutory Interpretation* (1976) pp 162-163; Alec Samuels, 'The Interpretation of Statutes' [1980] Stat LR 86 at 104-105.

Commission, which recommended the enactment of a general presumption to the effect that such an action would lie unless the particular Act expressly provided to the contrary.[1] The Commission put forward a draft Bill which was subsequently introduced into Parliament as the Interpretation of Legislation Bill 1980. The relevant provision was cl 4, which provided as follows:

> 'Where any Act passed after this Act imposes or authorises the imposition of a duty, whether positive or negative and whether with or without a special remedy for its enforcement, it shall be presumed, unless express provision to the contrary is made, that a breach of the duty is intended to be actionable (subject to the defences and other incidents applying to actions for breach of statutory duty) at the suit of any person who sustains damage in consequence of the breach.'

The Bill was subsequently withdrawn.[2] Nevertheless, it is in practice increasingly common for individual statutes to provide expressly for the presence or absence of civil liability.[3] On balance, however, it would be over-optimistic, for the reasons given in the next paragraph, to believe that a general presumption along the lines proposed by the Law Commission would effect a significant improvement in the quality of the law relating to damages for breach of statutory duty.

Difficulties with the Law Commission's proposal

[13.20] Whether the granting of a civil action would further the purposes of the particular legislation is a question to which the answer may sometimes vary according to the circumstances of the breach.[4] And it will often be quite unrealistic to expect the legislature (or the parliamentary draftsman) to foresee all such circumstances in advance. It may therefore be perfectly rational for Parliament to wish to leave the matter, in some contexts at least, to the courts. Accordingly, in this context – as elsewhere in the law – a degree of ex post facto reasoning will sometimes be unavoidable and the achievement of total predictability will not be possible. Moreover, if a statutory presumption along the lines proposed had been introduced there might have been a danger that Parliament would 'play safe' in subsequent enactments by expressly excluding it virtually as a matter of routine. Since the Commission was apparently anxious not to see the scope of the action for breach of statutory duty unduly narrowed, this would mean that their proposal would have turned out to be counter-productive.

1 See Law Com No 21 (1969), para 38. The Commission favoured a presumption in *favour* of liability, rather than the other way round, in order to 'avoid any danger of the civil action being restricted in practice by a failure to provide for it in express terms'.
2 For a recent suggestion that a statutory presumption to the *opposite* effect should be created, see KM Stanton *Breach of Statutory Duty in Tort* (1986) p 152: 'The best way to improve the law would be for an Interpretation Act to provide that the tort is not to be inferred. The judicial task would then be merely to put flesh on the bones of the expressly created species of the tort.'
3 See, eg the Mineral Workings (Offshore Installations) Act 1971; Fair Trading Act 1973; Counter-Inflation Act 1973; Guard Dogs Act 1975; Safety of Sports Grounds Act 1975.
4 Cf *Gorris v Scott* (1874) L R 9 Exch 125, discussed above.

Chapter 14

Employers' liability to their employees

The common law duty

Introduction

[**14.01**] The common law relating to the duty which an employer owes to his employees consists largely of the application of the ordinary principles of negligence in a special context. These principles include, where a plaintiff has been injured by the carelessness of a fellow-employee, the normal operation of a master's vicarious liability for the negligence of one of his servants.[1] This is in practice often the route by which persons injured at work obtain damages from their employer: a route which only became available in relatively recent times when the old doctrine of common employment was finally abolished by statute.[2] Ordinary negligence and straightforward vicarious liability are not, however, the whole of the story. There is still an area of uncertain ambit within which an employer will be held liable to an employee for injuries carelessly inflicted even though the employer was not himself personally at fault, and the person who inflicted the injuries was not one of his servants for the purposes of vicarious liability as generally understood. This area of so-called 'non-delegable duty', in which the employer is under a primary duty not merely to take reasonable care but to see that reasonable care is taken, was limited but not eradicated by the decision of the House of Lords in *Davie v New Merton Board Mills Ltd*.[3] It was at least hinted in that case that the concept was largely a historical relic of attempts to circumvent the doctrine of common employment.[4] Nevertheless, its survival appears to be due at least in part to valid contemporary considerations of convenience: the employer being an appropriate and

---

1 See ch 18 below.
2 See the Law Reform (Personal Injuries) Act 1948, s 1(1).
3 [1959] AC 604, [1959] 1 All ER 346, HL.
4 See ibid per Lord Simonds at 618 and 350.

Tort and contract

[**14.02**] In *Johnstone v Bloomsbury Health Authority*[2] the plaintiff, a junior hospital doctor, contended that he had been required by his employers to work such long hours as foreseeably to damage his health. His employers argued that his claim, even if true, was unsustainable, since his contract expressly required him to work long hours and that this express provision took priority over any duty in tort, or implied term of the contract, to protect his health. The Court of Appeal accepted that the express terms of the contract took priority over any tortious or implied contractual duty but, by a majority,[3] refused to strike out the claim holding that, on the proper construction of the contract of employment, the express and implied duties were not inherently in conflict. The defendants had therefore not established beyond argument that they had in fact acquired a contractual right to work the plaintiff so hard as to damage his health. The implication, however, that if the contract unambiguously so provides an employer can at common law[4] acquire the right foreseeably to injure the health of his employees seems, to say the least, profoundly unattractive.[5]

Duty does not extend to pure economic loss

[**14.03**] In *Reid v Rush & Tompkins Group plc*[6] the plaintiff was sent by his employers to work abroad in a country in which third party motor insurance was not compulsory. He was seriously injured in a road accident for which the other driver, who was uninsured and unable to pay damages, was to blame. The plaintiff sought, in effect, to recover compensation for his injuries from his employers arguing that the duty of care in the master-servant relationship extended, in the circumstances, either to insuring the plaintiff against accident themselves or to advising him of the deirability of taking out his own insurance. His claim failed. The Court of Appeal held that an employer's duty at common law extended only to protection of his servant against physical injury and not to protection against the

---

1 Cf the Employers' Liability (Defective Equipment) Act 1969, discussed below.
2 [1991] 2 All ER 293, CA.
3 Sir Nicolas Browne-Wilkinson V-C and Stuart-Smith LJ. Leggatt LJ dissented on the ground that 'those who cannot stand the heat should stay out of the kitchen': [1991] 2 All ER 293 at 303.
4 But cf s 2(1) of the Unfair Contract Terms Act 1977: 'A person cannot by reference to any contract term or to a notice given to persons generally or to particular persons exclude or restrict his liability for death or personal injury resulting from negligence.' The plaintiff in *Johnstone*'s case was held also to have an arguable case on the basis of this provision (the Court of Appeal being unanimous on this point).
5 It is submitted that the reasoning of Stuart-Smith LJ, who appeared in effect to dissent on this point, is to be preferred.
6 [1989] 3 All ER 228, [1990] 1 WLR 212, CA.

incurring of economic loss. In the absence of a specific legislative enactment only an express term in the contract would extend the liability of the employer in this way.

Safe system of work

[14.04] It was at one time usual to subdivide the employer's own common law duty to his employees into a three-fold classification relating to the need for competent fellow-employees, safe equipment, and appropriate methods of work.[1] More recently, however, the tendency has been to adopt a unified approach since 'all three are ultimately only manifestations of the same duty of the master to take reasonable care so to carry out his operations as not to subject those employed by him to unnecessary risk'.[2] The House of Lords has emphasised that this is essentially a question of fact in each case, and that care should be taken not to convert reasons given by judges when deciding such questions into propositions of law capable of general application.[3] The headings which follow are therefore adopted merely for the convenience of exposition in highlighting the more prominent types of issue with which the courts have had to deal.

Appropriate equipment and supervision

[14.05] If the work which an employee is required to do involves a known risk the employer is obliged to devise a method of working which, as far as possible, minimises the risk, and also to provide appropriate safety equipment or facilities. Thus in *General Cleaning Contractors v Christmas*[4] the House of Lords held the defendant employers liable for failing to take suitable precautions which could have prevented their employee from falling and suffering serious injuries, while cleaning the windows of a building from the outside. Lord Reid expressed himself as follows:[5]

> 'Where the problem varies from job to job it may be reasonable to leave a great deal to the man in charge, but the danger in this case is one which is constantly found and it calls for a system to meet it. Where a practice of ignoring an obvious danger has grown up I do not think that it is reasonable to expect an individual workman to take the initiative

---

1 See *Wilsons & Clyde Coal Co Ltd v English* [1938] AC 57 at 78, [1937] 3 All ER 628 at 640 per Lord Wright.
2 Per Pearce LJ in *Wilson v Tyneside Window Cleaning Co* [1958] 2 QB 110 at 121, [1958] 2 All ER 265 at 271, CA; see also *Wingfield v Ellerman's Wilson Line* [1960] 2 Lloyd's Rep 16 at 22, CA, per Devlin LJ; *McDermid v Nash Dredging and Reclamation Co Ltd* [1986] QB 965 at 974, [1986] 2 All ER 676 at 681, CA per Neill LJ (see also *McDermid*'s case in the House of Lords [1987] AC 906, [1987] 2 All ER 878, discussed below.
3 See *Qualcast (Wolverhampton) Ltd v Haynes* [1959] AC 743, [1959] 2 All ER 38, HL.
4 [1953] AC 180, [1952] 2 All ER 1110. See also *Drummond v British Building Cleaners Ltd* [1954] 3 All ER 507, [1954] 1 WLR 1434, CA. Cf *Wilson v Tyneside Window Cleaning Co* [1958] 2 QB 110, [1958] 2 All ER 265, CA.
5 [1953] AC 180 at 194, [1952] 2 All ER 1110 at 1117.

in devising and using precautions. It is the duty of the employer to consider the situation, to devise a suitable system, to instruct his men what they must do, and to supply any implements that may be required...'

The safety equipment or facilities should also be reasonably accessible where the employees who need them are actually working. In *Clifford v Charles H Challen & Son Ltd*[1] the defendants kept barrier cream, to protect against the risk of their employees contracting dermatitis from the substance with which they worked, in the factory store but not in the workshop itself. Cohen LJ said:[2]

> 'Where an employer is making use of a dangerous process, it is not enough for him to have available somewhere in the factory the appliances necessary to minimise the danger. The system of working must be one in which the appliances are available at the place where they are needed...'

[14.06] If, however, the appropriate facilities *were* properly made available, to the knowledge of the workforce, a plaintiff employee who argues that insufficient pressure was put upon him actually to make use of those facilities will understandably find it much harder to succeed than plaintiffs in cases where the defendants failed to provide safety equipment at all. In *Qualcast (Wolverhampton) Ltd v Haynes*[3] the plaintiff was an experienced foundry worker who was injured when molten metal splashed on to one of his feet. He was aware that spats and boots were available to protect against this risk but failed to wear them. He nevertheless claimed that the defendants had failed to provide him with a safe system of work in that he had not actually been ordered or advised to wear spats. His claim failed. Lord Radcliffe said:[4]

> '... though, indeed, there may be cases in which an employer does not discharge his duty of care towards his workmen merely by providing an article of safety equipment, the courts should be circumspect in filling out that duty with the much vaguer obligation of encouraging, exhorting and instructing workmen, or a particular workman, to make regular use of what is provided.'

In one case a plaintiff who had failed to use safety equipment which was available was unsuccessful in his claim even though, being unable to read, he had not understood a notice in the factory drawing attention to the equipment and urging that it should be used.[5] On the other hand, it would be wrong to suppose that it will always be sufficient for an employer to do no more than merely provide proper safety equipment and make known its availability to the workforce. Particularly if disregard for the safety measures becomes widespread, the employer may be held liable if he acquiesces passively in this

1 [1951] 1 KB 495, [1951] 1 All ER 72, CA. Cf *Woods v Durable Suites Ltd* [1953] 2 All ER 391, [1953] 1 WLR 857, CA.
2 [1951] 1 KB 495 at 500, [1951] 1 All ER 72 at 76, CA.
3 [1959] AC 743, [1959] 2 All ER 38, HL.
4 Ibid at 753 and 40.
5 See *James v Hepworth & Grandage Ltd* [1968] 1 QB 94, [1967] 2 All ER 829, CA.

disregard and takes no steps at all to pressurise his employees into protecting themselves.[1] Thus in *Bux v Slough Metals Ltd*[2] the defendants were held liable when one of their employees suffered serious eye injuries. Goggles, which would have prevented the accident, were available but members of the workforce generally were notoriously reluctant to wear them as they considered that they impeded their work. Stephenson L J said:[3]

> 'There was evidence which justified the judge's finding that the employers acquiesced in the universal rejection of goggles in the die-casting foundry . . .That acquiescence came too early and too easily for the employers to rely on Lord Radcliffe's warning in *Qualcast* . . and I agree with the judge that there was a clear breach of their duty to take reasonable precautions in relation to their employees, including the plaintiff, about the wearing of goggles by making it a rule and trying to enforce it by supervision.'

Standard of care

[14.07] In *Stokes v Guest, Keen & Nettlefold (Bolts and Nuts) Ltd*[4] Swanwick J 'perused some of the standard line of authorities dealing with the duties of employers towards their workmen' and expressed his conclusions as follows:[5]

> 'From these authorities I deduce the principles, that the overall test is still the conduct of the reasonable and prudent employer, taking positive thought for the safety of his workers in the light of what he knows or ought to know; where there is a recognised and general practice which has been followed for a substantial period in similar circumstances without mishap, he is entitled to follow it, unless in the light of common sense or newer knowledge, it is clearly bad; but, where there is developing knowledge, he must keep reasonably abreast of it and not be too slow to apply it; and where he has in fact greater than average knowledge of the risks, he may be thereby obliged to take more than the average or standard precautions. He must weigh up the risk in terms of the likelihood of injury occurring and the potential consequences if it does; and he must balance against this the probable effectiveness of the precautions that can be taken to meet it and the expense and inconvenience they involve. If he is found to have fallen below the standard to be properly expected of a reasonable and prudent employer in these respects, he is negligent.'[6]

That reliance upon 'general practice' will not absolve defendants, if that practice involves an obvious risk, is illustrated by the leading

---

1 Cf *Pape v Cumbria County Council* [1992] 3 All ER 211.
2 [1974] 1 All ER 262, [1973] 1 WLR 1358, CA.
3 [1974] 1 All ER 262 at 274, [1973] 1 WLR 1358 at 1371, CA.
4 [1968] 1 WLR 1776.
5 Ibid at 1783.
6 In *Thompson v Smiths Shiprepairers (North Shields) Ltd* [1984] QB 405 at 415, [1984] 1 All ER 881 at 889 Mustill J described this as a 'succinct and helpful statement of the law'.

case of *Morris v West Hartlepool Steam Navigation Co Ltd*,[1] in which the plaintiff seaman fell into the hold of a ship and suffered serious injuries. The House of Lords, by a majority, effectively condemned as negligent a general practice of not guarding or covering access to the hold from the inside of a vessel while the ship was at sea. Although the practice was long-established the patent nature of the risk, and the ease with which precautions could have been taken, meant that it failed to come 'up to the standard required from a reasonably prudent employer whose duty it is to take reasonable steps to avoid exposing his servants to unnecessary risks'.[2]

[**14.08**] Difficult questions may arise where negligence is alleged in a situation involving, in the words of Swanwick J in the *Stokes* case, 'developing knowledge'. In *Thompson v Smiths Shiprepairers (North Shields) Ltd*[3] the plaintiffs hearing had been adversely affected by excessive noise over the course of 30 years' employment in the shipbuilding and shiprepairing trades. Some appreciation of the undesirability of continuous subjection to noise had existed throughout the plaintiffs' working lives, but it was only during the later years that research established the full seriousness of the risk and effective protective devices began to be developed. Mustill J expressed himself as follows:[4]

> '[There] is a type of risk which is regarded at any given time (although not necessarily later) as an inescapable feature of the industry. The employer is not liable for the consequences of such risks, although subsequent changes in social awareness, or improvements in knowledge and technology, may transfer the risk into the category of those against which the employer can and should take care.'

His Lordship awarded damages to the plaintiffs, not for their whole loss, but only for the extent to which they had suffered injury after the date at which 'a reasonable employer, with proper but not extraordinary solicitude for the welfare of his workers, [would] have identified the problem of excessive noise in his yard'.[5]

[**14.09**] The process of weighing up a risk in terms of its likelihood, seriousness and the cost and effectiveness of possible precautions, is as relevant in this area as in the rest of the law of negligence. In *Latimer v AEC Ltd*[6] the House of Lords refused to hold the defendants liable for failing to take the 'drastic step'[7] of closing down their factory rather than allow their employees to run the risk of slipping on a floor across which oil had spread. Lord Tucker considered that it had not been proved 'that the floor was so slippery that, remedial steps not

---

1   [1956] AC 552, [1956] 1 All ER 385, HL. See also *Cavanagh v Ulster Weaving Co Ltd* [1960] AC 145, [1959] 2 All ER 745, HL.
2   Per Lord Tucker in [1965] AC 552 at 576.
3   [1984] QB 405, [1984] 1 All ER 881.
4   Ibid at 415-416 and 889.
5   Ibid at 423 and 894. See also *McSherry v British Telecommunications plc* [1992] 3 Med LR 129 (repetitive strain injury).
6   [1953] AC 643, [1953] 2 All ER 449, HL.
7   Per Lord Porter, ibid, at 643 and 451, and Lord Tucker at 659 and 455.

being possible, a reasonably prudent employer would have closed down the factory rather than allow his employees to run the risks involved in continuing work'. The plaintiff, who incurred injuries when he fell on the slippery floor, therefore failed in his claim for damages.

Duty owed to each employee individually

[14.10] The employer's duty is one 'which is owed to each employee individually', observed Neill LJ in one case,[1] 'and accordingly account has to be taken of the . . . [particular] employee whose safety may be at risk'. In the well-known case of *Paris v Stepney Borough Council*[2] the plaintiff, who was already blind in one eye, became totally blind when a piece of metal entered his other eye. The wearing of goggles would have prevented the accident, and the House of Lords held the defendant employers liable in negligence for failing to provide them for the plaintiff. This was notwithstanding the fact that the risk of any such injury occurring in the occupation in question was so low that it was neither usual nor necessary to provide goggles for two-eyed employees. But the gravity of the injury, if the risk should materialise, required that special steps should have been taken to protect a one-eyed employee.[3] Similarly the level of skill and experience of the individual employee will often be relevant in determining the precise extent to which safety measures, and supervision with respect to such matters, may be necessary.[4]

Duty does not extend to paternalism

[14.11] The proposition, illustrated by *Paris v Stepney Borough Council*, that an employer must take an employee's individual susceptibilities into account, does not imply that the employer must refuse to employ someone who is anxious to work for him even though the existence of special susceptibilities, combined with the nature of the job, will put the employee at some risk even if all proper care is taken. As Edmund Davies LJ put it in one case:[5]

> 'It requires no authority to illustrate the cogency of the proposition that the duty of reasonable care does not impose upon an employer the

---

1 See *McDermid v Nash Dredging and Reclamation Co Ltd* in the Court of Appeal: [1986] QB 965 at 974, [1986] 2 All ER 676 at 681, CA. (*McDermid's* case itself, in which the decision of the Court of Appeal was subsequently affirmed by the House of Lords, is discussed below.)
2 [1951] AC 367, [1951] 1 All ER 42, HL.
3 See also per Stuart-Smith LJ in *Johnstone v Bloomsbury Health Authority* [1991] 2 All ER 293 at 299-300, CA.
4 'An experienced workman dealing with a familiar and obvious risk may not reasonably need the same attention or the same precautions as an inexperienced man who is likely to be more receptive of advice or admonition': per Lord Radcliffe in *Qualcast (Wolverhampton) Ltd v Haynes* [1959] AC 743 at 754, [1959] 2 All ER 38 at 40E, HL. See also per Lord Keith of Avonholme in the same case (at 755 and 42E).
5 *Kossinski v Chrysler United Kingdom Ltd* (1973) 15 KIR 225. See also *Bailey v Rolls-Royce (1971) Ltd* [1984] ICR 688, CA.

necessity of saying to an employee: "You are not fit for this properly-planned and entirely safe work because of your own physical condition, and therefore, despite your own desire to continue at it, we must dismiss you."'

Thus in *Withers v Perry Chain Co Ltd*[1] a plaintiff who willingly and deliberately continued to do work which unavoidably involved some risk of dermatitis, even though she knew that she was susceptible to the disease, completely failed in her claim against her employers when it materialised. Of course the rule in this case presupposes that the employee is fully apprised of all the relevant circumstances. There might, as Devlin LJ observed, be liability 'if the employee were to conceal the risk or fail to give the employee information which he had and which might help her to evaluate it properly'.[2]

Dangerous fellow-employees negligently left in post

[**14.12**] Since the abolition of the doctrine of common employment a plaintiff injured by a fellow-employee will, of course, be able to hold the employer liable vicariously if the fellow-employee was acting in the course of his employment. Cases occasionally arise, however, in which that employee caused injury while playing a practical joke which misfired with serious consequences. In one case of this type the 'joke' was so closely connected with the tortfeasor's actual work that it was held to come just within the course of his employment for the purposes of vicarious liability.[3] More usually, however, deliberate activities of this kind cannot plausibly be regarded as coming within the course of employment.[4] It might then be alleged by the plaintiff victim that, by allowing a state of affairs to occur in which practical jokes could take place, the employer was himself negligent as being in breach of his own primary duty to provide a safe system of work. Such a claim succeeded in *Hudson v Ridge Manufacturing Co Ltd*.[5] In this case the plaintiff was tripped up by a fellow-worker who had persistently engaged, for several years, 'in horse-play and skylarking', and who had an 'almost incurable habit of tripping people up'. The defendants had frequently reprimanded him but to no effect; and they continued to employ him notwithstanding his behaviour. Streatfeild J observed that 'there existed . . . in the system of work, a source of danger' for which the defendants should be held liable. His Lordship emphasised, however, that if the incident had been an isolated one or had, perhaps, occurred once before and been followed by a reprimand

---

1 [1961] 3 All ER 676, [1961] 1 WLR 1314, CA. See also *Jones v Lionite Specialities (Cardiff) Ltd* (1961) 105 Sol Jo 1082, CA.
2 [1961] 3 All ER 676 at 680, [1961] 1 WLR 1314 at 1320. But cf *White v Holbrook Precision Castings* [1985] IRLR 215, CA (no duty to warn of possibility of developing trivial condition causing minor discomfort).
3 See *Harrison v Michelin Tyre Co Ltd* [1985] 1 All ER 918, [1985] ICR 696.
4 See *Coddington v International Harvesters of Great Britain Ltd* (1969) 6 KIR 146.
5 [1957] 2 QB 348, [1957] 2 All ER 229.

giving reasonable grounds for supposing that there would be no recurrence, liability could not be imposed on the employer.[1]

Defective equipment

[**14.13**] The Employer's Liability (Defective Equipment) Act 1969 s 1(1) provides as follows :

> 'Where after the commencement of this Act —
> (a) an employee suffers personal injury in the course of his employment in consequence of a defect in equipment provided by his employer for the purposes of the employer's business; and
> (b) the defect is attributable wholly or partly to the fault of a third party (whether identified or not),
> the injury shall be deemed to be also attributable to negligence on the part of the employer (whether or not he is liable in respect of the injury apart from this subsection), but without prejudice to the law relating to contributory negligence and to any remedy by way of contribution or in contract or otherwise which is available to the employer in respect of the injury.'

The purpose of this provision was to reverse the decision of the House of Lords in *Davie v New Merton Board Mills Ltd*.[2] In this case apparently sound equipment, obtained from a reputable source, turned out to be defective, due to negligence in its manufacture, and injured an employee of the defendants. The latter were held not liable on the ground that the employer had discharged his duty by taking reasonable care when acquiring the equipment: the employee's remedy was to proceed against the manufacturer under *Donoghue v Stevenson*. This decision was felt to be inconvenient since the employee might in practice have difficulty in pursuing the third party supplier or manufacturer. Accordingly, providing the employee can show that the defect which caused him injury was due to carelessness, the Act enables him to recover against his employer regardless of whether or not he is able even to identify the negligent third party. Of course if the employer has himself been negligent with respect to the equipment, eg by failing to inspect it or to remove it from use when he knew, or should have known, of the defect, then he will be liable to his injured employee at common law.[3] The word 'equipment', for the purposes of the Act, is to be construed broadly, and even includes ships.[4]

---

1 See ibid at 350 and 230. See also *Smith v Crossley Bros Ltd* (1951) 95 Sol Jo 655, CA ('a wicked act which the defendants had no reason to foresee').
2 [1959] AC 604, [1959] 1 All ER 346, HL.
3 See, eg *Pearce v Round Oak Steel Works* [1969] 3 All ER 680, [1965] 1 WLR 595, CA; *Taylor v Rover Co Ltd* [1966] 2 All ER 181, [1966] 1 WLR 1491; *Condo v South Australia* (1987) 47 SASR 584.
4 See *Coltman v Bibby Tankers Ltd, The Derbyshire* [1988] AC 276, [1987] 3 All ER 1068, HL: ('The purpose of the Act was manifestly to saddle the employer with liability for defective plant of every sort with which the employee is compelled to work in the course of his employment and I can see no ground for excluding particular types of chattel merely on the ground of their size or the element upon which they are designed to operate.' per Lord Oliver).

[**14.14**] It should be noted that an employer is required by statute to be insured 'against liability for bodily injury or disease sustained by his employees ... arising out of and in the course of their employment'. This provision is to be found in the Employers' Liability (Compulsory Insurance) Act 1969, s 1(1). It obviously includes in its scope an employer's liability under the Employers' Liability (Defective Equipment) Act as well as his common law liability for failure to provide a safe system of work. Accordingly, an injured employee should now be able to recover compensation even if the defect in the equipment had been due to the negligence of a third party who subsequently turned out to be insolvent: a situation in which *Davie v New Merton Board Mills* would in practice have left him remediless.

Non-delegable duty

[**14.15**] The approach reflected by the legislature, in the Employer's Liability (Defective Equipment) Act 1969, to the problem of employer's liability for injuries suffered by their employees, is similar to that adopted by the common law as it was perceived to be[1] prior to the decision in *Davie v New Merton Board Mills Ltd.*[2] In that case, however, the House of Lords was apparently of the opinion that there should be some narrowing in the scope of an employer's liability for injuries with respect to which neither he, nor other servants of his, had been negligent. But the considerations of policy and convenience underlying the imposition of so-called 'non-delegable duties' upon employers continue to exercise influence, even at common law, notwithstanding the decision in *Davie*'s case. Accordingly an employer might still find himself liable, beyond the normal confines of vicarious liability, for the fault of someone else. That this is so has been strikingly demonstrated by another, much more recent, unanimous decision of the House of Lords. In *McDermid v Nash Dredging and Reclamation Co Ltd*[3] the defendants were held liable for injuries suffered by one of their employees as a result of the negligence of a tugboat captain, who was not their servant. The plaintiff had, however, been instructed by the defendants to work on a project in which both they and the tugboat captain were involved; and this had the effect of putting the plaintiff under the supervision of the captain, whose method of working was found to be unsafe and which caused the injury. Lord Brandon spoke as follows:[4]

> '... an employer owes to his employee a duty to exercise reasonable care to ensure that the system of work provided for him is a safe one ... The essential characteristic of the duty is that, if it is not performed, it is no defence for the employer to show that he delegated its performance to a person, whether his servant or not his servant, whom he reasonably

---

1 See *Wilsons & Clyde Coal Co Ltd v English* [1938] AC 57, [1937] 3 All ER 628, HL.
2 [1959] AC 604, [1959] 1 All ER 346, HL.
3 [1987] AC 906, [1987] 2 All ER 878, HL. See also *Sumner v William Henderson & Sons Ltd* [1964] 1 QB 450, [1963] 1 All ER 408.
4 [1987] AC 906 at 919, [1987] 2 All ER 878 at 887.

believed to be competent to perform it. Despite such delegation the employer is liable for the non-performance of the duty'.[1]

Lord Brandon's speech also included a reference to a 1984 decision of the High Court of Australia, *Kondis v State Transport Authority*,[2] in which a similar decision had been reached and which had been heavily relied on by the Court of Appeal in *McDermid*'s case.[3] Mason J, in that case, stated what he understood to be the reason for the imposition of liability upon employers in these circumstances, and also put the scope of that liability on a wide basis. He said:[4]

> 'The employer has the exclusive responsibility for the safety of the appliances, the premises and the system of work to which he subjects his employee and the employee has no choice but to accept and rely on the employer's provision and judgment in relation to these matters. The consequence is that in these relevant aspects the employee's safety is in the hands of the employer; it is his responsibility. The employee can reasonably expect therefore that reasonable care and skill will be taken. In the case of the employer there is no unfairness in imposing on him a non-delegable duty; it is reasonable that he should bear liability for the negligence of his independent contractors in devising a safe system of work. If he requires his employee to work according to an unsafe system he should bear the consequences.'[5]

Duty discharged on the facts

[**14.16**] *McDermid v Nash Dredging and Reclamation Co Ltd* was distinguished on the facts in *Cook v Square D Ltd*.[6] In this case the plaintiff was sent by his employers in the UK to work in Saudi Arabia at premises occupied by another firm, where he suffered injury due to a hazard on those premises. The Court of Appeal accepted that the duty owed by the UK employers could not be delegated but held that that duty, which was only to do what was reasonable in all the circumstances, had not been breached merely by the presence of a hazard on a site abroad occupied by supposedly competent international contractors. 'The suggestion that the home-based employer', observed Farquaharson LJ,[7] 'has any responsibility for the daily events of a site in Saudi Arabia has an air of unreality'. In *McDermid*'s case the relationship between the tugboat captain and the main employers had been much closer. Although the plaintiff in *Cook*'s case therefore failed Farquaharson LJ emphasised that, as the contrast with *McDermid* indeed illustrated, decisions in other cases could well be different even where the facts were superficially similar. He said:[8]

---

1 See also *Wingfield v Ellerman's Wilson Line* [1960] 2 Lloyd's Rep 16 at 22, CA, per Devlin LJ.
2 (1984) 55 ALR 225.
3 See [1986] QB 965, [1986] 2 All ER 676, CA.
4 (1984) 55 ALR 225 at 235.
5 See also *Morris v Breaveglen Ltd* (1992) 137 Sol Jo LB 13, CA.
6 [1992] IRLR 34, CA.
7 [1992] IRLR 34 at 38.
8 Ibid, at the same page.

'Circumstances will, of course, vary, and it may be that in some cases where, for example, a number of employees are going to work on a foreign site or where one or two employees are called upon to work there for a very considerable period of time that an employer may be required to inspect the site and satisfy himself that the occupiers were conscious of their obligations concerning the safety of people working there.'

Statutory duties

Introduction

[**14.17**] It has long been established that an action for damages for breach of statutory duty can subsist in favour of an employee, injured due to contravention by his employer of one or more of the numerous statutory provisions or regulations relating to safety at places of work. It is intended that all these measures should eventually be replaced by regulations and approved codes of practice promulgated under the Health and Safety at Work etc Act 1974. This is in order to improve the law in this area and also to give it a more unified and coherent structure. The process is a gradual one, however, and until they are superseded the duties imposed by 'existing statutory provisions', as they are referred to in the 1974 Act, remain in force according to the terms of those provisions. Moreover, the replacement regulations, to be made under powers conferred by the Health and Safety at Work etc Act,[1] will also give rise to the action for damages for breach of statutory duty, except in so far as they themselves provide otherwise.[2]

[**14.18**] In 1992 the process of replacement was carried significantly forward by the Workplace (Health, Safety and Welfare) Regulations 1992.[3] Although these regulations will only come into force, as far as existing workplaces are concerned, on 1 January 1996, they came into effect on 1 January 1993 as far as new workplaces are concerned. When fully in force they will have the effect of superseding a number of the 'existing statutory provisions'[4] contained in the Factories Act 1961, and equivalent measures to be found in the Offices, Shops and Railway Premises Act 1963, which are dealt with below.[5] Of necessity, comprehensive treatment of the detailed provisions relating to particular trades, much of it also contained in delegated legislation, cannot be attempted in a work of this kind. What follows should therefore be supplemented, as appropriate, by reference to additional original sources and relevant specialist works[6].

1   See s 15.
2   Health and Safety at Work etc Act, s 47(2).
3   SI 1992/3004.
4   See the Health and Safety at Work etc Act, s 53(1) and Sch 1.
5   Sections 1 to 7, 18, 28, 29, 57 to 60 and 69 of the Factories Act 1961, and ss 4 to 16 of the Offices, Shops and Railway Premises Act 1963 are repealed: Workplace (Health, Safety and Welfare) Regulations 1992, Sch 2.
6   See, eg Munkman *Employer's Liability at Common Law* (11th edn, 1990).

Dangerous machinery and the duty to fence

[**14.19**] In *F E Callow (Engineers) v Johnson*[1] Lord Hailsham LC concisely summarised the statutory provisions relating to the statutory duties of employers with respect to the fencing of factory machinery,[2] and also highlighted some of the difficulties to which those provisions have given rise. He said:[3]

> 'My Lords, this appeal is another example of litigation arising from s 14 of the Factories Act 1961. Section 14 forms part of a group of five sections (ss 12 to 16) which deal with the liability of an employer in a factory to fence parts of the machinery for the protection of his employees. These sections are clearly intended to form, as it were, a single code and should be read together. Section 12 deals with prime movers. Section 13 deals with transmission machinery. Section 14 deals with dangerous parts of machinery, other than prime movers and transmission machinery. The obligation cast on the employer is not unqualified, and s 15 deals with the operation of machinery which, under the exceptions to the preceding sections, is unfenced. Section 16 deals with the construction and maintenance of fences in cases where the duty to fence applies under the preceding sections. It provides (in language which may be material to this appeal) that the fences are to be kept in position while the parts required to be fenced are "in motion or use", thereby implying that there may be cases in which the parts are in motion but not in use and equally cases in which the parts required to be fenced are in use but not in motion.
>
> At first sight the code provided by this group of five sections is deceptively simple. In point of fact, however, its provisions, especially those of s 14 which are now under discussion, have given rise to a considerable degree of difference of opinion. In some ways the duty cast on employers has seemed at times unduly harsh. In others the protection afforded to the worker has seemed illusory and unreal.'

'Prime movers' and 'transmission machinery'

[**14.20**] 'Prime movers' are the devices which propel the machinery of the factory. The expression is defined in the Act itself[4] as meaning 'every engine, motor or other appliance which provides mechanical energy derived from steam, water, wind, electricity, the combustion of fuel or other source'. Section 12(1) of the Act provides that the moving parts of such equipment 'shall be securely fenced', except that certain electrical machinery need not be fenced if its particular position or construction renders it as safe as it would be if it were fenced.[5]

[**14.21**] Section 13 of the Act contains similar fencing requirements for 'transmission machinery',[6] whereby the 'prime movers' activate the working equipment or appliances of the factory. Such machinery has

---

1 [1971] AC 335, [1970] 3 All ER 639, HL.
2 For similar provisions relating to machinery in offices see the Offices, Shops and Railway Premises Act 1963, s 17.
3 [1971] AC 335 at 341-342, [1970] 3 All ER 639 at 641.
4 Ie Factories Act 1961, s 176(1).
5 See s 12(3).
6 For definition see s 176(1).

to be 'securely fenced' unless its position or construction renders it equally safe without fencing.[1] In order to be 'securely fenced' the machinery must be made safe against foreseeable risks.[2] The relevant risks are, however, those which involve an employee's body coming into contact with the working parts of the machinery. The section does not require protection against the risk of the machinery itself breaking and parts of it flying out and causing injury. Only complete encasement of the machinery would normally be effective against that particular hazard; and such extreme measures are not contemplated by an obligation merely to 'fence'.[3]

'Other machinery'

[**14.22**] Whereas 'prime movers' and 'transmission machinery' are in effect deemed automatically to be dangerous, and to require fencing, 'other machinery' is required by s 14 to be fenced only if it is in fact 'dangerous'. For this purpose 'machinery is to be regarded as dangerous if it is a reasonably foreseeable cause of injury to anybody acting in a way in which a human being may be reasonably expected to act in circumstances which may be reasonably expected to occur'.[4] Once machinery comes within this test, and hence within the section, the obligation to 'securely fence' is 'unambiguously absolute'.[5] Although there is power to modify this obligation by delegated legislation,[6] in the absence of such a modification it is no defence to the factory owner that secure fencing would be so impractical as to render the machine commercially unusable.[7]

[**14.23**] The scope of the protection afforded to employees by s 14 has been narrowed by a controversial series of decisions of the House of Lords. The section has been treated as only requiring fencing against the risk of injury being caused directly by the operator's body coming into contact with the machine. In *Nicholls v F Austin (Leyton) Ltd,*[8] the plaintiff was injured when part of a piece of wood, which she was

---

1 For a case in which the defendants argued unsuccessfully that their machinery was within the exemption see *Hodkinson v H Wallwork & Co Ltd* [1955] 3 All ER 236, [1955] 1 WLR 1195, CA.
2 See *Burns v Joseph Terry & Sons Ltd* [1951] 1 KB 454, [1950] 2 All ER 987, CA.
3 *Carroll v Andrew Barclay & Sons Ltd* [1948] AC 477, [1948] 2 All ER 386, HL. Of course there might be liability on the employer at common law in such a case if negligence could be proved.
4 Per Lord Goff in *Mailer v Austin Rover Group plc* [1989] 2 All ER 1087 at 1089, HL. The formulation is based on wording propounded by du Parcq J in *Walker v Bletchley Flettons Ltd* [1937] 1 All ER 170 at 175 and amended by Lord Reid in *John Summers & Sons Ltd v Frost* [1955] AC 740 at 766, [1955] 1 All ER 870 at 883, HL.
5 Per Lord Simonds in *John Summers & Sons Ltd v Frost* [1955] AC 740 at 752, [1955] 1 All ER 870 at 873.
6 See *Automatic Woodturning Co Ltd v Stringer* [1957] AC 544, [1957] 1 All ER 90, HL; *Miller v William Boothman & Sons* [1944] KB 337, [1944] 1 All ER 333, CA. Cf *Benn v Kamm & Co Ltd* [1952] 2 QB 127, [1952] 1 All ER 833, CA; *Quinn v Horsfall & Bickham Ltd* [1956] 2 All ER 467, [1956] 1 WLR 652, CA.
7 See, generally, *John Summers & Sons Ltd v Frost* [1955] AC 740, [1955] 1 All ER 870, HL.
8 [1946] AC 493, [1946] 2 All ER 92, HL.

putting through a circular saw, flew off and injured her. The House held that the section did not require fencing to be effective against the risk of injury by material being ejected from the machine, and the plaintiff's claim failed. In *Close v Steel Co of Wales Ltd*,[1] a claim under the section similarly failed even though it was part of the machine itself, a fragment from the shattered bit of a drill, which flew out and injured the plaintiff, by entering his eye. Moreover, although contact between the plaintiff's *clothing* and the machine, giving rise to injury, can give rise to a valid claim, injury caused by contact between the machine and a *tool* held by the plaintiff cannot.[2] On the other hand it has been judicially stated in the House of Lords that the ambit of these restrictive decisions will not be extended further than their own facts require;[3] and parts of machinery not in themselves dangerous can nevertheless attract the fencing provision if they give rise to danger, eg by creating 'nips' by virtue of proximity to each other[4] or to materials being worked on the machine.[5]

Plaintiff's conduct

[14.24] The fact that the plaintiff acted carelessly, indolently, or even frivolously in coming into contact with the machine will not absolve his employer from liability for any failure to comply with the fencing provision: such actions by employees are reasonably foreseeable and fencing should guard against them.[6] Nor does it matter that the employee was not actually acting in the course of his employment at the time when he was injured. The expression 'a frolic of his own', which is relevant to a master's vicarious liability for the torts of his servants, is not relevant here.[7] In *Uddin v Associated Portland Cement Manufacturers Ltd*[8] the plaintiff left his allotted place of work, entered a part of the factory where he was not authorised to be, and only came into contact with the unfenced machine which caused him injury when he leaned over it in order to catch a pigeon. He was nevertheless held able to sue his employers for breach of their statutory duty under the section. Moreover, provided that the accident

---

1   [1962] AC 367, [1961] 2 All ER 953, HL. See also *Eaves v Morris Motors Ltd* [1961] 2 QB 385, [1961] 3 All ER 233, CA.
2   See *Sparrow v Fairey Aviation Co Ltd* [1964] AC 1019, [1962] 3 All ER 706, HL.
3   Per Lord Hailsham LC in *F E Callow (Engineers) Ltd v Johnson* [1971] AC 335 at 343, [1970] 3 All ER 639 at 642, HL. See also *Wearing v Pirelli Ltd* [1977] 1 All ER 339 at 346, [1977] 1 WLR 48 at 56, HL, per Lord Edmund-Davies.
4   *F E Callow (Engineers) Ltd v Johnson* [1971] AC 335, [1970] 3 All ER 639, HL. But cf *Pearce v Stanley Bridges Ltd* [1965] 2 All ER 594, [1965] 1 WLR 931, CA.
5   See *Midland and Low Moor Iron & Steel Co Ltd v Cross* [1965] AC 343, [1964] 3 All ER 752, HL; *Hoare v M & W Grazebrook Ltd* [1957] 1 All ER 470, [1957] 1 WLR 638. See also *Dairy Farmers Co-operative Ltd v Azar* (1990) 95 ALR 1 (Aust HC).
6   *Smith v Chesterfield and District Co-operative Society Ltd* [1953] 1 All ER 447, [1953] 1 WLR 370, CA. Of course, the plaintiff's damages may be reduced for contributory negligence in such a case.
7   See per Diplock LJ in *Allen v Aeroplane and Motor Aluminium Castings* [1965] 3 All ER 377 at 379, [1965] 1 WLR 1244 at 1248, CA.
8   [1965] 2 QB 582, [1965] 2 All ER 213, CA.

would not have happened had not the defendant employers failed to fence in breach of the section, it is irrelevant that the way in which the accident actually happened was unforeseeable or unexplained.[1]

Construction and position of fencing: 'in motion or use'

[**14.25**] The Factories Act 1961, s 16, reads, where material, as follows:

> 'All fencing or other safeguards . . . shall be of substantial construction, and constantly maintained and kept in position while the parts required to be fenced or safeguarded are in motion or use, except when any such parts are necessarily exposed for examination and for any lubrication or adjustment shown by the examination to be immediately necessary . . .'

The words 'in motion or use', in this provision, have given rise to a number of reported cases. It is clear that a machine can be 'in motion' even though not actually undertaking, at the time, the actual task for which it was designed and commercially intended.[2] But it does not follow that *any* movement constitutes 'motion' for the purposes of the provision. In *Richard Thomas & Baldwins Ltd v Cummings*[3] the plaintiff crushed his finger when he manually rotated a machine in the course of repairing it. While the repairs were in progress the fencing had been removed and the power switched off. The House of Lords held that the manual rotation had not constituted 'motion' for the purposes of the section, and that the defendant employers had therefore not been in breach of their statutory duty. The House considered that to have decided otherwise could have led to absurdity since, as Lord Reid observed, 'there must be many occasions in the course of repairing and readjusting machinery when it is necessary to expose parts which in ordinary use must be fenced and to move them to an appreciable extent'. His Lordship could therefore 'see no answer to the argument' that if, on the facts in question, the provision were construed in favour of the plaintiff it would be 'practically impossible in such cases to make the necessary repairs and readjustments without committing an offence by contravening the provisions of section 16'.[4] On the other hand, in *Stanbrook v Waterlow & Sons Ltd*[5] the plaintiff, in order to load a printing machine with paper before printing commenced, had to remove the guard and switch the machine on and off very quickly: this was because slight rotation was necessary in order to feed in the paper and the machine could not be rotated by hand. The plaintiff suffered injury in the process and the Court of Appeal held that the machine was in 'motion' and that the defendants

---

1 See *Millard v Serck Tubes Ltd* [1969] 1 All ER 598, [1969] 1 WLR 211, CA. See also *F E Callow (Engineers) Ltd v Johnson* [1971] AC 335 at 347, [1970] 3 All ER 639 at 645, HL, per Lord Hailsham LC.
2 See *Irwin v White, Tomkins and Courage Ltd* [1964] 1 All ER 545, [1964] 1 WLR 387; see also *Horne v Lec Refrigeration Ltd* [1965] 2 All ER 898.
3 [1955] AC 321, [1955] 1 All ER 285, HL. See also *Knight v Leamington Spa Courier Ltd* [1961] 2 QB 253, [1961] 2 All ER 666, CA.
4 [1955] AC 321 at 334, [1955] 1 All ER 285 at 290; see also per Lord Oaksey at 330 and 287.
5 [1964] 2 All ER 506, [1964] 1 WLR 825, CA.

were accordingly in breach of the fencing provision: the Court therefore held in effect that the machine was inherently dangerous in that as it stood it could not be loaded without contravening the section.[1] But it does not follow that very brief rotation of a machine in this way by connection and disconnection of the power automatically constitutes 'motion' for the purposes of the section and that only manual movement, with the power cut off, does not do so. In appropriate cases such brief powered movement for repair purposes can be permissible, when the fence is removed, without constituting a breach of the section.[2]

Floors and access

[**14.26**] Two sections of the Factories Act 1961 deal with the physical condition of places of work. Section 28 (1) provides as follows: 'All floors, steps, stairs, passages and gangways shall be of sound construction and properly maintained and shall, so far as is reasonably practicable, be kept free from any obstruction and from any substance likely to cause persons to slip.'[3]

Section 29(1) reads thus:

> 'There shall, so far as is reasonably practicable, be provided and maintained safe means of access to every place at which any person has at any time to work, and every such place shall, so far as is reasonably practicable, be made and kept safe for any person working there.'

Although the word 'safe' appears in s 29(1) but not in s 28(2) this does *not* imply that s 28 imposes a more onerous obligation in that a floor in fact 'safe' could nevertheless be said to involve a breach of the section by having been improperly 'maintained'. An argument to this effect was rejected by the Court of Appeal in *Payne v Weldless Steel Tube Co Ltd*,[4] in which the court held that a floor could only be said to have been improperly maintained for the purposes of the section if it was in fact unsafe for persons using it.

Transient dangers

[**14.27**] In the case of s 28(1) the second limb of the sub-section, requiring the relevant areas to 'be kept free from any obstruction, and from any substance likely to cause persons to slip' imposes a distinct obligation from the first limb. The phrase did not, in fact, appear in the equivalent provision of the Factories Act 1937 and was inserted in order to provide a remedy in situations in which normally sound, and

---

1 But see per Dankwerts LJ in the *Stanbrook* case, ibid, at 508 and 829.
2 See *Mitchell v Westin* [1965] 1 All ER 657, [1965] 1 WLR 297, CA. Cf *Knight v Leamington Spa Courier Ltd* [1961] 2 QB 253, [1961] 2 All ER 666, CA; *Kelly v John Dale Ltd* [1965] 1 QB 185, [1964] 2 All ER 497.
3 See also the Offices, Shops and Railway Premises Act 1963, s 16 and *Bell v Department of Health and Social Security* (1989) Times, 13 June.
4 [1956] 1 QB 196, [1955] 3 All ER 612, CA.

properly maintained, floors had temporarily become obstructed or slippery.[1] Similarly, it is now clear that in the case of s 29(1) the requirement that areas within that section should be 'kept safe for any person working there' also creates a separate obligation from the section's first limb. In *Cox v Angus*[2] Lloyd J held 'as a matter of law' that there could 'be a breach of the occupier's obligation under the second half of section 29(1) even though the danger [was] transient or temporary'. It should also be noted that, in appropriate cases, the provision of 'safe means of access' within s 29(1) might require the employer to take precautions such as clearing or gritting a factory car park during icy conditions in winter.[3] But, providing he has established a proper system for the taking of such precautions, an employer will not be in breach of his statutory obligation merely because, in severe winter conditions, not every part of the area had been gritted by the start of the working day.[4]

'Reasonably practicable'

[**14.28**] Both ss 28(1) and 29(1) include the phrase 'so far as is reasonably practicable'. The onus of proving, for the purposes of this provision, that the taking of precautions was *not* reasonably practicable lies upon the defendant: it is not necessary for the plaintiff to prove that such precautions *were* reasonably practicable.[5] A defendant who seeks to rely on the excuse must raise it specifically in his pleading.[6] In *Jenkins v Allied Ironfounders Ltd*,[7] Lord Reid said that in order to determine reasonable practicability it was necessary to balance 'any expense, delays or other disadvantages involved in adopting the preventive system' against 'the nature and extent of the risks involved if that system was not adopted'.[8] In the case itself precautions which 'would certainly have been possible'[9] were held nevertheless not to have been 'reasonably practicable'. But it would be wrong to suppose that the availability of the defence has the effect of reducing the level of the duty which the sections impose upon

---

1   See, eg *Dorman Long (Steel) Ltd v Bell* [1964] 1 All ER 617, [1964] 1 WLR 333, HL. Cf *Latimer v AEC Ltd* [1953] AC 643, [1953] 2 All 449, HL (decided under the Factories Act 1937, s 25).
2   [1981] ICR 683 at 687. Cf *Levesley v Thomas Firth & John Brown Ltd* [1953] 2 All ER 866, [1953] 1 WLR 1206, CA (decided under the Factories Act 1937, s 26).
3   See *Woodward v Renold* [1980] ICR 387. Cf *Thomas v Bristol Aeroplane Co Ltd* [1954] 2 All ER 1, [1954] 1 WLR 694, CA.
4   *Gitsham v CH Pearce & Sons plc* (1991) Times, 11 February, CA.
5   See *Nimmo v Alexander Cowan & Sons* [1968] AC 107, [1967] 3 All ER 187, HL.
6   See *Bowes v Sedgefield District Council* [1981] ICR 234, CA. See also *Johnston v Caddies Wainwright* [1983] ICR 407, CA; *Larner v British Steel plc* (1993) Times, 19 February, CA.
7   [1969] 3 All ER 1609, [1970] 1 WLR 304, HL.
8   Ibid at 1612 and 307. See also per Lord Goff in *Mailer v Austin Rover Group plc* [1989] 2 All ER 1087 at 1090: 'If, for example, the defendant establishes that the risk is small, but that the measures necessary to eliminate it are great, he may be held to be exonerated from taking steps to eliminate the risk on the ground that it was not reasonably practicable for him to do so.'
9   Per Lord Reid in *Jenkins v Allied Ironfounders Ltd* [1969] 3 All ER 1609 at 1612, [1970] 1 WLR 304 at 307, HL.

defendants so as to make it no higher than the ordinary common law duty of care imposed by the tort of negligence. In particular the degree of probability of the hazard manifesting itself, which if it is very low can sometimes exonerate a defendant from negligence liability, does not appear to be relevant. In *Bennett v Rylands Whitecross Ltd*[1] Kilner Brown J said that the fact that a danger 'was unwittingly created, or was a fluke, or a million to one chance, does not absolve the defendants from an obligation which is absolute unless they can show that it was not reasonably practicable for them to have prevented or removed' it. It also appears to be the case that a defendant who proves that he had established a reasonable system for the taking of precautions will nevertheless incur liability if that system broke down due to a non-negligent momentary lapse on the part of one of his employees in operating it. 'If it is reasonably practicable for steps to be taken by anyone', said Denning LJ in one case,[2] 'they must be taken'.[3]

Ventilation and extraction of fumes and dust

Ventilation

[**14.29**] The Factories Act 1961, s 4(1) provides as follows:

> 'Effective and suitable provision shall be made for securing and maintaining by the circulation of fresh air in each workroom the adequate ventilation of the room, and for rendering harmless, so far as practicable, all such fumes, dust and other impurities generated in the course of any process or work carried on in the factory as may be injurious to health.'[4]

The word 'ventilation' is the key to the whole of this provision, and therefore qualifies the words 'rendering harmless' in the latter part of the section. Accordingly, those words do not impose a separate and additional obligation even though a literal reading might have suggested otherwise. In the 1984 case of *Brook v J & P Coates (UK) Ltd*[5] Boreham J, summarising the effect of earlier authorities,[6] expressed himself as follows: 'Put broadly, that section, in my judgment, relates to the securing of effective ventilation by the circulation of fresh air. It does not . . . enjoin the fitting of exhaust appliances to extract dust at source.'

Although there are *dicta* to the contrary apparently favouring strict liability,[7] the better view is 'that knowledge (actual or constructive in

---

1 [1978] ICR 1031 at 1034.
2 *Braham v J Lyons & Co Ltd* [1962] 1 WLR 1048 at 1051, CA. See also per Pearson LJ (at 1053). Cf per Donovan LJ, dubitante, (at 1052-1053).
3 See also *Williams v Painter Bros Ltd (1968)* 5 KIR 487 at 490, CA, per Winn LJ.
4 See also the Offices, Shops and Railway Premises Act 1963, s 7(1).
5 [1984] 1 All ER 702 at 717g.
6 See *Ebbs v James Whitson & Co Ltd* [1952] 2 QB 877, [1952] 2 All ER 192, CA and *Graham v Co-operative Wholesale Society Ltd* [1957] 1 All ER 654, [1957] 1 WLR 511.
7 See *Ebbs v James Whitson & Co Ltd* [1952] 2 QB 877 at 882, [1952] 2 All ER 192 at 193, CA, per Singleton LJ and at 886 per Hodson LJ.

the sense that the dutiful occupier should have known) of the danger must be there before the occupier can be in breach of his duty under section 4'.[1] The speeches in the House of Lords in *Nicholson v Atlas Steel Foundry*,[2] in which an action based on it succeeded, provide a useful example of the application of s 4(1) to a particular factual situation.

Positive measures

[**14.30**] The taking of positive measures actually to remove dust or fumes, although not covered by s 4, is among the matters dealt with by s 63(1) of the Act. This section provides as follows:

> 'In every factory in which, in connection with any process carried on, there is given off any dust or fume or other impurity of such a character and to such extent as to be likely to be injurious or offensive to the persons employed, or any substantial quantity of dust of any kind, all practicable measures shall be taken to protect the persons employed against inhalation of the dust or fume or other impurity and to prevent its accumulating in any workroom, and in particular where the nature of the process makes it practicable, exhaust appliances shall be provided and maintained, as near as possible to the point of origin of the dust or fume or other impurity, so as to prevent it entering the air of any workroom.'

It is to be noted that there is a dichotomy in the opening part of the section between 'injurious' dust on the one hand and '*any* substantial quantity of dust' on the other.[3] In the former case there has to be knowledge, or means of knowledge, of the harmful propensity before liability can arise.[4] But in the latter case there is an obligation to take measures even though the dust is not known actually to be harmful.[5] In both situations, however, the obligation is only to take measures which are 'practicable'. In one case, in which the section was successfully relied upon, Boreham J said that he took ' "practicable" in this context to mean a precaution which could be undertaken without practical difficulty'.[6] The expression should, however, be contrasted with one found elsewhere in the Act: 'so far as is reasonably practicable'. This expression seems to import a lower duty than that in s 63(1).[7] In *Wallhead v Ruston and Hornsby Ltd*[8] Bagnall J

---

1 Per Latey J in *Cartwright v CKN Sankey Ltd* [1972] 2 Lloyd's Rep 242 at 246 (revsd on other grounds in (1973) 14 KIR 349, CA). See also *Wallhead v Ruston and Hornsby Ltd* (1973) 14 KIR 285 at 291-292 per Bagnall J.
2 [1957] 1 All ER 776, [1957] 1 WLR 613.
3 See *Richards v Highways Ironfounders (West Bromwich) Ltd* [1955] 3 All ER 205 at 209, [1955] 1 WLR 1049 at 1054, CA, per Evershed MR.
4 See *Cartwright v G K N Sankey Ltd* (1973) 14 KIR 349 at 355, CA, per Edmund Davies LJ. But cf per Megaw LJ in the same case at 365-366.
5 See *Gregson v Hick Hargreaves & Co Ltd* [1955] 3 All ER 507 at 515-516, [1955] 1 WLR 1252, CA.
6 *Brooks v J & P Coates (UK) Ltd* [1984] 1 All ER 702 at 718.
7 See *Gregson v Hick Hargreaves & Co Ltd* [1955] 1 WLR 1252, CA, at 1267 per Parker LJ.
8 (1973) 14 KIR 285 at 292.

suggested that 'one difference . . . between the two . . . expressions is that questions of cost may be taken into account in deciding what is reasonably practicable but not in deciding what is practicable'.[1] It is clear, however, that even this higher level of duty requires reference 'to the state of knowledge at the time, and particularly to the knowledge of scientific people'.[2] In *Adsett v K & L Steelfounders and Engineers*[3] the defendants themselves were the first in the field in the development of a particular protective device which would have been effective in the case in question. The plaintiff suffered injury, however, before this development took place, but argued that he should nevertheless recover on the ground that the subsequent advances had shown that it would have been 'practicable' to provide protection at the time. The Court of Appeal rejected this argument and the plaintiff's claim failed. In the later case of *Richards v Highways Ironfounders (West Bromwich) Ltd*[4] Evershed MR expressed himself as follows:

> 'The nature of the obligation has been epigrammatically expressed as being that the measures taken must be possible in the light of current knowledge and according to known means and resources. It is clear then, in my judgment, that the matter must be judged in the light of the state of the relevant knowledge at the time of the alleged breach. Thus the fact that at some later date some method of protection has been discovered which was not dreamed of at the date of the alleged breach, even though all the individual materials therefor were known and available, will not suffice. On the other hand, I must not be taken to be saying that the state of knowledge, or absence of knowledge, within the limited scope of a particular industry, or branch of an industry, is by any means necessarily conclusive. It must be a question of fact and of the weight of all the material evidence in any particular case to assess what was in truth known, or what ought to have been known, by the employers charged at the relevant dates.'

[**14.31**] The general obligation under s 63(1) 'to protect the persons employed against inhalation' is not confined to extraction methods in themselves, but may extend to the provision of suitable masks to be worn by those at risk.[5] The specific obligation imposed towards the end of the section to provide 'exhaust appliances . . . as near as possible to the origin of the dust' cannot apply where there are 'no "points" which are definable and fixed and which can be said to be the origin of the dust'.[6] The primary application of this limb of the provision will, as Evershed MR put it in the *Highway Ironfounders* case, be to cases in which 'the dust or fume is emitted at some fixed

---

1 Cf per Edmund Davies LJ in *Cartwright v GKN Sankey Ltd* (1973) 14 KIR 349 at 363, CA.
2 *Adsett v K & L Steelfounders and Engineers Ltd* [1953] 2 All ER 320 at 323, [1953] 1 WLR 773 at 780, CA, per Singleton LJ.
3 [1953] 1 WLR 773 at 780, CA, per Singleton LJ.
4 [1955] 3 All ER 205 at 210, [1955] 1 WLR 1049 at 1054, CA.
5 *Crookall v Vickers-Armstrong Ltd* [1955] 2 All ER 12 at 16, [1955] 1 WLR 659 at 655.
6 Per Evershed MR in *Richards v Highways Ironfounders (West Bromwich) Ltd* [1955] 3 All ER 205 at 213, [1955] 1 WLR 1049 at 1059, CA.

point or points on a machine and the exhaust appliance is intended
... to be fixed in such a manner that the dust, instead of being emitted
into the atmosphere, is drawn off outside or elsewhere'.[1]

Injury caused by lifting heavy loads

[**14.32**] Section 72(1) provides as follows: 'A person shall not be employed to lift, carry or move any load so heavy as to be likely to cause injury to him.'[2] The section was considered and applied by the House of Lords in *Brown v Allied Ironfounders Ltd*.[3] In this case the plaintiff suffered injury when lifting a heavy load by herself. It was the normal practice for two employees to lift such loads together, but the defendant employers knew that some workers attempted to do it by themselves. Nevertheless no express instruction was given to the plaintiff that she should seek help with the lifting, even though such help would have been available had she sought it. In these circumstances the House of Lords held that the plaintiff had been 'employed' to move a load likely to injure her, for the purposes of the section, and she recovered damages.[4] The House emphasised, however, that the question whether the section had been contravened was one of fact which would turn upon 'the particular circumstances of each particular case'.[5] In the later case of *Black v Carricks (Caterers)*[6] a plaintiff manageress, who found herself alone in the defendant's shop due to the illness of her assistants, complained over the telephone to her supervisor that certain trays of bread were too heavy for her to lift by herself. In reply she was told to do the best she could and to obtain the assistance of a customer if she needed it. Her claim for damages for breach of statutory duty[7] in respect of a back injury, suffered when she in fact lifted one of the trays, was unsuccessful. The Court of Appeal held that the telephone instructions were only 'in the nature of guidance rather than directive' and that 'in trying to do better than was called for, [the plaintiff] became the victim of her own conscientiousness'.[8] In the 1984 case of *Bailey v Rolls Royce (1971) Ltd*[9] the Court of Appeal rejected, on its facts, a claim based on s 72(1) after the court had construed the word 'likely' in the subsection. May LJ said:[10]

---

1 Per Evershed MR in *Richards v Highways Ironfounders (West Bromwich) Ltd* [1955] 3 All ER 205 at 213, [1955] 1 WLR 1049 at 1059, CA.
2 Cf the Offices, Shops and Railway Premises Act 1963, s 23(1): 'No person shall, in the course of his work in premises to which this Act applies, be required to lift, carry or move a load so heavy as to be likely to cause injury to him.'
3 [1974] 2 All ER 135, [1974] 1 WLR 527, HL.
4 Cf *Peat v N J Muschamp & Co Ltd* (1969) 7 KIR 469, CA.
5 [1974] 2 All ER 135 at 137, [1974] 1 WLR 527 at 529H per Lord Morris. See also per Lord Kilbrandon (at 141 and 534E) : '... this is not the class of case in which the multiplication of citations is profitable.'
6 [1980] IRLR 448, CA.
7 The case was decided under the Offices, Shops and Railway Premises Act 1963, s 23(1). Although the wording of this section is slightly different from that of s 72(1) Megaw LJ did not think this implied any difference in meaning: see [1980] IRLR 448 at 454. But cf per Shaw LJ at 452.
8 [1980] IRLR 448 at 452 per Shaw LJ.
9 [1984] ICR 688, CA.
10 Ibid at 699.

'In my opinion, one has to approach the construction of this subsection, and the meaning of its provision, giving the words their ordinary and natural English meaning. In my view, "likely" is the equivalent of "probable" or "more probable than not"; it is certainly more than merely "possible".'

Two members of the Court of Appeal in *Bailey's* case did emphasise, however, that the test for 'likelihood' is related to each individual employee so that an employer might incur liability under the subsection even though other employees, in a healthier condition than the particular plaintiff, would not have been likely to suffer injury.[1] In the same case the view was also expressed that the test for likelihood was objective in the sense that it would be applied 'irrespective of the question whether the defendants knew, or ought to have known'[2] of a particular plaintiff's predisposition to injury. These dicta were, however, not followed by the Court of Appeal in the recent case of *Whitfield v H & R Johnson (Tiles) Ltd*.[3] In this case a congenital back condition, of which her employers were wholly unaware, made the plaintiff susceptible to injury from lifting loads which would not normally have caused injury to a person not suffering from her condition. Her claim based upon breach of the subsection was unsuccessful. Beldam LJ expressed himself as follows:[4]

> 'Lifting or moving an object of virtually any weight would have been likely to cause injury to the plaintiff sooner or later. So it is said that, because of the use of the word "to him", the occupier of a factory or an employer would be in breach of s 72 if he employed a person on work which involved lifting even the lightest of loads if, for example, the employee suffered from an unsuspected aneurism and the strain of lifting caused it to burst . . . I am unable to agree that Parliament, by adding those two words, intended so unreasonable or unlikely a result. I consider that full meaning can be given to those words read in the context of the section as a whole by holding that they were intended to make sure that the weight of the load was appropriate to the sex, build and physique, or other obvious characteristic, of the employee in question.'

Thus 'if the injury is occasioned because of some latent condition', said Purchas LJ,[5] 'then the load could not be said to be "likely to cause injury" because the word "likely" imports a reasonable anticipation that the event will happen'.

Provision of safety equipment

[**14.33**] Various sections of the Factories Act 1961 require the provision of safety equipment in particular circumstances. For example 'suitable goggles or effective screens' for eye protection are obligatory when certain processes are being carried out;[6] and if a

---

1   See per Slade LJ in ibid at 700, and per Stephenson LJ at 702.
2   Per Stephenson LJ in ibid at 702. See also per Slade LJ at 701.
3   [1990] 3 All ER 426, CA.
4   [1990] 3 All ER 426 at 434-435.
5   [1990] 3 All ER 426 at 439.
6   See s 65 and *Hay v Dowty Mining Equipment Ltd* [1971] 3 All ER 1136. See also *Rogers v George Blair & Co Ltd* (1971) 11 KIR 391, CA. Cf *Daniels v Ford Motor Co* [1955] 1 All ER 218, [1955] 1 WLR 76, CA.

person who fell from his workplace could fall more than two metres then, depending upon the circumstances, safety precautions such as the provision of safety-belts may be necessary.[1] Similarly, the provision of masks may be necessary if dust or fumes are present.[2] Specific safety requirements may also be imposed by delegated legislation.[3] Although each case will depend upon its own circumstances,[4] a statutory duty to provide safety devices is unlikely to be fulfilled if the equipment is not immediately and readily available at the place where it is needed. In one case it was held that to have a pair of goggles hanging in the foreman's office, from where they could be fetched if desired, was not sufficient.[5] If the appropriate equipment is *not* provided, however, a plaintiff employee will still fail if the evidence suggests that the plaintiff would probably not have worn or used the devices even if they had been provided: in such a case it will be taken that the breach of duty was not a cause of the plaintiff's loss.[6]

Causation and contributory negligence

[**14.34**] In *Westwood v Post Office*[7] Lord Kilbrandon expressed himself as follows:

> 'My Lords, the defence of contributory negligence as an answer, even as nowadays only a partial answer, to a claim arising out of breach of statutory duty is one which it must always be difficult to establish. The very existence of statutory safety provisions must be relevant to the consequences which a man may reasonably be expected to foresee as arising from his own conduct; his foresight as to that will be to some extent governed by what he may reasonably be expected to foresee as arising from his master's statutory obligations.'

Nevertheless, if the circumstances so warrant the courts will not shrink from holding that a workman claiming for breach of statutory duty was contributorily negligent. Cases of this type, in which an apportionment is made under the Law Reform (Contributory Negligence) Act 1945 are an every-day occurrence in the courts. But the well-known warning of Lord Tucker in *Staveley Iron & Chemical*

---

1 See s 29(2) (as amended by the Factories Act 1961 etc (Metrication) Regulations 1983 (SI 1983/978).
2 See s 63(1), discussed above.
3 See, eg the Construction (Working Places) Regulations 1966 (SI 1966/94).
4 Cf per Pearson J in *Ginty v Belmont Building Supplies Ltd* [1959] 1 All ER 414 at 422G: 'I do not think that there is any hard and fast meaning of the word "provided"; it must depend on the circumstances of the case as to what is "provided" and how what is "provided" is going to be used.'
5 *Finch v Telegraph Construction and Maintenance Co Ltd* [1949] 1 All ER 452. See also *Nolan v Dental Manufacturing Co Ltd* [1958] 2 All ER 449, [1958] 1 WLR 936.
6 See *Cummings (or McWilliams) v Sir William Arrol & Co Ltd* [1962] 1 All ER 623, [1962] 1 WLR 295, HL. See also *Wigley v British Vinegars* [1964] AC 307, [1962] 3 All ER 161, CA.
7 [1974] AC 1 at 16G-H, [1973] 3 All ER 184 at 193, HL.

Co Ltd v Jones[1] is often quoted in cases[2] in which contributory negligence by a workman is in issue. His Lordship said:

> '... in cases under the Factories Acts, the purpose of imposing the absolute obligation is to protect the workmen against those very acts of inattention which are sometimes relied on as constituting contributory negligence, so that too strict a standard would defeat the object of the statute.'

Accident entirely plaintiff's fault

[**14.35**] The question of contributory negligence cannot arise until the plaintiff has discharged the burden of showing that the defendant's breach of statutory duty was a cause of his loss. 'In my judgment', said Lord Reid in *Bonnington Castings Ltd v Wardlaw*,[3] 'the employee must in all cases prove his case by the ordinary standard of proof in civil actions: he must make it appear at least that on a balance of probabilities the breach of duty caused or materially contributed to his injury'.[4] It follows that a plaintiff whose employers have been in breach of statutory duty may, nevertheless, in an extreme case, be wholly defeated on causal grounds due to his own negligence and fail even to achieve an apportionment under the 1945 Act. In *Rushton v Turner Bros Asbestos Co Ltd*,[5] the plaintiff's fingers were crushed when he attempted, in defiance of a clear instruction never to do so, to clean an unfenced machine while it was working. Ashworth J held that the claim would fail completely and expressed himself as follows:[6]

> 'I have been pressed, and rightly pressed, by counsel for the plaintiff, with the submission that this accident does not differ in kind from many other accidents reported in the books in which the defendant employers have been found guilty of a breach of the Factories Act, and none the less the plaintiff has succeeded in spite of considerable contributory negligence on his own part. It seems to me that in each case it is a question of degree, looking at the whole of the circumstances, fairly and broadly, to see whether a breach of the Factories Act is of itself an operative cause of the accident or is more truly in a sense the circumstances in which the accident happened.'[7]

---

1 [1956] AC 627 at 648, [1956] 1 All ER 403 at 414, HL.
2 See, eg *Mullard v Ben Line Steamers Ltd* [1971] 2 All ER 424 at 428, CA; *Westwood v Post Office* [1974] AC 1 at 17, HL.
3 [1956] AC 613 at 620, [1956] 1 All ER 615 at 618, HL.
4 The earlier case of *Vyner v Waldenberg Bros Ltd* [1946] KB 50, [1945] 2 All ER 547, which appeared to suggest that the onus of disproving causation would be on the employer once breach of statutory duty was established, was disapproved by the House of Lords in *Bonnington Castings v Wardlaw*.
5 [1959] 3 All ER 517, [1960] 1 WLR 96.
6 [1959] 3 All ER 517 at 521, [1960] 1 WLR 96 at 101.
7 See also *Jayes v IMI (Kynoch) Ltd* [1985] ICR 155, CA, in which the Court of Appeal reached the same result by making a finding of 100 per cent contributory negligence against the employee (see per Goff LJ at 159). This method would, however, no longer be regarded as appropriate: see *Pitts v Hunt* [1991] 1 QB 24, [1990] 3 All ER 344, CA, and, generally, ch 4 above.

Volenti non fit injuria

[**14.36**] It is also possible in exceptional circumstances for the defence of volenti non fit injuria to defeat a claim by a servant against his employer involving breach of statutory duty. In addition to the need to satisfy all the normal requirements of the defence,[1] however, it is possible that the scope of the maxim will in practice be confined in this context to situations in which the employer was not personally at fault and was only responsible vicariously for the breach of duty.[2]

Coterminous fault

[**14.37**] In one type of case the employee injured as the result of a breach of a statutory duty may himself have been the person properly entrusted by his employer with the task of seeing that the particular provision was complied with. It is well established that a defendant employer can defeat a claim by the plaintiff in such circumstances, even though the former may have been technically in breach of the statute due to the latter's failure to discharge the task which had been allotted to him.[3] At one time the question sometimes asked in these cases was whether the master had 'delegated' the performance of the statutory duty to his servant.[4] In *Ginty v Belmont Building Supplies Ltd*,[5] however, Pearson J adopted a supposedly more straightforward test which has since been generally accepted as the better approach. In finding against the plaintiff in the case before him his Lordship expressed himself as follows:[6]

> 'There has been a number of cases ... in which it has been considered whether or not the employer delegated to the employee the performance of the statutory duty. In my view, the law which is applicable here is clear and comprehensible if one does not confuse it by seeking to investigate this very difficult and complicated question whether or not there was a delegation. In my view, the important and fundamental question in a case like this is not whether there was a delegation, but simply the usual question: Whose fault was it?'[7]

---

1 See above, ch 4.
2 See, generally, *ICI Ltd v Shatwell* [1965] AC 656, [1964] 2 All ER 999, HL.
3 'I would deem it incongruous and irrational if ... the plaintiff could, in effect, say to his employer: "Because of my disregard of your reasonable instructions I have brought about the position that you are in breach of your statutory obligations, and so I claim damages from you because of such breach" ': per Morris LJ in *Man-Waring v Billington* [1952] 2 All ER 747 at 750, CA.
4 See *Smith v Baveystock & Co Ltd* [1945] 1 All ER 531, CA.
5 [1959] 1 All ER 414. Cf *Nicol v Allyacht Spars Pty Ltd* (1987) 163 CLR 611 (Aust HC).
6 Ibid at 423-424.
7 In *Ross v Associated Portland Cement Manufacturers Ltd* [1964] 2 All ER 452 at 455, [1964] 1 WLR 768 at 777, Lord Reid quoted this passage and added: 'If the question is put in that way one must remember that fault is not necessarily equivalent in this context to blameworthiness. The question really is whose conduct caused the accident.'

The principle of 'coterminous fault', as it is sometimes called,[1] will not enable a defendant totally to defeat the plaintiff's claim if the latter can show that there was additional illegality on the defendant's part, in which the plaintiff was not implicated, and which was also a factor in causing the accident.[2] In particular, an employer who fails to provide proper safety equipment cannot avoid all liability merely because his employee makes the most of a bad job, and goes ahead knowing that in so doing he is acting improperly. 'The respondents cannot escape liability by saying', observed Lord Guest in *Ross v Associated Portland Cement Manufacturers*,[3] ' "You worked in a place which was obviously unsafe. You cannot therefore recover"'. Fault will also clearly not be 'coterminous' if the plaintiff was not sufficiently experienced or senior to have been properly entrusted with the performance of the statutory duty in the first place.[4]

Relationship between statutory and common law duties

Separation

[14.38] The courts have, in general, been anxious to keep separate from each other the questions of whether an employer has been in breach of his statutory duty and whether he has been negligent at common law. In *Bux v Slough Metals Ltd*[5] defendants who had been exonerated from breach of statutory duty, but held liable for negligence at common law, unsuccessfully contended on appeal that, in the circumstances, these findings were inconsistent and that compliance with their statutory duty constituted fulfilment of their common law duty also. In rejecting this argument Stephenson LJ expressed himself as follows:[6]

> 'There is, in my judgment, no presumption that a statutory obligation abrogates or supersedes the employer's common law duty or that it defines or measures his common law duty either by clarifying it or by cutting it down – or indeed by extending it. It is not necessarily exhaustive of that duty or co-extensive with it and I do not, with all due respect to counsel for the defendants' argument, think it possible to lay down conditions in which it is exhaustive or to conclude that it is so in this case. The statutory obligation may exceed the duty at common law

---

1 See *Ross v Associated Portland Cement Manufacturers Ltd* [1964] 2 All ER 452, [1964] 1 WLR 768, HL; *Leach v Standard Telephones and Cables Ltd* [1966] 2 All ER 523, [1966] 1 WLR 1392.
2 See, eg *Jenner v Allen West & Co Ltd* [1959] 2 All ER 115, [1959] 1 WLR 554, CA; *Leach v Standard Telephones and Cables Ltd* [1966] 2 All ER 523, [1966] 1 WLR 1392.
3 [1964] 2 All ER 452 at 458, [1964] 1 WLR 768 at 781.
4 See, eg *Ross v Associated Portland Cement Manufacturers Ltd* [1964] 2 All ER 452, [1964] 1 WLR 768, HL.
5 [1974] 1 All ER 262, [1973] 1 WLR 1358, CA.
6 Ibid at 272 and 1369-1370.

or it may fall short of it or it may equal it. The court has always to construe the statute or statutory instrument which imposes the obligation, consider the facts of the particular case and the allegations of negligence in fact made by the particular workman and then decide whether, if the statutory obligation has been performed, any negligence has been proved.'

Preservation of the distinction

[**14.39**] Of course, there can be situations in which the relevant statutory provision imposes an obligation no higher than that of reasonable care, and in such circumstances the case will usually resolve itself into a single inquiry into whether or not such care was in fact taken.[1] More usually, however, separate treatment of the two issues will be necessary.[2] This will either be because of the imposition by statute of a stricter duty,[3] or because of the limited scope of the statutory provisions. In the latter type of case the courts have insisted on preserving the distinction between the two heads of liability by, inter alia, refusing to allow statutory provisions to be relied on by analogy in support of a common law claim. Thus in *Chipchase v British Titan Products Co Ltd*[4] the plaintiff was injured when he fell while painting at a point six feet above the ground. Had he been working just six inches higher statutory provisions requiring additional safety precautions would have been applicable. In acquitting his employers of negligence at common law the court rejected the proposition that the precautions required by the statute could be relevant in determining what constituted reasonable care at common law.[5]

1 See, eg *Thomas v Bristol Aeroplane Co Ltd* [1954] 2 All ER 1, [1954] 1 WLR 694, CA.
2 See, eg *Larner v British Steel plc* (1993) Times, 19 February, CA.
3 Cf *Quintas v National Smelting Co Ltd* [1961] 1 All ER 630, [1961] 1 WLR 401, CA in which the Court of Appeal (Willmer LJ dissenting) held that the appropriate apportionment for contributory negligence would differ depending upon the nature of the defendant employer's liability.
4 [1956] 1 QB 545, [1956] 1 All ER 613, CA. See also *Kimpton v Steel Co of Wales Ltd* [1960] 2 All ER 274, [1960] 1 WLR 527, CA.
5 See also per Lord Reid in *Smith v National Coal Board* [1967] 2 All ER 593 at 596, [1967] 1 WLR 871 at 875G, HL. But cf per Somervell LJ in *Franklin v Gramophone Co Ltd* [1948] 1 KB 542 at 558, [1948] 1 All ER 353 at 360, CA.

Part five

Special areas of liability

Chapter 15

Professional negligence[1]

General principles

Standard of care

[15.01] In *Bolam v Friern Hospital Management Committee*[2] McNair J said the following in relation to professional negligence:

> 'The test is the standard of the ordinary skilled man exercising and professing to have that special skill. A man need not possess the highest expert skill; it is well established law that it is sufficient if he exercises the ordinary skill of an ordinary competent man exercising that particular art.'

As the two expressions 'professing' and 'exercising' in this quotation imply, the question whether a particular defendant complied with the 'standard of the ordinary skilled man' potentially involves two related, though separate, issues. The first is whether the defendant in fact possessed the *knowledge* to be expected of a competent professional person in the particular field.[3] The second is whether his *judgment* and, where relevant, his physical prowess in the discharge of a practical task, were lacking in quality. The first of the two questions is, understandably, usually easier to answer than the second.

State of knowledge

[15.02] The body of professional knowledge in any field increases in size as time goes by, and the court will endeavour to avoid hindsight in determining whether the defendant's state of knowledge was such

---

1   See Jackson and Powell *Professional Negligence* (3rd edn, 1992); Dugdale and Stanton *Professional Negligence* (2nd edn, 1989).
2   [1957] 2 All ER 118 at 121, [1957] 1 WLR 582 at 586. See also *Chin Keow v Government of Malaysia* [1967] 1 WLR 813, PC; *Wimpey Construction UK Ltd v Poole* [1984] 2 Lloyd's Rep 499.
3   Cf *Wimpey Construction UK Ltd v Poole* [1984] 2 Lloyd's Rep 499 at 506-507, per Webster J.

as could reasonably have been expected of him prior to the accident. Thus in *Roe v Minister of Health*[1] the plaintiffs were paralysed after being injected, for minor operations, with an anaesthetic solution which had been contaminated. The possibility of such contamination, through invisible cracks in the containers in which the solution had been kept, was not known to the medical profession before this tragic case brought it to light; and an appropriate warning was then inserted into the textbooks. The defendants were acquitted of negligence but, as Denning LJ pointed out, 'nowadays it would be negligence not to realise the danger, but it was not then'.[2]

[**15.03**] If the knowledge which would have prevented the accident which occurred to the plaintiff did exist, but only buried in relatively obscure professional literature, difficult questions of fact may arise as to the extent of the professional person's duty to delve into such literature before giving advice or embarking on a course of action. In *Vacwell Engineering Co Ltd v BDH Chemicals Ltd*[3] an explosion occurred which could have been avoided if the defendants' chemists had consulted pre-war textbooks which contained a warning of the particular risk, based on experiments carried out by a nineteenth-century French chemist. Unfortunately, the leading modern textbooks, which were consulted, omitted any reference to the risk. The trial judge nevertheless held the defendants liable for negligence for failing to 'carry out an adequate research into the scientific literature'.[4]

'Errors of judgment'

[**15.04**] It is a hallmark of many, if not most, kinds of professional expertise that their exercise often calls for the making of fine judgments. Merely because such a judgment subsequently turns out to have been 'wrong', in the sense that, with hindsight, it can be seen that adopting a different course would have produced a better result, does not of itself constitute negligence. In attempting to express this with clarity, Lord Denning MR once drew a sharp distinction between mere 'errors of judgment' on the one hand and 'negligence' on the other.[5] When what is now the leading case on the subject, *Whitehouse v Jordan,* reached the House of Lords, however, the distinction was condemned as a 'false antithesis'.[6] Lord Fraser expressed himself as follows:[7]

> 'Merely to describe something as an error of judgment tells us nothing about whether it is negligent or not; it depends on the nature of the

---

1 [1954] 2 QB 66, [1954] 2 All ER 131, CA. See also *McLean v Weir and Goff* [1980] 4 WWR 330 (Can).
2 [1954] 2 QB 66 at 86, [1954] 2 All ER 131 at 139, CA.
3 [1971] 1 QB 88, [1969] 3 All ER 1681.
4 Ibid at 109 and 1698. An appeal by the defendants was subsequently settled on terms broadly favourable to the plaintiffs: see [1971] 1 QB 111n.
5 See *Whitehouse v Jordan* [1980] 1 All ER 650 at 658, CA.
6 See [1981] 1 All ER 267 at 276, [1981] 1 WLR 246 at 257-258. See also per Donaldson LJ in the Court of Appeal: [1980] 1 All ER 650 at 662.
7 [1981] 1 All ER 267 at 281, [1981] 1 WLR 246 at 263.

error. If it is one that would not have been made by a reasonably competent professional man professing to have the standard and type of skill that the defendant held himself out as having, and acting with ordinary care, then it is negligent. If, on the other hand, it is an error that a man, acting with ordinary care, might have made, then it is not negligence.'

The concept of an 'error of judgment' as a term of art is therefore now discredited. Nevertheless, the practical importance of the approach which that expression was used, albeit perhaps misleadingly, to denote remains unchanged. The court will not attempt to 'second-guess', nor will it lightly condemn, a competent professional person doing his best to exercise his judgment in an uncertain situation.[1] To some this may appear as an unjustifiable indulgence towards professional people,[2] particularly since it not infrequently has the effect of leaving uncompensated those who may have incurred grievous suffering. But until the at least nominally fault-based tort system is reformed[3] it is not easy, even in personal injury cases, readily to condemn the prevailing judicial attitude. The approach of the courts appears realistic in its appreciation of the circumstances within which professional people often have to work.

Medical negligence[4]

Difficulties of proof

[**15.05**] Although the standard of proof to be applied in cases of alleged medical negligence is in theory no different from that applicable elsewhere, the courts do appear particularly reluctant to hold that a doctor has been careless unless the evidence is exceptionally clear.[5] Where obvious blunders have been made, such as the administration of wrong drugs or dosages with fatal

---

1 Cf *Stafford v Conti Commodity Services Ltd* [1981] 1 All ER 691, [1981] 1 Lloyd's Rep 466.
2 See Joseph *Lawyers Can Seriously Damage Your Health*, (1985) chs 2 and 3.
3 Cf per Lawton LJ in the Court of Appeal in *Whitehouse v Jordan* [1980] 1 All ER 650 at 661-662: 'I have come to this conclusion [ie against the imposition of liability] with sorrow, knowing as I do what anguish the parents have suffered and the grave disabilities which the infant plaintiff will have to bear until death. As long as liability in this type of case rests on proof of fault judges will have to go on making decisions which they would prefer not to make. The victims of medical mishaps of this kind should, in my opinion, be cared for by the community, not by the hazards of litigation.'
4 See Michael A Jones *Medical Negligence* (1991).
5 See Michael A Jones 'Medical Negligence – The Burden of Proof' (1984) 134 NLJ 7. See also the Report of the *Royal Commission on Civil Liability and Compensation for Personal Injury (Pearson)* (Cmnd 7054-I) para 284: 'The proportion of successful claims for damages in tort is much lower for medical negligence than for all negligence cases. Some payment is made in 30-40% of claims compared with 86% of all personal injury claims.'

results,[1] compensation will invariably be forthcoming without resort to litigation.[2] But if a case is sufficiently uncertain to be remotely worth fighting, the plaintiff faces an uphill struggle.[3] Even if the trial judge can be persuaded to find a case proved there is some indication that the appellate courts will be more generous, than they usually are to defendants, in allowing what are essentially questions of fact to be ventilated afresh on appeal.[4] Nor will the maxim res ipsa loquitur readily be invoked to assist the plaintiff.[5] There appear to be three reasons for this judicial reluctance to find negligence proved in medical cases. The first is a recognition of the fact that the response of the human body to treatment can rarely be predicted beyond all doubt, and that 'medical science has not yet reached the stage where the law ought to presume that a patient must come out of an operation as well or better than he went into it'.[6] The second reason is one of policy: anxiety to discourage the development of excessive 'medical malpractice' litigation along the lines perceived to exist in America, with its supposed disadvantages including causing doctors to practise 'defensive medicine' through constant fear of lawsuits.[7] The third reason is a particular solicitude for the standing of individual doctors who are alleged to have transgressed.[8]

1 See, eg *Strangeways-Lesmere v Clayton* [1936] 2 KB 11, [1936] 1 All ER 484; *Collins v Hertfordshire County Council* [1947] KB 598, [1947] 1 All ER 633; *Bovenzi v Kettering Health Authority* [1991] 2 Med LR 293; See also *Kralj v McGrath* [1986] 1 All ER 54 ('. . . horrific treatment, completely unacceptable, breaking all the rules. . . '). Cf *Prendergast v Sam and Dee Ltd* (1989) Times, 14 March, CA (doctor liable, along with pharmacist, where bad handwriting on a prescription caused pharmacist to supply wrong drug).
2 Nevertheless, proving *causation* of harm may still be an insurmountable obstacle even if carelessness was undoubted. See, eg *Kay's Tutor v Ayrshire and Arran Health Board* [1987] 2 All ER 417, HL: no liability for administration of dose of penicillin 30 times greater than that prescribed to patient suffering from meningitis; causal link with subsequent brain damage not proved. See also *Wilsher v Essex Area Health Authority* [1988] AC 1074, [1988] 1 All ER 871, HL. See, generally, ch 2 above.
3 Cf Lord Ackner 'The doctor in court-victim or protected species?' (1992) 8 PN 54.
4 See the majority decision of the Court of Appeal in *Whitehouse v Jordan* [1980] 1 All ER 650, CA, and its affirmation by the House of Lords: [1981] 1 All ER 267, [1981] 1 WLR 246. See also *Maynard v West Midlands Regional Health Authority* [1985] 1 All ER 635, [1984] 1 WLR 634, HL. For criticism of *Whitehouse v Jordan* see Gerald Robertson in (1981) 44 MLR 457.
5 See *Girard v Royal Columbian Hospital* (1976) 66 DLR (3d) 676. But cf *Cassidy v Ministry of Health* [1951] 2 KB 343, [1951] 1 All ER 574, CA.
6 *Girard v Royal Columbian Hospital* (1976) 66 DLR (3d) 676 at 691. See also per Lawton LJ in *Whitehouse v Jordan* [1980] 1 All ER 650 at 659, CA: 'Medical practice these days consists of the harmonious union of science with skill. Medicine has not yet got to the stage, and maybe it never will, when the adoption of a particular procedure will produce a certain result.'
7 See, eg per Lord Denning MR in *Whitehouse v Jordan* [1980] 1 All ER 650 at 658, CA. See also per Lawton LJ at 659.
8 'In my opinion allegations of negligence against medical practitioners should be considered as serious . . . the defendant's professional reputation is under attack. A finding of negligence against him may jeopardise his career and cause him substantial financial loss over many years': per Lawton LJ in *Whitehouse v Jordan* [1980] 1 All ER 650 at 659, CA.

Standard of care

[15.06] Notwithstanding the sympathetic approach of the court to defendants in medical negligence cases, no qualification is made to the principle that the care taken must be evaluated against a generally established standard of reasonableness. A doctor must show the degree of skill appropriate to his post and the duties required of him, even though the tradition of 'learning on the job' may mean that an unrealistically high level of competence is thereby required of junior medical staff. 'To my mind', observed Mustill LJ in *Wilsher v Essex Area Health Authority*,[1] 'it would be a false step to subordinate the legitimate expectation of the patient that he will receive from each person concerned with his care a degree of skill appropriate to the task which he undertakes to an understandable wish to minimise the psychological and financial pressures on hard-pressed young doctors'.[2] At the same time, however, 'the standard of care required', as Pill J said in *Knight v Home Office*,[3] 'will vary with the context. The facilities available to deal with an emergency in a general practitioner's surgery cannot be expected to be as ample as those available in the casualty department of a general hospital, for example'. Thus in *Knight*'s case itself, which involved an unsuccessful claim with respect to a suicide by a mentally ill prisoner, Pill J was 'unable to accept that the practices in a prison hospital are to be judged in all respects by the standard appropriate to a psychiatric hospital outside prison. There may be circumstances in which the standard of care in a prison falls below that which would be expected in a psychiatric hospital without the prison authority being negligent'.[4]

Relevance of common practice

[15.07] The difficulties of plaintiffs in medical negligence cases are increased by the understandable reluctance of the courts, on the ground of their lack of competence to do so, to condemn as careless methods of treatment which the defendant may be able, with the assistance of expert witnesses, to show was not unusual. 'A doctor is not guilty of negligence', said McNair J in *Bolam v Friern Hospital Management Committee*,[5] 'if he has acted in accordance with a practice accepted as proper by a responsible body of medical men skilled in

---

1 [1987] QB 730 at 751, [1986] 3 All ER 801 at 813, CA.
2 See also per Glidewell LJ in [1986] 3 All ER 801 at 831. Sir Nicolas Browne-Wilkinson V-C dissented on this point: see [1986] 3 All ER at 833. *Wilsher*'s case subsequently went to the House of Lords (see [1988] AC 1074, [1988] 1 All ER 871), but this aspect of the opinions expressed in the Court of Appeal was not considered.
3 [1990] 3 All ER 237 at 243.
4 Ibid.
5 [1957] 1 WLR 582 at 587. See also *Sidaway v Bethlem Royal Hospital Governors* [1985] AC 871, [1985] 1 All ER 643, HL.

that particular art'.[1] Accordingly, attempts to persuade the court that a generally accepted practice was itself negligent, which may occasionally succeed in other contexts,[2] are unlikely to assist a plaintiff in this area.[3] Nor will *deviation* from a generally accepted practice be in itself enough even to shift the burden of proof on to the defendant doctor.[4]

Administrative practices

[**15.08**] Where the alleged negligence relates not to clinical practices as such, but rather to the *administrative system* within which those practices were carried out, the position is slightly different. Claims have, for example, succeeded on the basis of inadequate supervision by senior medical staff of their juniors.[5] It has been recently suggested, obiter, by two members of the Court of Appeal,[6] that the overall management position of a hospital might be made the basis of negligence liability towards individual patients. In so far as the underlying problem is one of lack of resources, however, such plaintiffs are likely to have difficulty in persuading the court that the matter does not raise non-justiciable policy questions if the hospital authority is a statutory body as under the National Health Service.[7] The funding of that Service is currently a matter of major political controversy, the rational resolution of which is unlikely to be furthered by the application of negligence concepts.[8]

---

1 The *Bolam* test is also applicable to situations involving mental patients not competent to give consent to treatment: *F v West Berkshire Health Authority* [1989] 2 All ER 545, HL (see, especially, per Lord Brandon at 560, disagreeing with the Court of Appeal which had favoured a special, more stringent, test for such cases).
2 See, eg *Morris v West Hartlepool Steam Navigation Co* [1956] AC 552, [1956] 1 All ER 385, HL; *Cavanagh v Ulster Weaving Co* [1960] AC 145, [1959] 2 All ER 745, HL.
3 But the *Bolam* test clearly can have no place in determining questions of *causation* which must ultimately be decided by the court, albeit with the assistance of expert witnesses, as a question of fact: see *Cavanagh v Bristol and Weston Health Authority* [1992] 3 Med LR 49 at 56, per Macpherson J.
4 See *Wilsher v Essex Area Health Authority* [1987] QB 730, [1986] 3 All ER 801, CA, overruling a dictum of Peter Pain J in *Clark v MacLennan* [1983] 1 All ER 416.
5 See *Jones v Manchester Corpn* [1952] 2 QB 852, [1952] 2 All ER 125. See also *Collins v Hertfordshire County Council* [1947] KB 598, [1947] 1 All ER 633.
6 Sir Nicolas Browne-Wilkinson V-C and Glidewell LJ in *Wilsher v Essex Area Health Authority* [1987] QB 730, [1986] 3 All ER 801, CA. For discussion see Montgomery, 'Suing Hospitals Direct: What Tort?' (1987) NLJ 703. See also ch 18 below.
7 Cf *Department of Health and Social Security v Kinnear* (1984) 134 NLJ 886.
8 Cf per Pill J in *Knight v Home Office* [1990] 3 All ER 237 at 243: 'It is not a complete defence for a government department any more than it would be for a private individual or organisation to say that no funds are available for additional safety measures ... In making the decision as to the standard to be demanded the court must, however, bear in mind as one factor that resources available for the public service are limited and that the allocation of resources is a matter for Parliament.' For discussion of the negligence liability of public bodies see, generally, ch 12 above.

Where there are differing professional schools of thought

[**15.09**] It may sometimes be the case that professional opinion is divided as to the most appropriate procedure to adopt in a particular situation. In such a case the court will not see its function as being to decide which of the rival contentions is the better. On the contrary, a doctor will normally succeed in negating liability if he shows that his approach is regarded as proper by one well-established school of thought, notwithstanding that there exists an equally well-established school of thought to the opposite effect. The leading case is now *Maynard v West Midlands Regional Health Authority*.[1] The defendants carried out an operation for diagnostic purposes which, although properly conducted, carried the inherent risk of permanent impairment of the patient's power of speech. The risk unfortunately materialised and the plaintiff alleged that the operation had been unnecessary, in that ample evidence on which to make a diagnosis had existed without it. This contention was supported by a powerful expert witness whose evidence the trial judge preferred to that of the defendants' expert witnesses. He accordingly found for the plaintiff, but his decision was reversed by the Court of Appeal and this reversal was upheld by the House of Lords. The House held, in effect, that the judge had been wrong to seek to make a choice between the views expressed by the expert witnesses on the two sides.[2] Lord Scarman put it as follows:[3]

> 'A case which is based on an allegation that a fully considered decision of two consultants in the field of their special skill was negligent clearly presents certain difficulties of proof. It is not enough to show that there is a body of competent professional opinion which considers that theirs was a wrong decision, if there also exists a body of professional opinion, equally competent, which supports that decision as reasonable in the circumstances ... [A] judge's "preference" for one body of distinguished professional opinion to another also professionally distinguished is not sufficient to establish negligence in a practitioner whose actions have received the seal of approval of those whose opinions, truthfully expressed, honestly held, were not preferred.'[4]

The duty to warn

[**15.10**] In *Sidaway v Governors of Bethlem Royal Hospital*[5] a risk of paralysis, which was attendant upon an operation properly conducted

---

1 [1985] 1 All ER 635, [1984] 1 WLR 634, HL. See also *Bolam v Friern Hospital Management Committee* [1957] 2 All ER 118, [1957] 1 WLR 582.
2 See also *Hughes v Waltham Forest Health Authority* [1991] 2 Med LR 155, CA.
3 [1985] 1 All ER 635 at 638-639, [1984] 1 WLR 634 at 638-639.
4 See also per Slade LJ in the non-medical case of *Luxmoore-May v Messenger May Baverstock* [1990] 1 All ER 1067 at 1076: 'The valuation of pictures of which the artist is unknown, pre-eminently involves an exercise of opinion and judgment, most particularly in deciding whether an attribution to any particular artist should be made. Since it is not an exact science, the judgment in the very nature of things may be fallible, and may turn out to be wrong. Accordingly, provided that the valuer has done his job honestly and with due diligence, I think that the court should be cautious before convicting him of professional negligence.'
5 [1985] AC 871, [1985] 1 All ER 643, HL.

upon the plaintiff in the vicinity of her spinal cord, unfortunately materialised. This particular risk had not been explained to her prior to the operation, and she contended that she would not have gone ahead if it had been. She sued the surgeon alleging that the absence of such a warning constituted negligence.[1] It was accepted that in omitting the warning the defendant had been 'following a practice accepted as proper by a responsible body of competent neurosurgeons'.[2] But the plaintiff argued that the test in *Bolam v Friern Hospital Management Committee*[3] should be confined to cases involving criticism of a doctor's *treatment*, as distinct from his explanation and discussion with the patient beforehand. She sought to introduce into English law the doctrine of 'informed consent', with its special emphasis upon a person's autonomy of decision over his own body,[4] which has found favour in North America including the Supreme Court of Canada.[5] By a majority, Lord Scarman dissenting, the House of Lords rejected the plaintiff's argument and her claim failed. Their Lordships considered that it would be undesirable and unrealistic to draw the suggested distinction in the context of the doctor's overall duty to care for his patient, and expressly affirmed the applicability of the *Bolam* test to allegations of negligence in the context of the doctor-patient relationship generally.[6]

[**15.11**] The *Sidaway* decision has been criticised on the ground that it is paternalistic in its approach,[7] but it should be noted that there are important indications in the speeches that in two respects fuller disclosure of risks may be required of doctors than an unqualified application of the *Bolam* test might have indicated. Firstly, a patient who asks specific questions must be given full and accurate answers to them:[8] the 'common practice' approach is only relevant as to the appropriateness of *volunteering*

---

1 Attempts to base claims against doctors in *trespass*, alleging that inadequate disclosure vitiated consent, have met with strong judicial disapproval in England: see, eg *Chatterton v Gerson* [1981] QB 432, [1981] 1 All ER 257; *Hills v Potter* [1983] 3 All ER 716, [1984] 1 WLR 641n. For discussion of the relationship between trespass and negligence in this context see Tan Keng Feng, 'Failure of Medical Advice: Trespass or Negligence?' (1987) 7 LS 149.
2 [1985] AC 871 at 896, [1985] 1 All ER 643 at 660, per Lord Bridge.
3 [1957] 2 All ER 118, [1957] 1 WLR 582.
4 For discussion see, generally, Gerald Robertson 'Informed Consent to Medical Treatment' (1981) 97 LQR 102; Margaret Brazier 'Patient Autonomy and Consent to Treatment: the Role of the Law?' (1987) 7 LS 169. See also Ian Kennedy 'The Patient on the Clapham Omnibus' (1984) 47 MLR 454.
5 See *Reibl v Hughes* (1980) 114 DLR (3d) 1, and especially at 13, per Laskin CJC.
6 See also *Gold v Haringey Health Authority* [1988] QB 481, [1987] 2 All ER 888, in which the Court of Appeal held that the *Bolam* test applied to contraceptive advice, and rejected a suggestion that a distinction should be drawn between 'therapeutic' and 'non-therapeutic' medical advice so as to exclude the *Bolam* test from the latter.
7 See Teff 'Consent to Medical Procedures: Paternalism, Self-Determination or Therapeutic Alliance?' (1985) 101 LQR 432.
8 But cf *Blyth v Bloomsbury Area Health Authority* (1987) Times, 11 February, CA. (unsuccessful claim by patient who had sought further information before administration of a drug which subsequently caused her harm: no obligation on the hospital to give the patient all the information at its disposal in response to such an inquiry).

information.¹ Secondly, the court reserves the overriding power to hold that the common practice with respect to disclosure in a given situation may be inadequate. In theory, of course, this power always exists, but as far as actual treatment is concerned it is in practice hardly ever exercised. But there is reason to suppose that in the case of disclosure of risk, where ethical considerations are obviously prominent and the issue itself is not so immediately technical, the court may be rather more ready to exercise the power. Thus Lord Bridge was 'of opinion that the judge might in certain circumstances come to the conclusion that disclosure of a particular risk was so obviously necessary to an informed choice on the part of the patient that no reasonably prudent medical man would fail to make it'.² Both Lord Bridge and Lord Templeman approved of the decision (though not the reasoning) of the Canadian Supreme Court in *Reibl v Hughes*³ in which a neurosurgeon who failed to warn his patient of a 10% risk of a stroke, which materialised, was held liable.

Warning and causation

[**15.12**] If a plaintiff does succeed in proving that a proper warning was not given he will still need to show that treatment would in fact have been declined if one had been given. In *Reibl v Hughes*⁴ the Supreme Court of Canada favoured an objective rather than a subjective test to decide this question: ie the plaintiff's claim will fail if a reasonable person in his position (and free, of course, of hindsight) would not have declined treatment if he had received a full disclosure even if the plaintiff himself would have done so.⁵ But this was in the overall context of the existence of a doctrine of 'informed consent', whereby failure to make full disclosure is itself deemed negligent. This doctrine is more favourable to the plaintiff than the English approach within which the *Bolam* test remains influential. If the plaintiff succeeds in establishing prima facie liability even under this less favourable regime, it is submitted that the defendant should at least be subjected to a heavy burden of proof to show that a reasonable patient would still have gone ahead if he had been provided

---

1   '. . . when questioned specifically by a patient of apparently sound mind about risks involved in a particular treatment proposed, the doctor's duty must, in my opinion, be to answer both truthfully and as fully as the questioner requires': per Lord Bridge in [1985] AC 871 at 898; see also per Lord Diplock at 895 and per Lord Templeman at 902. See also Simon Lee, 'Operating under Informed Consent' (1985) 101 LQR 316.
2   [1985] AC 871 at 900. See also per Lord Templeman at 904-905. It has also been suggested that *Sidaway* principles imply the existence of a 'duty of candour' requiring doctors to be frank about what occurred *after* treatment has been given and a mishap has taken place: see *Naylor v Preston Area Health Authority* [1987] 2 All ER 353 at 360, [1987] 1 WLR 958 at 967, CA per Sir John Donaldson MR, reiterating the views expressed by himself and Mustill LJ in *Lee v South West Thames Regional Health Authority* [1985] 2 All ER 385 at 389-390, [1985] 1 WLR 845 at 850, CA.
3   (1980) 114 DLR (3d) 1.
4   (1980) 114 DLR (3d) 1.
5   This is the approach favoured by Professor Kennedy: see (1984) 47 MLR 454 at 471.

with all the requisite information.[1] Moreover, where the plaintiff proves a breach of duty by virtue of the doctor's failure to answer specific questions put by the patient himself, it would seem logically impossible to apply a strictly objective test. In any event, even an objective test will take into account the patient's individual situation in so far as non-medical factors might have made a decision to decline treatment rationally justifiable.[2] Thus Lord Scarman in *Sidaway v Governors of Bethlem Royal Hospital*[3] referred to the patient's need 'to consider and balance the medical advantages and risks alongside other relevant matters, such as, for example, his family, business or social responsibilities of which the doctor may be only partially, if at all, informed'. Although his Lordship was dissenting there is no reason to suppose that the majority would have disagreed with him on this point.

Contractual negligence

[**15.13**] If the patient was treated privately, so that he entered into a contractual relationship with his doctor, the question may arise as to whether his chances of success are higher in contract than in tort. In theory this could be so if the contract was a most unusual one in which the doctor guaranteed that his treatment would succeed. In practice, however, such guarantees are seldom, if ever, given and the court will lean strongly against implying any term to that effect. In *Thake v Maurice*[4] the plaintiff had a sterilisation operation which was properly carried out. Subsequently, however, he regained his fertility and his wife became pregnant. Although his contention that the surgeon had, albeit inadvertently, contractually guaranteed sterility was upheld by the trial judge[5] that decision was reversed by the Court of Appeal.[6] In the similar case of *Eyre v Measday*,[7] in which the Court of Appeal reached the same result, Slade LJ put it as follows:[8]

> '... in my opinion, in the absence of any express warranty, the court should be slow to imply against a medical man an unqualified warranty as to the results of an intended operation, for the very simple reason

---

1 See the Australian case of *Ellis v Wallsend District Hospital* (1989) 17 NSWLR 553 in which the New South Wales Court of Appeal adopted a subjective test in preference to the objective test favoured in Canada. See, especially, per Samuels JA at 581 and Kirby P (dissenting but not on this point) at 560.
2 Cf *Videto v Kennedy* (1981) 125 DLR (3d) 127 (patient anxious to avoid scarring after sterilisation operation which she had wished to keep secret from her Catholic parents). See also *Reibl v Hughes* (1980) 114 DLR (3d) 1 at 6.
3 [1985] AC 871 at 886, [1985] 1 All ER 643 at 652.
4 [1986] QB 644, [1986] 1 All ER 497.
5 See [1984] 2 All ER 513. For discussion see, generally, Rogers 'Legal Implications of Ineffective Sterilization' (1985) 5 LS 296. See also Grubb 'Failed Sterilisation: Is a Claim in Contract or Negligence a Guarantee of Success?' [1986] 45 CLJ 197.
6 It should be noted, however, that the defendant's appeal itself was dismissed and the plaintiff retained the judgment in his favour. This was because, on the facts, the doctor had failed to give an adequate *warning* of the possibility of the return of fertility.
7 [1986] 1 All ER 488, CA.
8 Ibid at 495.

that, objectively speaking, it is most unlikely that a responsible medical man would intend to give a warranty of this nature. Of course, objectively speaking, it is likely that he would give a guarantee that he would do what he had undertaken to do with reasonable care and skill; but it is quite another matter to say that he has committed himself to the extent suggested in the present case.'

As this quotation illustrates, the term usually to be implied in medical contracts is that the doctor will act with reasonable care and skill,[1] and hence the result on any given set of facts should normally be the same irrespective of whether or not there was a contractual relationship between doctor and patient.

Lawyers

Advocate's immunity

[**15.14**] It is clear that advocates enjoy, for reasons of public policy, immunity from suit for any alleged negligence in the conduct of a case in court.[2] This applies irrespective of whether the advocate is a solicitor or a barrister.[3] But it is apparent that the immunity will now be construed narrowly and that it is unlikely to extend, even in relation to contentious business, much beyond things said or done in the courtroom itself. In *Saif Ali v Sydney Mitchell & Co*[4] the House of Lords held, albeit by a bare majority, that a barrister could be liable for negligence in advising the plaintiff on the selection of defendants in anticipated litigation arising out of a motor accident. On the other hand in *Somasundaram v M Julius Melchior & Co (a firm)*[5] the Court of Appeal held that there could be no liability in circumstances in which the plaintiff alleged that he had been wrongly over-persuaded by his solicitor and counsel to plead guilty to a criminal charge. Since the plea had been followed by a conviction his claim would be struck out on the ground that it involved an attack on a decision of a court of competent jurisdiction and was therefore an abuse of process. The question of immunity from liability, of advocates and others, on grounds of public policy is considered at greater length in Chapter 5 above, to which reference should be made for further discussion.

Types of claim

[**15.15**] Because the facts of each of the cases and matters with which they deal are themselves unique, the circumstances in which solicitors or barristers might find themselves facing allegations of negligence

---

1   See also *Thake v Maurice* [1986] QB 644 at 684-685, [1986] 1 All ER 497 at 510, CA per Neill LJ.
2   See *Rondel v Worsley* [1969] 1 AC 191, [1967] 3 All ER 993, HL.
3   See the Courts and Legal Services Act 1990, s 62, quoted in ch 5 above.
4   [1980] AC 198, [1978] 3 All ER 1033, HL. Cf *Welsh v Chief Constable of the Merseyside Police* [1993] 1 All ER 692.
5   [1989] 1 All ER 129, [1988] 1 WLR 1394, CA.

admit of infinite variety.[1] Obviously, legal advice cannot be deemed 'negligent' merely because a court eventually adopts a different view of the law from that which the legal adviser originally propounded to his client.[2] On the other hand, if, for instance, counsel's opinion carelessly overlooked a recent decision of the House of Lords or Court of Appeal, which any practitioner in that speciality would without question have regarded as being directly in point, the imposition of liability in negligence would be appropriate. The most straightforward cases, however, are those in which obvious slips have been made, such as failing to register a land charge,[3] or failing to start proceedings in time so that they become statute-barred. The existence of liability, on the part of the solicitor responsible, will normally be virtually self-evident in cases of this kind. Rather more difficult to decide, depending upon the facts, will be cases in which it is alleged that a solicitor failed adequately to investigate the factual circumstances surrounding a particular matter. At the easier end of the spectrum of this type of case will be situations in which complex documents, such as commercial leases,[4] have been perused (or drafted) with insufficient care and some aspect vital to the client's interest has simply been overlooked.[5] It may also be negligent, even in an apparently simple conveyancing transaction,[6] to accept the word of the other party on some crucial question of fact without making further checks.[7] Less straightforward, however, will be situations in which some precaution has been omitted, perhaps in investigating title, which with hindsight it would have been prudent to take, but expert witnesses differ as to whether they would in fact have taken the precaution in the circumstances.[8] If the defendant can establish that he followed common practice[9] this will obviously be of great assistance to him in

1 Examples of successful claims against solicitors, in addition to other cases cited below, include *Crossan v Ward Bracewell* [1986] NLJ Rep 849 and *McLellan v Fletcher* [1987] NLJ Rep 593.
2 See, eg *Ormindale Holdings v Ray, Wolfe, Connel, Lightbody & Reynolds* (1980) 116 DLR (3d) 346. See also per Lord Salmon in *Saif Ali v Sydney Mitchell* [1980] AC 198 at 231: 'Lawyers are often faced with finely balanced problems. Diametrically opposite views may and not infrequently are taken by barristers and indeed by judges, each of whom has exercised reasonable, and sometimes far more than reasonable, care and competence. The fact that one of them turns out to be wrong certainly does not mean that he has been negligent.' See also per Lord Wilberforce at 214 and per Lord Diplock at 214-221.
3 See, eg *Midland Bank Trust Co Ltd v Hett, Stubbs & Kemp* [1979] Ch 384, [1978] 3 All ER 571; *Bell v Peter Browne & Co* [1990] 2 QB 495, [1990] 3 All ER 124, CA. Cf *Griffiths v Dawson & Co* (1993) Times, 5 April.
4 For a case in which negligence liability was established against a solicitor with respect to an unusual clause in a commercial lease see *County Personnel (Employment Agency) Ltd v Alan R Pulver & Co* [1987] 1 All ER 289, [1987] 1 WLR 916, CA.
5 See, eg *Sykes v Midland Bank Executor & Trustee Co Ltd* [1971] 1 QB 113, [1970] 2 All ER 471, CA. See also *Hill v Harris* [1965] 2 QB 601, [1965] 2 All ER 358, CA. Cf *Ford v White & Co* [1964] 2 All ER 755, [1964] 1 WLR 885.
6 On which see, generally, HW Wilkinson 'Negligent Conveyancing, One Thousand Ways of Erring' (1986) NLJ 887 at 911.
7 See, eg *Goody v Baring* [1956] 2 All ER 11, [1956] 1 WLR 448.
8 See, eg *G & K Ladenbau (UK) Ltd v Crawley and de Reya* [1978] 1 All ER 682, [1978] 1 WLR 266.
9 See, eg *Simmons v Pennington & Son* [1955] 1 All ER 240, [1955] 1 WLR 183, CA.

such a case but, for obvious reasons, the court will be less ready than in cases of alleged medical negligence to accept the legitimacy of the existing practice without some analysis of its desirability.[1] Indeed, in one case Oliver J even cast doubt upon the propriety of expert evidence in cases of this kind. In *Midland Bank Trust Co Ltd v Hett, Stubbs & Kemp*[2] he said:

> 'I have heard the evidence of a number of practising solicitors ... I must say that I doubt the value, or even the admissibility, of this sort of evidence, which seems to be becoming customary in cases of this type. Clearly, if there is some practice in a particular profession, some accepted standard of conduct which is laid down by a professional institute or sanctioned by common usage, evidence of that can and ought to be received. But evidence which really amounts to no more than an expression of opinion by a particular practitioner of what he thinks he would have done had he been placed, hypothetically and without the benefit of hindsight, in the position of the defendants is of little assistance to the court, whilst evidence of the witnesses' view of what, as a matter of law, the solicitor's duty was in the particular circumstances of the case is, I should have thought, inadmissible, for that is the very question which it is the court's function to decide.'

Adequacy of explanation

[15.16] Perhaps the most difficult kind of negligence claim against a solicitor to resolve, because it involves subjective personal interaction, is one in which it is alleged that he failed adequately to *explain* to his client the legal implications of a particular document or situation.[3] In such cases much will necessarily depend upon the level of education and expertise of the client himself. 'An inexperienced client', Donaldson LJ once observed,[4] 'will need and will be entitled to expect the solicitor to take a much broader view of the scope of the retainer and of his duties than will be the case with an experienced client'. It would, for example, normally be necessary clearly to explain to someone providing security for loans to a relative the exact nature and extent of the commitment being undertaken.[5] On the other hand it is hardly likely to be necessary to spell out to an experienced property developer the obvious fact that he could be sued if he did not comply with the clear terms of a proposed contract.[6] Nor is a barrister always obliged to ensure that his lay client fully understands the

---

1 Cf *Edward Wong Finance Co Ltd v Johnson, Stokes & Master* [1984] AC 296, [1984] 2 WLR 1, PC.
2 [1979] Ch 384 at 402, [1978] 3 All ER 571 at 582.
3 Cf *County Personnel (Employment Agency) Ltd v Alan R Pulver & Co* [1987] 1 All ER 289, [1987] 1 WLR 916, CA.
4 See *Carradine Properties Ltd. v DJ Freeman & Co* (1982) 126 Sol Jo 157, CA (the passage in the text was quoted from the transcript by Staughton J in *R P Howard Ltd v Woodman Matthews & Co* [1983] BCLC 117 at 121-122).
5 Cf *Forster v Outred & Co* [1982] 2 All ER 753, [1982] 1 WLR 86, CA. See also *Fox v Everingham* (1983) 50 ALR 337 (Federal Court of Australia).
6 See *Aslan v Clintons* (1984) 134 NLJ 584 Cf *Sykes v Midland Bank Executor and Trustee Co* [1971] 1 QB 113, [1970] 2 All ER 471, CA.

implications of his advice; depending upon the circumstances counsel may well be entitled to leave that task to the solicitor involved.[1]

Tort and contract

Coexistence of tort duty

[**15.17**] In *Midland Bank Trust Co Ltd v Hett, Stubbs & Kemp*[2] Oliver J held that, alongside the contractual relationship existing between them, a solicitor owes to his client a duty of care in tort. This marked a radical departure from the position as previously understood, based upon a well-known decision of the Court of Appeal in 1938, that a solicitor's duty to his client was in contract only.[3] In the *Hett* case itself the effect of the decision of Oliver J was that the plaintiff client was able to take advantage of a more favourable limitation period, than he would otherwise have been able to do, in an action against his solicitor for loss caused by the latter's carelessness. *Hett*'s case was not mentioned in *Tai Hing Cotton Mill Ltd v Liu Chong Hing Bank Ltd*,[4] in which Lord Scarman doubted whether 'there is anything to the advantage of the law's development in searching for a liability in tort where the parties are in a contractual relationship'.[5] The better view, however, is that the correctness of the decision of Oliver J on the relationship of solicitor and client is not affected by this dictum. Lord Scarman was dealing with the relationship of banker and customer and emphasised that his remarks were directed 'particularly' at situations in which the parties were 'in a commercial relationship'.[6]

Solicitors and third parties

[**15.18**] Shortly after the decision in *Hett*'s case came the famous case of *Ross v Caunters*,[7] in which Sir Robert Megarry V-C held that a solicitor owed a duty of care in tort not only to his own client but also, in certain circumstances, to third parties who might be adversely affected by his negligence in advising or acting on behalf of his client. In that case a solicitor was held liable to the proposed beneficiary under a will whose gift was rendered void due to the failure of the testator, as a result of the solicitor's negligence when advising and acting for him, to comply with the formalities of the Wills Act 1837.[8]

---

1 See *Mathew v Maughold Life Assurance Co* (1987) 3 PN 98, CA.
2 [1979] Ch 384, [1978] 3 All ER 571. See also *Aluminium Products Pty Ltd v Hill* [1981] Qd R 33 (Full Court of Supreme Court of Queensland).
3 See *Groom v Crocker* [1939] 1 KB 194, [1938] 2 All ER 394, CA.
4 [1986] AC 80, [1985] 2 All ER 947, PC.
5 Ibid at 106 and 957.
6 But cf per Mustill LJ in *Bell v Peter Browne & Co* [1990] 3 All ER 124 at 134, quoted in ch 11 above, regretting the existence of concurrent rights of action in contract and tort.
7 [1980] Ch 297, [1979] 3 All ER 580. See also *Smith v Claremont Haynes & Co* (1991) Times, 3 September.
8 See also the decision of the New Zealand Court of Appeal in *Gartside v Sheffield, Young & Ellis* [1983] NZLR 37 in which many of the Commonwealth cases on this point, some of them conflicting, are referred to.

In the 1993 case of *White v Jones*[1] the defendant solicitors had, due to their negligence, wholly failed to comply with the request of the testator that a will should be drawn up to benefit the plaintiffs. Imposing liability, the Court of Appeal asserted that *Ross v Caunters* had been correctly decided, notwithstanding the recent narrowing in the scope of liability for pure economic loss generally, and duly applied it. The decisions in *Ross v Caunters* and *White v Jones* do not imply that solicitors owe a *general* duty of care to devisees: for example they clearly do not owe them a duty when acting for the testator, during his lifetime, in a transaction subsequent to the will which adversely affects the subject matter of the devise.[2] Nevertheless, the decisions in *Ross*[3] and *Hett* have clearly effected a significant change in the law relating to professional negligence by solicitors. Moreover, although it has not gone uncriticised,[4] it should be noted that the correctness of the *Hett* case has also been assumed by the Court of Appeal.[5] As far as the principle in *Ross v Caunters* is concerned, however, its importance in practice is limited by the fact that its applicability will necessarily be confined to situations in which the client and the third party were both, as Sir Robert Megarry himself put it, 'on the same side'.[6] But the recent case of *Al-Kandari v JR Brown & Co*[7] indicates that these words should not be taken too literally. In this case the defendant firm of solicitors, who were acting for the husband in a matrimonial matter, undertook to retain their client's passport. He nevertheless managed to get it back and to take the children of the marriage out of the country. The Court of Appeal held the solicitors liable in negligence to the plaintiff wife for failing to alert her to the fact that the passport had left their possession.[8] On the whole, however, situations in which solicitors will be liable to parties who are in dispute with their own clients are likely to remain relatively rare.[9] In *Ross v Caunters* itself Sir Robert Megarry said:[10]

'In broad terms, a solicitor's duty to his client is to do for him all that he properly can, with, of course, proper care and attention . . . The solicitor owes no such duty to those who are not his clients. He is no guardian of

---

1 [1993] NLJR 473, CA. See also *Kecskemeti v Rubens Rabin & Co* (1992) Times, 31 December.
2 See *Clarke v Bruce Lance & Co* [1988] 1 All ER 364, [1988] 1 WLR 881, CA.
3 Ie confirmed in *White v Jones*.
4 See, eg JM Kaye 'The Liability of Solicitors in Tort' (1984) 100 LQR 680. For judicial criticism see the dissenting judgment of Connolly J in *Aluminium Products Pty Ltd v Hill* [1981] Qd R 33 at 36ff.
5 See *Forster v Outred & Co* [1982] 2 All ER 753, [1982] 1 WLR 86, especially per Dunn LJ at 99: 'I find the reasoning of Oliver J . . . wholly convincing.' But cf *Bell v Peter Browne & Co* [1990] 3 All ER 124 in which the Court of Appeal implicitly criticised *Hett's* case and distinguished it narrowly on another point.
6 See [1980] Ch 297 at 310, [1979] 3 All ER 580 at 598
7 [1988] QB 665, [1988] 1 All ER 833, CA. Cf *Welsh v Chief Constable of Merseyside Police* [1993] 1 All ER 692.
8 The court reversed the decision of French J at first instance (reported in [1987] QB 514) who, while holding that a duty of care had existed, had rejected the plaintiff's claim essentially on grounds of remoteness.
9 Cf Markesinis 'Fixing Acceptable Boundaries to the Liability of Solicitors' (1987) 103 LQR 346.
10 See [1980] Ch 297 at 322, [1979] 3 All ER 580 at 599.

their interests. What he does for his client may be hostile and injurious to their interests; and sometimes the greater the injuries the better he will have served his client. The duty owed by a solicitor to a third party is entirely different. There is no trace of a wide and general duty to do all that properly can be done for him. Instead, in a case such as the present, there is merely a duty, owed to him as well as the client, to use proper care in carrying out the client's instructions for conferring the benefit on the third party.'

Of course these remarks were directed at cases, such as *Ross v Caunters* itself, in which the plaintiff never relied on the solicitor's advice. If a third party *did* actually rely on that advice, to the solicitor's knowledge, and did so to his detriment, then it might be thought that such a person should be able to claim against the solicitor simply on the principle in *Hedley Byrne & Co v Heller & Partners Ltd*[1] itself, without invoking the rule in *Ross v Caunters*. Thus where the client is a company, for example, the solicitor might also owe a duty in tort to the principal shareholder, if the latter was relying on him to protect his interests.[2] On the other hand if the situation is the much more usual one in which a solicitor is merely acting as agent for his own client in the latter's dealings with a third party, it has recently been held, in *Gran Gelato Ltd v Richcliff (Group) Ltd*[3] that liability for negligent misstatement will rarely be imposed on the solicitor. 'In normal conveyancing transactions', observed Sir Donald Nicholls V-C,[4] 'solicitors who are acting for a seller do not in general owe to the would-be buyer a duty of care when answering inquiries before contract or the like'.[5]

Nature of the contractual duty

[15.19] As far as a solicitor's relationship with his own client is concerned, the coexistence, since the decision in *Midland Bank Trust Co v Hett, Stubbs & Kemp,* of duties in contract and tort, has had an incidental effect on limitation and also, possibly, upon issues such as remoteness of damage.[6] It has not, however, altered the *scope* of the solicitor's duty to his client nor the standard of care which he must show to him. Oliver J emphasised in the *Hett* case itself that the scope of that duty is governed by the retainer.[7] Of course there may be factual disputes as to the scope of the retainer, particularly if it is unwritten.[8] But as far as the *standard* of care is concerned, it has long been accepted that it is to use reasonable care and skill. The

---

1 [1964] AC 465, [1963] 2 All ER 575, HL. See, generally, ch 5 above.
2 See *R P Howard Ltd v Woodman Matthews & Co* [1983] BCLC 117.
3 [1992] 1 All ER 865.
4 [1992] 1 All ER 865 at 872.
5 Sed quaere. For forceful criticism of the *Gran Gelato* decision see Peter Cane 'Negligent Solicitor Escapes Liability' (1992) 109 LQR 539 and Andrew Tettenborn 'Enquiries Before Contract – The Wrong Answer?' [1992] 51 CLJ 415.
6 Cf *H Parsons (Livestock) Ltd v Uttley Ingham & Co Ltd* [1978] QB 791, [1978] 1 All ER 525, CA.
7 See [1979] Ch 384 at 403.
8 See, eg *Griffiths v Evans* [1953] 2 All ER 1364, [1953] 1 WLR 1424, CA. Cf *Hall v Meyrick* [1957] 2 QB 455, [1957] 2 All ER 722, CA.

question whether a defendant solicitor complied with that standard will obviously be the source of most disputes in this area, but the principle involved will normally be clear. In one case, however, Megarry J questioned whether the contractual standard of care owed by a solicitor to his client might not in fact be *higher*, at least in some cases, than the approach adopted by the law of tort. 'The uniform standard of care postulated for the world at large', he observed in *Duchess of Argyll v Beuselinck*,[1] 'hardly seems appropriate when the duty is not one imposed by the law of tort but arises from a contractual obligation existing between the client and the particular solicitor or firm in question'. Without expressing a concluded view on the point his Lordship wondered whether the client who 'engages an expert, and doubtless expects to pay commensurate fees, is . . . not entitled to expect something more than the standard of the reasonably competent?' Megarry J made it clear that he was not thinking merely of the contrast between the general practitioner and the specialist but also of those of 'long experience and great skill as contrasted with those practising in the same field of the law but being of a more ordinary calibre and having less experience'.[2] The proposition that the duty of care, owed by a solicitor to his client and normally implied into the contract between them, might vary depending upon such factors as the reputation, expertise and cost of the particular firm seems, however, difficult to support.[3] The contrast with the 'uniform' test for negligence in the law of tort is also rather misleading, since so much depends upon the application of that test to the facts of each case.[4] The concept of reasonable care is an inherently flexible one and should preferably be regarded as the basic test to be applied, whether the solicitor is sued by his client in contract or in tort. Unless matters are to become excessively complicated there is, it is submitted, only one level of duty higher than that of reasonable care which should be afforded recognition by the law. That is strict liability. Although common elsewhere in the law of contract this would rarely be appropriate in the context of a contract between a solicitor and his client, except where the simplest matters of routine were concerned. Not only would the prudent solicitor be in practice most unlikely to undertake to produce a particular result irrespective of the circumstances, but there might conceivably also be objections on grounds of public policy to an officer of the court seeking to guarantee the outcome of a legal situation.

---

1 [1972] 2 Lloyd's Rep 172 at 183.
2 [1972] 2 Lloyd's Rep 172 at 183.
3 Cf *Greaves & Co (Contractors) Ltd v Baynham, Meikle & Partners* [1974] 3 All ER 666, [1974] 1 WLR 1261.
4 Cf *Wimpey Construction UK Ltd v Poole* [1984] 2 Lloyd's Rep 499 at 506-507 per Webster J.

Land, valuation and construction

The 'property' professions

[**15.20**] A number of related professions deal with various aspects of real property, including the valuation of land and buildings and the design and construction of the latter. Architects, civil engineers, and surveyors are the main groups involved, but the important function of valuation is often carried out by estate agents who will often, but not necessarily, also be qualified surveyors.

Valuation

[**15.21**] In *Singer & Friedlander Ltd v John D Wood & Co*[1] Watkins J said:[2]

> 'The valuation of land by trained, competent and careful professional men is a task which rarely, if ever, admits of precise conclusion. Often beyond certain well-founded facts so many imponderables confront the valuer that he is obliged to proceed on the basis of assumptions. Therefore, he cannot be faulted for achieving a result which does not admit of some degree of error.'

His Lordship went on to accept, on the basis of expert evidence, that the 'permissible margin of error' is 10 to 15% above or below the figure which at the time of valuation 'a competent careful and experienced valuer' would have arrived at 'after making all the necessary inquiries and paying proper regard to the then state of the market'. He concluded that any valuation falling outside this 'bracket' brought 'into question the competence of the valuer and the sort of care he gave to the task of valuation'. In *Singer & Friedlander Ltd v John D Wood* itself the defendant firm of surveyors and valuers was found to have been negligent, after the application of these criteria, and was held liable to the plaintiff bankers for losses suffered as a result of an excessive valuation. Defendant valuers were also held liable in two other reported cases decided round about the same time: *Kenny v Hall, Pain & Foster*[3] and *Corisand Investments Ltd v Druce & Co*.[4] Both of these cases, along with *Singer & Friedlander Ltd v John D Wood* itself, were produced by the crisis which affected the property market in 1973. In the judgments in all three of them, but particularly in the *Singer* and *Corisand* cases, the nature of the process of land valuation is considered at length, and the trio provides an important modern source of judicial authority on the approach of the law to negligence claims against surveyors and valuers.[5]

---

1 (1977) 243 Estates Gazette 212, [1977] EGD 569.
2 Ibid at 213 and 574.
3 (1976) 239 Estates Gazette 355, [1976] EGD 629.
4 (1978) 248 Estates Gazette 315, [1978] EGD 769.
5 For discussion see Brazier 'Surveyors' Negligence: A Survey' [1981] Conv 96; Follows 'Negligence in Relation to Land Valuations' (1982) 126 Sol Jo 752.

[15.22] Of course, in a case in which a surveyor simply overlooks obvious structural defects[1] in a property he is asked to value negligence will be easier to prove than in one in which the more abstract aspects of the process by which he arrived at his figure are called into question.[2] On the other hand, it has been held that a valuation is not to be confused with a structural survey, so that an estate agent asked to value a property for purchase as a retirement home was held not to have been negligent in failing to warn that the house had been built on peat and that settlement problems could lead to difficulties on resale.[3] But a valuer clearly does need to take care adequately to research the market in the area of the property in question;[4] and a qualified surveyor is also expected to keep abreast of changes in the law affecting land valuation.[5]

Liability to third parties

[15.23] In addition to his contractual duty to his own client to use reasonable care and skill, it is now established that a surveyor valuing property may also find himself liable in tort to third parties.[6] In *Smith v Eric S Bush*[7] the plaintiff bought a house on mortgage and, in common with the widespread practice of such purchasers, particularly at the lower end of the market, did not commission her own independent survey but relied on that carried out for the building society. Unfortunately, the building society's surveyor negligently failed to notice major defects in the property. The House of Lords held that he was liable to the plaintiff in tort. He should have known that the purchaser, as well as the building society, was likely to rely on his valuation.[8] Nor is a surveyor's liability to third parties necessarily

1 See, eg *Philips v Ward* [1956] 1 All ER 874, [1956] 1 WLR 471, CA; *Morgan v Perry* (1973) 229 Estates Gazette 1737; *Yianni v Edwin Evans & Sons* [1982] QB 438, [1981] 3 All ER 592; *Perry v Sidney Phillips & Son* [1982] 3 All ER 705, [1982] 1 WLR 1297, CA; *London and South of England Building Society v Stone* [1983] 3 All ER 105, [1983] 1 WLR 1242, CA.
2 See, eg *Roberts v J Hampson & Co* [1989] 2 All ER 504, [1990] 1 WLR 94 in which a surveyor was held liable for failing to spot dry-rot when carrying out a building society inspection of a home to be purchased by a couple of modest means. The judgment of Ian Kennedy J considers in some detail the extent of a surveyor's duty with respect to such matters as moving furniture and lifting carpets.
3 See *Sutcliffe v Sayer* [1987] 1 EGLR 155, 281 Estates Gazette 1452, CA. For criticism of this case on the ground that the distinction between a survey and a valuation is not tenable see Michael Harwood 'A Structural Survey of Negligent Reports' (1987) 50 MLR 588 at 594: 'Whether a house is bought to let, to live in or to die in, its valuation can only be related to its saleability.' But it should be noted that the defendant in *Sayer*'s case was not a qualified surveyor, and this could conceivably limit the applicability of the decision in other cases.
4 See *Baxter v FW Gapp & Co Ltd* [1939] 2 KB 271, [1939] 2 All ER 752, CA (overruled in *Swingcastle Ltd v Alastair Gibson* [1991] 2 AC 223, [1991] 2 All ER 353, HL, but not on this point).
5 See *Weedon v Hindwood, Clarke & Esplin* (1975) 234 Estates Gazette 121, [1975] EGD 750.
6 On the important question of the extent to which *disclaimers* of liability can be effective in such cases, see chs 4 and 5 above.
7 [1990] 1 AC 831, [1989] 2 All ER 514, HL.
8 Approving the decision of Park J in *Yianni v Edwin Evans & Sons* [1982] QB 438, [1981] 3 All ER 592.

restricted to those who themselves act in reliance on his valuation. Thus a surveyor who values a property on behalf of a mortgagee who is exercising his power of sale may also owe a duty to the mortgagor if, as will often be the case, it can be foreseen that his interests will suffer if the property is sold on the basis of an under-valuation.[1]

Design and construction

[**15.24**] It is beyond question that, on appropriate facts, an architect or engineer who is negligent in designing a structure, or in otherwise giving advice in the context of building operations, can be liable in tort to third parties, as well as in contract to his clients, for any loss or damage so caused. This was clearly established and illustrated by the 1963 case of *Clay v A J Crump & Sons Ltd*,[2] in which architects were held liable when their carelessness in the performance of their duties under a demolition contract was partly responsible for the collapse of a wall which killed two workmen on the site and injured a third. More recently, in *Rimmer v Liverpool City Council*,[3] the defendants were held liable when a panel of excessively thin glass, which had been negligently incorporated by their architects into the design of a council flat, broke and injured the plaintiff. Although it is obviously not in itself a defence to a claim by an injured third party that the defendant was acting under a contract with someone else, that contract may be relevant to tortious liability by determining the overall scope of the defendant's responsibilities in the operation. Thus in *Clayton v Woodman & Sons (Builders) Ltd*[4] and *Oldschool v Gleeson (Contractors) Ltd*,[5] which involved claims against architects and consulting engineers respectively, the defendants were absolved from liability on the ground that their alleged carelessness amounted to no more than a legitimate refusal to interfere with responsibilities which had been allocated not to them but to the building contractors themselves.

Contractual liability without negligence?

[**15.25**] Where professional people are sued by their own clients for breach of contract the usual implied term relating to the nature of the obligation undertaken is, as has already been indicated earlier in this chapter, merely that reasonable skill and care will be used. But where the contract is for the production of a specific chattel, or perhaps even a building, albeit by the use of professional skill, there is some authority for the proposition that a term familiar in contracts for the

---

1 See *Garland v Ralph Pay & Ransom* (1984) 271 Estates Gazette 106, [1984] EGD 867. Cf *Cuckmere Brick Co Ltd v Mutual Finance Ltd* [1971] Ch 949, [1971] 2 All ER 633, CA (see also *Tse Kwong Lam v Wong Chit Sen* [1983] 3 All ER 54, [1983] 1 WLR 1349, PC).
2 [1964] 1 QB 533, [1963] 3 All ER 687, CA.
3 [1985] QB 1, [1984] 1 All ER 930, CA. Cf *Kelly v City of Edinburgh District Council* 1983 SLT 593.
4 [1962] 2 QB 533, [1962] 2 All ER 33, CA.
5 (1976) 4 BLR 103.

sale of goods, namely that the object will be reasonably fit for its purpose, may be implied. If so, this will obviously put the professional person under a much more onerous obligation since he will be liable even if he was not careless. The Court of Appeal held in the 1943 case of *Samuels v Davis*[1] that this higher contractual duty applied to a contract between a dentist and his patient for the supply of dentures. The proposition by counsel for the dentist that the obligation was merely the usual professional one of reasonable skill and care was expressly rejected. Du Parcq LJ distinguished situations involving surgery, such as the extraction of a tooth, where that would indeed be the standard, and observed that 'the case is entirely different where a chattel is ultimately to be delivered'.[2] Much more recently, this view received powerful support, albeit obiter, in the House of Lords. In *Independent Broadcasting Authority v BICC Construction Ltd*[3] a television aerial mast, which had been designed by the defendant structural engineers, collapsed. Three members of the House[4] inclined to the view that the designers, who were held liable for negligence, would still have been liable even if they had not been negligent. The clearest statement to this effect was made by Lord Scarman. He referred with approval to *Samuels v Davis* and expressed himself as follows:[5]

> 'The extent of the obligation is, of course, to be determined as a matter of construction of the contract. But, in the absence of a clear, contractual indication to the contrary, I see no reason why one who in the course of his business contracts to design, supply, and erect a television aerial mast is not under an obligation to ensure that it is reasonably fit for the purpose which he knows it is intended to be. The Court of Appeal held that this was the contractual obligation in this case, and I agree with them ... Counsel for the appellants, however, submitted that, where a design, as in this case, requires the exercise of professional skill, the obligation is no more than to exercise the care and skill of the ordinarily competent member of the profession ... However, I do not accept that the design obligation of the supplier of an article is to be equated with the obligation of a professional man in the practice of his profession ... In the absence of any terms (express or to be implied) negativing the obligation, one who contracts to design an article for a purpose made known to him undertakes that the design is reasonably fit for the purpose.'

Financial services

Accountants[6]

[**15.26**] Accountants and auditors owe the usual professional duty of reasonable care and skill to their contractual clients. As in other

---

1 [1943] KB 526, [1943] 2 All ER 3, CA.
2 Ibid at 530 and 6. See also *Young & Marten Ltd v McManus Childs Ltd* [1969] 1 AC 454, [1968] 2 All ER 1169, HL (especially per Lord Upjohn at 473 and 1176ff).
3 (1980) 14 BLR 9. See also the decision of the Court of Appeal: (1978) 11 BLR 38.
4 See (1980) 14 BLR 9 at 26 (Viscount Dilhorne); and 44-45 (Lord Fraser of Tullybelton). For Lord Scarman's speech see next note.
5 Ibid at 47-48. See also per Roskill LJ in the Court of Appeal: 11 BLR at 51-52.
6 See, generally *Law and Accountancy* (Modern Law Review Special Issue, November 1991).

professions the standard required to satisfy this test is not static. In *Re Thomas Gerrard & Son Ltd*,[1] decided in 1967, Pennycuick J held auditors liable for negligence for accepting too readily explanations from the managing director of a company, relating to altered invoices, when they should have investigated further and might then have discovered a fraud being perpetrated on the company. His Lordship distinguished an 1896 decision in the Court of Appeal,[2] in which auditors had been held not liable on similar facts, on the ground that 'the standards of reasonable care and skill are, on the expert evidence, more exacting today than those which prevailed in 1896'.[3] But the most far-reaching change in the law relating to the liability of accountants has, of course, been the development of liability in tort to third parties for negligence under the *Hedley Byrne* principle. The expansion of the law effected by that case and subsequent decisions is obviously of particular importance to accountants, whose work will often foreseeably be relied on by other persons as well as their clients.[4] This aspect of negligence liability is considered at length in chapter 5 above, to which reference should be made for further discussion.

Investment advice

[**15.27**] Since their professional duties are usually relatively well-defined, accountants are, in a sense, at one end of the spectrum of those whose work involves giving advice and information in a financial context. At the other end are stockbrokers and others who advise generally on investment. Clearly, the more speculative the field in question the more difficult it will be to establish that advice which led to losses was in fact given negligently. In *Stafford v Conti Commodity Services Ltd*,[5] Mocatta J refused to hold a broker liable for advice given in respect of the commodities futures market, observing that 'in such an unpredictable market as this, it would require exceedingly strong evidence from expert brokers in relation to individual transactions to establish negligence on the part of the defendants'.[6] This decision was subsequently applied by the Court of Appeal in *Merrill Lynch Futures Inc v York House Trading Ltd*.[7] In this case the Court struck out a counterclaim by the defendant investors who alleged negligent advice, relying solely on the fact that they had incurred losses, when sued by the plaintiff commodity brokers for unpaid commission. On the other hand liability will be easier to establish if a broker carelessly gives advice based upon misleading factual information.[8]

1 [1968] Ch 455, [1967] 2 All ER 525.
2 See *Re Kingston Cotton Mill Co (No 2)* [1896] 2 Ch 279, CA.
3 [1968] Ch 455 at 475, [1967] 2 All ER 525 at 536.
4 Cf *Caparo Industries plc v Dickman* [1990] 2 AC 605, [1990] 1 All ER 568, HL.
5 [1981] 1 All ER 691.
6 Ibid at 698.
7 [1984] LS Gaz R 2544, CA.
8 See, eg *Elderkin v Merrill Lynch Royal Securities Ltd* (1977) 80 DLR (3d) 313.

Chapter 16

Liability of occupiers

The scope of 'occupation'

What can be 'occupied'?

[**16.01**] The majority of situations which give rise to questions concerning occupiers' liability inevitably concern land and premises. Nevertheless, it is important to realise that the scope of the two relevant statutes, the Occupiers' Liability Acts of 1957 and 1984, is not confined to such situations. The Acts also apply to 'any fixed or movable structure, including any vessel, vehicle or aircraft'.[1] Thus ships,[2] lorries,[3] ladders[4] and scaffolding,[5] for example, come within the legislation, as do empty houses which are no longer inhabited.[6]

Who is an 'occupier'?

[**16.02**] The Occupiers' Liability Acts provide that the question of who is an 'occupier', for their purposes, is to be answered by recourse to the common law.[7] In the leading case of *Wheat v E Lacon & Co Ltd*,[8] Lord Denning,[9] in the House of Lords, spoke as follows:

'In order to be an "occupier" it is not necessary for a person to have active control over the premises. He need not have exclusive occupation. Suffice it that he has some degree of control. He may share control with others. Two or more may be "occupiers". And whenever this happens, each is under a duty to use care towards persons coming lawfully on to

---

1 Occupiers' Liability Act 1957, s 1(3)(a). See also the Occupiers' Liability Act 1984, s 1(2) and (9).
2 See, eg *Ellis v Scruttons Maltby Ltd and Cunard Steamship Co Ltd* [1975] 1 Lloyd's Rep 64.
3 Cf *Lewys v Burnett and Dunbar* [1945] 2 All ER 555.
4 See *Wheeler v Copas* [1981] 3 All ER 405.
5 See *Kearney v Eric Waller Ltd* [1967] 1 QB 29, [1965] 3 All ER 352.
6 *Harris v Birkenhead Corpn* [1976] 1 All ER 341, [1976] 1 WLR 279, CA.
7 See the Occupiers' Liability Act 1957, s 1(2) and the Occupiers' Liability Act 1984, s 1(2)(a).
8 [1966] AC 552, [1966] 1 All ER 582, HL.
9 Ibid at 578 and 594.

the premises, dependent on his degree of control. If each fails in his duty, each is liable to a visitor who is injured in consequence of his failure, but each may have a claim to contribution from the other.'

In *Wheat v Lacon* a brewery company owned a public house which was run on their behalf by a resident manager who had living accommodation on the first floor. When a fatal accident occurred to a visitor in this accommodation, which was to all intents and purposes treated by the manager as his private dwelling, the House of Lords held that, on the facts, the brewery company retained sufficient control over the accommodation to qualify as an 'occupier' of it, in addition to the manager and his wife themselves.[1] The concept of dual occupation is also seen in cases in which even contractors, working only temporarily on premises, have been held to have sufficient control to qualify, along with others, as occupiers.[2] One consequence of the concept of dual occupation is that it is possible for a person to be a visitor in relation to one occupier but a trespasser in relation to another.[3]

[**16.03**] The fact that *control*, rather than physical presence on the premises, is the key to the concept of 'occupation' was strikingly illustrated in *Harris v Birkenhead Corpn*.[4] In that case the defendant corporation was held to have been the 'occupier' of a house which it owned, but which had been left empty when the tenant vacated it. The Court of Appeal held the corporation liable for failing to take steps to board up the premises and prevent them from becoming a hazard to child trespassers.[5]

Liability to visitors

Persons qualifying as 'visitors'

[**16.04**] The common law, prior to the passing of the Occupiers' Liability Act 1957, imposed a two-tier standard of care upon occupiers (except to trespassers and to persons who contracted with the occupier for a right of entry) corresponding to a distinction which was drawn between two types of entrant: invitees and licensees. Broadly speaking the occupier had to take reasonable care for the safety of his invitees,

---

1 The claim in respect of the accident ultimately failed due to lack of proof of any breach of the duty of care.
2 See, eg *Fisher v CHT Ltd*, [1965] 2 All ER 601, [1965] 1 WLR 1093. See also *AMF International Ltd v Magnet Bowling Ltd* [1968] 2 All ER 789, [1968] 1 WLR 1028.
3 See *Ferguson v Welsh* [1987] 3 All ER 777 at 785, [1987] 1 WLR 1553 at 1562-1563 per Lord Goff.
4 [1976] 1 All ER 341, [1976] 1 WLR 279, CA. See, especially, per Megaw LJ at 349 and 288: '[It is] clear that in law the quality of being in physical possession, or having been in actual physical possesion, is not in all cases – and is not in this case – a necessary ingredient of the legal status of occupier for the purposes with which we are concerned.'
5 See also *Collier v Anglian Water Authority* (1983) Times 26 March, CA (water authority 'occupier' of sea wall). Cf *Jordan v Achara* (1988) 20 HLR 607, CA.

with whom he had a shared interest in their entry on to his property, but a lower duty, merely to warn of concealed dangers of which the occupier was actually aware, to his licensees; the latter being those who had his permission to enter but shared no common purpose with him. One of the major changes in the law made by the 1957 Act was to abolish the distinction between invitees and licensees, and the separate duties of care associated with it, and to provide that entrants who would formerly have been members of either category would henceforth belong to a single, unified, category of ' visitors'.[1] It follows that as far as the scope of the new category is concerned, the common law only remains relevant in determining its outer frontier so as to exclude those, such as trespassers, who were neither invitees nor licensees. Prior to the passing of the Act there was a not inconsiderable body of case law in which the somewhat uncertain frontier *between* the two superseded categories was of importance.[2] But since the Act relatively little space has been taken up in the law reports, within the occupiers' liability context, by judicial consideration of which persons qualify as 'visitors' and most, but not all,[3] of it has been concerned with the question of whether or not the entrant was in fact a trespasser.[4] At the same time the number of reported decisions in which the *standard* of care imposed by the Act has been considered has also been fairly small. While arguments based on the absence of reported cases can never be conclusive, since they discount the possibility of an inconvenient level of uncertainty when cases are decided on their own facts,[5] it is perhaps not unreasonable to infer that the legislation has been successful in achieving a useful degree of simplification of the law in this area. The Act also clarified the position of persons who enter premises under a right conferred by law, whose precise status had apparently been uncertain while the invitee and licensee distinction prevailed. Such persons now enjoy at least the same rights as 'visitors'.[6]

The 'common duty of care'

[**16.05**] The Occupiers' Liability Act 1957, s 1(2) provides as follows:

> 'The common duty of care is a duty to take such care as in all the circumstances of the case is reasonable to see that the visitor will be reasonably safe in using the premises for the purposes for which he is invited or permitted by the occupier to be there.'

---

1 See the Occupiers' Liability Act 1957, s 1(2).
2 For discussion and criticism of the previous law see, generally, the Third Report of the Law Reform Committee ('Occupiers' Liability to Invitees, Licensees and Trespassers': Cmd 9305), which led to the passing of the 1957 Act.
3 Cf *Greenhalgh v British Railways Board* [1969] 2 QB 286, [1969] 1 All ER 114, CA.
4 See, eg *Stone v Taffe* [1974] 3 All ER 1016, [1974] 1 WLR 1575, CA (person staying on licensed premises after hours).
5 Cf the minority report of one member of the Law Reform Committee (the then Mr Kenneth Diplock Q C) in Cmd 9305 at pp 43-44.
6 See the Occupiers' Liability Act 1957, s 2(6).

It will be apparent that this formulation, guidance for the application of which is given in succeeding subsections, is virtually indistinguishable from the common law duty of care to 'neighbours' expounded in *Donoghue v Stevenson*.[1]

Activities on the land

[16.06] The similarity of the statutory formula to ordinary negligence, combined with the abolition of the elaborate distinction between the duties owed to invitees and licensees, has rendered less important a question which was sometimes significant at common law; namely, whether the rules relating to occupiers' liability were confined to injuries suffered due to the state of the premises or extended also to activities conducted by the occupier on them. There was some authority for the proposition that in the latter type of case the duty owed was the general one laid down in *Donoghue*'s case and that the entrants' status was irrelevant.[2] The reduction in the importance of this question, in the light of the formulation of occupiers' liability in the Act, is illustrated by the fact that no reported case since the Act has decided authoritatively whether that formulation does itself extend to the so-called 'activity' duty or is confined to the 'occupancy' duty.[3] The Act itself states that it is intended to regulate 'the duty which an occupier of premises owes to his visitors in respect of dangers due to the state of the premises *or to things done or omitted to be done on them*'.[4] But this wording does not itself settle the question since, having regard to the general background and context of the legislation, the phrase 'things done or omitted to be done' could not implausibly be confined to the erection of dangerous structures, or failure to repair, which would be within the scope of the 'occupancy' duty itself. Indeed, the majority of commentators do take the view that the Act is confined to situations in which the condition of the premises themselves is dangerous,[5] albeit perhaps as a *result* of some activity, and does not cover dangerous activities unrelated to the premises as such but which just happen to be carried on there.[6] It is submitted that this is in fact the better view.[7] To expand the law relating to occupiers' liability to cover everything which happened to occur on a defendant's land would be illogical, and would also be apt to introduce unnecessary vagueness into the law.

---

1 [1932] AC 562.
2 See *Dunster v Abbott* [1953] 2 All ER 1572, [1954] 1 WLR 58, CA; *Slater v Clay Cross Co Ltd* [1956] 2 QB 264, [1956] 2 All ER 625, CA. See also *Slade v Battersea and Putney Group Hospital Management Committee* [1955] 1 All ER 429, [1955] 1 WLR 207.
3 But cf *Videan v British Transport Commission* [1963] 2 QB 650, [1963] 2 All ER 860, CA.
4 Section 1(1) (italics supplied).
5 But cf dictum per Lord Keith in *Ferguson v Welsh* [1987] 3 All ER 777 at 783e-f, [1987] 1 WLR 1553 at 1560, HL (dealing with the position under s 2(4)(*b*) of the Act).
6 See, generally, the discussion in North *Occupiers' Liability* (1971) pp 71-87.
7 Cf *Railways Comr v McDermott* [1967] AC 169, [1966] 2 All ER 162, PC.

Children[1]

[**16.07**] According to s 2(3) of the Act the 'circumstances relevant' to establishing the content of the common duty of care in particular circumstances include 'the degree of care, and want of care, which would ordinarily be looked for in such a visitor'. The subsection then provides, by way of 'example', that 'an occupier must be prepared for children to be less careful than adults'. Whether an occupier has discharged his duty in a case in which a child visitor has been injured on his land will obviously be a question of fact in each case. Nevertheless, it is noteworthy that the courts have apparently been sensitive to the possible danger of imposing excessive burdens upon occupiers merely because they do not forbid children from playing on their land. In *Simkiss v Rhondda Borough Council*[2] a seven-year-old child, accompanied by a friend aged ten, suffered serious injury when she fell down a steep grassy slope, which was a natural feature of the locality, while playing on land owned by the defendant council. The trial judge held the council liable for not having fenced off the area, but his decision was reversed by the Court of Appeal. Dunn LJ observed that:[3]

> 'It is almost as if it were suggested that an occupier should fence off a climbable tree in case a child climbed too high up it and fell out of it, and as far as I know a climbable tree has never been held to be dangerous to children . . . There are many parts of the country with open spaces adjacent to houses where children play unattended, and this is to be encouraged.'

The primary responsibility for protecting small children from danger rests with their parents, and unless an area is so dangerous as to necessitate entry being forbidden in any event,[4] occupiers are entitled to assume, unless the known customs in the locality suggest the contrary, that parents will either warn their children of the existence of such hazards as are to be found there[5] or will prevent them from wandering on to the land in question unaccompanied.[6]

---

1 See Richard Kidner 'The Duty of Occupiers towards Children' (1988) 39 NILQ 150.
2 (1982) 81 LGR 460, CA.
3 Ibid at 470-471.
4 In which case the children would be trespassers, on which see the Occupiers' Liability Act 1984, discussed below. But it should, perhaps, still be noted that a child attracted on to the defendant's land by an 'allurement' may, in consequence thereof, be classified in effect as a lawful visitor: see, eg *Cooke v Midland Great Western Rly of Ireland* [1909] AC 229, HL. The importance of this doctrine is now, however, much reduced by virtue of the 1984 Act and the decision of the House of Lords in *British Railways Board v Herrington* [1972] AC 877, [1972] 1 All ER 749, HL.
5 See *Simkiss v Rhondda Borough Council* (1981) 81 LGR 460 at 471, per Dunn LJ.
6 See *Phipps v Rochester Corpn* [1955] 1 QB 450, [1955] 1 All ER 129.

Risks incident to plaintiff's calling

[**16.08**] A further 'example' of the circumstances relevant to a determination of whether a defendant has discharged his duty of care is given by s 2(3)(*b*) which provides as follows: 'an occupier may expect that a person, in the exercise of his calling, will appreciate and guard against any special risks ordinarily incident to it, so far as the occupier leaves him free to do so'. In *Roles v Nathan*[1] the Court of Appeal applied the principle in the subsection to deny liability to the widows of two chimney-sweeps who had been killed by dangerous fumes while working on a defective boiler.[2] They had, in fact, deliberately chosen to ignore the risk which they incurred by needlessly choosing to work in the manner which they did. On the other hand if the particular risk is one which all the skills of the plaintiff's calling do not enable him to avoid then the defendant, whose negligence created the dangerous situation, will be liable even if the plaintiff's calling is actually to deal with situations of the kind in question. Thus, in the important recent case of *Ogwo v Taylor*,[3] the House of Lords confirmed[4] that firemen foreseeably injured while fighting a fire, caused by the defendant's negligence, have a right to damages.

Entry pursuant to a contract

[**16.09**] The Occupiers' Liability Act 1957, s 3(1) provides that where an occupier is obliged by contract to allow people who are not parties to it to have access to his premises, such as workpeople who enter pursuant to a contract between himself and their employer, the common duty of care which the occupier owes to the entrants 'cannot be restricted or excluded by that contract'.[5] But the Act also provides that such persons can actually take the benefit of any provisions in the contract which have the effect of imposing on the occupier safety obligations more onerous than those required by the common duty of care.[6] If an entrant is entitled to access by virtue of a direct contract between himself and the occupier, but that contract contains no express term as to the latter's duty of care, the Act provides that a requirement for the common duty of care shall be implied into it.[7] If such an entrant is injured by breach of the duty, however, he is not obliged to sue in contract but can if he wishes elect to sue instead for breach of the duty in tort, as an ordinary visitor under the Act. In *Solle v W J Hallt Ltd*[8] Swanwick J held that the plaintiff's own

---

1 [1963] 2 All ER 908, [1963] 1 WLR 1117, CA. Cf *Epp v Ridgetop Builders Ltd* (1978) 94 DLR (3d) 505.
2 'These chimney sweeps ought to have known that there might be dangerous fumes about and ought to have taken steps to guard against them': [1963] 2 All ER 908 at 913, [1963] 1 WLR at 1123, per Lord Denning MR.
3 [1988] AC 431, [1987] 3 All ER 961, HL.
4 The House approved the earlier decision of Woolf J, on the same point, in *Salmon v Seafarer Restaurants Ltd* [1983] 3 All ER 729, [1983] 1 WLR 1264.
5 See also s 3(4) (entry pursuant to the terms or conditions of a tenancy).
6 See s 3(2).
7 See s 5(1).
8 [1973] QB 574, [1973] 1 All ER 1032.

contributory negligence would have had the effect of breaking the chain of causation if the defendant's breach of duty were treated as a breach of contract, and he would therefore have recovered nothing.[1] By suing in tort he was able to recover the appropriate proportion of his damages after allowance had been made for his contributory negligence.

Warnings, volenti, and contributory negligence

Warning

[**16.10**] The Occupiers' Liability Act 1957, s 2(4) provides, in limb (*a*), as follows:

> 'Where damage is caused to a visitor by a danger of which he had been warned by the occupier, the warning is not to be treated without more as absolving the occupier from liability, unless in all the circumstances it was enough to enable the visitor to be reasonably safe.'

The effect of this provision is to bring occupiers' liability into line with the law of negligence generally by ensuring that a defendant who has created a dangerous situation cannot absolve himself merely by giving a warning which is in reality inadequate. It reverses a majority decision of the House of Lords which had held that an occupier would be absolved from liability if the plaintiff entrant had known of the relevant hazard even if, in the circumstances, he could not be said to have been in a position freely to act on that knowledge so as to avoid danger.[2] Whether the warning will 'enable the visitor to be reasonably safe' will clearly be a question of fact in each case.[3] Thus insufficient detail in the warning,[4] or a significant alteration in the factual circumstances against the background of which it was given,[5] might result in its being held ineffective. Moreover inadequacy might now be due to the plaintiff's having little real option, despite the warning, but to negotiate the hazard.[6] It is to be noted that although the subsection refers to a warning given 'by the occupier' it will be sufficient if it is given by someone who is clearly acting on his behalf.[7]

Volenti non fit injuria

[**16.11**] The Occupiers' Liability Act 1957, s 2(5) provides as follows:

> 'The common duty of care does not impose on an occupier any obligation to a visitor in respect of risks willingly accepted as his by the visitor

---

1 Cf *Quinn v Burch Bros (Builders) Ltd* [1966] 2 QB 370, [1965] 3 All ER 801.
2 See *London Graving Dock Co Ltd v Horton* [1951] AC 737, [1951] 2 All ER 1.
3 See, eg *Roles v Nathan* [1963] 2 All ER 908, [1963] 1 WLR 1117, CA.
4 Cf per Lord Denning MR (dissenting) in *White v Blackmore* [1972] 2 QB 651, [1972] 3 All ER 158, CA.
5 Cf *Smith v Austin Lifts Ltd* [1959] 1 All ER 81, [1959] 1 WLR 100, HL; *Roles v Nathan* [1963] 2 All ER 908 at 915ff, [1963] 1 WLR 1117 at 1128ff, CA (per Pearson LJ dissenting).
6 Cf *A C Billings & Sons Ltd v Riden* [1958] AC 240, [1957] 3 All ER 1, HL.
7 See *Roles v Nathan* [1963] 2 All ER 908, [1963] 1 WLR 1117, CA.

(the question whether a risk was so accepted to be decided on the same principles as in other cases in which one person owes a duty of care to another).'

The purpose of this provision is, of course, to confirm that the maxim volenti non fit injuria is applicable in the sphere of occupiers' liability. It has been argued in an earlier chapter that volenti is best seen as a specific *defence* to a negligence action rather than as a denial that the defendant was in breach of duty.[1] By contrast a defendant who avoids liability on the ground that he gave a warning, which is held to have been adequate within s 2(4)(*a*), will in truth have *discharged* his duty rather than have contravened it but been able to rely on a 'defence'. There is thus no illogicality in the coexistence of 'warning' and volenti as separate concepts under the Act. In practice, however, there will of course often be a degree of overlap in the application of the two devices since knowledge of the risk is a necessary, albeit not a sufficient, condition of the applicability of the volenti defence. On the other hand a warning might be adequate to discharge the common duty of care even though, had it not done so, the defendant could not have succeeded in showing the requisite degree of consent to defeat the plaintiff on volenti grounds.[2] Conversely a defendant who gave an inadequate warning, or no warning at all, might still succeed in proving that the plaintiff had been volens if, eg he had acquired sufficient knowledge of the hazard from some source other than the occupier and could also be shown to have impliedly agreed to release the defendant from potential liability.

Contributory negligence

[**16.12**] Although the defence of contributory negligence is not expressly referred to in the Occupiers' Liability Act 1957 there is in practice no doubt that the defence is applicable to a claim based on breach of the common duty of care under the Act. There are several reported examples[3] of damages being reduced in such cases pursuant to the apportionment provisions of the Law Reform (Contributory Negligence) Act 1945.

Employment of independent contractors

[**16.13**] Section two subsection four of the Occupiers' Liability Act 1957 provides, in limb (b), as follows:

'where damage is caused to a visitor by a danger due to the faulty execution of any work of construction, maintenance or repair by an independent contractor employed by the occupier, the occupier is not to be treated without more as answerable for the danger if in all the circumstances he had acted reasonably in entrusting the work to an independent contractor and had taken such steps (if any) as he

---

1 See above, ch 4.
2 Cf *White v Blackmore* [1972] 2 QB 651, [1972] 3 All ER 158, CA.
3 See, eg *Stone v Taffe* [1974] 3 All ER 1016, [1974] 1 WLR 1575, CA; *Sole v Hallt Ltd* [1973] QB 574, [1973] 1 All ER 1032.

reasonably ought in order to satisfy himself that the contractor was competent and that the work had been properly done.'

This provision brings occupiers' liability broadly into line with vicarious liability in the law of negligence generally,[1] in which the employer of an independent contractor is not liable for damage caused by the latter's negligence except in special cases. The subsection removes doubts created by a case in which the House of Lords had held that an occupier had not discharged his duty of care by entrusting the performance of work on his premises to a reputable and competent independent contractor.[2] On the other hand, even apart from the restriction in the scope of the subsection itself to 'work of construction, maintenance or repair',[3] there is a limit to the extent to which the law relating to the vicarious liability of an occupier of premises for his independent contractors can be fully assimilated into the law governing employers of negligent contractors in other situations. Occupiers will often in practice have a higher degree of control over, and detailed awareness of, the activities of their independent contractors than is usual in other circumstances, particularly if the activity involved is a conspicuous one which lasts for a lengthy period of time. It would certainly be wrong for an occupier to suppose that simply by appointing a competent independent contractor he will effectively have divested himself of responsibility for the safety of his visitors with respect to dangers emanating from the work to be undertaken.[4] There are indications that the court will be scrupulous to ensure that the occupier has taken seriously his own obligation, under the wording of the subsection, 'to satisfy himself . . . that the work had been properly done'. In *AMF International Ltd v Magnet Bowling Ltd*,[5] which arose out of flood damage occurring during a major building operation, an attempt by the defendant occupiers to invoke s 2(4)(b) to avoid liability was unsuccessful. Mocatta J observed:[6]

'In the case of the construction of a substantial building I should have thought that the building owner, if he is to escape tortious liability for faulty construction, should not only take care to contract with a competent contractor . . . but also to cause that work to be supervised by a properly qualified professional man such as an architect or surveyor.'

Moreover his Lordship emphasised that this obligation applied not only to 'completed work' but also 'to precautions during the course of construction'. On the other hand, if the injury is suffered by one of the independent contractor's *own employees*, due to the contractor's using an unsafe system of work, the House of Lords has recently held that

---

1 See below, ch 18.
2 See *Thomson v Cremin* [1953] 2 All ER 1185, [1956] 1 WLR 103n, HL.
3 On the meaning to be attached to these words see North *Occupiers' Liability* (1971, London) pp 142-144.
4 Cf *Bloomstein v Railway Executive* [1952] 2 All ER 418.
5 [1968] 2 All ER 789, [1968] 1 WLR 1028.
6 Ibid at 803 and 1044.

the subsection will not normally provide a basis for the imposition of liability on the occupier, even if the latter is aware of the dangerousness of the system.[1]

Property damage

[16.14] The question whether occupiers can be liable under the 1957 Act for damage to, or loss of, property, as distinct from personal injury, cannot be answered as unequivocally as might be wished. This is due to a lack of clarity in the Act's own provisions combined with a degree of uncertainty in the common law background to them.[2] There is, however, no real doubt that the common duty of care may in appropriate circumstances extend to the protection of a visitor's property from *damage* while he is on the defendant's premises in person.[3] The wording of the Act also clearly implies that property belonging to third parties will similarly be protected,[4] but probably only if it is brought on to the defendant's premises by a visitor[5] (to whom, eg the property is on loan). What is far less clear is whether the Act can apply to situations in which the visitor's goods are not damaged, but *stolen* by a third party while on the defendant's premises. At common law the authorities seemed to lean against the imposition of liability on an occupier in such circumstances.[6] In practice it will often be difficult to prove that a defendant occupier was actually careless in failing to prevent the theft, so the question will not arise all that frequently.[7] It is submitted, however, that if thefts from the defendant's premises had been frequent he might be in breach of the common duty of care if he failed even to *warn* his visitors of this fact; and that in such circumstances theft of goods could come within the Act.[8]

---

1 See *Ferguson v Welsh* [1987] 3 All ER 777, [1987] 1 WLR 1553, HL. In special circumstances the occupier may, however, be liable at *common law* along with the independent contractor, as a joint tortfeasor: see ibid at 785 and 1562 per Lord Oliver and at 786 and 1564 per Lord Goff.
2 For discussion see, generally, North *Occupiers' Liability* (1971, London) pp 94-114.
3 See *AMF International Ltd v Magnet Bowling Ltd* [1968] 2 All ER 789, [1968] 1 WLR 1028.
4 See the Occupiers' Liability Act 1957, s 1(3)(*b*) ('property of persons who are not themselves his visitors').
5 See North, op cit, p 101. Cf *Drive-Yourself Lessey's Pty Ltd v Burnside* [1959] SRNSW 390.
6 See, eg *Tinsley v Dudley* [1951] 2 KB 18, [1951] 1 All ER 252, CA; *Edwards v West Herts Group Hospital Management Committee* [1957] 1 All ER 541, [1957] 1 WLR 415, CA.
7 Of course the defendant may be liable on some basis other than the 1957 Act: see, eg the strict liability of innkeepers now governed by the Hotel Proprietors Act 1956.
8 See Bowett 'Law Reform and Occupiers' Liability' (1956) 19 MLR 172 at 173: '... where the occupier of a store allows that store to become a hive of pickpockets, remaining negligently indifferent to their activities, he ought to be liable for the pecuniary loss of his lawful visitors resulting from the acts of these third persons on the same basis as he would be liable for bodily injury caused by a trap on his stairway.' Cf Goodhart (1957) 73 LQR 313.

Economic loss

[**16.15**] If a visitor's property is damaged, and he suffers additional financial loss which is foreseeably consequential on that damage, that loss is, consistently with the general law of negligence, recoverable under the 1957 Act. This was expressly decided by Mocatta J in *AMF International Ltd v Magnet Bowling Ltd*[1] where his Lordship expressed himself as follows:

> '... if the duty extends to the prevention of damage to property, I can see no reason in principle why the damages flowing from a breach of such duty should be limited or restricted (in the absence of express contractual provisions to that effect) other than by the ordinary rules as to the measure and remoteness of damage ... (F)inancial loss consequent upon personal injury is recovered every day in the courts and the same is frequently recovered in cases of damage to property.'

Liability to persons other than visitors

Persons covered by the Occupiers' Liability Act 1984[2]

[**16.16**] The Occupiers' Liability Act 1984 is complementary to the Act of 1957 since it deals with the relationship between an occupier and 'persons other than his visitors'. The most important category of such persons is that of trespassers, but the width of the formulation ensures that the benefit of the statutory duty under the Act is not confined to trespassers alone. The significance of this is that it also includes persons who enter pursuant to access agreements as well as users of private rights of way.

Trespassers

[**16.17**] The background to the 1984 Act was a belief that the law relating to liability towards trespassers needed to be clarified following the decision of the House of Lords in *British Railways Board v Herrington*.[3] In this case liability was imposed for injuries suffered by a six-year-old child trespasser when he was able to crawl through a fence, due to its dilapidated condition, on to an electrified railway line. Although the decision marked a major change in the approach of the law towards trespassers, and one significantly more favourable to them,[4] it was felt that the duty of 'common humanity' which it

---

1 [1968] 2 All ER 789 at 808, [1968] 1 WLR 1028 at 1050-1051.
2 For discussion of the Act see, generally, Michael Jones (1984) 47 MLR 713; R A Buckley [1984] Conv 413. (Permission granted by Sweet & Maxwell Ltd, to reproduce here material which formerly appeared in the latter article, is gratefully acknowledged.)
3 [1972] AC 877, [1972] 1 All ER 749, HL. See also *Pannett v P McGuinness & Co Ltd* [1972] 2 QB 599, [1972] 3 All ER 137, CA; *Harris v Birkenhead Corpn* [1976] 1 All ER 341, [1976] 1 WLR 279, CA.
4 For the harsher approach formerly adopted see *Robert Addie & Sons (Collieries) Ltd v Dumbreck* [1929] AC 358, HL.

enunciated, under which the occupier's duty would 'vary according to his knowledge, ability and resources',¹ was excessively vague and liable to lead to uncertainty. The matter was therefore referred to the Law Commission and their report,² which was published in 1976, formed the basis, eight years later, for the Occupiers' Liability Act 1984.

Access agreements

[**16.18**] Although persons entering land pursuant to an access agreement or order made under the National Parks and Access to the Countryside Act 1949, s 60 are not trespassers,³ they were exluded from the protection of the Occupiers' Liability Act 1957 since that Act expressly provided that they were not 'visitors' either.⁴ The Law Commission recommended that the new statutory duty which it proposed should apply for their benefit,⁵ and they are now clearly covered by the Occupiers' Liability Act 1984.

Users of private rights of way

[**16.19**] In *Holden v White*⁶ the Court of Appeal held that users of private rights of way were not 'visitors', and were therefore not owed the common duty of care laid down by the Occupiers' Liability Act 1957. The background to the decision was the doctrine of the law of easements that positive obligations are not imposed on the owner of the servient tenement.⁷ But it was not easy to see why this rule of property law should adversely affect the existence of liability in tort for carelessness,⁸ and the effect of the formula adopted by the Occupiers' Liability Act 1984 is clearly to bring users of private rights of way within the protection of the new statutory duty.⁹

The nature of the duty imposed by the 1984 Act

[**16.20**] The heart of the 1984 Act is to be found in s 1(3) and (4), which provide as follows:

---

1 [1972] AC 877 at 899, [1972] 1 All ER 749 at 758 per Lord Reid.
2 'Report on Liability for Damage or Injury to Trespassers and related questions of Occupiers' Liability' (Law Com No 75, Cmnd 6428).
3 See the 1949 Act, s 60(1).
4 See the 1957 Act, s 1(4).
5 See the Law Commission's Report, paras 37-41.
6 [1982] QB 679, [1982] 2 All ER 328, CA.
7 See ibid at 683 and 331 per Oliver LJ.
8 See Stanton 'Occupiers' Liability and Rights of Way' (1982) 98 LQR 541. Cf Griffith 'Easements and Occupiers' Liability' [1983] Conv 58. See also J R Spencer in [1983] CLJ 48 who argued that the decision was per incuriam on the ground that the right of way cases of *Thomas v British Railways Board* [1976] QB 912, [1976] 3 All ER 15, CA and *Skeen v British Railways Board* [1976] RTR 281 (in both of which the plaintiffs recovered damages) were not considered.
9 It should be noted that the Act does *not* apply to users of *public* rights of way since 'persons using the highway' are expressly excluded: see s 1(7). For discussion of the position of such persons, see below.

'(3) An occupier of premises owes a duty to another (not being his visitor) in respect of any such risk as is referred to in subsection (1)[1] above if—
(a) he is aware of the danger or has reasonable grounds to believe that it exists;
(b) he knows or has reasonable grounds to believe that the other is in the vicinity of the danger concerned or that he may come into the vicinity of the danger (in either case, whether the other has lawful authority for being in that vicinity or not); and
(c) the risk is one against which, in all the circumstances of the case, he may reasonably be expected to offer the other some protection.
(4) Where, by virtue of this section, an occupier of premises owes a duty to another in respect of such a risk, the duty is to take such care as is reasonable in all the circumstances of the case to see that he does not suffer injury on the premises by reason of the danger concerned.'

It is possible to criticise the wording of these provisions on the ground that the generalised approach adopted in them does not represent a significant advance upon the supposedly uncertain and unpredictable principles which *Herrington v British Railways Board* introduced into the common law.[2] On the other hand the insertion of specific guidelines into the legislation, referring expressly to categories such as child trespassers[3] or criminal entrants,[4] might well have produced excessive complication in an area where a degree of uncertainty is unavoidable due to the extent that each case must depend heavily on its own facts.

[16.21] In practice the general approach adopted by the courts to cases involving personal injury is unlikely now to differ substantially whether the claim is made by a 'visitor' under the Occupiers' Liability Act 1957, someone 'other than a visitor' under the Act of 1984, or someone relying on general *Donoghue v Stevenson* negligence at common law.[5] In particular, the duty owed to trespassers will no longer depend upon the actual occupier's individual resources, as was apparently the case under the highly subjective *Herrington* test. This does not, of course, imply that the precautions which an occupier will need to take to avoid liability will now be the same regardless of the

---

1 Ie 'any risk of their suffering injury on the premises by reason of any danger due to the state of the premises or to things done or omitted to be done on them'. This wording is almost identical to that in s 1(1) of the Occupiers' Liability Act 1957 discussed above.
2 See the criticism of the then Occupiers' Liability Bill by Lord Foot on Second Reading in the House of Lords: HL Deb, vol 443, ser 5, col 724.
3 Cf the American Law Institute's *Restatement of the Law of Torts* (2nd edn, 1965) para 339.
4 Quaere whether such entrants could be met, in any event, with a defence based on the maxim ex turpi causa non oritur actio. Cf *Ashton v Turner* [1981] QB 137, [1980] 3 All ER 870. When the then Occupiers' Liability Bill was before the House of Lords for Second Reading, Lord Mishcon felt that the maxim could apply to the criminal trespasser: HL Deb, vol 443, ser 5, col 724. Lord Hailsham LC, however, in reply, doubted whether the maxim could apply in the law of tort at all, and suggested that criminal trespassers would fare badly in any claim simply by virtue of the application of the Act's general reasonableness test to them on the facts: HL Deb, vol 443, ser 5, col 743.
5 Cf *Pannett v P McGuinness & Co Ltd* [1972] 2 QB 599, [1972] 3 All ER 137, CA.

nature of the potential plaintiff. Clearly the *content* of the duty may well continue to differ according to the status of the entrant. Not only will foreseeability of the presence of trespassers often be more difficult to establish than that of lawful visitors, but the extent to which an occupier can reasonably be expected to take steps to protect them from danger will frequently differ as well.

Warnings and assumption of risk

[**16.22**] The Occupiers' Liability Act 1984 provides that an occupier may discharge his duty 'by taking such steps as are reasonable in all the circumstances of the case to give *warning* of the danger concerned or to discourage persons from incurring the risk'.[1] The immediately-following subsection provides for the applicability of the doctrine of assumption of risk (ie volenti non fit injuria).[2] In making separate provision for the two related, but nevertheless distinct, concepts of warning and assumption of risk the Act does, of course, parallel the Occupiers' Liability Act 1957.[3]

No liability for damage to property

[**16.23**] A significant respect in which the scope of the duty owed to 'persons other than visitors' under the 1984 Act is narrower than that owed to 'visitors' under the Occupiers' Liability Act 1957, or that owed generally under the ordinary common law of negligence, is that claims under the 1984 Act are confined to personal injury or death; so that property damage is not recoverable.[4] Of course claims for lost earnings immediately consequential upon death or personal injury, in addition to pain and suffering, loss of amenities etc, will be recoverable in a claim under the Act in the usual way.

Exclusion of liability

Visitors and non-business occupiers

Possibility of excluding liability

[**16.24**] The Occupiers' Liability Act 1957, s 2(1) provides that an occupier owes the common duty of care to his visitors 'except in so far

---

1 Section 1(5) (emphasis added).
2 'No duty is owed by virtue of this section to any person in respect of risks willingly accepted as his by that person (the question whether a risk was so accepted to be decided on the same principles as in other cases in which one person owes a duty of care to another)': s 1(6).
3 See the Act of 1957, s 2(4)(a) and (5), discussed above.
4 See s 1(9) (defining 'injury'). The Law Commission considered recommending the making of a specific exception, so as to allow a trespasser to recover for damage to his clothes, but ultimately decided against it: see their *Report* (Cmnd 6428) para 30.

as he is free to and does extend, restrict, modify or exclude his duty to any visitor or visitors by agreement or otherwise'. It is therefore clear that unless death or personal injury suffered on business premises is involved,[1] or the situation is one in which the occupier is for some other reason not 'free to' do so, unilateral action by him, without the express agreement of the visitor in question,[2] can achieve exclusion of the liability which would otherwise be imposed upon him. By analogy with the learning on exemption clauses in the law of contract, the test of whether reasonable steps have been taken to inform visitors of the exclusion is an objective, and not a subjective, one. The cases show that a suitably prominent notice, displayed so as to impose the relevant condition upon entry, will suffice.[3] Indeed in one case such a notice was successfully relied upon even by an occupier who also gave a warning of the danger but one which was held to have been inadequate, a situation which Lord Denning MR, who dissented, considered anomalous.[4]

Where the occupier is not 'free to' exclude liability[5]

[16.25] Although actual agreement with his visitors may not be necessary to achieve exclusion of an occupier's liability, it appears that a visitor who is not in the circumstances able to exercise any real *choice* in the matter, since he is in reality inescapably committed to entering the occupier's premises, will not be bound by an exclusion clause even if he is actually aware of it.[6]

[16.26] There are two provisions of the Occupiers' Liability Act itself which, although the matter is not entirely free from doubt, probably amount to implicit restrictions on the freedom of occupiers to exclude their liability. Section 1(6) provides that 'persons who enter premises for any purpose in the exercise of a right conferred by law are to be treated as permitted by the occupier to be there for that purpose, whether they in fact have his permission or not'. Although this wording could be construed narrowly so as merely to confirm, for the avoidance of doubt, that persons exercising a right of entry cannot be forcibly removed or sued for trespass, it is submitted that the better view is that it also prevents exclusion by notice of the common duty of

---

1 See the Unfair Contract Terms Act 1977 ss 1(1)(c), 1(3)(b) and 2(1). But see also the Occupiers' Liability Act 1984, s 2. Both provisions are discussed below.
2 Cf the Occupiers' Liability (Scotland) Act 1960, s 2(1), in which only exclusion by agreement is contemplated (the words 'or otherwise' not appearing).
3 See *Ashdown v Samuel Williams & Sons Ltd* [1957] 1 QB 409, [1957] 1 All ER 35, CA; *White v Blackmore* [1972] 2 QB 651, [1972] 3 All ER 158, CA. For criticisms of the *Ashdown* decision (and, by implication, the post-Act position) see Gower (1956) 19 MLR 532; (1957) 20 MLR 181. Cf Odgers [1957] CLJ 39, 42ff.
4 See *White v Blackmore* [1972] 2 QB 651, [1972] 3 All ER 158, CA (Lord Denning attempted to remove the anomaly by denying that a disclaimer of liability could be effective unless it simultaneously satisfied the requirements relating to adequacy of warning: see pp 665-666).
5 See Symmons, 'How Free is the Freedom of the Occupier to Restrict or Exclude his Liability in Tort?' (1974) 38 Conv (NS) 253.
6 See *Burnett v British Waterways Board* [1973] 2 All ER 631, [1973] 1 WLR 700, CA.

care owed to them.¹ Similarly s 3(1) provides that 'where an occupier of premises is bound by contract to permit persons who are strangers to the contract to enter or use the premises, the duty of care which he owes to them as his visitors cannot be restricted or excluded by that contract'. If emphasis were placed upon the last three words quoted, the subsection could be taken to strike merely at the potential mischief of enabling liability to be restricted by a contractual provision which the visitor in question may never even have seen; but still leaving the occupier free to exclude liability by a notice which the visitor would see at the point of entry. Again, however, it is submitted that the better view is that such a notice would in fact be ineffective in this situation.² The visitors in question will often be employees of the contractor and will have no effective choice but to enter the occupier's premises if they are not to put their jobs in jeopardy.

Persons other than visitors

[**16.27**] The Occupiers' Liability Act 1984 does not include, unlike its 1957 predecessor, any provision contemplating exclusion of liability. Moreover its wording clearly requires the court to consider cases of injury to trespassers, and of others covered by it, on a broad basis of reasonableness. Any warning given, and its adequacy, will be taken into account along with such measures, if any, as were taken to try to prevent or discourage trespass.³ Thus if there is any kind of concealed or unusual hazard on the premises in question, a notice containing merely the time-honoured and inaccurate words 'Trespassers will be prosecuted' is most unlikely to be enough. To this extent it may be taken that the occupier does not enjoy the same freedom to exclude his liability to trespassers as he does to exclude his common duty of care to lawful visitors. It would also appear that the approach adopted by the later Act avoids the possibility of an occupier being able to rely upon a disclaimer to avoid the consequences of having given an inadequate warning.⁴

Visitors and business occupiers

[**16.28**] Provided the case concerns 'the occupation of premises used for business purposes of the occupier',⁵ the Unfair Contract Terms Act 1977 expressly prevents the exclusion of liability 'for death or personal injury'⁶ arising out of breach 'of the common duty of care imposed by the Occupiers' Liability Act 1957'.⁷ Moreover even 'in the case of other loss or damage' exclusion of liability is not permitted 'except in so far as the . . . notice satisfies the requirement of reasonableness'.⁸

1 Cf North *Occupiers' Liability* (1971, London) pp 130-131.
2 Cf North op cit, pp 148-152.
3 See s 1(5) of the Act.
4 Cf *White v Blackmore* [1972] 2 QB 651, [1972] 3 All ER 158, CA.
5 Unfair Contract Terms Act 1977 (hereafter referred to as 'UCTA'), s 1(3)(*b*).
6 UCTA, s 2(1).
7 UCTA, s 1(1)(*c*).
8 UCTA, s 2(2). On the 'requirement of reasonableness' see, further, s 11(3).

Unfortunately the Act does not attempt a definition of a 'business' for its purposes, except to stipulate that it 'includes a profession and the activities of any government department or local or public authority'.[1] While this omission will perhaps rarely be a source of serious difficulty, since it will probably usually be obvious whether or not the occupier's purposes bring him within the concept, there could still be difficult borderline cases involving prominent non-profit making institutions such as universities or private schools.

Entry for recreational or educational purposes

[16.29] In one specific area the freedom of business occupiers to exclude their liability, which was limited by the Unfair Contract Terms Act 1977, has subsequently been restored to them. The relevant provision is the Occupiers' Liability Act 1984, s 2 which, unlike the main body of that Act, is concerned with visitors as distinct from persons other than visitors. The section inserts additional words into the Unfair Contract Terms Act, which have the effect of providing that an occupier who allows visitors access to his premises for recreational or educational purposes shall not be subject to the limitations on exclusion of liability towards such visitors otherwise imposed by that Act.[2] The new provision, which does not apply if the occupier is actually in the business of providing recreational or educational facilities, reflects a policy decision designed to ensure that farmers, or others in similar circumstances, to whose land access for recreational or educational purposes might be desirable, should not be unduly discouraged from permitting such access by fear of potential legal liability.[3]

When the Acts do not apply

Relationship with ordinary negligence

[16.30] If the narrower interpretation of the scope of the Occupiers' Liability Act 1957, which was contended for earlier in this chapter, is correct the 'common duty of care' embodied in that Act will be confined to the static condition of the defendant's premises and will not apply to activities carried out on his land which are unrelated to the

---

1 UCTA, s 14.
2 The Occupiers' Liability Act 1984, s 2 provides as follows:
   'At the end of section 1(3) of the Unfair Contract Terms Act 1977 (which defines the liability, called "business liability", the exclusion or restriction of which is controlled by virtue of that Act) there is added—
      "but liability of an occupier of premises for breach of an obligation or duty towards a person obtaining access to the premises for recreational or educational purposes, being liability for loss or damage suffered by reason of the dangerous state of the premises, is not a business liability of the occupier unless granting that person such access for the purposes concerned falls within the business purposes of the occupier." '
3 See HL Deb vol 443, ser 5, col 721 (Lord Hailsham LC).

condition or safety of the land itself or any buildings upon it. Liability for such activities will therefore be regulated by the ordinary common law of negligence. The clearest statement of this view, since the passing of the Occupiers' Liability Act 1957, was by Lord Denning MR in *Videan v British Transport Commission*,[1] which concerned a fatal accident caused by the negligent driving, by one of the defendant's employees, of a powered trolly on a railway track. His Lordship stated that the general law of negligence applied and continued:

> 'The principle that I have stated applies only where an occupier or a contractor or anyone else conducts activities on land. It does not apply where an occupier has done no work on the land: for then his liability is as an occupier and nothing else. I am not disturbed by the suggestion that it is difficult to distinguish between a man's activities on land and the static condition of premises. I should have thought that whenever an occupier does things on land, whether he runs a moving staircase, or puts a bull into a field, or drives a railway engine, or uses land as a cinder tip, or even digs a hole, he is conducting activities on the land and he is under a duty of care, even to trespassers, if he ought to foresee their presence: and he is nonetheless under that duty because he is an occupier.'

[**16.31**] As far as lawful visitors are concerned it would not appear to make any difference in practice whether their claims are based upon the Occupiers' Liability Act 1957, alleging that the premises themselves were in a dangerous condition, or upon an allegation of ordinary *Donoghue v Stevenson* negligence in the conduct of an activity. Indeed the common duty of care is essentially a statutory exposition of negligence liability in the occupation context. It even seems clear that one respect in which a difference might possibly have been expected, that of exclusion of liability, it does not in fact do so. It appears that an occupier can exclude by notice liability for negligent activities on the land, and that the possibility of such exclusion is not confined to the occupancy duty in the narrow sense.[2]

[**16.32**] Since the material provisions of the two statutes use identical phraseology[3] it would appear reasonable to suppose that if the scope of the Occupiers' Liability Act 1957 is limited to the state of the land or premises then that of the Occupiers' Liability Act 1984 is similarly so limited. This means that the liability of occupiers to persons other than visitors, for the conduct of dangerous activities on the land, is still governed by the common law. If Lord Denning's contention is correct that the status of the entrant is wholly irrelevant where the activity duty is concerned, even if he is a trespasser, then the applicable common law will be the ordinary principles of negligence.[4] A somewhat surprising alternative possibility, however, would be to

---

1 [1963] 2 QB 650 at 667-668, [1963] 2 All ER 860 at 867, CA. See also per Harman LJ at 672-673. But cf Pearson LJ at 678.
2 Both the leading cases of *Ashdown v Samuel Williams & Sons* [1957] 1 QB 409, [1957] 1 All ER 35, CA, and *White v Blackmore* [1972] 2 QB 651, [1972] 3 All ER 158, CA, concerned activities.
3 Ie danger due to '. . . the state of the premises or to things done or omitted to be done on them': Occupiers' Liability Act 1957, s 1(1) and Occupiers' Liability Act 1984, s 1(1)(*a*).
4 Of course the fact of trespass could still be relevant on the issue of foreseeability.

hold that a trespasser's status affects the nature of the duty owed to him irrespective of whether it is an activity or the static condition of the premises which is in issue.[1] This reasoning would lead to the conclusion that the supposedly undesirably vague principles of 'common humanity', developed in *British Railways Board v Herrington*,[2] still apply if the claim is based upon a dangerous activity. It is submitted that Lord Denning's view that *Donoghue v Stevenson* applies is to be preferred. Nevertheless one paradoxical reason which a trespasser himself might have for supporting the opposite view is that it is at least arguable that, unlike ordinary negligence liability in this context, the doctrine of 'common humanity' represents an irreducible minimum of liability which it is impossible for an occupier to exclude by disclaimer.[3]

Liability of non-occupiers

[**16.33**] If injury is caused to a trespasser not by the occupier of the land in question, but by the carelessness of someone else such as a non-occupying independent contractor, the authorities on balance favour the view that the defendant cannot rely on the fact that the plaintiff is a trespasser, but owes to him the ordinary *Donoghue v Stevenson* duty in negligence. In *Buckland v Guildford Gas, Light and Coke Co*[4] a 12-year-old girl was electrocuted when she climbed a tree within the foliage of which the defendants had negligently allowed electric wires to be concealed. Morris J held that even if the deceased had been a trespasser on the tree that fact could not be relied upon by the defendants, who were not the occupiers, to reduce their ordinary foreseeability duty, and liability was imposed.[5]

[**16.34**] Since a non-occupier does not have the power to determine who enters the land and who does not, it is submitted that, unlike the occupier, he does not enjoy the latter's privilege of excluding his liability to visitors on the land by mere notice.[6] The justification for that privilege is arguably that the occupier confers a benefit on the visitor to which conditions can be attached,[7] but if no privilege is conferred there is no reason why the general duty of care imposed by

---

1 Cf per Lord Pearson in *British Railways Board v Herrington* [1972] AC 877 at 929, [1972] 1 All ER 749 at 785, HL. See also *Robert Addie & Sons (Collieries) Ltd v Dumbreck* [1929] AC 358, HL, which laid down the old law on liability to trespassers, and concerned an activity on the land.
2 [1972] AC 877, [1972] 1 All ER 749, HL.
3 See below.
4 [1949] 1 KB 410, [1948] 2 All ER 1086.
5 See also *Davis v St Mary's Demolition and Excavation Co Ltd* [1954] 1 All ER 578, [1954] 1 WLR 592; *Creed v McGeoch & Sons Ltd* [1955] 3 All ER 123, [1955] 1 WLR 1005. But cf per Lord Pearson in *British Railways Board v Herrington* [1972] AC 877 at 929, [1972] 1 All ER 749 at 785; *Perry v Thomas Wrigley Ltd* [1955] 3 All ER 243n, [1955] 1 WLR 1164.
6 Of course in practice the question will seldom now arise since a non-occupier carrying out an activity on the land will usually be an independent contractor who will be acting 'in the course of a business' and hence caught by the ban on the exclusion of liability for death or personal injury contained in the Unfair Contract Terms Act 1977.
7 See above, ch 4.

the law should not apply. Although not directly in point, it is suggested that support for this reasoning can be found by analogy in the speech of Lord Reid in *A C Billings & Sons Ltd v Riden*,[1] in which the appellant independent contractors were held liable for injuries suffered by an entrant. His Lordship said:

> 'The only reasonable justification I know of for the rights of a licensee being limited as they are is that a licensee generally gives no consideration for the rights which the occupier has given him and must not be allowed to look a gift horse in the mouth. That cannot apply to the appellants, who gave no concession to the respondent.'

Users of the highway

[**16.35**] In *Greenhalgh v British Railways Board*[2] the Court of Appeal held that users of public rights of way not maintainable at public expense are not 'visitors' of the occupier of the land in question, and so are not owed the common duty of care under the Occupiers' Liability Act 1957. In their Report, which preceded the Occupiers' Liability Act 1984, the Law Commission felt that to reverse this decision might impose undue burdens upon those whose land happened to be subject to public rights of way theoretically usable by unlimited numbers of people, and they were therefore not prepared to recommend it.[3] As far as users of public rights of way maintainable at public expense are concerned, existing statutory provisions[4] place such persons, if they happen to suffer injury, in at least as favourable a position as plaintiffs in an ordinary negligence action, and the Law Commission accordingly took the view that no further legislative action was needed.[5] As a result the Occupiers' Liability Act 1984 includes a general provision, relating to users of both types of public right of way, which preserves the decision in *Greenhalgh v British Railways Board*. Section 1(7) of the Act reads as follows: 'No duty is owed by virtue of this section to persons using the highway, and this section does not affect any duty owed to such persons.'[6]

A common law duty?

[**16.36**] Since the existing law is thus deliberately left unaltered by s 1(7) of the 1984 Act, a question immediately posed by the subsection is what duty *is* owed to users of non-maintainable public highways.

---

1 [1958] AC 240 at 249, [1957] 3 All ER 1 at 5, HL.
2 [1969] 2 QB 286, [1969] 2 All ER 114, CA.
3 See *Report on Liability for Damage or Injury to Trespassers and related questions of Occupiers' Liability* (Law Com No 75, Cmnd 6428) paras 48-51. The *Royal Commission on Civil Liability and Compensation for Personal Injury (Pearson)*, while acknowledging the apparent gap in the law, also felt unable to recommend any change: see Cmnd 7054-I, paras 1558-1562.
4 See the Highways Act 1980, especially s 58.
5 See their *Report*, paras 42-47.
6 It should be noted that users of *private* rights of way *are* brought within the umbrella of the 1984 Act, reversing *Holden v White* [1982] QB 679, [1982] 2 All ER 328, CA; see above.

Although, in the light of *Greenhalgh*, they are not to be treated as 'visitors' it surely cannot be the case that they are owed no duty at all at common law. If, for example, the owner or occupier of land subject to a public right of way, which he knows is constantly used by children on their journey to and from school, discovers an unexploded bomb just below the surface of the path in question, he surely cannot just sit back and do nothing at all. Although users of the right of way are not trespassers it would, prior to the 1984 Act, have been logical to expect that the duty of common humanity enunciated in *British Railways Board v Herrington*[1] would have applied to them. Indeed it can be argued that the decision of the Court of Appeal in *Thomas v British Railways Board*,[2] in which disrepair of a stile along a right of way enabled a small child to gain access to a railway line and thereby suffer injuries for which she was awarded damages, provides express authority for such a proposition.[3] If so, it would seem to follow from the preservation of the status quo by the 1984 Act that this is still the position. This result is not unattractive. Any fears of an unduly burdensome liability upon the occupier, which led to the preservation of the decision in *Greenhalgh*, are met by the emphasis in *Herrington* upon a subjective test related to the defendant's capacity, resources, and all the surrounding circumstances.[4] Thus, in the hypothetical case of the unexploded bomb, the occupier would not be expected to remove the bomb himself (any more than he would be, presumably, in a situation to which the common duty of care imposed by the Occupiers' Liability Act 1957 applied) but he could reasonably be expected to go to the trouble of issuing a warning and alerting the police. Despite its convenience, the position thus revealed is not without irony since one of the main reasons for the Law Commission's disapproval of *Herrington*, which led eventually to the passing of the Occupiers' Liability Act 1984, was dislike of a duty subjectively related to the occupier's resources.[5]

Where liability has been excluded

[**16.37**] A similar question to that concerning the duty, if any, owed to persons using non-maintained public rights of way, concerns the position of visitors where the common duty of care which would normally have been owed under the Occupiers' Liability Act 1957 has been validly excluded by notice of disclaimer.[6] In this context, as in the other one, it is difficult to believe that such persons are owed no

1 [1972] AC 877, [1972] 1 All ER 749, HL.
2 [1976] QB 912, [1976] 3 All ER 15, CA.
3 See, especially, per Scarman LJ (at 927): 'I think that the existence of a duty so to operate a railway that reasonable care is taken to reduce or avert danger to those who may reasonably be expected to be physically on the line, whether they be trespassers, visitors, or persons exercising their right to use a public highway, is to be deduced from the decision of the House of Lords in *British Railways Board v Herrington*.'
4 See [1972] AC 877 at 899, [1972] 1 All ER 749 at 758 (Lord Reid), 920 and 777(Lord Wilberforce) and 942 and 796 (Lord Diplock).
5 See the Law Commission's *Report* (Cmnd 6428), para 12.
6 See above.

duty *at all*. Since, moreover, the duty owed to trespassers under the Occupiers' Liability Act 1984 apparently cannot be excluded by disclaimer,[1] it would be remarkable if this meant that lawful visitors might be worse off than trespassers. The Law Commission itself noted that it would be 'extraordinary' if, in order to avoid being affected by an exclusion notice, a lawful visitor sought to argue that he was in truth a trespasser.[2] The Commission also observed, however, that:

> 'since the decision of the House of Lords in *Herrington's* case it has been suggested to us that the duty laid down in that case is incapable of exclusion, on the basis that the duty of humanity represents a minimum standard of conduct below which an occupier will not be permitted to go.'[3]

The Commission thought the argument an interesting one but their own recommendation for dealing with the problem,[4] which was however not implemented in the 1984 Act, made it unnecessary for them to express any view upon its validity. It is nevertheless submitted that the argument is indeed correct. The new statutory duty created by the Occupiers' Liability Act 1984 is expressly confined to 'persons other than visitors', so that obviously cannot provide the basis for a minimum duty to be owed to visitors who are subject to a disclaimer. Accordingly, as in the rights of way situation, the unexcludable minimum is presumably once again the common law doctrine of common humanity[5] laid down in *British Railways Board v Herrington*.

Landlords and the Defective Premises Act 1972, s 4

[**16.38**] Although the Occupiers' Liability Act 1957 was obviously mainly concerned with the liability of occupiers it did contain one provision, s 4, which in certain circumstances put the landlord of premises out of occupation in the same position as if he had actually been an occupier, and imposed the common duty of care upon him. Section 4 of the 1957 Act was in fact repealed by the Defective Premises Act 1972 and replaced by s 4 of *that* Act. The new provision is wider in scope than its predecessor. It also differs significantly from it in that it does itself define the duty which it imposes upon the

---

1 But cf Jones 'The Occupiers' Liability Act 1984' (1984) 47 MLR 713 at 723-725.
2 See the *Report*, para 66.
3 Ibid, para 60. The argument was apparently put to the Law Commission by Professor Jolowicz: see Symmons 'How Free is the Freedom of the Occupier to Restrict or Exclude his Liability in Tort' (1974) 38 Conv (NS) 253 at 268, note 70.
4 Ie that all attempts to exclude liability should be subjected to a 'reasonableness' test, irrespective of whether the entrant was lawful or unlawful, invited or uninvited: see the *Report*, paras 67-75. See also cl 3 of the Draft Bill annexed to the *Report*.
5 See Mesher 'Occupiers, Trespassers and the Unfair Contract Terms Act' [1979] Conv 58 at 64; Coote 'Exception Clauses and Common Humanity' (1975) 125 NLJ 752. See also North *Occupiers' Liability* (1971) p 132.

landlord, and does not adopt the technique of the earlier provision of treating him as if he were an occupier. Another respect in which the new provision moves beyond the original analogy of Occupiers' Liability, in the sense defined by the 1957 Act, is that it can apply in favour of persons who suffer damage while off the premises and is not confined to persons actually *on* the land or premises in question. In view of its legislative history, however, and since it can be relevant to claims for injury or damage suffered by persons who have entered upon the premises in question, it is convenient to set out s 4 of the Defective Premises Act 1972 here. The heart of the provision is to be found in the first two subsections and the first part of sub-s (3) as follows:

'(1) Where premises are let under a tenancy which puts on the landlord an obligation to the tenant for the maintenance or repair of the premises, the landlord owes to all persons who might reasonably be expected to be affected by defects in the state of the premises a duty to take such care as is reasonable in all the circumstances to see that they are reasonably safe from personal injury or from damage to their property caused by a relevant defect.

(2) The said duty is owed if the landlord knows (whether as the result of being notified by the tenant or otherwise) or if he ought in all the circumstances to have known of the relevant defect.

(3) In this section ' relevant defect' means a defect in the state of the premises existing at or after the material time and arising from, or continuing because of, an act or omission by the landlord which constitutes or would if he had had notice of the defect, have constituted a failure by him to carry out his obligation to the tenant for the maintenance or repair of the premises . . .'

Subsection (4) puts a landlord who has a *right* to enter the premises in the same position for the purpose of sub-s (1) as if the tenancy imposed an actual obligation on him to carry out those repairs.[1]

[**16.39**] It will be apparent that the section imposes a negligence-type liability upon landlords, if they are under an obligation to their tenants to repair the premises in question, in favour of anyone who suffers loss or damage as a result of the landlord's failure to keep the premises in repair.[2] No doubt the duty, in terms of the actual degree of care required, will be very similar in practice to that owed by occupiers to their visitors under the Occupiers' Liability Act 1957. It should be noted, however, that in contrast with the position relating to the

---

1   For a case in which the Court of Appeal *implied* the existence of a right of entry, thereby enabling the plaintiff tenant to benefit from the effect of sub-s (4) in activating sub-s (1) see *McAuley v Bristol City Council* [1992] 1 QB 134, [1992] 1 All ER 749, CA.

2   The use of the phrase 'all persons' in sub-s (1) means that tenants themselves can take advantage of the provision: see *Barrett v Lounova (1982) Ltd* [1989] 1 All ER 351 at 357-358, CA, per Kerr LJ following *Smith v Bradford Metropolitan Council* (1982) 44 P & C R 171, CA. See also, eg *McAuley v Bristol City Council* [1992] 1 QB 134, [1992] 1 All ER 749, CA.

common duty of care as defined in the 1957 Act, exclusion of liability under the 1972 Act is prohibited.[1]

---

[1] Section 6(3) provides as follows: 'Any term of an agreement which purports to exclude or restrict, or has the effect of excluding or restricting, the operation of any of the provisions of this Act, or any liability arising by virtue of any such provision shall be void.'

Chapter 17

Defective products

The common law

Introduction

[17.01] The common law of negligence relating to defective products is now less important than it formerly was. This is due to the introduction, by the Consumer Protection Act 1987, Part I, of a strict liability regime for harm caused by defective products. The new law, which is discussed later in this chapter, applies not only to personal injuries but also, in certain circumstances, to property damage[1]. The Act does, however, expressly preserve existing remedies so the common law of negligence is not superseded. Nevertheless in practice the role of the common law in this area will be considerably diminished, and it will therefore be dealt with here relatively briefly.

'Dangerous things'

[17.02] Until the celebrated landmark decision in *Donoghue v Stevenson*[2] the fallacious assumption, exploded by that case, that it would violate the doctrine of privity of contract to allow anyone, other than the person who had given value for it, to sue in respect of harm caused by a defective chattel, greatly obstructed the development of the law of tort in this context. Exceptions to the general rule of no liability outside contract tended to be confined, in an unsatisfactory manner, to specific categories. The concept of things 'dangerous in themselves' thus achieved prominence.[3] Although soon perceived to be artificial, since few things can be predicated in the abstract as being either inherently dangerous or completely safe, the concept even survived for some years after *Donoghue v Stevenson* should have been seen to have rendered it redundant. Thus, in the 1939 case of *Burfitt v*

---

1 The property must have been of a kind ordinarily used, and intended by the plaintiff to be used, for private consumption; and the damage must have amounted to at least £275 in value. See, s 5 of the Act, discussed below.
2 [1932] AC 562.
3 Cf *Longmeid v Holliday* (1851) 6 Exch 761.

343

A and E Kille,[1] the old terminology was used in imposing liability in tort upon a shopkeeper who sold a pistol to a 12-year-old boy, with which the latter shot and injured the plaintiff. The decision went the other way in the later case of *Ricketts v Erith Borough Council*,[2] which involved a claim against a shopkeeper in similar circumstances, except that the harm was caused by a bow and arrow: an object which was held not to be in itself dangerous. As late as 1949 the Court of Appeal, in the very doubtful case of *Ball v LCC*,[3] refused to impose liability for injuries caused by a negligently-installed boiler because the boiler was not in the category of things regarded as dangerous per se.

Donoghue v Stevenson

[17.03] Notwithstanding the apparent durability of the 'dangerous things' concept, the true starting point of the modern common law of tort relating to dangerous or defective chattels is the speech of Lord Atkin in *Donoghue v Stevenson*. Although its importance for the development of negligence liability in general obviously transcends its specific subject matter, the actual context of this case was, of course, a claim for personal injuries caused by a dangerous product: a bottle of ginger beer alleged to have contained a snail. Lord Atkin expressed the ratio decidendi of the decision in its narrower aspect in the following classic passage:[4]

> '. . . a maunufacturer of products, which he sells in such a form as to show that he intends them to reach the ultimate consumer in the form in which they left him with no reasonable possibility of intermediate inspection, and with the knowledge that the absence of reasonable care in the preparation or putting up of the products will result in an injury to the consumer's life or property, owes a duty to the consumer to take that reasonable care.'

[17.04] The years since *Donoghue v Stevenson* was decided have seen the principle of liability in negligence for defective products applied to an enormous range of differing fact-situations. Major early decisions which confirmed the significance of the newly-forged principle involved items such as underwear,[5] and substances such as hair dyes.[6] A particularly important development was recognition that Lord Atkin's use of the word 'manufacturer' was not to be taken literally. Thus the doctrine was extended to *distributors*[7] and, even more significantly, negligent *repairers* of chattels, such as motor vehicles[8] and lifts,[9] also began to be subjected to liability.

---

1 [1939] 2 KB 743, [1939] 2 All ER 372.
2 [1943] 2 All ER 629.
3 [1949] 2 KB 159, [1949] 1 All ER 1056, CA.
4 [1932] AC 562 at 599.
5 See *Grant v Australian Knitting Mills Ltd* [1936] AC 85.
6 See, eg *Watson v Buckley, Osborne, Garrett & Co* [1940] 1 All ER 174.
7 See, eg *Watson*'s case cited in the previous note.
8 See, eg *Stennett v Hancock and Peters* [1939] 2 All ER 578.
9 See *Haseldine v Daw & Son Ltd* [1941] 2 KB 343, [1941] 3 All ER 156, CA.

The duty

[**17.05**] Of course the duty of care owed at common law in respect of products is governed by the general principles of the law of negligence and might, indeed, be said to provide a paradigm instance of the applicability of those principles. Nevertheless the cases show that some issues occur fairly regularly in the application of the basic concepts to products claims, and it is convenient briefly to highlight these.

Warning

[**17.06**] Where substances such as potentially hazardous chemicals are concerned, a manufacturer may be under a duty to *warn* of his product's properties if he is not to be held liable in negligence. Thus in *Vacwell Engineering Co Ltd v BDH Chemicals Ltd*,[1] liability was imposed upon defendants who, because of their own inadequate research, failed to provide notification of the capacity of one of their substances to cause an explosion; such an explosion having occurred with fatal consequences. On the other hand, if a warning *is* given it may be effective, depending upon the particular circumstances, to discharge the manufacturer's duty of care even though not communicated to the injured plaintiff himself.[2] In *Holmes v Ashford*[3] the defendant maunufacturers marketed hair dye with a warning to hairdressers that it might be harmful to certain skins, and recommending that a test should be carried out before it was used. The plaintiff contracted dermatitis when her hairdresser disregarded this warning. Her claim against the manufacturers failed even though no warning had reached her as ultimate recipient of the product; the Court of Appeal held that the warning to hairdressers had constituted sufficient compliance with the duty.[4] The duty to warn is clearly not confined to potentially dangerous substances or individual objects; indeed it can be of great importance with respect to complex pieces of machinery such as cranes[5] or motor cars. If information about a particular hazard comes to light subsequently the manufacturer can even be under a duty to issue warnings, and perhaps take further steps, with respect to products already distributed and in use.[6] The practice of motor car manufacturers of 'recalling' vehicles for examination or repair in certain circumstances undoubtedly reflects, not merely a moral obligation and concern for public relations, but an actual legal duty as well.[7] Finally, a *warning* adequate to *discharge* the duty must be carefully distinguished from an *exemption* clause intended to *exclude* it; the enforceability of the

1 [1971] 1 QB 88, [1969] 3 All ER 1681 (subsequently varied in [1971] 1 QB 111, [1970] 3 All ER 553, CA).
2 See Pamela R Ferguson 'Liability for Pharmaceutical Products: a Critique of the "Learned Intermediary" Rule' (1992) 12 OJLS 59.
3 [1950] 2 All ER 76, CA.
4 See also *Kubach v Hollands* [1937] 3 All ER 907.
5 See *Rivtow Marine Ltd v Washington Iron Works* [1974] SCR 1189 (Can).
6 See ibid.
7 See *Walton v British Leyland UK Ltd* 1978 (2 July 1978, unreported) Willis J, see Miller and Harvey *Consumer Trading Law, Cases and Materials*, (1985) p 159.

latter might depend, subject to the particular circumstances, upon the provisions of the Unfair Contract Terms Act 1977.[1]

Testing

[17.07] In some circumstances even persons in the chain of distribution other than the original manufacturer may owe to the ultimate recipient a duty to test the product for safety. In *Andrews v Hopkinson*[2] a second-hand-car dealer was held liable for a collision caused by a dangerous steering defect in a vehicle which he had sold; the defect being one which could have been discovered by the defendant with the exercise of reasonable diligence. On the other hand, in *Sellars v Best*[3] Pearson J held that it would be taking *Donoghue v Stevenson* too far to hold an electricity board liable for failing to test the safety of electrical appliances, newly installed by a third party, before supplying electricity to a house and thereby enabling a defect in one of the appliances to cause a fatal electric shock.[4] If the situation is one in which a test by someone other than the original manufacturer is appropriate a failure to carry out the test may, depending upon the precise circumstances, exonerate the manufacturer provided he has taken all necessary steps to draw attention to the need for it. The hair dye case of *Holmes v Ashford*,[5] referred to in the previous paragraph, provides an obvious example.[6]

Intermediate inspection

[17.08] In the years following the decision in *Donoghue v Stevenson*, Lord Atkin's statement in his speech that liability for defective products was dependent, inter alia, upon the absence of any 'reasonable possibility of intermediate examination'[7] was often given special emphasis. It was described by Goddard LJ in one case as an 'all-important qualification';[8] and in two early reported cases at first instance negligent manufacturers of electrical equipment succeeded in avoiding liability precisely on the ground that there had been clear opportunities for intermediate inspection by the users of the equipment which, if taken advantage of, would have revealed the defects.[9] On the other hand it soon became clear that, as a weapon for defendants, the concept of intermediate examination had its limits. Thus an initial suggestion that the *Donoghue v Stevenson* principle should be confined to situations closely analogous to the facts of that

---

1 See, generally, ch 4 above.
2 [1957] 1 QB 229, [1956] 3 All ER 422.
3 [1954] 2 All ER 389, [1954] 1 WLR 913.
4 Cf *Hartley v Mayoh & Co* [1954] 1 QB 383, [1954] 1 All ER 375, CA.
5 [1950] 2 All ER 76, CA.
6 See also *Kubach v Hollands* [1937] 3 All ER 907.
7 [1932] AC 562 at 599.
8 *Haseldine v CA Daw & Son Ltd* [1941] 2 KB 343 at 376, [1941] 3 All ER 156 at 183, CA.
9 See *Dransfield v British Insulated Cables Ltd* [1937] 4 All ER 382 and *Paine v Colne Valley Electricity Supply Co Ltd* [1938] 4 All ER 803.

case, in which the bottle of ginger beer had been 'stoppered and sealed' by the manufacturer so as to remain in that state until opened by the consumer, was rejected by the Privy Council in *Grant v Australian Knitting Mills Ltd*.¹ In that case liability was imposed upon negligent manufacturers of underwear who had allowed their product to be contaminated by a chemical which caused dermatitis. 'The essential point', observed Lord Wright delivering the judgment of the Board,² 'was that the article should reach the consumer or user subject to the same defect as it had when it left the manufacturer'. It was accordingly irrelevant that the underwear had not been distributed in sealed packaging, nor was it an obstacle to liability that the plaintiff user had not considered it necessary to wash the garment before the first wearing. Similarly, even where there might have appeared to be ample opportunity for intermediate inspection a plaintiff will still succeed, if it becomes clear on the facts that the harm was suffered before that opportunity really existed.³ Even if the opportunity did exist the defendants will not be protected if they in truth never anticipated that there would be any intermediate inspection.⁴ Finally, in *Haseldine v CA Daw & Son Ltd*,⁵ Goddard LJ went so far as to suggest that the word 'probability' could be substituted for the phrase 'reasonable possibility' in Lord Atkin's dictum, and it is submitted that this proposition is correct. The careless creator of a source of danger should not escape liability at common law, except where he is entitled virtually to take it for granted that scrutiny by others of his work will take place before any harm can be expected to occur.

Relationship to causation and contributory negligence

[**17.09**] In the final analysis the notion of intermediate inspection appears merely to represent the application, in the particular context of defective products, of the general principles of the law of negligence relating to causation.⁶ It follows that in practice, since the broader approach to causal questions which has resulted from the passing of the Law Reform (Contributory Negligence) Act 1945,⁷ some decisions which before that Act ended in total defeat for the plaintiff might now be regarded as appropriate situations for apportionment if similar facts were to recur.⁸ Of course, this would not be the case directly if the intermediate inspection should have been carried out not by the plaintiff himself but by a third party. But in such cases the plaintiff will normally have a cause of action against the third party. Moreover, the broader modern approach to causation will still be relevant in such cases in so far as it might enable the third party to make a claim for contribution, on the ground that he was not alone in being liable to

---

1 [1936] AC 85.
2 Ibid at 106-107.
3 See *Barnett v H and J Packer & Co Ltd* [1940] 3 All ER 575.
4 See *Herschtal v Stewart & Ardern Ltd* [1940] 1 KB 155, [1939] 4 All ER 123.
5 [1941] 2 KB 343 at 376, [1941] 3 All ER 156 at 183, CA.
6 See *The Diamantis Pateras* [1966] 1 Lloyd's Rep 179 at 188 per Lawrence J.
7 See, generally, ch 4 above.
8 *Farr v Butters Bros & Co* [1932] 2 KB 606, CA is perhaps an example.

348 Defective products

the plaintiff.[1] If the case is one in which the allegation of contributory negligence is made against the plaintiff himself it does, of course, follow from the application of general principles that he must have failed to take reasonable care for his own safety before his damages can be reduced. Accordingly, even a plaintiff who inspected and discovered the defect might in some circumstances still recover in full, if the court is persuaded that he had no reasonable alternative but to take the risk.[2]

Proof of negligence

[**17.10**] Victims who claim to have suffered harm due to a defective product, in circumstances in which causation is not entirely clear, are apt to come up against either or both of two contrasting difficulties in discharging the onus of proof necessary to succeed in negligence. The first problem is that the longer the lapse of time since the product left the manufacturer, the more difficult it will be to show that the probabilities point to the attribution of fault to him rather than to subsequent interference with the product, or damage to it. Thus, in *Evans v Triplex Safety Glass Co Ltd*[3] a car windscreen suddenly shattered for no apparent reason, about a year after the date of manufacture. A claim for personal injuries suffered as a result was unsuccessful. Porter J observed that the question was one of degree rather than of law, but emphasised that he had 'to consider the question of time' and the possibility 'that the disintegration was due rather to the fitting of the windscreen than to faulty maunufacture having regard to its use on the road and the damage done to a windscreen in the course of use'.

Manufacturing process under the defendant's control

[**17.11**] The other main problem which can arise in products liability cases is that the manufacturing process will normally be under the defendant's control. He will therefore be the only party able in practice to furnish evidence as to the nature of that process, on the strength of which he may seek to contend that the best system reasonably possible had been operated and all proper precautions taken. In such cases, however, the plaintiff may benefit from a principle closely related to, if not identical with, that of res ipsa loquitur.[4] Thus in

---

1 See the Civil Liability (Contribution) Act 1978. It is to be noted that this Act, unlike its predecessor the Law Reform (Married Women and Tortfeasors) Act 1935, enables contribution to be sought between a defendant liable to the plaintiff in contract and one liable to him in tort and vice versa. This can obviously be of value in products liability cases where both retailer and manufacturer happen to be liable to the plaintiff. See, generally, ch 4 above.
2 Cf *Denny v Supplies and Transport Co Ltd* [1950] 2 KB 374, CA. See also *Rimmer v Liverpool City Council* [1985] QB 1 at 14, [1984] 1 All ER 930 at 938, CA.
3 [1936] 1 All ER 283.
4 See, generally, ch 2 above. But cf per Lord Macmillan in *Donoghue v Stevenson* [1932] AC 562 at 622: 'There is no presumption of negligence in such a case as the present, nor is there any justification for applying the maxim res ipsa loquitur.' Sed quaere.

Grant v Australian Knitting Mills, the facts of which have already been given, Lord Wright said:[1]

> 'According to the evidence the method of manufacture was correct; the danger of excess sulphites being left was recognised and was guarded against; the process was intended to be foolproof. If excess sulphites were left in the garment, that could only be because someone was at fault. The appellant is not required to lay his finger on the exact person in all the chain who was responsible or to specify what he did wrong. Negligence is found as a matter of inference from the existence of the defects taken in connection with all the known circumstances . . .'

It is implicit in this proposition that direct negligence by the maunufacturer himself is not the only route to the imposition of liability. This was emphasised by Mackenna J in the more recent case of *Hill v James Crowe (Cases) Ltd.*[2] In finding for the plaintiff his Lordship responded thus to defence evidence of the high standard of operation in their factory:[3]

> 'The manufacturer's liability in negligence [does] not depend on proof that he had either a bad system of work or that his supervision was inadequate. He might also be *vicariously* liable for the negligence of his workmen in the course of their employment. If the plaintiff's injuries were a reasonably foreseeable consequence of *such* negligence, the manufacturer's liability [is] established . . .'[4]

Danger of calling no evidence

[17.12] The readiness of the court in effect to apply the res ipsa loquitur approach in products liability negligence cases means that it is rarely safe, even for defendants who could not themselves be held responsible for the manufacturing process, to call no evidence when sued by someone harmed by the product, claiming that the plaintiff has not discharged the burden of proof. Relatively recent reported cases in both the Court of Appeal,[5] and the House of Lords,[6] have vividly illustrated the perilous nature of this course for defendants.

Economic loss

[17.13] The traditional approach of the common law was that, where defective products were concerned, the tort of negligence only provided redress in respect of personal injuries caused by the product, or in

---

1 [1936] AC 85 at 101.
2 [1978] 1 All ER 812, [1978] ICR 298.
3 Ibid at 816 and 303.
4 Italics supplied. The relevance of vicarious liability appears wrongly to have been overlooked in the earlier case of *Daniels v B White & Sons Ltd* [1938] 4 All ER 258, which Makenna J chose not to follow in *Hill's* case: the passage quoted is a direct criticism of the reasoning in *Hill.*
5 See *Pearce v Round Oak Steel Works Ltd* [1969] 3 All ER 680, [1969] 1 WLR 595, CA.
6 See *Henderson v Jenkins (H E) & Sons* [1970] AC 282, [1969] 3 All ER 756. Cf *Tan Chye Choo v Chong Kew Moi* [1970] 1 All ER 266, [1970] 1 WLR 147.

respect of damage to property *other* than the defective product itself.[1] That is to say, the owner or user of a defective chattel could not sue in *tort* merely because the chattel turned out to be less valuable or less useful than he had supposed it to be. Thus, he could not by claiming in negligence seek redress for his having incurred loss in repairing the product, in paying more for it than it had been worth, or in suffering a loss of profit in whatever activity he had sought to use it. This limitation on the scope of liability was simply an application of the conventional view that, for reasons of policy, losses purely financial in nature, unconnected with damage to person or property, should in general not be recoverable in negligence.[2] Redress for such losses had to be sought in *contract*: the owner or user of a defective chattel could look only to the person with whom he was in a contractual relationship with respect to the chattel, and the outcome would be governed by the terms of that contract.[3] The well-known decision of the House of Lords in *Junior Books Ltd v Veitchi Co Ltd*[4] did, however, cast doubt upon the correctness of the traditional view and indeed appeared to indicate that there was an exception to it, albeit of uncertain scope, whereby financial losses caused by a defective product could after all be recovered in tort. More recent cases, however, have seen a vigorous reassertion of the narrow conventional view. In the particular context of defective products, the decision of the Court of Appeal in *Muirhead v Industrial Tank Specialities Ltd*[5] suggests that *Junior Books v Veitchi* will be interpreted very narrowly. It would appear that this will confine liability in negligence, for financial losses flowing from a defect in the product in question itself, to situations in which a close relationship very similar to a contractual one in fact existed between plaintiff and defendant. The debate about the recovery of pure economic loss in negligence is, of course, far-reaching in scope and is not confined to the law relating to defective products. It is therefore considered at length elsewhere in this book.[6]

---

1   For the difficulties which the application of this principle can create by making it necessary to consider whether, for example, a package or container is to be considered a separate entity from its contents see *Aswan Engineering Co v Lupdine Ltd* [1987] 1 All ER 135, [1987] 1 WLR 1, CA.
2   It is possible that a limited exception to this general rule, which could have been relevant in some defective product cases, existed where the situation did originally involve a claim for actual physical damage: the success of which caused financial loss to be suffered by someone in the chain of distribution of the defective product. See *Lambert v Lewis* [1982] AC 225 at 278, [1981] 1 All ER 1185 at 1192 per Lord Diplock, and *Virgo Steamship Co SA v Skaarup Shipping Corpn* [1988] 1 Lloyd's Rep 352. But quaere whether this notion survived the decision of the House of Lords in *Murphy v Brentwood District Council* [1991] AC 398, [1990] 2 All ER 908.
3   Examination of the law of contract is, of course, outside the scope of the present work and reference should therefore be made to books dealing with that branch of the law for its application to defective products. See, eg Atiyah, *Sale of Goods* (8th edn, 1990 London).
4   [1983] 1 AC 520, [1982] 3 All ER 201, HL.
5   [1986] QB 507, [1985] 3 All ER 705, CA.
6   See, generally, ch 6 above.

Strict liability: The Consumer Protection Act 1987

Background

[**17.14**] The Consumer Protection Act 1987[1] received the Royal Assent shortly before the general election of that year. Part I of the Act, which is the only part relevant for present purposes, was passed in order to give effect to a Directive of the Council of the European Communities dated 25 July 1985.[2] The Directive was intended to bring about a regime of strict liability for defective products within the legal systems of the various member states of the EC. In view of the provenance of the Act it must be noted that sophisticated questions of EC law, relating to both vires and construction, may arise with respect to the scope of the Act and of the Directive which preceded it. Such questions are outside the scope of this book, which is concerned with the exposition of the Act in the context of English law, and examination of such issues must be sought elsewhere. Nevertheless attention must be drawn to an unusual provision to be found at the outset of the Act. Section 1(1) provides as follows: 'This Part shall have effect for the making of such provision as is necessary in order to comply with the product liability Directive and shall be construed accordingly.'

It is not altogether clear whether this subsection is only relevant, in accordance with conventional English rules of construction, where there is a perceived ambiguity in the wording of the Act as it stands, or whether it is of wider significance and permits reference to the Directive for the purposes of construction on a more general basis. In either event, it is clear that a knowledge of the content and wording of the Directive, as well as of the Act itself, is necessary for a satisfactory appreciation of the scope of the law.[3]

Strict liability

[**17.15**] Article 1 of the Directive states simply: 'The producer shall be liable for damage caused by a defect in his product.' Article 3 makes clear that the liability imposed upon producers is not limited to actual manufacturers and provides also for the imposition of liability, on the same basis as for producers, or *importers* of goods. The strict liability provided for by the Directive is set out in the 1987 Act, albeit by means of a rather different drafting technique, in the first two subsections of s 2, as follows:

> '(1) . . . where any damage is caused wholly or partly by a defect in a product, every person to whom subsection (2) below applies shall be liable for the damage.

---

1 For comment see Clark (1987) 50 MLR 614.
2 85/374/EEC:L 210/29.
3 It is perhaps unfortunate that, while the Bill was going through Parliament, the Government rejected a suggestion that the Directive should be set out in a schedule.

(2) This subsection applies to –
(a) the producer of the product;
(b) any person who, by putting his name on the product or using a trade mark or other distinguishing mark in relation to the product, has held himself out to be the producer of the product;
(c) any person who has imported the product into a member State from a place outside the member States in order, in the course of any business of his, to supply it to another.'

The section thus makes clear that, in addition to manufacturers, the strict liability regime will also apply to those who sell goods within EC countries which they themselves have acquired from outside the community, and to retailers who put their own brand name on the goods which they sell even though those goods were in fact manufactured by others. In view of the widespread nature of this latter practice in the retail trade this provision is of particular importance. Of course it must not be forgotten that even within a strict liability regime for defective goods the plaintiff will still have to prove *causation*,[1] and in some cases, particularly perhaps in cases where drugs have been taken for some pre-existing condition,[2] this will not necessarily be by any means an easy task.

Liability of suppliers

[17.16] The Act contains an important provision protecting consumers who are unable themselves to *identify* the relevant defendant potentially liable to them under s 2(1). They are able to call upon the person who *supplied* them with the goods to provide them with the identity of the producer, or other person to whom s 2(2) applies in relation to the product. If the supplier fails to comply with a request for that information within a reasonable time the Act provides that the supplier himself will be liable for the damage.[3]

Joint and several liability

[17.17] It will be apparent that, by virtue of s 2 of the Consumer Protection Act, there may be a number of defendants against whom a plaintiff may be able to seek redress for damage caused to him by a defective product. Subsection (5) of the section therefore makes clear that their liability is joint and several.

'Products' and 'producers'[4]

[17.18] Section 1(2) of the 1987 Act provides, inter alia, that: ' "product" means any goods or electricity and . . . includes a product

1 Art 4 of the Directive emphasises the point: 'The injured person shall be required to prove the damage, the defect and the causal relationship between defect and damage.'
2 See Christopher Newdick, 'Strict Liability for Defective Drugs in the Pharmaceutical Industry' (1985) 101 LQR 405 at 420ff.
3 See s 2(3), giving effect to Art 3.3 of the Directive.
4 See Arts 2 and 3 of the Directive. See also Simon Whittaker 'European Product Liability and Intellectual Products' (1989) 105 LQR 125.

which is comprised in another product, whether by virtue of being a component part or raw material or otherwise.' Thus, the manufacturer of a defective component cannot escape products liability merely because he did not manufacture the finished article.[1] By virtue of s 2, however, the 'producer' of a product rendered defective by a defective component will be liable along with the manufacturer of that component. On the other hand mere suppliers of assembled goods are given a measure of protection by s 1(3) which provides as follows: '. . . a person who supplies any product in which products are comprised, whether by virtue of being component parts or raw materials or otherwise, shall not be treated by reason only of his supply of that product as supplying any of the products so comprised.'[2]

'Producers'

[**17.19**] It will be apparent from the foregoing provisions that, where assembled goods are concerned, the precise definition of 'producer' may well be crucial. On this point, s 1(2)(c) enacts the following:

> ' "producer", in relation to a product, means-in the case of a product which has not been manufactured, won or abstracted but essential characteristics of which are attributable to an industrial or other process having been carried out . . . the person who carried out that process.'

A person who merely provides a container within which a defective item is housed may, for example, be able to invoke this definition of 'producer', so as to avoid liability on the ground that his activity did not confer 'essential characteristics' on the finished product.

Agricultural products

[**17.20**] The Directive provided that member states should be free to exclude 'primary agricultural products' from the strict liability regime if they so chose, or free to include them.[3] According to art 2 of the Directive ' "primary agricultural products" means the products of the soil, of stock-farming and of fisheries, excluding products which have undergone initial processing'.[4] The UK opted for exclusion and s 2(4) of the Act provides as follows:

> 'Neither subsection (2) nor subsection (3) above [ie the sub-sections imposing the strict liability] shall apply to a person in respect of any defect in any game or agricultural produce if the only supply of the game or produce by that person to another was at a time when it had not undergone an industrial process.'

---

1 Conversely a components manufacturer is not liable simply because the finished article itself is defective: see s 4(1)(f).
2 But note that a product will be defective, for the purpose of the imposition of liability upon its actual producer, and the other persons to whom s 2(2) applies, even if the defect arises out of a defect in a component part: see s 3(1).
3 See Arts 2 and 15(a).
4 The definition in s 1(2) of the Act uses almost identical wording.

354 Defective products

Since agricultural produce are only exempt from the strict liability so long as they are not subjected to an 'industrial process' the meaning of this latter phrase, which does not appear to be defined by the Act, will clearly be crucial in the agricultural context. The wider the interpretation put upon the phrase the narrower will be the scope of the exemption enjoyed and vice versa. Obviously processed, and presumably frozen, foods will attract the strict liability, but if, for example, crop-spraying were held to be an 'industrial process' a high proportion of 'fresh' fruit and vegetables might also be a potential source of liability.

'Defect'[1]

[**17.21**] 'Defect' is defined in s 3 of the Act.[2] A product is defective if its safety 'is not such as persons generally are entitled to expect'.[3] Inevitably there will often be scope for debate over questions of fact and degree in deciding whether or not a particular product was defective. Whether that adjective would be appropriate to describe a useful drug, which gives rise to dangerous side-effects, is but one example of the kind of context in which such issues might arise. Section 3(2) provides that 'all the circumstances are to be taken into account' in assessing safety and refers, inter alia, to the following: 'the manner in which, and purposes for which, the product has been marketed, its get-up . . . and any instructions for, or warnings with respect to, doing or refraining from doing anything with or in relation to the product.' 'Get-up' refers to the general presentation and packaging of the product. Where *warnings* are concerned their scope and effectiveness in any particular situation may unavoidably give rise to controverted questions of fact. A warning given to a doctor by a drug company might not, for example, be passed on to the patient. If there is no possibility of direct communication between patient and drug company it is submitted that, other things being equal, the warning given to the doctor should be effective to exonerate the drug company. The patient would be left to seek a remedy if possible against the doctor, in negligence or contract.

'comprised in'

[**17.22**] Section 3(1) of the Act includes the words that ' "safety" in relation to a product, shall include safety with respect to products comprised in that product'. In the case of composite pieces of equipment the notion of 'comprised in' is presumably a potential source of dispute. Are the tyres supplied with a new car 'comprised in' the car so as to render the manufacturer of the car liable in addition to

---

1 See Alessandro Stoppa 'The concept of defectiveness in the Consumer Protection Act 1987: a critical analysis' (1992) 12 L S 210.
2 See also Art 6 of the Directive.
3 Section 3(1). The concept of safety is not confined to the context of death or personal injury but includes risks of damage to property, ibid.

the manufacturers of the tyres themselves?[1] It is submitted that an affirmative answer should be given to this particular question, but difficult borderline cases are almost bound to arise in other situations.

Defences

'State of the art'[2]

[17.23] The scope of any defences available under a supposed 'strict liability' regime will necessarily be crucial in determining how strict the liability really is, or to what extent it in truth approximates to a fault based system. By far the most significant defence under the Consumer Protection Act, Part I in this respect, is that sometimes referred to as the 'state of the art' defence, which is to be found in s 4(1)(e) of the Act as follows:

> '... it shall be a defence ... to show that the state of scientific and technical knowledge at the relevant time was not such that a producer of products of the same description as the product in question might be expected to have discovered the defect if it had existed in his products while they were under his control.'

The wording of this provision is significantly different from that of the Directive, which is apparently less favourable to producers than the Act. Instead of exonerating a producer who could not have been 'expected' to discover the defect, the Directive uses an ostensibly objective formula based upon whether the state of knowledge was in fact such as to have 'enabled' the existence of the defect to have been discovered.[3] But even under the Directive's formula, and a fortiori under that of the Act, the 'state of the art' defence is controversial on the ground that it will facilitate the application of negligence criteria inconsistent with the rationale of strict liability. Ironically, it is even arguable that the Thalidomide tragedy, which provided part of the impetus for products' liability reform,[4] might be an example of the kind of situation in which the defence could be successfully invoked. Clearly, much will depend in practice upon whether the courts are disposed to put a wide or a narrow interpretation upon the scope of the defence.[5] Difficulties are, however, likely to result in either event.

---

1 Cf *Aswan Engineering Establishment Co v Lupdine Ltd* [1987] 1 All ER 135 at 152, [1987] 1 WLR 1 at 21 per Lloyd LJ, and see also s 5(2) of the Act (no liability for damage to the whole or any part of the product in question itself).
2 See Christopher Newdick, 'The Development Risk Defence of the Consumer Protection Act 1987' [1988] 47 CLJ 455.
3 See Art 7(e). Following complaints to the European Commission its Vice President wrote to the UK Government, early in 1988, contending that the Act had indeed failed fully to implement the Directive. It is possible that the matter will ultimately be referred for resolution to the European Court of Justice.
4 Of course another, rather different consideration, behind the EC initiative was a desire to harmonise competition within the Community.
5 Paradoxically, negligence cases have taken quite a severe view against defendants of what they ought to have discovered, which might be thought to approach strict liability: see eg *Vacwell Engineering Co Ltd v BDH Chemicals* [1971] 1 QB 88, [1969] 3 All ER 1681 (failure to consult forgotten literature published at the turn of the century).

Defective products

If a wide view is adopted the strict liability will be eroded, but if a narrow view is favoured inappropriate and abstruse debate, almost epistemological in nature, could arise in construing 'knowledge'. Thus, Dr Stapleton has asked, in her powerful analysis of the reforms envisaged by the European Directive itself, whether the defence could be negated on the basis of suggestions 'only aired by a junior scientist at an informal, obscure and unpublicised seminar in Siberia'.[1] Nevertheless, it is submitted that, on balance, a narrow interpretation of the defence is to be preferred. This would be more consistent with the rationale of strict liability and would be of greater assistance tactically to plaintiffs, making it easier for them to obtain favourable settlements without litigation.

Other defences

[17.24] Section 4 of the Act also provides that it shall be a defence to show that the supposed defect was attributable to compliance by the defendant with a statutory requirement imposed upon him,[2] or in the case of a component, wholly attributable to the design of the product of which the component formed a part or to constraints which the specification of that product necessarily imposed[3] An important limitation on the scope of the liability is that liability is not to be imposed if the supply of the product by the defendant 'was otherwise than in the course of a business'[4] or 'otherwise than with a view to profit'.[5] Presumably, trading companies operated by charitable organisations would not be able to invoke these provisions in their defence, but borderline cases in which the applicability of the provisions is uncertain could no doubt arise.

Contributory negligence, exclusion and limitation of liability

[17.25] The Act provides that the provisions of the Law Reform (Contributory Negligence) Act 1945 will apply, where appropriate, to products' liability claims.[6] Section 7 of the Act makes clear that liability cannot 'be limited or excluded by any contract term, by any notice or by any other provision'.[7] The normal three-year limitation period applies to claims under the Act,[8] but there is also an important special provision which extinguishes liability ten years after the putting into circulation of the product which caused the damage.[9]

---

1 Stapleton, 'Products Liability Reform-Real or Illusory ?' (1986) 6 OJLS 392 at 418.
2 See s 4(1)(a).
3 See s 4(1)(f).
4 See s 4(1)(c)(i).
5 See s 4(1)(c)(ii).
6 See s 6(4) and Art 8(2).
7 See also Art 12.
8 See Sch 1 adding an additional section, s 11A to the Limitation Act 1980. See also Article 10.1 of the Directive.
9 See the Limitation Act 1980, s 11A(3), inserted by the Consumer Protection Act 1987, Sch 1. See also Art 11 of the Directive.

Damage

[17.26] It is very important to note that the Act is not confined to death or personal injury but extends to 'any loss of or damage to any property (including land)'.[1] But loss or damage to the product *itself*,[2] in whole or in part[3] cannot be made the basis of a claim.[4] The Act imposes a threshold on all claims relating to loss of or damage to property of £275.[5] This means that plaintiffs whose loss is below that figure can recover nothing but those whose loss exceeds it can recover the full amount including the first £275. The intention is to discourage excessive litigation over small sums. In the case of damage to property, liability will not be imposed if the object lost or damaged was not of a kind 'ordinarily intended for private use, occupation or consumption' and was not 'intended by the person suffering the loss or damage mainly for his own private use, occupation or consumption'. The introduction of the concept of 'intention' here would appear to be a potential cause of uncertainty. What of damage to a sophisticated computer system which is used by the plaintiff partly in the operation of his business, which he runs from home, and partly used by him for playing games?

Consequential losses

[17.27] It is unclear whether financial losses consequential upon loss of or damage to any property will be recoverable under the Act. Such losses are, of course, recoverable in negligence (unlike pure economic loss), subject to the operation of the normal rules relating to remoteness of damage. But since the basic objective of the Act and the Directive is consumer protection, perhaps it would be appropriate to conclude that such losses are excluded since they are typically, although obviously not exclusively, commercial in nature. If this is correct it means, as Paul Dobson has suggested, that:

> 'if . . . a toaster catches fire and the fire badly damages the plaintiff's house, the plaintiff will be entitled to claim the cost of repairing the house and replacing the burnt contents but will not be able to claim the cost of alternative accommodation rendered necessary because the house was uninhabitable until repaired'.[6]

In the case of death or personal injury, however, consequential losses such as loss of income will be recoverable just as in negligence.[7]

---

1 See s 5(1), giving effect to Art 9 of the Directive.
2 Cf *Murphy v Brentwood District Council* [1991] 1 AC 378, [1990] 2 All ER 908, HL.
3 Cf *D & F Estates Ltd v Church Commissioners* [1989] AC 177, [1988] 2 All ER 992, HL.
4 See s 5(2).
5 See s 5(4) and Art 9(b) of the Directive.
6 Annotation to the Consumer Protection Act 1987, s 5 (*Current Law Statutes Annotated*).
7 Fatal Accidents Act claims can be based on the new liability: see the Consumer Protection Act 1987, s 6.

Evaluation

[17.28] It remains to be seen how far the Consumer Protection Act will improve the protection of those who suffer injury or loss as a result of defective products, beyond that already afforded to them by the law of negligence. It is certainly possible to argue that at a theoretical level the Act, and indeed the Directive itself, is vulnerable to criticism on the ground that, while purporting to introduce strict liability, it uses concepts which are fundamentally inconsistent with such liability and which reflect negligence criteria.[1] But it is probably wrong to see the 'reforms' as a cynical or cosmetic attempt to confer benefits upon consumers which in reality will turn out to be nugatory. In practice, the absence of the need formally to prove negligence should be of substantial assistance to plaintiffs in settlement negotiations in situations to which the Act applies. And wholesale abrogation of existing concepts, in the development of the new liability, could well have led to confusion rather than to greater clarity. As Christopher Newdick, in his valuable study of the reform has written:[2]

> 'The most significant effect of this measure of reform may be educative. For those who never seriously considered the possibility of litigation following an accident, and for those practitioners who hesitated to follow the example of their American colleagues, Product Liability may serve to enlarge the scope of cases considered appropriate for litigation and settlement. To this extent, albeit in a more orderly and consistent manner, it may incline the law of Tort to expand its boundaries to include areas which have received little attention hitherto . . . Developments of this nature may be expected to contribute much to the evolution of Tort in the long-run, but the path on which such growth may take place is likely to originate from sources with which existing law is already familiar.'

[17.29] The very choice of products liability in isolation, as a subject for legislative action, can be criticised in so far as it confers upon one class of plaintiffs a privilege of strict liability not enjoyed by others.[3] The radical reformer who wishes to see civil liability in the personal injuries field replaced, by general uniform state provision, is inevitably likely to be impatient with concentration upon product liability. At this level, however, the debate necessarily acquires political overtones. In the view of the present writer there is much to be said for reforming our admittedly flawed system of liability for accidental damage along lines which still preserve some notion of attribution of responsibility, and which do not increase unnecessarily

---

1 See, especially, Stapleton, 'Products Liability Reform-Real or Illusory ?' (1986) 6 OJLS 392 who argues that the concept of 'defect' itself introduces the kind of cost-benefit considerations which underly negligence (and could prove particularly unsatisfactory where a product's *design* has caused damage) irrespective of specific defences such as 'state of the art'. Cf Christopher Newdick, 'The Future of Negligence in Product Liability' (1987) 104 LQR 288.
2 'The Future of Negligence in Product Liability' (1987) 104 LQR 288 at 310.
3 See Stapleton 'Products Liability Reform – Real or Illusory ?' (1986) 6 OJLS 392 at 421. See also the same writer on 'Three Problems with the New Product Liability' in *Essays for Patrick Atiyah* Cane and Stapleton (eds) (1991).

the role of the state. It is therefore submitted that the extension of strict liability by the identification and isolation of areas of special risk, in so far as this can be done with some degree of coherence, provides an attractive route forward.

Chapter 18

Vicarious liability

Introduction

Background

[**18.01**] 'It is a rule of law', observed Lord Reid in *Staveley Iron & Chemical Co v Jones Ltd*,[1] 'that an employer, though guilty of no fault himself, is liable for damage done by the fault or negligence of his servant acting in the course of his employment'. This is a succinct statement of what may be termed 'true' vicarious liability. It is apparent that such liability constitutes a major exception, as far as the employer is concerned, to the principle of no liability without fault. At one time a rival, or 'master's tort' theory had its adherents.[2] This attempted to explain the cases seemingly based on vicarious liability by postulating that the employer had in some sense been in breach of a duty imposed by the law upon himself. This approach was sometimes useful, particularly in enabling the unfortunate doctrine of common employment, which until 1948 prevented fellow-workers from suing each other for negligence at the workplace, to be circumvented.[3] Indeed, the concept of duties which cannot be delegated remains important in several areas of the law of negligence: in particular, of course, that concerned with liability for independent contractors. It is also relevant to the liability of hospitals, and bailees. As far as situations involving what could be termed 'ordinary' acts of carelessness by workpeople in the course of their duties, however, a superficial attraction of the 'master's tort' theory was that it purported to obviate the need to admit the existence of a major exception to the fault principle.[4] But this implausible doctrine, manifestly based on

1 [1956] AC 627 at 643, [1956] 1 All ER 403 at 409, HL.
2 See, eg per Uthwatt J at first instance in *Twine v Bean's Express Ltd* [1946] 1 All ER 202, criticised by Newark in (1954) 17 MLR 102 (the decision of the Court of Appeal, reported in 175 LT 131, proceeded on different grounds).
3 See, eg *Wilsons & Clyde Coal Co Ltd v English* [1938] AC 57, [1937] 3 All ER 628, HL. The doctrine of common employment was abolished by the Law Reform (Personal Injuries) Act 1948.
4 For a suggestion of another supposed attraction of the theory, in a certain type of defamation case, see per Lord Denning MR in *Riddick v Thames Board Mills Ltd* [1977] QB 881 at 893, [1977] 3 All ER 677 at 685, CA.

legal fiction, could not be counted a success. Accordingly, in the case from which Lord Reid's quotation is taken, the House of Lords explicitly rejected the theory and it can safely be regarded as having been buried.[1] It is therefore now generally accepted that a straight exception to the fault principle is here being made for reasons of policy. In *ICI Ltd v Shatwell*[2] Lord Pearce put it as follows:

> 'The doctrine of vicarious liability has not grown from any very clear, logical or legal principle but from social convenience and rough justice. The master having (presumably for his own benefit) employed the servant, and being (presumably) better able to make good any damage which may occasionally result from the arrangement, is answerable to the world at large for all the torts committed by his servant within the scope of it.'

Where the servant has a defence

[18.02] It is implicit in rejection of the 'master's tort' theory that, for the employer to be liable, there must have been carelessness on the part of his servant which would normally constitute actionable negligence. This was the basis of the actual decision of the House of Lords in *Staveley Iron & Chemical Co Ltd v Jones*.[3] Similarly, in *ICI Ltd v Shatwell*,[4] the House of Lords held that a master not in breach of any duty of his own could not incur vicarious liability for the negligence of one of his servants where that servant would have had a complete defence of volenti non fit injuria to any claim made against him personally by the plaintiff. On the other hand, there will occasionally be rare situations where the servant enjoys some peculiar procedural defence which protects him from liability.[5] The master may nevertheless incur liability in such cases, but the better view is that they do not constitute genuine exceptions to the proposition that the master's liability is vicarious rather than personal. The technical defence enjoyed by the servant does not detract from the proposition that his conduct has been in substance tortious, and the 'social convenience and rough justice', to which Lord Pearce referred,[6] make it appropriate that the master should be liable on the same basis as if the technical defence did not exist.

Who is a servant?

Control no longer conclusive

[18.03] Over the years the approach adopted by the courts in determining whether one person was the 'servant' of another, whether

1 But cf Glanville Williams 'Vicarious Liability: Tort of the Master or of the Servant' (1956) 72 LQR 522. See also Barak 'Mixed and Vicarious Liability – A Suggested Distinction' (1966) 29 MLR 160.
2 [1965] AC 656 at 685, [1964] 2 All ER 999, at 1011-1012, HL.
3 [1956] AC 627, [1956] 1 All ER 403, HL.
4 [1965] AC 656, [1964] 2 All ER 999, HL.
5 See, eg *Broom v Morgan* [1953] 1 QB 597, [1953] 1 All ER 849, CA (the facts of this case, involving the inability at one time of husband and wife to sue each other in tort, can no longer recur in view of the Law Reform (Husband and Wife) Act 1962).
6 See above.

362 Vicarious liability

in relation to the imposition of vicarious liability in tort or for some other purpose, has inevitably undergone modification as the world of work has become more complex and sophisticated. It is necessary to distinguish someone employed under a contract of *service* from someone employed under a contract *for services* whose carelessness, as an independent contractor of his employer, will not result in the imposition of liability on the latter save in exceptional circumstances. The traditional test for the existence of a contract of service was whether the alleged servant was under the 'control' of his employer. But if this had been insisted upon in an age of increasing professionalism, and technical skill, the result would have been greatly to diminish the scope of vicarious liability. In *Stevenson, Jordan and Harrison Ltd v MacDonald and Evans*[1] Denning LJ put it thus:

> 'There are many contracts of service where the master cannot control the manner in which the work is to be done, as in the case of a captain of a ship... It is often easy to recognize a contract of service when you see it, but difficult to say wherein the difference lies. A ship's master, a chauffeur, and a reporter on the staff of a newspaper are all employed under a contract of service; but a ship's pilot, a taxi-man, and a newspaper contributor are employed under a contract for services. One feature which seems to run through the instances is that, under a contract of service, a man is employed as part of the business, and his work is done as an integral part of the business; whereas, under a contract for services, his work, although done for the business, is not integrated into it but is only accessory to it.'

Recognition that the control test must be modified in modern circumstances has enabled vicarious liability to be imposed on hospital authorities for the negligence of doctors and other skilled medical staff,[2] whereas the literal application of that test would obviously have made the imposition of such liability impossible.[3] Moreover, it is apparent that, as was judicially observed in a case in which a market research interviewer was held to be a servant, the 'opportunity to deploy individual skill and personality is frequently present in what is undoubtedly a contract of service'.[4]

Relevance of commercial risk

[18.04] In the important case of *Ready Mixed Concrete (South East) Ltd v Minister of Pensions and National Insurance*[5] MacKenna J decided that a lorry-driver who was required to wear the uniform of the Ready Mixed Concrete company, and to be available whenever that company required, was nevertheless a self-employed haulage contractor rather than a servant of the company. The fact that his

---

1 [1952] 1 TLR 101 at 111, CA.
2 See, eg *Cassidy v Ministry of Health* [1951] 2 KB 343, [1951] 1 All ER 574, CA and the note by Kahn-Freund, 'Servants and Independent Contractors' in (1951) 14 MLR 504. The liability of hospital authorities is discussed more fully below.
3 Cf *Hillyer v St Bartholomew's Hospital (Governors)* [1909] 2 KB 820, CA.
4 *Market Investigations Ltd v Minister of Social Security* [1969] 2 QB 173 at 188, [1968] 3 All ER 732 at 740, per Cooke J.
5 [1968] 2 QB 497, [1968] 1 All ER 433.

contract declared his status to be that of an independent contractor was not conclusive in itself.[1] But the fact that he owned his own lorry, was responsible for its maintenance, and depended for his overall profitability on the use which he made of this asset and the extent to which he safeguarded it, led to the conclusion that he was indeed such a contractor and not a servant. The judge quoted[2] an important passage from the judgment of Lord Wright in a 1947 Privy Council case, reported only in Canada,[3] in which his Lordship observed that in the 'complex conditions of modern industry' determination of the master-servant relationship had to take into account 'ownership of the tools ... chance of profit' and 'risk of loss'. Although each case will depend upon its own facts, it is submitted that these considerations of commercial risk will often be of central importance in modern cases.

Possible relevance of nature of claim

[18.05] A number of the recent authorities on determination of the existence of a contract of service, including the *Ready Mixed Concrete* case itself, have not in fact involved tort claims at all. They have more often been concerned with attempts to gain the taxation advantages of self-employed status.[4] In one case, the Court of Appeal took the view that the appellant could not seek to have himself classified as self-employed for that purpose and yet seek to be re-classified as a servant when *that* would be to his advantage because he wished to bring a claim for unfair dismissal.[5] On the other hand, in a later unfair dismissal case, this decision was distinguished on its facts and re-classification was achieved.[6] Moreover, it is significant that in one case which *did* involve a tort claim, for injuries suffered at the plaintiff's place of work, the Court of Appeal held, albeit by a majority, that a master-servant relationship *had* existed in substance despite the plaintiff's original agreement to function as a self-employed building worker.[7] Accordingly, if a situation were to arise involving a vicarious liability tort claim by a *third party* it would seem a fortiori that the court would be prepared to resolve any doubts which existed, about the presence of a master-servant relationship, in favour of the plaintiff. It is submitted that such flexibility of approach would certainly be desirable.[8]

---

1 '... whether the relation between the parties to the contract is that of master and servant or otherwise is a conclusion of law dependent upon the duties imposed by the contract. If these are such that the relation is that of master and servant, it is irrelevant that the parties have declared it to be something else': [1969] 2 QB 497 at 513, [1968] 1 All ER 433 at 439.
2 [1969] 2 QB 497 at 520, [1968] 1 All ER 433 at 443.
3 *Montreal v Montreal Locomotive Works* [1947] 1 DLR 161 at 169. (The case was exhumed by Atiyah in his *Vicarious Liability in the Law of Torts* (1967).
4 A practice which became notorious in the building industry with the so-called 'labour-only sub-contract' or 'lump'.
5 See *Massey v Crown Life Insurance Co* [1978] 2 All ER 576, [1978] 1 WLR 676, CA.
6 See *Young and Woods Ltd v West* [1980] IRLR 201, CA.
7 See *Ferguson v Dawson & Partners (Contractors) Ltd* [1976] 3 All ER 817, [1976] 1 WLR 1213, CA.
8 Cf Ewan McKendrick 'Vicarious Liability and Independent Contractors – A Re-examination' (1990) 53 MLR 770.

Borrowed servants

[**18.06**] An employer may sometimes lend one of his employees to another organisation, for which that person will work temporarily. Such an arrangement often arises in situations in which a piece of heavy machinery, such as a crane, is hired out along with its operator.[1] But it is not confined to such situations.[2] If a third party is injured as a result of the negligence of the 'borrowed' servant the original, or 'general', employer may in theory seek to show that, instead of himself, the *other* organisation is vicariously liable to the victim. In modern law, however, the possibility appears to be academic. It is clear from the leading case of *Mersey Docks and Harbour Board v Coggins and Griffith (Liverpool) Ltd*,[3] that the burden of proving that the negligent person has become *pro hac vice*,[4] the servant of the hirer is on the general employer, and that it is a heavy one to discharge. It would be necessary to prove, inter alia, that the servant had consented to the change of employer and that, in so far as *control* still has some relevance to the establishment of a master-servant relationship, this rested with the temporary 'employer'. In practice the burden is so heavy that there appears to be no reported case since 1893 in which it has been successfully discharged.[5] Considerations of policy, such as convenience and certainty, clearly favour the imposition of vicarious liability upon the general employer, who is responsible for the administration of the relevant employer-employee relationship including such matters as payment of social security contributions.

Need to distinguish hirer's duty to the servant

[**18.07**] The hirer may, of course, himself incur liability in tort *to* the borrowed servant, and this may even include liability for breach of certain aspects of an employer's duty to provide a safe system of work.[6] But, in general, the courts are reluctant to hold that the general employer has effectively transferred legal reponsibility for the

---

1 See, eg *Mersey Docks and Harbour Board v Coggins and Griffith (Liverpool) Ltd* [1947] AC 1, [1946] 2 All ER 345, HL.
2 See, eg *Bhoomidas v Port of Singapore Authority* [1978] 1 All ER 956, [1978] 1 WLR 189, PC.
3 [1947] AC 1, [1946] 2 All ER 345, HL.
4 'which I would translate *for the time being*': per Lord Denning MR in *Savory v Holland Hannen & Cubitts (Southern) Ltd* [1964] 3 All ER 18 at 20, [1964] 1 WLR 1158 at 1162, CA.
5 Per Lord Salmon in *Bhoomidas v Port of Singapore Authority* [1978] 1 All ER 957 at 956, [1978] 1 WLR 189 at 191-192. The 1893 case is *Donovan v Laing, Wharton and Down Construction Syndicate* [1893] 1 QB 629, CA which has been heavily criticised: see eg per Lord Macmillan in *Mersey Docks and Harbour Board v Coggins and Griffiths* [1947] AC 1 at 14, [1946] 2 All ER 345 at 350. In *Denham v Midland Employers' Mutual Assurance Ltd* [1955] 2 QB 437 at 444, CA Denning LJ apparently indicated obiter that the facts supported discharge of the burden in the case before him: sed quaere.
6 See, eg *Garrard v AE Southey & Co and Standard Telephone and Cables Ltd* [1952] 2 QB 174, [1952] 1 All ER 597; *Gibb v United Steel Companies Ltd* [1957] 2 All ER 110, [1957] 1 WLR 668. For Employers' liability see, generally, ch 14 above.

safety of his servants to another party¹ The fact that they are occasionally prepared so to hold, however, means that particular care is needed in reading some of the cases in which *Mersey Docks and Harbour Board v Coggins and Griffith* has been cited and discussed. The principles enunciated in that case have sometimes been relied on to justify decisions in which the hirer has been held to owe some of the duties of employers' liability to the borrowed servant,² but these decisions are not authorities on the separate question of vicarious liability to third parties for carelessness *by* the servant.

General employer may be entitled to contractual indemnity

[18.08] 'As between himself and the public', observed Lord Pearce in *Arthur White (Contractors) Ltd v Tarmac Civil Engineering Ltd*,³ 'the general master cannot divest himself of responsibility for the servant ... But the parties to the hiring contract may determine liability inter se'. Thus, it is perfectly possible for the general employer to stipulate in the contract of hiring that he is to be indemnified against the consequences of any carelessness on the part of the servant who is loaned. Such a provision obviously leaves the rights of the victim unaffected, but can clearly be of value to the general employer once he has settled the victim's claim. In the *Tarmac* case a point on the construction of such a contract was fought up to the House of Lords, and ended in the general employers securing a full indemnity from the hirers.⁴

The course of employment

Wrongful method of performance

[18.09] In *Kooragang Investments Pty Ltd v Richardson and Wrench Ltd*,⁵ Lord Wilberforce said of the authorities on the course of employment:

> 'These cases have given rise to a number of fine distinctions, the courts in some cases struggling to find liability, in others to avoid it. ... It remains true to say that, whatever exceptions or qualifications may be introduced, the underlying principle remains that a servant, even while performing acts of the class which he was authorised, or employed, to do, may so clearly depart from the scope of his employment that his master will not be liable for his wrongful acts.'

1   See, eg *O'Reilly v ICI Ltd* [1955] 3 All ER 382, [1955] 1 WLR 1155, CA. Cf *Savory v Holland Hannen & Cubitts (Southern) Ltd* [1964] 3 All ER 18, [1964] 1 WLR 1158, CA. See also *McDermid v Nash Dredging and Reclamation Co Ltd* [1987] AC 906, [1987] 2 All ER 878, HL and *Morris v Breaveglen Ltd (t/a Anzac Construction Co) (1992)* 137 Sol Jo LB 13, CA. See, generally, ch 14 above.
2   See *Garrard* and *Gibb* cases cited above.
3   [1967] 1 WLR 1508 at 1520, HL.
4   See also *Herdman v Walker (Tooting) Ltd* [1956] 1 All ER 429, [1956] 1 WLR 209.
5   [1981] 3 All ER 65 at 70, PC.

Situations in which servants employed to drive their employer's vehicles took those vehicles off on journeys for purposes of their own, on routes wholly different from those required by the business of the employers in question, provided early examples of departure from the scope of employment such as negated the imposition of vicarious liability.[1] A clear but remarkable recent example of employees acting outside the course of employment is provided by *General Engineering Services Ltd v Kingston and St Andrew Corpn*.[2] In this case a fire brigade which was operating a 'go slow' policy as part of industrial action drove literally on a stop and go basis (ie constantly stopping and starting to prolong their journey), so as to reach a fire at the plaintiffs' premises only after they had burned down. The Privy Council had no hesitation in affirming the decision of the Court of Appeal of Jamaica that this conduct was outside the course of employment of members of the fire brigade. On the other hand even deliberate criminal acts have sometimes been treated, in particular circumstances, as coming within the course of employment, albeit as improper modes of performance of the servants' duties.[3] As far as acts of pure negligence on the part of servants are concerned, however, perhaps the most striking example of a case in which the court may be said to have 'struggled to find liability' is the well-known decision of the House of Lords in *Century Insurance Co Ltd v Northern Ireland Road Transport Board*.[4] The driver of a petrol tanker, while watching the process of discharging his cargo at a garage, lit a cigarette and threw the match on the floor. For the purposes of a liability insurance policy taken out by the Road Transport Board the driver's carelessness, which not surprisingly produced an explosion and a conflagration, was held to come within the course of his employment. Viscount Simon LC invoked Milton as an authority on the course of employment: 'In circumstances like these, "they also serve who only stand and wait".'[5] Although the question of whether a particular act was or was not in the course of employment is one of law, its solution will obviously depend very much on the facts of each individual case. Accordingly the creation of the 'fine distinctions' to which Lord Wilberforce referred was perhaps inevitable. For the purposes of exposition it is convenient to group the decisions in certain broad categories of similar fact-situations. But it is not suggested that these categories reflect significant differences in the underlying principles involved.

The moving of vehicles

[**18.10**] A number of cases have concerned accidents caused by employees not qualified or permitted to drive vehicles in the course of their duties nevertheless doing so. In *Iqbal v London Transport*

---

1 See, eg *Storey v Ashton* (1869) LR 4 QB 476. Cf *Aitchison v Page Motors Ltd* (1935) 154 LT 128.
2 [1988] 3 All ER 867, [1989] 1 WLR 69, PC.
3 See below.
4 [1942] AC 509, [1942] 1 All ER 491, HL.
5 [1942] AC at 514 quoting the last line of Milton's 'Sonnet On His Blindness'.

Executive[1] the Court of Appeal held the defendants not vicariously liable when one of their conductors, despite being expressly forbidden from doing so,[2] drove a bus in an attempt to move it so as to allow another bus to secure egress from the depot.[3] 'The driving of a bus', said Megaw LJ,[4] 'was not within the sphere of employment'. On the other hand, in *Kay v ITW Ltd*[5] the defendants' servant, who was employed to drive a fork lift truck, found a five-ton diesel lorry blocking the path of his truck. He promptly climbed into the empty cab of the lorry and, in attempting to drive it, caused it to reverse into the plaintiff causing him severe injuries. The Court of Appeal held the defendant employers vicariously liable.[6] The case was, in the words of Sellers LJ, 'near the borderline' but the servant's 'exceptional and excessive conduct' was not 'so gross and extreme as to take his act outside what he was employed to do'.[7] Sachs LJ perhaps came closest to formulating a working presumption that could be of use in cases of this kind and similar situations:[8]

> 'Once ... it is conceded that [the employee] was doing something in his working hours, on his employers' premises, and when seeking to act in his employers' interests, and that, moreover, his act had a close connection with the work which he was employed to do, it seems to me that the onus shifts to the employers to show that the act was one for which they were not responsible.'

Work, rest and play

[18.11] It is a long-established principle that accidents which occur on the highway, when the servant is merely travelling to or from work, do not come within the course of employment for the purposes of vicarious liability.[9]

> 'So a bank clerk who commutes to the City of London every day from Sevenoaks is not acting in the course of his employment when he walks across London Bridge from the station to his bank in the City. This is because he is not employed to travel from his home to the bank: he is employed to work at the bank, his place of work, and so his duty is to arrive there in time for his working day.'[10]

The correctness of this principle was affirmed, but its applicability distinguished on the facts, in the leading case of *Smith v Stages*.[11] Two employees working in the Midlands were sent by their employer to do an urgent job in Wales. They were paid for their journey time and also

---

1 (1973) 16 KIR 329.
2 On prohibited acts generally, see below.
3 See also *Beard v London General Omnibus Co* [1900] 2 QB 530, CA.
4 (1973) 16 KIR 329 at 336.
5 [1968] 1 QB 140, [1967] 3 All ER 22, CA.
6 See also *LCC v Cattermoles (Garages) Ltd* [1953] 2 All ER 582, [1953] 1 WLR 977.
7 [1968] 1 QB 140 at 154, [1967] 3 All ER 22 at 27.
8 Ibid at 156 and 28.
9 See *Vandyke v Fender* [1970] 2 QB 292, [1970] 2 All ER 335, CA.
10 Per Lord Goff in *Smith v Stages* [1989] AC 928 at 936, [1989] 1 All ER 833 at 836, HL.
11 [1989] AC 928, [1989] 1 All ER 833, HL.

given the equivalent of the rail fare, although there was no stipulation that they should travel by train. The plaintiff was injured in a road-accident caused by the negligence of his fellow-employee when the two of them were returning from Wales in the latter's car. The House of Lords held that the accident had occurred in the course of employment. Lord Goff said:[1]

> 'In my opinion [the plaintiff] was required by the employers to make this journey, so as to make himself available to do his work ... and it would be proper to describe him as having been employed to do so. The fact that he was not required by his employer to make the journey by any particular means, nor even required to make it on the particular working day made available to him, does not detract from the proposition that he was employed to make the journey.'[2]

Similarly, accidents on the highway which occur *during* the working day, when employees are travelling to or from particular sites, have been held to come within the course of employment even if the particular journey in question was undertaken simply in order to procure lunch.[3] But a journey to a cafe for tea undertaken when the servants concerned, having 'taken the view that they had done enough work to pass muster, were filling in the rest of their time until their hours of work had come to an end' was held to be outside the course of employment.[4] Even a lorry-driver who had, perfectly properly, stopped for lunch in the course of the working day, but carelessly caused an accident while crossing the road as a pedestrian having just climbed down from his cab, was held to have been 'a stranger to his master from the moment when he left the lorry'.[5] Again, a servant who overstayed his ten-minute tea-break by 50% was held to be outside the course of employment when injured during the extra five minutes.[6] Nevertheless, a servant on his employer's premises purely to collect his wages, and after his work has ceased, can still be within the course of employment.[7] Moreover, a servant who carelessly and improperly delegated his own duties to someone else was held to have been acting in the course of his employment in so doing, so as to lead to the imposition of vicarious liability on his employers when a third party was injured as a result.[8] Even a practical joke may be in the course of employment if it takes the form merely of an eccentric manner of discharging prescribed duties,[9] but not if it is a quite unrelated act of isolated misbehaviour.[10]

1 [1989] AC 928 at 938, [1989] 1 All ER 833 at 838.
2 See also per Lord Lowry in [1989] AC 928 at 955-956, [1989] 1 All ER 833 at 851 for a valuable summary of the general principles applicable in these cases.
3 See, eg *Harvey v R G O'Dell Ltd* [1958] 2 QB 78, [1958] 1 All ER 657.
4 *Hilton v Thomas Burton (Rhodes) Ltd* [1961] 1 All ER 74 at 77, [1961] 1 WLR 705, at 708-709 (Diplock J).
5 *Crook v Derbyshire Stone Ltd* [1956] 2 All ER 447 at 450, [1956] 1 WLR 432 at 436 (Pilcher J).
6 See *R v Industrial Injuries Comr, ex p Amalgamated Engineering Union (No 2)* [1966] 2 QB 31, [1966] 1 All ER 97, CA.
7 *Staton v National Coal Board* [1957] 2 All ER 667, [1957] 1 WLR 893.
8 *Ilkiw v Samuels* [1963] 2 All ER 879, [1963] 1 WLR 991, CA.
9 See *Harrison v Michelin Tyre Co* [1985] 1 All ER 918, [1985] ICR 696.
10 See *O'Reilly v National Rail and Tramway Appliances Ltd* [1966] 1 All ER 499.

Prohibited acts

[18.12] It seems to be established that, as Stephenson LJ, put it in *Stone v Taffe*,[1]

> 'a prohibition by an employer of what his servant may do is not by itself conclusive of the scope of his employment against third parties injured by the servant, but ... the injured person cannot make the employer liable where he himself knows of the prohibition, and has the opportunity to avoid the danger of injury from the prohibited act, before he exposes himself to the danger.'[2]

On the other hand, even where the injured person does *not* know of the prohibition the overall situation may still be analysed as one in which the servant acted outside the course of his employment, and the existence of the prohibition, while not conclusive by itself, could be highly relevant to the determination of that issue.[3] Another factor to which the court will attach importance, in deciding whether the servant's act took him outside the course of his employment, is the *purpose* for which it was done. This is certainly not a conclusive factor, however, and there are decided cases which indicate that the mere fact that the servant perceived himself as acting for his master's purposes is neither a necessary[4] nor a sufficient[5] condition for the imposition of vicarious liability. But in a case which might otherwise be regarded as marginal, purpose can be the factor which ultimately tips the scales.[6] This was emphasised in *Rose v Plenty*[7] in which the Court of Appeal, by a majority,[8] held the employers of a milk roundsman vicariously liable when the latter's carelessness caused injury to a boy whom he had taken on his van to help him in his deliveries, despite being explicitly forbidden by his employers from so doing. 'In considering whether a prohibited act was within the course of the employment', said Lord Denning MR, 'it depends very much on the purpose for which it is done. If it is done for his employers'

---

1 [1974] 1 WLR 1575 at 1581, CA (certain passages in parenthesis in the original are omitted from the quotation in the text).
2 In strict logic it is not easy to see why knowledge of the prohibition on the part of the plaintiff should be relevant, if the act of the servant would otherwise have been in the course of his employment. But the presence or absence of such knowledge does seem to help to explain the actual decisions (although not the reasoning) in some of the earlier cases. See, especially, Newark in (1954) 17 MLR 102 discussing *Twine v Bean's Express Ltd* [1946] 1 All ER 202 (affd on other grounds 62 TLR 458, CA). But it should be noted that on the facts of *Twine*'s case (which involved a notice to passengers in the cab of the defendants' vehicle in which their servant gave a lift to the plaintiff) the particular argument which Newark put forward would no longer be valid in view of the Road Traffic Act 1988, s 149(2).
3 See, eg *Conway v George Wimpey & Co Ltd* [1951] 2 KB 266, [1951] 1 All ER 363, CA.
4 See *Lloyd v Grace, Smith & Co* [1912] AC 716, HL.
5 See, eg *Iqbal v London Transport Executive* (1973) 16 KIR 329, CA.
6 See, eg *Canadian Pacific Rly Co v Lockhart* [1942] AC 591, [1942] 2 All ER 464, PC; *LCC v Cattermoles (Garages) Ltd* [1953] 2 All ER 582, [1953] 1 WLR 977, CA.
7 [1976] 1 All ER 97, [1976] 1 WLR 141, CA.
8 Lord Denning MR and Scarman LJ. Lawton LJ dissented.

business, it is usually done in the course of his employment, even though it is a prohibited act.'[1]

Assaults and criminal acts[2]

[**18.13**] In the famous case of *Lloyd v Grace, Smith & Co*[3] the House of Lords imposed vicarious liability upon an employer for loss caused by a deliberate fraud which had been perpetrated by his servant purely for the latter's own benefit. It is possible, however, that the case really turned upon a non-delegable duty imposed on the employer by the law of agency, as a result of his having clothed the dishonest servant with apparent authority, rather than upon true vicarious liability in the modern sense.[4] This interpretation is perhaps supported by cases in which liability has been imposed upon bailees for theft by their servants.[5] It is certainly true that in situations in which the servant's act resembles negligence more closely than it does in the cases of deliberate dishonesty, namely physical assaults committed in a perceived emergency or the heat of the moment, the question whether the servant believed himself to be acting for the benefit of his master, or on his own account, appears to be highly material in determining whether or not vicarious liability will be imposed upon the employer for the injuries suffered by the victim. Thus in *Poland v John Parr & Sons*[6] an assault by a servant upon someone he thought was stealing his master's property gave rise to the imposition of vicarious liability, when the assault had unexpectedly serious physical consequences for the victim. On the other hand, assaults by garage hands[7] and bus conductors,[8] not as a result of misconceived attempts to promote their employers' interests but due simply to their having been overcome by sudden outbursts of loss of temper in their dealings with members of the public, have been held to fall outside the course of employment.

The master's indemnity

[**18.14**] In the well-known case of *Lister v Romford Ice & Coal Storage Co Ltd*,[9] the House of Lords, by a bare majority, established that a

1 [1976] 1 All ER 97 at 100-101, [1976] 1 WLR 141 at 144. Quaere, however, whether Lord Denning's formulation is not too wide. Cf per Scarman LJ at 103ff and 146ff. (Lord Denning's approach is incidentally, as he acknowledges in his judgment, not really consistent with *Iqbal v London Transport Executive*, discussed above.)
2 See Rose 'Liability for an Employee's Assaults' (1977) 40 MLR 420.
3 [1912] AC 716, HL.
4 Cf *Armagas Ltd v Mundogas SA, The Ocean Frost* [1986] AC 717, [1986] 2 All ER 385, HL. See also *Kooragang Investments Ltd v Richardson & Wrench Ltd* [1982] AC 462, [1981] 3 All ER 65, PC and comment by Tettenborn, 'Authority, Vicarious Liability and Negligent Misstatement' [1982] 41 CLJ 36.
5 See *Morris v CW Martin & Sons Ltd* [1966] 1 QB 716, [1965] 2 All ER 725, CA. Cf *United Africa Co Ltd v Saka Owoade* [1955] AC 130, [1957] 3 All ER 216, PC.
6 [1927] 1 KB 236, CA.
7 *Warren v Henleys Ltd* [1948] 2 All ER 935.
8 *Keppel Bus Co Ltd v Sa'ad Bin Ahmad* [1974] 2 All ER 700, [1974] 1 WLR 1082, PC.
9 [1957] AC 555, [1957] 1 All ER 125, HL.

master who has been held vicariously liable to a third party for the negligence of his servant can obtain an indemnity from the servant by virtue of an implied contractual obligation that the latter will use due care in the performance of his duties on the master's behalf.[1] The same result can be reached by awarding the master 100% contribution under the Civil Liability (Contribution) Act 1978, master and servant being joint tortfeasors.[2] In *Lister*'s case the House of Lords refused to countenance the implication into contracts of service of a term in favour of the employee that he would be indemnified by his master against the consequences of his own negligence, even though the master could be expected to carry insurance against the risk of liability to third parties brought about by carelessness on the part of his employees. The potentially disastrous consequences for employees in particular, and for industrial relations in general, if employers, or in practice their insurers exercising the right of subrogation, were to invoke the *Lister* principle led to legislation being considered to change the law as laid down by the House of Lords. In the event this was averted by a 'Gentlemen's Agreement'[3] whereby employers' liability insurers agreed that they would not seek to claim against employees under *Lister*. Interestingly the existence of this agreement, and the industrial realities which it reflected, has had repercussions on the *law itself* outside the immediate area of insurance with which it deals; and as a result it has had an impact upon subrogation claims by persons who were not themselves insurers and were therefore not parties to the agreement. In *Morris v Ford Motor Co*[4] it enabled the Court of Appeal, in a situation to which *Lister v Romford Ice & Cold Storage* did not directly apply, to avoid extending that decision and instead to imply a term into a contract between a negligent servant's employers, and another company. The indirect effect of that implication was, in the particular circumstances of the *Morris* case, to confer a degree of actual *legal* protection upon the servant from his being called upon to pay the damages which his carelessness had caused.

Independent contractors and non-delegable duties

The concept of non-delegable duty

[**18.15**] In *Salsbury v Woodland*,[5] Widgery LJ said:

'It is trite law that an employer who employs an independent contractor is not vicariously responsible for the negligence of that contractor. He is

---

1 For dicta suggesting that a relatively narrow interpretation be placed upon the precise scope of this implied contractual obligation, see *Harvey v R G O'Dell Ltd* [1958] 2 QB 78 at 106, [1958] 1 All ER 657 at 667 per McNair J.
2 See, eg *Semtex Ltd v Gladstone* [1954] 2 All ER 206, [1954] 1 WLR 945; *Harvey v RG O'Dell Ltd* [1958] 2 QB 78, [1958] 1 All ER 657 (both decided under the earlier Law Reform (Married Women and Joint Tortfeasors) Act 1935).
3 See *Morris v Ford Motor Co Ltd* [1973] QB 792, [1973] 2 All ER 1084, CA.
4 [1973] QB 79, [1973] 2 All ER 1084, CA.
5 [1970] 1 QB 324 at 336-337, [1969] 3 All ER 863 at 867, CA.

not able to control the way in which the independent contractor does the work, and the vicarious obligation of a master for the negligence of his servant does not arise under the relationship of employer and independent contractor. I think that it is entirely accepted that those cases - and there are some - in which an employer has been held liable for injury done by the negligence of an independent contractor are in truth cases where the employer owes a direct duty to the person injured, a duty which he cannot delegate to the contractor on his behalf.'

Although this statement, including its assertion that the general rule is one of non-liability for independent contractors, accurately represents the broad approach of the law in this area, a major unresolved problem is the precise delineation of the situations in which non-delegable duties are in fact owed by the employers of independent contractors. To hold the employer liable is effectively to make an exception to the general principle of no liability without fault.[1] One might therefore have expected that the situations in which non-delegable duties would be held to exist would simply be the same as those in which the law imposes strict liability even where independent contractors are not involved.[2] There are three reasons, however, why this test does not in fact provide a straightforward indication of the state of the law. First, the scope of strict liability itself is still the subject of considerable uncertainty and lack of clarity. Secondly, the courts have not, in fact, limited liability for independent contractors to established strict liability situations but have sometimes not hesitated to extend it, so as to give the plaintiff a further defendant,[3] in a manner which from the point of view of principle seems arbitrary and difficult to support.[4] Thirdly, the concept of non-delegable duty has sometimes been invoked by the courts in cases turning mainly upon 'true' vicarious liability for actual servants; particularly in situations involving alleged medical negligence in hospitals, and claims by employees against their employers for injuries suffered at work. The aim has been to overcome difficulties of various kinds within the law of vicarious liability itself; but the resulting overlap with, and use of concepts more familiar in, the independent contractor field has inevitably been a source of added complexity. As a result of the overall lack of clarity and principle in the law relating to liability for independent contractors it is necessary to consider separately the main types of situation within which the courts have invoked the concept of non-delegable duty.

---

1 Obviously, if the employer has been careless in choosing to employ a contractor whom he should have known was incompetent he will be personally liable for his own negligence in so choosing.
2 It is sometimes forgotten that *Rylands v Fletcher* (1868) LR 3 HL 330 itself involved carelessness on the part of the defendant's independent contractor. But the case was rightly treated as turning solely upon the presence or absence of strict liability, since the defendant had not himself been at fault.
3 Clearly the independent contractor will be liable for his own negligence; the temptation to hold the employer liable as well arises where the contractor is not worth suing or is already actually insolvent.
4 See Glanville Williams 'Liability for Independent Contractors' [1956] CLJ 180.

(i) Highways

[18.16] This is a context in which the general law relating to the imposition of strict liability is itself uncertain. In one much criticised decision of the Court of Appeal on the law of nuisance it was held that where 'premises on a highway become dangerous' the owner, if he is contractually obliged or entitled to repair, will be responsible for any resulting loss or injury 'whether he knew or ought to have known of the danger or not'.[1] In fact, however, most of the better known 'highway' cases have themselves actually involved independent contractor situations,[2] so that the scope for comparing such cases with those involving strict liability simpliciter, so to speak, is limited. But given that, for good or ill, it is established beyond doubt at common law that there is no liability without proof of fault for accidents actually occurring in the course of travel on the highway, it is far from obvious why other activities on or near the highway should warrant the imposition of a non-delegable duty upon the employers of independent contractors. Indeed when the matter was considered by the Court of Appeal in *Salsbury v Woodland*,[3] a restrictive approach to the scope of liability was adopted. The defendants employed an independent contractor to fell a tree in their garden. Due to the contractors' carelessness the tree fell against some telephone wires, which in turn fell on to the nearby road and caused an accident. The court refused to hold the defendants liable for the negligence of the contractors. Their Lordships indicated that only work undertaken actually on the highway itself, or work of an inherently dangerous nature, should lead to the imposition of liability.

(ii) Dangerous activities

[18.17] The concept of 'extra-hazardous' activity has been used to impose liability upon the employers of independent contractors. In the 1934 case of *Honeywill & Stein Ltd v Larkin Bros*[4] independent contractors were employed to photograph the interior of a cinema; a procedure which in those days required the ignition of magnesium powder on a metal tray. Owing to the contractors' negligence a fire was caused which damaged the cinema. The Court of Appeal held that the employers of the independent contractors would be liable to the cinema owners.[5] Their Lordships accepted that it was 'well established as a general rule of English law that an employer is not liable for the acts of his independent contractors' but asserted the existence of 'special rules which apply to extra-hazardous or dangerous operations'.[6] Of course if a situation which is perceived as one of special hazard happens to fit into a recognised category of strict

---

1 *Wringe v Cohen* [1940] 1 KB 229 at 223, [1939] 4 All ER 241 at 243, CA.
2 See, eg *Tarry v Ashton* (1876) 1 QBD 314; *Holliday v National Telephone Co* [1899] 2 QB 392, CA.
3 [1970] 1 QB 324, [1969] 3 All ER 863, CA.
4 [1934] 1 KB 191, CA.
5 See also *The Pass of Ballater* [1942] P 112. Cf *Brook v Bool* [1928] 2 KB 578.
6 [1934] 1 KB 191 at 196 and 200 per Slesser LJ delivering the judgment of the court.

liability, such as the rule in *Rylands v Fletcher* itself, then the imposition of liability for the negligence of independent contractors will be unexceptionable. Thus in *Balfour v Barty-King*[1] the Court of Appeal imposed such liability upon an occupier, from whose premises independent contractors had caused fire to escape resulting in damage to a neighbouring property. But in the well known case of *Read v J Lyons & Co*[2] the House of Lords expressly decided that the mere fact that an activity could be described as 'ultra hazardous' was not *by itself* sufficient to justify the imposition of strict liability. The elaborate factors which operate to limit the scope of such liability, such as the requirement of 'escape' under the rule in *Rylands v Fletcher*, also had to be satisfied. Since hazard depends upon context it would in any event, in the words of Lord Macmillan,[3] 'be impracticable to frame a legal classification of things dangerous and things not dangerous'. The proposition that employers should be liable for the negligence of their independent contractors, merely because the context is one of particular danger, therefore seems difficult to support.[4] No doubt powerful arguments can be advanced for the extension of strict liability, but such extension can only be achieved with a degree of certainty (which is particularly desirable so that potential defendants can know their insurance position) by some statutory mechanism.[5] Covert extension of what amounts to strict liability, by fastening on to the fortuitous employment of an independent contractor in the particular case, would appear in principle to be undesirable. It is accordingly submitted that the decision in *Honeywill & Stein v Larkin Bros*, which did not coincide with an independently recognised head of strict liability, is inconsistent with *Read v Lyons* and no longer represents the law.

(iii) Nuisance

[18.18] The scope of liability for independent contractors in nuisance is not altogether clear.[6] Such authorities as exist on the point do indicate, however, that this is an area in which the general negligence rule of non-liability is at least qualified if not rejected.[7] Thus, in *Matania v National Provincial Bank*[8] the defendants, who employed independent contractors to make alterations to their flat, were held liable by the Court of Appeal when dust and noise caused a nuisance

---

1 [1957] 1 QB 496, [1957] 1 All ER 156, CA.
2 [1947] AC 156, [1946] 2 All ER 471, HL.
3 Ibid at 172 and 477. See also Stallybrass, 'Dangerous Things and the Non-Natural User of Land' 1929 CLJ 376.
4 The proposition has been rejected by a majority of the High Court of Australia: *Stevens v Broadribb Sawmilling Co* (1985-86) 160 CLR 16.
5 See, eg the recommendations of the *Royal Commission on Liability for Personal Injury and Accident Compensation* (Pearson) (Cmnd 7054 vol) I ch 31.
6 For further discussion see Buckley *Law of Nuisance* (1981) pp 80-82.
7 Cf *Spicer v Smee* [1946] 1 All ER 489 at 495 per Atkinson J: 'usually a man is not liable for the default of an independent contractor . . . [but] in the law of nuisance an exception exists.'
8 [1936] 2 All ER 633, CA.

to a neighbour. The true principle is probably that the employer will only be liable either if nuisance is inevitable from the nature of the work which his contractor is employed to do, or if he fails to restrain the contractor when an obvious and continuing nuisance is being caused. The making, in such circumstances, of an exception to the general rule of no liability for the acts of independent contractors is not necessarily anomalous. The majority of nuisance cases involve, as did *Matania* itself, a continuing activity, unlike the typical negligence situation of sudden accidental damage. Since the defendant would be liable in nuisance if he did the work in the same objectionable way himself, the imposition of liability for his contractor would seem to accord with principle.

(iv) Hospitals[1]

[18.19] In *Cassidy v Ministry of Health*[2] Denning LJ expressed the view that a hospital owes a non-delegable duty of care to its patients. He was anxious to establish that hospital authorities would be liable when negligence occurred, especially in situations in which *teams* of medical staff had been involved: some members of which had been employed under contracts of service while others had been outside consultants acting in effect as independent contractors. Lord Denning's objective was to circumvent the possibility of hospitals avoiding vicarious liability either by invoking the 'control' test, so as to deny that such liability was capable of arising at all out of the carelessness of skilled professional people such as doctors,[3] or by exploiting the difficulty which plaintiffs in such cases will often have of identifying which individual member of the medical staff had actually been negligent; and hence of showing that the person concerned had been a 'servant' as distinct from an 'independent contractor'. Although the other members of the Court of Appeal, Somervell and Singleton LJJ, agreed with Denning LJ in finding for the plaintiff in *Cassidy*'s case, they actually based their decision on the narrower ground of orthodox vicarious liability. Nevertheless it seems not unlikely that Lord Denning's concept of a non-delegable duty does now represent the law where treatment in National Health Service hospitals[4] is concerned.[5]

[18.20] Related to, but not identical with, the question of whether hospitals should be subjected to a non-delegable duty giving rise to liability when normally competent doctors perform negligently, is the question whether hospital authorities can also be directly liable for

1   See Bettle 'Suing Hospitals Direct: Whose Tort Was It Anyhow' (1987) 137 NLJ 573.
2   [1951] 2 KB 343 at 359-365, [1951] 1 All ER 574 at 584-588, CA. See also *Roe v Minister of Health* [1954] 2 QB 66 at 82, [1954] 2 All ER 131 at 137, CA.
3   Cf *Hillyer v St Bartholomew's Hospital (Governors)* [1909] 2 KB 820, CA.
4   Different issues may arise where private hospitals are involved: cf *Yepremian v Scarborough General Hospital* (1980) 110 DLR (3d) 513.
5   The *Cassidy* approach has been followed in Australia: see, eg *Albrighton v Royal Prince Alfred Hospital* [1980] 2 NSWLR 542, CA.

inadequate treatment resulting from the underfunding and understaffing of their institutions. As has already been indicated in an earlier chapter,[1] in *Wilsher v Essex Area Health Authority*,[2] two members of the Court of Appeal expressed the view, albeit obiter, 'that there seems to be no reason in principle why . . . a hospital management committee should not be held directly liable in negligence for failing to provide sufficient qualified and competent medical staff'.[3] If, however, the alleged failure simply reflected overall financial difficulties any such claim would appear to face formidable problems relating to the justiciability of resource allocation decisions.[4]

(v) Injuries at work

[18.21] In certain circumstances an employer's duty with respect to the safety of his employees at their place of work may be non-delegable. This has recently been authoritatively reaffirmed by the House of Lords,[5] and has been discussed in an earlier chapter.[6]

(vi) Bailees

[18.22] It is sometimes said that the responsibility of bailees for reward towards the owners of the property bailed is capable of amounting to a non-delegable duty of care.[7] Thus garages entrusted with plaintiffs' motor cars have been held liable for damage caused by their servants in circumstances in which the servants in question were at least arguably acting outside the course of their employment, so that ordinary vicarious liability could not have been imposed.[8] The fact that bailment will often involve a contractual relationship between bailor and bailee, and that bailment is a concept of some antiquity in the law,[9] might account for what in terms of contemporary principle could appear anomalous. On the other hand, it has been forcefully argued that the concept of non-delegable duty is not in fact necessary to explain the relevant decisions. A servant wrongfully making use, on a journey of his own, of a car bailed to his master may legitimately be regarded as acting *inside* the course of his employment

---

1   Ie ch 15 above.
2   [1987] QB 730, [1986] 3 All ER 801, CA.
3   [1987] QB 730 at 775, [1986] 3 All ER 801 at 831 per, Glidewell LJ. His Lordship was agreeing expressly on the point with Sir Nicolas Browne-Wilkinson V-C. Mustill LJ found it unnecessary to express an opinion (see at 748 and 811). The point was not considered when *Wilsher's* case went to the House of Lords (see [1988] AC 1074, [1988] 1 All ER 871).
4   See, generally, ch 12, above.
5   See *McDermid v Nash Dredging and Reclamation Co Ltd* [1987] AC 906, [1987] All ER 878, HL.
6   Ie ch 14 above.
7   See *Morris v CW Martin & Sons Ltd* [1966] 1 QB 716, [1965] 2 All ER 725, CA, per Lord Denning MR at 722ff and 730ff.
8   See, eg *Aitchison v Page Motors Ltd* (1935) 154 LT 128, as explained by Lord Denning MR in *Morris v CW Martin & Sons Ltd* [1966] 1 QB 716 at 724-725, [1965] 2 All ER 725 at 730, CA. Cf *Chowdhary v Gillot* [1947] 2 All ER 541.
9   See, generally, Palmer *Bailment* (2nd edn, 1991).

with respect to the care of the vehicle itself, even if he would be acting *outside* it with respect to any damage caused to a third party in a road accident.[1]

'Collateral negligence'

[18.23] In *Penny v Wimbledon UDC and Iles*[2] the Court of Appeal imposed liability upon the employers of independent contractors in a case which involved the creation of a dangerous situation on the highway. Romer LJ said obiter, however, that he wished 'to point out that accidents arising from what is called casual or collateral negligence cannot be guarded against beforehand'[3] and that employers would not be liable for such negligence even in non-delegable duty situations. This 'principle' was apparently made the basis of the decision of the Court of Appeal in the difficult case of *Padbury v Holliday and Greenwood Ltd*.[4] The defendant builders employed sub-contractors to put in window-frames. One of the sub-contractors' servants carelessly left a tool on a window sill, from which it was blown by the wind on to the unfortunate plaintiff who was a pedestrian in the street below. The defendants were held not liable on the ground

> 'that before a superior employer could be held liable for the negligent act of a servant of a sub-contractor it must be shown that the work which the sub-contractor was employed to do was work the nature of which, and not merely the performance of which, cast on the superior employer the duty of taking precautions'.[5]

It is submitted, however, that this reasoning is difficult to follow.[6] If it be assumed, as it appears to have been in the *Padbury* case itself, that potentially dangerous activities on or very close to the highway are capable of giving rise to non-delegable duties, it is not easy to see why the employer should be exonerated from liability in the circumstances which arose. Providing that the person whose carelessness caused injury was acting in the course of his employment as a servant of the independent contractor, as he presumably was in the situation in *Padbury*, it should surely follow that the employers of the independent contractor will be liable. To hold otherwise is effectively to define the non-delegable duty out of existence in negligence cases. This is because independent contractors will normally be firms rather than individuals and hence will only be capable of negligence through the acts of their servants.[7] Significantly, in *Salsbury v Woodland*[8] Sachs LJ

1 See *Clerk and Lindsell on Torts* (16th edn, 1989) pp 219-220.
2 [1899] 2 QB 72, CA.
3 Ibid at 78.
4 (1912) 28 TLR 494, CA.
5 Per Fletcher Moulton LJ (as reported in the indirect speech of the Times Law Reports).
6 But cf *Street on Torts* (8th edn, 1988) p 455.
7 In *Padbury v Holliday and Greenwood Ltd* itself an action against the sub-contractors themselves, to which it is difficult to see that there could have been any defence, was discontinued (perhaps on grounds of insolvency).
8 [1970] 1 QB 324 at 348, [1969] 3 All ER 863 at 878, CA.

observed that he 'derived no assistance at all from any distinction between "collateral and casual" negligence and other negligence' and that 'such a distinction provide[d] too many difficulties for [him] to accept without question'. It is indeed submitted that the concept of 'collateral negligence' in this context is incoherent and that its use should be abandoned.[1]

'Agents'

Special type of non-delegable duty upon car-owners in certain cases

Terminology

[18.24] Vicarious liability for the negligence of others is not confined to situations involving servants acting in the course of their employment, and those involving independent contractors in the exceptional situations which have been outlined above. In a special line of cases liability has been imposed upon the owners of motor cars for the carelessness of persons whom they have permitted to drive their vehicles, in circumstances in which that driving was undertaken at least in part for the benefit of the owner in question and at his request.[2] Somewhat confusingly, the careless drivers have sometimes been termed the 'agents' of the owners for the purposes of this principle.[3] The cases typically involve social or domestic situations so that the drivers could not appropriately be labelled as servants or as independent contractors of the owner, but it is not obvious that the term 'agent' is any more appropriate. It is true that there is some *overlap* between the concept of agency as used in the law of contract, and that of vicarious liability in the law of tort. Thus an employer cannot be vicariously liable for his servant's deceit under the rule in *Lloyd v Grace, Smith & Co*[4] unless the servants act fell within his actual or ostensible authority as defined by the law of agency.[5] Nevertheless the two concepts are essentially different. As Eveleigh J observed in one case:[6]

> 'There is no general rule that a principal is liable for the acts of an agent performed for his benefit even though the acts are performed solely in the course of carrying out the project which the principal has commissioned. If that were the case, an independent contractor would involve his employer in liability as a general rule rather than exceptionally.'

---

1 But cf *Walsh v Holst & Co Ltd* [1958] 3 All ER 33 at 42, [1958] 1 WLR 800 at 814, CA per Sellers LJ (sed quaere).
2 Two of the earliest examples are *Samson v Aitchison* [1912] AC 844, PC and *Pratt v Patrick* [1924] 1 KB 488.
3 See, eg *Samson v Aitchison* [1912] AC 844.
4 [1912] AC 716, HL, discussed above.
5 *Armagas Ltd v Mundogas SA, The Ocean Frost* [1986] AC 717, [1986] 2 All ER 385, HL.
6 *Nottingham v Aldridge* [1971] 2 QB 739 at 749, [1971] 2 All ER 751 at 757.

Lord Denning MR put it in this way in *Launchbury v Morgans*:[1]

> 'The words "principal" and "agent" are not used here in the connotation which they have in the law of contract (which is one thing), or the connotation which they have in the business community (which is another thing). They are used as shorthand to denote the circumstances in which vicarious liability is imposed.'

Scope

[18.25] Until the more recent case of *Launchbury v Morgans* the best-known post-war decision concerning the 'agency' liability of motor-car owners was probably the decision of the Court of Appeal in *Ormrod v Crosville Motor Services Ltd*.[2] The defendant car owner, who was in Monte Carlo, arranged for a friend to drive the car to Monte Carlo to meet him. The driver was to visit friends of his own en route, but after he reached Monte Carlo the plan was for him and the defendant to go off on holiday together using the car. The driver was involved in an accident at the outset of his journey to Monte Carlo, before he had even left England, which was caused partly by his negligence. The defendant was held vicariously liable. Denning LJ said:[3]

> 'The law puts an especial responsibility on the owner of a vehicle who allows it out on to the road in charge of someone else, no matter whether it is his servant, his friend, or anyone else. If it is being used wholly or partly on the owner's business or for the owner's purposes, then the owner is liable for any negligence on the part of the driver.'

The *Ormrod* case was subsequently applied by the Court of Appeal in *Carberry v Davies*[4] in which a father anxious that his son, who was too young to drive, should gain some enjoyment from the family car, arranged for a friend to act as chauffeur. The father was held liable for the driving of the 'chauffeur' when the car was being used to take the son on a trip with his girl-friend. On the facts of the case the interest and involvement of the father in the particular expedition was not very immediate, to say the least, and Harman LJ was indeed moved to remark that the case was 'very near the line'.[5] More typical are cases in which the scope of this particular doctrine of vicarious liability has received a narrower interpretation. The mere fact that the driver is using the car with the owner's permission is certainly not enough in itself to make the latter liable.[6] In *Hewitt v Bonvin*[7] the Court of Appeal refused to hold a car owner liable for his son's negligent driving in circumstances in which the father had consented to the use of the car to take home two of the son's girl-friends.[8]

1 [1971] 2 QB 245 at 255, CA (the later reversal of the Court of Appeal in this case by the House of Lords does not affect the terminology).
2 [1953] 2 All ER 753, [1953] 1 WLR 1120.
3 [1953] 2 All ER 753 at 755, [1953] 1 WLR 1120 at 1123.
4 [1968] 2 All ER 817, [1968] 1 WLR 1103, CA.
5 Ibid at 819 and 1108.
6 A fortiori if the owner's permission was not obtained: see *Klein v Caluori* [1971] 2 All ER 701, [1971] 1 WLR 619.
7 [1940] 1 KB 188, CA.
8 See also *Rambarran v Gurrucharran* [1970] 1 All ER 749, [1970] 1 WLR 556, PC.

Launchbury v Morgans

[18.26] The line of cases extending vicarious liability to the owners of motor cars, albeit in limited circumstances, was prompted by the fact that the owner was more likely than the driver to be insured. In *Launchbury v Morgans*[1] Lord Denning MR,[2] in the Court of Appeal, attempted to take this underlying rationale nearer to its logical conclusion, by extending the scope of liability to cases in which the car was merely being driven with the owner's permission; thereby effectively eliminating the restrictive conditions relating to the owner's involvement in, and request that, the car be used for the particular purpose. The defendant wife permitted her husband to use her car. On one occasion it was involved in a serious accident while the wife was at home and the car had been taken by her husband on a 'pub crawl'. When the crash actually occurred the driving had been taken over by a friend of the husband, the latter having become too intoxicated. Imposition by the Court of Appeal of liability on the wife was unanimously overturned by the House of Lords. The House refused to sanction what would have amounted to a radical extension, on policy grounds, of vicarious liability. The potentially far-reaching implications in terms of insurance and resources meant that such a change in the law could only appropriately be made by the legislature, not by the courts.[3] On the other hand, none of the earlier cases, including *Ormrod v Crosville Motor Services Ltd*[4] itself, was actually overruled so it must presumably be taken that they are still good law, especially as the House undertook a fairly thorough general review of the authorities in this area. Nevertheless, it is clear that the principle in the earlier cases is unlikely to be extended. Thus in the 1981 case of *Norwood v Navan*,[5] the Court of Appeal refused to hold the owner liable for his wife's driving when she had taken the car out on a shopping expedition, notwithstanding that the purpose of the trip was partly to buy food for the family.

Other situations?

[18.27] In so far as the 'agency' cases can be said to be based upon any coherent principle, that principle would, at least in theory, appear to be capable of extending beyond situations involving the ownership of motor cars.[6] Indeed, the principle was used to impose liability in one

---

1 [1973] AC 127, [1972] 2 All ER 606, HL; rvsg [1971] 2 QB 245, [1971] 1 All ER 642, CA.
2 Edmund Davies LJ agreed with Lord Denning as to the result, but adopted somewhat narrower reasoning. Megaw LJ dissented.
3 See [1973] AC 127 at 137, [1972] 2 All ER 606 at 610 (Lord Wilberforce); 142-143 and 615-616 (Lord Pearson) and 151 and 622 (Lord Salmon).
4 [1953] 2 All ER 753, [1953] 1 WLR 1120, CA.
5 [1981] RTR 457, CA.
6 'The law ... is the same whether the chattel being used with the permission of its owner is a car or, for example, a gun or a tennis racquet': per Edmund Davies LJ in *Launchbury v Morgans* [1971] 2 QB 245 at 260, [1971] 1 All ER 642 at 651. See also per Eveleigh J in *Nottingham v Aldridge* [1971] 2 QB 739 at 750, [1971] 2 All ER 751 at 758: '... the motor vehicle is not in ... a special category.'

case in which, although it involved a motor car, the defendant was not the vehicle's owner but merely a willing passenger and contributor to the cost of petrol, the car having been stolen.[1] In another case, albeit one in which the claim failed on the facts, the application of the principle to careless driving of a luggage trolly was considered.[2] But given the hostility of the House of Lords to the creation of new categories of vicarious liability,[3] applications of the principle in fresh contexts will presumably in practice be extremely rare.

1 See *Scarsbrook v Mason* [1961] 3 All ER 767.
2 See *Norton v Canadian Pacific Steamships Ltd* [1961] 2 All ER 785, [1961] 1 WLR 1057, CA.
3 Ie in *Morgans v Launchbury* [1973] AC 127, [1972] 2 All ER 606, HL.

Part six

Tort, the state and the future

Chapter 19

Insurance and state provision

Introduction

[19.01] Although proof of negligence is usually a necessary condition, under the tort system, for the making of a monetary award to an accident victim, it is obvious that a wholly traditional account of the operation of the fault principle, in isolation from its broader social and financial context, would nowadays be seriously incomplete. There are two main reasons for this. Firstly, even where a plaintiff is successful in his negligence claim the damages, in the vast majority of cases, will not be paid by the defendant himself but by an insurance company. Indeed, uninsured defendants are seldom worth suing. A brief account of the impact of insurance in this area, with reference to the main statutory provisions in the road traffic and employment spheres, in which insurance is compulsory and which account for the great majority of tort claims, is therefore essential. The second reason for a broader account is that, looking at the problem of compensation for personal injury and disability as a whole, it is important to recognise that tort claims provide the background to only about one-quarter of the total amount of money paid out to accident victims. Apart from other sources (including victims' *own* insurance policies) which account for another quarter, the lion's share, *half* of the overall total, is provided by the state in various forms of welfare benefit.[1]

[19.02] It is obviously beyond the scope of a textbook on the law of negligence to give a full account of our now highly developed and complex social security system.[2] Moreover since, in the great majority of situations with which that system deals, the *manner* in which the injury or disability occurred is irrelevant, the very *basis* of the system

---

1 See the Report of the *Royal Commission on Civil Liability and Compensation for Personal Injury (Pearson)* Cmnd 7054-I, pp 12-13. It should be stressed that these proportions concern money actually paid out. As a percentage of all accident victims the figure for successful tort claimants is very much lower: about 6 ½%. See the Report, vol 1, p 24.
2 The leading work is Ogus and Barendt *The Law of Social Security* (2nd edn, 1982).

is fundamentally different from that of negligence.[1] There are, however, a number of areas of state provision in which the manner in which an injury or disability was *caused*, or at least the context in which it occurred, is of relevance to the making of an award. Since these could therefore be perceived as having a degree of similarity with tort, and because they are likely to be particularly relevant to situations in which the making of tort claims may also be considered, they require at least outline mention in a work of this kind. Those to be looked at will be the industrial injuries scheme, the vaccine damage payments scheme, and the criminal injuries compensation scheme. But the first topic to be considered will be the relevance of insurance to negligence cases.

The role of insurance

Negligence: appearance and reality[2]

[**19.03**] Until relatively recently it was considered to be improper for the court even to be told whether the parties to a negligence action were insured. Although it is probably safe to assume that this is no longer the case, due at least in part to the insistence of Lord Denning upon considering overtly the relevance of insurance in such cases during his long and influential judicial career,[3] it is noteworthy that the adoption of a more traditional reticence on the matter by leading counsel in one case received favourable judicial comment from the Court of Appeal as late as 1973.[4] On the other hand it is almost certainly true that, even when the presence or absence of insurance was supposedly shrouded in secrecy, its existence influenced covertly the development of the law.[5] For example, the objective, or 'reasonable man' test, for the presence of negligence means that liability will not infrequently be imposed upon defendants who have merely been unlucky, rather than blameworthy in any real sense.[6] If motorists and doctors, for example, had to look to their own resources to pay the huge sums often awarded against them, the imposition of liability would be both impracticable and morally objectionable. There is

---

1 Some critics argue that the social security approach is inherently preferable, and that it should be allowed to replace the tort of negligence altogether. For discussion, see ch 20, below.
2 See Martin Davies 'The end of the affair: duty of care and liability insurance' (1989) 9 LS 67.
3 See, eg *Lamb v Camden London Borough Council* [1981] QB 625 at 638, [1981] 2 All ER 408 at 414-415, CA.
4 See *Launchbury v Morgans* [1971] 2 QB 245 at 263, [1971] 1 All ER 642 at 654, CA, per Megaw LJ.
5 See Fleming James 'Accident Liability Reconsidered: The Impact of Liability Insurance' (1948) 57 Yale LJ 549.
6 See, eg *Nettleship v Weston* [1971] 2 QB 691, [1971] 3 All ER 581, CA (learner driver) and *Roberts v Ramsbottom* [1980] 1 All ER 7, [1980] 1 WLR 823 (stroke victim).

another reason why insurance can sometimes have the effect of causing the reality of negligence liability to differ markedly from its appearance. The exercise of the right of *subrogation*, whereby a plaintiff's own insurers can use his name even against his wishes[1] to sue the defendant who caused his injury, once they have recompensed him for his losses in accordance with the terms of his policy, is capable of producing in some cases an unreal situation in which neither of the nominal parties to the action is in truth conducting the litigation or is even interested in its outcome.[2]

New approaches?

[19.04] The factors outlined in the previous paragraph are among those which lend some support to the view that society should seek to move towards greater use of *first party* insurance, whereby people would be encouraged primarily to insure themselves and their income *directly* against losses arising through injury. Such insurance, whereby the premiums can be geared more precisely to the particular risk, is commonly supposed to be more efficient and less wasteful than *liability* insurance, the use of which underpins negligence: the latter being apt to give rise to high transaction costs, through settlement negotiations or litigation.[3] On the other hand it appears that liability insurance is not necessarily inefficient, given the right market circumstances.[4] Nor should the possibility that increased premiums, imposed through the medium of liability insurance, may have a beneficial effect upon accident prevention and safety, be wholly discounted or ignored.[5] Moreover, insurers, whose expertise lies in developing products in response to demand, created by such factors as the incidence of legal liability, can sometimes appear unsure what is required of them when invited by legal reformers to use their experience to make suggestions as to how the law itself should be changed.[6] As far as the existing common law is concerned there is an almost paradoxical sense in which the attitude of the judiciary towards insurance matters has come full circle. Instead of refusing to admit even the existence of insurance, the courts will now sometimes insist on deciding cases in such a way as to avoid disturbing the existing insurance framework; on the ground that any changes in that framework can only appropriately be achieved by legislative

---

1 See, eg *Lister v Romford Ice and Cold Storage* [1957] AC 555, [1957] 1 All ER 125, HL.
2 For a recent example see *Mark Rowlands Ltd v Berni Inns Ltd* [1986] QB 211, [1985] 3 All ER 473, CA. Cf *Hobbs v Marlowe* [1978] AC 16, [1977] 2 All ER 241.
3 For discussion see, generally, Atiyah *Accidents, Compensation and the Law* (Cane ed) (4th edn, 1987).
4 See Furmston (ed) *The Law of Tort* (1986) p 199 (E W Hitcham on 'Some Insurance Aspects'). See also 'The Law of Tort and Non-Physical Loss: Insurance Aspects' (1972) 12 JSPTL (NS) 119 at 174 (report of discussion of a paper presented to a Ford Foundation Workshop by A V Alexander).
5 See P J Sherman in 'The Pearson Report and Insurance' , pp 129-130, published in Allen, Bourn and Holyoak (eds) *Accident Compensation after Pearson* (1979).
6 See, generally, the papers of Hitcham and Alexander cited above, note 4. See also that by Sherman, cited in previous note.

intervention.[1] By far the most prominent sphere of existing legislative intervention is, of course, that of motor transport, to which we now turn.

Road Traffic Act

[**19.05**] The Road Traffic Act 1988, s 143(1) provides that:

> '(a) a person must not use a motor vehicle on a road unless there is in force in relation to the use of the vehicle such a policy of insurance ... in respect of third party risks as complies with the requirements of this Part of this Act, and
> (b) a person must not cause or permit any other person to use a motor vehicle on a road unless there is in force in relation to the use of the vehicle by that other person such a policy of insurance ... in respect of third party risks ...'

This well-known provision is intended to ensure that victims of negligence in motor accident cases do not go uncompensated, due to inability on the part of the driver responsible to meet the claim out of his own resources. Although the carrying of liability insurance by motorists has been compulsory for nearly 60 years[2] it was not until 1972 that it became obligatory for the cover to include *passengers* in the driver's own vehicle.[3] Since that year it has no longer been possible for drivers, and their insurance companies, to seek to exclude liability to passengers by causing a notice of disclaimer to be exhibited in the vehicle.[4] Nevertheless the statutory requirement does not extend to the carrying of liability insurance for injuries suffered by the driver himself. In *Cooper v Motor Insurers' Bureau*,[5] the owner of a motor cycle asked the plaintiff to road test it for him. Due to the owner's negligence the brakes failed and the plaintiff was very seriously injured. The question arose whether the owner had been under a statutory obligation to be insured against his liability to the plaintiff in such circumstances. The Court of Appeal held that, on the true construction of the Act, he had not. Cumming-Bruce LJ said:[6]

> '... it is clear that the obligation on the insured is to take out a policy covering him in respect of third party risks which, whatever ambiguity the phrase may have, clearly does not include the actual driver of the vehicle at the time of the use of the vehicle which gives rise to the damage.'

[**19.06**] If the situation is one to which the statutory obligation to insure applies, the Road Traffic Act 1988, s 151 provides, by way of a statutory exception to the doctrine of privity of contract, that the insurer will become directly liable to the victim to satisfy a judgment

1 See, eg *Morgans v Launchbury* [1973] AC 127, [1972] 2 All ER 606, HL.
2 It was originally introduced by the Road Traffic Act 1930.
3 See the Road Traffic Act 1988, s 145 (the provision originated in the Motor Vehicles (Passenger Insurance) Act 1971, s 1).
4 See the Road Traffic Act 1988, s 149.
5 [1985] QB 575, [1985] 1 All ER 449, CA.
6 Ibid at 580 and 452.

obtained against the policy-holder.[1] In certain circumstances this can apply even if the insurer would have had a valid defence if sued on the policy by the customer himself.[2] In such a case, however, the insurer is entitled to seek recoupment, of any damages which he has been compelled to pay, from the policy-holder. Accident victims are even protected, by virtue of an extra-statutory scheme which must now be considered, if the driver was uninsured or even unidentified.

The Motor Insurers' Bureau

[19.07] Making it a criminal offence for drivers to drive while uninsured, and also giving accident victims a direct statutory right against the driver's insurance company where he is insured, does not of itself assist the victims of drivers who, albeit in breach of the criminal law, in fact failed to take out insurance policies as required by the legislation. This gap is met by the extra-statutory device of an agreement between the Motor Insurers' Bureau, which is a body set up by insurers transacting motor vehicle business, and the Secretary of State for the Environment.[3] The agreement originally dates from 1946 but the version currently operative dates from 1988. The heart of it is to be found in the first two clauses as follows:

> '1. In this Agreement ... "relevant liability" means a liability in respect of which a policy of insurance must insure a person in order to comply with Part VI of the Road Traffic Act 1972.[4]
>
> SATISFACTION OF CLAIMS BY MIB
> 2. If judgment in respect of any relevant liability is obtained against any person or persons in any Court in Great Britain whether or not such a person or persons be in fact covered by a contract of insurance and any such judgment is not satisfied in full ... then MIB will ... satisfy ... the judgment ... '

Since this agreement is between the Bureau and the Secretary of State the doctrine of privity of contract could in theory be invoked to prevent accident victims, who are necessarily third parties, from enforcing it. But the Bureau has resolved never to take the point so that, notwithstanding occasional murmurs of judicial disquiet at being asked to give judgment in favour of parties who have no cause of

---

1 It is important to note that the insurer has to be given notice of the claim by the victim, if this right is to arise, within seven days of proceedings being commenced against the policy-holder: s 152(1).
2 See s 151(5) of the 1988 Act, but note that s 152(2) does entitle the insurer to avoid liability to the victim if the policy is voidable for non-disclosure or false representation. In the event of such avoidance the victim would have to claim from the Motor Insurers' Bureau, see below.
3 See D B Williams *Hit and Run and Uninsured Driver Personal Injury Claims* (4th edn, Chichester, 1983). See also Andrew Geddes 'Difficulties Relating to Directives Affecting the Recoverability of Damages for Personal Injury' (1992) 17 ELR 408 on issues, relevant to the Motor Insurers' Bureau, which arise out of attempts to harmonise the law relating to damages for personal injury within the European Community.
4 See now Pt VI of the Road Traffic Act 1988.

action,[1] the agreement in practice provides effective protection for accident victims in the situation with which it deals. It is important to note that the Bureau can and does take *other* defences which would have been available to an insurer sued directly by the policy-holder's victim under the Road Traffic Act.[2] In fact the Bureau is able to get itself added as a defendant in appropriate cases to ensure that relevant points are taken.[3] Of course, the effect of a victim's direct rights, under the Road Traffic Acts, against insurers will sometimes prevent the Bureau, just as it prevents insurers, from taking certain defences against the victim which could have been taken against an attempt by an actual policy-holder to sue his insurer. Thus in *Gardner v Moore*[4] the House of Lords confirmed that the Bureau would be liable where an uninsured driver *deliberately* injured his victim since, on the true construction of the Road Traffic Act, this risk was one against which drivers were obliged to be insured; nevertheless the principle that no one can profit from his own wrong would have prevented an insured driver from himself enforcing his liability policy in such circumstances.[5] The decision of the House on this point confirmed the well-known decision of the Court of Appeal, reached twenty years earlier, in *Hardy v Motor Insurers' Bureau*.[6] Finally, it is important to note that, just as in claims against insurers under the Road Traffic Act, the Motor Insurers' Bureau must be given notice of proceedings arising out of an accident within seven days of their commencement.[7] In one recent case the Bureau actually took the point by way of defence that such notice had not been given.[8]

Hit and run drivers

[**19.08**] It is somewhat surprising that, although the Bureau sometimes made ex gratia payments to victims in such cases, it was not until 1969 that the agreement between the government and the Bureau covered the serious problem of 'hit and run' drivers who are untraced. Until that year the contractual obligations of the Bureau were confined to situations in which an identified driver was either uninsured or in which his insurer had been able to deny liability. Now, however, a separate Agreement, which in its currently operative form dates from 1972, provides that the Bureau will also cover 'hit and run' situations.

---

1 See, eg per Viscount Dilhorne in *Albert v Motor Insurers' Bureau* [1972] AC 301 at 320, [1971] 2 All ER 1345 at 1354, HL.
2 See, eg *Randall v Motor Insurers' Bureau* [1969] 1 All ER 21, [1968] 1 WLR 1900.
3 See, eg *Gurtner v Circuit* [1968] 2 QB 587, [1968] 1 All ER 328, CA. Cf *White v London Transport Executive* [1971] 2 QB 721, [1971] 3 All ER 1, CA.
4 [1984] AC 548, [1984] 1 All ER 1100, HL.
5 Cf *Gray v Barr* [1971] 2 QB 554, [1970] 2 All ER 702; *Meah v Creamer (No 2)* [1986] 1 All ER 943.
6 [1964] 2 QB 745, [1962] 2 All ER 742, CA.
7 See cl 5(1) of the 1988 Agreement.
8 See *Cooper v Motor Insurers' Bureau* [1985] QB 575, [1985] 1 All ER 449, CA and see per Cumming-Bruce LJ at 581 and 452: 'I ventured in argument to describe that defence as meritorious but unattractive. But there is no answer to it.'

Employers' liability

[19.09] The Employers' Liability (Compulsory Insurance) Act 1969, s 1(1) provides as follows:

> 'Except as otherwise provided by this Act, every employer carrying on any business in Great Britain shall insure, and maintain insurance, under one or more approved policies with an authorised insurer or insurers against liability for bodily injury or disease sustained by his employees, and arising out of and in the course of their employment in Great Britain in that business . . .'

With the passing of this Act of 1969 the principle of compulsory liability insurance was extended to include employers.[1] Unlike the case of motor-accident victims, however, the injured employees are not given a direct statutory right of action against the employer's insurer, nor is there any institution similar to the Motor Insurers' Bureau to protect the employees of uninsured employers.[2]

Where the holder of a liability policy is insolvent

[19.10] If the holder of a liability insurance policy becomes bankrupt, or makes a composition order with his creditors, or if a company with such a policy is wound up or has a receiver appointed, 'his rights against the insurer in respect of the liability shall . . . be transferred to and vest in the third party to whom the liability was . . . incurred'. These words are contained in the Third Parties (Rights Against Insurers) Act 1930, s 1. This Act ensures that anyone who had a claim against an insolvent policy-holder, which comes within the terms of the liability policy, can claim directly from the insurance company. The object is to ensure that the proceeds go to the victim and do not simply become part of the general assets of the insured, and hence lost in the distribution to his creditors. It is important to realise that this valuable provision is not confined to situations in which the taking out of liability insurance is compulsory, but extends to all situations in which such a policy has in fact been taken out by a tortfeasor who becomes insolvent. Unlike the road traffic situation, however, the victim can never be in a better position against the insurance company than the policy holder himself would have been, so that any defences which would have been available to the insurance company against him will also be available against his victim.[3] Moreover, in *Bradley v Eagle Star Insurance Co Ltd*[4] the House of Lords held, by a majority,

---

1 For comment see Hassan (1974) 3 ILJ 79.
2 But employees are indirectly protected if the insurer who provided their employer's compulsory cover is in liquidation: see the Policyholders Protection Act 1975, s 6.
3 *McCormick v National Motor and Accident Insurance Union* (1934) 49 Ll L Rep 361, CA; *Post Office v Norwich Union Fire Insurance Society* [1967] 2 QB 363, [1967] 1 All ER 577, CA.
4 [1989] AC 957, [1989] 1 All ER 961, HL.

that the victim did not acquire any rights under the section against the insurers until the existence and amount of the tortfeasor's liability had been established.[1] In the case itself, which concerned an industrial disease, this had not been done and could not now be done directly since the company in question had been wound up many years before.[2] The plaintiff's claim was therefore not allowed to proceed even though trial of it would have been indistinguishable in practice from the great majority of such cases in which the effective defendant is an insurance company and the alleged tortfeasor is defendant in name only.[3]

Injury at work[4]

Background and structure

[19.11] The Workmen's Compensation Act of 1897 introduced a special scheme of compensation for those injured at work. It was originally paid for by employers themselves and had the great advantage over the common law, whose deficiencies no doubt helped to account for its introduction, that it was not necessary to prove negligence. With the expansion of general welfare provision made by the Labour government after the second world war, in the light of reforms recommended by the Beveridge Report, compensation for industrial injuries and diseases became part of what is now known as the Social Security system. The so-called 'industrial preference', whereby more generous treatment is accorded to work victims than to others, has been greatly eroded over the years consistently with the criticism of those who consider it wrong in principle that a welfare system should distinguish between recipients according to the context in which their particular misfortunes arose. Nevertheless, it has not yet been found politically practicable wholly to abolish the preservation, as a separate category, of compensation for industrial accidents and diseases and it still remains the case that certain work victims can enjoy a degree of preferential treatment within the social security system.

---

1 Ie in litigation or by agreement.
2 Since the decision of the House of Lords in *Bradley v Eagle Star Insurance Co* the position of claimants in such cases has been assisted by a change in company law which enables companies to be revived for the purpose of personal injury claims if they were dissolved up to 20 years earlier: see the Companies Act 1989, s 141. This provision, which is retrospective in effect, amends the Companies Act 1985, s 651 which only permitted revival within two years of dissolution.
3 Cf per Lord Templeman dissenting: 'The dissolution of the . . . company has no significance in the present case save that it enables the [insurers] to argue that they are not bound to pay in respect of a liability which they accepted and for which they were paid premiums.' [1989] AC 957 at 970, [1989] 1 All ER 961 at 968.
4 See, generally, Lewis *Compensation For Industrial Injury: A Guide To The Revised System Of Benefits For Work Accidents And Diseases* (1986, Abingdon).

Accidents and diseases

[**19.12**] The Social Security Contributions and Benefits Act 1992, s 94(1), re-enacting earlier legislation, provides that entitlement to benefit is dependent upon the employee suffering 'personal injury caused . . . by accident arising out of and in the course of his employment'. Over the years a large body of case law has been built up by decisions of National Insurance Commissioners as to which situations come within this phrase and which do not.[1] To establish that someone contracted a disease at work will usually be less straightforward than proving that he had an 'accident',[2] and diseases are therefore dealt with separately. Schedule 1 to the Social Security (Industrial Injuries) (Prescribed Diseases) Regulations 1985[3] provides a list of prescribed diseases and the occupations with which they are associated. There is then a rebuttable presumption that a claimant thus employed, who has developed a prescribed disease, did so at work.

Disablement benefit

[**19.13**] In recent years significant changes have been made to the industrial injuries compensation scheme, which have had the effect of further eroding the 'industrial preference' and of promoting an even closer relationship between the scheme and the mainstream of social security. With the abolition in 1990 of reduced earnings allowance, which provided compensation for those whose earning capacity had been reduced by injury at work, the main benefit peculiar to the scheme which still survives is Disablement Benefit. This represents what is, for social security, an unusual concept since it provides financial compensation for what is, at least in the way in which it is calculated, non-pecuniary loss. It is a benefit payable to industrially disabled people to reflect the loss of faculty caused to them by their disability, and is therefore not dissimilar in principle from the damages for loss of amenity recoverable in negligence at common law. An assessment is made on a percentage basis by comparing the claimant's condition with the position enjoyed by an able-bodied person,[4] and weekly payments are then made accordingly subject to a statutory maximum. Formerly assessments could be made of

---

1   For examples of cases in which such decisions have been considered by the High Court by way of judicial review see *R v Industrial Injuries Comr, ex p Amalgamated Engineering Union (No 2)* [1966] 2 QB 31, [1966] 1 All ER 97, CA and *R v National Insurance Comr, ex p Michael* [1977] 2 All ER 420, [1977] 1 WLR 109, CA.
2   But much difficulty has arisen in this field in distinguishing an 'accident' (or 'event') from a 'process': the latter not providing the basis for a claim unless it gives rise to a prescribed industrial disease. See Ogus and Barendt *The Law of Social Security* (3rd edn, 1988) p 259.
3   SI 1985/657.
4   See the Social Security (General Benefit) Regulations 1982 (SI 1982/1408).

disabilities as low as 1%, with the payments made for the lower degrees of disability usually being paid as lump sum gratuities rather than as weekly pensions. But the Social Security Act 1986 has provided that,[1] henceforth, there will be no entitlement to benefit for those injured in the future whose degree of disability is rated as being lower than 14%. Those whose disability is rated at between 14 and 20% will automatically receive the same level of benefit as those rated at 20%. The effect of this is that the making of lump sum payments will disappear.

Vaccine damage

[**19.14**] As a result of public concern over the plight of certain vaccination victims, on whose behalf it would be difficult if not impossible to prove negligence at common law, the Vaccine Damage Payments Act 1979 introduced an ad hoc scheme whereby tax-free lump sums can be paid to those whom vaccination in respect of certain diseases has left with very serious brain damage.[2] The 1979 Act itself fixed the level of the lump sum at £10,000, but the Social Security Act 1985, s 23 provided that that figure can be increased by delegated legislation, and it is currently £20,000.

Criminal injuries[3]

Basis of compensation

[**19.15**] Since 1964 there has been in existence a body known as the Criminal Injuries Compensation Board which administers an ad hoc scheme, not part of the social security system.[4] As originally set up,

---

1 See now the Social Security Contributions and Benefits Act 1992, s 103.
2 It should be noted that claimants are still required to prove *causation*, on a balance of probabilities, before a vaccine damage tribunal; and the figures for successful claims suggest that there may be disturbing discrepancies in the criteria adopted on this point by different tribunals: see Christopher Newdick 'Strict Liability for Dangerous Drugs in the Pharmaceutical Industry' (1985) 101 LQR 405 at 429 and references there given. Cf *Loveday v Renton* [1990] 1 Med LR 117, in which the High Court held in a negligence action that it had not been proved that pertussis whooping-cough vaccine was capable of causing brain damage.
3 It is appropriate to consider this topic briefly, notwithstanding that it concerns intentionally, rather than carelessly, inflicted injury. The fact that the criminal injuries sphere involves state provision based on the manner in which the injuries were *caused* makes it significant for present purposes (but intentional harm will, of course, usually be actionable within the tort of negligence on an a fortiori basis).
4 See David Miers *Compensation for Criminal Injuries* (1990); Desmond Greer Criminal *Injuries Compensation* (1991).

the Criminal Injuries Compensation Scheme was non-statutory and provided what was described as ex gratia compensation, but which came out of government funds included in the Home Office Vote.[1] In 1988, however, legislation was passed enabling the Board to be put on a statutory basis.[2] The Board entertains applications from victims, or the dependants of victims, of personal injury which is directly attributable to the commission, broadly speaking, of violent criminal activity.[3]

Nature of awards

[19.16] Compensation is assessed in accordance with the principles for the time being applicable to the assessment of damages[4] at common law. Awards are therefore made in respect of both pecuniary and non-pecuniary loss, although for the purposes of calculating pecuniary loss the earning capacity of the person who sustained the injury is 'taken not to be or to have been in excess of one-and-a-half times the gross average industrial wage'.[5] During the year 1991-92 the Board paid out in total more than £144 million in compensation.

Is the Scheme justifiable?

[19.17] The existence of the Criminal Injuries Compensation Scheme has been criticised[6] as being characteristic of the piecemeal approach to provision for the victims of personal injury, which is sometimes considered to have undesirably impeded the development of a system capable of dealing with victims in a manner unrelated to how their injuries were caused. On this view it might be considered irrational to single out the victims of criminal violence for especially generous treatment, distinct from that accorded by the welfare state to other victims of personal injury.[7] In the absence, however, of greatly improved state provision for all sufferers, it is submitted that the existence of the Criminal Injuries Compensation Board is justifiable. What is unusual about situations involving criminal violence is the particularly acute sense of grievance apt to be felt by the victim, combined with the exceptionally low degree of probability that compensation will in practice be recoverable from the criminal for

---

1   Even as a non-statutory body the Board was subject to the supervisory jurisdiction of the High Court exercised by judicial review: see *R v Criminal Injuries Compensation Board, ex p Lain* [1967] 2 QB 864, [1967] 2 All ER 770.
2   See the Criminal Justice Act 1988, ss 108-114, and Schs 6 and 7. See also Peter Duff 'Criminal Injuries Compensation: the Scope of the New Scheme' (1989) 52 MLR 518.
3   See the Criminal Justice Act 1988, s 109.
4   See the Criminal Justice Act, 1988, Sch 7, para 8.
5   See the Criminal Justice Act, 1988, Sch 7, para 10(1).
6   See Atiyah's *Accidents, Compensation and the Law* (Cane ed) (4th edn, 1987) ch 13.
7   Some victims of crime have another advantage over other sufferers from injury, in that they may benefit from the power of a criminal court to order compensation to be paid by the offender: see the Powers of Criminal Courts Act 1973 (as amended by the Criminal Justice Acts 1982 and 1988).

396 Insurance and state provision

what is obviously serious tortious conduct.[1] It is significant that a research study on the Scheme reported that 'victims saw compensation, whatever its source, as symbolic - a judgment about their offence and their suffering'.[2]

---

1 If the victim does succeed in obtaining common law damages any award from the Board has to be repaid.
2 See Appendix B (summarising research by J Shapland) to *Compensation and Support for Victims of Crime*, H C 43, Session 1984/85 (First Report of the House of Commons Home Affairs Select Committee, quoted in Hepple and Mathews *Tort Cases and Materials* (4th edn, 1991) p 929).

Chapter 20

Reform?

Criticisms of the existing system

Introduction

[**20.01**] Although the most radical proponents of reform of the law of tort occasionally suggest that the redress which it affords to those who suffer *property damage* should be abolished,[1] by far the greatest attention and criticism is focused upon compensation through the tort of negligence for *personal injury*. It is indeed beyond question that the operation of the law in this area is vulnerable to powerful criticism. While the various objections overlap, they can nevertheless be conveniently grouped under three main heads. The first is that tort is an extremely inefficient and wasteful system for compensating victims of personal injury. The second is that its operation, both in theory and in practice, is arbitrary and capricious. The third is that the spread of liability insurance, which shields tortfeasors in many situations from the financial consequences of their actions, has effectively deprived the tort of negligence of any moral basis which it might once have had.[2]

Inefficiency

[**20.02**] Probably the most striking condemnation of the law of negligence are the astonishing figures for the cost of its administration. Paragraph 83 of the first volume of the report of Lord Pearson's *Royal Commission on Civil Liability and Compensation for Personal Injury*[3] reads as follows:

> 'We estimate that the operating costs of the tort system amount to about 85 per cent of the value of tort compensation payments, or about 45 per cent of the combined total of compensation and operating costs.

---

1 See, eg Ison *The Forensic Lottery* (1967) ch 6. See also Atiyah's *Accidents, Compensation and the Law* (Cane ed) (4th edn, 1987) ch 25, pp 576-577.
2 Cf Donald Harris 'Evaluating the Goals of Personal Injury Law: Some Empirical Evidence' in *Essays for Patrick Atiyah* (Cane and Stapleton, eds) (1991).
3 Cmnd 7054-I.

Of these operating costs, about 40 per cent is accounted for by the costs of insurers in handling claims and on general administration. The remaining elements are the commissions paid by insurers to brokers and agents, claimants' legal fees, and profit. Each represents about a fifth. On small claims, the expenses can be greater than the damages paid.'

The same Commission reported,[1] by contrast, that the 'cost of administering social security benefits for injured people is about 11 per cent of the value of compensation payments, or 10 per cent of the cost of payments and administration'.

Arbitrariness

Great majority of accident and disease victims excluded

[**20.03**] The basic flaw in the law of negligence, if it is evaluated purely as a compensation system and without regard to other considerations, is the concentration, which by definition is central to it, upon the way in which a given injury or disability was *caused*. The overwhelming majority of disabled persons, possibly as high as 90%, are sufferers from disease and congenital handicap rather than victims of accidental injury.[2] Moreover, even among accident victims, 35 to 40% of the total have their mishaps in their own homes so that the making of negligence claims will rarely be feasible. The investigations of the Pearson Royal Commission revealed that the proportion of accident victims (themselves only a very small proportion of the disabled) which actually succeeds in obtaining tort compensation is the remarkably low figure of 6½%.[3]

Difficulties of proof

[**20.04**] In addition to the arbitrariness inherent in distinguishing between sufferers from disability on the ground of causation, the law of negligence can also operate capriciously between claimants, even within its legitimate sphere of operation, due to the differing degrees of difficulty which discharging the onus of proof may provide for plaintiffs. The difficulties are particularly acute where the accident happens very quickly, but it has recently been forcefully pointed out that they can also be severe where the disability occurs very slowly. The problems experienced where an accident takes place suddenly are, of course, typified by mishaps involving motor vehicles. The point was made vividly in para 991 of the Pearson Royal Commission,[4] which reads as follows:

---

1 See vol 1, para 121.
2 See Atiyah's *Accidents, Compensation and the Law* (Cane ed) (4th edn, 1987) ch 1.
3 See the Report of the Royal Commission (Cmnd 7054-I), para 78, Table 5.
4 Cmnd 7054-I, p 211.

'A retired county court judge told us that his "main difficulty in trying running down cases was the lack of certainty of the evidence. This uncertainty is largely attributable to the very nature of the accidents, the split second timing and the fallibility of the human brain in grasping accurate detail in a moment." Often the victim is in no position to look for witnesses himself. As one road accident victim, interviewed in a BBC television "Man Alive" report broadcast in May 1976, put it, "It's rather awkward if you're lying on the road with your leg sticking through your trousers".'

[20.05] The problems of proof presented by situations which develop very slowly are of a rather different kind. Stapleton has demonstrated, however, that the orientation of tort towards traumatic incidents means that it fails to deal adequately with a type of situation which should, in theory at least, be within its scope. The situation in question is that concerning industrial and other man-made diseases. The latency of many diseases, and the gradualness of their contraction, pose particular difficulties for the tort system as far as proof of causation, and problems such as limitation of actions, are concerned.[1]

Insurance and the moral basis of negligence

[20.06] Were it not for the existence of liability insurance the usefulness in practice of the tort of negligence would long ago have been reduced to vanishing point. There is little point in suing a defendant who would be unable to pay damages even if the litigation were successful. But once it is conceded that the defendant will not be obliged to pay the damages himself the justification for predicating liability only upon fault becomes less apparent. Indeed, as was pointed out in the previous chapter, use of the notion of the 'reasonable man' so as to render the test for fault 'objective' would in many cases be unacceptable; were it not for recognition of the fact that the defendant will not have to pay the damages himself, and that little or no stigma of personal culpability will attach to him. Only on this basis is it acceptable that accidents caused by learner drivers,[2] or stroke victims,[3] which the defendants in question could not have avoided causing, can give rise to tortious liability. The consequences of liability insurance for the conceptual integrity of the tort of negligence, and its associated effects upon the substantive law, have been well summarised by Professor J A Jolowicz:[4]

> 'The essential justification for the principle of liability for fault and its apparent logical corollary that, special cases apart, there should be no liability without fault, is to be found in ... ideas ... which belong to a morality which, for better or worse, is no longer capable of being given practical effect in any but exceptional cases.'

1 See Stapleton *Disease and the Compensation Debate*, (1986) chs 1–4.
2 See *Nettleship v Weston* [1971] 2 QB 691, [1971] 3 All ER 581, CA.
3 See *Roberts v Ramsbottom* [1980] 1 All ER 7, [1980] 1 WLR 823.
4 See 'Compensation for Personal Injury and Fault' in Allen (Bourn and Holyoak, eds) *Accident Compensation after Pearson* (1979, London) p 40.

Various proposals for reform

The Pearson Commission

Terms of reference

[**20.07**] The Royal Commission on *Civil Liability and Compensation for Personal Injury*, chaired by Lord Pearson, was set up in 1973, partly as a result of public concern over the Thalidomide tragedy, and reported in 1978. Its terms of reference were as follows:

> 'To consider to what extent, in what circumstances and by what means compensation should be payable in respect of death or personal injury (including ante-natal injury) suffered by any person–
> a. in the course of employment;
> b. through the use of a motor vehicle or other means of transport;
> c. through the manufacture, supply or use of goods or services;
> d. on premises belonging to or occupied by another or
> e. otherwise through the act or omission of another where compensation under the present law is recoverable only on proof of fault or under the rules of strict liability,
> having regard to the cost and other implications of the arrangements for the recovery of compensation, whether by way of compulsory insurance or otherwise.'

For the purposes of exposition in outline, the main recommendations of the Royal Commission can be divided into two parts. Firstly, their proposal for a special statutory scheme to compensate road accident victims and, secondly, their proposals for reform of the law of tort itself.

(i) Road accident scheme

[**20.08**] The Commission recommended that a special scheme should be introduced, within the social security system, to provide compensation, without the necessity of proving fault required by the common law of tort, for victims of road accidents. The scheme would have been modelled on the industrial injuries scheme,[1] which at that time provided more generous earnings-related benefits for those injured at work than are obtainable under ordinary social security welfare provisions, and which includes compensation for non-pecuniary loss in the form of payments for loss of faculty. The Commission proposed that the scheme should be paid for by all motorists through the medium of a levy on the cost of petrol. In 1991 the Lord Chancellor's Department outlined proposals for a limited scheme of no-fault compensation for victims of minor road accidents, in response to a suggestion made by the Civil Justice Review in 1988, but the proposals bore little resemblance to the Pearson

---

1 See ch 19 above.

recommendations. They would be funded not by a levy on petrol but through higher motor insurance premiums, and they would only allow victims to claim for personal injuries without proving fault up to a very modest limit of £2,500.[1]

(ii) Reform of tort

[20.09] The Commission recommended that benefits received by plaintiffs from the social security system should henceforth be fully offset against any damages in tort which they subsequently recovered. In effect the substance of this proposal was implemented, as far benefit entitlement for five years after the accident is concerned, by the Social Security Act 1989.[2] This implementation was *not*, however, combined with the introduction of a major scheme of greatly increased social security payments for victims of road accidents which Pearson had recommended. If it had been the result would have been a substantial disincentive to the mounting of litigation for negligence at common law in such cases. Two further recommendations were intended to deal with a widely held view that there is an unfortunate weighting in the tort system, whereby the less seriously injured are over-compensated and the victims of serious injury are under-compensated. The Commission proposed that, in order to help to remedy these difficulties, no damages for non-pecuniary loss (ie pain and suffering and loss of amenity) should be recoverable for the first three months after the injury. In the case of the seriously injured, changes should be made in the method of calculating their future pecuniary loss so as to ensure that the amounts which they were awarded would be more generous. The Commission also made the recommendation, which could if implemented have had the potential significantly to alter the operation of the law of tort, that unless he could satisfy the court that in his special circumstances a lump sum would be more appropriate, a plaintiff should be obliged to receive compensation for future pecuniary loss in the form of periodic payments. As has already been explained in an earlier chapter,[3] periodic payments made by way of out of court 'structured settlements' have become increasingly common in recent years so that part of the thinking behind this proposal has, in a sense, begun to be implemented in practice, albeit by a fortuitous route very different from that envisaged by Pearson. In addition the Commission recommended that certain situations should be identified by statute as involving exceptional risk, and that provision should be made for the imposition in such cases of strict rather than fault-based liability.

1 See Evlynne Gilvarry in (1991) Law Soc Gaz, 22 May.
2 See now the Social Security Administration Act 1992 and ch 8 above.
3 See ch 8 above.

Finally, it should be mentioned that the Commission also proposed the introduction of a system of strict liability for defective products.[1]

Criticism of the report

[**20.10**] Unfortunately, the report of the Pearson Commission met with a hostile reception from critics of many differing persuasions.[2] Such critics found common ground in perceiving that the report was fundamentally flawed by the lack of a coherent overall strategy. Those opposed to the preservation of tort as a compensation system for personal injury at all regretted the fact that the Commission placed a narrow interpretation upon its terms of reference; thereby preventing itself from considering the possibility of implementing a comprehensive accident compensation scheme, along the lines of that in New Zealand,[3] involving the abolition of tort in this area. Others considered that the somewhat casually advanced proposals for the extension of strict liability in tort had not been thought through, and that they had profound implications for the whole structure and philosophy of civil liability. The Commission seemed to be unaware of these implications, and indeed of their doubtful consistency with the main body of the report which contemplated the preservation of negligence as a necessary condition for the imposition of tort liability in the majority of cases. The singling out of road accident victims for a special compensation scheme, based on a generous regime of increased social security benefits, was criticised as an undesirably ad hoc proposal, unfair to those who suffer in other situations. It would increase rather than simplify the complication of the overall picture as regards compensation, and retard rather than advance progress towards comprehensive reform. The earnings-related benefits under the proposed scheme, to be paid for by a flat rate levy on petrol, would also have unduly favoured the better off at the expense of the less well off.[4] Although some of the less radical proposals have been put into effect,[5] albeit in modified forms, it is hardly surprising that, in view of the reception which the report received, the main thrust of the Commission's recommendations have not been implemented and the report seems destined to gather dust.

---

1 For the system ultimately introduced see ch 17 above.
2 See, generally, the papers collected in Allen, Bourn and Holyoak (eds) *Accident Compensation after Pearson* (1979), especially those by Professor J A Jolowicz and Professor P S Atiyah. See also Fleming 'The Pearson Report: Its "Strategy"' (1979) 42 MLR 249.
3 See below.
4 See D R Harris 'An Appraisal of the Pearson Strategy' in Allen, Bourn and Holyoak (eds) *Accident Compensation after Pearson* (1979).
5 See the Administration of Justice Act 1982, and chs 7, 8, and 9 above. Of course a system of strict liability for defective products has now also been introduced: see ch 17 above.

The New Zealand Scheme

[**20.11**] By far the most radical reform in this area, in any common law country, was introduced in New Zealand in 1972.[1] It took the form of a comprehensive state compensation system for those who suffer personal injury as a result of accidents, provided compensation for both pecuniary and non-pecuniary loss, and actually abolished the common law tort action for such accident victims. The relevant legislation is now to be found in the country's Accident Rehabilitation and Compensation Insurance Act of 1992. This Act makes substantial changes to the nature of the scheme, which in its relatively generous original form was apparently proving difficult to fund, and reduces the benefits which it provides. The new scheme in practice resembles a compulsory insurance system. Premiums are paid by drivers, medical personnel, employers and earners. The scheme also derives income from a levy on the price of petrol and from general taxation. Claimants who suffer lost earnings as a result of their injuries are awarded 80% of their losses, on a periodic payments basis, up to a statutory maximum. But the lump sum payments for non-pecuniary loss such as pain and suffering, which the Scheme originally provided, have been abolished and replaced by an 'Independence Allowance' where a claimant suffers a degree of disability of at least 10%. The scheme is administered by the Accident Rehabilitation and Compensation Insurance Corporation and is relatively straightforward to operate; the victim making his claim by seeing a doctor and filling out an official form, copies of which are readily available. It is possible to challenge, ultimately in the courts, rejection of a claim.

[**20.12**] Even in its modified form the New Zealand Scheme represents a bold experiment,[2] but it is limited in its scope: being largely confined to 'accidents'[3] and 'medical misadventures'[4] and not extending to those who suffer disability as a result of disease, except through 'occupational disease'.[5] The cost implications of extending it to all disabled people proved prohibitive even for the Scheme in its original form. Moreover, the funding difficulties which the Scheme has experienced only serve to highlight the obvious point that providing compensation to everyone affected by injury or illness, on the same scale as tort provides for a 'lucky' few accident victims, is always likely to be beyond the capacity of any country's economy. But in so far as the New Zealand Scheme preserves discrimination between the

---

1 See Harris 'Accident Compensation in New Zealand: A Comprehensive Insurance System' (1974) 37 MLR 361. See also vol 3, ch 10 of the Report of the Royal Commission on *Civil Liability and Compensation for Personal Injury (Pearson)* (Cmnd 7054-III) vol 1, ch 10 and Holyoak in Allen, Bourn and Holyoak (eds) *Accident Compensation after Pearson* (1979) pp 180-196.
2 For a review of the early years of the Scheme's operation see Ison, *Accident Compensation. A Commentary on the New Zealand Scheme* (1980).
3 See the Accident Rehabilitation and Compensation Insurance Act 1982, s 3.
4 See ibid, s 5.
5 See the Accident Rehabilitation and Compensation Insurance Act 1982, s 7.

disabled, based on the *cause* of their disabilities, it necessarily falls short of the ideal of those who wish to see such discrimination disappear. On the other hand, the more conservatively minded will have doubts about the wisdom, or acceptability in this country, of outright abolition of the common law action for negligence in the majority of personal injury cases. It is to be noted that one member of the Pearson Commission has observed that, even if it had not felt constrained by its terms of reference, it is doubtful whether the Commission would have recommended a scheme along the New Zealand lines for the United Kingdom.[1] Even in New Zealand itself concern has been expressed about the 'moral hazard' effect upon those who would otherwise be defendants, of removing the right to sue for negligence, particularly in the area of medical mishaps.[2]

Proposals by members of the Oxford Centre for Socio-Legal Studies

[**20.13**] In the period 1976-79 the Centre for Socio-Legal Studies at Wolfson College, Oxford (a research unit of the Economic and Social Science Research Council) carried out a major survey of victims of illness and injury, involving several thousand such people. The results of the survey, and the recommendations of the research team, were published by Oxford University Press in 1984 in a volume entitled *Compensation and Support for Illness and Injury*. Unlike that of the Pearson Royal Commission, the Oxford inquiry was frankly intended from its inception to shift the focus of attention away from the causes of *accidents* and towards 'the *consequences* of mental and physical disabilities, whether temporary or permanent'.[3] Although it was already well known that those disabled by illness greatly outnumber those who suffer serious accidental injury, the inquiry produced results which highlighted the differing long-term effects of the two kinds of misfortune: victims of illness being overall more likely than accident victims to suffer long-term incapacity. It also produced striking evidence of the inbalance within the tort system itself as regards different categories of accident victim. It to some extent weakened the case for singling out road accident victims for specially generous treatment, as Pearson had recommended, by emphasising that they are already the most successful category of accident victims under tort. Thus, between one quarter and one third of those injured in road accidents recover tort damages. The equivalent proportion of those injured at work is around one fifth. But the proportion of victims of other types of accident who succeed in tort, albeit including those who would presumably have had little or no chance of proving negligence, is less than one in fifty. As far as the relative consequences

---

1   See Marsh 'The Pearson Report on Civil Liability and Compensation for Death or Personal Injury' (1979) 95 LQR 513 at 517.
2   See citations in Margaret A McGregor Vennell and Joanna Manning 'Accident Compensation' [1992] NZ Recent Law Review 1, pp 6-7.
3   Harris et al *Compensation and Support for Illness and Injury* (1984) p 3.

of accident and illness are concerned it appears that victims of illness, consistent with their greater tendency to suffer from long-term incapacity, use the 'benefits in kind' provided by social services, such as help in the home, nearly three times as much as do victims of accident; the elderly, inevitably, make particular use of these services. It also appears that illness is responsible for twice as much absence from work as is accident.

[20.14] On the basis of their findings, the Oxford group recommended that 'the future policy-maker should plan to phase out all existing compensation systems which favour accident victims (or any category of them) over illness victims',[1] and hence that the tort action should be abolished in this area. Thus *cause* should cease to be a relevant factor in awarding compensation for illness and injury, and benefits should instead be based entirely on *need*. The *financing* of the compensation scheme should, however, 'incorporate some measure of risk relationship',[2] possibly by differential levies on employers with bad accident records for example. The administration of the compensation system would inevitably be primarily a matter for the state, but there could still be scope for the private sector both in financing parts of the scheme, particularly where relatively short-term losses were involved, and in providing top-up insurance for those who wanted it. In particular the private market could have a role in insuring against non-pecuniary losses such as pain and suffering; since the group assumed that public funds would not be available to compensate for such losses, at least for the foreseeable future. The essential strategy of the Oxford group was therefore to press for *income-support*, for all victims of illness and accident, as the highest public priority in this area. Thus benefits would be earnings-related for earners; particular importance being attached to restricting 'the extent to which disabled people are forced to rely on means-tested (supplementary) benefits'.[3] The new scheme should also be weighted to ensure a greater concentration of resources on the provision of benefits to the relatively few long-term disabled rather than those whose losses are short-term. The group thus concluded as follows: 'We believe that the damages system for death and personal injury should be abolished as soon as improvements in sick pay and social security provision produce a rational, coherent, and integrated system of compensation for illness and injury.'[4]

Focus upon disease

[20.15] An important contribution to discussion of reform in the present area is that by Dr Stapleton in her book, *Disease and the Compensation Debate*, published by Oxford University Press in 1986. Stapleton powerfully demonstrates the deficiencies of tort in dealing

1 Ibid, p 327.
2 Ibid, p 341.
3 Ibid, p 338.
4 Ibid, p 328.

with cases of man-induced disease where, in theory at least, a negligence remedy should sometimes be available. She agrees with the long-term goal of the Oxford group, discussed above, that a needs-based scheme providing for all victims of disablement regardless of cause should be introduced. She does, however, make the ingenious tactical suggestion that, in the short-term, this goal could be promoted by increasing the social security benefits paid to victims of disease and leaving in place, for the time being, the existing tort system and other benefits for victims of traumatic injury. This strategy, 'which turns conventional reform wisdom on its head',[1] would be designed to avoid offending vested-interests and eventually to generate public pressure for a comprehensive scheme. The idea is to overcome the difficulty which faces those who press for the *immediate* implementation of such schemes: namely that the inevitable *reduction* in compensation paid to successful claimants in tort, is likely to generate opposition. Since she adopts *needs-based* comprehensive reform as the ultimate objective Stapleton believes that compensation for non-economic losses, such as pain and suffering and loss of amenity, should ultimately be phased out.[2] She does, however, also face up rigorously to the implications of adopting an approach to reform which is devoted to compensation for pecuniary losses. Just as distinguishing between the *disabled* by focussing upon causation has come to seem arbitrary, if relief of poverty is to be the primary objective of the compensation system might not distinguishing between the *poor* according to whether or not they happen to be disabled also be perceived as arbitrary? Disablement is certainly not the only source of poverty. Stapleton hints that a widespread intuitive belief that preference should be given to the disabled probably exists but concedes that, logically, to a reformer intent on rationality that cannot, in itself, be a justification.[3] Indeed, the possible existence of an intuitive attraction in distinguishing between traumatic and non-traumatic injury, and drawing the line at *that* point, is of course one of the arguments which can be advanced by the conservatively-minded in favour of preserving some kind of tort system.

Possible changes in the burden of proof

[**20.16**] A reform sometimes proposed by those who wish to see the operation of the law of tort improved rather than abolished is to alter the burden of proving negligence in certain situations. Thus the Pearson Commission noted[4] that as early as 1932 a Bill was introduced into Parliament, with government support, to reverse the burden of proof in situations in which cyclists or pedestrians were killed or injured in accidents involving motor vehicles. The Bill did

---

1 Op cit, p 155.
2 Ibid, pp 157-158.
3 See ibid, pp 178ff.
4 See the Royal Commission on *Civil Liability and Compensation for Personal Injury* Cmnd 7054-I, paras 1069-1075.

not, of course, become law but some members of the Royal Commission were apparently impressed by the arguments in favour of such a measure. It is in the road accident field that the operation of the law of negligence is popularly supposed to be particularly unsatisfactory. A considerable proportion of the notoriously high administration costs of tort are probably probably accounted for by the problems of proof in such cases, and the scope for dispute to which they give rise. It would be reasonable to suppose that a reversal of the burden of proof against drivers of motor vehicles, in cases involving collisions causing injury to other road users, would increase the number of claims settled without trial and promote settlements on terms more favourable to the non-motorist accident victim. Ultimately, the Pearson Commission came down against recommending such a change, however, on the ground that it would cut across their plan for introducing a comprehensive scheme of compensation for road accident victims outside tort. But the Commission nevertheless noted that such 'a reversal of the burden of proof appears to operate satisfactorily in more than one European jurisdiction'.[1] Moreover, such a reversal also operates in the common law jurisdiction of Ontario. Section 167 of Ontario's Highway Traffic Act[2] is worth setting out in full:

'(1) When loss or damage is sustained by any person by reason of a motor vehicle on a highway, the onus of proof that the loss or damage did not arise through the neglect or improper conduct of the owner or driver of the motor vehicle is upon the owner or driver.

(2) This section does not apply in case of a collision between motor vehicles . . . nor to an action brought by a passenger in a motor vehicle in respect of any injuries sustained by him while a passenger.'

It is submitted that, notwithstanding the view of the Pearson Commission, the possibility of introducing a provision of this kind into England merits further consideration.[3]

Extension of strict liability

[20.17] A more far reaching attempt to preserve and yet radically reform the law of tort, than merely altering the burden of proof in some cases, might be to extend and restructure the incidence of strict liability. This ought to reduce the amount of litigation caused in negligence by the need to prove fault, at least provided the fault issue was not allowed too readily to re-enter through the back door via defences such as contributory negligence.[4] But a badly structured regime of strict liability could lead to an increase in litigation if too much scope existed for demarcation disputes as to which situations

---

1 Ibid, para 1072.
2 RSO 1980, ch 198. See now RSO 1990 ch 8, s 193.
3 See Fleming 'The Pearson Report: Its "Strategy" ' (1979) 42 MLR 249 at 262.
4 See Jolowicz 'Compensation for Personal Injury and Fault' in Allen, Bourn, and Holyoak (eds) *Accident Compensation after Pearson* (1979) pp 60-61.

did, and which did not, attract the liability.[1] A rationale for the extension of strict liability has been put forward by a number of economic analysts, in particular Professor Calabresi[2] in America, who advocate it as a vehicle for helping to ensure that the full costs of risk-creating activities are 'internalised': that is to say, placed on the shoulders of those who benefit from the activities in question. In theory, it is argued, such an approach could help to deter the creation of avoidable danger through the operation of the price mechanism. There are, however, considerable obstacles in the path of full acceptance of this particular justification for the imposition of strict liability, not least the many other factors which can influence the operation of the market and thereby greatly diminish the significance of the imposition of legal liability for damage caused.[3] Moreover, any regime of strict liability based on presumed attribution of risk, or 'enterprise liability' as it is sometimes called, could raise difficult questions of causation and of which risks should be attributed to which activities.[4] The Pearson Commission[5] put forward proposals for the introduction by statute of schemes of strict liability for activities and situations regarded as particularly hazardous, but these have not been implemented. Nevertheless the recent introduction by statute of a strict liability regime for defective products[6] constitutes a major reform of the law away from negligence principles. Indeed, despite the potential difficulties involved, and without subscribing to the intricate economic theories advanced by some of its supporters, it is possible to see considerable attractions in the extension of strict liability as an appropriate strategy for reform of the law, in a manner fundamentally different from the abolition of tort and its replacement by state welfare provision. As Professor JA Jolowicz has written:[7]

> 'Accidents will continue to happen despite the exercise of care by all concerned; it is essential that we learn to accept responsibility for the consequences of our decisions and our actions, not only of our faults, and that lesson a properly constructed system of civil liability, but not a system of social security, can help to teach us.'[8]

---

1 See Atiyah 'What Now?' in Allen, Bourn, and Holyoak, (eds) *Accident Compensation after Pearson* (1979) pp 234-238.
2 *The Cost of Accidents: A Legal and Economic Analysis* (1970, Yale University Press).
3 See, generally, Atiyah's *Accidents, Compensation and the Law* (Cane ed) (4th edn, 1987) ch 24
4 See Stapleton *Disease and the Compensation Debate* (1986, Oxford) chs 5 and 6. She writes: 'Ironically . . . the distinction between risks to be ascribed to the enterprise and those which are not, still falls to be decided in complex and costly case by case assessments of attribution/responsibility, etc. comparable to those which the shift to strict liability was designed to avoid.'(ibid, p 95). See also Ison, *The Forensic Lottery* (1967, London) pp 37-41; Henderson 'The Boundary Problems of Enterprise Liability' (1982) 41 Maryland LR 659.
5 Royal Commission on *Civil Liability and Compensation for Personal Injury*, (Cmnd 7054-I) ch 31.
6 See ch 17 above.
7 'Compensation for Personal Injury and Fault' in Allen, Bourn, and Holyoak (eds) *Accident Compensation after Pearson* (1979) p 78.
8 See also Professor Jolowicz's article, 'Liability for Accidents' [1968] CLJ 50.

Conclusions

[20.18] In one respect the law of negligence resembles the House of Lords in its legislative capacity. Almost everyone agrees that reform is necessary, but agreement as to what form it should take is infinitely more difficult to achieve. Apart from any other considerations the appallingly high administrative costs of tort in personal injury cases render the status quo indefensible. More fundamentally, however, two questions underly the reform debate. First, is it ever legitimate to distinguish between victims of misfortune according to the manner in which their plight was *caused*? Secondly, is it desirable to *abolish* civil liability (whether fault-based or not) for personal injury? The answers to both questions will necessarily be subjective and that to the second, in particular, is likely to reflect political preferences.

[20.19] It is clear from the way in which public pressure has led to the creation of ad hoc compensation schemes in particular situations, and the response to charitable appeals following major disasters, that greater sympathy is felt for some sufferers from misfortune than for others. Admittedly this is probably due in part to the publicity given by the media to particularly dramatic cases. Nevertheless, it seems not improbable that the sudden trauma of disability through accident is genuinely more likely to evoke feelings of anger and concern, on the part of the immediate victim and others, than the slower development of equivalent disabilities by natural causes. Part of this reaction may be due to a retributive instinct[1] which some reformers are apt to regard as primitive, or even attempt unconvincingly to explain away by arguing that it is a response which reflects the concepts of the legal system rather than the other way round.[2] Obviously, the law should not give effect to all the prejudices, for want of a better expression, which may be discernible in the popular will. But nor can it afford wholly to ignore public opinion on matters which arguably reflect fundamental intuitions. In the view of the present writer it remains appropriate for the law to distinguish, broadly speaking, between 'accident' victims and others.[3]

[20.20] The fallacy inherent in the 'abolitionist' thesis is the assumption that the provision of compensation is the sole social

---

1 Cf Ehrenzweig 'A Psychoanalysis of Negligence' (1953) 40 Northwestern Univ LR 855.
2 See, eg Lloyd-Bostock 'Fault and Liability for Accidents: the Accident Victim's Perspective' in Harris et al *Compensation and Support for Illness and Injury* (1984, Oxford) ch 4.
3 The impossibility of wholly eliminating intuitive preferences in this area is intriguingly illustrated by the fact that the Oxford group, which otherwise favoured uniform treatment for all the disabled, was prepared to admit that *one* exception might be justified, namely 'battle casualties, that is, the provision of special pensions for those injured in actual armed hostilities, which is the exceptional situation where society may compel citizens to be the front-line of defence against large-scale, organized attack'. Harris et al *Compensation and Support for Illness and Injury* (1984, Oxford) p 336.

function, or at any rate the only one of any value, served by the law of negligence. The fact that only tiny numbers of cases reach trial, and that in many instances insurance companies can effectively choose which ones will do so,[1] does not detract from the fundamental importance of the preservation in a free society of the right of any citizen for his own purposes to sue, or even with appropriate attendant publicity merely to *threaten* to sue, in the independent courts of the country, the government itself or any individual or organisation whose actions he believes have caused him harm.[2] Moreover, even on specific issues such as the quantum of damages in personal injury cases, decisions reached by the courts can provide a valuable benchmark against which the levels of benefit provided by the welfare state can be judged, even though the impossibility of providing compensation at tort levels for all is admitted. It is noteworthy that the abolition of tort is usually opposed by trades unions. This is sometimes derided as simply reflecting a desire to preserve an inducement to membership by providing legal services. But this reaction seems too cynical; it has been rightly dismissed as 'turning history on its head'.[3] The arguments were well put by in 1979 by the Legal Officer of the General and Municipal Workers' Union as follows:[4]

> 'The practical advantages ... of retaining the right to make a common law claim alongside a satisfactory state system are at least three-fold. First, it is usually difficult to make breakthroughs in a state scheme to include illnesses not previously accepted as employment-caused, e.g. radiation cases. The advantage of a tort claim is that individuals backed by their unions can establish a causal link, get publicity and thus put pressure on the state scheme to keep it up-to-date. This may be particularly necessary when the state or a state corporation is the employer concerned. Secondly, a worker may want to establish that his employer was to blame for his illness or disability. Even a good state system of compensation with some degree of differential contributions is unlikely to apportion blame to an individual employer. Thirdly, in cases of unjust refusal of benefit a worker has another avenue through which he or she may obtain compensation.'

[**20.21**] What then is to be done? It is submitted that the main objective of reform of the law itself should be to bring about some reduction in the role of negligence, by development of strict liability for personal injuries in various defined categories. Attention might also usefully be given to the possibility of reversing the burden of proof in negligence for some situations. In a few special areas, of which that involving medical accidents is perhaps the most conspicuous, it may be appropriate to develop compensation systems

---

1 See, generally, Hazel Genn *Hard Bargaining* (1987).
2 Cf Linden 'Tort Law as Ombudsman' (1973) 51 Can Bar Rev 155.
3 See Tess Gill 'Pearson: Implications for Victims of Industrial Accidents' in Allen, Bourn, and Holyoak (eds) *Accident Compensation after Pearson* (1979) p 158.
4 See previous note, and the page reference there given.

independent of legal process.[1] At the same time efforts should be made to improve the *accessibility* of legal services by, for example, more energetic development of insurance schemes to cover the expense involved and, possibly, by the development of other forms of private sector funding. As far as the welfare state itself is concerned, the prevailing political and economic climate seems currently to favour radical re-thinking on the allocation of available resources. The focus upon the relationship between tort and the social security system, which has been a feature of much writing upon accident compensation in recent times, has left tort lawyers better equipped to contribute to this important debate than would have been their forbears of a couple of generations or so ago.

---

1   In 1989 the British Medical Association published proposals for a 'no fault' scheme for medical mishaps, and the possibility of reform in this area received further public attention in 1990 when a Private Member's Bill (sponsored by Ms Rosie Barnes, then Independent SDP MP for Greenwich) also put forward proposals. In addition the government announced in 1991 that it would examine the feasibility of introducing a limited arbitration scheme for medical cases, but this would be negligence-based: see Michael Jones 'Arbitration for Medical Negligence Claims in the NHS' (1992) 8 PN 142.

Index

Accidents
 compensation–
  medical accidents, for, 20.21
  proportion of victims obtaining, 20.03
 fatal. *See* DEATH
 industrial injuries compensation scheme, 19.12
 road, disclaimer of liability for, 4.04
 victims, social security paid to, 19.01
Accountants
 reasonable skill and care, professional duty of, 15.26
Administrative law
 unreasonableness in, 12.16
Advocates
 immunity, 1.13, 1.17, 5.08, 15.14
 abuse of process, 5.11
 Bar, not confined to, 5.09
 narrow interpretation of, 5.10
Agricultural products
 defective products, exclusion from, 17.20
Arbitrators
 negligent misstatement, immunity from, 5.13
Assault
 vicarious liability for, 18.13
Assumption of risk. *See* VOLENTI NON FIT INJURIA
Auditors
 negligent misstatement, third party claims in, 5.19-5.22
 reasonable skill and care, professional duty of, 15.26

Bailees
 non-delegable duty of care, 18.22
Breach of statutory duty
 Act, scope of–
 class, protection of, 13.06
 risk, need for harm to be within, 13.07
 statutory undertakers, protection of, 13.08
 actions for damages–
  existing law of negligence, not confined to, 13.04, 13.05
  old cases, 13.02
  presumption as to lying of, 13.13
  scope of law, 13.01
  social issues, 13.01
  tort of negligence applying to, 13.01
 assumption of existence of civil liability, 13.12
 background, 13.02
 civil liability, legislative intention as to, 13.03
 contributory negligence, defence of, 13.17
 employers' liability. *See* EMPLOYERS' LIABILITY
 fault, relevance of–
  appropriate imposition of liability, 13.15
  avoidance of liability, 13.14
  strict liability distinguished, 13.16
 no offence committee, imposition of civil liability on, 13.18
 penalty–
  criminal sanction, 13.10
  no provision for, 13.11, 13.12
  relevance of provision for, 13.09
 reform of–
  express provisions in Acts, 13.19
  Law Commission proposal, 13.19, 13.20
 special damage approach, 13.02
 statutory negligence doctrine, 13.04, 13.05
 volenti, defence of, 13.17
Buildings
 defective construction of, 1.14
 vendor, duty of care as to state of premises, 1.14
Burden of proof
 mitigate, breach of duty to, 7.08
 possible changes in, 20.16

Carelessness
 general presumption of liability, 1.04
 injury or damage, causation of, 2.12

statutory powers, in exercise of, 1.09
subsequent adoption of protective
   measures, not inferred from, 2.10
test for liability, application as, 1.07

Causation
burden of proof–
   balance of probabilities, 2.12
   possible and actual causes, of,
     2.14
careless ultra vires decision, effect of,
   12.17
causative factor impossible to isolate,
   2.13
dilemma situations, in, 3.16
employers' liability, 14.34
more than one, some damage caused
   by, 2.13
philosophical issues, 3.02
remoteness, and, 3.01
res ipsa loquitur–
   absence of fault, hypotheses
     consistent with, 2.16, 2.17
   covert strict liability, as, 2.16
   defendant's evidence,
     incompleteness or inadequacy
     of, 2.18
   evidence, defendant offering, 2.15
   fault principle, survival of, 2.17
   initial presumption, 2.15
   reasonable care, failure to take,
     2.18
   rebuttal of, 2.17

Child
contributory negligence by–
   age of child, relevance of, 4.15
   circumstances of, 4.14
   subjective test, 4.14
duty owed by, 2.02
future lost earnings, compensation
   for, 8.13
limitation of actions, time limit for,
   11.03
'lost years', claim for, 8.16
mother, loss of services of, 9.19
occupiers' liability to, 16.07
parental duty owed to, 2.03

Common practice
relevance of, 2.09

Compensation. *See also* DAMAGES
accidents, for–
   medical, 20.21
   proportion of victims obtaining,
     20.03
ad hoc schemes, establishment of,
   20.19
criminal injuries, for. *See* CRIMINAL
   INJURIES COMPENSATION SCHEME
industrial injuries. *See* INDUSTRIAL
   INJURIES COMPENSATION SCHEME
medical accidents, for, 20.21
negligence–
   scheme, acceptability as, 8.29
   social function of, as, 20.20
   reasonable, approach to, 8.03

Contract
breach, apportionment under
   contributory negligence
   provisions, 4.16
exclusion of liability by, 4.26
tort–
   rigid demarcation with, 4.16
   term taking priority over, 14.02

Contribution
assessment of–
   contributor's limited liability to
     plaintiff, where, 4.25
   statutory provisions, 4.24
claim for–
   circumstances for, 4.18
   conclusiveness of judgments, 4.21,
     4.22
   defendant no longer liable to
     plaintiff, against, 4.19
   defendant who has settled claim,
     by, 4.20
   sanction in damages, abolition of,
     4.23
   statutory provisions, 4.18
   tortfeasor and person liable in
     contract, between, 4.18
contributory negligence, relation to,
   4.01
covenants not to sue, and, 4.18
dismissal of action, 4.22
exemption, power of court, 4.24
joint and several tortfeasors
   distinguished, 4.17
more than one person liable, where,
   4.17
release of cause of action, 4.18

Contributory negligence
apportionment–
   basis of, 4.09-4.11
   blameworthiness and causation,
     taking into account, 4.09, 4.10
   contribution, of, 4.11
   damages, of, 4.11
   doctrine of, 4.07
   negligent misstatement cases,
     5.33
assumption of risk, relation to, 4.01,
   4.03
background, 4.07
breach of contract, and, 4.16
breach of statutory duty, defence to,
   13.17
causation doctrine, 4.07
child, by–
   age of child, relevance of, 4.15
   circumstances of, 4.14
   subjective test, 4.14
contribution, relation to, 4.01
duty of care, not relying on, 4.08
employers' liability–
   apportionment, 14.34
   plaintiff, accident entirely fault

of, 14.35
intermediate inspection of products, and, 17.09
negligent misstatement, in case of–
  apportionment provisions, 5.33
  not easily established, 5.34
  relevance of, 5.32
occupiers' liability, in context of, 16.12
pleading, 4.07
product liability, in relation to, 17.25
severity of damage, plaintiff contributing to–
  crash helmets, failing to wear, 4.12
  drunk driver, knowingly riding with, 4.13
  risk, general exposure to, 4.13
  safety precautions, failure to take, 4.12
  seat-belts, failure to wear, 4.12

Counsel
advocates' immunity, 1.13, 1.17, 5.08
  abuse of process, 5.11
  Bar, not confined to, 5.09
  construction of, 15.14
  narrow interpretation of, 5.10
non-litigious work, liability for, 1.13

Criminal injuries compensation
alternative remedy of, 1.24
assessment of, 19.16
basis of, 19.15
scheme, justification of, 19.17

Damages
assessment, postponement of, 7.12
contingencies, allowance for, 7.09
death, on. *See* DEATH
events before trial, occurrence of, 7.10
general–
  distress, for, 7.03
  itemisation, 7.04
  overall sum, 7.04
  overlap of, 7.05
  post-trial pecuniary losses and non-pecuniary loss, consisting of, 7.03
heads of, 7.01
insurance companies, paid by, 19.01
interest on, 7.13
measure of, and remoteness of damage, 3.03
mitigation–
  medical treatment, refusal of, 7.07
  onus of proof, 7.08
  plaintiff's state of knowledge, 7.06
  social security benefits, claim of, 7.06
parasitic, doctrine of, 6.12
personal injury, for. *See* PERSONAL INJURY, DAMAGES FOR
property damage, for. *See* PROPERTY DAMAGES
provisional, 7.11
special–
  meaning, 7.02
  pre-trial lost earnings, for, 7.02
structured settlements, 8.28, 20.09
tortious and non-tortious intervening events, 7.10

Death
bereavement, damages for–
  Administration of Justice Act 1982, law before, 9.27
  fixed sum, 9.26
  nature of award, 9.28
causes of action, survival of–
  another cause, injured person dying from, 9.03
  statutory provisions, 9.01
dependents, claims by–
  background, 9.04
  criminal action, death in, 9.24
  damages, assessment of–
    apportionment, 9.21
    benefits, disregard of, 9.22, 9.23
    capital sum, 9.13
    contingencies, 9.14
    division of awards, 9.10
    existing support not legally enforceable, where, 9.16
    family, possibility of deceased and plaintiff starting, 9.17
    future, degree of likelihood as to, 9.15
    global sum approach, 9.21
    interest on, 9.20
    lost benefit, for, 9.12
    lost earnings, for, 9.11
    mother, loss of services of, 9.19
    multiplier, 9.13
    non-material benefits, effect of, 9.23
    promotion prospects, taking into account, 9.17
    remarriage or prospects not taken into account, 9.18
    stages in, 9.10
  defined relationship, loss flowing from, 9.07
  dependents, list of, 9.06
  extent of dependency, amounts included in, 9.07
  joint operations, loss of, 9.09
  life of crime, earnings as proceeds of, 9.25
  persons claiming, 9.05
  public policy, falling on ground of, 9.24, 9.25
  shared expenses, loss of, 9.08
  statutory provisions, 9.04

funeral expenses—
  recovery of, 9.29
  scope of, 9.30
limitation of actions, 11.01. *See also* LIMITATION OF ACTIONS
lost years' loss of income not surviving, 9.02
personal injuries claims, time limit for, 11.20

Defective premises
  negligence-type liability, 16.39
  repairs, duty to carry out, 16.38

Defective products
  common law liability—
    dangerous things, for, 17.02
    decreasing importance of, 17.01
    distributors, of, 17.04
    Donoghue v Stevenson, case of, 17.03
    duty of care, 17.05
    economic loss, redress for, 17.13
    intermediate inspection—
      causation, relationship to, 17.09
      contributory negligence, relationship to, 17.09
      possibility of, 17.08
    negligent repairers, of, 17.04
    principle, application of, 17.04
    proof of negligence—
      defendant's control, manufacturing process under, 17.11
      no evidence, danger of calling, 17.12
      onus of, 17.10
      res ipsa loquitur, 17.12
    testing, duty of, 17.07
    warning, duty of, 17.06
  defect, meaning, 17.21
  other products comprised in, safety of, 17.22
  producer, meaning, 17.18, 17.19
  products, meaning, 17.18
  strict liability—
    agricultural products, exclusion of, 17.20
    Consumer Protection Act 1987—
      background to, 17.14
      EC Directive, implementing, 17.14
      evaluation of, 17.28
    contributory negligence, 17.25
    damage—
      consequential losses, 17.27
      scope of, 17.26
    defences—
      state of the art, 17.23
      statutory requirement, defect attributable to, 17.24
      supply other than in the course of business, 17.24
    exclusion clauses, 17.25
    introduction of regime, 17.01
    joint and several, 17.17
    legislative action, choice for, 17.29
    statutory provisions, 17.15
    suppliers, of, 17.16
    warnings, 17.21

Defendant
  conduct, utility of, 2.06

Disabled persons
  cause of disability, 20.03

Dismissal for want of prosecution
  limitation period, within, 11.06
  pre-limitation delay, relevance of, 11.07

Duty of care
  child, of, 2.02
  child, owed to by parents, 2.03
  common practice, relevance of, 2.09
  defendant's conduct, utility of, 2.06
  errors of judgment, 2.11
  harm, precautions to prevent, 2.05
  just and reasonable, 1.10
  minorities, protection of, 2.08
  precautions necessary for protection, extent of, 2.07
  subsequent adoption of protective measures, effect of, 2.10
  volenti, relationship with, 4.06

Economic loss
  act or statement, carelessness as, 6.23
  common law approach to, 6.01
  consequential on injury or damage to third party—
    avalanche of claims, fear of, 6.13
    Canada, liability imposed in, 6.21
    exceptions to general rule, rejection of possibility of—
      Aliakmon case, 6.17, 6.18
      contract, priority of, 6.20
      House of Lords, view of, 6.15
      plaintiff and owner of damaged property, commercial relationship between, 6.16
      pre-*Aliakmon* cases, 6.16
      transferred loss, principle of, 6.19
    older approach to, 6.12
    orthodox view, confirmation of, 6.14
    parasitic damages, doctrine of, 6.12
  damage to property not owned by plaintiff, consequential to, 6.01
  defective product, caused by, 17.13
  employers' duty not extending to, 14.03
  failure to insure, due to, 6.25
  family breadwinner, death of, 9.04

floodgates argument, 6.04
Hedley Byrne, effect of, 6.03
justification, 1.04
loss of services, abolition of action for, 6.27
lost income, claim for, 6.01
negligent misstatement, caused by, 1.12, 6.03. *See also* NEGLIGENT MISSTATEMENT
occupiers' liability, 16.15
physical damage distinguished, 1.04
policy as to, 1.04
property damages, 10.17
public nuisance, in case of, 6.26
'pure' loss and loss consequential on damage to property distinguished–
    importance of, 6.01
    pragmatic approach to, 6.02
purpose, concept of, 6.23
recovery for, 6.22
reduction in value of plaintiff's property due to defendant's negligence–
    building cases–
        Anns, rejection of, 6.06
        builder, loss of, 6.07
        complex structure theory, 6.07-6.10
        contract, relevance of, 6.11
        evaluation, 6.11
        general rule, exception to, 6.09
        health and safety, emphasis on, 6.05
        Junior Books decision, 6.09, 6.10
        plaintiff and defendants, proximity of, 6.10
        statutory provisions, interaction with, 6.06
        structural elements of buildings, defects in, 6.08
reversal of trend on, 6.04
scope of recovery for, 1.03
statutory bodies, negligence of. *See* STATUTORY BODIES
statutory powers, 6.24
'Egg-shell skull' rule
foreseeability principle, modification of, 3.10, 3.11
Employer
liability. *See* EMPLOYER'S LIABILITY
vicarious liability. *See* VICARIOUS LIABILITY
Employers' liability
causation, 14.34
common law duty–
    contract, under, 14.02
    negligence, principles of, 14.01
    non-delegable duty, 14.01, 14.15
    pure economic loss, not extending to, 14.03
    statutory duties, relationship with–
        distinction, reservation of, 14.39
        separation, 14.38
compulsory insurance, 14.14, 19.09
contributory negligence–
    apportionment, 14.34
    plaintiff, accident entirely fault of, 14.35
coterminous fault, principle of, 14.37
dangerous machinery, duty to fence–
    construction and position of fencing, 14.25
    other machinery, meaning, 14.22
    parts in motion or in use, 14.25
    plaintiff, conduct of, 14.24
    prime movers, meaning, 14.20
    scope of protection, 14.23
    statutory provisions, 14.19
    transmission machinery, 14.21
defective equipment–
    compulsory insurance, 14.14
    injury due to, 14.13
    non-delegable duty, 14.15
delegation of duty to employee, 14.37
floors and access–
    reasonably practicable precautions, taking, 14.28
    statutory provisions, 14.26
    transient dangers, 14.27
fumes and dust–
    inhalation, protection against, 14.31
    positive measures for removing, 14.30
    ventilation, 14.29
heavy loads, injury caused by lifting, 14.32
insurance, compulsory, 19.09
non-delegable duty–
    concept of, 14.01
    discharge on the facts, 14.16
    policy considerations, 14.15
safe system of work, provision of–
    appropriate equipment and supervision, 14.05, 14.6
    dangerous fellow-employees, 14.12
    developing knowledge, situation of, 14.08
    each employee, duty owed to, 14.10
    encouragement of use of facilities, 14.06
    paternalism, not extending to, 14.11
    principle of, 14.04
    risk, weighing up, 14.09
    standard of care, 14.07-14.09
safety equipment, provision of, 14.33
statutory duties–
    breach of, 14.17
    common law duties, relationship with–

418 *Index*

distinction, reservation of,
14.39
separation, 14.38
existing provisions, 14.18
replacement of measures, 14.17
volenti as defence, 14.35
Errors of judgment
negligence, not necessarily
constituting, 2.11
Exclusion of liability
contract, by, 4.26
disclaimers, non-contractual–
circumstances for, 4.27
privity of contract, and, 4.28
survey report, in, 4.31
Unfair Contract Terms Act, and,
4.30, 4.31
volenti, relationship with, 4.29

Fatal accidents. *See* DEATH
Foreseeability
acts and omissions, distinction
between, 1.05
nervous shock cases, in, 1.25
omissions, in case of, 1.06
probability, and, 2.04
remoteness of damage, test for. *See*
REMOTENESS OF DAMAGE
rise and fall of, 1.01
statement of law of negligence by
reference to, 1.01
sufficient condition of liability, not,
1.04
test, width of, 1.01
Wilberforce doctrine–
criticisms in context, 1.03
rejection of approach, 1.02
statement of, 1.01
utility, loss of, 1.07
Funeral expenses
damages for–
recovery of, 9.29
scope of, 9.30

Government decisions
justiciability of–
economic loss, claim for, 12.07
liability, imposition of, 12.07
ordinary negligence concepts, use
of, 12.08, 12.09
trend in, 12.09

Harm
precautions to prevent, 2.05
Highway
dangerous situation, independent
contractors causing, 18.23
strict liability for, 18.16
users of–
common law duty to, 16.36
visitors, not, 16.35
Hospitals
inadequate treatment resulting from

underfunding and understaffing,
liability for, 18.20
non-delegable duty of care, 18.19

Immunity
advocates', 5.08-5.11, 15.14
arbitrators, of, 5.13
barristers, of, 1.13, 1.17, 5.08-5.11
buildings, in relation to, 1.14
mutual valuers, of, 5.13
progressive erosion of, 1.11
statutory bodies, of. *See* STATUTORY
BODIES
witnesses, of, 5.12
**Industrial injuries compensation
scheme**
accidents and diseases, for, 19.12
background, 19.11
disablement benefit, 19.13
structure, 19.11
Insurance
bankrupt, holder of policy becoming,
19.10
companies, damages paid by, 19.01
employers' liability, in respect of,
14.14, 19.09
failure to insure, loss due to, 6.25
financial loss, not taken into account
for, 8.17
first party, 19.04
judiciary, attitude of, 19.04
law of negligence, influence on, 19.03
legal liability, incidence of, 19.04
moral basis of negligence, and,, 20.06
Motor Insurers' Bureau–
defendant, added as, 19.06
ex gratia payments by, 19.08
hit and run situations, covering,
19.08
notice of proceedings given to,
19.06
Secretary of State, agreement
with, 19.06
new approaches to, 19.04
payment of, 19.01
reality and appearance of negligence,
in, 19.03
relevance of, 19.03
Road Traffic Act–
privity of contract, exception to
doctrine of, 19.06
required by, 19.05, 19.06
spread, effect of, 20.01
subrogation, right of, 19.03
third party, rights transferred to,
19.10
Interest
damages, on, 7.13
Fatal Accidents Acts awards, on,
9.20
Investment advice
negligent, 15.27

Just and reasonable
use of phrase, 1.10

Land
non-occupiers, liability of, 16.33, 16.34
occupiers, liability of. *See* OCCUPIERS' LIABILITY

Latent damage
background, 11.23
building cases, in, 11.23
cause of action already accrued, not resuscitating, 11.28
concurrent liability, 11.29
doomed from the start, meaning, 11.24
extension of limitation period, 11.26
'long stop' provision, 11.27
negligent design, 11.24
purchasers of property, protection of, 11.25
statutory provisions, 11.25

Lawyers' negligence
advocates' immunity. *See* ADVOCATES; COUNSEL
claims against, types of, 15.15
explanation, adequacy of, 15.16
practice, evidence of, 15.15
tort and contract–
coexistence of duty, 15.17
contractual duty, nature of, 15.19
third parties, duty to, 15.18

Legislation
rights and duties, delineation of, 1.23

Limitation of actions
accrual of cause of action, 11.05
concealment of cause of action–
start of period, postponement of–
requirements, 11.22
statutory provisions, 11.21
damage occurring before party conscious of, 11.05
dismissal for want of prosecution, and, 11.06, 11.07
latent damage. *See* LATENT DAMAGE
personal injuries claims–
date of knowledge–
expert advice, relevance of, 11.13, 11.14
identity of defendant, of, 11.12
significant, that injury was, 11.10, 11.11
statutory provisions, 11.09
special time limit for–
death, where resulting, 11.20
discretion to override, 11.15- 11.20
guidelines, not fettered by, 11.18, 11.19
lapse of proceedings, 11.17
relevant factors for, 11.16
statutory provisions, 11.08
procedure, 11.04

time limits–
computation of dates, 11.02
discretion of court, 11.01
person under disability, for, 11.03
statutory provisions, 11.01

Local authorities
building control, cases airing from, 12.13
public policy, attempts to avoid negligence liability by, 12.11

Marriage
claim by dependant on death, relevance of remarriage, 9.18
prospects, loss of, 8.09

Medical negligence
common practice, relevance of–
administrative practices, 15.08
principle of, 15.07
contractual, 15.13
differing professional schools of thought, effect of, 15.09
policy, 15.05
proof, difficulties of, 15.05
risk in treatment, duty to warn of–
causation, and, 15.12
common practice, 15.11
informed consent, doctrine of, 15.10
paternalism, 15.11
questions, answering, 15.11
standard of care, 15.06

Minorities
protection of, 2.08

Mutual valuers
negligent misstatement, immunity from, 5.13

Negligence
acceptability of as compensation scheme, 8.29
causation, concentration on, 20.03
cost of administration, 20.02
criticisms of system, 20.01
moral basis of, 20.06
novel situation, extension of liability to–
alternative remedy more appropriate for, 1.24
conflicting interests, 1.17
court, decision of, 1.15
'floodgates' argument, 1.16
illegal or anti-social conduct by plaintiff, 1.20
legislative or administrative solution more suitable for, 1.23
police activity, in case of, 1.18
sanctity of life, policy as to, 1.19
ordinary principles, justification or explanation for exclusion of, 1.22
proof, difficulties of, 20.04, 20.05

reform, proposals for–
  agreement, lack of, 20.18
  burden of proof, possible charges in, 20.16
  disease, focus on, 20.15
  New Zealand scheme, 20.11, 20.12
  objectives of, 20.21
  Oxford Centre for Socio-Legal Studies, of, 20.13, 20.14
  Pearson Commission, 20.07-20.10. *See also* PEARSON COMMISSION
  strict liability, extension of, 20.17
social function of, 20.20

Negligent misstatement
breach of duty, proof of–
  knowledge or skill, reference to, 5.06
  prediction, advice taking form of, 5.05
  professional judgments, in case of, 5.05
business, in course of, 5.29
contributory negligence–
  apportionment provisions, 5.33
  not easily established, 5.34
  relevance of, 5.32
development of liability for, 5.16
difficulties arising with, 5.04
disclaimers of liability–
  exclusion by, 4.27
  Hedley Byrne case, in, 5.27
  replies to inquiries, as to, 5.27
  requirements, 5.28
  Unfair Contract Terms Act, effect of–
    business, statement in course of, 5.29
    denial of duty, 5.31
    reasonableness, 5.30
    where possible, 5.27
economic loss, and, 1.12
Hedley Byrne, case of, 5.01
omissions. *See* OMISSIONS
public policy issues–
  advocate's immunity, 5.08-5.11
  arbitrators' immunity, 5.13
  mutual valuers' immunity, 5.13
  witnesses' immunity, 5.12
reliance on, 5.01
social occasions, on–
  exceptional cases, in, 5.14, 5.15
  opinions by professional people at, 5.15
special relationship, concept of, 5.01
special skills, whether required, 5.02
standard of care, 5.07
third party claims–
  auditors, extent of liability of–
    assumption of responsibility, meaning, 5.22
    class, notion of, 5.21
    narrow view of, 5.19
    purpose of statement, 5.23
    indeterminate liability, fear of, 5.16
    recipient of advice, in negotiation with, 5.18
    references, in relation to, 5.19
  solicitors, against, 5.17
  surveyors, against, 5.17
types of, 5.03
underlying principles, questions concerning, 5.04

Nervous shock
extent of liability for, 1.09
Hillsborough cases, 1.25
potential situations, 1.25
test of reasonable foreseeability applying to, 1.25

Nuisance
independent contractors, liability of, 18.18
public, recovery of economic loss, 6.26

Occupiers' liability
Acts not applying, where–
  dangerous activities, conduct of, 16.32
  exclusion of liability, on, 16.37
  highway, users of–
    common law duty to, 16.36
    visitors, not, 16.35
  non-occupiers, liability of, 16.33, 16.34
  ordinary negligence, relationship with, 16.30-16.32
Defective Premises Act, under, 16.38, 16.39
disclaimer, exclusion by, 4.27
exclusion of–
  Acts not applying, where, 16.37
  persons other than visitors, to, 16.27
  visitors and business occupiers, to– recreational or educational purposes, entry for, 16.29
  Unfair Contract Terms Act, 16.28
  visitors and non-business occupiers, to–
    implicit restrictions on, 16.26
    occupier not free to exclude, 16.25, 16.26
    possibility of exclusion, 16.24
non-occupiers, liability of, 16.33, 16.34
occupier–
  control by, 16.03
  meaning, 16.02
persons other than visitors, to–
  exclusion of liability, 16.27
  Occupiers' Liability Act 1984, covered by–
    access agreements, 16.18
    cases involving personal

Index

injury, approach to, 16.21
nature of duty, 16.20
private rights of way, users of, 16.19
property damage, no liability for, 16.23
trespassers, 16.17
volenti, 16.22
warnings, 16.22
width of, 16.16
structures capable of being occupied, 16.01
visitors, to–
  children, 16.07
  common duty of care, 16.05
  common law standard of care, 16.04
  contributory negligence, 16.12
  entry pursuant to contract, duty of care, 16.09
  independent contractors, employment of, 16.13
  land, activities on, 16.06
  persons qualifying as, 16.04
  plaintiff's calling, risks incident to, 16.08
  property damage, for–
    economic loss, 16.15
    theft of property, 16.14
    uncertainty as to, 16.14
  volenti non fit injuria, 16.11
  warnings, 16.10

Omissions
acts distinguished in law, 1.05
control, failure to exercise, 1.06
foreseeability–
  criterion of, 1.05
  test, application of, 1.06
liability, imposition of, 1.05
statement, to make–
  contract, relevance of, 5.25
  duty of care, existence of, 5.26
  pre-contractual situation, in, 5.25
  property, concept of title in, 5.26
  question of law in relation to, 5.24
statutory powers, in exercise of, 12.20

Parents
children, duty owed to, 2.03

Pearson Commission
recommendations–
  road accident scheme, 20.08
  tort, reform of, 20.09
report, criticisms of, 20.10
terms of reference, 20.07

Personal injury, damages for
care, cost of–
  general calculation, 8.23
  living expenses, deductibility of, 8.25
  National Health Service facilities, use of, 8.24
  private medical sector, expenses of, 8.24
  reasonableness of remaining at home, 8.24
  relatives, care by–
    calculation of award, 8.27
    payment for, 8.26
criticism of, 20.01
financial loss, for–
  calculation of future lost earnings–
    actuarial tables not used for, 8.10
    children, in case of, 8.13
    future unemployment due to injury, risk of, 8.12
    higher rates of tax, ignoring, 8.11
    inflation, ignoring, 8.11
    loss of marriage prospects, effect of, 8.09
    method of, 8.08
  gains, relevance of–
    charitable payments, 8.17
    entitlements not paid for by plaintiff, 8.18
    ex gratia payments, 8.17
    pensions, 8.17
    private insurance policies, 8.17
incidence of tax, taking into account, 8.21
'lost years', for–
  amount of damages, 8.15
  children, for, 8.16
  death, not surviving, 9.02
  statutory provisions, 8.14
pension scheme contributions, taking account of, 8.22
state benefits, relationship with–
  full deductibility, 8.20
  new and old regimes, 8.20
  statutory provisions, 8.19
guidelines for, 8.04
limitation of actions, 11.01, 11.08. See also LIMITATION OF ACTIONS
non-pecuniary loss–
  amenity, loss of, 8.03
  awards in other cases, relevance of, 8.04
  catastrophic injury cases, 8.05
  inflation, effect of, 8.07
  pain and suffering, 8.01
  reduced life expectancy, 8.02
  unconscious plaintiffs, of, 8.06
plaintiff's home, adaption or purchase of, 8.23
reasonable compensation, approach to, 8.03
reform, scope for–
  compensation scheme, tort as, 8.29
  computation of damages, 8.30
  specific, 8.31

structured settlements, 8.28, 20.09
Plaintiff
  illegal or anti-social conduct by, 1.20
Police
  negligence liability, negation of, 1.18
Probability
  degree of, 2.04
Product liability. See DEFECTIVE PRODUCTS
Professional negligence
  accountants. See ACCOUNTANTS
  auditors. See AUDITORS
  investment advice, giving, 15.27
  lawyers, of. See LAWYERS' NEGLIGENCE
  losses, calculation of, 10.17
  medical. See MEDICAL NEGLIGENCE
  property professions–
    aspects of property dealt with, 15.20
    design and construction–
      contractual liability, 15.25
      third parties, liability to, 15.24
    valuation–
      liability for, 15.21
      permissible margin of error, 15.21
      structural defects, overlooking, 15.22
      third parties, liability to, 15.23
    standard of care–
      errors of judgment, 15.04
      state of knowledge, 15.02, 15.03
      test of, 15.01
Property damages
  assessment of value, 10.03
  diminution in market value, for, 10.07
  gains by plaintiff, relevance of, 10.08
  hire of substitute, for, 10.06
  land and buildings–
    additional losses for, 10.16
    betterment, allowance for, 10.10
    business, interruption of, 10.16
    date of assessment, 10.14, 10.15
    gains on, 10.11
    negligent surveys of–
      lenders, liability to, 10.13
      liability for, 10.12
    notional cost of reinstatement, 10.10
    reinstatement or difference in value, 10.09, 10.10
  loss of use, for, 10.04, 10.5
  new areas of recovery, 10.17
  'no-claims' bonus, for loss of, 10.07
  other work during period of repair, 10.05
  remoteness, 10.07
  repair or difference in value, for, 10.02
  restitutio in integrum, principle of, 10.01, 10.07

Proximity
  policy factors behind, 1.08-1.10
  use of term, 1.08
Public policy
  dependents' claims falling on ground of, 9.24, 9.25
  justiciable issues, 1.09
  local authority, attempts to avoid negligence liability by, 12.11
  negligent misstatements, issues as to–
    advocate's immunity, 5.08-5.11
    arbitrators' immunity, 5.13
    mutual valuers' immunity, 5.13
    witnesses' immunity, 5.12
  non-delegable duty, considerations as to, 14.15
  police activity, as to, 1.18
  proximity, in relation to, 1.08-1.10
  public servants, cases involving, 1.17
  sanctity of life, and, 1.19
  statutory bodies, and. See STATUTORY BODIES
  suicide, as to, 1.21

Reasonable man
  objective test of, 2.01
  standard of, 2.01
References
  negligent misstatement, third party claims in, 5.19
Remoteness of damage
  causation, and, 3.01
  foreseeability test–
    artificiality and hindsight, 3.08
    background to, 3.04
    extraneous circumstances, effect of–
      'egg-shell skull' rule, 3.10, 3.11
      impecuniosity of plaintiff, 3.12, 3.13
      pre-existing condition, 3.10, 3.11
    liability, spectrum of, 3.09
    mitigation of damage, opportunity for, 3.12, 3.13
    necessary, not sufficient, as, 3.15, 3.20
    present state of law, 3.07-3.09
    uncertainty of, 3.06
    universal panacea, not, 3.05
  intervening act–
    plaintiff, by–
      dilemma situations, in, 3.16
      relevance of remoteness, 3.14, 3.15
      rescue cases, 3.18
      suicide cases, 3.17
    third parties, by–
      deliberate and mischievous, 3.19-3.21

medical treatment, inadequate, 3.23
negligent, 3.22, 3.23
probability, high degree of, 3.20, 3.21
measure of damages, and, 3.03
proper scope of, 3.02
Res ipsa loquitur
absence of fault, hypotheses consistent with, 2.16, 2.17
covert strict liability, as, 2.16
defective products, proof of negligence as to, 17.12
defendant's evidence, incompleteness or inadequacy of, 2.18
evidence, defendant offering, 2.15
fault principle, survival of, 2.17
initial presumption, 2.15
reasonable care, failure to take, 2.18
rebuttal of, 2.17
Rescue
injury in course of, 3.18
Road accidents
disclaimer of liability for, 4.04
Road traffic
insurance, requirement of, 19.05, 19.06
Motor Insurers' Bureau–
defendant, added as, 19.06
ex gratia payments by, 19.08
hit and run situations, covering, 19.08
notice of proceedings given to, 19.06
Secretary of State, agreement with, 19.06

Sanctity of life
public policy as to, 1.19
Service, loss of
abolition of action for, 6.27
Social security
accident victims, money paid to, 19.01
basis of system, 19.02
disablement benefit, 19.13
Solicitors
negligence. *See* LAWYERS' NEGLIGENCE
negligent misstatement, third party claims in, 5.17
third parties, duty to, 15.18
Standard of care
child, of, 2.02
developing knowledge, situation of, 14.08
employers' liability, for, 14.07-14.09
medical negligence, 15.06
negligent misstatement, in case of, 5.07
professional negligence,
errors of judgment, 15.04
state of knowledge, 15.02, 15.03
test of, 15.01
reasonable man, of, 2.01
skill and care, degree of, 2.01
Statutory bodies
administrative decisions, challenges to, 12.03
factors bearing on liability–
competing public interests–
efficiency and thrift, balance between, 12.11
imposition of liability, 12.11
police, liability of, 12.10
private law duty of care not arising, 12.10
regulatory functions, 12.12
resource implications, 12.11
policy–
administrative law, unreasonableness in, 12.16
causation, 12.17
misconstruction of statute, 12.15
'overkill', danger of, 12.15
statutory purpose–
building control, 12.13
economic loss, claim for, 12.14
government decisions, justiciability of–
economic loss, claim for, 12.07
liability, imposition of, 12.07
ordinary negligence concepts, use of, 12.08, 12.09
trend in, 12.09
just and reasonable, use of phrase, 1.10
negligence, liability in, 12.01
statutory powers–
carelessness in exercise of, 1.09
negligence in exercise of–
buildings, inspection of, 12.04
Canadian case on, 12.18
clarification of decisions, 12.04
decisions on, 12.02
flood damage, dealing with, 12.02
House of Lords decisions on, 12.03
ordinary claims, and, 12.01
policy and operational spheres distinguished, 12.04, 12.06, 12.09
policy 'immunity'–
applicability, 12.05
Diplock test, 12.05
omissions, liability for, 12.20
presumption, 12.06
public and private law, in, 12.19
street lighting, provision of, 12.02
Sterilisation
failure of, 10.17
Strict liability
defective products, for. *See* DEFECTIVE PRODUCTS

development of concept, retarded
  development of, 2.01
extension, proposals for, 20.17
fault distinguished, 13.16
highway, for, 18.16
res ipsa loquitur rule, imposition by, 2.16

Suicide
dependents, claims by, 9.25
public policy as to, 1.21
remoteness of damage issues, 3.17

Surveyors
negligent misstatement, third party claims in, 5.17
negligent surveys–
  lenders, liability to, 10.13
  liability for, 10.12
valuation–
  liability for, 15.21
  permissible margin of error, 15.21
  structural defects, overlooking, 15.22
  third parties, liability to, 15.23

Tax
damages for lost earnings, taken into account for, 8.21

Tort
contract–
  rigid demarcation with, 4.16
  term taking priority over, 14.02

Tortfeasor
contribution by. See CONTRIBUTION

Vaccine damage
lump sum payments for, 19.14

Vicarious liability. See also EMPLOYERS' LIABILITY
agency cases–
  car-owners, 18.24-18.26
  fresh contexts, application in, 18.27
background, 18.01
car-owners, non-delegable duty of–
  agents, for, 18.24
  cases extending liability, 18.26
  permission, car driven with, 18.26
  scope of, 18.25
  terminology, 18.24
doctrine of, 18.01
employment, course of–
  employee acting outside, 18.09
  master's indemnity, 18.14
  performance, wrongful method of–
    assaults, 18.13
    authorities on, 18.09
    criminal acts, 18.13
    prohibited acts, 18.12
    vehicles, moving, 18.10
  practical jokes in, 18.11
  stopping in, 18.11
  travelling to and from work, 18.11
independent contractors–

acts of servants, negligence through, 18.23
collateral negligence, 18.23
general rule for, 18.15
non-delegable duty–
  bailees, of, 18.22
  concept of, 18.15
  dangerous activities, concept of, 18.17
  highways, contract of, 18.16
  hospitals, of, 18.19, 18.20
  injuries at work, for, 18.21
  nuisance, liability in, 18.18
principal, of, 18.24
servant–
  borrowed–
    contractual indemnity, employer entitled to, 18.08
    hirer's duty to, 18.07
    imposition of liability for, 18.06
  defence, having, 18.02
  persons being, determining–
    commercial skill, relevance of, 18.04
    control, test of, 18.03
    nature of claim, possible relevance of, 18.05
true, statement of, 18.01

Volenti non fit injuria
agreement, objective test of, 4.05
all or nothing concept of, 4.03
breach of statutory duty, defence to, 13.17
continuing activity, in case of, 4.04
contributory negligence, relation to, 4.01
duty of care, relationship with, 4.06
employers' liability, defence to, 14.36
exclusion of liability, and, 4.01
by disclaimer, relationship with, 4.29
knowledge, insufficiency of, 4.02
occupiers' liability, in context of, 16.11, 165.22
other defences, relationship with, 4.03
specific defence, as, 4.06
understanding, evidence of, 4.02
vicarious liability, effect on, 4.03

Witnesses
immunity, 5.12